The BOOK of *REVELATION*
Mysteries Revealed

Don T. Phillips

Second Edition

"The Book of Revelation: Mysteries Revealed," by Don T. Phillips. ISBN 978-1-62137-119-9.

Published 2012 by Virtualbookworm.com Publishing Inc., P.O. Box 9949, College Station, TX 77842, US. ©2012, Don T. Phillips. All rights reserved. No part of this publication may be reproduced, stored in a retrieval system, or transmitted in any form or by any means, electronic, mechanical, recording or otherwise, without the prior written permission of Don T. Phillips.

Manufactured in the United States of America.

Table of Contents

Acknowledgements	i
Preface	v
Overview	xi

Chapter	**Page**
1: The Call from Heaven	1
2: Letters to the Seven Churches	15
3: The Throne of God	87
4: The Scroll and the Lamb of God	97
5: Biblical Chronology: Adam to Christ	105
6: The Sabbatical and Jubilee Years	131
7: Daniel's 70 Week Prophecy	155
8: Finding Daniel's 70th Week	197
9: The Seven Feasts of Israel	213
10: Seals, Trumpets and Bowls: Exposition	249
11: Seals, Trumpets and Bowls: Chronology	297
12: The Little Scroll	325
13: The Two Witnesses	331
14: The Sun Clothed Woman, the Man Child and the Dragon	339
15: The Two Groups of 144,000	359
16: The Great Multitude	377
17: The Beasts of Revelation	381
18: The Antichrist	397
19: The Three Angels	421
20: The Harvests of the Earth	427
21: Mystery: Babylon the Great	437
22: Commercial Babylon	457
23: Rapture of the Saints on Rosh Hashanah	469
24: Marriage of the Lamb	479
25: The Wedding Supper: Wise and Foolish Virgins	497
26: The Three Invasions of Jerusalem	525
27: The Millennial Kingdom	547

Chapter	Page
28: Resurrections and Judgments.............................	563
29: A New Heaven and a New Earth........................	595
30: Come Quickly, Lord Jesus.....................................	601
Bibliography...	607

Acknowledgments

There are many people that I would like to thank who have contributed to this book. Above all there are three individuals that without their help, I would have never completed this manuscript: God the Father, God the Son and the Holy Ghost. Each has comforted me, encouraged me, chastised me and given me wisdom beyond my normal understanding at one time or another. In the physical realm, there are several individuals who have helped me in various ways. Without a doubt, the one person most responsible for my interest, examination and understanding of basic scriptural principles has been Pastor Dan Cummins. Dan has been my friend and mentor for over 20 years. Long ago he introduced me to the Seven Feasts of Israel in a revival, and later showed me the significance of the Pattern of the Harvest. In the Old and New Testaments, people lived completely off of the land and were farmers, sheepherders and hunters. In the New Testament, Christ often spoke in agricultural terms and used these principles as a basis for many of His parables and miracles. Understanding both the Seven Feasts of Israel and the Pattern of the Harvest is crucial to understanding the Book of Revelation. Both are used extensively in this book. Dan has been a valued friend, spiritual advisor and theologian ... thank you Dan. In the early 1990's Dr. Mark Rutland, now president of Oral Roberts University called me out during one of his sermons and anointed me to teach the gospel. I have heeded his call, and have taught and intensely studied prophecy for over 25 years. I am also grateful to Dr. Terry Tekyl, who was my pastor at Aldersgate United Methodist Church in College Station, Texas and taught me to wait on the Lord. Dr. Tekyl allowed me to teach Sunday school classes for many years under his covering. His ministry of prayer left an enduring mark on my faith and teaching ministry. I am also grateful to Danny Green, pastor of Covenant Family Church in College Station for allowing me to teach in his church for several years. Pastor Green is a fine theologian and was a strong role model. Finally, I would like to acknowledge the influence that Dr. Bruce Wood has had on my spiritual maturity. Dr. Wood is currently my pastor at Aldersgate United Methodist church, where I am now a member.

There have been many, many individuals who have joined me in countless hours of fellowship and study of the word. Without their continually asking *why,* I would never have found the profound hidden meanings in many scriptures. I would like to thank Jim Beard for his early encouragement. Of course, it almost goes without saying that some of the most influential, respected and well known biblical scholars have *fed me meat* when I was *chewing on bread.* Some are still alive, but many have passed into eternity in the hands of Jesus…. A position that I am confident I will achieve not by any works that I have done, but because of the Grace of my Lord Jesus Christ. I want to thank Dr. Clarence Larkin, A.W. Pink, Robert Thomas, Sir Isaac Newton, James Ussher, Dr. Floyd Nolan Jones, Hal Lindsey, Jack Finnegan , S. H. Horn, L. H. Wood, Dr. Edwin R. Thiele, Donald Salerno, Dr. John MacArthur and Dr. John Walvoord to name a few. Without a doubt, there are two people who have had the most influence on my views of the rapture and my intense examination of the structure of the Book of Revelation: Marvin Rosenthal and Robert Van Kampen…. both visionaries and outstanding Biblical researchers.

I have saved my most sincere and heartfelt thanks for the last. My main supporter in writing this book; my severest critic; and the person who continually challenged my scriptural understanding of prophecy; is my wife: Candyce J. Phillips. She suffered through countless hours of editing, reading, challenging and inquiring the pages of this manuscript. She encouraged me to write this book and by her faith in me it is now contained herein.

I would like to reserve very special thanks to Pat Marvenko Smith for allowing me to use five of her artwork collection: One in each of Chapters 10, 16, 17, 21 and 27. Duncan Long is thanked for allowing me to use one of his pictures in Chapter 10.

Finally, I am very aware of the following warning considering what I have written in trying to provide a new and biblically based interpretation of the Book of Revelation.

> *"And the Spirit and the bride say, Come. And let him that heareth say, Come. And let him that is athirst come. And whosoever will, let him take the water of life freely. For I testify unto every man that heareth the words of the prophecy of this book, If any man shall add unto these things, God shall add unto him the plagues that are written in this book: And if any man shall take away from the words of the book of this prophecy, God shall take away his part out of the book of life, and out of the holy city, and from the things which are written in this book."*   Rev 22:17-19

I have tried to reveal the scriptures without compromising either content or meaning. I hope that in some way, the words in this book will lead a soul to Christ, and for others strengthen their understanding of prophecy. I encourage anyone who reads this book to seek the Holy Spirit in forming their own opinions; take nothing as an absolute truth without intense investigation; and always… always… let the scriptures themselves speak the truth. God will hold me accountable for what I have written and knows that I have done the best I can. I can only believe in His Grace to save me, wretched creature that I am. In future years I will no doubt look at some of my words and realize that they could be better…or even wrong. Scriptural understanding is a life long journey. For now, I place my future in the large, capable hands of my Savior… the Son of God…..Jesus Christ.

                                           Don T. Phillips
                                           September, 2012

To those that matter most in my life………..

    Candy Phillips

    Ronald Alan Phillips (Ron)

    Don T. Phillips, III (Donnie)

    …….and *"The Mouse"*

Preface

The first thing to settle is my unwavering belief in God's word. The very existence of Jesus Christ is accepted by simple faith, and that existence is revealed in every book of the bible. I believe in the complete and perfect transmission of God's word between Him and His people He chose ordinary people to write the Holy Scriptures under the influence and guidance of the holy spirit. I believe that there are no contradictions or fables in the Holy Bible. I am aware that well-meaning Christians spend an enormous amount of time identifying biblical errors in both composition and in translation. The modern mantra seems to be that when scripture cannot be easily resolved, there is a *scribal error*. I completely reject such a conclusion. If an equal amount of time…and more…was devoted to resolving biblical conflicts, I am persuaded that a solution to any conundrum can be found. I have chosen with good reason to principally rely upon the Authorized King James Version of God's Holy Word in this book. I am well aware that the original Aramaic and ancient Hebrew versions of the Holy Bible are without a doubt God inspired and without error, but I believe that the King James Bible was equally inspired by the Holy Spirit. When in doubt of any verse or word, I believe that the original meanings of each should be sought out and if possible studied in the context of the words of an original manuscript. Unfortunately, laymen such as I have no access to such documents. Strong's Concordance, Vines Dictionary and other sources of translation are invaluable. The King James Bible was the only readily available source of God's word for centuries, coming to the world in the fullness of time when the printing press was passed from God to the earth. I am persuaded that with so many souls at stake the Authorized King James Version is not inerrant in key concepts or translation. I must point out that other modern bibles such as the NIV study bible and the Ryrie New King James Bible are easier to read and provide valuable information. I have not abandoned these holy documents, but have sought further understanding in their translations. In summary, all in-line scriptural references in this book… and there are many…will be from the Authorized King James Bible.

Having stated apologetics, I will now address an important and relevant question: ***Why yet another book on the Revelation Record?"*** The answer reflects my acquired beliefs that there has been widespread misunderstanding on how the Book of Revelation is structured and how it is organized and presented. In addition, other important topics such as the Rapture and the Wrath of God have been core to my investigation of prophecy for some time. Long ago, I taught a ***pre-tribulation*** rapture theology with the tribulation period being 7 years long. After investigating the scriptural support of a pre-tribulation rapture and the associated 7 year duration of the Tribulation Period, I began to seriously question that position. I read hundreds of articles, books and papers searching for the truth. Finally, after many years of frustrated investigation I decided to do the only thing which could lead to the truth… look at the Holy Scriptures and ask the Holy Spirit for wisdom and understanding. Of course, because of all of the time that I had spent trying to unravel scholarly explanations of scripture by learned theologians, I had seen all of the available theories and support for the pre-post-mid tribulation rapture theories. In 1990 Marvin Rosenthal published his landmark book entitled *The Pre-Wrath Rapture of the Church*. This made sense to me and squared with most scripture, but there were still some nagging questions regarding timing and position. In 1992 Robert Van Kampen published a new book on the pre-wrath rapture called *The Sign*. This convinced me that a pre-wrath rapture made more sense than a pre-tribulation, mid- tribulation or post-tribulation position. However, I was still not convinced that the pre-wrath rapture presented by both Rosenthal and Van Kampen passed scriptural scrutiny. I was always haunted by Rev 11:15-19, which if carefully examined without any preconceived bias demanded a rapture, resurrection and rewards at the 7th trumpet. Finally, I realized that the seals, trumpets, and bowls were not lock stepped sequential across a 7 year time span: The seals only provide a general overview of the tribulation period, just like the preface to any good book. Almost simultaneously, I developed an intense interest in building a Biblical Chronology from Adam to the death of Christ. I did not realize that this was the key to unlocking the duration of the tribulation period, which I am now convinced is only 3.5 years. Finally, I began to realize that the Seven Feasts of Israel were not just historical events ordained by God after the Exodus, but collectively they provide a *blueprint* of all the events in the life of Jesus Christ (His first advent) and the Book of Revelation leading up to His second coming (the second advent). All of the pieces then came together, and the result is this manuscript.

It should again be noted that the key to understanding the Book of Revelation is to recognize that the seals, trumpets and bowls do not constitute a continuous sequence of events which transpire in lock step across a fixed period of time. Structurally, both the Book of Daniel and the Book of Revelation have much in common. They are both constructed in such a way as to first reveal a great prophetic truth without complete detail, and then later to reveal more details in parallel descriptions. Without devoting a great deal of time to this issue, it should be stated that the book of Revelation is organized along **three** great themes.

> ➢ A description of God's heavenly kingdom (Rev 4) and of the risen Christ (Rev 1:1-19): **The things that thou hast seen** (Rev 1:19).
> ➢ A description of: **The things which are** (Rev 1:19). Letters to the Seven Churches in Asia Minor (Rev 2-3 and Rev 5).
> ➢ A description of: **The things which shall be hereafter** (Rev 1:19 through Rev 6-22)

The **things which shall be hereafter** are composed of four main sub-groups of scripture.

- A description of the *tribulation period… the seals, bowls and trumpets (Rev 6-19)*
- The Millennial Kingdom (Rev 20)
- The New Heavens and the New Earth (Rev 21-22:1-5)

- Closing remarks and warnings (Rev 22:6-21)

The descriptions of: ***things which will be hereafter*** (Rev 6-22) are further subdivided into what is called a ***bifed*** in the English literature. The ***seals*** span the entire tribulation period of 3.5 years, and predict conditions or general events which will occur...They are not precursors to the trumpet and bowl judgments as is erroneously taught (Rev 6:1-15, Rev 8:1). The tribulation period of 3.5 years contains the trumpet and bowl judgments which are released sequentially (Rev 8, 9 11:1-14, 16:1-21). Parenthetical events are described in Rev 7 (144,000 sealed and a great multitude seen in heaven): Rev 10 (the Little Scroll) and Rev 11 (the Two Witnesses) The ***bifed*** occurs at Rev 12. Between Rev 12:1 and 18:24, things which take place on heaven and earth during the same 3.5 year tribulation period are presented in greater detail. The Tribulation Period is initiated by a great war in Heaven, concluding with Satan and his angels being cast down to the earth.
(Rev 12):1-17

The rise of the Antichrist (Rev 13:1-10) and the false prophet (Rev 13:11-18) are detailed in Rev 13. Three more interludes are then recorded which describe special events. In rapid sequence, 144,000 overcomers are seen in heaven (Rev 14:1-5): Three angels who warn the people of imminent tribulation (Rev 14:6-13): And the Harvest of the earth (Rev 14).The first Harvest is to gather the saints to meet Christ in the air at the rapture (Rev 14:14-16), and the second Harvest is to gather all of Satan's armies to the great Battle of Armageddon (Rev 14:14-20). The Wrath of God, which is the 7 Bowl judgments (Rev 16:1), is described in Rev 15 and Rev 16. Rev 17 and Rev 18 describes both the *content* and the *collapse* of the Religious Empire of the Antichrist (Rev 17), and the Commercial Empire of the Antichrist (Rev 18). These two systems will exist over the entire tribulation period. After describing the Religious and Commercial empires of the Antichrist, the Apostle John is now shown how the Church Age (the Age of Grace) will end. Rev 19:1-10 describes heavenly praise because the end of Satan and his influence over this world has arrived. The *second advent* of

Christ is described in Rev 19:11-21, which includes the Battle of Armageddon and the ultimate fate of the Antichrist and the False Prophet. Rev 20:1-6 describes the binding of Satan for 1000 years in the Abyss; the 1000 year Millennial Kingdom and the Great White Throne judgment of all unbelievers. Finally, the New Heavens and the New Earth are described in great detail in Rev 21:1-27 and Rev 22:1-5. The Book of Revelation ends with a doxology that issues a warning to all who refuse to heed the words of this great, prophetic book (Rev 22:6-21).

I would like to tell the reader about a few literary rules which I have purposely violated and why. *First*, every **scripture** used in text is indented and in bold-italics. All scriptural references are taken from the Authorized King James Bible. *Second*, even though my wife complained bitterly, I have liberally used italics to emphasize **key concepts** in the narratives. In general, these highlighted words or terms are excerpts from a Biblical scripture, but some quote noted authorities on the subject at hand. On many occasion, I chose to use only *italics* to simply *emphasize* a word or term, and usually these referred to historical or secular concepts.... there are exceptions to both rules. However, when you see highlighted text, it is a sign to pay close attention to the concept being presented. Finally, out of utmost respect for God the Father and Christ the Son: I have tried to capitalize any word which directly refers to either. In fact, one of the forgotten literary conventions of the Original King James Bible was that any reference to **God** which applied to God the Father was capitalized. I have extended this convention to the **Son** of God out of respect for his holy name.

What a glorious journey it will be for all of those who take the time to read and study the things which were recorded by the Apostle John in the Book of Revelation. It may come as a surprise to many to know that God has placed a special set of blessings upon you for studying these things. A special blessing (beatitude) has been promised for all who read and study these words.

> **Blessed** is *he that readeth, and they that hear the words of this prophecy, and keep those things which are written therein* (Rev 1:3)

The world is captivated by people like Nostradamus and Edgar Casey who have claimed that they can see into the future; and who would not like to be able to predict the future with certainty? For sure, there have been men (prophets) of old that have accurately prophesied about future events. But, in all cases their words of prophesy were inspired and guided by God's thoughts.

> *"Knowing this first, that no prophecy of the scripture is of any private interpretation. For the prophecy came not in old time by the will of man: but holy men of God spake as they were moved by the Holy Ghost. But there were false prophets also among the people, even as there shall be false teachers among you, who privily shall bring in damnable heresies, even denying the Lord that bought them, and bring upon themselves swift destruction. And many shall follow their pernicious ways; by reason of whom the way of truth shall be evil spoken of "*   II Peter 1:19-21, 2:1-2

Do not be lured into the snare of buying books that tell of the future. Avoid soothsayers and fortune tellers. There is only one book ever written that will accurately and faithfully teach you what the future holds. Saints, I can assure every one of you reading this preface that the Book of Revelation is the only book which has ever been written or will ever be written that describes things which will surely come to pass. John the revelator wrote:

> *"The angel said to me, "these sayings are faithful and true: and the Lord God of the holy prophets sent His angel to shew unto His servants the things which must shortly be done"*   Rev 22:6

Enjoy your journey and prepare for the Lord…. He is coming again soon.

                         Don T. Phillips
                         September, 2012

Overview

This book presents evidence to support that the Tribulation Period is 3.5 years, 1260 days, 42 Months long and not 7 years as commonly taught. The 7 seal judgments are not time sequenced, but provide an overview of the tribulation period. The 1260 days are divided into two major time periods: (1) One of 1250 days during which the Antichrist and the False Prophet persecute those who refuse to worship Satan and the Antichrist. The 7 Trumpet judgments take place over this 1250 day period of satanic persecution. (2) A period of 10 days in which the 7 bowl judgments are poured out upon the earth and the kingdom of the antichrist. The 7 bowl judgments are the *Wrath of God*.

We will present strong evidence that the rapture and resurrection of all saints takes place as the 7th trumpet sounds, just before God pours out His wrath in the the 7 bowl judgments. Hence, this book presents sound scriptural arguments for a *new* **Pre-Wrath Rapture** theory. The final defeat of Satan and his followers takes place at the Battle of Armageddon which will occur after the 1260 days (The last half of Daniel's 70th week) have run their course. The following diagram provides a graphic and time sequenced overview of the Book of Revelation. Welcome to the future! The following topics are all discussed in this book. The topics described are in a logically consistent and chronological order, but we would never break faith over the

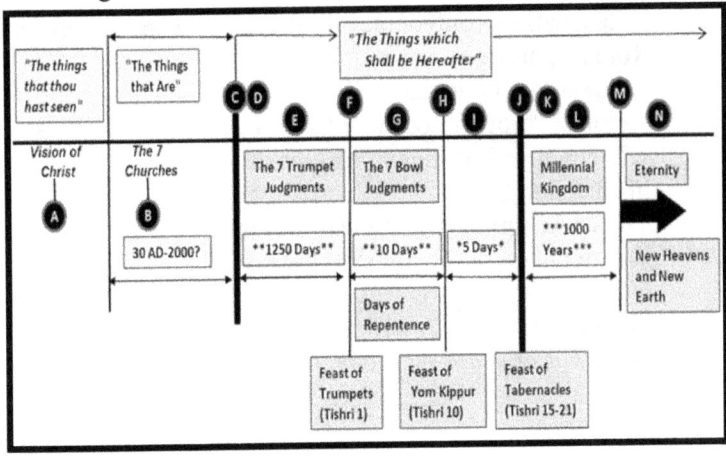

exact sequence in which they are presented. The previous diagram has ⬤ circles containing the letters A-N positioned across the timeline. The key events which will occur either at these points in time, are summarized in the following paragraphs.

A John is a prisoner on the Island of Patmos when he is called to see the future.
- The Heavenly Throne of God
- Vision of Christ

B John is told to record and deliver 7 letters addressed to the 7 Churches in Asia.
- Ephesus
- Smyrna
- Pergamum
- Thyatira
- Sardis
- Philadelphia
- Laodicea

C Before the 1260 day tribulation period can begin, the following things must take place.
- A ten nation confederacy will arise out of the ancient Roman Empire.
- A great world leader will arise from among these 10 nations. Through political, oratory and military skills he will conquer 3 of the tan nations, then unify all ten under his dictatorship.
- The exact timing is not clear, but this great world leader will manage to establish peace in Israel and rebuild Herod's Temple. He will then likely be proclaimed as the long awaited Jewish Messiah. He will establish a ***covenant of death*** with Israel.

D It is not clear exactly what prophesied event will actually start the last 3.5 years of Daniel's 70th week. There are two possibilities, and both are very close to one another chronologically. (1) The tribulation period will begin with a great heavenly war (Rev 12: 1-9) or (2) it will begin just *after* Satan and his angels are cast down to earth. We believe that the Tribulation period will begin just after Satan is defeated and cast down. The immanency of the tribulation period will be signaled to all who have studied Rev 12 with a *sign* in the heavens. This *sign* will be a great heavenly conflict between Satan and his angels and Michael and his angels. We believe that the entire world will see this battle, possibly as a great cosmic disturbance. Over some unknown period of time, Satan will be defeated and cast to the earth with 1/3 of all the angelic beings (Rev 12:4)

- Just before Satan is cast down, a *Man Child* is raptured to the Heavenly Mt. Zion. These are the *firstfruits* unto God.
- The world leader will be wounded with a knife unto death; he will be revived by Satan and become the hated Antichrist.

The Tribulation Period now begins. In rapid succession, the following events occur.

- The Beast out of the Sea emerges, which will rule over the world leaders mind and body. This is the Antichrist.
- The Beast out of the Earth arises to support the Antichrist with a worldwide religious system called Babylon the Great…. This is the False Prophet.
- The Antichrist and his armies will turn on Israel and attack Jerusalem. This will be called *The Jerusalem Campaign*.
- The Antichrist and his forces will be supernaturally turned away.
- 144,000 from 12 tribes of Israel will be sealed
- The *Little Scroll* is shown to John

- ➤ Two Witnesses stand in the temple to warn everyone: *Do not take the mark of the beast.*

E The 7 trumpet judgments are unleashed.
   Trumpets 5-7 are called the *Three Woes*

F The first 1250 days of the tribulation period will come to a close with two major events which will occur in close proximity to one another.

- ➤ The two witnesses are slain and lie dead in the street.
- ➤ The rapture of all saints (living) and the resurrection of all saints (dead) occur as the 7th trumpet sounds on the Feast of Trumpets (Tishri 1). Every believer in Christ has been removed from the earth at the 7th trump.

G The next 10 days bring the Wrath of God: The 7 Bowl Judgments. Four major heavenly events also take place over this short period of time.

- ➤ The Bema Seat Judgment of believers takes place in Heaven.
- ➤ The Two Witnesses are raised and taken to heaven
- ➤ The Marriage of the Lamb takes place in Heaven
- ➤ The 7 Bowl Judgments are poured out over a short period of time (10 days).

H The 10 day period of God's Wrath ends on Nisan 10: The Feast of Yom Kippur. The most important battle in the history of the world takes place on this day.

- ➤ The Battle of Armageddon ends the Tribulation period

I Between the Feast of Yom Kippur on Nisan 10 and the Feast of Tabernacles on Nisan 15, the following events occur.
- The 144,000 sealed Jews will be assembled with those that survived the Tribulation Period to live in the land. This is the fulfillment of God's Covenant with Abraham.
- The Antichrist and the False Prophet are cast into the Lake of Fire
- Satan is cast into the Bottomless Pit for 1000 years (The Millennial Kingdom).
- The Rod Judgment takes place in the wilderness
- The Judgment of the Sheep and Goat Nations takes place in Jerusalem

J The *Joyous Feast of Tabernacles* (Tishri 15-22) takes place in Jerusalem to celebrate the defeat of Satan and the Antichrist.

K Following the last great day of Tabernacles on Tishri 22, establishing the reign of Christ will be initiated, and a Period of Restoration will take place. It is likely that the 1000 year Millennial Kingdom begins on Tishri 23; but this is speculation. It might begin on Tishri 11 or Tishri 15…. The exact day is unimportant.

L The millennial Kingdom of 1000 years will now be established and run its course.

- The Throne where Christ will rule and reign over the nations is set in place
- The land is cleansed
- The Temple is cleansed and restored in Jerusalem
- The temple is Dedicated 75 days after the Feast of Yom Kippur on the Feast of Dedication.

- King David is set upon his throne to rule over Israel
- The land is divided, and Israel inherits the Land

Israel will live in the Promised Land for 1000 years. Everyone will prosper, and the life span of man will be very long.... some possibly 1000 years or longer. However, Adam's curse will overcome some and they will rebel against Christ. The earth will need to be destroyed and all sin purged as in the Days of Noah.

M After the 1000 years have passed, the following events will take place.

- Satan will be loosed for a *short while*. He will gather all rebels and unbelievers out of the world
- The last great battle which we call *Satan's Last Stand* will take place in Jerusalem.
- Satan and all evil in the world will finally be destroyed at the last great battle: *Satan's Last Stand*
- Satan is cast into eternal punishment in the Lake of Burning Fire
- Death and Hell are cast into the Lake of Burning Fire
- The judgment of all unbelievers from all ages now takes place: The **Great White Throne Judgment**.

N The earth is now completely renovated and all things on it destroyed by Fire. Eternity now begins.

- A new Heaven and New Earth appears for eternal habitation
- The eternal throne of God and Christ is set in place on this earth, and eternity has arrived

Each of these things will be discussed in detail in the next 22 chapters. May God bless you as you study his Holy Word. The journey to eternity will be exciting!!

Chapter 1

The Call from Heaven

Introduction

"The Revelation of Jesus Christ, which God gave unto him, to shew unto his servants things which must shortly come to pass; and he sent and signified it by his angel unto his servant John: Who bare record of the word of God, and of the testimony of Jesus Christ, and of all things that he saw. Blessed is he that readeth, and they that hear the words of this prophecy, and keep those things which are written therein: for the time is at hand."   Rev 1:1-3

The Greek word for Revelation is *apokalupsis* which means to *unveil* or to *uncover*. The Book of Revelation is meant to complete the record of the Church Age which started in 30 AD at the Feast of Pentecost. The end of this age is the 1000 year millennial kingdom and then eternity, when new heavens and a new earth will be formed. It also completes the reign of sin over the earth and of that old serpent Satan who brings sin and eternal damnation to mankind. The book of Revelation is the only book ever written that predicts with certainty things that will occur in the future. It may come as a surprise to many Christians, but it is also the only book ever written in which all that *read or hear the words* will be blessed. In fact, the blessing promised is threefold: (1) anyone who *reads* it will be blessed, (2) anyone who *hears* it will be blessed, and (3) anyone who *keeps the commandments* in this book will be blessed. I suspect that everyone can use blessings from God, so be prepared to be spiritually and intellectually blessed. There are those who teach and believe that the book is just a collection of fictitious symbols and symbolism. Those who say that the book is not describing real events have not even read and understood the first verse! Pity those people, for the events of this book *will come to pass*. As we will show in later chapters, those unprepared Christians will have to go through most of the tribulation period. We are immediately told that John did not dream these things nor was it revealed to him in a vision, he actually *saw* these things with his own eyes. In Rev 4:1, we are told that John saw a door standing open in heaven, a voice *like a trumpet* told him to *Come up here, and I will show you things*. We are told in Rev 1:1 that the message is to *his servants*. The Greek word translated servants is *doulos*. It is used 120 times in the New Testament, and is used by the apostle Paul in Romans Chapter 6.

> *"For sin shall not have dominion over you: for ye are not under the law, but under grace. What then? shall we sin, because we are not under the law, but under grace? God forbid. Know ye not, that to whom ye yield yourselves* servants *to obey, his* servants *ye are to whom ye obey; whether of sin unto death, or of obedience unto righteousness? But God be thanked, that ye were the* servants *of sin, but ye have obeyed from the heart that form of doctrine which was delivered you. Being then made free from sin, ye became the* servants *of righteousness. I speak after the manner of men because of the infirmity of your flesh: for as ye have yielded your members* servants *to uncleanness and to iniquity unto iniquity; even so now yield your members* servants *to righteousness unto holiness."*
> Romans 6:14-19

It is clear that the servants to whom this revelation is given are those who are sanctified, justified and glorified under the new covenant.

The Salutation

> *"John, to the seven churches which are in Asia: Grace be unto you, and peace, from him which is, and which was, and which is to come; and from the seven Spirits which are before his throne; And from Jesus Christ, who is the faithful witness, and the first begotten of the dead, and the prince of the kings of the earth. Unto him that loved us, and washed us from our sins in his own blood, And hath made*

us kings and priests unto God and his Father; to him be glory and dominion for ever and ever. Amen." Rev 1:4-6

John reaffirms that he is the author of the book. We are now told where the book is to be initially read; in the seven churches of Asia (Roman Asia Minor). The seven churches to be addressed are Ephesus, Smyrna, Pergamum, Thyatira, Sardis, Philadelphia and Laodicea. It is believed that the apostle Paul established all seven churches on his visits to Asia. There were, of course, many other churches outside of Israel. These seven were chosen because they were representative of all the churches which would be formed during the church age. The book of Revelation is a book of *sevens,* seven being the biblical number of *completion or perfection*.

- There are 7 churches (Rev 1:4)
- There are 7 Spirits at God's throne (Rev 1:4, 3:1, 4:5 and 5:6)
- There are 7 candlesticks (Rev 1:12, 1:13, 1:20 and 2:1)
- There are 7 stars (Rev 1:16, 1:20, 2:1 and 3:1)
- There are 7 lamps (Rev 4:5)
- There are 7 Seals (Rev 5:1, 5:5)
- There are 7 Trumpets (Rev 8:2, 8:6)
- There are 7 Bowls (Rev 15:7, 17:1, 21:9)
- There are 7 Horns (Rev 5:6)
- There are 7 Eyes (Rev 5:6)
- There are 7 Angels standing before God (Rev 8:2, 8:6)
- There are 7 Thunders (Rev 10:3, 10:4)
- There are 7 Thousand People Killed (Rev 11:13)
- There are 7 Heads (Rev 12:3, 13:1, 17:3, 17:7, 17:9)
- There are 7 Crowns (Rev 12:3)
- There are 7 Angels with 7 Bowls (Rev 15:1)
- There are 7 Mountains (Rev 17:9)
- There are 7 Kings (Rev 17:10-11)

The repetition of the number *seven* indicates that God has a perfect plan for His earth, and that everything has been predetermined. The number seven persists throughout the holy writ; there are seven dispensations or ages, there are seven Holy

Feasts of Israel, there are seven High Holy Days, a week has seven days, the last three prophetic feasts which herald the second coming of Christ are in the seventh Jewish month, creation took six days and on the seventh day God rested... etc.

The salutation continues by citing from whom it is spoken: ***him which is, and which was, and which is to come.*** The identification of *him* has caused much controversy. Some say this salutation is from God the Father and some say it is from Christ. However, there is really no controversy since Christ is identified in the very next verse. Christ is described in three ways: (1) He is the *faithful witness,* (2) He is the *first begotten from the dead,* and (3) He is the *Prince of the Kings of the earth.* Notice that Christ is identified as a separate personage from God in the salutation. This confirms the *mystery* of the Trinity; Father, Son and Holy Ghost. Yet, they are unity in operation and holiness. The Holy Trinity is prominently displayed in the first chapter of the book of Revelation; they are the triune Godhead. Christ is our *faithful witness*. He sits at the right hand of God on His throne and faithfully intercedes for us; He was faithful in all that God gave Him to do; He was faithful to the death; and He will never forsake us. It is reaffirmed that the real rulers of this earth are not Satan's princes, not kings, not presidents, and not dictators, but our Lord Jesus Christ.

> *"For he hath put all things under his feet. But when he saith, all things are put under him, it is manifest that he is excepted, which did put all things under him."*
> I Corinthians 15:27

Christ loves us and *washed* our sins away with His own blood on the cross of Calvary. Oh how He loves us!

> *"Who shall separate us from the love of Christ? Shall tribulation, or distress, or persecution, or famine, or nakedness, or peril, or sword? Nay, in all these things we are more than conquerors through him that loved us. Nor height, nor depth, nor any other creature, shall be able to*

> *separate us from the love of God, which is in Christ Jesus our Lord."* Romans 8:35-39

Christ's love for us transcends time as we know it. He has declared that we will reign forever as **Kings and Priests**.

> *"And they sang a new song, saying, Thou art worthy to take the book, and to open the seals thereof: for thou wast slain, and hast redeemed us to God by thy blood out of every kindred, and tongue, and people, and nation; And hast made us unto our God kings and priests: and we shall reign on the earth."* Rev 5:9-10

The Coming and Character of Christ

> *"Behold, he cometh with clouds; and every eye shall see him, and they also which pierced him: and all kindreds of the earth shall wail because of him. Even so, Amen. I am Alpha and Omega, the beginning and the ending, saith the Lord, which is, and which was, and which is to come, the Almighty."* Rev 1:7-8

Suddenly with no transition, the apostle John presents the first prophetic revelation in the book. The opening word *behold* reinforces the fact that John *saw* all of the things he is about to record. The impact of the opening statement frames the entire message put forth in the book of Revelation; the triumphant Second Advent of our Lord Jesus Christ. The scene is projected all the way to the end of the tribulation period when Christ returns to fight the battle of Armageddon.

> *"And I saw heaven opened, and behold a white horse; and he that sat upon him was called Faithful and True, and in righteousness he doth judge and make war. His eyes were as a flame of fire, and on his head were many crowns; and he had a name written, that no man knew, but he himself. And he was clothed with a vesture dipped in blood: and his name is called The Word of God. And the armies which were in heaven followed him upon white horses, clothed in fine*

linen, white and clean. And out of his mouth goeth a sharp sword, that with it he should smite the nations: and he shall rule them with a rod of iron: and he treadeth the winepress of the fierceness and wrath of Almighty God. And he hath on his vesture and on his thigh a name written, KING OF KINGS, AND LORD OF LORDS."   Rev 19:11-16

The triumphant return of Jesus Christ is the culmination of God's plan for all mankind which started in the Garden of Eden, and it is the fulfillment of what was foretold by the prophets of old.

"I saw in the night visions, and, behold, one like the Son of man came with the clouds of heaven, and came to the Ancient of days, and they brought him near before him. And there was given him dominion, and glory, and a kingdom, that all people, nations, and languages, should serve him: his dominion is an everlasting dominion, which shall not pass away, and his kingdom that which shall not be destroyed."   Daniel 7:13-14

This prophecy recorded by Daniel reaffirms that at His second advent, Christ will be seen by everyone, particularly the Jews who crucified Him and the Romans who pierced His side while on the cross of Calvary. At that time there will not only be a great celebration (Rev 19:6), but great lamentations and wailing(Rev 18:19). We will show in subsequent chapters that the second advent of Christ is likely to take place on the *Feast of Yom Kippur*. Unlike the joyous rapture of the Church, when all living Saints will rise to meet Him in the air at the Feast of Trumpets, at the second advent of Christ, **all kindred's of the earth shall wail**. The time for salvation has ended, and the time for vindication has come. Those who will be left will have universally rejected salvation through Christ, and now those who are alive at His second advent must pay the consequences. The angel says **amen**, let it be so.

The next utterance is in the first person and is undoubtedly from *Jesus Christ*. He declares Himself to be **Alpha and Omega**. This phrase is used by Christ here in the first chapter, and also in the last chapter, Rev 22.

> *"And, behold, I come quickly; and my reward is with me, to give every man according as his work shall be. I am Alpha and Omega, the beginning and the end, the first and the last."* Rev 22:12-13

Finally, we are reassured that the Lord we serve is not dead, but lives forever. The Muslims, Buddhists and other man-made religions serve dead gods, but we serve a *living God*! He **was, and is, and is to come.** Like Christ, we proclaim *amen!* Let it be so; come quickly Lord Jesus.

The Messenger and the One Who Sends the Message

> *"I John, who also am your brother, and companion in tribulation, and in the kingdom and patience of Jesus Christ, was in the isle that is called Patmos, for the word of God, and for the testimony of Jesus Christ. I was in the Spirit on the Lord's day, and heard behind me a great voice, as of a trumpet, Saying, I am Alpha and Omega, the first and the last: and, What thou seest, write in a book, and send it unto the seven churches which are in Asia; unto Ephesus, and unto Smyrna, and unto Pergamos, and unto Thyatira, and unto Sardis, and unto Philadelphia, and unto Laodicea. And I turned to see the voice that spake with me. And being turned, I saw seven golden candlesticks; And in the midst of the seven candlesticks one like unto the Son of man, clothed with a garment down to the foot, and girt about the paps with a golden girdle. His head and his hairs were white like wool, as white as snow; and his eyes were as a flame of fire; And his feet like unto fine brass, as if they burned in a furnace; and his voice as the sound of many waters. And he had in his right hand seven stars: and out of his mouth went a sharp two edged sword: and his countenance was as the sun shineth in his strength. And when I saw him, I fell at his feet as dead. And he laid his right hand upon me, saying*

unto me, Fear not; I am the first and the last: I am he that liveth, and was dead; and, behold, I am alive for evermore, Amen; and have the keys of hell and of death. Write the things which thou hast seen, and the things which are, and the things which shall be hereafter; The mystery of the seven stars which thou sawest in my right hand, and the seven golden candlesticks. The seven stars are the angels of the seven churches: and the seven candlesticks which thou sawest are the seven churches."   Rev 1: 9-20

Although there has been theological debate on who actually wrote the book of Revelation, we have no doubts whatsoever that the author is the apostle John who has been exiled by the Roman Emperor to the island of Patmos. John had been boldly preaching the gospel, and he was arrested and exiled as a political agitator. John was the last of the original 12 disciples, all of whom had been martyred for preaching the gospel. We should take note that even the inner circle that Jesus chose, his beloved disciples, were not spared from horrible deaths. The apostle Paul wrote in many places how he had suffered and was persecuted for Christ's sake. We should take careful note that if these founding fathers were not spared from tribulation, why should we casually wait around for a pre-tribulation rapture and escape tribulation? We will see later that there will be a group of saints who will *escape all of these things* (Luke 2:16); they are called the *overcomers* in each of the seven churches But the majority of Christians will have the privilege, *yes* the privilege, of going through what has been called the tribulation period and winning many souls to Christ.

John was *in the spirit* on *the Lord's Day*. This phrase has also sparked considerable controversy. The context has been confused with the concept that John had been transformed into a spirit-state to receive the revelation. There is no license or indication that this is inferred here. It is more likely that John is in a state of deep prayer in which as Lenski put it, *"A state in which the ordinary faculties of the flesh have been suspended and the inner senses opened"*. John is probably regularly praying in this state; he is seeking a closer communication and state of intimacy with his Lord Jesus Christ whom he longs to see again. The *Lord's Day* has been interpreted to mean either the Jewish Sabbath (Saturday) or Sunday. In the context of how the modern Sabbath day emerged as Sunday, and the theme of Christ renewing his covenant with the church throughout this book, we believe that the best interpretation is Sunday and not Saturday. By the end of the second century AD, the *Day of the Lord* in reference to the Sabbath was almost universally accepted as Sunday because Christ rose from the dead early on Sunday. The gospel accounts also record how the disciples observed the Jewish Sabbath on Saturday, even after the death of Christ, but also worshipped on Sunday to make that day holy unto Christ. The *voice of a trumpet* is a common theme throughout the entire book of Revelation. It heralds the calling of John to record what he is shown; John is told to come to heaven to **see these things** by a **voice** which was penetrating and loud **like the sound of a trumpet** (Rev 4:1). When the period of tribulation begins to run its course, there are seven trumpet judgments which will be announced by a loud trump (Rev 8:2, 6, 13); the four demonic angels loosed from the Euphrates are told to come forth by a trumpet (Rev 9:14); and the rapture of the church will be initiated by the sound of a trumpet (I Thess 4:16-18, I Cor 15:51-52).

John is next commanded to **write in a book**, what he sees, and to send the book to the **seven churches in Asia** (Rev 1:11). It seems clear that John is commissioned to write an entire book, and to also send a personal letter to each of the seven churches. It appears that the seven letters to the seven churches in Rev 2-3 are separate, personal messages from Christ, but they are all meant to be read by each church. The issue is not important; it is only important to know that this is not a secret book but one which was to be read and shared in all the churches. We should heed this message today and hear more sermons from the pulpit on the contents and messages of these 7 letters.

Christ next reaffirms that he is eternal and that He is **alpha and omega.** The strength of this phrase is that alpha is the first letter in the Greek alphabet and omega is the last. Christ is reaffirming that in Him all things are complete. He is *the first and the last* and *the beginning and the end* (Rev 22:12).

John next hears a *voice like thunder* and he turns to see *seven golden lampstands*. The Greek translation in the KJV of *lampstands* is best interpreted as candlesticks. We are not confused as to what these represent. We are told in Rev 1:20 that the seven candlesticks represent the *seven churches* of Rev 2-3. The symbolism is clear. The 7 Churches to whom these letters are directed represent all of the churches today; 7 being the biblical number of completeness. However, the *church* is only a building; the real church is its *members*. All Christians are to *let their light shine*. Christ said that we are to be the *light of the world* (Mat 5:14). The simile comes from the *menorah*. The menorah was a lampstand with seven pipes that stood in Herod's Temple in Jerusalem. However, there is likely a deeper spiritual symbolism implied since the menorah was a Jewish artifact in the Tabernacle of Moses under the old economy. The menorah received its oil from a common reservoir, and the seven pipes were of no use without that source. Oil in the new covenant often represents the Holy Spirit, and the seven pipes are symbolic of the witness of salvation through Jesus Christ in each of the seven churches. John immediately recognizes Christ standing *in the midst of the seven candlesticks*. What a glorious picture of how Christ operates through his people. He is in the midst of the seven churches, constantly moving about to minister to and through His saints. In each of the letters to the seven churches, He constantly speaks, saying; *I know*, *I know*. Christ *knows* what is going on; He is constantly watching and waiting; He is moving through the Body of Christ… *HE KNOWS*.

The personage which John now sees evidently surprised him and overcame him with awe. In Rev 1:17 we are told that *he fell at His feet as if dead*. The last time John saw Christ on the day of Pentecost he appeared as the *suffering servant*. Now, he is dazzling and majestic. He is clothed with a garment (likely white) *from head to foot,* He is girded with a *golden sash about His waist,* His hair was *white like wool*, His feet like *fine brass* and his voice like the sound of *many waters*; deafening and majestic like Niagara Falls. He is called *like the Son of Man*, Christ's favorite expression of Himself when He was on this earth. The dress is characteristic of those garments worn by the High Priest in their service in the temple. His appearance is the same as that seen by Daniel.

> *"...the Ancient of days did sit, whose garment was white as snow, and the hair of his head like the pure wool: his throne was like the fiery flame, and his wheels as burning fire."*
> Daniel 7:9

> *"Then I lifted up mine eyes, and looked, and behold a certain man clothed in linen, whose loins were girded with fine gold of Uphaz: His body also was like the beryl, and his face as the appearance of lightning, and his eyes as lamps of fire, and his arms and his feet like in colour to polished brass, and the voice of his words like the voice of a multitude."* Daniel 10:5-6

The mental picture is certainly one of *righteousness and majesty*, but it also a picture of the eternal character of the Son. He existed when the world was framed, He existed in Daniel's day, and He exists today. He is the one *which is, which was and which is to come* (Rev 1:2). His *feet of burning bronze* almost certainly stand for *judgment,* and ultimately the eternal separation of the righteous from the unrighteous. In ancient times, the precious wheat was brought to the *threshing floor* where oxen shod with brass feet would trample the wheat. The husks would be separated from the precious grains of wheat, and then the wind *(Holy Spirit)* would separate the wheat from the chaff; then the precious wheat would be stored in the barn. This is a beautiful picture of the **Parable of the Wheat and the Tares** (Mat 21:3) and how Christ will separate His elect (the wheat) from the *tares of the world*. It is also beautifully and prophetically acted out in the Old Testament by the story of *Ruth and Boaz*, and how Ruth came to the threshing floor at midnight seeking the kinsman redeemer (Ruth 2:1-23).

Continuing what John saw, he *fell at His feet as if Dead*. Our merciful King then said *fear not* to John. Oh Saints, these two simple words bring tears to our eyes as we pen this book. I pray and hope that anyone reading this book will understand these two words: *Fear not*. Are we not fearful that we have all sinned and fallen short of the glory of God? Have we not all cast our doubts and fears upon our Lord and Savior? Have we not all been fearful that Christ does not hear our prayers? Will we not all be fearful that when we finally stand before God at the *Bema Seat Judgment* that we will be found unworthy to enter into His presence? (Rev 11:15-18) Listen to these words and believe them. Christ said **FEAR NOT**. Praise His name forever and ever for saving us by grace and not by works. We have all sinned and fallen short of the Glory of God, but *fear not*.

Christ next reassures John and each of us that He *IS* the risen Christ. He also assures us that He will lay His mighty right hand, the hand of judgment and wrath, on us, and will say: ***I am the first and the last; I am He that liveth and was dead; and behold I am alive forevermore***; ***behold I live and through My resurrection and power over death you shall live also***. No exposition can do His words justice. He has conquered death and is alive forevermore. Because we believe that He is the Son of God, that He was dead, buried and resurrected to the Father, we will be also. *Fear not*, He says.

Having reassured John that He is alive forevermore and ruling over all creation, He now commands John to **write the things which thou hast seen, and the things which are, and the things which will be hereafter.** These simple words provide us with an outline of the book of Revelation. The *things which thou hast seen* clearly refer to what we have just examined Rev 1:1, Rev 1:20. The *things which are* refer to the seven churches which existed when John is called to record the assessment of each church as it is given to him. This is found in Rev 3-4. The *things which shall be hereafter* are the things which are recorded in Rev 4:1, Rev 22:21. In fact, we will hold to the belief that not one thing that John sees after Rev 6:1 has yet occurred; they are all future. The reader might note that we break with traditional commentaries to characterize the things which John sees in Rev 4:1-4:9 as not being in the future. John is taken through an open door in Rev 4:1, and this happened when he was on the Island of Patmos. He immediately sees heaven and God's throne in all of its glory. We suggest that the throne of God, the four living creatures and the 24 elders surrounding the throne were there in circa 90-93 AD and are there today, just as John saw them. This will be the subject of Chapter 3. Finally, a *mystery* is revealed to John. The concept of a biblical mystery is not what we understand as a modern mystery novel or something that we cannot immediately understand. A biblical mystery is something that has been either unknown or concealed until it is explained by a message from God. The *mystery* revealed at this point in time is that: **The seven stars are the angels of the seven churches: and the seven candlesticks which thou sawest are the seven churches**. Here a wonderful and comforting message is given to every church, every pastor and every congregation. There is a *star* assigned to each church and that star is an *angel*! Imagine that!! Every group of Christians gathered together in His holy name has a guardian angel assigned to them who will help the body of Christ (the church) through god times and bad times. Stay the course… stay in the word… and stay in God's care.

This concludes *the things which John saw*; it is now time to discuss the *things which are*, or the Letters to the Seven Churches in Asia.

Thoughts and Things.........

Chapter 2

Letters to the Seven Churches

In Revelation Chapter 1, the prophet John was *in the spirit* on the Lord's Day and was called to the presence of our Lord Jesus Christ by a *great voice as the sound of a trumpet*. John was permitted to see Christ in his post-resurrection glory, and was told to *write the things which thou hast seen*, which he did. The second command was to *write the things which are*, which is an assessment by Christ of the seven Churches which existed at that time in Asia, which today would be known as Greece. Recall in Rev 1:13 we saw the risen Christ walking among the seven *lampstands*, which represented these seven churches in Asia. It should be clearly understood that Christ was watching each of the seven churches then, and He is watching every church today. As He walks among His Churches, any deed good or bad will not go unnoticed. Denominational churches who think that apportionments and gifts to abortion clinics, leadership given to sexually abusive pastors and teachings that depart from the everlasting gospel will go unnoticed are sadly mistaken. Although each church received a personal letter which clearly revealed that Christ knew everything that was going on in that church, it is clear that Christ intended each letter to be circulated and read at every church. Although there were seven distinct churches, each was simply a geographical manifestation of the

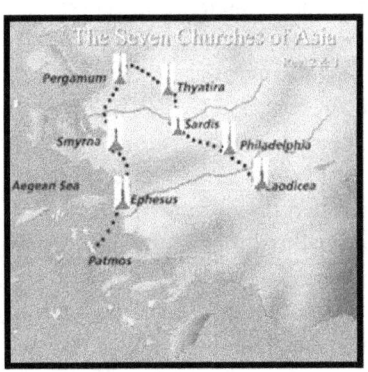

body of Christ. It is incorrect to state as some have that these were the only churches in Asia that Christ was watching. For example, a strong church founded by Paul in Collossi has been omitted. The force of the seven letters is not one of total completeness, but everything that Christ condemned and hated then, he will condemn and hate today. Each individual letter and the set of seven letters provide to us a *template* by which each church today can judge themselves. Hence, we must carefully and prayerfully also scrutinize each letter and examine both the corporate and private relationship to the risen savior. The seven churches were all in close proximity to one another in Western Asia Minor, and starting with Ephesus on the Western seacoast they were arranged in a roughly circular pattern moving North, East, South and back to the West. Each of the seven churches existed in a city of the same name. It is interesting that God never intended to have multiple denominations and different theologically chartered churches in every city. The church which Jesus Christ founded was to be universal, and each was to preach the same saving gospel of Jesus Christ. In the New Testament, every time a church is mentioned it corresponded to a city and not a local denomination. For example, the founding church was simply the church at Jerusalem. The time at which the seven churches in Asia existed was approximately 90-93 AD, about 60 years after the day of Pentecost. As we will see, in this short amount of time each church existed under a different vision of our Lord Jesus Christ, and that vision generally reflected the need of each city to receive the unique blessings which was required in that local community. We will also see that except for the churches at Philadelphia and Smyrna, in that very short period of time each church had already apostatized into some sinful practice or worldly compromise that Christ hated. Today as we prepare for the second coming of Jesus Christ, each church regardless of denomination needs to be a full-gospel church striving to fully understand and follow the full counsel of the Holy Scriptures. Fortunately, our salvation does not depend upon our full and complete knowledge of our Savior, which is impossible to comprehend in its fullness, but we can rest in his grace and the finished work of the cross. The seven churches are not only identified by name, but also by the meaning of the name. The church names represented the seven churches to which a letter was addressed, but the fundamental message conveyed to each Church is characterized by the meaning of each name.

Ephesus......... Desirable
Smyrna......... Offering of Sacrifice
Pergamum... Much married, adulterous
Thyatira... .... Sacrifice of Labor
Sardis............ Remnant
Philadelphia...Brotherly Love
Laodicea......... Judgment and Justice

We will see that each of the seven letters is uniquely directed to the individual Church, but each of the letters was not meant to be confined in either meaning or presentation to each individual church. In each letter, John records the words of Christ which are *He that hath an ear, let him hear what the spirit says to the churches*. It is certain that each letter was initially delivered to and read by each church initially, then transmitted to the next church in the circular pattern of churches until it returned. Each letter is addressed to the angel of each church...*Unto the angel of the Church*. The English word *angel* comes from the Greek work ***angelos***, which can be interpreted as either an angel or a messenger. Since each letter is written to the ***Hagios*** (*saints)* or the *ecclesia* (*chosen ones*) in each church and not to an angel, the best interpretation is that the letters were sent to the *messenger* of each church or by implication to the pastor of each church, who then read it to the congregation. Each of the letters reveals an important characteristic of our Lord Jesus Christ.

To the church at Ephesus he says *I know*…. to the church at Smyrna he says *I know*… to every church he says *I know*. In Rev 1, John's first vision of Christ saw him walking in the midst of the **seven candlesticks** which are the seven churches (Rev 1:13, 20). In his right hand he held the **seven stars** which are the *angelos* of every church (Rev 1: 20). His eyes were seen as a *flame of fire* (Rev 1: 14). Christ knows everything, sees everything, watches everything, he *knows*. The pastor of every church today and the members of each congregation who attend each church should note these things with fear and trembling, but also with thanksgiving for God's grace. We all fall short of the glory of God, but: **For unto whomsoever much is given, of him shall there be much required** (Luke 13:48). The business of God's kingdom here on Earth is not just the job of the pastor or of the lay leaders, but to each of us is expected much. Everyone has a gift to offer, in proportion to that which has been given to him.

Each of the seven letters is unique in their message to the Church, but with a few exceptions each has a common format.

Concept of who Christ is and how the Church sees Him
Commendation of works
Condemnation of those things that Christ hates
Counsel to the Church and its members
Comments on other things going on in the Church
Covenant to those that **Overcome**…*A covenant is a promise*
Conclusions and **Warnings** to those who will not hear His voice

The purpose of each letter has been suggested under three different scenarios. First, it is obvious that each of the letters were addressed to seven actual churches which existed at the time the Revelation was received. The purpose of each letter was to summarize the things that Jesus liked about each church, state the practices that Jesus hated at each church, and encourage each church to redeem itself and to warn that if the church does not repent the consequence will be the removal of its candlestick. Second, it became popular in the 19th century to identify each church with a period of time during the Church Age that each church represented, from the day of Pentecost until the tribulation period commences. Third, the letters were written to both the seven churches which existed then, and to each church which exists today. Since God is the same *yesterday, today, and tomorrow*, the things which He hated then, He would hate now; the things which He commended then, He would commend now. We should carefully note that God cannot and will not accept any form of sin or sinful practices. There are churches today that tolerate abortion, adultery and poor doctrine. These practices are hated by God, and they will eventually *have their candlestick removed* if they do not repent. After considering these three positions, we have decided that the first and third are correct but cannot fully support the second. It is certainly possible that one could point to the characteristics of a particular period in time and match those to one of the churches. However, there are certain observations which suggest that this may be coincidental and possibly meaningless. The main problem is that each of the seven churches which existed in John's day describe issues and problems that could not only fit the churches then, but at any time in the past 2000 years. Second, if there are specific time periods associated with each of the seven churches there would be considerable overlap, and in all cases the problems which existed then in each church continue to undermine the churches of today. Third, the entire book of Revelation is primarily directed to events that are yet future to the current time. From Rev 4 to Rev 22, all of the events revealed to the prophet John are yet to come. If each church to which a letter is addressed represents a past period of time, the basic message of the book is out of sorts. Even if a positive identification of each church description to a particular period of time could be firmly established, what would it mean as epochs of time passed? For one thing, the premise of each passing generation to be watchful and the clearly relevant principle of eminency would be completely destroyed. Third, if one takes the time to characterize and assess the wide range of denominational beliefs that exist today, it is clear that each of the seven churches that existed in John's day exist today in one form are another. Finally, it would be irresponsible to the body of Christ today to ignore the things which Christ commended and condemned in the collective set of letters. There has been too much theological debate and focus on which church best represents which era of time, and not enough focus on what is the central message that was sent to the churches in the first century, and the message to be heard in all the churches which exist today. Hence, when we discuss each of the seven letters to the seven churches, we will first describe the physical setting in which the church existed, and the beliefs and practices which dominated the culture of each community. Each individual letter will then be analyzed, and conclude with what is being said to the churches of today in the context of each letter. We will see that like the denominational focus of many congregations and pastors of today, each church had only a partial knowledge of Jesus Christ, and each was tolerating some form of local spiritual corruption from the community in which it existed. The true church will not tolerate anything which our Lord Jesus Christ hates, and recognize that the corrupting influence of Satan that was in each of the churches of Asia is also in the churches today. Jesus specifically warned us about not heeding His words when he said:

> *"For I testify unto that every man heareth the words of the prophecy of this book, if any man shall add unto these things, God shall add unto him the plagues that are written in this book."* Rev 22:18

> *"For without are dogs and sorcerers and whoremongers, and murderers and idolaters, and whosoever loveth and maketh a lie."* Rev 22:15

Surely, *"He who hath an ear let him hear what the spirit says to the churches."* Rev 3:22

As we examine each of the seven letters, we will observe that:

- There are 23 descriptions of the risen Christ.
- Jesus specifically describes what he will do or can do 26 times.
- There are 33 things mentioned which he commends.
- There are 23 things specifically mentioned which he hates.
- There are 22 rewards or blessings mentioned to those who will heed his word.
- There are 16 warnings to follow his directions with consequences for not doing so.

While somewhat subjective, based upon the commendations and condemnations to each church, the best church to the worst church in descending order are:

- Church at Philadelphia
- Church at Smyrna
- Church at Ephesus
- Church at Pergamum
- Church at Thyatira
- Church at Sardis
- Church at Laodicea

There are two churches for which there was not one word of condemnation: the church at *Philadelphia* and the church at *Smyrna*. There is one church for which there was not one redeeming quality and no commendation: the church at *Laodicea*. The second coming of Jesus Christ is specifically mentioned in the letters to the churches at Thyatira, Sardis and Philadelphia. Finally, there are specific promises to ***him that overcometh*** in each of the seven letters. This last observation points out a fundamental principle of salvation by grace and not by works. The gift of eternal life is offered to any who would freely accept it from our Lord and Savior, and is conditioned only upon the personal belief that Christ died for our sins, redeemed us by his precious blood on the cross of Calvary and rose from the dead to be our advocate. He is sitting at the right hand of God the Father and continually intercedes for us in our behalf. To those who accept our savior and believe these things, there are wonderful promises to members of each church, but these are also corporate promises to the body of Christ. We will be extremely concerned with what Christ promised to the *overcomer* in each church. A summary of these promises are as follows.

*I will give to eat of the tree of life….***Ephesus**
*He…shall not be hurt of the second death….***Smyrna**
I will give thee a Crown of Life.
*I will give to eat of the hidden manna….***Pergamum**
I will give him a white stone, and in the stone a new
    name written
I *will give power over the nations* …**Thyatira**
He shall rule with a rod of iron
I shall give him the Morning Star
*Shall be clothed in white raiment …….***Sardis**
I will not blot his name from the book of life
I will confess his name
Will I make a pillar in the temple of my god…
    Philadelphia

Write upon him the name of my God
Write upon him the name of the city of my God
Write upon him my new name
*Grant to sit with me in my throne…..***Laodicea**

It is obvious that regardless of the condition of each church, there will be overcomers which will rule and reign as kings and priests with Jesus through all eternity. This reaffirms the fact that each individual must come to Christ in his own way, and that no one can make that choice for him. Certainly the myth that there is only *one true denomination*; whether Catholic, Pentecostal, Baptist or Methodist is a lie of Satan. Jesus previously said during his earthly ministry: **My sheep hear my voice, and I call my own sheep by name, and I will lead them out** (John 10:3). There is only one body of Christ with many members.

We will now examine each church separately in the order that John receives the message.

The Church at Ephesus….*The church that had lost its first love*

Characteristics of the Community
Under Caesar Augustus, Ephesus was named the capital of a Roman province of Asia, which was then called Asia minor and is now modern Greece. The word Ephesus means *the desired one* in Greek. It was known as a *free city*, and possessed the *right of asylum* for those who committed involuntary or non-premeditated murder. The *blood avenger* could not follow such people into the city. This reminds us of the *Cities of Refuge* established by Joshua after the Exodus from Egypt. Ephesus was the first church to which a letter was addressed, and it was also the crown jewel of the seven churches. Ephesus, Smyrna and Pergamum were the largest and richest cities of the seven, but Ephesus was by far the most magnificent and famous city. It was an important port

on the Aegean Sea and a major trade center where eastern and western commerce met. All of the seven cities had large and ornate temples dedicated to various Greek gods and goddesses. All were important cities in the Roman Empire, and all were major trade centers; but Ephesus outshone them all. Ephesus was one of the favorite cites visited by the apostle Paul on his missionary journeys, and is described in the 18th and 19th chapters in the book of Acts. The apostle John was there for many years, and it is recorded that after the crucifixion of Jesus Christ that he took Mary the mother of Jesus there to live out her days. Her tomb is said to be there today. The most magnificent and beautiful temple in Asia might have been the temple of Artemis, dedicated to the Greek love goddess, Diana. The temple was a massive structure that was one of the seven wonders of the ancient world. The temple was 225 feet long, 220 feet wide and 65 feet high. It is reported that the temple was supported by 127 pillars covered with gold and adorned in precious stones. The Geek goddess Diana was a grotesque person shown in a seated position with many breasts. She was the goddess of fertility, and the temple of Diana was frequented by many prostitutes who offered love for money and gifts. The temple had hundreds of priestesses who functioned as sacred prostitutes.

The women of Ephesus were required to visit the temple at least once a year and fornicate with a complete stranger as an act of worship. Another outstanding feature of Ephesus was a large library called Celsius which housed ancient manuscripts from a wide variety of scholars. Ephesus was a learned and educated city, but like Rome they never fully embraced the knowledge of Christ and his eternal kingdom to come.

"Add to your faith virtue, and to virtue knowledge. And to knowledge temperance, and to temperance patience, and to patience godliness; and to godliness

> *brotherly kindness, and to kindness charity. For if these things be in you and they abound, they make you that you will never be barren or unfruitful in the knowledge of our Lord Jesus Christ."*
> II Peter 1: 5-7.

A hill called Mt. Pion overlooked the city and from there one could clearly view an impressive harbor which was visited by ships from all over the Mediterranean Sea. On the western side of Mt. Pion there stood an amphitheater which could seat over 25,000 people. However, there were two problems which continually plagued the city. The first was that the area was subject to frequent earthquakes; one in 23 AD almost destroyed the city, and one in 262 AD virtually leveled the city and destroyed the temple of Artemis. Second, the magnificent harbor was at the mouth of the river Kayster. The river carried sediment to the harbor from all of western Asia, so that it was constantly in need of dredging. Eventually it completely filled up with silt and sand, and today is nothing more than a large flood plain. Like the shifting sands of the harbor at Ephesus, the church which was once so active and full of works eventually was sifted in God's hands and found wanting; it had lost all of its spirit and its first love. Today there is nothing left but ruins.

Concept of Christ

> *"And unto the angel of the church at Ephesus write... These things saith he that holdeth the seven stars in his right hand, who walketh in the midst of the seven golden candlesticks."* Rev 1:1

This is a personal reference to the risen Lord as seen by John in Rev 1:12-13, 16. As we pointed out in Chapter 1, the proper Greek rendering of the word *candlestick* is *lampstand*. This revelation of the resurrected Jesus Christ is reminiscent of what the prophet Zachariah saw in Zach 4:2: *What seest thou? And he said, I have looked and behold a candlestick all of gold, with a bowl upon the top of it, and his seven lamps thereon, and seven pipes to the seven lamps which are on the top thereof.* The candlestick was one of the ordained pieces in the tabernacle of Moses. It was made of pure gold, which spoke of the purity and worth of Jesus Christ. It was beaten into its form which speaks of the beating that our Lord suffered on the day of his crucifixion. It had three branches out of each side, and one in the middle, through which the oil flowed to provide light. This was a shadow and type of the oil of the Holy Spirit, and of our Lord Jesus who is the light of the world. The lampstand provided light for the Levitical priesthood as they administered their intercessory duties, which speaks of the anointing of the pastor in each church today. From Rev 1:20 the mystery of the seven stars are that they are the angels of the seven churches, and the seven candlesticks are the seven churches. Christ is seen holding all of the *angelos* assigned to each church in his right hand, the hand of authority and strength. Carefully note that Christ *walks in the midst of the seven candlesticks*. He watches, He knows, He anoints, and He is in our midst. In any assembly today just as then, He walks among the worshippers, nourishing, healing and revealing Himself to each individual. Size of the church is not an issue: *For where two or three are gathered together in my name, there am I in the midst of them* (Mat 18:20).

Commendation and Credits

> *"I know thy works, and thy labor and thy patience, and how thou canst not bear them which are evil: and thou hast tried them which say they are apostles, and are not, and found them liars. And hast borne, and hast patience, and for my name's sake hast laboured, and hast not fainted."*   *Rev 1:2-3*

The church at Ephesus evidently had many outreach programs and was working hard to spread Christianity. They patiently endured the persecution of traditional Jews and the immoral followers of the goddess Diana. They boldly proclaimed Christ in the face of evil opposition. Evidently, some had entered the church at Ephesus claiming to be apostles. The word apostle means *one sent forth with authority*. In the New Testament, there were two types of apostles that were recognized as genuine and sent with the specific authority and commission of Jesus Christ. The original 12 apostles, plus Matthias who replaced Judas after the crucifixion, were universally accepted as apostles of our savior. Paul called himself an apostle after he was personally chosen and converted on the road to Damascus, and afterward became the greatest missionary in history. Others were often accepted as apostles if they were personally instructed and taught by Christ during his 3.5 years of earthly ministry.

One or more persons claiming apostolic authority had evidently infiltrated the church at Ephesus and were teaching false doctrine. Beyond that, we know little of what had transpired but we do know that they were tried in the spirit and found wanting: ***But, beloved remember ye the words which were spoken before of the (true) apostles of our lord Jesus Christ, how that they told you there should be mockers in the last time, who should walk after their own ungodly lusts. These are they who separate themselves, sensual, having not the (Holy) spirit*** (Jude 17-19). False doctrine was being recognized and expunged in the church at Ephesus, and false teachers were being called liars. The members of the church at Ephesus were laboring hard, yet they were not fainting or faltering. There was another great work which was taking place in the church, and it was fully recognized by Christ.

> *"But this thou hast, that thou hatest the deeds of the Nicolaitanes, which I also hate."*   *Rev 2:6*

Not a great deal is known about the Nicolaitanes, but they were reported to be a religious cult which evolved from the false teachings of a heretic named Nicolaos. The name itself is derived from two Greek words; *Niko,* which means *to conquer or overthrow* and *Laos,* which means *the people or the laity.* The Nicolaitanes practiced a theology based upon the separation of the physical body from the spiritual man. Since the physical body is born under the curse of Adam, it is wicked from the beginning and anything done in the flesh is of no consequence. Since the spiritual body is unseen and undefiled, it is the only enduring part of man's eternal existence. Since Christ ended the curse of the law, it did not matter what the body did or did not do. They practiced sexual immorality, adultery and all manner of sins of the flesh. The apostle Paul specifically addressed this heresy in his letter to the Romans: ***What then? Shall we sin because we are not under the law but under grace? God forbid. Let not sin therefore reign in your mortal body, that ye should obey it in the lusts thereof*** (Rom 6: 15, 12). It is obvious that sin would flourish in a community which worshipped the sex goddess Diana. However, an alternate meaning of the name *Nico* is *ruler,* so that an alternate meaning would be *ruler of the Laity*. The Nicolaitanes established a *denomination* that chose to follow Satan and not our Lord Jesus Christ. This belief sprung from the ordination of the Aaronic priesthood in the Old Testament, and later manifested itself fully in the supreme worship and deity in the personage of the Pope in the Roman Catholic Church. As time went on, the clergy in many churches have assumed themselves to be the absolute spiritual and personal rulers of their congregation. There is nothing wrong with establishing pastors, elders and other church leaders as long as it does not produce theological contradictions, idol worship, individualized divine rights and man-made theological beliefs. The church at Ephesus recognized and hated these practices, just as the Lord Jesus Christ did then and today.

"If any man preach any other gospel unto you than that ye have received, let him be accursed." Gal 1:9.

Even though the Church at Ephesus was enduring patiently and fighting the good fight, there was something which was undermining the faith and was a growing cancer to the church.

Condemnation and Chastening

"Nevertheless, I have somewhat against thee, because thou hast left thy first love." Rev 1:4

There are many reasons for the members of a church body to serve Christ. Immediately after receiving Christ as one's personal savior, a new Christian usually has a fervent desire to do something in the church. This is a Christian's first love. Often this leads to reckless, immature service but it is sincere and dedicated. As time goes by, the deep initial love can become routine and later a habit. Some Christians simply burn out, drop out and then just hang out in Sunday's service. Others find a renewal and rejuvenation of their first love, followed by fervent service, evolving into routine service, and then another renewal and return to first love. The renewal of first love is sometimes the result of a church revival, and sometimes a result of a personal experience in Christ. Service to Jesus Christ should be based upon pure and perfect love for him; any other motivation is not what Christ expects. In I Kings, the story is told of how King Solomon died and the 12 tribes of Israel split into the northern kingdom and the southern kingdom which was led by the tribe of Judah. The fist king of the southern kingdom was Rehoboam, the son of Solomon (I King 14:21). Under Rehoboam the southern kingdom apostatized, engaging in idol worship and sodomy. For these practices, God allowed Egypt to invade the southern kingdom; ransack the temple, pillage the treasures and take away the shields of gold which Solomon had made to please the Lord. Instead of repenting and returning to the fist love that his father Solomon had for God, Rehoboam instead made shields of brass and placed them in the temple. They shown like gold, they looked like gold and they functioned as gold, but they were not gold, they were brass. This was what was happening in the church at Ephesus. The *gold* love of their first works was being replaced by brass, and God will not accept anything but the real thing. The *gold* of sincere, dedicated and fervent service was being replaced by the *brass* of legalistic, ritualistic and dead works. Paul called works based on anything but the foundation of the true gospel of Jesus Christ ***wood, hay and stubble*** (1 Cor 3:12). The church of Ephesus and the church of today have been told: ***I have somewhat against thee, because thou hast left thy first love.*** The condemnation is immediately followed by counsel.

Counsel to the Church

> *"Remember therefore from whence thou are fallen, and repent, and do the first works; or else I will come unto thee quickly, and I will remove thy candlestick out of his place, except thou repent."*
> Rev 2:5

Our lord Jesus Christ now issues a stern warning: **Remember** and **Repent.** *Remember* the love that you once had for the first works and apply that love to those that are now ongoing. *Recall* your first love and restore the dedication and joy that you once had in serving Christ: *Renew* your first love and your faithfulness: *Re-establish* the personal relationship that we once shared: *Reestablish* your works established in love: *Re-evaluate* your works and take inventory of your motives and your spiritual desires: *Repent* or I will come quickly and remove your candlestick. These are stern words and a stern warning; **repent,** or I will remove your candlestick. Evidently the social, personal and community pressure was too much, because today there is nothing left of the church at Ephesus except for ruins; the candlestick was removed.

Covenant to the Overcomer

> *"He that hath an ear, let him hear what the Spirit says to the churches. To him that overcometh will I give to eat of the tree of life, which is in the midst of the Paradise of God."*   *Rev 2:7*

The first thing to note is that Christ is speaking to the *churches*; all of them. The letter to Ephesus was read to the church at Ephesus, and then taken to each of the other six churches in Asia Minor. The second thing to note is that the *spirit* is speaking also. *And without controversy, great is the mystery of Godliness: God was manifest in the flesh, justified in the spirit, seen of angels, preached unto the Gentiles, believed in the world, received up unto glory* (I Tim 3:16). Christ promises to him that overcomes he will be able to eat of the tree of life. Who is the overcomers who will eat of the tree of life?

For whatsoever is born of God overcometh the world: and this is the victory that overcometh the world, even our faith. Who is he that overcometh the world, but he that believeth that Jesus is the Son of God?

(I John 5:4-5). In each church there will be those who will overcome the world. The Greek word for *overcometh* is *nikao*, which means to subdue, conquer or get the victory. Nikao is used 19 times in the New Testament and 18 times by the apostle John. Nikao is used eight times to qualify the recipient of the overcomer promises to the seven churches in the book of Revelation. It is interesting that the same word is used in Rev 17:14 to describe the victory of Christ at the battle of Armageddon when he defeats the beast and his 10 nation confederacy. ***...and the Lamb shall overcome them for he is Lord of Lords and King of Kings; and those that are with him are called, and chosen and faithful.*** The promise to the overcomer concerns the *tree of life*, and the right to eat of its fruit. This is the same tree of life that fed Adam and Eve in the Garden of Eden before the fall of Adam and Eve. When Adam and Eve were expelled from the Garden of Eden, they lost the privilege of living forever. After the millennial kingdom is established and Satan is cast into the lake of fire and brimstone to deceive man no more, the right to eat of the tree of life will be restored for those who overcome. ***In the midst of the street of it (the New Jerusalem) and on either side of the river (which flows out of the throne of the Lamb and God) there was the tree of life.*** Imagine that! We who believe on the Lord Jesus Christ will be sustained by a *tree of life*, and we will rule and reign with him. ***For if we be dead with him, we shall also live with him: if we suffer we shall also reign with him*** (*(*II Tim 2:12). ***He that hath an ear, let him hear what the Spirit says to the churches.***

The Church at Smyrna... *The Persecuted Church in Poverty*

Characteristics of the Community
The word Smyrna means *the offering of sacrifice*. Smyrna was a poor church that existed under great persecution from the Jewish people that lived there. Smyrna was about 35 miles from Ephesus, and like Ephesus the city had a large magnificent harbor at the entry to the Hermus Valley. The city was probably founded by Alexander the Great. Its main street was built from local rock which contained gold dust and was called *the street of gold*. It connected two great temples:

a temple dedicated to the Greek god Zeus, and another built to honor Cybele. Zeus was the chef of all Olympian gods. Zeus is the god that Antiochs Epiphanes offered as a deity to the Jews when he desecrated their temple of worship (II Macc. 6). Cybele was the Greek mother of all gods and corresponded to Mary the mother of Jesus in pagan worship. Smyrna was also the object of something called the *10% rule*. Persecutors of the church at Smyrna reported the Christians to the emperor of Rome and demanded that they worship the emperor in a third temple dedicated to Julius Caesar. All citizens including Christians were required to appear at the temple once a year and participate in offering pagan sacrifices of wild animals. Failure to do so resulted in a person being declared an enemy of Rome, and they could be hunted down and murdered. A reward of 10% of their estate was offered to the executioner. Is no wonder that Christ said: ***I know your poverty and your suffering***. Satan had unleashed powerful forces against the church at Smyrna, but in spite of all their hardships they managed to survive. Smyrna also had *labor guilds*, or what we now call labor unions. No one could work for wages unless they were in a labor guild, and no one could be in a labor guild without declaring Caesar lord and master. In contrast to the extreme poverty being experienced by the church at Smyrna, we note that the word Smyrna in the Greek can also mean *myrrh*. The city was famous for its large quantities of myrrh which were imported and sold. Myrrh had a sweet aroma when burned, and at the birth of Jesus it was brought to honor him. Myrrh was also used by those who could afford it in the embalming process. Nicodemus came to Jesus after the crucifixion and brought about a hundred pounds of myrrh and aloes (John 19:39). Myrrh is associated with death, and it is appropriate to the great suffering and persecution that the church was going through, even unto death under the 10% rule. Smyrna was also known throughout the Roman Empire as the leader in the emerging science of medicine.

In the letter to Smyrna, there was not a single rebuke or condemnation, not one! It is interesting to compare the spiritual development of Smyrna to that of Ephesus. Paul called Ephesus his pastoral home. Ephesus was also called pastoral home by Paul, Timothy and John. They each visited Smyrna on a regular basis. Smyrna also had a well-known pastor called *Polycarp*. According to legend, he died a martyr. He was bound and placed on a stake and surrounded by wood. When his persecutors set the wood on fire, Polycarp was engulfed in flames but was never burned at all. The people were so enraged that they stabbed him repeatedly with a sword until he died. Polycarp is regarded as a saint in the Roman Catholic Church.

In tragic contrast, the church at Ephesus now lies in ruins while a large Christian community at Smyrna still exists today in the modern city called Izmir. True to his promise, Jesus is still walking among his lampstands, supplying the oil of the Holy Spirit and watching his sheep. The church at Smyrna was under great suffering and persecution, but this is part of God's mysterious plan to bring his followers to maturity. Paul knew this when he said: *for I reckon that the sufferings of this present time are not worthy to be compared with the glory which shall be revealed in us* (Rom 8:18). The letter to the Church at Smyrna is the shortest of all the letters, but it is full of praise for the group of Christians that gathered there.

Concept of Christ

> *"And unto the angel of the church at Smyrna write… These things saith the first and the last, which was dead and is alive."* Rev 2:8

In Chapter 1, Christ was seen saying that *I am Alpha and Omega, the first and the last* (Rev 1:13). Christ earlier greeted the prophet John by saying: *from him which is, and which was and which is to come* (Rev 1:4). Jesus Christ is *the firstborn of every creature* (Col 1:15). *He is the head of the body, the church: who is the beginning, the firstborn from the dead; that in all things he might have the preeminence* (Col 1:18). The first man was Adam, the last man Jesus Christ. Every person is first born into the sinful nature of Adam; when one accepts Christ as their savior, that person is born a second time into the body of Christ. *The first man Adam was made a living soul, the last Adam was made a quickening spirit* (I Cor 15:45). The parallel reference to *Alpha and Omega* refers to the first (*alpha*) and last (*omega*) letters in the Greek alphabet. There is nothing that can be expressed in the Greek vocabulary which has not already been revealed by our Lord Jesus Christ; Christ has been revealed to all by his life, death and resurrection to eternal life. He *was dead*, descended into hell, preached to those in prison, and rose from the dead to eternal life. He is the *firstfruits* of all those who will rise from the dead at the *last trump* (I Cor. 15: 52).

Commendation and Credits

> *"I know thy works, and tribulation, and poverty, (but thou art rich) and I know the blasphemy of them which say they are Jews and are not, but are the synagogue of Satan."* Rev 2:9

Christ again says. *I know* that you are doing my works, and that you are poor. I also know that you are being severely persecuted for me. Poverty follows persecution, and is a direct result of great affliction. In spite of being poor, the church was carrying on the work of Christ. There is a message here to the church of today. It is increasingly true that the church is a showplace for modern architecture and beauty. Enormous debt usually accompanies such splendor, eating up the dollars that could be used for outreach and missions. The church at

Smyrna was said to be poor, but it was spending all it had for the cause of Christ. However, social rejection and societal persecution were not the only things that were causing their great affliction. There was evidently a group of people there that claimed to be Jews, but in fact were neither Jewish nor Christian in belief or practice. Whether they were Jews in the sense of being descendents of Abraham or proselytes is not the issue here. They had apostatized and were following Satan in his spiritual synagogue. The *street of gold* connected the temples of Cybele and Zeus, and both practiced adulterous, sinful and immoral practices centered on the worship of Greek gods. If these persecutors were Jews, they may have been by birth but not by practice. In another sense, the church of Jesus Christ is not a building at all but the body of Christ. Hence, the *synagogue* mentioned here could well represent the group of the persecutors themselves. In any case, Satan was in control of their body and soul, and they were actively opposing Christ and the church at Smyrna.

Condemnation and Chastening
Not one Word!!!!

Counsel to the Church

> *"Fear none of these things which thou shalt suffer: behold the devil shall cast some of you into prison, that ye may be tried; and ye shall have tribulation ten days: be thou faithful unto death, and I will give thee a crown of life."*   Rev 2:10

Christ now reveals a frightening truth to the church. Although they were under great persecution, tribulation and poverty, the worst is yet to come. Satan is going to increase his persecution and the prospects are not good. Some will be cast into prison and some will be killed. In this revelation Christ brings trepidation, but he also brings comfort: **Fear none of these things**. Our Lord

Jesus Christ has never promised any Christian exemption from persecution. On the contrary, Christ exhorted them to continue in the faith: **we must through great tribulation enter into the kingdom of God** (Acts 14:22). Christ identifies the agent of this persecution: it is Satan himself. Satan evidently has a death grip on this community since we have already been told that he has a *synagogue* here. The phrase *ye may be tried* is poorly translated from the Greek word *peirasthete* which means *ye may be tested*. This word does not carry the weight of being tested in a sense of persecution, but tested with the purpose of falling away from the faith. The same word is used in I Peter 2:7: **that the trial of your faith, being much more precious than gold which perisheth, though it be tried with fire, might be found unto praise and honor and glory at the appearance of Jesus Christ**. A particular period of tribulation is identified as *ten days*. This period of time has been the subject of various interpretations by a wide range of expositors. A widely-held interpretation is that the church at Smyrna represented the period of time between 90 AD and about 300 AD, in which ten Roman emperors exerted great affliction upon the Christians. This position is weak, since the first emperor was actually Nero, circa 54 AD and the second Domitian around 81 AD. To equate the 10-day future period of persecution with two dead Nero's would make no sense, since at the time this letter was written the third ruler would have already been on his throne. Another position is to use the *year-day* theory to predict an intense 10-year period of persecution yet future. A third interpretation is that this is a symbolic number only, and represents an indefinite period of time, perhaps the entire time the church existed. If this is so, why would this number even be used in the first place? I believe that in the course of studying our interpretation of the entire book of Revelation, a natural and straightforward interpretation can be adopted. We will cover the details later, but a strong case based upon Matthew 24, the sequence of trumpets and bowls, Jewish

Messianic expectations and scriptural consistency will place the rapture of the church at the seventh trump; exactly as identified by the apostle Paul and in Rev 11:15-18. This will occur on the Jewish Feast of Trumpets (***Rosh Hashanah***) on the Jewish date Tishri 1. The *Wrath of God* which is the ***Bowl Judgments*** (Rev 15:1, 16:1) will follow the rapture of the church (Chapter 23) and they will be poured out over a 10-day period of time, just as our Lord warned. The ***Battle of Armageddon*** (Christ's Second Advent) will occur on the *Feast of Yom Kippur*, Tishri 10 (Rev 19:19). This will last one day and is the ***Lord's Day*** (Zep 2:1-3).

Remember that this letter is directed to the church at Smyrna, but is to be read by and applies to all of the seven churches. Christ then assures this same group that if they are ***faithful unto death*** that he will reward them with a ***crown of life.*** The Greek phrase used here is ***ton stephanon tes zoes***. There are two types of crowns that are used in the book of Revelation. There is a *stephanos* crown and a *diadem* crown. The *stephanos* crown is that which will be awarded to those who competed in the Olympic Games and emerge victorious. It is also used in the context of a ruler of an earthly kingdom. The diadem crown is reserved for those who accept Christ as their Savior. This is the same crown worn by Christ at His second advent (Rev 19:11-14). It is the crown which is promised to the saints whose names are inscribed in the Book of Life Rev 2:10, 3:5). Imagine that! Christ has reserved for each of those who accept him as Lord and Savior an eternal crown which is a symbol of eternal life! ***He who has an ear to hear... let him hear.***

Covenant to the Overcomer

> *"He that hath an ear, let him hear what the Spirit saith unto the churches; He that overcometh shall not be hurt of the second death."* Rev 2:11

In each of the seven letters, Christ provides us with a glimpse of a reward which has been reserved by him for those who overcome. The promise now revealed here is that: **He that overcometh will not be hurt of the second death.** What is this *second death* that Christ refers to? The first death is a *physical* death which all but a few that survives the tribulation period will have to experience. The second death is a *spiritual* death that is reserved for all unbelievers. There is an old saying: *A Christian is born twice, but dies only once. A non-christian is born once but dies twice.* Being a Christian simply means accepting the Lord Jesus Christ as your savior and being born again. In today's church, the message of eternal separation from God is not often preached. The message of love, rewards, and promises to the believer dominate sermons today. However, the second death is very real. It is reserved for those who refuse to accept the gift of eternal life by believing that Christ suffered and died for our sins, was buried dead and resurrected on the third day, and now sits at the right hand of God the Father serving as our great high priest and advocate. The unbeliever will be condemned to the *second death* at the White Throne Judgment of God following the 1000-year millennial reign of Christ here on this earth (Rev 20:14 and 21:8). The result of this second death is to be cast into the lake of fire and brimstone (Rev 20:14-15). It is sad but true; the decision to reject the free gift of salvation and the Holy Spirit is eternal. Our primary mission in life is to bring the unbeliever into a covenant relationship with Jesus Christ and to rescue unbelievers from the second death. Oh that we might each take this responsibility seriously and work while we can, for our Lord Jesus Christ will return soon to claim and reward those that are his at his coming. Christ has given us a wonderful, sure promise:

> *"I am the good Shepherd and know my sheep, and I am known of mine. As the Father knoweth me, even so I know the Father: and I lay down my life for my sheep."* John 10:14-15
>
> *" My sheep hear my voice, and I know them, and they follow me: and I give unto them eternal life; and they shall never perish, neither shall any man pluck them out of my hand."* John 10:27-28

The Church at Pergamum... *The Church with Corrupted Theology and Adulterous Practices*

Characteristics of the Community

The city of Pergamum is known today as Bergama. The church at Pergamum was founded by the apostle Paul, but the city seems to have been established by Alexander the Great in his early years of conquest. After the death of Alexander, it became the capital city of the Seleucid Kingdom, which was one of the four divisions of the Grecian Empire given to the Greek general Seleucus I. The reign of Pergamum then passed to Attalus III, and after his death in 133 BC it became part of the Roman Empire. Rome called this area Asia Minor, and Pergamum became the official capital city. Pergamum was connected to Smyrna by a highway that ran north along the coast for about 40 miles, and then turned inland in a northeast direction about 15 more miles. There the city sat on a high hill from which one could see the Aegean Sea on a clear day. The Caucus Valley lay before the city and a scenic curved road wound around the steep hill until it reached a large plateau upon which the city was built. At the height of its splendor, it housed about 150,000 people. Pergamum was not on a major trade route, but it became famous as a center of academic excellence and culture. It was in the city of Pergamum that scholars invented parchment, which was used to record the written word. Parchment was made from the cured skin of animals: dried, smoothed and polished. It was an excellent media for recording information, far superior to papyrus which was developed in Egypt and used throughout the known world. Pergamum had a library which rivaled the great library at Alexandria. The library was said to have housed over 200,000 roles of parchment. Pergamum became the best medical center in the Roman Empire. It had a large medical school with operating rooms and medical care facilities. It was here that the symbol of medicine arose: a serpent twisted around a long rod. Ascleplos was the Greek god of healing, and to honor him the people built the temple of Ascleplos. A road connected the temple of Ascleplos to the temple of Athena, which was one of the seven wonders of the ancient world. It contained an image of Zeus which was over 40 feet high. Surrounding its base stood carvings and statues of other Greek gods. The city was full of temples dedicated to the worship of Greek gods. In addition to the temples of Ascleplos and Athena, another major place of idol worship was the temple of Dionysus. Dionysus was dedicated to animal worship, particularly snakes and serpents. The city was also a center of *Caesar worship*. Once a year all of the citizens were required to come to the temple, offer which means *Caesar is Lord*. The provincial governor assigned to Pergamum had a rare ***Ius gladii***, which is translated as having *the right of the sword*. Those who possessed the power of *Ius Gladii* had the right to pronounce death to anyone without a trial. The proconsul at Pergamum possessed this power. It was in the midst of all of this paganism and satanic activity that the church at Pergamum existed. That great Christian scholar Donald G. Barnhouse once wrote: ***Ephesus had been the church of wheat sown on good ground, bringing forth fruit, but the first love had been lost. In the church at Smyrna, corruption had begun to set in, and the risen Lord saw the synagogue of Satan existing at Pergamum.*** In the Church at Smyrna, the ***Parable of the Mustard Seed*** had been fulfilled in type. The tree had come to maturity but *the birds of the air, the Devil's birds*, had come to lodge in its branches. It is from the word Pergamum that we get the English word for polygamy. The church at Pergamum had apostatized to the point where it was trying to be married to both the world and to Jesus Christ. We will see that this would not be tolerated by Christ and the church was in serious trouble by the time that this letter was written.

Concept of Christ

> *"And unto the angel of the church at Pergamum write... These things saith he which has the sharp sword with two edges."* Rev 2:12

Christ introduces himself as: *he which has the sharp sword with two edges.* Two questions which naturally arise are: (1) what sword? and (2) what are the two edges? Paul revealed that the sword is the *Word of God*.

> *"for the word of God is quick, and powerful, and sharper than any two edged sword, piercing even to the dividing asunder of soul and spirit, and of the joints and marrow, and is a discerner of the thoughts and intents of the heart."* Heb 4:12.

The word of God has two edges, and both are eternal in nature. John boldly proclaimed that the word *is* God: *and the Word was made flesh and* (Christ*) dwelt among us* (John 1:14) and: *In the beginning was the Word, and the Word was with God, and the Word was God.* (John 1:1). But this sword cuts both ways, those who hear and reject the word and the gift of eternal life will perish by the sword and be condemned to eternal separation from God. Christ will slay all of his enemies at the battle of Armageddon with this sword. *And he was clothed with a vesture dipped in blood, and his name is called the Word of God. And out of his mouth goeth a sharp*

sword, that with it he should smite the nations (Rev 19: 13, 15). The members of the church at Pergamum would well understand this imagery, living under the threat of *Ius Gladii*.

Commendation and Credits

> ***"I know thy works, and where thou dwellest, even where Satan's seat is: and thou holdest fast my name, and hast not denied my faith, even in those days wherein Antipas was my faithful martyr, who was slain among you where Satan dwelleth."***
> Rev 2:13

Christ is walking among his lampstands, observing their works. ***I know thy works***. The eyes are like flames of fire (Rev 1:14). Nothing is missed, nothing is overlooked, and nothing is hidden. He knows exactly where his church is located, and he ***knows where Satan's seat is***. Various interpretations of this phrase have been proposed, but we see no reason to spiritualize or allegorize the statement of Christ. Since the time that Satan and one third of all the angels (Rev 12: 4), were cast out of the third heaven where God dwells, Satan has been the ruler of a large army of demons, fallen angels and princes of this world. But a ruler must have a place from which to rule, and Christ says that the seat of Satan was in Pergamum. The Greek word used here is *thorax* and is only used three times in the New Testament, all in the book of Revelation, and each time referring to satanic activity. In Rev 16:10 the fifth bowl of God's wrath is poured out upon the ***seat of the Beast***, and the beast is identified in Rev 12 as the satanic-controlled antichrist. The seat of the beast is *Babylon*, which will be rebuilt and serve as the economic and false religious capital of Satan during the tribulation period (Rev 17-18). At the time that Christ wrote this letter to the church at Pergamum, the ***seat of Satan*** was evidently in Pergamum, possibly in the temple of Dionysus where the image most worshipped was a serpent. It appears that the original image of a serpent was of beauty before Adam fell and the serpent was cursed by God. It is not unreasonable to think that Satan was trying to elevate himself once again to a position of authority and beauty. He is the ***prince of the air*** today (Eph 6:12) and also the ***prince of this evil world*** (John 12:31). In any case, there is no reason to doubt that Satan's *seat* was spiritually in Pergamum. Today it is somewhere else but we have no idea where it might exist. During the tribulation period Satan will attack Jerusalem, overrun the city and establish his religious seat in the rebuilt Herod's temple. In the midst of Satan's activity, Christ recognizes that: ***thou holdest fast my name, and hast not denied my faith***. In spite of living under great persecution and coexisting with the very seat of Satan, these Christians were remaining faithful to the name of Jesus Christ. There is a question of just what it means in this context to remain *faithful*. There are two interpretations: (1) to remain faithful in a personal context, continuing their belief that Jesus Christ was crucified, buried and rose from the grave. There was evidently no wavering from this truth and from the gift of eternal life to all of those who believe and remain faithful: ***Holding fast the faithful word as he has taught, that he may be able by sound doctrine both to exhort and to convince the gainsayers*** (Titus 1:9), and (2) to remain faithful in a public forum, and to not deny Christ even in the face of death. Even Peter abandoned his faithfulness, denying Christ not once, not twice but three times. In the tribulation period to come, both will be a test of one's faith. Satan will demand that all people worship images of him, and to also take the mark of the beast on either their right hand or their forehead (Rev 13: 14-17). The failure to do so will result in physical death. However, there is more. Anyone who worships the beast and takes his mark will be tormented by fire and brimstone forever (Rev 14:10-11). The reward for being faithful is worth the price. After the Second Advent of Christ, John saw:

the souls of them that were beheaded for the witness of Jesus, and for the word of God, and which had not worshipped the beast, neither his name, neither had not received his mark upon their foreheads, or in their hands; and they lived and reigned with Christ a thousand years (Rev 21:4). This is surely the meaning of not denying faith in Jesus Christ, for the threat of death was certainly present in Pergamum. This interpretation is made more certain by the immediate reference to *Antipas*. Antipas was thought to be one of the first pastors in the church at Pergamum, and he was publicly martyred. Church tradition has it that Antipas was taken before a statue of Caesar and told to worship him as lord. Antipas boldly proclaimed that there was only one Lord, his Lord Jesus Christ. It is recorded that a Roman soldier stood over him with a sword and said: *Antipas do you not know that the entire world is against you?* To which he was said to reply: *Then Antipas is against the whole world, I will not deny my Christ.* It is further recorded that Antipas was stripped naked, beaten, and placed in a brass cauldron shaped like a bull. He was then boiled alive. The word that is translated martyr is *martus*, which is usually translated *witness*, and was used in Rev 1:5 to describe the glorified Christ as our *faithful witness*. Imagine that! Christ is giving Antipas the same title he gives himself! To every Christian who might have to experience tribulation: ***He who has an ear let him hear***. Although the church at Pergamum was holding up under severe persecution, there was something terribly wrong.

Condemnation and Chastening

> *"But I have a few things against thee, because thou hast there them that hold the doctrine of Balaam, who taught Balac to cast a stumbling block before the Children of Israel, to eat things sacrificed onto idols, and to commit fornication. So hast also them*

that hold the doctrine of the Nicolaitanes, which thing I hate."   Rev 2:14-15

Here we see a congregational tragedy. Even though there were some in the church at Pergamum who were holding fast even unto death, there were others who had submitted to Satan and were only going through the motions. In a direct statement, Christ says: *I have a few things against thee*. Two major doctrinal errors emerge which Christ says he hates: the doctrine of Balaam, and the doctrine of the Nicolaitanes. In the church at Ephesus the deeds of the Nicolaitanes had surfaced and were corrupting the body of Christ. Here at Ephesus, these deeds had taken root and had become false doctrine. Our Lord Jesus Christ not only condemns the doctrine, but also *them that hold* that doctrine. We have already discussed the Nicolaitanes in the letter to the church at Ephesus. Recall that this was a religious sect founded by a proselyte named Nicole, who apostatized and promoted two practices which the Lord hates. The first was a rigid hierarchy of church leaders who interpreted the scriptures according to their own way. Nicholas promoted a hierarchy of infallible and rigid church leaders who failed to challenge societal sins. The second doctrine was to adopt and accept idolatry, prostitution and homosexuality. It is likely that both practices existed in some form or another in the church at Pergamum, and the Lord hated it. The writer of Hebrews addressed the apostasy in Rome by saying: *It is a fearful thing to fall into the hands of the living God. But call to remembrance the former days, in which after you were illuminated, ye endured a great fight of afflictions* (Heb 10:31-32).

The other scathing condemnation addressed the doctrine of Balaam. What is this *Doctrine of Balaam*, which the Lord also hates? Balaam was the son of Beor and was raised in Mesopotamia. He was a powerful and influential sorcerer. It is likely that he descended from the Magi, who were soothsayers from Babylonia. We hear of Balaam in Numbers 20-24 and Deut 23:4. Moses was about to die and Joshua would be anointed by God to lead Israel across Jordan into the Promised Land. King Balak of Moab was assembling his armies to take on the Israelites. With a battle imminent, Balak summoned Balaam to curse the army of Israel and gain him a great victory. In Numbers 22:12 we are told that the Lord appeared to Balaam and warned him not to do so. Disappointed, Balak offered Balaam a great deal of riches to reconsider. Again the Lord appeared to Balaam, but this time permitted him to visit Balak under the condition that Balaam would not say anything except what the Lord tells him to say. On the journey to see King Balak, a strange story of the Angel of the Lord appearing on the road and of the ass he was riding speaking to Balaam is recorded in Numbers 22. When Balaam reached King Balak, he was repeatedly enjoined to curse the God of Israel and the Israelites, but Balaam only spoke blessings according to the Lord's instructions. It is here that for some strange reason, Balaam turned aside and hatched a plan for which Balak would be greatly rewarded. Balaam told King Balak to go and get all of his beautiful women to seduce the men of Israel, causing them to commit adultery and intermarry against God's specific instructions. The second plan was to get the men of Israel to worship idols and pagan gods, and to eat food that had been sacrificed to those gods. The result was to be swift and sure: God would destroy his own people in anger, and Balak would have no trouble defeating their armies. Here we have two things which are condemned over and over again in both the Old and New Testaments: ***idol worship and adultery***. The plan was simple; corrupt God's people, make them abandon and ignore God's laws, and become a part of Satan's world. It is an age old story, and one that should be regularly visited by the pastors in today's pulpits. In contrast, we see the modern church in many cases being led by adulterers, homosexuals and men who promote satanic practices such as serpent worship, idol worship and sexual immorality. We need to see a return to God's Word. If it is condemned by God, it should not become a part of church doctrine. Peter warned against these practices when he said:

> *"spots they are and blemishes, sporting themselves with their own deceivings while they feast with you; having eyes full of adultery, and that cannot cease from sin; beguiling unstable souls… which have forsaken the right ways , and are gone astray, following the way of Balaam… who loved the wages of unrighteousness."* II Peter 2:13-15.

Counsel to the Church

> *"Repent; or else I will come unto thee quickly, and I will fight against them with the sword of my mouth."* Rev 2:16

Our Lord Jesus Christ now issues a stern warning: *If they do not repent, he will come quickly and fight with them with the sword of his mouth*. What is this sword? We have already discussed the meaning of this term.

> *"For the word of God is quick, and powerful, and sharper than any two edged sword, piercing even to the dividing asunder of soul and spirit, and of the joints and marrow, and is a discerner of the thoughts and intents of the heart."* Heb 4:12.

This sword appears three times in the Revelation. In John's earlier vision, he saw the risen Christ: *holding in his right hand seven stars, and out of his mouth went a sharp two edged sword* (Rev 1:16). In Rev 1:9: *and out of his mouth goeth a sharp sword that with it he should smite the nations* (Rev 19:15). There have been theological debates as to whether the Lord was threatening eradication and judgment of the church at

Pergamum, or whether this is a near-far prophecy that has to do with the Second Advent of Jesus Christ. It is clear from scripture that both are operative here. The church at Pergamum eventually fell to the sword of Jesus Christ. Satan's army, the antichrist and the false prophet will also fall at the battle of Armageddon (Rev 19:21).

Covenant to the Overcomer

> *"He that hath an ear, let him hear what the Spirit saith unto the churches; He that overcometh will I give to eat of the hidden manna, and I will give him a white stone, and in the stone a new name written which no man knoweth saving he that receiveth it."*
> Rev 2:17

The promise to those who believe in the Lord Jesus Christ and are overcomers is in two parts: (1) They will be given the **hidden manna**, and (2) they will be given a **white stone with a new name written upon it**. The word manna means *what is it?* It was food created and delivered by God on a daily basis. The manna had three characteristics. On Sunday through Thursday, it was picked every morning and was to be consumed during that day and evening. It would spoil if kept for more than one day. On Friday, a double portion was provided to feed the people both Friday and Saturday which would last two days without spoiling. It is recorded that Moses placed three items inside of the Ark of the Covenant as a memorial to Yahweh; the *Rod of Aaron* which budded, the *Tables of the Law*, and a *Pot of Manna*. The pot of manna which was placed in the ark was said to have never spoiled. The Ark of the Covenant disappeared after the destruction of the first temple, and the Bible does not tell us anything about where it went. Jewish tradition holds that the prophet Jeremiah hid the ark and its contents before the temple and Jerusalem was destroyed; and that it will not reappear until the nation of

Israel is restored and the Abrahamic Covenant is fulfilled. Some modern archaeologists maintain that the ark is hidden in a monastery in Ethiopia. We do know that the ark of Moses was a copy of the original ark in heaven. In Rev 11:19, we see the true ark is seen in the Temple of God. This is called the **Temple of the Tabernacle of the Testimony** in Rev 15: 6. It is interesting that the Children of Israel were eating the manna when Balaam came on the scene, and it ceased as soon as they crossed over the Jordon River. It miraculously appeared; the time it appeared was unknown until it happened and it sustained the Children of Israel in all of its wilderness journeys. It is our interpretation that this symbolism refers to the personage of Jesus Christ as the true manna from heaven, and refers to the invitation of Jesus Christ to **eat of the bread of life**. The manna which we now receive is *spiritual manna*, and it sustains us in times of trials, persecution and tribulation.

The second promise to the overcomer is a **white stone**. This stone has a new name written upon it which no one knows but the one who receives it. This white stone is difficult to identify, but we are inclined to believe that it is the equivalent of a stone that was kept under the breastplate of the High Priest. In ancient times when a decision had to be made which affected God's people, the **"urim"** and the **"thummin"** was employed to seek God's will. The urim and the thummin were two identical stones in size and shape, but one was white and one was black. The question or decision was always framed such that a *yes or no* would render the answer. The High Priest would reach into a pocket which held the two stones, and extract only one. The decision was irrevocable and final. This speaks of the Bema Seat Judgment (Rev 20:4) (Rev 11:15-18) in which all believers must appear before the throne of God. The implication of this promise is an eternal one; there is only a white stone that says "yes". Jesus Christ has given us that stone which will save us by faith in him from eternal damnation and separation from God. Imagine that! Jesus Christ is our advocate and intercessor, and he says **YES**. Praise God forever for the glorious work which was accomplished on the cross. We can't earn that stone by works; we cannot buy that stone with gold or silver; and we don't deserve that stone. *Thank you Jesus forever and ever.*

The Church at Thyatira... *The Church which Compromised*

Characteristics of the Community

The letter to the church at Thyatira was the fourth written in a series of seven. It is the longest of the seven letters, and is a mixture of praise and condemnation. Thyatira is the least famous of all the seven churches but provides a contrast between good works and tolerance of pagan practices. The name Thyatira is formed from two root words; **Thira** which means *sacrifice* and **tira** which means *continual*. Thyatira was carrying on good works, but it had fallen into three great apostasies: (1) the worship of idols and graven images, (2) indulgence in immorality and adulterous practices, and (3) falling away from grace into work-based practices.

The city of Thyatira lay in a long, fertile valley between the Hermus and the Caicus rivers. It was not a coastal town, but lay about 50 miles north and east from Pergamum. It was founded to protect the coastal cities from invaders advancing east to west. The hills surrounding the city were not high enough to afford great protection, and the city was attacked and destroyed on several occasions. It was always rebuilt and always returned to a state of prosperity. The city was not a major center of idol or Caesar worship, but had pagan temples dedicated to Apollo and Artemis. One of the most impressive structures in Thyatira was a large central temple dedicated to a famous female oracle and fortune teller called *Sambathe*. The temple of Sambathe was a center of adulterous practices and prostitution. Once a year all female citizens of Thyatira were required to enter the temple and engage in sexual relations with a complete stranger. While known for its adulterous practices, Thyatira was most famous for its work guilds and commercial trade. The various trade guilds functioned quite differently from what we would call labor unions today. A citizen of Thyatira could not work at all unless they were a member of the guild which governed that vocation. Wool producers, cloth manufacturers, leather workers, potters and bronze metal workers were among the most powerful working groups. Guilds not only controlled the commerce and wealth of Thyatira, but also formed the basis for the social structure of the city. Each guild had its own pagan god which was worshipped as a deity. Festivals were held on a regular basis, and great feasts were held in which food dedicated to the pagan god was eaten as an offering. Following each feast, an immoral sexual orgy was held in which open sexual acts were engaged by all. Participation in these acts of sexual immorality was required by all present, and to exit prematurely resulted in ridicule and rejection by those present. It is clear that the church members at Thyatira were struggling with the issues of idol worship and adultery, and that they had apostatized to the point of tolerance and participation. The doctrinal errors in the church at Thyatira were similar to those in the church at Pergamum, but were much worse. Not only did the church compromise sound doctrine in yielding to idol worship and adulterous practices, but either overtly or covertly accepted and failed to condemn these practices.

Perhaps the best known commercial product sold in Thyatira was purple cloth that has been attributed to a woman named Lydia. Lydia was the first known Asian convert to Christianity on Paul's first journey to Asia Minor. Paul converted Lydia in Philippi, but she practiced her trade in Thyatira (Acts 16:18). Purple was a very costly die extracted from a small shellfish called *Mulex Trunculus*. It contained a gland that once punctured would yield a single drop of fluid, which when then exposed to air would turn a deep shade of purple. Because of its beauty and difficulty to obtain, it became the color of choice for royalty.

It was in the midst of these practices that the church of Thyatira existed. The problem with the church was that they preached the gospel message but tolerated pagan practices. Worldly tolerance, idol worship and immorality were both within and without the church. Christ said;

> *"No man can serve two masters: for either he will hate the one, and love the other; or else he will hold to the one, and despise the other. Ye cannot serve God and mammon."* Mat 6:24.

God will not be mocked; the candlestick at Thyatira ran out of oil, and today nothing is left of the old city or the once vibrant church except rubble.

Concept of Christ

> **"And unto the angel of the church at Thyatira write….. These things saith the Son of God who has his eyes like unto a flame of fire, and his feet are like fine brass."** Rev 2:18

The risen Christ presents himself to the church at Thyatira in three ways. The *first* is as the **Son of God**. This can be contrasted to John's earlier vision of Christ in which He was walking among the candlesticks (churches) as one like unto the Son of man. This assertion of his deity is necessary as he pronounces judgment upon a church that had strayed far from the holy calling under which it was founded. In all the other letters presented so far, Christ revealed himself through a descriptive identification, but here he clearly asserts himself as the true and only son of God. Jesus had clearly revealed himself in this way during his earthly ministry (Mat 11:27, Luke 10:22, John 11:24). It was this proclamation that caused him to be condemned and executed (Mat 26:63, John 19:7). Only the son of God is capable of discerning the true motives of service. The *second* identification Christ reveals is that he has ***eyes like unto a flame of fire*** through which he sees the church at Thyatira. This also reflects John's first vision of Christ in Rev 1:14. Christ's first earthly appearance was as a *suffering servant*, but he will come again soon as a conquering *King of Kings* to execute righteous judgment and holy justice. In Rev 19:11 we will see Christ at the Second Advent, with the same eyes as a flame of fire, destroying all who have refused his gift of eternal life and slaying those who oppose him. If this identification was not enough to strike fear into the Thyatirians, the third identification will. The *third* way in which Christ presents himself is as one with ***feet of brass***. In the scriptures, brass is often used as a symbol of judgment. The parable of the wheat and tares clearly illustrates that there will be a time of judgment in which the righteous (*wheat*) will be separated from the unrighteous (*tares*). After the harvest, the wheat was always separated from the chaff by oxen treading the grain with shoes of polished brass. The precious wheat was then brought into the storehouse, and the chaff scattered to the four winds. Christ is the one who will discern all things and separate the wheat from the tares. ***In righteousness he doth judge all things and make war… and he treadeth the winepress of the fierceness and wrath of almighty God***. But before judgment is pronounced, Christ first shows his grace by a series of commendations.

Commendation and Credits

> *"I know thy works, and charity, and service, and faith, and thy patience and thy works; and the last to be more than the first."* Rev 2:19

There are five commendations with a qualification, two short of seven; the number of completeness. Again Christ asserts that *he knows*: He always knows, He always sees with eyes of flaming fire, and He always knows our (1) *works,* (2) *charity,* (3) *service,* (4) *faith,* and (5) *patience.* Works is repeated twice, possibly to emphasize that even though the church at Thyatira was in danger of having its candlestick removed; this was not an entirely dead church. It did have works, and the latter works seem to be more than when the church was first founded. The conjunction *and* seems to connect *charity, service and faith* to works. While faith without works is a dead and nonproductive faith, works without charity, service and faith is dead in both intent and execution. It is true that service is a natural outgrowth of faith, but one should compliment and undergird the other. Having recognized the good things in this church, Christ now launches into a severe statement of condemnation and chastening.

Condemnation and Chastening

> *"Not withstanding I have a few things against thee, because thou sufferest that woman Jezebel, which calleth herself a prophetess, to teach and to seduce my servants to commit fornication, and to eat things sacrificed unto idols."* Rev 2:20

Christ will now state that he has only a *few things against thee,* but they are severe and disastrous. They *sufferest that woman Jezebel.* The title of Jezebel is the feminine counterpart to that of Judas, and indicates the highest level of apostasy. What does this statement mean?

First, it is unlikely but possible that this is the actual name of a woman who was a member of the church. Jezebel was the pagan wife of King Ahab (I Kings 16-21). Her goal was to seduce the northern kingdom into three practices that God consistently condemns in the scriptures: (1) worship of other gods; (2) indulgence in adulterous, sexual and immoral practices; and (3) teaching heretical doctrine. We have already discussed how the city of Thyatira promoted and enforced immoral practices in the work guilds, and maintained several temples in which Greek gods were worshipped. Evidently the church had chosen to accept these social pressures, simply look the other way, or fail to preach against these practices. It is certain that some important church member referred to as Jezebel was actually ***teaching and seducing my servants*** into participation or indulgence of these practices. Although the apostle Paul (I Tim 2:12) consistently taught against women teaching in the church, that in itself is not a thing that God seems to forbid. Lydia was obviously very influential in the early church days. Anna was a prophetess who recognized Christ in the temple at his dedication and boldly proclaimed Him to be the promised Jewish Messiah (Luke 2:36-38). Mary Magdalene was undoubtedly a vocal and outspoken supporter of her Christ after she was freed from 7 demonic spirits (Luke 8:3).

The problem was not one of teaching, but teaching the wrong things. She was seducing church members to ***commit fornication, and to eat things sacrificed unto idols***. To what degree the false doctrines of this woman Jezebel were connected to those being taught and tolerated in nearby Pergamum is unknown, but Pergamum was only about 25-30 miles away and the Nicolaitan influence there promoted both eating meat sacrificed to idols and sexual immorality.

Correction by Christ

> *"And I gave her space to repent of her fornications and she repented not. Behold, I will cast her into a bed, and them that commit adultery with her into great tribulation, except they repent of their deeds. And I will kill her children with death; and all the churches shall know that I am he which searcheth the reins and hearts: and I will give unto every one of you according to your work."*   Rev 2:21-23

While not specifically stated here, Christ has already indicated that *He knows*, and at this point He clearly indicates that He has tolerated this long enough; if the church does not immediately cease these practices there will be immediate consequences. Christ has given her, and by association the church members who follow her teachings, *space to repent* and she has *repented not*. The declaration is stark and real. He will cast her and them that follow her and commit adultery into a *bed* (of suffering); their children will be put to death; and they will be given judgment consistent with their works.

Here we must state a fundamental belief that is completely consistent with the scriptures that we hold regarding works and salvation. There are good works and bad works; God-inspired works are *good works* and man-inspired works are *bad works*. The good works will be rewarded, but the bad works will not. Paul addressed this doctrine in his second letter to the Corinthians.

> *"Every man's work shall be made manifest, for the day (of judgment) will declare it, because it will be revealed by fire; and the fire will try every man's work of what sort it is. If any man's work abide which he has built thereupon, he shall receive a reward. If any man's work shall be burned, he shall suffer loss but he himself shall be saved."*
>   I Cor. 3: 12-14

Salvation cannot be earned but is by grace; service and rewards in the hereafter are for those works that are holy and acceptable to the Lord. One reason why the letters to the seven churches should be closely studied is to discern between these two truths. Christ himself verifies this truth in declaring that: *I will give unto every one of you according to your works.*

Counsel to the Church

> *"But unto you I say, and unto the rest in Thyatira, as many as have not this doctrine, and which have not known the depths of Satan, as they speak; I will put upon you none other burden. But that which you have already: hold fast till I come."*
> Rev 2:24-25

In this passage Christ clearly relates the sins of Jezebel to what he calls the *depths of Satan*. Make no mistake about it; these are the works of Satan. In a remarkable statement, Christ acknowledges that there are some in the church of Thyatira who have not accepted or followed the doctrines of Jezebel or the tremendous societal and social pressures in the city. They are speaking out against this heresy. Christ says that: *I will not put upon you any other burden, but that which you have already*. Such grace and compassion our Savior has! He will ask no more of those that suffer under the teachings of Jezebel but to stay the course. What a glorious promise! They are doing the work of the Lord and carrying on the faith; he will ask no more. How long? Christ says to *hold fast until I come*. So much for the teaching that this letter is a historical artifact and that it has no meaning today. It has been almost 2000 years since Christ made this statement, and he has not come yet. Christ says to watch, wait, do not retreat but *conquer the land*, do not faint but *run strong*. *Surely I come quickly, Amen Even so, come Lord Jesus* (Rev 22:20).

Covenant to the Overcomer

> *"He that hath an ear, let him hear what the Spirit saith unto the churches; He that overcometh, and keepeth my works unto the end, to him will I give power over the nations: and he shall rule them with a rod of iron; as the vessels of a potter shall they be broken to shivers; even as I received of my Father. And I will give him the morning star."*
> Rev 2:29, 26-28

As in all the seven letters, Christ concludes with a promise to the overcomers. Here Christ gives a total of three promises to those who are patiently fighting the good fight: (1) *I will give power over the nations*, (2) those to whom power is granted will *rule with a rod of iron*, and (3) I *will give him the morning star*. This is paradoxically the only church to receive three promises. The force of the word *power* is given by the Greek word **Exousian**, which implies that the class of Christians who are referred to as overcomers will physically rule over people. That a group of the Messiah's followers will join him in ruling and reigning in the hereafter is a common theme of prophecy (Rev 1:6, 12:5, 19:15). In the *Parable of the Talents*, Christ said: **Well done thy good and faithful servant: thou hast been faithful over a few things, I will make thee ruler over many things** (Mat 25:21). This is a *Kingdom Parable* and is prophetic of things to come. Those Christians who will have to be martyred for Christ's sake during the last 3 ½ years of the tribulation period will rule and reign with Christ during the 1000-year millennial kingdom (Rev 20:4). Ruling with a *rod of iron* is a direct reference to Psalms 2:8-9. The implication is that the overcomer will also rule with a rod of iron. The reference to the phrase *as the vessels of a potter shall they be broken to shivers* is a powerful Greek phrase which carries the meaning of violence and destruction. It is probably a reference to the

Second Advent of Christ when the saints will join Christ in his victorious and righteous destruction of Satan and all of his followers at the battle of Armageddon (Rev 19:11-16). The third promise is that in some mystical and wonderful way we will receive Christ himself as part of who we will be for all eternity. *I am the Root and the offspring of David, the bright and morning star* (Rev 22:16). *He that hath an ear, let him hear what the spirit sayeth unto the churches* (Rev 2:29).

The Church at Sardis... *The Dead Church*

Characteristics of the Community

The name Sardis means *the escaping ones* or *those who came out*. The city was situated about 50 miles East of Smyrna in the middle of a large plain which was split by a high hill rising to just over 1500 feet. Sardis was a transition point between the plains of *Hermus* and the mountain of *Tmolus*. Tmolus was an ancient King of Lydia. Mount Tmolus towered over Sardis to a height of 2200 meters. Greek mythology records that it was on Mt. Tmolus that the musical contest between Pan and Apollo was decided. To the north of this high hill the rise splintered into a series of long narrow fingers, one of which formed a steep outcropping descending into a flat plateau. It was here that Sardis was built. The geographical location of Sardis formed a natural fortification on three sides which made the city almost impregnable to foreign invaders.

The city appears to have been founded around 1200 BC. Sardis was on a main trade route from east to west, and was the object of frequent invasions. Although well protected, it had fallen on two different occasions. On each occasion, the city fell due to complacency and the belief that they were impregnable. Cyrus the Mead and Alexander the Great both conquered the city by descending the steep outcropping to the east of the city at night without opposition. On both occasions, there was not a single guard posted to alert the city at the point of descent. The city of Sardis was very affluent and rich and it is reported that the nearby River Pactolus contained gold. Ancient writings attest that gold coins were struck there for Roman emperors using the gold from the Pactolus River. When the apostle John penned the book of Revelation, the city was famous for its performing arts and had a massive amphitheatre which could seat over 1000 participants. However, the city was best known for its ability to both manufacture and dye wool products. Sardis was the center of wool trade in Asia Minor. Woolen garments for kings and noblemen were manufactured in Sardis. It is said to be the first city to master the art of dying wool purple and scarlet, which was universally recognized as the attire of royalty. The city was not a major center of pagan worship, but a large number of residents worshipped the goddess Cybele, who was said to have the power to restore the dead to life. These characteristics of Sardis were representative of the spiritual fiber of the church at Sardis. This church was a rich church, which like the city had fallen into spiritual lethargy and dead works. It had everything worldly but nothing spiritually. The church at Sardis was dead in works, deeds and witness. The rebuke by Christ is scathing and final, there was nothing worth saving.

Concept of Christ

> *"And unto the angel of the church at Sardis write... These things saith he that hath the seven Spirits of God, and the seven stars; I know thy works, that thou hast a name that thou livest, and art dead.:*
> Rev 3:1

After addressing this letter to the ***angel of the church at Sardis,*** Christ offers two characteristics of his preeminence and immediately states his view of the church. Christ identifies himself as: ***he that has the seven spirits of God and the seven stars.*** We have previously seen this description in Rev 1:4 and 1:20. The seven stars are almost certainly identified as the *angels or messengers* at each church to which the seven letters are addressed. The **seven spirits of God** have been the source of much controversy, and have been suggested as either the seven-fold nature of Christ or as seven angels who stand waiting and ready for special service. Neither seems to fit the current context. The most satisfactory explanation seems to be a reference to the manifold works of the Holy Spirit revealed in Is 11:1-3. These are the spirit of (1) *wisdom,* (2) *understanding,* (3) *counsel,* (4) *might,* (5) *power,* (6) *fear,* and (7) *knowledge.* These seven spirits speak to the omniscient character of Christ and his perfect knowledge of all things. Christ now states as He has before that *He knows*. He knows *thy works*, but their works are not in the name of our Savior which is eternal, but in another name that they live by. The name of Jesus Christ is power; it is love; and it is the only name by which salvation can be granted. Christ now utters a terrible condemnation: **Thou hast a name *(by which)* thou livest and *(thou)* art dead.** Not decaying or dying but *dead*. It was outwardly rich and alive, but inwardly it was pronounced *dead*.

Commendation and Credits

> *"Thou hast a few names even in Sardis which have not defiled their garments; and they shall walk with me in white: for they are worthy."*   Rev 3:4

Although Christ had pronounced that the Church at Sardis was dead, he now acknowledges that there were a precious few who have not yet **defiled their garments**. Sardis was famous for woolen clothes of scarlet and purple, but these are the clothes of man and not the raiment that Christ wants us to wear. Christ will clothe his chosen ones in raiment of pure white as we will see in his promise to the overcomers. At the Second Advent of Christ, those who Christ calls will follow him into battle clothed as a *wife which hath made herself ready*. On that day, the *Day of the Lord*, **Let us be glad and rejoice and give honour to him; for the marriage of the Lamb is come, and his bride hath made herself ready** (Rev 19:7).

Condemnation and Chastening

> *"Be watchful, and strengthen the things which remain, that are ready to die; for I have not found thy works perfect before God."*   Rev 3:2

Christ now addresses the faithful few, and counsels them to be vigilant and strong: Be **watchful and strengthen the things which remain, that are ready to die.** Evidently, although Christ has already pronounced the church at Sardis to be spiritually dead, there were some good works remaining which should be strengthened immediately. Christ asserts that *they are ready to die*, as it is clear that those who hold fast and continue with some good works are on the verge of dying. Good and acceptable works which please God must come forth from a basis of love and faith, and these two fundamental properties of good works were evidently missing and dead in the church at Sardis. As already pointed out, the outward appearance of this church was wealth, prosperity and greatness; but God does not base his judgment upon outward appearances of the flesh but the inward qualities of the heart. This church is spiritually dead.

Counsel to the Church

> *"Remember therefore how thou hast received and heard, and hold fast, and repent. If therefore thou shalt not watch, I will come on you as a thief, and thou shalt not know what hour I will come upon thee."*   Rev 3:3

To those who Christ has found worthy, he offers a counsel of redeeming grace and redemption: ***Remember therefore how thou hast received and heard.*** Christ points out in a definite manner that it is not so much *what* has been heard but *how* it has been heard. What does this mean? According to the book of Acts, at this time the apostles had succeeded in preaching the gospel throughout the known world. It is not *what* we hear, but *how* we hear, and how we respond to the call. Today the gospel is transmitted by books, television and the internet 24 hours a day, but an unbelieving world refuses to accept the gift of eternal life. The gospel of Jesus Christ and the gift of eternal life must be received in spirit and truth by the heart and not the ear. The next counsel is to *hold fast and repent*. The Greek word for repent is ***metanoeo*** which means to think differently, to understand and react accordingly. The message is clear: ***Wherefore come out from among them, and be ye separate, saith the Lord, and touch not the unclean thing; and I will receive you*** (2 Cor. 6:17). This is reminiscent of the command in the Old Testament that no one could touch a dead person without being defiled, and to be cleansed required a blood sacrifice and atonement. Christ now asserts the immanency of his council. ***If therefore thou shalt not watch, I will come on you as a thief, and thou shalt not know what hour I will come upon thee.*** This statement by Christ is almost identical to that recorded by Luke in his record of the Olivet Discourse (Luke 13):

> *"Watch ye therefore for the master of the house cometh, at evening, or at midnight, or at the cockcrowing or in the morning, lest suddenly he finds you (spiritually) sleeping. And what I say unto you (his disciples) I say unto all, watch."*
> Luke 13:35-37

Covenant to the Overcomer

> *"He that overcometh, the same shall be clothed in white raiment; and I will not blot his name out of the book of life, but I confess his name before his angels. He that hath an ear, let him hear what the Spirit saith unto the churches."* Rev 3:5-6

Be reminded that the promise given to the overcomer in each church is also for every church. Christ promises three things: (1) *the same shall be clothed in white raiment.* We have already discussed the meaning of this promise. The eternal clothing of the resurrected saints appears to be white, symbolic of truth, purity and the righteous acts of the saints (Rev 19:8). (2) *I will not blot his name out of the Book of Life.* There are many books mentioned in the Bible and a study of each is both informative and rewarding. Two specific books are here in view. God appears to have in his possession a *Book of Life* which contains the names of every person who will be born. The existence of such a book can be traced to the book of Exodus (Exodus 32:32). The exact term *Book of Life* is recorded in Phil 4:3. The second Book of Life is identified only in the apocalypse, and is referred to as the **Lamb's Book of Life** (Rev 13:8, 21:27). Since the source of the message to the church at Sardis is Christ himself, the reference here is rightly implied to be his book, the *Lamb's Book of Life*. Careful exegesis of the Holy Scriptures will result in the following possible interpretation. God's Book of Life at creation contained the name of every person who was ever to be born of woman. This includes the Old Testament saints and the New Testament saints. The Lamb's Book of Life appears to be one that is kept by Jesus Christ. A name is entered into that book when a sinner is saved and accepts Christ as his/her Savior. The names recorded in the Lamb's Book of Life can never be erased. The two books are not identical. (3) *I will confess his name before his angels.* The third promise is directly related to the second, and implies that at the final judgment, Christ will *acknowledge* all whose names are written in his Lamb's Book of Life to both God the Father and his angelic hosts. The implication of such a promise is that if we who are in Christ acknowledge him before other men and do not deny his holy name, Christ will faithfully do the same for each of us before God and his angels. At the Feast of Dedication in Jerusalem (Feast of Hanukah), Christ affirmed this glorious promise. *My sheep hear my voice, and I know them, and they follow me. And I will give unto them eternal life; and they shall never perish, neither shall any man pluck them out of my hand* (John 10:27-28).

The Church at Philadelphia... *The Strong Church*

Characteristics of the Community

The word Philadelphia means *one who loves his brother*. The American city of Philadelphia, Pennsylvania assumed this name and is known as the City of Brotherly Love. The church at Philadelphia was called the gateway to the east, and was situated on a road connecting Smyrna to Asia and all points east. The road from Rome to Pergamum also crossed at Philadelphia. The city was active in trade, but was not as wealthy as Smyrna. Greece designated the city as a center of Greek culture and language arts. The citizens of Philadelphia were obviously well educated. Philadelphia was about 30 miles south and southeast of Sardis in the lower reaches of the Hermus valley, but it was founded on the edge of a great plateau rising 1500 feet above the valley floor. Philadelphia was famous for its wine, and might be considered to be the *Napa Valley of Asia Minor*. The patron god of Philadelphia was the Greek god Bacaas, the god of wine and liquid spirits. The soil was ideally suited to growing wine, having been deposited over the centuries by ancient volcanic activity. The city was well protected from invading armies, but could not protect itself from periodic earthquakes. It was on the edge of an unstable geographic region called *Katakekaumene*, which means *I burn down*. The city had been severely damaged on one occasion, and almost totally destroyed on another. Each time it was rebuilt stronger than before. The town of Philadelphia still exists under the name of *Alaseher*, which means *City of God*. It has thousands of Christians that worship and live there. Although the town itself was naturally unstable, the church at Philadelphia was rock solid. Christ's message to this church had *not one criticism*. He was pleased with its mission, its message and its merits.

Concept of Christ

> *"And unto the angel of the church at Philadelphias write… These things saith he that is holy, he that is true, he that hath the Key of David, he that openeth, and no man shutteth, and no man openeth."*
> *Rev 3:7*

After the common salutation to the *angel* of the church at Philadelphia, Christ reveals himself in a way quite different from any of the previous five churches. He declares himself as: (1) **holy**, (2) **true**, and (3) **he that hath the key of David**. He ends by asserting that: **he that openeth, and no man shutteth, and no man openeth**. The *Holy One* in the Old Testament always referred to the Holy God, *Jehova*, and any Jew would readily discern that here Christ is equating his holiness to that of the Father. To any Jew, this is blasphemy, but throughout the New Testament this title is associated with the *Lamb of God* (Mark 1:24, Luke 1:35, 4:34, John 6:69, Acts 4:27, 30 and I John 2:20 to cite a few). The Greek word used here for holy is **alethinos** and is coupled with the adjective **hagios**, being translated *He that is holy*. This phrase does not only bring the force of someone who is sinless, but one who is holy in the sense of being chosen and set apart. Since Christ is holy by his own declaration, his words are also holy and true. The phrase, ***holy one*** comes from the Latin word *alethinas*, which also carries with it the context of one who is real as opposed to unreal. In Christ, the Church at Philadelphia is being addressed by God himself as a part of the Holy Trinity. Jesus in his earthly ministry declared himself to be: ***the way, the truth and the life*** (John 14:6). The wages of sin are death, but the payment for accepting Jesus Christ as one's personal Savior is eternal life. Christ next reveals himself as the one who has ***the Key of David***. To any devout Jew living at that time, King David was expected to come again, purge all evil from the earth, restore all things and establish an eternal kingdom that would last forever. This statement is in direct reference to Isa 22:22. Christ was from the royal line of David, and his linage and authority have already been established in Rev 1:5 and is given in Mat 1:1-17. According to Messianic Jewish expectation, the eternal earthly kingdom awaited by the Jews would not be established until David returns. In looking ahead, it is obvious from the full context of this letter that in Rev 3:9 Satan had attacked the church using a group of church members who declared themselves to be Jewish Christian converts, but they were not: They were trying to discredit the works and words of the Messiah. They were trying to persuade the church that there was yet another Messiah to come, and that he would hold the keys to the kingdom. In his opening remarks, Jesus makes it clear that He alone held the ***Key of David***. The central message of the Old Testament was that a greater seed of Abraham, from the lineage of David, would arise to save all mankind, Christ is that *key*. He holds the key to the bottomless pit (Rev 20:1-3); He holds the keys to Death and Hades (Rev 1:18); and He holds the key to the Kingdom of Heaven (Mat 16:17-18). No man can shut the door of salvation that He opens; and no man can open it once it is shut at the end of the age.

Commendation and Credits

> *"I know thy works: behold, I have set before thee an open door, and no man can shut it for thou hast a little strength, and hast kept my word, and hast not denied my name."*   Rev 3:8

In the previous verse, Christ has identified himself as having the Key of David, which opens a door that no one can shut. Here he affirms as in previous letters that: *I know thy works*. Christ has been walking around in this church and watching their dedication and works to him. These works are fully acceptable, and for their labor he now sets before them an open door that he reaffirms no man can shut. Jesus Christ himself is the door (John 10:7). Once any person has accepted Jesus Christ as their Savior the door to salvation is opened to that person, and no one can shut that door. Christ is pleased with this church and now offers three reasons why their continuing works are acceptable: (1) ***thou hast (only) a little strength*** (2) thou ***hast kept my word*** and (3) ***thou hast not denied my name***. The Greek word used for strength is ***dunamis*** and is best translated *power*. After Christ was baptized of John in the Jordon River, he resisted the temptations of Satan for 40 days and: ***he returned in the power (***dunamis***) of the*** (Holy) ***spirit*** Paraclete)into Galilee (Luke 4:14). At his second coming he will return with all of his holy angels with *dunamis*, and his saints will be with him. The strength that they possess is now explained. ***They have kept his word and not denied his name***. Evidently they have experienced a confrontation in which they had been commanded to deny the deity of Jesus Christ and they had not. As in the gospel accounts, it is likely that some Jews had attempted to persuade the church members to deny Christ, but they had remained strong.

Condemnation and Chastening

Not a single word!!!

Correction by Christ

> *"Behold, I will make them of the synagogue of Satan, which say they are Jews and are not, but do lie; behold I will make them to come and worship before thy feet, and to know that I have loved you. Because thou hast kept the word of my patience, I also will keep thee from the hour of temptation which shall come upon all the world, to try them that dwell upon the earth."* Rev 3:9-10

The previous conjecture that a group of Jews were trying to undermine the church now becomes a near certainty, since Christ says he will: **make them of the synagogue of Satan, which say they are Jews and are not** to **worship before thy feet.** The reason given is that Jesus loves those who have kept his word and not denied his name. The synagogue is not the church, but the teaching center in which the scriptures are taught and debated. Evidently some false Messianic Jews or a group of the Jewish population was preaching some form of heresy, religion without Jesus Christ. Today we see the same sort of satanic attack from a much broader set of religious zealots: Hindus, Buddhists, Muslims and other religious groups. Jesus here warns us that these teachings are from Satan, and must be rejected. According to Jude 3-4, 12-17 this sort of religious assault on the gospel of Jesus Christ will not only increase but prosper.

> *"For there are certain men crept in unawares, who were before of old ordained to this condemnation, ungodly men, turning the grace of our God into lasciviousness, and denying the only Lord God, and our Lord Jesus Christ"*

"These are spots in your feasts of charity, when they feast with you, feeding themselves without fear, clouds that are without water, carried about of winds, trees without fruit withereth, twice dead."

These heretics in the Church at Philadelphia are declared by Christ to be a member of the **Church of Satan**. Satan was said to dwell in the city of Pergamum (Rev 2:13), but he had also infiltrated the churches at Smyrna and Philadelphia. At this point Christ interjects a *promise* to every member of this church: **Because thou hast kept the word of my patience, I also will keep thee from the hour of temptation which shall come upon all the world, to try them that dwell upon the earth.** This promise must be examined in light of what is yet to come. What is the *hour of temptation* that shall come upon the entire world? First note that the word *hour* is the Greek word **hora** which is used 86 times in the New Testament, and every time it is used to denote a relatively short period of time (Rev 3:3, 8:1, 9:15, 11:13, 14:7, 17:12, :10, 18:17, and 18:19.). It evidently is a period of time that the entire world will be tried and tested. The central theme of the book of Revelation is that Satan will be given 3.5 years to persecute and tempt those that dwell upon the earth, and kill those who refuse to worship his image. **And he** (the false prophet) **had power to give life to the image of the beast** (Satan) **, that the image of the beast should both speak, and cause that as many as would not worship the image of the beast should be killed.** During that period of time, many followers of Christ who **hast kept my word and not denied my name** (Rev 3:8) will be martyred (Rev 6:4, 6:11, 20:4). This is the *tribulation period* (Mat 24:21). We will later show that this period of time is the last 3.5 years of Daniel's 70th week. Christ here promises that the church body of Philadelphia, for whom he had no rebuke, will not have to go through this period of persecution. This conclusion is reinforced by examining

Rev 17:12, in which a 10-nation confederacy will receive power for *one hour* under the dictatorship of the antichrist; which will last exactly 3.5 years.

Counsel to the Church

> *"Behold, I come quickly: hold that fast which thou hast, that no man take thy crown."*   Rev 3:11

While this counsel is given to the members of the church at Philadelphia, it is also offered to all of the churches, with special emphasis to the church at Philadelphia: ***He that hath an ear, let him hear what the Spirit says unto the churches.*** This is a promise to anyone who follows the examples and practices set by the church body at Philadelphia. No requirement is placed upon this church except to *hold fast*. Many a church has started strong with good programs and good works, only to falter and fail as time goes on. It is difficult to stay the course set before us, and requires much prayer and dedication. We are best to remember that our Lord and Savior Jesus Christ held fast even unto death. We must not falter or fail if we are to follow him. The next statement is prophetic and discloses the fate of all Christians who will not be faithful to him and his gospel message: ***Hold fast to which thou hast, that no man take thy crown***. We must realize that this letter contained no rebuke at all, nothing but praise. It is clear that in shadow and type, all members were being praised and were not in danger of losing the Crown of Life promised to those who were faithfully enduring severe persecution in the church at Smyrna (Rev 2:10). The crown referred to in this letter is undoubtedly the Crown of Righteousness. ***I have fought the good fight, I have finished my course, I have kept the faith: Henceforth there is laid up for me a Crown of Righteousness, which the Lord, the righteous judge, shall give me at that day: and not to me only, but unto all of them that love his appearing*** (I Tim 4:7-8). Christ is the righteous judge, and the place is the Bema Seat

Judgment, at which time all whose names are found in the Lamb's Book of Life will be rewarded for works done. We appear before Christ not to receive God's wrath of condemnation, but our Crown of Righteousness. None of those who have accepted Christ as their Lord and Savior will ever lose their Crown of Life.

Covenant to the Overcomer

"Him that overcometh will I make a pillar in the temple of my God, and he shall go no more out: and I will write upon him the name of my God, and the name of the city of my God, which is New Jerusalem, which cometh down from out of Heaven from my God; and I will write upon him my new name. He that hath an ear, let him hear what the Spirit saith unto the churches." Rev 12:13

As in each of the other churches, there are promises made to a group of Christ's followers which are called overcomers. They are not a group of *Phi Beta Kappa* Christians, but simply individuals who have sold out to Christ and have chosen to follow after Him rather than what the world has to offer. These are the individuals of whom the writer of the book of Hebrews referred when exhorting the Christians in Rome: ***Therefore, leaving the principles of the doctrine of Christ, let us go on unto perfection"***(Heb 6:1). We can never hope to achieve any form of perfection in this life, but on that day we will be like imputed to us through his abundant grace. This is a message to every Christian today to move on to maturity and to stop wasting time and opportunities to serve Christ.

To the faithful church at Philadelphia, three promises are made to the overcomer: (1) ***I will make*** (him) ***a pillar in the temple of my God, and he shall go no more out***, (2) ***I will write upon him the name of my God, and the name of the city of my God, which is New Jerusalem,*** *which cometh down from out of Heaven from my God,* and (3) *I will write upon him my new name.* Consistent with the fact that there is no rebuke whatsoever for this church, the promises found here reflect how this class of overcomers will spend eternity. The promise to make the overcomer a *pillar in the temple of my God* is clearly a metaphor. What is a pillar? It is something that provides great support to the structure in which it stands. Since the use of *pillar* is a metaphor, it is best to interpret the *temple* in which the pillar is housed to be a metaphor also. This conclusion is also theologically correct, since in Revelation 21:22 we are told that in the New Jerusalem where all of the saints will reside that there is no temple. **And I saw no temple therein: for the Lord God Almighty and the Lamb are the temple of it.** This passage also reveals to us that the Son of God *is the temple.* The overcomers from the Church at Philadelphia are promised that they will be forever in the presence of our Lord Jesus Christ. They will stand with him forever. They are given the strong assurance that they will be with him forever. Members of the church at Philadelphia would have no trouble understanding the meaning of this promise. In the city of Philadelphia, when a new magistrate for the city was named by Rome, a pillar honoring him was placed in one of the temples of the city. The overcomer is also assured that *he shall go no more out.* Once joined to Christ, no one can separate them from Christ Jesus. *Who can separate us from the love of Christ? ...for I am persuaded that neither death, nor life, nor angels, nor principalities, nor powers, nor things present or those to come... shall be able to separate us from the love of God, which is in Jesus Christ our Lord* Rom 8:35-39.

The second promise is that: *I will write upon him the name of my God, and the name of the city of my God, which is New Jerusalem, which cometh down from out of Heaven from my God.* Our dual relationship to God the Father and God the Son is emphasized by associating our identity three times with God. In the Old Testament, the name of God could not even be spelled out. In our new relationship with him, He will have written upon us the name of God to assure our identity with him. Second, we will have the name of our eternal dwelling place, the New Jerusalem written upon us. This will *be an eternal visible sign of our right* to inhabit that city. Christ said;

> *"In my Father's house are many mansions: if it were not so, I would have told you. I go to prepare a place for you. And if I go and prepare a place for you, I will come again, and receive you unto myself; that where I am, you may be also."* John 14:2-3.

Finally, Christ asserts that: *I will write upon him my new name.* When Jesus Christ returns to rule as King of Kings, he will be called by a new name that no one can know until that time. Imagine that! We will be given a new name, and will be identified with not only the name of God himself, but of Christ's new name and the name of the New Jerusalem. Revelation Chapter 21 provides a detailed description of the New Jerusalem. *He that hath an ear, let him hear what the Spirit says to the churches*

The Church at Laodicea... *The Lukewarm Church*

Following the glorious description of the church at Philadelphia, in which there was no rebuke whatsoever, we now come to the seventh and final letter to the church at Laodicea. In stark contrast, the church at Laodicea has fallen so far that Christ has not one thing good to say about its existence, not a single commendation. Laodicea is a prime example of what can happen to any church that abandons the gospel of Jesus Christ and chooses to follow the world.

Characteristics of the Community

The city of Laodicea was almost due west of Ephesus, and about 40 miles southeast of Philadelphia. Like most of the other six cities, it was on a main trade route connecting Ephesus to the Far East. It was in close proximity to some of the best agricultural farmland in all of what is now called Greece. It was famous for growing sheep with glossy black wool and the textile industry that built up around this product. Laodicea was the center of medical practices and was famous for the knowledge of how to package and dispense medicinal supplies. Perhaps the most famous medical discovery was a salve which had been developed to treat eye diseases. The majority of the Laodiceans were very wealthy, and lived in lavish villas, some of which had hot water baths fed by nearby volcanic springs. In 60 AD a major earthquake almost totally destroyed the city. Rome offered funds to rebuild the city, but the residents of Laodicea refused the offer and rebuilt the city themselves. Both the city and its residents lacked for nothing. They were wealthy, self-sufficient and needed no one. Wealth and power lead to worldly living, and the love of money can lead one to complacency and eventually replace one's love for Christ. To be strong in Christ is to be weak. To be pure in Christ is to be persecuted by the world. In his second letter to the Corinthians, Paul spoke of this: *I take pleasure in infirmities, in reproaches, in necessities, in persecution, in distresses for Christ's sake: for when I am weak, then I am strong* (II Cor. 12:10). The church at Laodicea was rich and dressed in fine black woolen clothing with salve to sooth their eyes, but Christ said they were: *wretched, miserable, poor, blind and naked.* They had lost their candlestick (Rev 1:20) and were as good as dead.

Concept of Christ

"And unto the angel of the church of the Laodiceans write... These things saith the Amen, the faithful and true witness, the beginning of the creation of God." Rev 3:14

In the opening statement of this letter the Authorized King James Version has an interesting play on words. ***Unto the... Church of the Laodiceans***. All other letters begin with a salutation to the *angelos* of the church to whom the letter is addressed. Here the implication is that the church at Laodicea does not belong to Christ, but to the world. They have become disconnected from Christ and his eternal purpose for the body of Christ. Christ asserts himself as the ***Amen***. The word *amen* is a word picture which means *let it be so*. Christ has weighed them in the balance and they have been found wanting. His final judgment: *let it be so*. He is the one faithful and true witness. He cannot and will not lie; he is the Son of God. Jesus said: **I *am the way, the truth and the life*.** He is the firstborn of all creation, and the first to rise from the grave to everlasting glory.

Commendation and Credits

Not one….not even one!

Condemnation and Chastening

"I know thy works, that thou art neither cold nor hot: I would thou wert cold or hot. So then because thou art lukewarm, and neither cold nor hot, I will spue thee out of my mouth. Because thou sayest, I am rich, and increased with goods, and have need of nothing; and knowest not that thou art wretched, and miserable, and poor, and blind, and naked."
Rev 3:15-17

Again Christ asserts that *I know*. He wastes no time in revealing what He knows about this church: *I know thy works*. Christ has made this statement to four of the six churches which precede Laodicea (Ephesus, Thyatira, Sardis and Philadelphia). The phrase used here as in all the previous cases can imply works that are acceptable or unacceptable to Christ. The proper usage is in context. Christ minces no words here: *Thou art neither cold nor hot*. The displeasure with this church is not the lack of works, but the manner in which they are being conducted. Sincerity is something that can always be discerned when people do things. The world today is full of people who work for a living and hate what they are doing. They are just going through the motions. Such people seldom excel at what they are doing, and they usually achieve only the minimum goals required. They are just leaves in the wind, with neither fervent direction nor purpose. They are neither *cold nor hot*. The Christians at Laodicea have avoided complete absence of works, but have failed to achieve spiritual fervor. The Greek word for hot used here is *zestos*. Its root derivative means *to boil*. It was translated *fervent* in both Acts 18:25 and in Romans 12:11. The Greek word for cold used here is **psychros** which means *cold to the point of absence of any heat*. It is very interesting that in the city of Laodicea, its water supply came from a number of large springs which had been created by subterranean pressure from volcanic activity. At the surface, the water was not cool or hot, but tepid and lukewarm. Most people have enjoyed an ice cold soda pop and a piping hot cup of coffee. But, lukewarm coffee and soda pop is worse than none at all. In contrast, Christ expects nothing less than sincere, *boiling* fervor in going about the work of proclaiming His gospel and promoting His Kingdom. Those Christians that are *cold* at least have a chance to become hot, but lukewarm service is worse than being cold to Christ. Christ said:

> *"No man can serve two masters: for either he will hate the one, and love the other; or else he will hold to the one, and despise the other. Ye cannot serve God and mammon."* Matthew 6:24

In a scathing rebuke of what is happening spiritually and in their works, Christ asserts that: *because thou art lukewarm, and neither cold nor hot, I will spue thee out of my mouth.* The disgust of Christ with this behavior is reflected in the meaning of the Greek word which is used for *spue*. It literally means to *vomit*. The phrase *spew you out of my mouth* only occurs here in the entire New Testament. While this rebuke is scathing, it pales in comparison to the scorn which is indicated in the next judgment of Christ. *Because thou sayest, I am rich, and increased with goods, and have need of nothing; and knowest not that thou art wretched, and miserable, and poor, and blind, and naked.* Christ wants to clothe all of his believers in pure white robes of righteousness, but He asserts here that the people in the church of Laodicea are *naked*. Recall that the town of Laodicea was a wealthy community that was a large commercial and trade center. The wealth of a congregation is not reflected in how beautiful the sanctuary might be or in how majestic the building appears, it is in the inward wealth and beauty of the people who serve Him in goodness and in truth. The church at Smyrna was living in poverty, but Christ said that *I will give you a Crown of Life*. The churches of today should take heed of this message; too many churches have beautiful, expansive buildings and luxurious sanctuaries, but their works are *lukewarm*. The congregation in the upper room was likely eating only cold figs and reclining on the floor, but the Holy Spirit fell on them in power and they went forth to preach the gospel *on fire* for Christ. The statement that the congregation of Laodicea was *blind* would have great meaning. Recall that the great center of healing in this town had developed a salve which when put on the eyes would heal the effects of all the sand and winds that blew in that area. Ironically, the Laodiceans could heal inflamed eyes but could not heal themselves. *And why beholdest thou the mote that is in thy brother's eye, but perceivest not the beam that is in thine own eye?* (Luke 6:41).

Counsel to the Church

> *"I counsel thee to buy of me gold tried in the fire, that thou mayest be rich; and white raiment, that thou mayest be clothed, and that the shame of thy nakedness do not appear; and anoint thine eyes with eye salve, that thou mayest see. As many as I love, I rebuke and chasten: be zealous therefore, and repent. Behold, I stand at the door, and knock: if any man hear my voice, and open the door, I will come into him, and will sup with him, and he with me."* Rev 3:18-20

As complacent as this church was in its works, and in spite of Christ's scathing rebukes, there is apparently some hope yet. The phrase *I counsel* is best interpreted as *I advise*, and it is a strong grammatical construction. Christ advised this church to do three things: (1) *buy of me gold tried in the fire*, (2) be clothed in *white raiment*, and (3) *anoint thine eyes*. What is this *gold* of which Christ speaks? This is not the earthly gold by which men mark their success in this world, but *spiritual gold*. Gold becomes more precious the more it is carefully refined. It must be heated, melted and in its purist form separated from all impurities. The analogy of seeking to be Christ-like through fleshly works is not a thing of value to the Lord, nor is a long list of works. We are made pure as gold by the redeeming grace of Jesus Christ, and our submission to Him as the Master refiner. Our faith in Him and how we respond to His calling is much more valuable to Him than all of the gold in the world. We were not redeemed and reconciled to God by gold and silver, but by the sacrificial death of our Lord Jesus Christ on the Cross of Calvary.

> *"That the trial of your faith, being much more precious than of gold that perisheth, though it be tried with fire, might be found unto praise and honour and glory at the appearing of Jesus Christ: Forasmuch as ye know that ye were not redeemed with corruptible things, as silver and gold, from your vain conversation received by tradition from your fathers."*   I Peter 1:7-8

The *white raiment* of which Christ speaks here is usually associated with the resurrection of our sinful body. However, this cannot be the case here. Christ is speaking to a group of living Christians in this church. The nakedness referred to here is often used as to represent spiritual nakedness. This is the clothing of Christians who have outwardly professed to put on the righteousness of Christ, but inwardly they are naked. *For as many of you as have been baptized into Christ have put on Christ* (Gal 3:27). Christ again uses a simile that reflects their worldly wealth. *Anoint thine eyes with eye salve, that thou mayest see.* We have already pointed out that this city is famous for its eye salve. Christ now enjoins them to find the salve of salvation and apply it to their spiritual condition. Christ now provides the salve of grace. *As many as I love, I rebuke and chasten: be zealous therefore, and repent.* This humbly reminds us of how we may have disciplined and counseled our own children. How many of us have severely rebuked our children and executed punishment on them for their own good, and then later shown our love and concern for them. Christ now shows His abundant grace. He assures them that while He is losing His patience with this church and is ready to remove their *candlestick*, He provides them redemption: *be zealous therefore, and repent.* This grace is not passive but requires them to be *zealous*. This is a message to many of the saints today; do not be lukewarm; do not be lethargic; do not work with complacency. Christ calls us to be *zealous* and *hot*; not lukewarm. In one of the great affirmations of Christ's love for us He now utters a remarkably passionate call.

> ***"Behold, I stand at the door, and knock: if any man hear my voice, and open the door, I will come into him, and will sup with him, and he with me."***
> Rev 3:20

The picture of Christ standing at the door and knocking is identical to the Jewish groom who has come to claim his bride. He stands at the door and knocks, waiting for the opportunity to rush inside and claim his bride. The *door* is likely a simile which represents the heart. The Holy Spirit is constantly knocking on the door of our heart, and asking to come in. Another possible reference is to the Second Advent of Christ when He returns for His saints. The door of salvation is open now, but it will closed when He returns, Christ is offering us His open door, but He stands ready to close the door to salvation to all those who refuse His free gift of salvation while they are still alive on this earth. The offer is conclusive and sure: *if any man hear my voice, and open the door, I will come into him.* Here we are given another wonderful promise; *I will sup with him, and he with me.* What an intimate and wonderful promise! Christ is inviting us to come and dine with Him! When Christ held His last supper with His disciples he made the following statements and promise:

> ***"And as they were eating, Jesus took bread, and blessed it, and brake it, and gave it to the disciples, and said, Take, eat; this is my body. And he took the cup, and gave thanks, and gave it to them, saying, Drink ye all of it; For this is my blood of the new testament, which is shed for many for the remission***

> *of sins. But I say unto you, I will not drink henceforth of this fruit of the vine, until that day when I drink it new with you in my Father's kingdom."* Mat 26:26-29

That Day is at the marriage supper of the Lamb. We will *sup with Him and He with me.* Oh what a glorious promise! Oh what a wonderful promise! *Oh Lord Jesus, come quickly!*

Covenant to the Overcomer

> *"To him that overcometh will I grant to sit with me in my throne, even as I also overcame, and am set down with my Father in his throne."* Rev 3:21-22

There is only one promise given to the overcomer in this letter, but it is a majestic and unbelievable one. We are going to be allowed to set with Jesus and God Himself on His holy throne. This is a reaffirmation of the promise given to the lukewarm church of Laodicea. Christ also gave this promise to His 12 disciples while He was here on this earth. *And Jesus said unto them, Verily I say unto you, That ye which have followed me, in the regeneration when the Son of man shall sit in the throne of his glory, ye also shall sit upon twelve thrones, judging the twelve tribes of Israel* (Mat 19:28). The pattern of Christ sharing His throne with the overcomers follows the relationship of Jesus Christ to His Father, who is now sitting on the throne of God and constantly interceding for us. *Now of the things which we have spoken this is the sum: We have such a high priest, who is set on the right hand of the throne of the Majesty in the heavens* (Heb 8:1). However, we see in this promise that Christ will also have a throne which is different from the one He now shares with the Father. The existence of two thrones provides us information about the millennial kingdom and the economy in which it will operate. Christ's throne will exist here on the earth in Jerusalem during the millennial kingdom. He will share this throne with not only the overcomers but also with David who will rule and reign over the 12 tribes of Israel. Following the 1000 year millennial kingdom, God and His Son will once again share the same throne (Rev 22:3). In a final appeal to not only the seven churches in Asia Minor, but to all of the churches today Christ closes all of the letters with a familiar directive. ***He that hath an ear, let him hear what the Spirit saith unto the churches.***

Conclusions

There are those who teach that these seven letters to each of the seven Churches in the Roman province of Asia Minor are strictly historical and that the warnings and praises only apply to that period of time over which each church existed. For all practical purposes, all seven churches have disappeared into history, but the spirit in each lives on. That spirit is either from Christ or from Satan, and sometimes a mixture of both. However, it is generally agreed among church scholars that two of these seven churches represent the two main types of churches that will exist in the end times. Those two churches are *Philadelphia and Laodicea*. The Church at Philadelphia *has kept his word and not denied his name*. It *has little strength* but it *has persevered*. There is absolutely no rebuke at all! Laodicea is *rich but spiritually poor*; it is *neither hot nor cold but has lukewarm faith*. In a scathing rebuke, Christ says that this church is wretched, poor, miserable blind and naked. There is absolutely no commendation or redeeming qualities. This is how it will be just before Christ comes in many churches, and this is what we see happening today. Some churches will remain true to Jesus Christ and resist the world; the rest will be in a religious system which teaches compromise and false doctrine.

> ***"Now the Spirit expressly says that in the latter times some will depart from the faith, giving heed to***

> *deceiving spirits and doctrines of demons. Speaking lies in hypocrisy, having their own conscience seared with a hot iron."*   I Timothy 4:1-2

It is both instructive and beneficial to carefully review and heed what Christ has said to the seven churches. The following tables summarize these important messages.

The Seven Churches in Asia Minor				
Unto the angel of the Church of...	Commendations	Credits	Condemnation	Counsel
Ephesus The Apostolic Church	Works, labor and patience. You cannot bear them that are evil. Have tried & rebuked Those who claim to be apostles but are liers	Hate the Nicolaitans	Forgotton your first love.	Remember from where you have fallen. Repent and do your first works
Smyrna The Persecuted Church	Works, tribulation & poverty Blasphemy of those who say they are Jews, but are not.	I know your afflictions & poverty	None at all !!!	Fear none of these things that you will suffer
Pergamus The Tolerant Church	I know your works... I know the seat of Satan is where you live	You hold fast to my name and not denied your faith	Tolerate doctrines of Balaam. You hate the Nicolaitans	Fear nothing & be faithful
Unto the angel of the Church of...	Commendations	Credits	Condemnation	Counsel
Thiatira The Apostate Church	Works, charity, faith and patience Thy works(now) are more than at first	Since some do not hold to doctrine of Jezrbel..I will put no other Burden	You allow Jezebel to teach false doctrine and adultery. Repent now or be judged according to works	Hold fast until I come
Sardis The Dead Church	You have some works	There are a few who have not defiled their garments	I have not found your works perfect before God You have a name and you live, but you are dead	Watch, remember, hold fast & repent Strengthen your works.
Philadelphia The Church that followed Christ	I know your works	You have little strength, but not denied my name	None at all !!!	Hold fast to what you have so no one can take your crown
Laodicea The Church that had no zeal	I know your faith and zeal...but you are neither hot or cold	None at all !!!	You say you are rich but you are naked, miserable, blind & poor	Be zealous and repent... Buy gold tried in fire.. Annoint your eyes

of the Church of...	Promises To him who overcomes	Personality You exist under	Punishment Repent quickly or..	Picture of Christ I am He that...
Ephesus The Apostolic Church	Right to eat of tree of life in Paradise of God	Wicked men	..I will remove your lampstand	Holds the 7 stars in My right hand & walks among the lampstands
Smyrna The Persecuted Church	I will give you a crown of life	The memory of the martyr Antipas	None at all !!!	Am the First & the Last...was dead but now alive
Pergamus The Tolerant Church	You will not be hurt by the second death	Pagan practices & Seat of Satan	I will fight with you using the sword in my mouth	Has a sharp sword with two edges
Thyatira The Apostate Church	I will give the hidden manna & a white stone with a new name	Ritualism & worldly compromise	Those who are adulterous must repent or face much tribulation	Is the Son of God, has eyes like flaming fire & feet like fine brass
Sardis The Dead Church	I will not blot your name from Book of Life Will confess your name before My father Will give you rainment of white	Forgetfulness of what you have seen & heard	I will come suddenly like a theif, & you will not know the hour	Has the seven spirits of God & the seven stars

of the Church of...	Promises To him who overcomes	Personality You exist under	Punishment Repent quickly or..	Picture of Christ I am He that...
Philadelphia The Church that followed Christ	I will make a pillar in the temple of my God I will give him My name I will give him the name of My God	The synagogue of Satan Them that say they are Jews... but are not	No punishment whatsoever !!!	Is holy & true Has the Keys of David in My hand Opens a door that cannot be shut... Shuts a door that cannot be opened
Laodicea The Church that had no zeal	You will sit with me upon my throne	Apostacy & dead theology	I will spew you out of my mouth	Is the Amen The faithful & true witness The beginning of God's creation I stand at the door and knock

He who has an ear....Let him hear what the Spirit says to the churches........

This concludes the command that the apostle John had received to *write the things which are* concerning the seven churches (Rev 1:19-b). It is now time for John to faithfully record ***the things which will take place after this*** (Rev 1:19-c).

Chapter 3

The Throne of God

Revelation 4 is generally recognized as the beginning of prophetic revelation to John concerning future events. In Rev 1, John had seen Christ and his majesty. Rev 2 and 3 were concerned with the seven letters to seven churches in the Roman province of Asia Minor; churches which actually existed in John's day. Rev 4 now transitions John to a state of *being in the spirit,* and he is transported into the heavenly realms to see and record end-time events: the *things which must shortly take place* (Rev 1:1). In reality, the apocalyptic visions which John will receive do not begin until Rev 5. Revelation Chapter 4 contains a description of what John immediately sees as he enters into the very presence of God through a *door*. What John sees is a rare picture of the throne of God and what surrounds that throne. We will now examine this beautiful vision.

> *"After this I looked, and, behold, a door was opened in heaven: and the first voice which I heard was as it were of a trumpet talking with me; which said, Come up hither, and I will shew thee things which must be hereafter. And immediately I was in the spirit: and, behold, a throne was set in heaven, and one sat on the throne. And he that sat was to look upon like a jasper and a sardine stone: and there was a rainbow round about the throne, in sight like unto an emerald. And round about the throne were four and twenty seats: and upon the seats I saw four and twenty elders sitting, clothed in white raiment; and they had on their heads crowns of gold. And out of the throne proceeded lightnings and thunderings and voices: and there were seven lamps of fire burning before the throne, which are the seven Spirits of God. And before the throne there was a sea of glass like unto crystal: and in the midst of the throne, and round about the throne, were four beasts full of eyes before and behind. And the first beast was like a lion, and the second beast like a calf, and the third beast had a face as a*

man, and the fourth beast was like a flying eagle. And the four beasts had each of them six wings about him; and they were full of eyes within: and they rest not day and night, saying, Holy, holy, holy, Lord God Almighty, which was, and is, and is to come. And when those beasts give glory and honour and thanks to him that sat on the throne, who liveth for ever and ever, The four and twenty elders fall down before him that sat on the throne, and worship him that liveth for ever and ever, and cast their crowns before the throne, saying, Thou art worthy, O Lord, to receive glory and honour and power: for thou hast created all things, and for thy pleasure they are and were created." Rev 4: 1-11

Immediately following the messages given to the apostle John for each of the seven churches, he is transitioned into a completely new state of existence. He sees an **open door** in heaven and the *voice which he first heard* commands him to **come up hither**. This voice which calls John forth is evidently that of God the Father. It is likely not that of Jesus Christ since he does not appear until Rev 5:6. The purpose of John's transformation and of his spiritual journey is to be told of the things which **must take place after this.** The fact that John is called to enter into the presence of God through an **open door** in the **Spirit** has caused much theological confusion and diverse interpretation. The classic *pre-tribulation* rapture proponents have identified this event as being synonymous with the rapture of the church described by Paul in I Cor. 15:51-54. The door which is mentioned here is unique to the New Testament. Whether it is a literal or symbolic door is unknown.

Any pre-tribulation rapture teacher will say that this door and the spiritual state that John is in is a definite reference to what must occur when the church is raptured. This position cannot be defended in our view. (1) John was called into heaven over 2000 years ago. If it was meant to represent the framework of a rapture of the saints in the end time, there is no hint in this passage. (2) When the rapture does occur, the dead in Christ will precede those who are alive; there is no indication that the dead are involved here at all. (3) John sees and is transported through a door in the third heaven. There is no door associated with any of Paul's teachings or in Rev 11:15-18. (4) The raptured saints, dead and alive, will meet Christ in the air; Christ is not even in view until Revelation Chapter 5. (5) John immediately sees the Throne of God, the 24 elders and the two living creatures. This imagery and these participants are nowhere mentioned in the scriptures by Paul or in the Book of Revelation at the gathering of the saints. (6) The raptured saints will be gathered to our Lord Jesus Christ by angels. Christ made that quite clear in the Parable of the Wheat and the Tares (Mat 13: 39, 43). The angels of heaven are not involved here at all. (7) John is taken to heaven *in the spirit*, but his body remains on Patmos. At the *rapture*, the dead shall be raised and we in our own bodies will rise to meet Christ in the air. (8) John is being called to heaven to receive revelation knowledge; this is completely out of context to the rapture. (9) John is specifically greeted with: ***I will show you***. There is no such command in the Scriptures related to the rapture of the body of Christ. (10) John ascended to heaven at the command of a voice which *was like a trumpet speaking*; the saints will be raised at the rapture by the sound of an actual trumpet (shofar). (11) There is no indication that John receives crowns or a white robe; at the rapture, the saints will receive both. (12) In Rev 11:18 the rapture is described as occurring at the seventh trumpet. The scroll has not yet been opened and no previous trumpets have been sounded. (13) In Rev 11: 15, the rapture is preceded by a heavenly declaration that ***The kingdoms of this world have become the kingdoms of our Lord Jesus Christ***. The kingdoms of this world will be under the command and authority of Satan and the antichrist for 3.5 more years, until he and his fallen angels are defeated by Christ at the Battle of Armageddon.

In summary, there is no scriptural authority for connecting the ascension of John to heaven with the rapture of the church. The fact that John had to be *in the spirit* is inconsistent with the teachings of Scripture on the rapture of the saints. Paul said: ***Now this I say, brethren, that flesh and blood cannot inherit the kingdom of God; neither doth corruption inherit incorruption***. Flesh and blood are earthly things which make up our earthly body. John had to be *in the spirit* to ascend into heaven, for man's flesh is corrupted; and no corrupted flesh or blood can be in the very presence of God. That is precisely why that when the rapture occurs, every saint (live or dead) will receive new resurrection bodies. After his experience, John returned to Patmos and resumed his fleshly existence. The popular belief that Rev 4:1 represents the rapture of the church is a myth that has been concocted to support a pre- tribulation rapture.

John immediately sees a magnificent throne in heaven and **One sat on the throne**. The throne of God is a part of many key events in the book of Revelation. In fact, it is seen in every chapter in the Book of Revelation except Chapters 2, 9, 10, 15, 17 and 18. The *one* who is sitting on the throne is no doubt God the Father. This is virtually assured by comparing this scene to Rev 6:16 and Rev 7:10. His appearance was like a ***jasper and a sardis stone***. The ancient Jasper stone was *clear as crystal* (Rev 21:11), and the sardis stone is *blood red in appearance*. It is not likely that these stones have any hidden meaning; they simply represent the glory of God. His raiment is **white as snow** (Dan 7:9); His train fills the temple (Is. 6:1); and He is standing on a sea of sapphire (Exodus 24:10). A *rainbow* is around the throne that must be colored multiple shades of green (Emerald). This rainbow is likely a symbol of deliverance, protection and mercy to those that *fear God*, and remind us of the covenant He made with Noah to never again destroy the world with water. He is surrounded by 24 elders and four living creatures, which continually serve and praise God (Rev 4:8-9). *Who are these 24 elders and four living creatures?* Their identification has sparked considerable controversy. Since we are not told who they actually are, we can only provide a *best guess*, based upon scriptural clues. The 24 thrones are occupied by *elders*. There is no definitive word in the Scriptures used to identify elders in both the Old and the New Testament; but they are always seen as leaders or people in positions of service (Mat 21:23, 26:3, Mark 11:27, Acts 4:8, 4:23, 15:6, Tit 1:5, Jas 5:14) This is insufficient to identify this group. However, we know that they have nine key identifying characteristics.

- They are on ***thrones*** (Rev 4:4)
- They are dressed in ***white robes*** (Rev 4:4)
- They are wearing ***crowns*** (Rev 4:4)
- They continually ***worship God*** (Rev 4:10)
- They each have ***harps and golden bowls*** full of the prayers of the Saints (Rev 5:8)
- They are ***redeemed*** to God by ***your*** (Christ's) ***blood*** (Rev 5:9)
- They were redeemed from ***every tribe and tongue*** (Rev 5:9)
- They are ***kings and priests*** (Rev 5:10)
- They will eventually ***reign on the earth*** (Rev 5:10)

These are not characteristics of angels, but of redeemed saints. They appear to be former human beings which are now in heaven. ***Thrones*** (Rev 3:21), ***white garments*** (Rev 3:5), ***crowns*** (Rev 2:10, 3:11), and the ***right to rule*** (Rev 2:27) are all promises given to the *overcomer*. The crowns that they wear are *diadems* and not *stephanos* crowns. Stephanos crowns are those awarded to victors in the Greek games or those athletes who win gladiator matches or Olympic events. Diadems are those crowns that are given to believers when they come into the presence of Christ to receive rewards. Crowns throughout the book of Revelation should be carefully noted as type, because they clearly indicate earthly rewards or eternal rewards. Finally, angels were never ***redeemed by God's blood***; they are created beings. It seems to be inescapable that these 24 *elders* are redeemed saints and overcomers. But who is this group of overcomers and where did these elders come from? We believe that the maximum sacrifice that a Christian can make for Jesus Christ is to give their life as a martyr. We believe that these are a select and chosen group of martyrs who have been caught up to heaven sometime before the tribulation period begins. This is not so hard to believe if we relate these elders to another group of martyrs which has also been caught up to heaven *during* the tribulation period and is seen waiting impatiently to be avenged under God's throne.

"And when he had opened the fifth seal, I saw under the altar the souls of them that were slain for the word of God, and for the testimony which they held: And they cried with a loud voice, saying, How long, O Lord, holy and true, dost thou not judge and avenge our blood on them that dwell on the earth? And white robes were given unto every one of them; and it was said unto them, that they should rest yet for a little season, until their fellow servants also and their brethren, that should be killed as they were, should be fulfilled." Rev 6: 9-11

The similarity of this group of martyrs is unmistakable, but not definitive. A second possibility, which has been proposed by some, is that these elders are Old Testament saints. This view is bolstered by the fact that King David appointed 24 courses of priests to assist in the temple services. The courses and their service were still serving according to their scheduled times when Herod's Temple fell in 70 AD. Each of the twenty four elders would appropriately represent each of the 24 courses. They would be a part of the firstfruits resurrection that occurred just after Christ rose from the grave (Mat 27:52-53). A third possibility which has been proposed is that this is a select group of high ranking angels which have been placed in God's service. Considering all the scriptural clues, we believe that the 24 elders are martyred Christians and not angelic beings or Old Testament Hebrews; but we would not be dogmatic about our conclusion that they are martyrs.

The four living creatures are easier to identify. They are most certainly a class of angelic beings. They are *full of eyes, front and back* (Rev 4:6): They do not rest day or night singing *Holy, holy, holy, Lord God Almighty, who was and is and is to come* (Rev 3:8). They seem to have some form of superiority over the 24 elders, because whenever the living creatures give glory and honor to God, the elders **fall down before Him (God) and cast their crowns before the throne;** singing:

"You are worthy, O Lord, to receive glory, honor and power; for You created all things, and by Your will they exist and were created."   Rev 3:11.

These four living creatures are very close to the Seraphim which Ezekiel saw in Ez. 1:1-28. A comparison between what Ezekiel and John saw is given in the following table.

Seraphim	4 living creatures
4 in number	4 in number
4 Faces of a man	4 Faces of a man
4 wings	6 wings
Full of eyes	Wings full of eyes
Under the throne	Around the throne
Each had the face of a man, an oxen, a lion, and an eagle	One creature was like a lion One creature was like a calf One creature was like a man One creature was like an eagle

In Isaiah 6, he (Isaiah) had a vision in which he saw God sitting on his throne, and standing there were **seraphim.** They also cried **Holy, Holy, Holy.** Comparing the angelic beings in Rev 4:4 to those in Isaiah 6:2, these four living creatures are not *seraphim*, but they are very much like them in appearance. They are no doubt angelic beings of the highest order, who serve God day and night. They are high-ranking angelic beings which cannot be identified. From the throne of God proceeded **Lightnings, thunderings and voices.** The manifestations of signs in the form of *lightnings, thunderings and voices* are common to ensuing events in the apocalypse. **Thunderings**: Rev 6:1, Rev 8:5, Rev 10:3-4, Rev 11:19, Rev 14:2, Rev 16:8. **Lightning**: Rev 8:5, Rev 11:19, Rev 16:18. **Voices**: Rev 8:5, 13, Rev 10:3, 4, Rev 11:15, 19, Rev 16:18. These signs seem to accompany a presence or apocalyptic declaration of action by God.

There are **seven lamps of fire burning before the throne.** These are immediately identified as the **seven Spirits of God.** What or who are these seven spirits? The book of Revelation refers to these seven spirits four times.

> *"Grace and peace to you from Him who is, and who was, and who is to come, and from the seven spirits before His throne, and from Jesus Christ, who is the faithful witness....."*   Rev 1:4-5

> *"To the angel of the church in Sardis write: These are the words of him who holds the seven spirits of God and the seven stars. I know your deeds; you have a reputation of being alive, but you are dead."*   Rev 3:1

> *"From the throne came flashes of lightning, rumblings and peals of thunder. Before the throne, seven lamps were blazing. These are the seven spirits of God."*   Rev 4:5

> *"Then I saw a Lamb, looking as if it had been slain, standing in the center of the throne, encircled by the four living creatures and the elders. He had seven horns and seven eyes, which are the seven spirits of God sent out into all the earth."*   Rev 5:6

There have been a variety of interpretations as to whom or what these seven spirits might represent. One position is to equate them to seven angels, but this seems to be impossible from the above description. Some have been so bold as to assume that the Holy Spirit is actually ten spirits. When confusion reigns, always seek scriptural precedence. An appealing explanation is found in Isaiah 11.

> *"And the Spirit of the LORD shall rest upon him, the spirit of wisdom and understanding, the spirit of counsel and might, the spirit of knowledge and of the fear of the LORD."*   Is 11:2.

Many have identified the seven spirits with this passage. However, careful exegesis of this verse will only yield six specific spirits referenced, all of which constitute the multiple work of the Holy Spirit in every believer. We believe that the most consistent and logical explanation is to refer to Zach 4.

> *"And said unto me, What seest thou? And I said, I have looked, and behold a candlestick all of gold, with a bowl upon the top of it, and his seven lamps thereon, and seven pipes to the seven lamps, which are upon the top thereof... For who hath despised the day of small things? for they shall rejoice, and shall see the plummet in the hand of Zerubbabel with those seven; they are the eyes of the LORD, which run to and fro through the whole earth."*
> Zach 4:2, 10

Zachariah speaks of seeing *seven lamps*. In Rev 4:5 John has already seen **seven lamps which are the seven spirits of God**. Rev 5:6 equates seven spirits to **seven eyes, which are the seven spirits of God sent out into all the earth.** This is almost identical to Zachariah seeing: **they are the (seven) eyes of the LORD, which run to and fro through the whole earth.** So we have the seven spirits equated to (1) seven lamps, (2) seven eyes, and (3) seven spirits.

"God is telling us that the seven lamps of fire burning before His throne and the seven horns including the seven eyes on the lamb are the seven Spirits of God. So in all reality the seven Spirits are all three of these things. The simplicity in this amazes me. In Ephesians 4 it tells us that there is one Spirit. It also says that there is one body referring to the Church" (Tommy Spurgeon).

> **"There is one body, and one Spirit, even as ye are called in one hope of your calling; One Lord, one faith, one baptism, One God and Father of all, who is above all, and through all, and in you all."** Eph. 4:4-6

Here is a *mystery* that is not explained. The best explanation seems to be the simplest. Scriptures attest to the fact that there is only one Holy Spirit. In Rev 2-3 there were seven letters written to seven churches, but in reality there is only one church, and the one body of Christ who makes up the one universal church is multitudes of believers. In Rev 5:6, John tells us that seven spirits of God are sent forth into *all the earth*. The manifold spirit of Christ is in fact everywhere in the form of the Holy Spirit. But the Holy Spirit is also in multitudes of believers. The seven lamps burning with fire is a simile projecting the same truth. The fire coming from the lamp represents every individual moving to maturity by tribulation. Recall that when John the Baptist saw Christ coming he said: ***There is one coming who will baptize you with water and with fire***. No lamp can burn without oil, and this speaks of spiritual anointing. In Rev 5:6, John sees Jesus portrayed as a *lamb* with *seven eyes*. Hence, John is shown with symbolism that the seven eyes, the seven lamps and the seven spirits all portray our Lord Jesus Christ as moving, watching and walking among His church (believers). This seems to be the most satisfactory interpretation of these difficult verses taken collectively.

John now turns his attention to a seven sealed scroll and who is worthy to open that scroll.

Chapter 4

The Scroll and the Lamb of God

The apostle John has just been shown the throne of God; the four living creatures and the 24 elders that are continuously administering praise to God the Father. In Rev 5:1, John once again assures us that: *I saw* these things. The current revelation is in two parts: (1) John sees a scroll in the right hand of God and a search is made of who can open it. (2) Our Lord Jesus Christ is worthy to open the scroll and is charged with doing so.

> *"And I saw in the right hand of him that sat on the throne a book written within and on the backside, sealed with seven seals. And I saw a strong angel proclaiming with a loud voice, Who is worthy to open the book, and to loose the seals thereof? And no man in heaven, nor in earth, neither under the earth, was able to open the book, neither to look thereon. And I wept much, because no man was found worthy to open and to read the book, neither to look thereon. And one of the elders saith unto me, Weep not: behold, the Lion of the tribe of Judah, the Root of David, hath prevailed to open the book, and to loose the seven seals thereof. And I beheld, and, lo, in the midst of the throne and of the four beasts, and in the midst of the elders, stood a Lamb as it had been slain, having seven horns and seven eyes, which are the seven Spirits of God sent forth into all the earth."*
> Rev 5:1-6

The first part of John's vision is concerned with a *mysterious scroll* which he sees in the right hand of God. The content of this scroll is not at this time known or revealed, but it is real and obviously holds the written word of God. It is not unusual for God to maintain written records of importance. There is a **Book of Remembrance** (Mal. 3:16), a **Book of Life** (Rev 3:5), a **Lamb's Book of Life** (Rev 17:8, 21:27), a **Little Book** (Rev 10:2), and other books (Rev 20:12). In Ezekiel 2, Ezekiel is handed a ***book*** (scroll) by a heavenly hand and told to eat and digest its contents. This scroll is unusual by the standards of man, since it contains *seven seals* and is written *on the front and back*. Extremely important Roman documents were sometimes

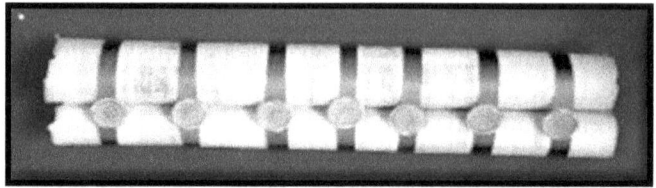

sealed with multiple seals, but to have one with seven seals, and be written on both sides seems to be rare. Seven being the number of perfection, we can state that the contents are final and complete. We know from subsequent chapters that this scroll contains a written account of the apocalypse and everything that will occur over the last 3.5 years of this age, the millennial kingdom and finally a description of the eternal realm. Another angel now enters the scene who is a *strong angel*. We know from other Scriptures that Gabriel and Michael are called *strong angels* and carry out special missions for God. It is not likely that this angel is either one, or it would have been called by name. We are best to only acknowledge that this is an angelic being who has great authority and of a higher order who carries out God's instructions. The ensuing proclamation is authoritative and *loud*: **Who is worthy to open the book, and to loose the seals thereof?** The question of being worthy is not related to physical or mental capabilities, but who is worthy to comprehend and relate the thoughts of God? In this context, the *worthiness* demanded is far beyond any qualification that a mortal human could bring forth. Since a *strong angel* is uttering this request, it is evident that lower ranks of angelic beings cannot muster to the call. The qualification is immediately addressed by a lamentation uttered by the strong angel: **And no man in heaven, nor in earth, neither under the earth, was able to open the book, neither to look thereon.** The scope of who is worthy is severe; no one in heaven, or on the earth or under the earth is deemed worthy. John is overwhelmed by the failure to identify who is worthy to open the scroll. He is evidently aware of the fact that its contents are very important to his mission. He is so distraught that his human qualities, even in his spiritual state, are overtaken by emotion: **He wept much**. How foolish and human John was at this point in time. He is standing in the very presence of God almighty that created the heavens and the earth, and formed man out of His spit and His dirt. God is in control of all things…. the heavens and earth are under His control. Here is a strong object lesson for each of us: believe that no matter how desperate the situation might seem to be, God is in command. Place your burdens and cares upon Him and His Son and everything will be ok. The strong angel is unable to intervene, but one of the 24 elders puts the situation under control: **Do not weep**, he said. How poignant, how loving, how touching. Christ has assured us that in His future kingdom there will be no tears, and no sorrows. He is worthy to give us a place to live that no one else could ever do. The elder immediately assures John that there is indeed someone who is worthy to open the scroll: it is ***the Lion of the tribe of Judah; the root of David.*** It is interesting that the elder immediately qualifies our Lord Jesus Christ because of who He is and his lineage. Christ is of the tribe of Judah from His ancestral lineage, and He is of the Davidic line of kings. Both qualify Him to be the long-awaited Jewish Messiah. But the real reason why He is worthy is that He has ***prevailed***. Prevailed over what? While the physical qualifications to be the long awaited Jewish Messiah were to be from the Tribe of Judah and to be the greater Son of David, the spiritual qualifications are more important to all who believe upon His name. Christ prevailed over Satan when he stood against him for 40 days in the wilderness: Christ prevailed over the Scribes and the Pharisees, making a mockery out of their theology: Christ prevailed over death itself, having been raised from the grave and He now sits on the right hand side of God the Father. He alone is worthy to hold the scroll, to break the seals, and to reveal its content. As if *scales had been lifted from his eyes*, John looked and saw standing in the midst of the throne, in the midst of the four living creatures, and in the midst of the 24 elders, a ***Lamb as if it had been slain***. The location of this *Lamb* in the throne room is identical with that later observed by John in Rev 7:17. The fact that the risen Christ appears as a Lamb is consistent with His exalted position as ***the Lamb of God*** who was obedient to His father in His sacrificial death. He was the perfect, acceptable sacrifice to please the Father; He was our sacrificial Passover lamb. The appearance of Christ as a Lamb *slain* is in direct contrast to His appearance at His second advent (Rev 19:11-16) where He appears as a *conquering King*. The duality of Christ, as a suffering servant (Lamb) and also as a conquering warrior (King) can be related to the belief by the Hebrews that two Messiah's will appear to save them. They do not see or understand that these two Messiahs they so fervently seek are the one Messiah, Jesus Christ. His appearance in this scene is to reveal the future actions of His Father. The most important point may be that John has seen in the flesh the wounds of Christ both when He was pierced in His side on the cross of Calvary, and when Christ appeared to His disciples in the upper room. Here He appears again, just at the right time and in the right place. Christ always *appears* to us and *comforts* us just when we need Him. However, a further description enhances and adds to the mere picture of a Lamb. John also sees that He has **seven horns and seven eyes, which are the seven spirits of God**. Horns in prophetic Scripture usually represent power and authority. They are seven in number because seven is the number of perfection and completeness. Christ, even as a Lamb, is all-powerful and His authority comes from God His Father; He is the consummate warrior and King. The *seven eyes and seven spirits* have already been discussed. The eyes of the Lord see everything, penetrating the body and the soul of man. Nothing escapes the sight of the Lamb.

After describing the scroll and being shown who is worthy to disclose its contents, John now sees the scroll being transferred by God the Father to His Son, the Lamb of God (Rev 5:7). He then experiences the rejoicing of *every creature which is in heaven and on the earth, and under the sea and such as are in the sea* (Rev 5:13).

> *"And he came and took the book out of the right hand of him that sat upon the throne. And when he had taken the book, the four beasts and four and twenty elders fell down before the Lamb, having every one of them harps, and*

> *golden vials full of odours, which are the prayers of saints. And they sung a new song, saying, Thou art worthy to take the book, and to open the seals thereof: for thou wast slain, and hast redeemed us to God by thy blood out of every kindred, and tongue, and people, and nation; And hast made us unto our God kings and priests: and we shall reign on the earth. And I beheld, and I heard the voice of many angels round about the throne and the beasts and the elders: and the number of them was ten thousand times ten thousand, and thousands of thousands; Saying with a loud voice, Worthy is the Lamb that was slain to receive power, and riches, and wisdom, and strength, and honour, and glory, and blessing. And every creature which is in heaven, and on the earth, and under the earth, and such as are in the sea, and all that are in them, heard I saying, Blessing, and honour, and glory, and power, be unto him that sitteth upon the throne, and unto the Lamb for ever and ever. And the four beasts said, Amen. And the four and twenty elders fell down and worshipped him that liveth for ever and ever."*
> Rev 5:7-14

The scroll that has caused John such anguish because no one could be found that was worthy to reveal its contents is now taken from the hand of God the Father and placed in the hand of the Son. This exchange authorizes the Son to reveal His father's eternal plan for reclaiming the earth and vanquishing His enemies. Of all living creatures, only Christ is worthy to redeem the earth and reveal the contents of the scroll. He is worthy because He has conquered death, He has conquered sin, and He has conquered the power of Satan. There is an immediate response from the four living creatures and the 24 elders. They all fall before Christ and began to praise Him. The 24 elders and by extension possibly the four living creatures have harps and bowls full of *the prayers of the Saints*. In the Old Testament, the sound of harps is associated with joy and gladness. When David went to retrieve the Ark of the Covenant from the Philistines, his journey home was accompanied by harps and cymbals as he danced. In Rev 14:2 and Rev 15:2 we will again encounter the use of harps to herald important events. The bowls contain the prayers of the Saints. Two interpretations have been offered; the first is that the elders are holding the prayers of Saints throughout the ages, and the second is that these are specific prayers directed toward the final destruction of evil men and Satan's kingdom. The first is not appropriate, since the elders seem to be redeemed saints (martyrs), and they were not put into place until after Christ's resurrection. The second is appealing since every Christian looks forward to the day when Satan will be vanquished and removed from this earth. It is possible, however, that these are the accumulated prayers of all New Testament saints for Christ to finally arise from the throne and fulfill all the promises of His Second Advent. In any case, we cannot and should not go into further speculation. It is sufficient to say that our prayers *are* heard and evidently some are divinely stored and protected by heavenly beings. The elders and the four living creatures now burst forth in a **new song**. The *old song* was a song of praise (Rev 4:8) to God the Father, but this *new song* is directed to Jesus Christ and is a song of *redemption*. But angels do not need redemption, so who is singing this song and who is being redeemed? Here we have a strong indication that our previous conjecture is true; that The 24 elders are martyrs from the church age. These elders are 24 in number but they represent every believer from every generation of believers. The 24 elders are leading this new song, and it proclaims three things of importance.

- They (the elders) have been **redeemed.**
- They have been redeemed from every **tribe and every tongue and all people and all nations.**
- They have been made **Kings and Priests.**
- They will reign **on the earth.**

A promise has been given to those who believe in Jesus Christ that we will rule and reign with Him. This will be during the millennial kingdom when the nation of Israel will finally inherit the land and Christ will reign supreme as King of Kings and Lord of Lords from Jerusalem. In the letter to the Church at Thyatira, a promise was made by Christ that the overcomer will rule with a ***rod of iron*** (Rev 2:27). Peter affirmed that the body of Christ is a chosen generation of royalty.

> ***"But ye are a chosen generation, a royal priesthood, an holy nation, a peculiar people; that ye should shew forth the praises of him who hath called you out of darkness into his marvellous light."*** I Peter 2:9

The first song of *praise* was from the four living creatures (Rev 4:8), the second from both the 24 elders and the four living creatures. A crescendo of praise now rises from this same group, joined by a multitude of angels who have assembled before the throne. The number of angels is ***ten thousand times ten thousand, and thousands of thousands.*** This number is not meant to be calculated, but rather to indicate that this is an extremely large group which God has numbered. The number of angels before God's throne defies number. This gives us an idea of how many angels were created by God to carry out His business in this world. These are only 2/3 of all the angels that originally inhabited the heavenly realm (Rev 12:3-4). This third song of praise is again directed to Christ being *worthy*. It is sung in a ***loud voice***.

> ***"Worthy is the Lamb that was slain to receive power, and riches, and wisdom, and strength, and honour, and glory, and blessing."*** Rev 5:12

Christ is declared to be worthy to receive seven different gifts : seven being the number of perfection. (1) He receives ***Power,*** (2) He receives ***Riches,*** (3) He receives ***Wisdom,*** (4) He receives ***Strength,*** (5) He receives ***Honor,*** (6) He receives ***Glory,*** and (7) He receives ***Blessing.*** The reason He alone is worthy is because He came down from Heaven; He walked on this earth in a physical body subject to temptations and tears; He lived a sinless life, and He died on the cross of Calvary for our sins. Yes! *He is Worthy*! Finally, the crescendo of song rises to unprecedented heights. All of creation now begins to praise both God and our Lord Jesus Christ.

> **"every creature which is in heaven, and on the earth, and under the earth, and such as are in the sea, and all that are in them, heard I saying, Blessing, and honour, and glory, and power, be unto him that sitteth upon the throne, and unto the Lamb for ever and ever."** Rev 5:13

Here we have a very interesting description of those who offer praise, blessings and honor. We are told that every creature *in heaven, on the Earth and in the sea* joins the crescendo. I sometimes ask the following question to friends of mine: *"Do you think that fish can think and speak?"* After they look at me as if I was crazy, they usually say, *no*. That is when I tell them to read Rev 5:13! Those who offer up this third doxology are no longer representative, but exhaustive. The totality of those who now offer praise is reminiscent of God's omnipotent power, for *(He) made heaven and earth, the sea and all that are in them* (Psalm 146:6). In the gospel of John, he affirmed that Jesus Christ as the second member of the Godhead was also present when all things were created.

> *"In the beginning was the Word, and the Word was with God, and the Word was God. The same was in the beginning with God. All things were made by him; and without him was not any thing made that was made. In him was life; and the life was the light of men."* John 1: 1-4

It is fitting and proper that this momentous event is brought to a close by the four living creatures that continually stand by God, who rest neither day nor night, and sing **Holy, Holy, Holy** (Rev 4:8). They conclude this scene by saying *Amen*, and this causes the 24 elders to fall down and worship Him. The adoration is directed to the throne, and considering the plurality of God and Christ that we just discussed, it is likely addressed to both deities. This properly brings to a close all of ***those things which are*** (Rev 1:19). John is about to see far into the future and record ***Things which must shortly take place***"(Rev 1:1, 19). The seals are now about to be opened, but first we need to examine biblical chronology and the role of Daniel's 490-year prophecy in determining how long the Tribulation lasts.

Chapter 5

Biblical Chronology: Adam to Christ

The Romance of Biblical Chronology (Anstey)

The Book of Revelation as transcribed by the apostle John is not just the last book in the Bible; it is the culmination of God's eternal plan for mankind. It is the revelation of how the world as we now know it will be transformed into a place where there will be no sadness, no tears, and a perfect place to live forever with our Lord Jesus Christ. This transformation will not take place until three things are accomplished: (1) The Jewish people, the *apple of God's eye*, will finally accept Jesus Christ as their savior and be restored into a covenant relationship with God; (2) the *times of the Gentiles* will finally end; (3) the *age of the church* will be over; (4) the *Bride of Christ* will be complete, and (5) Satan and all of his minions will be conquered and cast into the Lake of Fire and Brimstone (Rev Rev 19:20, 20:10). Sin will reign no more and all prophecy will have been fulfilled.

God's plan for mankind has never changed. It started with a personal, sinless relationship with Adam and Eve in the Garden of Eden and it will end in the same way between Christ and all who accept Him as their personal Savior. Since the Holy Bible is divinely inspired and recorded by men of God under the guidance of the Holy Spirit, one would certainly expect to find an inerrant record of the sequence of events which are recorded between the first book of the Bible (*Genesis*) and the last (*Revelation*). We believe that this is true, and that by carefully studying and following the Scriptures, a continuous sequence of key events that have occurred between the creation of Adam and the last day in the Great Tribulation Period can be constructed.

This chapter will show this to be true, and in the process of reconstructing such a chronology, we will determine when the Exodus occurred, the sequence of Sabbatical and Jubilee years, the year Christ was crucified and other interesting and important dates. However, the main purpose of this chapter is to show that based upon the biblical chronological records, the final period of great tribulation; which is incorrectly called the *Lord's Day* and is usually identified as the 70th Week of Daniel is *not* seven years in duration as commonly taught, but only 3.5 years .

Biblical Chronology

Many biblical scholars have attempted construction of a biblical chronology. Those of James Ussher, Martin Anstey and Sir Isaac Newton represent initial efforts going back to the 16th century AD. More recently, Floyd Nolan Jones, Daniel Gregg, Willis Beecher, M.J. Agee and others have published various chronologies. The work presented here is largely the result of independent investigations and biblical research by the author, but there is general agreement within certain periods of time across all other chronologies, particularly in the sequential ordering and yearly counts of the Old Testament patriarchs between Adam and Joseph. The basic premise accepted by this offered chronology is that the biblical records are sequential, complete, and without error. The basis of all biblical records in this book is the Authorized King James Bible. A fundamental point of contention, and one that differentiates one offered chronology from another, is where the chronology should start. All complete biblical chronologies start with the first man, Adam. There are three fundamental constructions that have been offered. The *first* is that the calendar of years starts with the creation of the world. The *second* is that the calendar of years starts with the birth of Adam. The *third* is that the calendar of years starts from the year in which Adam was expelled from the Garden of Eden. The problem with each starting point is that nowhere in the Holy Scriptures are we told when these events occurred. In fact, the way years are distinguished today (2011 AD, for example) is a creation of man and not God. Years are divided into two categories: BC and AD. It is commonly taught that BC stands for *before Christ* and AD stands for *after death*. This is only partially correct. How could the year 1 BC have been *before Christ* and 1 AD been after death? BC does stand for before Christ, but AD actually stands for the Latin phrase *anno domini*, which means *in the year of our Lord*. The BC/AD dating system is not taught in the Bible. A monk named

Dionysius Xiguus invented the BC/AD terminology. The issue of where to start a chronology is further complicated by the fact that we are not told how long that Adam and Eve spent in Eden before the fall. Some chronologists have used 40 years, the biblical period of trial and testing: Others have used seven years, the biblical number of completeness: Others seem to have a particular reason for choosing one number or another. However, as we will demonstrate, it is possible to start at some known modern *anchor event* or secular date, and work backwards through the biblical records to a reasonable starting point. Many chronologists have been confounded in the quagmire of having to calculate the time span consumed by the *period of the judges* and the *period of the Kings of Judah and the Northern Kingdom*. To show how these problems can influence a particular chronology (Jones), the following table shows what is often referred to as the *Date of Creation* by several respected chronologists, although this may not be strictly true as previously discussed.

Name	Year (BC)	Name	Year (BC)	Name	Year (BC)
J. Africanus	5501	H. Spondanus	4051	Becke	3974
G. Syncellus	5492	M. Anstey	4042	Krentzeim	3971
J. Jackson	5426	M. Lange	4041	W. Dolen	3971
W. Hales	5411	E. Reinholt	4021	E. Reusnerus	3970
Eusebius	5189	J. Cappellus	4005	J. Claverius	3968
M. Scotus	4192	J. Ussher	4004	P. Melanchthon	3964
L. Condomanus	4141	E. Greswell	4004	J. Haynlinus	3963
L. Lydiat	4103	F. Jones	4004	A. Salmeron	3958
M. Maestlinus	4079	E. Faulstich	4001	J. Scaliger	3949
J. Ricciolus	4062	D. Petavius	3983	M. Beroaldus	3927
J. Salianus	4053	F. Klassen	3975	A. Helwigius	3836

In order to avoid making an assumption as to when God created the earth, or how long that Adam and Eve were in the Garden of Eden, the chronology which we offer will begin in the first year that Adam and Eve left the Garden of Eden. All years after that year will be called an AY (Adam's Year) year, and the first year will be *AY=1*. Some may wish to call the first year *"Year 0"*, but we will not. Because we do not know from the biblical record how long that Adam was in the Garden of Eden, and we choose to make the year of expulsion equal to AY=1, this is called a *relative chronology*. This will result in our AY count being one year longer than those that start at Year 0. In the Holy Scriptures, Genesis Chap 2 is where the chronology will begin its journey.

> ***"This is the book of the generations of Adam."***   Gen 5:1

> ***"And Adam lived an hundred and thirty years, and begat a son in his own likeness, after his image, and called his name Seth."***   Gen 5:3

Starting in Genesis Chapter 2, there are references to the generations and events which follow Adam. Genealogies are detailed throughout Genesis, Exodus and Leviticus. Of particular interest are Gen 5 and Gen 11, which lists the generations of Adam to Noah. From Noah to Joseph requires a bit more detective work, but the information is in the Holy Scriptures. From the biblical records, one can construct the following Table which reconstructs the AY year that every patriarch was born.

Name	Lived (Yrs)	Had Son	At Age	Key Events	AY YEAR Year Born	Biblical Reference
Adam	930	Seth	130	Key Events	1	Gen 5:3
Seth	912	Enosh	105		131	Gen 5:6
Enosh	905	Cainan	90	Methuselah	236	Gen 5:9
Cainan/Kenan	910	Mahalalel	70	Dies	326	Gen 5:12
Mahalalel	895	Jared	65	1657	396	Gen 5:15
Jared	962	Enoch	162	Creation	461	Gen 5:18
Enoch	365	Methuselah	65	Year of Flood	623	Gen 5:21
Methuselah	969	Lamech	187	1657	688	Gen 5:25
Lamech	777	Noah	182	Shem Birth	875	Gen 5:28
Noah-600 @ Flood	950	Shem	502	1559	1057	Gen 5:32
Shem-Gen 11:10-Lived 600 yrs	600	Arphaaxed	100	Arphaaxed Birth	1559	Gen 11:10
Arphaaxed-Born 2Yrs after flood	438	Salah	35	1659	1659	Gen 11:12
Selah	433	Eber	30	Abram Covenant	1694	Gen 11:14
Eber	464	Peleg	34	1729	1724	Gen 11:16
Peleg	239	Reu	30	Abram 75 when	1758	Gen 11:18
Reu	239	Serug	32	enters Canaan	1788	Gen 11:20
Serug	230	Nabor	30	2024	1820	Gen 11:22
Nahor	148	Terah	29	Terah died in	1850	Gen 11:24
Terah	205	Abraham	70	2084	1879	Gen 11:26
Abraham...75 entered Canaan	175	Isaac	100	Abram 100 when	1949	Gen 21:5
Isaac	180	Jacob & Esau	60	Issac born	2049	Gen 25:26
Jacob	147	Joseph	91	2049	2109	See Below
Joseph	110				2200	Gen 50:22

Again note that Adam is shown to leave in *Year 1*. Observe that Adam had a son called Seth at age 130. We choose to use the convention that the first year that Adam was cast out of the Garden of Eden was his *birth year into the world*. This is because that while he was in the Garden of Eden, and ate of the Tree of Life; his body would never decay or die. God intended that he would walk and talk with Adam forever (Gen 1: 15-17). When Adam sinned, he began to die (Gen 2:17). This is how every man is born of the flesh. From the moment he exits the womb of a woman, his body starts to function and die until the actual time of his death. Consistent with accepted convention, the *birth year of his life* is counted as *Year 0*, not year one. So when Adam had a son Seth at age 130 (Gen 5:3), it was in AY year 131, and not AY year 130. By following the sequence of birth dates recorded in Genesis, one easily arrives at the birth of Joseph in AY 2200. The Table on the right depicts the years between when Joseph was sold into slavery by his jealous brothers at age 17 and when the exodus occurred in terms of AY years. The AY dates shown are determined as follows. After being sold into slavery, the KJV records that Joseph was brought before the pharaoh at age 30 and asked to interpret a dream.

God showed him the meaning of the dream after all of Pharaoh's soothsayers had failed. The dream depicted an immediate period of seven years of plenty, followed by seven years of extreme famine. The Pharaoh was so pleased he put Joseph in charge of all the grain in Egypt, and

Biblical Event	AY Year
Joseph sold into slavery at age 17	2217
13 Yrs later at age 30 he is called before Pharoh (Gen 41:46)...............	2230
7 Years of Plenty follow	2237
Followed by 7 by years of famine	2244
Jacob moves to Egypt at age 130 in second year of famine..........	2239
Jacob lives for 17 Yrs in Egypt, then dies at age 147 [enters at 130, (130 +17)]=147	2256
Joseph lives to age 110, and then dies in Yr	2310
Now, Abram left at age 75	2024
It is exactly 430 years to the day that the Exodus starts............................	2454
Since Exodus was in year	2454
Moses was born in year........................	2374
The number of years between Josephs death & Moses birth is........	64
Aaron was 3 Years younger, Born in.....	2371
Note that Terah, Abram's father died in Yr ..	2084
Abraham died at age 175 in year.............	2124
So when Terah died, Abraham was age...	135

instructed him to stockpile grain for the seven years of famine. In the second year of famine, Joseph's father Jacob (Israel) moved himself and his entire family to Egypt at age 130. Jacob then divinely became the *kinsman redeemer*, a type of Jesus Christ. Jacob remains in Egypt until he died at age 147 (AY 2256). Joseph dies at age 110 in AY Year 2310. At this point many chronologists falter, since there is no continuing linkage to the Exodus from Egypt. Here we must do some detective work to find the AY Year of the Exodus. The key is found in Exodus 12: 40-41.

> ***"Now the sojourning of the Children of Israel, who dwelt in Egypt, was 430 years. And it came to pass at the end of the 430 years, even the selfsame day it came to pass, that all the hosts of the Lord went out from the land of Egypt."***
> Exodus 12: 40-41.

Paul affirmed this period of time in Gal 3:15-17. This passage clearly states several facts. The *Children of Israel* is the nation of Israel, starting with Abraham, Lot and those that came with him to the land of Canaan, continuing to those who followed Jacob into Egypt. The 430 years apply to the Total Sojourn of Abraham and his descendants from when Abraham left Mesopotamia to the Exodus from Egypt. The first day of the 430-year period of time was the same day that the Exodus occurred, which was Nisan 15 on the Hebrew Calendar. This passage might also imply that the starting day of the 490-year period and the day of the Exodus was the same day, Thursday.

The offered chronology clearly shows that the Exodus occurred in AY 2454. It can also be stated with certainty that the Exodus occurred shortly after midnight, Nisan 15 (Hebrew days start and end at 6:00pm, not at midnight). Hence, we can calculate that the 430-year period started in the Year AY 2024 (AY 2454-430 years). Is this date significant in our chronology? *YES*, it is the year that Abraham answered the call of God to leave Haran at age 75.

"Now the Lord had said onto Abram, get thee out of thy country (Haran), and from thy kindred, and from thy father's house, unto a land that I will show thee (Land of Canaan). And I will make of thee a great nation, and I will bless thee and make thy name great; and thou shalt be a blessing (Gen 12:1-2). So Abram departed, as the Lord had spoken unto him, and Lot went with him, and Abram was seventy and five years old when he departed out of Haran."
Gen 12:1-4

So how long did the *Children of Israel* spend in Canaan? That is easily determined. Abraham left Haran at age 75 in AY 2024. Jacob moved the nation of Israel to Egypt in AY 2239. Hence, the nation of Israel spent 215 years in Haran (AY 2239-AY 2024). Since the total sojourn of Israel in both Canaan and Egypt was 430 years, this solves a problem that has long been debated. Israel spent *exactly 215 years in Egypt* (AY 2454 - AY 2239). As a second witness, we can calculate the 215 years spent in Egypt another way. The 430-year period began when Abram was 75 years old. From the call of Abram to the birth of Isaac is 25 years (Gen 12:4). From the birth of Isaac to Jacob's birth is 60 years (Gen 25:26). From Jacob's birth to his death is 147 years (Gen 47:28). From the death of Jacob to the death of Joseph is 54 years (Gen 41: 46- Gen 50:22). The total of all these years is 286 years. Subtracting 286 from the total of 430 years we obtain 144 years to the Exodus. Note that since Moses was 80 years old at the Exodus, there is $(144-80) = 64$ years from Joseph's death to the birth of Moses, and 61 years to the birth of Aaron. Now, Jacob came to Egypt with his family and stayed 17 years before his death at age 147 (Gen 47:9, Gen 47:28). Seventeen years to the death of Jacob plus 54 years to the death of Joseph plus 144 years from the death of Joseph to the Exodus totals 215 years. Hence, the sojourn of Abraham and his descendants in Canaan was also 215 years. This information will allow us to interpret a *hard scripture*. Gen 15:16 records that **they** (the seed of Abraham) *will come hither again in the 4th generation*. This implies that the Children of Israel must leave Canaan and then return again. They left Canaan when Jacob came to Egypt with his family. When did they return again? They left at the exodus;

which was 215 years later. The four generations were Jacob to Levy, Levy to Kohath, Kohath to Amran, and Amran to Moses (Gen. 35:23, Exod. 6:16, 6:18, and 6:20). There are two other biblical clues which can now lead to a complete chronology from Adam's departure out of the Garden of Eden to the exodus out of Egypt.

> ***"Then he said to Abram: Know certainly that your descendants will be strangers in a land that is not theirs, and will serve them, and they will afflict them four hundred years."*** Genesis 15:13

We have shown that the Israelites spent only 215 years in Egypt, so this length of time (400 years) cannot be equivalent to that period of time. The key to interpreting this verse is that it pertains to *Abraham's descendants*, and not to Abraham. We now need to notice that Abraham entered the land of Canaan at age 75 (Gen 12:4). He was 86 years old when Ishmael was born to Hagar, but Ishmael was not the child of promise (Gen 17:21). Isaac was the offspring who would begin the line of descendants which would lead to Jesus Christ (Mat 1:2-16). Isaac was born to Sarah when Abraham was 100 years old (Gen 21:5). Many biblical chronologists state that Isaac was weaned at age 5, and that event started the 400 year count in Gen 5:13. The following logic is often stated.

Isaac was born in AY 2049; 25 years after Abram left Haran for the land of Canaan. When Isaac is age 5, there was a great feast held in Canaan (Gen 21:8). Ishmael was jealous of Isaac and *scoffed him*. Hearing this, Sarah said to Abraham: ***cast out this bondwoman*** (Hagar) ***and her son (Ishmael) for the son of this bondwoman shall not be heir with my son, even with Isaac*** (Gen 21:10). At this point in time, Ishmael lost any claim to his birthright as the oldest son. This event occurred 30 years after Abraham left Haran and it was at this point in time that the 400 year period of time given in Gen 15:13 started. The *seed* referred to in Gen 15:13 and Acts 7:6 are Isaac and later Jacob, starting when Isaac became heir to the promise when Ishmael was cast out for mocking Isaac (Gen 21:8-10). This turn of events was a fulfillment of Gen 17:21 when God told Abram that Isaac was to be heir to the promises, and not Ishmael. The *terminus* of the 400 years in Gen 15:13 is the Exodus. This then solves the problem of correctly identifying the 400 year period as part of the 430-year period. Starting with the birth of Joseph in AY 2200, we can now accurately trace the 215 year sojourn of the Children of Israel in Egypt. The sequence of events and when they occurred are again summarized in the following Table.

Biblical Event	AY Year
Joseph sold into slavery at age 17	2217
13 Yrs later at age 30 he is called	
before Pharoh (Gen 41:46)...............	2230
7 Years of Plenty follow	2237
Followed by 7 by years of famine	2244
Jacob moves to Egypt at age 130 in	
second year of famine..........	2239
Jacob lives for 17 Yrs in Egypt, then dies	
at age 147 [enters at 130, (130 +17)]=147	2256
Joseph lives to age 110, and then dies in Yr	2310
Now, Abram left at age 75	2024
It is exactly 430 years to the day that	
the Exodus starts...........................	2454
Since Exodus was in year	2454
Moses was born in year........................	2374
The number of years between	
Josephs death & Moses birth is.........	64
Aaron was 3 Years younger, Born in.....	2371
Note that Terah, Abram's father died in Yr ..	2084
Abraham died at age 175 in year...............	2124
So when Terah died, Abraham was age...	135

Chronology: From the Exile of Joseph to the Exodus

At this point, we need to clarify a key biblical fact concerning the chronology offered in the King James Bible. A controversy exists as to when Terah birthed his son Abram (later called Abraham). In the King James Bible it is recorded that ***Terah lived 70 years and begat Abram, Nahor and Haran*** (Gen 11:26). But can we verify that Terah was 70 years old when

Abram was born? The KJV text seems to *indicate* that Abram was born first when Haran was 70 years old, but this is not conclusively stated. In the book of Acts, Stephen stated that ***Then he*** (Abram) ***came out of the land of the Chaldeans*** (Mesopotamia); ***and dwelt in Charan*** (Haran); ***and from thence, when his father was dead, he removed him into this land*** (Canaan) ***wherein you*** (Israel) ***now dwell*** (Acts 7:4). In Genesis, Moses recorded that ***and the days of Terah were 205 years; and Terah died in Haran*** (Gen 11:32).Using these two passages, it might be concluded that Terah died when Abram was 75 years old and Abram immediately left for the land of Canaan. Terah did died at the age of 205, and this would be in AY 2084. It follows that Terah would be 130 years old when Abram was born. The problem is that in the King James Bible, it is clearly stated that: ***Terah lived 70 years and begat Abram, Nahor and Haran*** (Gen 11:26). Using this passage, other scholars have taken Abram to be born when Terah was age 70: This would make Terah age 145 when Abram left at age 75, and he would have been alive 20 years later when Isaac was born. Note that the birth of Abram when Terah was only 70 years old or when he was 130 years old is only important for properly liking the birth and death AY dates of a particular chronology.

The assumption that Haran was 130 years old at the birth of Abram simply pushes all AY dates after AY 1879 forward 60 AY years. Nevertheless, we would like to know if Abram was born in year AY 1949 or in year AY 2009. To justify our choice (other than the fact that KJV implies age 70 in Gen 11:26); Can we find other support to justify the *short chronology*? One source of additional information is the ancient book of Asher. Asher is not just one of many non-canonical biblical records; it is mentioned twice in the Old Testament.

"Is it not written in the Book of Asher?"   Josh 10:13
"Behold, it is written in the Book of Asher"
II Samuel 1:18

These two references in the KJV seem to lend credibility to the witness of Asher. The Book of Asher contains a remarkably detailed record of the generations of the patriarchs from Adam to the death of Joseph. It also contains information not found anywhere else, including the names of other wives and sons. The following statement is interesting: **Terah was 70 years old when he begat Abram** (Jasher 7:51). This is a second witness to the same statement in KJV, but is very specific and unambiguous. We have taken the time to carefully study the Book of Jasher and traced the following sequence of AY years for events which emerge using AY 1949 as the birth date of Abram when his father Haran was 70 years old.

Terah Age	The Book of Jasher		KJV AY Year	Abram's Age	Noah's Age
	Terah Born in...		1879		
70	Terah's age when Abram is born..	70	1949	0	892
80	Abram hides for 10 Yrs in a cave from Nimrod................................		1959	10	902
80	Sarah is born this same Year..................		1959	10	902
119	Abram now moves to Noah's house in Shinar and stays 39 Yrs.........		1998	49	941
120	Abram leaves Noah at age 50, returns to father Terah in Shinar.................		1999	50	942
122	Abram stays in Shinar 2 Yrs, at which time Nimrod threatens his life. He moves back to Noah's house.....................		2001	52	944
122	After one month in Noah's house, Terah comes to see Abram and Abram convinces him to go to Canaan with him........		2001	52	944
125	But they stop in Haran and remain 3 Yrs.......		2004	55	947
125	After these three Yrs, God appears to Abram for the first time and tells him to move on to Canaan..		2004	55	947
128	Abram & Terah dwell in Canaan for 3 Yrs, then Noah dies at age 950...350 Yrs after the flood occurred. Abram is 58 Yrs old. when Terah returns to Haran........................		2007	58	950
140	After 12 more Yrs (15 Yrs in Canaan), God gives all the promised land to Abram........		2019	70	
145	"At that time"...Abram returns to Haran to tell his father Terah...He stays 5 Yrs.........		2024	75	

Terah Age		AY Year	Age of Abram	
145	The lord now appears to Abram a second time and says, " 20 years ago I told you to go to Canaan…now you do it". Abram now leaves a SECOND TIME for Canaan. Before leaving he takes Sarah as his wife and convinces his brother Lot to come with him…	2024	75	
169	Abram lives with Lot in Canaan for 24 years, then God institutes the ritual of circumcism..	2048	99	
169	The same Year, the destruction of Sodom and Gomorah occur……………………..	2048	99	
				Age of Issac
170	One year later, Issac is born…Abram is 100 years old…………………………………..	2049	100	0
175	Issac becomes the child of promise at age 5 and Terah attends a great feast	2054	105	5
205	Terah dies at age 205 when Issac is 35 years old. He is buried in Haran…………………..	2084	135	35
	Two years later when Issac is 37 years old, the "binding of Issac" occurs……………..	2086	137	37

Jacob Age		AY Year	Age of Abram	Age of Issac
	Issac takes a wife (Rebecca) 3 yrs later at age 40…………………………..	2089	140	40
0	When Issac is 60 yrs old, Rebecca has Jacob & Esau……………………….	2109	160	60
15	15 Yrs later, Abraham dies at age 175……….	2124	175	75
16	1 yr later (Jacob & Esau are 16), Esau goes hunting…he is attacked by Nimrod, and Esau kills Nimrod…Nimrod is 215 yrs old, and has reigned for 185 years………………	2125		76
18	2 years later, Selah son of Arphaxad dies at age 483 yrs old………………………………	2127		78
50	"at that time", Jacob is sent to the house of Shem where he stays for 32 years…………………………..	2159		110
50	"at that time" Shem dies at age 600. Jacob then returns home to Hebron…………………	2159		110

Note ….Shem was born 98 years before the flood, and was 100 years old when Arphaxed was born. (Gen 11:10). He died exactly 500 yrs after the birth of Arphaxed (Gen 11:11)

Jacob		AY Year		Issac
63	13 years after the death of Shem, Rebecca & Jacob "steal" the birthright from Esau. Jacob and Esau now 63 yrs old………………………	2172		123
64	Ishmael dies one yr later………………………….	2173		124
77	Esau vows to kill Jacob, and he flees to Eber's house where he hides for 14 years…………………………………………..	2186		137
77	After hiding for 14 yrs, Jacob finally returns to Hebron but Esau still wants to kill him, so he now flees to Laban's house in Canaan….	2186		137
79	2 yrs later, Eber son of Shem dies at age 464..	2188	Age of Joseph	139
91	Joseph is born when Jacob is 91 yrs old	2200	0	151
97	Jacob spends 20 yrs at Laban's house. He marries both Leah & Rachel during this period of time. ………………………………..	2206		157
107	When Jacob is age 107, in 10th yr after leaving Laban's house Leah dies at age 51….	2216		167
108	In the following year, Joseph is sold into Egyptian slavery at age 17………………….	2217	17	168

Note….If Jacob is now age 108, and Joseph is age 17, Jacob had son Joseph at age 91.

Event	AY Year	Joseph	Issac	Jacob
At age of 18, he encounters the sexual advances of Potifar's wife. He is accused of attacking her & thrown in prison............	2218	18	169	109
Issac dies at age 180................................	2229	29	180	120
Joseph stays in prison for 12 yrs..................	2230	30		121
At age 30, Joseph is called before the Pharoh to interpret his dreams.................	2230	30		121
7 Yrs of plenty follow.............................	2237	37		128
After 2 yrs of famine, Jacob moves his entire family to Egypt....................................	2239	39		130
5 more yrs of famine follow........................	2244	44		135
Jacob lives in Egypt for 17 yrs, and then dies. He is 147 yrs old............................	2256	56		147
Joseph dies at age 110.............................	2310	110		
Abram leaves Haran at age 75.....	2024			
430 years later: Exodus occurs.....	2454			
Moses was therefore born in........	2374			
Joseph died in creation year........	2310			
Years between death of Joseph and birth of Moses...	64 Years			

Jasher Chronology

It was amazing to find that the sequence of events recorded in the book of Jasher between when Terah was born and the exodus occurred exactly coincided with the AY dates independently determined from the KJV records. The Jasher Chronology is therefore accepted as being valid to this study. There are several interesting details that emerge from the Book of Jasher that are not recorded in the KJV narrative, but none contradict the KJV records.

- Terah was born when Noah was age 822 years old, and Abram was able to learn from him until Noah's death when Abram was age 58.
- Abram actually stayed in Noah's house for 39 years as a young adult.
- Abram is told to leave Mesopotamia and go to Canaan at age 70. He leaves but stops in Haran for 5 years.
- Abram is told a SECOND time to go to Canaan at age 75. This time he leaves with Lot and Sarah. His father Terah refuses to go and stays in Haran. Abram is 75 years old when he leaves Haran for Canaan.
- Terah lives another 60 years and dies in Haran.

> - Acts 7:4 seems to imply that Abraham moves his body to Canaan and buries him there.
> - Isaac is anointed the child of promise at age 5; not at his weaning ceremony but at a great feast. This is a result of jealousy by Ishmael which resulted in his expulsion.
> - Isaac is 60 years old when Jacob and Esau are born.

All indications are that the chronological sequence, and the sequence of events recorded in the Book of Jasher, can be accepted as authentic when synchronized to the KJV narrative. If this premise is accepted, then Jasher provides much more detail to the KJV chronology. It is particularly interesting to now realize that Abram did not leave for the promised land of Canaan at his father Terah's death. In addition, the age of Terah at the birth of Abram is now firmly established as 70; not 130. It is also interesting to know that God had to tell Abram to leave for the promised land twice before he finally obeyed God.

The additional information brought to light by the Jasher Chronology seem to conclusively show that the Exodus occurred in AY 2454 and that the 40-year exile and wanderings in the deserts ended 40 years later in AY 2494. We are now ready to project these dates forward using a remarkable set of biblical clues. The following passage is key to our study.

> *"And it came to pass in the 480th year after the Children of Israel had come out of the land of Egypt, in the 4th year of Solomon's reign over Israel, in the month of Ziv, which is the second month, that he (King Solomon) began to build the house of the Lord."* I King 6:1

King Solomon was the third king of Israel, following Saul (40 years) and David (40 years). This verse states that the first temple, known as Solomon's Temple, was started 480 years after the Exodus occurred, in the Month of Ziv (May/June) on the second day. The Hebrew calendar referred to in this passage is shown on the next page.

Hebrew Month	Civil Month	Religious Month	Days	Calendar Month
Nisan	7	1	30	March/April
Iyar	8	2	29	April/May
Sivan	9	3	30	May/June
Tammuz	10	4	29	June/July
Av	11	5	30	July/August
Elul	12	6	29	August/September
Tishri	1	7	30	September/October
Cheshvan	2	8	29	October/November
Kislev	3	9	30	November/December
Tevet	4	10	29	December/January
Shevat	5	11	30	January/February
Adar 1	6	12	29	February/March
Adar 2			30	

The Jewish Calendar

In ancient times, the first of each month was determined by the first crescent of the new moon, reported by two witnesses. In the month of Nisan, the priesthood would examine the Barley and Wheat crops. If mature enough to collect a firstfruit offering in two weeks, then the month of Nisan would start. If the crop was not mature enough a new month called Adar 2 was added. In this way, the Hebrew lunar calendar would stay in synch with the Seasonal Solar calendar. This method was replaced after the Babylonian exile with a calendar that was regulated by rules, including adding 7 extra months every 19 years. With minor adjustments, this calendar is still in use today.

The reader should mark this calendar for future reference. It will be used many times in this book. Recall that the Exodus occurred in AY 2454. Using I Kings 6:1, Solomon's Temple was started in AY 2933. This occurred in the 4th year of King Solomon's reign. The first AY year of Solomon's first year of reign is easily determined as AY 2930 and his last year of reign in AY 2969. Solomon died sometime during AY 2969 (we will later give evidence that it was in the summer of AY 2969). During the last year of King Solomon's reign, a prophet named Elijah arose and told Jeroboam, the son of Nebat, that God had chosen him to rule over 10 tribes of Israel (I Kings 11:31). The other two tribes of Israel would remain in the Davidic line and Rehoboam, Solomon's son, would reign over them (I Kings 11:32-39). When Solomon heard of this, he *sought to kill Jeroboam*, But Jeroboam arose and fled to Egypt (I Kings 11:40). He remained there until the death of King Solomon. At that time, the nation of Israel split into two kingdoms; *the Kingdom of Judah* (Southern Kingdom) and the *Kingdom of Israel* (Northern kingdom). The capital city of Judah became Jerusalem, and the capital city of Israel became Shechem, which was in the mountains of Ephraim (I Kings 12:1-33). We will show later that the Southern Kingdom of Judah lasted exactly 390 years from the death of King David, and the Northern Kingdom of Israel lasted 255.5 years. For now, we need to first ask how we know that the Southern Kingdom of Judah lasted 390 years. To answer this question, we turn to the prophet Ezekiel. In Ezekiel 4 he is told by God to *act out* the misery and affliction that would befall Jerusalem. He was then told that this affliction would last 390 years. God's instructions were as follows.

> *"You also, son of man, take a clay tablet and lay it before you, and portray on it a city, Jerusalem. Lay siege against it, build a siege wall against it, and heap up a mound against it; set camps against it also, and place battering rams against it all around. Moreover, take for yourself an iron plate, and set it as an iron wall between you and the city. Set your face against it, and it shall be besieged, and you shall lay siege against it. This will be a sign to the house of Israel. Lie also on your left side, and lay the iniquity of the house of Israel against it. According to the number of the days, 390 days, so you shall bear the iniquity of the house of Israel. I have laid upon you a day for each year."*
> Ezekiel 4: 1-2, 4-5, 6-b.

Over a period of the last 400 years, many prominent scholars have believed that the 390 years depicted in this scene began with the death of Solomon and the divided kingdom, and terminated with the total destruction of both Jerusalem and Solomon's temple at the hands of the Babylonians. In the 19th year of Nebuchadnezzar (King of Babylon), the walls of Jerusalem were destroyed and the temple burned to the ground. All of the city's treasurers were taken to Babylon. The remaining leaders of Judah were killed, and the rest of the people were carried into Babylonian captivity. Only the very poorest and afflicted people remained in the hills of Judah, and the rest fled to Egypt (2 Kings 25:23-30).

We are now in a position to determine in what AY year this occurred. We have shown that the last year of King Solomon's reign was AY 2969. Hence, the 390 years that the Southern Kingdom of Judah existed started in AY 2970 and ended in AY 3359. It is now time to ask an important question: In what BC year did all of these events occur? The Holy Bible never records either a BC or an AD date in which any event occurred. If we could determine exactly what BC year that Judah fell in AY 3359, then all other events could also be given a BC year date by simply backtracking to AY 1. Here we must rely upon archeological discoveries and ancient manuscripts to provide such a date. Fortunately, over the past 100 years there has been a great deal of historical records recovered and interpreted.

The Fall of Jerusalem and the Temple Destruction

The fall of Jerusalem in AD 3359 was to the Babylonian Empire, which flourished between the fall of the Assyrian Empire (612 BC) and the rise of the Medo-Persian Empire. Its capital city was Babylon. The Babylonians kept excellent records, including detailed lists of solar and lunar eclipses. Using modern computers, it is relatively easy to determine a modern date for recorded events by correlating any event referenced to any ancient eclipse. All eclipses occur in a very predictable and unchanging pattern. The only problem is to establish these dates on the ancient Julian calendar. Yearly designations and calendar dates were represented by the Julian calendar after it was first introduced in 45 BC. When historians date events prior to that year, they normally extend the Julian calendar backward in time. This extended calendar is known as the *Julian Proleptic Calendar*. In the year 1582, the modern Gregorian calendar was introduced to correct minor errors in the Julian calendar. Similarly, it is possible to extend the Gregorian calendar backward in time before 1582. However, use of the *Gregorian Proleptic Calendar* is not recommended. It has been suggested that in order to compare and assess different chronological schemes before 1582, that all dates be converted to Julian calendar dates. Unless noted otherwise, we have used Julian dates in this book for events that come before 70 BC. The Babylonian Empire was prophesied to destroy Jerusalem long before it ever happened. In Jeremiah 25:11-12, the prophet said that the Jews would suffer 70 years of Babylonian domination. Jeremiah also said Babylon would be ruled after the 70 years had run its course by the Medo-Persians, and that the Israelites would be allowed to return to their own land. Both parts of this prophecy were fulfilled. About 2620 years ago, Babylon captured the last Assyrian king and ruled over a vast part of what had been the Assyrian Empire, to which the land of Israel previously had been subjugated. The date of the fall of the Assyrian Empire to a Babylonian King called Naboplasser is well known and occurred in 609 BC. A scroll called the Babylonian Chronicle contains a detailed record of what happened next. We extract the following narrative from Finnegan.

> *"The chronicle puts the death of Naboplasser on Abu 8 (Aug 15, 605 BC) in the 21st year of his reign. Naboplasser was succeeded by Nebuchadnezzar on Elulu 8 (Sept 7, 605 BC). It is certain that Nebucadnezzar began his official reign on Nisanu 1 (April 12, 604 BC. Two elipses are recorded during the reign of King Nebuchadnezzar, the first on April 22, 621 BC in the 5th year of Nebuchadnezzar, and the second on July 4, 568 BC in the 37th year of Nebuchadnezzar. These two elipse dates secure the above date for the first year of Nebuchadnezzar's reign. Edwin Theil, a highly respected chronological expert, wrote: "No dates in ancient history are more firmly established than these dates".*

In the 19th year of Nebuchadnezzar's reign, Nebuzaradan, who was captain of Nebuchadnezzar's bodyguard, came against Jerusalem. He burned Solomon's temple, ransacked the city of Jerusalem, destroyed the walls of the city and carried away all of the temple treasures. He left behind only the oldest and poorest people (II King 25: 3-7 and Jer 52:12-16). This date is recorded in Jer 52:12 as *the 10th day of the 5th month,* and in II Kings 25:8 as the *seventh day of the fifth month*". The difference in two days is likely due to the fact that the deportation obviously took several days. Jewish Rabbinic tradition recorded the date as either Av 7 or Av 10, respectively. It was later recorded that the *official* fall of Solomon's temple was designated as AV 9 (July/August), the same date that Herod's temple was destroyed in 70 AD! Solomon's Temple evidently was breached on AV 7, set fire and burned for two days, and actually fell on AV 9. It is generally taught by Jewish historians that both temples fell on the exact same day on AV 9. The 19th year of Nebuchadnezzar's reign was from Nisan 1 (April 13), 586 BC to Adar 30 (April 1) 586 BC. The most likely date for the final fall of Jerusalem and the end of the Kingdom of Judah was July 18, 586 BC (Finnegan) in AY 3359. The Israelites continued to rebel against Babylonian domination for several years, until Babylon asserted its dominance by taking many Jews as captives to Babylon, and by destroying Jerusalem. Domination of the Babylonian Empire ended in 539 BC, when Cyrus, a leader of Persians and Medes, conquered Babylon and brought an end to its rule. Cyrus later offered the captive Jews their freedom and allowed them to return to their homeland.

Calendar Dates for the Chronology

We have spent a lot of time establishing that the final fall of Jerusalem occurred in the 19th year of King Nebuchadnezzar on *July 8, 586 BC*. We have also shown that the first year of the Divided Kingdom occurred in AY 2970, and that the end of the Kingdom of Judah came 390 years later in AY 3359. We will now assume that 586 BC is the *anchor year* from which we can work backward from AY 3359 and determine the calendar year of every other AY year in the offered chronology. Recall that AY years started with AY=1, which was the first year that Adam and Eve lived on the Earth after being expelled from the Garden of Eden.

The last question to be asked is: What months should be used to start and end each AY year? There are two positions held as to what month should start each AY year. The first is that the Jewish calendar month of Nisan (March/ April) should start each AY year. The second is that Tishri 1 (Sept/ Oct) should start each year. We prefer to use a Tishri 1 date to begin each AY year for three reasons. The *first* is that Jewish Rabbinical tradition teaches that the world was created in Tishri. Quoting Rabbi Eleazar;

> *"In Tishri the world was created, In Tishri the patriarchs Abraham and Jacob were born; in Tishri the patriarchs died."* Tractate Rosh Hashanah, 10b-11a

The *second* reason is based upon what God instructed Moses to do following the Exodus from Egypt which occurred in the month of Nisan (Nisan 15) in March or April.

> *"This month (Nisan) shall be unto you the beginning of months; it shall be the first month of the year to you."* Exodus 12:2

By this command, God did not restart the sequence of years; he simply instructed the nation of Israel to start their life anew from this point on and call the month of Nisan *Month 1*. The Jews recognized and followed this command by adopting and observing two types of yearly sequences. The first is called the *Civil Year* and is Tishri 1 to Tishri. The second is called the "Religious Year" and runs from Nisan 1 to Nisan 1. This is shown in Table 5.3. Before the exodus, if a biblical verse referenced *Month 1*, it was always referring to the month of Tishri. In any biblical verse after the Exodus, *Month 1* would always refer to the month of Nisan. It should be remembered that regardless of how the month of Nisan was numbered, it *always* started in the modern month of March or April in the spring; the month of Tishri always started in September or October

The question to be asked is why God would instruct Moses to renumber the months so that Nisan would be remembered as the first month, *if it was already the first month*? The answer seems to be obvious. The month of Tishri was always the first month from creation to AY 2454. The Exodus had to occur in the seventh month of a Tishri year, or God's instruction to Moses makes no sense whatsoever. Third, it has been noticed that since the first word in Genesis, which means *beginning,* is translated *in the beginning*. The Hebrew letters in this first word can be rearranged to mean the first day in the month of Tishri, an interesting observation. In any case, we choose to start each AY Year on Tishri 1. Each AY year would then run from Tishri 1 to the end of the 12th month, Elul. For simplicity, we will simply use the duration of each year to be Tishri 1- Tishri 1. Similarly, a Nisan1 to the end of Adar 1 (or Adar 2) will be simply Nisan 1- Nisan 1. Equating AY 3359 to the year Sept, 587-Sept, 586 BC, and working backward through time, we can determine the Jewish civil calendar year for every AY year between AY 1 and AY 3359. The following table shows dates for important events.

Event	AY Year	Julian Years
Adam & Eve Leave Garden of Eden	1	Sept/Oct, 3945 BC-Sept/Oct, 3944 BC
The Great Flood (Adam is 600 Yrs Old)	1657	Sept/Oct, 2288 BC-Sept/Oct, 2287 BC
Abraham Leaves Haran @ Age 75	2024	Sept/Oct, 1922 BC-Sept/Oct, 1921 BC
Jacob Dies	2256	Sept/Oct, 1691 BC-Sept/Oct, 1690 BC
Joseph Dies	2310	Sept/Oct, 1637 BC-Sept/Oct, 1636 BC
Moses Born	2374	Sept/Oct, 1572 BC-Sept/Oct, 1571 BC
Exodus From Egypt	2454	March/April 1491 BC
Law is Given @ Mt. Sinai	2454	April/May 1491 BC
Moses Dies at Age 120	2494	Feb/March 1491 BC
Exodus Ends & Jordan River Crossed	2494	March/April 1491 BC
First Year of King Solomon's Reign	2930	Sept/Oct, 1016 BC-Sept/Oct, 1015 BC
Fourth Year of King Solomon's Reign	2933	Sept/Oct, 1013 BC-Sept/Oct, 1012 BC
Temple Started in Month of Ziv	2933	April/May, 1012 BC
Last Year of King Solomon's Reign	2969	Sept/Oct, 977 BC-Sept/Oct, 976 BC *
First Year of Divided Kingdom (Judah)	2970	Sept/Oct, 976 BC-Sept/Oct, 975 BC
Jerusalem Falls to Babylonian Empire	3359	July 8, 586 BC **

*This is a well-established date, verified by solar ellipse dates and the Babylonian chronicles.
**We will later show that King Solomon likely died in the summer of 976.

Dates from Adam to the Fall of Judah

The following graphic is easily understood, and is given to show how the anchor date of 586 BC is linked to AY 1.

AY Year		Hebrew Year
1	Year Adam left Eden:	Sept, 3945-Sept, 3944
		2454 years
2454	Year of the Exodus:	Sept, 1492-Sept, 1491
2454	Exodus:	Sept, 1492-Sept, 1491
		480 years
2933	Solomon's 4th Year:	Sept, 1013-Sept, 1012
2930	Solomon's 1st Year:	Sept, 1016-Sept, 1015
		4 years
2933	Solomon's 4th Year:	Sept, 1013-Sept, 1012
2930	Solomon's 1st Year:	Sept, 1016-Sept, 1015
		40 years
2969	Solomon's 40th Year:	Sept, 977-Sept, 976
2970	Divided Kingdom	Sept, 976-Sept, 975
		390 years
3359	Fall of Judah:	Sept, 587-Sept, 586
Judah fell on July 8, 586 BC (Finnegan)		
Solomon (likely) died in Summer of 976 BC		
Kingdom Of Judah lasted 390 years to fulfill Ezekiel 4:1-8		

Summary

We have shown that a relative chronology of key biblical events can be constructed without compromising the Holy Word. Most important, the method used did not necessitate that neither the time period of the Kings between the death of Joshua and the reign of King Solomon, or the 390 years of the divided kingdom, be accurately mapped out. Using nothing but the *clues* found in Scripture and a secure Julian calendar date for the fall of the Kingdom of Judah to the Babylonian Empire, the AY dates and

Julian dates for a sequence of all important biblical historical events were determined. The AY year and the Julian year are the Tishri-Tishri years in which the events occurred, unless a date is clearly given. For example, the Exodus was in AY 2454; March/April 1491 BC. AY years start on Tishri 1 (Sept/Oct) and end on Tishri 1 (Sept/Oct) for convenience.

This has been a long and complicated journey from when Adam and Eve were driven from the Garden of Eden in AY 1 (3945-3944 BC) until the Kingdom of Judah fell to the Babylonian Empire on AY 3359; July 8, 586 BC. Using these results, we will subsequently show how to identify the crucifixion of Christ and the duration of the tribulation period.

Comment: The established chronology with associated AY and Julian year dates were originally determined based solely upon the biblical records. It was not discovered until later that James Ussher, a 17th Century Archbishop, had meticulously constructed an amazingly similar Chronology but using a different line of reasoning. The Ussher Chronology was constructed by tracing biblical dates all the way from Genesis to the final fall of the Southern Kingdom by the Babylonian empire. He reconstructed the duration of the *Period of the Monarchs*; the *Period of the Kings*; and the duration of the *Northern and Southern Kingdoms* after Solomon's death. Working backward, he arrived at 4004 BC as a creation date. In an interesting coincidence, if one takes the age of Terah to be 130 years old at the age of Abram's birth, and start the AY count at zero (not at AY 1 as in the offered chronology).... The offered sequence of AY dates will coincide with Ussher's creation year of 4004 BC. Ussher's chronology has both strong advocates and strong objectors. It is generally conceded that his date of the final fall of Jerusalem in 588 BC is two years in error. The date we use here is now widely accepted (Finnegan). Of course, the method used in this chapter did not require that the time of the Judges or the Kings be calculated year to year. The linkage in I Kings 6:1 and the anchor date of July 8, 586 BC rendered this unnecessary. This leads to two necessary assumptions. The first is to accept the clear and unambiguous statement in I Kings 6:1 at face value that from the exodus to the start of Solomon's Temple was 480 years. Several AY Year dates for the exodus have been proposed by other chronologists. The difference in proposed dates hinges upon (1) the age of Haran at the birth of Abram; (2) The use of zero or one as the first AY Year; (3) Interpretation of I Kings 6:1; (4) a chronology of both the Judges and the Kings; and (5) whether or not the KJV Bible is the biblical record used to establish the chronology proposed. In reality, by working backward from an anchor point of 586 BC to a date of the exodus, the AY year used by working down from Adam through the biblical record will only change the AY count and the BC date used to begin the chronology. The most important assumption is that from Solomon's death to the final fall of Judah in 586 BC was 390 years using the Ezekiel prophecy.

Between 1951 and 1982 Edwin R. Thiel published three editions of a landmark book called *The Mysterious Numbers of the Hebrew Kings.* Thiel was a brilliant biblical researcher who contributed many things to the understanding of ancient Hebrew history, including proof of how Hebrew regnal years were determined following Solomon's death and through the divided kingdom. However, he was obsessed with trying to match the biblical record with Assyrian Records and could not rationalize or determine a 390 year chronology of the divided kingdom. It is now clear to some researchers (including myself) that Thiel made a serious error. He compromised and invalidated the biblical records recorded in the Holy Writ; changing, overlapping, and correlating the reigns of Kings to force Assyrian record confirmation. In doing so, he forced a much shorter time period for the divided kingdom than 390 years. Using his assumptions, the exodus would have occurred in the spring of 1446. We will not address his errors here, but for the interested reader we recommend that the critical assessment of Floyd Nolan Jones be studied. In the body of work presented in this chapter, I was able to accurately and completely reconstruct the 390 year duration of the divided kingdom, and the reign of every King in the Northern and Southern kingdom. The start date of every King's reign has been double dated and in every case confirms the biblical records. This is a separate study available from the author if requested.

In the words of Dr. Nolan Jones, we have two choices: Believe the biblical records and the inspired word of God, or believe the secular and historical records of the Ancient Assyrian Empire. Being a biblical literalist… I have elected to follow the records recorded in the King James Bible. I have no reason not to believe that my entire chronology will be rejected by scholars who accept Thiel's work… So be it. There is always room for scholarly debate on biblical principles, as long as God's word is not rejected in favor of historical and secular records. The chronology I offer will now be used to determine when the Sabbatical and Jubilee years *would* occur within the same chronology. Using Jewish tradition, biblical records and the *History of the Jews* by Josephus, we will show their validity. Having determined the validity of the chronology, we will then show when Jesus Christ was crucified and present solid evidence that the tribulation period is only 3.5 years in duration. Before we can do this, we will need to establish the correct sequence of years for both the Jewish Sabbatical and Jubilee years.

Thoughts and Things…..

Chapter 6

The Sabbatical and Jubilee Years

In order to fully understand the prophecy of Daniel's 70th week, we need to understand the concepts of a Sabbatical year, a Sabbatical cycle and the year of Jubilee. Using the chronology developed in Chapter 5 and doing a little *biblical detective work*, we can identify when the Sabbatical and Jubilee years occurred.

Sabbatical Years

God ordained and established the sabbatical year, and instructed Moses and Israel to honor these years. The command to observe Sabbatical years is found in Lev 25.

> *"And the LORD spake unto Moses in Mount Sinai, saying, Speak unto the Children of Israel, and say unto them, When ye come into the land which I give you, then shall the land keep a sabbath unto the LORD. Six years thou shalt sow thy field, and six years thou shalt prune thy vineyard, and gather in the fruit thereof; but in the seventh year shall be a sabbath of rest unto the land, a sabbath for the LORD: thou shalt neither sow thy field, nor prune thy vineyard. That which groweth of its own accord of thy harvest thou shalt not reap, neither gather the grapes of thy vine undressed: for it is a year of rest unto the land. And the sabbath of the land shall be meat for you; for thee, and for thy servant, and for thy maid, and for thy hired servant, and for thy stranger that sojourneth with thee, And for thy cattle, and for the beast that are in thy land, shall all the increase thereof be meat."* Lev 25:1-7

In the Torah, it was written that no trees could be planted, pruned or harvested during a Sabbatical year. However, irrigation was permitted to keep trees alive. During the time that Herod's temple was standing, rabbinical law forbade Jews to work in the fields one month before a Sabbatical year. This was not a part of the *Law*, but an attempt by the rabbis to *fence in the law* to keep it from being violated. The Sabbatical year has three primary aspects. The *first* is religious; The Sabbath Year was to be a *Sabbath unto the Lord*. It is a holy convocation ordained by God. The *second* aspect is agricultural; the seventh year is to be a *Sabbath for the land*, in which the land would rest and renew itself. A *third* aspect is added to the agricultural principles in Deuteronomy 15:1-11. All debts are to be forgiven during that year, and those to whom money is owed no longer have the right to demand it back. This aspect of the commandment is designed to enable the impoverished to make a fresh start.

Since the land could not be planted and harvested in a Sabbatical year, the question arises as to how the Children of Israel were to eat during that year. Not only that, since the land could not be planted until the planting season of the eighth year, there were about two years without produce. God provided for these two years in a miraculous way.

> *"And if you say "what shall we eat in the 7th year, since we have not sown or gathered in our produce?" Then I will command my blessing on you in the 6th year, and it will bring forth produce enough for three years. And you shall sow in the 8th year, and eat old produce until the 8th year, until its produce comes in you shall eat of the old harvest."*
> Lev 25: 20-21.

The Lord is faithful and true, and he will take care of those whom he calls and those who respond. This covenant promise was unconditional. The Sabbatical year has many Messianic overtones, and has a direct relationship to the second coming of Christ as we will see later. The Sabbatical years were to continue forever (as long as the Children of Israel were in the land).

Year of Jubilee

The Sabbatical year was to be observed every seventh year. The sabbatical year (just as the Jewish civil year) started on Tishri 1, (Sept-Oct). A sequence of seven Sabbatical years was 49 complete years. The 50th year was to be both a Year of Jubilee and the start of the next Sabbatical year cycle. Interestingly, the

Year of Jubilee started on Tishri 10 on the Feast of Atonement. This unusual start date has Messianic and prophetic implications. The last year of Jubilee will start at the end of Daniel's 70th week, and will begin the 1000-year millennial kingdom. We will have more to say about this later.

> *"And thou shalt number seven Sabbaths of years unto thee, seven times seven years; and the space of the seven Sabbaths of years shall be unto thee forty and nine years. Then shalt thou cause the trumpet of the Jubilee to sound on the tenth day of the seventh month, in the Day of Atonement shall ye make the trumpet sound throughout all your land. And ye shall hallow the fiftieth year, and proclaim liberty throughout all the land unto all the inhabitants thereof: it shall be a jubilee unto you; and ye shall return every man unto his possession, and ye shall return every man unto his family. A jubilee shall that fiftieth year be unto you: ye shall not sow, neither reap that which groweth of itself in it, nor gather the grapes in it of thy vine undressed. For it is the jubilee; it shall be holy unto you: ye shall eat the increase thereof out of the field. In the year of this jubilee ye shall return every man unto his possession. Wherefore ye shall do my statutes, and keep my judgments, and do them; and ye shall dwell in the land in safety."*
> Lev 25 8-55

In the year of Jubilee; the land shall rest; it shall not be planted, pruned or harvested. The English word *jubilee* comes from the Hebrew word *yobel* meaning a trumpet or a horn. A rams' horn was to be blown on the Day of Atonement to announce the start of the year of Jubilee. It is interesting to this study that the rabbinical teachings agree that there were two *sacred yobels* to be sounded on two other occasions. In Genesis 22:1-14, Abraham was asked by God to sacrifice his only son, Isaac, on Mount Moriah. But before Abraham could harm his son, God saw Abraham's faith and rewarded it by instead providing a *ram* to be used as the *sacrifice*. The ram was totally consumed in a burnt offering, except for the two horns. It is traditionally believed that God took *one horn* to be sounded when *Moses* was to give the *law on Mt. Sinai*. The *second* ram's *horn* was reserved to be sounded when their long awaited *Jewish Messiah* will finally redeem Israel and call them all (living or dead) home. This Jewish belief clearly has parallel applications to the Christian *rapture*. This story is not biblically supported, but it is a widely-held belief in some Jewish circles. Our interpretation and parallel to this widespread Jewish belief is that **Jesus Christ will return in the air to rapture the body of Christ away from God's Wrath, which are the seven bowl judgments, at some future Feast of Trumpets (Rosh Hashanah).** This event will also signal the approaching final redemption of Israel and their final gathering to Jerusalem, just 10 days later at the final battle of Armageddon on the Feast of Yom Kippur. The final Rosh Hashanah will occur on Tishri 1 and the final Feast of Yom Kippur will occur on Tishri 10. The 10 days between these two feasts are known as the *days of awe* or the *days of redemption* in Jewish liturgy. They will signal the gathering of the remnant of Israel, those who will come through the Great Tribulation Period sometimes called the *Time of Jacob's Trouble*; these are those who have finally recognized Jesus Christ as their messiah and savior.

The year of Jubilee is a Sabbath of Sabbaths. It is a special year among special years. The year of Jubilee is unique to all other Sabbatical years in that it is initiated on Tishri 10. This is a feast day, a high Sabbath, and a fast day. Tishri 10 represents the most holy day of the year for Jews. It is also the great *Day of Atonement* (Lev. 23:26-32). There were three things which happened on that day in ancient Israel:

- ➢ All Hebrews slaves were set free.
- ➢ All land returned to its original owner or owner's family.
- ➢ All debts are to be forgiven.   Deut 15:1-23

For 215 years before the Exodus, the Israelites had been slaves in the land of Egypt, without freedom and without possessions. Everything in Egypt belonged to the Pharaoh. After the Exodus, the Children of Israel wandered in the desert for 40 years as a result of disobedience to the Lord. After crossing the river

Jordan we will shortly show that it took Joshua and his army between 5 years, 3 months; and 6 years, 3 months; to conquer the land. Once the land was conquered, the land of Canaan was divided among the 11 tribes (the Levites had no land inheritance). Every adult male among them became a land owner. This land could not be permanently sold. If a man became poor he could sell part or all of his land, but *only temporarily.* It would *always* revert to him or his descendants at the year of *Jubilee*. If he became poor and was unable to pay his debts, he could sell himself into slavery, and work to pay off his debts. Again that slavery could only be temporary. When the great *Day of Atonement* in the *Year of Jubilee* came, he became a free man once again and repossessed his inheritance. What a wonderful promise this was! How many hopeless slaves to debt in the poorest countries of the world today would wish they lived under such laws! The lord said that *the land is mine*; you are only a sojourner on *my land* (Lev 25:23). This inheritance was intended to never depart from the Children of Israel; the land was to be handed down from generation to generation. Oh how Israel failed God! The raging wars today between the Palestinians and the Jews should have never happened. The controversy of who owns the land of Israel today is forever settled; all the land belongs to God. But God has not turned his back on Israel forever, for after Jesus Christ returns in glory (Rev 19:11-21) the land will once again become the inheritance of God's children, the Jewish nation. Surely we say, *Come quickly Lord Jesus.*

When did Sabbatical and Jubilee years start to be observed? Over the last 2500 years, there have been many debates and interpretations of this question. Most have been based upon a complete misunderstanding of when Sabbatical years were to be *initiated.* One of the most recent hypotheses has been based upon an ancient non-canonical manuscript called the *Book of Jubilees*. The Book of Jubilees is generally recognized as one of the oldest manuscripts in existence. The Book of Jubilees contains a comprehensive chronology and record of the generations that were born between when Adam and Eve were created, to the giving of the law on Mt. Sinai. The chronology given in the *Book of Jubilees* is based on multiples of seven years duration. A Jubilee is a period of 49 years or seven *weeks of years*, into which all of time has been divided. The Book of Jubilees defines a *Jubilee* to be the 49th year in a 49-year cycle. According to the book, Adam and Eve were in the Garden of Eden for exactly seven years. At the end of the seventh year they sinned, and were expelled. The concept of every seventh year being a *Sabbatical Year* and the 50th year being a *Year of Jubilee* is never defined or used. Several biblical scholars have insisted that the Sabbatical and Jubilee years *started* when Moses led the Exodus out of Egypt. At that time, the concept of a Sabbatical year was not even known scripturally. An even larger group of chronological researchers have proposed that the year Joshua crossed the river Jordan after a 40-year Exodus was both a year of Jubilee and the first year in the first seven-year Sabbatical cycle. The basis for this assumption is rooted in Lev 25:2.

> *"When you come into the land which I give you, then shall the Land keep a Sabbath onto the Lord."*   Lev 25:2-b

This interpretation demonstrates a complete misunderstanding of why a Sabbatical year was dictated by God to Moses. The primary purpose of a Sabbatical year is to *rest the land from cultivation and harvest by the Jewish land owner*. When Joshua crossed the river Jordan after Moses had led the Israelites through the wilderness for 40 years, the *land* did not belong to Israel (although it did belong to God and had been promised to Israel as an inheritance). Joshua shortly embarked on a campaign to conquer the land and then give it to the 11 tribes of Israel (excluding the Levites). It is impossible to initiate any Sabbatical year cycle until the land has been conquered, the land divided, and the land cultivated (planted and harvested). Remember that both the Sabbatical years and the subsequent year of Jubilee is a *corporate commandment to all of Israel* and both are intended to *let the land rest* from six consecutive years of planting and harvesting. The 50th or Jubilee year is an extra year of rest for the land, and involves forgiving debts.

A large number of chronologists has determined from Jewish Rabbinical records, the Works of Josephus, and the Holy Bible when several Sabbatical years might have occurred, and built a sequence of Sabbatical years around those records. There are no definitive records anywhere as to when Jubilee years might have occurred. By all indications, Israel *never* observed a single year of Jubilee. However, we do know that if an initial set of seven seven-year Sabbatical cycles could be discovered, then the 50th year would be a Jubilee, and all other 49-year Sabbatical cycles and Jubilee years would follow. Before we attack this problem, we should note that exactly when a Jubilee cycle occurs is a debated topic. The debate is not that the Jubilee is the 50th year following a 49-year (seven-seven's) Sabbatical cycle, but how the 50th year is to be counted. The first interpretation is that the 50th (Jubilee) year is the *first year* of the next Sabbatical cycle. The second interpretation is that the 50th year is a *separate year*, and that the next Sabbatical cycle starts following the 50th year. Rabbi Judah states: *"The Jubilee year counts both ways"*, meaning it is counted as both the 50th year and the first year of the next seven-year cycle. We agree with Rabbi Judah. This assumption will be proven correct when we compare our derived sequence of Sabbatical years to historical records, and when the Jewish people seemed to observe Sabbatical years. In order to determine the chronological ordering of Sabbatical years, it is necessary to trace the Exodus from when Moses left Egypt in 1491 BC to when the Jordan River was crossed 40 years later in 1451 BC.

The Exodus Journey

The Chronology of the 40-year exodus sojourn is clearly recorded in the Books of Genesis, Exodus, Leviticus and Joshua. The nation of Israel left on the night following Nisan 14 which began Nisan 15 at 6:00 pm. The journey from leaving Egypt until the river Jordan was crossed 40 years later consisted of two major time periods: The *first* was the departure from Egypt, followed by the giving of the law at Mt Sinai and construction of the tabernacle. The *second* was the failure at Kadesh-barnea to trust God, followed by 38 years of wandering in the wilderness. The following sequence of events was recorded in the Holy

Scriptures. Recall that the Jewish day starts at 6:00pm and the Jewish Sabbath day is Saturday.

Timeline	Event	Reference
1st Day....Nisan 15	Exodus starts just after midnight	Ex 12:40-42, Num 33:3
47 Day journey	Arrival at Mt Sinai	Ex 19:1
50th day after departure	God speaks the 10 commandments	Ex 20:1-20, Deut 5:22
2nd year, 1st Month, 1st Day	Tabernacle set up after 7 Months, 3 days Construction	Ex 40:2, 40:17
2nd year, 2nd month, 20th Day	Depart from Mt. Sinai 50 days after tabernacle is completed	Num 10:11
2nd year, 3rd Month, 8th Day	Arrive at Kadesh-barnea after a 18 day journey including a 7 day delay to heal Miriam. Spies sent out to Promised Land	Deut 1:2 Num 12:15
2nd year, fourth Month, 18th Day	Spies return. Only Joshua & Caleb give a good report. God condemns them to wander 40 years (total since Exodus) in the wilderness......One year for each day.	Num 13:25
	Moses stays at Kadesh-barnea for almost 9 Months	Deut 1:46 Deut 2:14
3rd year, 15st Day, 1st Month	Moses departs Kadesh-barnea for 38 years in the Wilderness	Deut 2:14
40th year, 5th Month, 1st Day	Aaron dies and is buried on Mt. Hor	Num 33:38
40th year, 12th month, 1st Day	Moses dies and is taken to Mt. Nebo by God. He recites all of the law to Israel before he is taken away. He anoints Joshua as the new leader	Deut 34:1, Deut 34:7-8 Josh 1:1-5
41st year, Month 1, Day 1	Camp at River Jordan....Spies sent out a second time	Deut 34:8 Josh 2:1
41st year, Month 1, Day 10	River Jordan is crossed on Nisan 10	Josh 4:19
	All men circumcised	Josh 5:2-5
41st year, Month 1, Day 14	Exodus completed....Manna ceases	Josh 5:12

We are now ready to prove that under the leadership of Joshua, the land was conquered in less than seven years. To prove this, we need to do a little *detective work*. It is amazing how many different time periods (years) have been proposed for Joshua and the army of God to conquer the various nations and Kings in Canaan. Of course, the land was never fully conquered and after the initial period of conquest, the Children of Israel became complacent and failed to fully fulfill their destiny. The author has seen estimates ranging from seven years to more than 40 years required to conquer the land, division of the land and the release of the 12 tribes to their allotted inheritance. If studied carefully, the biblical record is quite clear on how long this actually took. Looking at the previous diagram we can trace the main events of the Exodus from Egypt. The time period required to conquer the land of Canaan can also be determined with scriptural help. Moses led the nation of Israel out of Egyptian bondage starting shortly after midnight (Exodus 12:29-30) on Nisan 15, a Thursday. This was the first day of the *Feast of Unleavened Bread* (Ex 12:17). They crossed the Red Sea (Sea of Reeds) three days later and emerged a new, free nation (a type of rebirth which was a shadow and type of our Lord's resurrection). On the 47th day after they left Egypt, they arrived at Mt. Sinai and on the 50th day (Exodus 19:1) God gave them the law (a shadow and type of when the New Covenant was ratified as the Holy Spirit fell on the day of *Pentecost*). The tabernacle was finished on the 20th day of the second month in the second year, and on that day Moses and the Children of Israel departed for the Promised Land. They arrived at Kadesh-barnea one year, one month and 23 days after leaving Egypt (Num 10:11). The journey took 40 days included a 3 day delay, and days for Miriam to be cleansed (Num 12:15). Moses immediately sent 12 men to spy the land (Lev 13:2-3), and after 40 more days they returned. Upon their return, 10 of the spies gave a bad report, and only Joshua and Caleb gave a good report (Num 13:25-33). In one of the most tragic events in biblical history, the 10 spies who gave the bad report were killed by a plague; the Lord sentenced the nation of Israel to wander a total of 40 years in the wilderness (Deut 2:7); none of the generation that rebelled were allowed to see the promised land (Num 26:64-65); and only Joshua and Caleb would enter Canaan of all those who were at Kadesh-barnea (Num 14:22-24, 30, 37-38, Deut 1:1-38). This is a stark testimony to anyone who refuses to trust in the Lord and not respond to a sacred calling. Moses stayed at Kadesh-barnea for about eight months and 5 days (Deut 2:14). He finally departed near or on the first day of the third year after leaving

Egypt (Deut. 2:13). He then led the nation of Israel through the wilderness for 38 more years. In the 40th year, on the first day of the 12th month, Moses gathered all the people to him. He reviewed all of the events that had transpired since they had left Egypt, and he read all of the Law. Moses was 120 years old that very day (Deut 31:1-2). Having been instructed by God, he inaugurated Joshua as the new commander-in-chief (Deut 31:23), recorded the law in a *book* (Deut 31:24), and was then taken to Mt. Nebo by God where he died (Deut 32: 48-50). The entire nation of Israel wept for 30 days (Deut 34:8) and on Nisan 1, 39 years, 11 months and 15 days after leaving Egypt they broke camp and prepared to cross the river Jordan. They crossed the river Jordan; Joshua circumcised every male; and then they pitched camp at Gilgal on Nisan 14; exactly 40 years after leaving Egypt (Josh 5:1-12). Manna ceased the next day (Nisan 15) and Joshua began the conquest of Canaan at Jericho (Josh 5:12-15, Josh 6). It was necessary to examine in detail the Exodus journey to establish how long it took to conquer the land. The duration of the conquest, which terminated in a division of the Promised Land, is determined as follows.

Joshua, Caleb and the other 10 men were sent to spy on the enemy one year one month and 23 days after leaving Egypt. They were gone for 40 days, and returned one year three months and 3 days after leaving Egypt. Most chronologist stumble on this next point; but after God passed judgment on the nation of Israel for their unbelief, Moses remained at Kadesh-barnea for eight months and 27 days. At this point, Moses broke camp and began 38 additional years wandering in the wilderness. When Caleb was sent to spy the land, he was 40 years old. Caleb said:

> *"I was 40 years old when Moses the servant of the Lord sent me from Kadesh Barnea to spy out the land."* Josh 14:7

We now move forward to the Division of Canaan by Joshua.

> *"So Joshua conquered* **all the land:** *the mountain country and the lowland and the wilderness slopes, and all their Kings.; he left none remaining, but* **utterly destroyed all**

that breathed, as the Lord of Israel had commanded. Then Joshua returned, and all Israel with him, to the camp at Gilgal (Josh 10:43). So Joshua took the whole land, according to all that the Lord had said to Moses; and Joshua gave it as an inheritance to Israel, according to their divisions by tribes. Then the land rested from war."
Josh 11:15-23

Note carefully that the tribes did not inherit the land until this point in time. In the Book of Numbers the Lord's instructions are given as to when the land was to be divided and inherited by the tribes of Israel.

"Speak to the Children of Israel, and say to them: When you have crossed the Jordan into the land of Canaan… you shall dispossess the inhabitants of the land and dwell in it…and* (then*) you shall divide the land by lot, as an inheritance among your families." Num 33:51-54.

God gave these instructions for possessing the land just before Joshua crossed the river Jordan. Many chronographers have assumed, based upon this passage, that this first year in the land was both a Jubilee year and a Sabbatical year. Nowhere is this implied in these instructions. The land was not to be inherited until (1) the land was conquered and (2) the land is divided by lots. When was the land divided? Chapter 13 in the book of Joshua is dedicated to a detailed account of how the land was to be divided. At that time: "***Joshua was old*** (between 90-100 years old), ***and stricken in years*** (Josh 24:29). The narrative continues as the Lord admonishes Joshua for not fully completing the conquest (Josh 13:2-5). But the Lord said, ***I will drive (all them) out before the Children of Israel; only divide it by lot to Israel as I have commanded you*** (Josh 13:6). Here is another great object lesson. Even though we are weak and sometimes falter, when God has a plan he will bring it to completion. When the Lord calls, he will see you through. So Joshua divided the land as recorded in Joshua 13:1-33 and Joshua 14:1-6. But here something unusual happens. Caleb approaches Joshua and says:

> *"Then the children of Judah came unto Joshua in Gilgal: and Caleb the son of Jephunneh the Kenezite said unto him, Thou knowest the thing that the LORD said unto Moses the man of God concerning me and thee in Kadesh-barnea. Forty years old was I when Moses the servant of the LORD sent me from Kadesh-barnea to spy out the land; and I brought him word again as it was in mine heart. Nevertheless my brethren that went up with me made the heart of the people melt: but I wholly followed the LORD my God. And Moses sware on that day, saying, Surely the land whereon thy feet have trodden shall be thine inheritance, and thy children's for ever, because thou hast wholly followed the LORD my God. And now, behold, the LORD hath kept me alive, as he said, these forty and five years, even since the LORD spake this word unto Moses, while the children of Israel wandered in the wilderness: and now, lo, I am this day fourscore and five years old."*
> Josh 14:6-10

Can you just imagine this confrontation between Caleb and Joshua, who was the most powerful and respected man in all of Israel. Caleb is saying to Joshua, *Moses promised me a piece of this land and I want it now!* Caleb now provides the following justification.

> *"And now, behold, the Lord has kept me alive, as he said, these forty and five years, even since the LORD spake this word unto Moses, while the children of Israel wandered in the wilderness: and now, lo, I am this day fourscore and five years old."*   Joshua 14:10-11

There you have it! On that very day, Caleb is 85 years old. It is now time to do a little math.

- ➢ Joshua was sent to spy on the land one year, three months, and 25 days after leaving Egypt.
- ➢ Joshua is 40 years old.
- ➢ It is 45 years until Caleb's confrontation with Joshua
- ➢ Caleb is exactly 85 years old when he confronts Joshua

- The time between when Joshua is sent to spy the land and when the river Jordan is crossed is 38 years, eight months and five days.
- The children of Israel remained at Kadesh–barnea for eight months and five days before leaving on a 38-year wilderness journey (Deut 2:14)

If Caleb has *just turned* 40 years old when he returned from spying the land, and was promised an inheritance by Moses, there were 45 years between this event and his confrontation with Joshua. This leaves six years, three months and 25 days that were spent conquering the land. If, in fact, Caleb was 40 years old when he was sent to spy the land, but *one day later* he would be 41 years old, the conquest of the land would have taken five years, three months and 25 days. We do not know exactly how old Caleb was when he was sent to spy the land, but following scriptural clues we can state with certainty that the average time to conquer the land can be determined as five years, nine months and 25 days. The following Table gives a snapshot of the years between the Exodus and when the land was divided.

5 yrs, 3 Mos, 25 days ≤ time to conquer the land ≤ 6 yrs, 3 Mos, 25 days

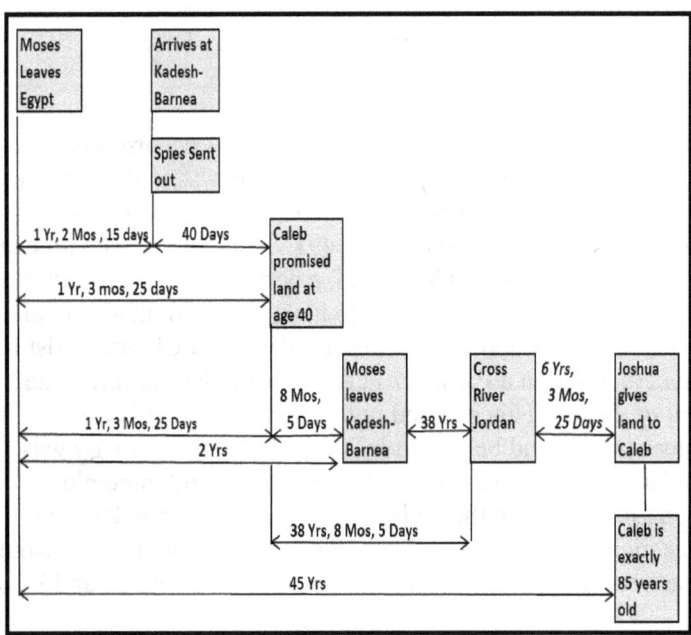

> The Jordan River was crossed in March/April of 1451 BC.
> Joshua took about 6 years to conquer the land.
> He then moved all of his armies and the Tabernacle to Shiloh;
> he then built his living quarters and erected the Tabernacle.
> In order to divide the land fairly, he sent men throughout
> the entire land to determine its suitability to support an
> agricultural economy and to raise sheep. He then divided the
> land to each of the tribes and sent them home to their
> alloted portions. The Children of Israel then "possesed the land
> and dwealt therein" (Josh 21:43, Josh 22:4).

- The Exodus lasted 40 years exactly
  (Nisan 15, 1491 - Nisan 14, 1451)

- Conquest of land took less than seven years
  (6 years, 3 months and 25 days maximum)

- The land was divided sometime in Summer of 1444 AD

- The tribes of Israel inherited land and returned home.
  The first Sabbatical year count started in Sept, 1444

- First Sabbatical year was seven years later
  (Tishri 1, 1438 – Tishri 1, 1437).

We have shown in Chapter 5 that the Exodus occurred in AY 2454 in the Julian year 1491. Note that this was in the Jewish civil calendar year of Tishri 1, 1492 – Tishri 1, 1491. The Exodus took place on Nisan 15, 1491. The Exodus account can be traced from Egypt to Mt. Sinai, a period of 47 days, and it can be verified that the Exodus had to have occurred on a Thursday. This is a shadow and type of the crucifixion of Christ. Christ had to be crucified on a Passover Feast; Wednesday; to fulfill the *Sign of Jonah*. This resulted in the first day of the Feast of Unleavened Bread being Nisan 15, a Thursday. The *sign* was that He would lie in the grave for three days and three nights, just as Jonah was in the belly of the whale for three days and three nights. After exactly three days and three nights, He would arise from the grave. Christ was crucified on Nisan 14 and He would arise three days and three nights later. In 30 AD, the Passover Lamb was slaughtered on the afternoon of Wednesday, Nisan 14, just as Christ was also crucified on that same day at the same time. Christ is *our* Passover Lamb, and the Firstfruit of all who will rise from the grave. The first day that Christ had departed from this earth was Nisan 15, which was the first day the Children of Israel departed from Egypt. Chapter 9 will provide a more detailed discussion of the crucifixion of Christ.

The Jordan River was crossed in 1451 BC (AY 2494) and conquest of the land was started in the same year. We have shown that conquering the land took a minimum of about 5 years, 3 months, 25 days; a maximum of about six years, 3 months and 25 days; the shortest and longest time periods yield an average of about five years and nine months. The land would be divided in AY 2501, most likely in the fall of 1445 BC. At that point in time, the tribes would all inherit the land as God promised, return home, and start to work the land. Of course, there was never an end to wars because of Israel's rebellion. But God's promise had been fulfilled under Joshua. It is now almost certain that the conquest of the land took less than God's number of completeness, seven years. It was not the number of completeness, because the Children of Israel never fully possessed all of the land that God gave to them. The first year of the first Sabbatical cycle occurred as soon as the tribes began to inherit and work the land. Sabbatical Years ran from Tishri 1 to Tishri 1, and coincided with both the Jewish traditional civil year and our AY years. The first Sabbatical year count started on Tishri 1 in the Hebrew Year 1444 BC. The first *week of years* ended on Elul 29, 1437 BC; so 1438 BC to 1437 BC was the *first Sabbatical year*. This is shown below.

AY	1	AY	2	AY	3	AY	4	AY	5	AY	6	AY	7
2464	1492 1491	2455	1491 1490	2456	1490 1489	2457	1489 1488	2458	1488 1487	2459	1487 1486	2460	1486 1485
2461	1485 1484	2462	1484 1483	2463	1483 1482	2464	1482 1481	2465	1481 1480	2466	1480 1479	2467	1479 1478
2468	1478 1477	2469	1477 1476	2470	1476 1475	2471	1475 1474	2472	1474 1473	2473	1473 1472	2474	1472 1471
2475	1471 1470	2476	1470 1469	2477	1469 1468	2478	1468 1467	2479	1467 1466	2480	1466 1465	2481	1465 1464
2482	1464 1463	2483	1463 1462	2484	1462 1461	2485	1461 1460	2486	1460 1459	2487	1459 1458	2488	1458 1457
2489	1457 1456	2490	1456 1455	2491	1455 1454	2492	1454 1453	2493	1453 1452	2494	1452 **1451**	2495	1451 1450
2496	1450 1449	2497	1449 1448	2498	1448 1447	2499	1447 1446	2500	1446 1445	2501	1445 1444	2502	*1444 1443*
2503	*1443 1442*	2504	*1442 1441*	2505	*1441 1440*	2506	*1440 1439*	2507	*1439 1438*	2508	1438 1437	2509	*1437 1436*

Having determined when the Sabbatical years started, it is now easy to determine when all other Sabbatical years occurred, or at least when they were supposed to occur. Since the first sabbatical cycle of seven years has been determined, it is also easy to determine when all the *Jubilee years* were to be observed. The following Table shows the Sabbatical years between 1438 BC-1437 BC and 222 AD-223 AD. The year

First Sabbatical Year..1438-1437							First Jubilee Year..1396-1395										
Sabbatical Years							Jubilee	Cycle	Sabbatical Years							Jubilee	Cycle
1	2	3	4	5	6	7			1	2	3	4	5	6	7		
1438	1431	1424	1417	1410	1403	1396	1395	1	1389	1382	1375	1368	1361	1354	1347	1346	2
1340	1333	1326	1319	1312	1305	1298	1297	3	1291	1284	1277	1270	1263	1256	1249	1248	4
1242	1235	1228	1221	1214	1207	1200	1199	5	1193	1186	1179	1172	1165	1158	1151	1150	6
1144	1137	1130	1123	1116	1109	1102	1101	7	1095	1088	1081	1074	1067	1060	1053	1052	8
1046	1039	1032	1025	1018	1011	1004	1003	9	997	990	983	976	969	962	955	954	10
948	941	934	927	920	913	906	905	11	899	892	885	878	871	864	857	856	12
850	843	836	829	822	815	808	807	13	801	794	787	780	773	766	759	758	14
752	745	738	731	724	717	710	709	15	703	696	689	682	675	668	661	660	16
654	647	640	633	626	619	612	611	17	605	598	591	584	577	570	563	562	18
556	549	542	535	528	521	514	513	19	507	500	493	486	479	472	465	464	20
458	451	444	437	430	423	416	415	21	409	402	395	388	381	374	367	366	22
360	353	346	339	332	325	318	317	23	311	304	297	290	283	276	269	268	24
262	255	248	241	234	227	220	219	25	213	206	199	192	185	178	171	170	26
164	157	150	143	136	129	122	121	27	115	108	101	94	87	80	73	72	28
66	59	52	45	38	31	24	23	29	17	10	3	5	12	19	26	27	30
33	40	47	54	61	68	75	76	31	82	89	96	103	110	117	124	125	32
131	138	145	152	159	166	173	174	33	180	187	194	201	208	215	222	223	34

shown is the first year. Note that the years of Jubilee are also shown in the *columns* labeled *Jubilee*, and that each Sabbath and Jubilee Year always spans two Julian calendar years. As previously stated, there is no indication that *any* Jubilee Years were ever observed. It is also true that the failure to observe 70 Sabbatical and Jubilee years resulted in God destroying Jerusalem, Solomon's temple, and deporting the entire nation of Israel to Babylon for 70 years. The critical question that begs to be asked is: *do historical, biblical and written records support these dates?* The answer is convincingly, YES. We offer only a few verifications as follows.

> ➢ Jack Finnegan, one of the most-respected chronographers of our time and author of the *Handbook of Biblical Chronology* has proposed that the beginning of the Bar Kokhba rebellion and the first year of Israel's

liberation was 131-132 AD. He proposes that this was a Sabbatical year. We agree.

➢ August Strobel and others have suggested that 458-457 BC was a Sabbatical year. Jewish tradition and rabbinical opinion also hold that this was a Sabbatical year (The Shemitah). Maimonides, a respected and reliable ancient historian wrote: *"With Ezra, the Shemitah (Sabbatical years) began to be counted, and after seven Sabbatical years they sanctified the 50th year; for even though the Jubilee year(s) were not observed, these years were nevertheless counted in order to satisfy the Shemitah"*. We concur with 458-457 BC being a Sabbatical year, and in Chapter 8 we will show that 458 BC-457 BC is in fact the year referred to by Maimonides.

➢ The historian Josephus has identified several Sabbatical years in his history of the ancient world. 136 BC-135 BC (Antiq. Book 13:8:1); 45 BC-44 BC (Antiq. Book 14:10:5) and 38 BC-37 BC (Antiq. Book15:1:2)

Antiq Book13:8:1
said 177th yr of Secluid Dynasty was a Sabbatical Yr...Yr1 was Oct 312-Oct 311 BC..Hence, Sabbatical Yr was 136 BC-135 BC

Antiq Book14:10:5
Sabbatical Yr was 45 BC-44 BC

Antiq Book 15:1:2
38 BC-37 BC

…… We concur with all of these Sabbatical years.

➢ In the first full year of the Ministry of Jesus Christ, He attended a temple service in his home town of Nazareth He opened the Book of Isaiah the Prophet and read the following passage:

"The Spirit of the Lord is upon me, because he hath annointed me to preach the gosple of the poor; he hath sent me to heal the brokenhearted, to preach deliverance to the captives, recovering of sight to the blind, to set at liberty them that are bruised. To preach the acceptable year of the Lord." Luke 4:18-19

This passage was taken from Isa. 61:1-2(a). He stopped reading in the middle of verse 61:2 because the first part of Verse 61:2 dealt with the message of *preaching the acceptable year of the Lord*, while the second part of 61:2 dealt with *the Day of Vengence of our Lord*. The Day of Vengence is the *second coming of Jesus Christ*, when he will fight the battle of Armageddon (Revelation Chapter 19). He chose not to announce that event at that time. The Jubilee year was to be observed as a Sabbatical year, but with the added condition to: *"proclaim a release through the land to all its inhabitants"* (Lev. 25:10). All land would be returned to its original owner, and all slaves would be set free. It is the proclaiming of release in the Jubilee that is tied to proclaiming release to the captives in the words of Isaiah and Jesus. Therefore, the Jubilee is equated with the *favorable year of the Lord*. Did Jesus read this passage on a Jubilee year at the tabernacle in Nazareth? In Chapter 8, we will show that Jesus Christ began his 3.5-year ministry at the river Jordan in September of 26 AD. From our list of Sabbatical years, 26-27 AD is a Sabbatical year and 27-28 AD is a year of Jubilee. The proclamation of Isa 61:1-2 is to be read on the Day of Atonement, Tishri 10. Since in 26 AD, after his baptism, Jesus went to be tempted by Satan for 40 days; he could not have been in Nazareth in 26 AD, so *it must have been in 27AD, and 27-28 AD was a year of Jubilee as we have previously shown.*

AD 26-27 is held to be A Sabbatical Year, and 27-28 a Year of Jubilee.

> In 70 AD the Roman general Titus attacked Jerusalem and on Av 9, August 4 (Julian date). Herod's temple as burned to the ground. Josephus was an eye witness. He and others record that 70 AD was a year immediately following a Sabbatical year. Since we use Jewish years from Tishri 1-Tishri 1, the year Tishri 1, 69-Tishri 1, 70

Ab 9, Aug 5 AD 70 was fall of temple to Titus...This was a year immediately following a Sabatical year.

AD was the year that Herod's temple was destroyed. The previous year is Tishri 1, 68-Tishri 1, 69 AD, and we show this as a Sabbatical year!

➢ Finnegan has researched several papyrus fragments recently found at a place called Murabba'at, and known collectively as the Mur 24 papyri. They are written in Hebrew, and reflect what is equivalent to a sequence of *bank notes* in today's economy. The Bar Kokhba revolt was a revolutionary revolt against the oppression of the Roman Empire. This was a critical battle in Hebrew history, for after the Roman Empire put down the rebellion, there was never another insurrection of the Hebrew nation until Israel became a country in the 20th century. Assembling data from these papyri Finnegan has constructed the following table.

Date	Description
131-132 AD	Year of the revolt... A Sabbatical Year
132-133 AD	"First year of the liberation of Israel"
133-134 AD	"Second year of the liberation of Israel"
134-135 AD	"Third year of the liberation of Israel"
135-136 AD	"Fourth year of the liberation of Israel"
136-137 AD	"Fifth year of the liberation of Israel"
137-138 AD	"Sixth year of the liberation of Israel"
138-139 AD	Seventh Year....A Sabbatical Year

We agree with Finnegan: both 131 AD-132 AD and 138 AD-139 AD are Sabbatical years.

➢ It has been suggested that by divine appointment, Alexander the Great conquered Jerusalem and began to reign in 331 BC. This appears to be true since 332-331 BC was a Sabbatical year.

> 332 BC-331 BC was believed to be a Sabbatical Year Alexander the Great started to rule Jerusalem in 331 BC

All of the Evidence presented suggests that our list of Sabbatical years is correct. This would also make our sequence of Jubilee years correct.

Scholarly Support

In 1856, Benedict Zukermann published a table of sabbatical years based upon both historical and biblical evidence. His table of Sabbatical years has been recognized as a standard since that time. One objector to the Zuckermann dates was Ben Zion Wacholder; who in 1973 published a study on the same subject. He concluded that the Zuckermann dates were all one year early. In 2007, Bob Pickel published a scholarly investigation of both the Zuckermann and Wacholder dates. Using ten reference points, he showed convincingly that the Zuckermann dates were correct. Both Pickel and Zuckermann conclude that 458 BC-457 BC was a Sabbatical year (the Wacholder date would be 457 BC-456 BC). Finally, Jack Finnegan... who is one of the most respected chronographers of the modern era... concluded in his widely acclaimed *Handbook of Biblical Chronology* that the Zuckermann dates were verifiable and correct. It should be easily recognized that the sequence of Sabbatical years produced by Zuckermann are identical to those determined in this book, but we derived the Sabbatical years based upon strictly biblical evidence. Our sequence of Jubilee years and when they occur appear to be unique to the offered chronology in this book.

The Consequence of Failure

The Lord had made incredible provisions for his people as part of the Sabbatical and Jubilee years. Sadly, it is not known how many of these years were actually observed by the corporate nation of Israel. The Bible only hints at several of these years being observed, and there is no undisputed biblical record of when they were observed. Leviticus 26:34-35 says the land will take her Sabbath even if the nation of Israel ignored God's word. Prophets and leaders regularly called Israel to account for neglecting the demands of the Sabbatical and Jubilee ordinances (Neh. 5:1-13, Jer. 34:8-18, Amos 2:6-7, 8:5-6, Eze.18: 7-9, Isaiah 58). Whether the Sabbatical and Jubilee years were ever adequately observed is a secondary question; we are called to accountability, regardless. This is a basic Christian principle today. God will not be mocked, nor will he sleep. We will all be held accountable for our deeds, good and bad, at the *Judgment Seat of Christ*. Thank God that we are living under the grace of our Lord Jesus Christ. We may suffer loss for bad works, but we will all be saved, all of those who accept Jesus Christ as their Savior. What is known for sure is that *God was keeping track* of his holy years, and that the house of Israel refused to observe a combination of 70 Sabbatical and Jubilee years between when they were started and the final fall of Judah in 586 BC.

> *"Yet ye have not hearkened unto me, saith the LORD; that ye might provoke me to anger with the works of your hands to your own hurt. Therefore, thus saith the LORD of hosts; Because ye have not heard my words, behold, I will send and take all the families of the north, saith the LORD, and Nebuchadnezzar the king of Babylon, my servant, and will bring them against this land, and against the inhabitants thereof, and against all these nations round about, and will utterly destroy them, and make them an astonishment, and an hissing, and perpetual desolations. Moreover I will take from them the voice of mirth, and the voice of gladness, the voice of the bridegroom, and the voice of the bride, the sound of the millstones, and the light of the candle. And this whole land shall be a desolation, and an astonishment; and these nations shall serve the king of Babylon seventy years. And it shall come to pass, when seventy years are accomplished, that I will punish the king of Babylon, and that nation, saith the LORD, for their iniquity, and the land of the Chaldeans, and will make it perpetual desolations."*
>   Jeremiah 25:9-12

> *"For thus saith the LORD, That after seventy years be accomplished at Babylon I will visit you, and perform my good word toward you, in causing you to return to this place".*   Jeremiah 29:10.

This is an *amazing* prophecy made by Jeremiah. He received his prophetic call in the thirteenth year of King Josiah's reign around

626 BC (Jer. 1:2-3). This prophetic word proclaimed that the nation of Israel would be conquered by a Babylonian king named Nebuchadnezzar, and that the entire Jewish nation would serve the nation of Babylon for a period of 70 years. After the 70 years had been fulfilled, Babylon would be punished (fall to the nation of Assyria), and the Jews would be allowed to return to their land. All of this came true starting in 605 BC with the deportation of a large number of Jews; including Daniel, Shadrach, Meshach and Abednego by King Nebuchadnezzar of the Babylonian Empire. There were actually three deportations:

- 605 BC - This is when Daniel and other members of Judah's elite were taken into captivity (Daniel 1:1 & 2 Kings 24:1-2),

- 597 BC - Jehoiakim was taken into captivity (2 Chron. 36:5-6). Three months and ten days later Jehoiachin, along with other members of the royal family, were taken into captivity (2 Chron 36:9-10 & 2 Kings 24:15-17),

- 586 BC - After a 3-year siege, Jerusalem was conquered and destroyed, and most of the remaining people were taken into captivity, along with articles from the temple. Only the poorest people remained. This is widely accepted as the final fall of Judah and the Nation of Israel (2 Kings 25).

The final fall of the Northern Kingdom, which was all that remained of the original 12 tribes ruled by David and Solomon, was in 586 BC. The following passage is taken from Finnegan who references Thiele.

"In King Zedekiah's ninth regnal year, in the 10th month, on the tenth day of the month, Nebuchadnezzar came against his faithless appointee, and with his whole army laid siege to Jerusalem (I King 25:1). The 9th year of Zedekiah was Tishri 1, 589 BC (Oct 10) to Elul 30, 588 BC (Sept, 28).The siege went on for slightly more than two and one-half years until at last famine was unbearably severe in the city. A

breach was made in the city (wall). The king and men of war fled by night, but was overtaken in the plains of Jericho. Zedekiah was captured and taken to Nebuchadnezzar at Riblah, where his sons were slain before his eyes and he was blinded and taken off to Babylon to prison until the day of his death (II King 25:3-7, Jer 52:5-11).The date of the final fall of Jerusalem was in the 11th year of Zedekiah, on the 9th day of the 1st month (II King 25:2-3, Jer 52:5-6). The 11th year of Zedekiah was from Tishri 1, 587 BC (Oct 18) to Elul 30, 586 BC (Oct 30). The 4th month is Tammuz (June/July), and in 586 BC the 9th day is equivalent to July 18, and is determined to be a Saturday. This, then, is the highly probable date of the final fall of Jerusalem... **July 18, 586 BC.**

This is chosen to be our ***anchor date*** from which working backward (or forward) all Julian years can be determined from the AY years previously derived from the Biblical records.

Conclusion

We will not go into any great detail concerning the 70 years of servitude under the Babylonian Empire. It is stated in the scriptures that the 70 year exile of the children of Israel were a direct result of not allowing the land to rest for some combination of Sabbatical and Jubilee years. The starting and ending dates of the exile are not important to our study,nor when the holy years were failed to be observed, but the fact that Daniel was carried into Babylon and remained there throughout the full 70 years is important. While Daniel was in Babylon, he was given a series of prophetic visions which would originate in the reign of King Nebuchadnezzar, and terminate at the Second Advent. The story of Daniel and his prophetic revelations are given in the Book of Daniel. It is impossible to understand the book of Revelation without understanding Daniel, and any serious student of prophecy should spend a great deal of time studying the Book of Daniel. As we will see, the sequence of Sabbatical and Jubilee years determined in this chapter will prove to be important components of when the 490 year prophecy of Daniel's 70th week started, and will help to verify the correct dates for the earthly ministry of Christ, His crucifixion, and His Second Advent. We will now turn our attention to the most important prophecy in the Old Testament: the *70 weeks of Daniel*.

Thoughts and Things......

Chapter 7

Daniel's 70 Week Prophecy

Daniel's Prophecy of 70 Weeks

Daniel is one of the most remarkable persons in the entire Bible. He was never rebuked or criticized for departing from the Word of the Lord. He was deported from Jerusalem by Nebuchadnezzar in the first group of exiles in 605 BC, along with Shadrach, Meshach and Abednego. God gave him the gift of interpreting visions and dreams, and he became the third most powerful man in Babylon. After the Persians conquered Babylon in 539 BC under Darius I, he continued to serve in the King's palace. In the first year of Darius, he *understood by books* that the Jewish Babylonian exile would last for 70 years. The *books* were the writings of the prophet Jeremiah. Jeremiah began prophesying at age 20 during the 13th year of the reign of King Josiah. At the age of 33 (23 years later), he predicted that the southern kingdom of Judah would come to an end, and that Israel would serve the king of Babylon for 70 years (Jer 25:11-12, II Chron 36:20-21)). As Daniel studied the books of Jeremiah, he realized that 70 years had almost passed since he was deported. Daniel began a remarkable prayer (Dan 9:1-18) in which he petitioned the Lord to end the captivity as prophesied, and **turn (His) fury from the Holy City of Jerusalem** (Dan 9:16). His prayer was answered by the Archangel Gabriel (Dan 9:20). The response from Gabriel should be carefully noted: ***Oh Daniel, I am now come forth to give thee skill and understanding.*** Gabriel clarified his mission: ***I am come to show you; for thou art greatly loved: therefore understand the matter and consider the vision.*** (Dan 9:23). Oh what a wonderful greeting! Daniel is said to be *greatly loved* by the Lord. The vision was then presented.

> *"Seventy weeks are determined upon thy people and upon thy holy city, to finish the transgression, and to make an end of sins, and to make reconciliation for iniquity, and to bring in everlasting righteousness, and to seal up the vision and*

> *prophecy, and to anoint the most Holy. Know therefore and understand, that from the going forth of the commandment to restore and to build Jerusalem unto the Messiah the Prince shall be seven weeks, and threescore and two weeks: the street shall be built again, and the wall, even in troublous times.*
>
> *And after threescore and two weeks shall Messiah be cut off, but not for himself: and the people of the prince that shall come shall destroy the city and the sanctuary; and the end thereof shall be with a flood, and unto the end of the war desolations are determined.*
>
> *And he shall confirm the covenant with many for one week: and in the midst of the week he shall cause the sacrifice and the oblation to cease, and for the overspreading of abominations he shall make it desolate, even until the consummation, and that determined shall be poured upon the desolate."* Dan 9:24-27

This prophecy is considered to be one of the most important in the entire Holy Bible. It spans a period of time from when it was issued to the second coming of Jesus Christ. It also predicts when the Messiah will be crucified. Note that this prophecy begins with the ***going forth of the commandment to restore and to build (rebuild) Jerusalem.*** We will examine these verses in some detail. They form the cornerstone for all of prophecy. The revelation is directed to (1) *thy people*, the nation of Israel, and (2) *thy holy city*, Jerusalem. There are six things to be accomplished:

1. Finish the transgression,
2. Make an end to sins,
3. Make reconciliation for iniquity,
4. Bring in everlasting righteousness,
5. Seal up the vision and prophecy,
6. Anoint the most Holy.

These six things to be accomplished seem to be arranged in two groups of three. The first three are dealing with the *issue of sin*, and the second three with a *state of righteousness*. Here we must be careful to rightly divide and discern the word of God. Many students of prophecy firmly state that Jesus Christ accomplished all of these things when He went to the cross. Others teach that the first three were accomplished at the cross (first advent of Christ), and the second three will be accomplished at the end of the age (Second Advent of Christ). This is certainly true, and many scriptural references can be found to support this position. However, we must not ignore the simple and straightforward words of the angel: ***Seventy weeks are determined upon thy people and upon thy holy city***. This prophecy concerns *thy people* (plural) and *thy holy city*. Daniel's people are the people of Israel, Jews…. and the city is Jerusalem. The ***mystery*** of this is that Christ was an Israelite from the tribe of Judah…He was both the Son of God and a Hebrew by birth. As we will see, His work on the cross put an end to transgression, made a permanent atonement for sins and made reconciliation for iniquity. His work when He returns at the end of this age will bring in everlasting righteousness, seal up vision and prophecy and anoint the most holy. Jesus Christ is the only person born of woman who could fully accomplish these things. The important thing to understand is that through Christ ***all*** can share in these accomplishments by believing upon His holy name and accepting Him as their savior. The beneficiaries are both Jews and Gentiles. However, this prophecy concerns the Jewish people and how long it will take them to corporately fulfill this prophecy. The concept of anyone other than the Jewish people being addressed was completely unknown to Daniel. Hence, to assert that all of these things will be accomplished by Jesus Christ is correct… but the prophecy is concerned also with when the Jewish people will fulfill these six things. Individually, there have been many Jews who have accepted Christ as their Savior and Messiah. However, the nation of Israel as a whole will only accomplish these things in the last days of the tribulation period. Paul affirmed this in his letter to the Romans.

> ***"For I would not, brethren, that ye should be ignorant of this mystery, lest ye should be wise in your own conceits; that blindness in part is happened to Israel, until the fulness of the Gentiles be come in. And so all Israel shall be saved:***

> *as it is written, There shall come out of Sion the Deliverer, and shall turn away ungodliness from Jacob: For this is my covenant unto them, when I shall take away their sins."*
> Romans 11:25-27

Finally, we need to address the meaning of *Jerusalem* fulfilling these six things. It would be foolish to state that a city of wood and stones could fulfill this prophecy. However, notice what Christ said:

> *"O Jerusalem, Jerusalem, thou that killest the prophets, and stonest them which are sent unto thee, how often would I have gathered thy children together, even as a hen gathereth her chickens under her wings, and ye would not!"* Mat 23:37

Here Christ is obviously relating the sins of the people of Jerusalem with the city itself. The *city* of Jerusalem never killed anyone. The broader meaning seems to be that there will be Jews from every nation and every city worldwide that will come to Christ up until His second advent, but before the tribulation period ends and the Battle of Armageddon is fought, the Jews in Jerusalem will finally turn to Christ as their Messiah. It is also true that the city of Jerusalem will be completely destroyed before Christ will return there to rule and reign during the millennial kingdom. Hence, the City of Jerusalem will in a real sense be *born again*. Equating a selected group of people (Israel) with a city (Jerusalem) is not unique to this prophecy. In Rev 21:9-10 an angel tells John that he will now see the bride, the Lambs wife, which is a city called the ***New Jerusalem***. Keeping these truths in mind, we will now briefly discuss each of these six things which have been determined upon *thy people* and *thy city*.

Finish the Transgression

The word translated *transgression* has a root meaning *to rebel*. In this context, it refers to the Jews specific sin of rebellion against God. This rebellion was the root cause of Israel's other sins. Gabriel was relating to Daniel that Israel would not stop its rebellion against God and His holy laws until these 490 years would run their course. Scriptures reveal that Israel will not repent, turn to God and be saved until the second coming of Christ at the end of the final tribulation period. At that time, *all of Israel will be saved.* This is a corporate decree, and not an individual decree (Zech 12:10-13:1; Rom 11:25-27). It is true that each individual must come to Christ on a personal basis, but just as the body of Christ is one unit, the believing Children of Israel will constitute one unit of individual believers (Lev. 26:40-42; Jer. 3:11-18, Hos. 5:15). *At that time,* Israel's national transgression, the rejection of her Messiah, will be brought to an end.

> *"And it shall come to pass in that day, that I will seek to destroy all the nations that come against Jerusalem. And I will pour upon the house of David, and upon the inhabitants of Jerusalem, the spirit of grace and of supplications: and they shall look upon me whom they have pierced, and they shall mourn for him, as one mourneth for his only son, and shall be in bitterness for him, as one that is in bitterness for his firstborn." ….." In that day there shall be a fountain opened to the house of David and to the inhabitants of Jerusalem for sin and for uncleanness"*   Zach 2:9-10, 13:1

Make an End to Sins
The Greek word used here for *sins* is *chatta'ath*. It refers to the permanent end of the acts of sin. It cannot refer to the end of the problem of original sin as some maintain, or of how Christ dealt with sin on the cross. The sacrificial death of Christ on the cross of Calvary did not put an end to sins at all; it enabled our sins to be permanently forgiven by grace. Nothing is conveyed in the words of this phrase which convey the end of original sin. At the cross, Christ dealt with the sin issue in the context that they are to be *remembered* no more and are *forgiven* by grace. The phrase *put an end to sins* means exactly what it says, to put an end of sin forever. The national sin of Israel will come to an end when they accept Christ as their Messiah and the only Son of God at His second coming.

Make Reconciliation for Iniquity

The Hebrew word *kapher* is translated *reconciliation in* Daniel 9:24, but in the Authorized King James Bible, it is sometimes translated as *atonement*. Atonement in the Old Testament always carries the force of a *covering*. The Levitical sacrificial system could never permanently reconcile Israel to God, only the work of Jesus Christ at the cross could do that. *Kapher* carries the meaning of *cleanse, forgive, and reconcile*. This is the work of Jesus on the cross of Calvary. The apostle Paul revealed that Jesus Christ fully reconciled all sinners to salvation.

> *"God was in Christ, reconciling the world to Himself, not imputing their transgressions unto them; and hath committed unto us the word of reconciliation"* (II Cor. 5:19). *"For when we were enemies, we were reconciled to God by the death of his Son"* (Rom 5:10).

Bring in Everlasting Righteousness

It is written that: ***There is none righteous, no, not one*** (Rom 3:10). The only righteous person that ever existed on earth is Jesus Christ our Lord. Any righteousness attributed to man is imputed to him by Christ. The argument concerning the phrase *bring in everlasting righteousness* is usually that righteousness was ushered in forever when Christ died on the cross. There is no denying that through his sacrificial death that we can now claim righteousness by accepting Christ as our savior, but we are not righteous until victory over this life is claimed at death, and we stand *without spot or wrinkle*, blameless before the throne of God. Sin and unrighteousness will continue to exist until we are fully transformed into the righteousness of Christ. The apostle John saw this.

> *"And I heard as it were the voice of a great multitude, and as the voice of many waters, and as the voice of mighty thundering, saying, Aleluuia: for the Lord God omnipotent reigneth. Let us be glad and rejoice, and give honor to Him: for the marriage of the Lamb is come, and his wife hath made herself ready. And to her it was granted that she*

should be arrayed in fine linen, clean and white: for the fine linen is the righteousness of saints." Rev 19:6-8.

For those alive and dead at the rapture of the saints, everlasting righteousness will be brought in at the **Marriage of the Lamb** in heaven.

*"And to her (*the Bride of Christ) *was granted that she should be arrayed in fine linen, clean and white: for the fine linen is the righteousness of saints."* Rev 19:8

The Bride of Christ will be in the Wedding Chamber of Christ between Tishri 1 and Tishri 10 (Rev 19:9). On the Day of Atonement (Feast of Yom Kippur, Tishri 10) the second advent of Christ will take place as He returns to fight Satan, the antichrist, the false prophet and all of their followers at the battle of Armageddon. After the Battle of Armageddon, the Marriage Supper of the Lamb will take place on the earth. We will devote two entire Chapters (25 & 25) to this glorious event.

Seal up Vision and Prophecy

The subject of biblical prophecy is a lifelong journey. Prophecy probably takes up more verses in the Holy Scriptures than any other subject. The book of Revelation is future prophecy between Rev. Chapter 6 and Chapter 23. Contrary to what some may teach, prophecy and prophets exist in the church today; and will continue to exist until the end of the church age.

"And God hath set some in the church, first apostles, secondarily prophets, thirdly teachers, after that miracles, then gifts of healings, helps, governments, diversities of tongues." I Corinthians 12:26

When one reads the directive to *seal up the vision and prophecy, the vision* is the collective content of the entire prophecy given to Daniel. If one reads this verse without bias or preconceived notions, then the issue of a *gap* between the death of Christ and his second coming should be uncontested. The only question to be answered is how long is this *gap* or *period of time*? Christ himself answered this question when he gave the Olivet Discourse shortly before his crucifixion: ***But of that day and hour knoweth no man, no, not the angels of heaven, but my Father only*** (Mat 24:36). At the end of the age of grace when Christ appears, vision and prophecy will be sealed up forever. No one knows when this will occur. Prophecy will not be sealed up until there is no need for prophecy…and this will only happen when Christ returns at His second advent.

Anoint the Most Holy

This is a difficult passage. The word *anoint* is from the Hebrew word *mashiyach*, which means to *set aside or consecrate for a holy purpose.* There have been two primary interpretations. The first interpretation is that the *most holy* refers to our *Lord Jesus Christ*. This interpretation has little merit, since Jesus Christ needs no anointing. He was and is the only Son of God, and has already been anointed by the Father.

> ***"How God anointed Jesus of Nazareth with the holy ghost and with power: who went about doing good, and healing all that were oppressed of the devil; for God was with Him."***
> Acts 10:38

The second interpretation is that the *Most Holy* refers to the *millennial temple*. In both the Old and New Testament, the *Most Holy* would be clearly understood to be the *Holy of Holies,* where God came to visit with the High Priest once a year on the Feast of Yom Kippur. Man was separated from God (symbolically) by a curtain that separated the Holy Place from the Holy of Holies. This curtain was rent from top to bottom when Christ cried out ***it is finished*** as he died on the cross of Calvary. The temple and the Holy of Holies were completely destroyed in 70 AD by Titus and his Roman army. However, it will be rebuilt. The 3rd temple is clearly shown in Rev 11:1 with Jewish people worshipping there prior to the rise of the antichrist. Over 2000 years ago Zachariah predicted that all the nations would ***worship*** Jesus Christ during the 1000 year millennial kingdom.

> *"And it shall come to pass, that everyone that is left of all of the nations which came against Jerusalem (at the battle of Armageddon) shall even go up from year to year to worship the King, the Lord of hosts, and to keep the Feast of Tabernacles."* Zechariah 14:16.

The phrase Most Holy is taken from the Hebrew words *qodesh qoddashem*, which means *the Holy of Holies*. It is therefore concluded that this part of the prophecy refers to the cleansing, anointing and dedication of the cleansed temple to be used for worship in the millennial kingdom.

The Commandment to Restore and Rebuild Jerusalem

It is crucial that we determine exactly when this commandment went forth. There are two basic things to consider. The *first* is that we are able to look back in time and determine the most likely time and place that this commandment occurred. *Second*, the decree which will initiate the 70 week prophecy of Daniel must lead to the beginning of the ministry of Christ when he came to the River Jordan to be baptized by John at the end of 483 years. There are four decrees to consider.

The Decree of Cyrus

In 536 BC, the Persian King Darius conquered Babylon and installed Cyrus (a Mede) to act as king. This happened after the 70 weeks of exile had been fulfilled as recorded by Jeremiah (Jeremiah 29:10). In Ezra 1:1 we read: *Now in the first year of Cyrus king of Persia, that the word of the Lord by the mouth of Jeremiah might be fulfilled, the Lord stirred up the spirit of Cyrus, king of Persia, that he made a royal proclamation*. This proclamation authorized the return of Israel to Jerusalem to *build (rebuild) the house (temple) of the Lord*. From 536 BC, a span of 483 years *unto the Messiah the Prince* (Jesus Christ), would take us to 53 BC. This is way too early, so we must look elsewhere.

The Decree of Darius

The rebuilding of the temple authorized by Cyrus did not go well. The *people of the land* (Ezra 4:1-5) resisted the project, and it is recorded in Ezra 4:24 that the work *ceased until the second year of the reign of Darius, king of Persia.* Darius succeeded Cyrus in 518 BC. The work resumed in 520 BC under Haggai and Zechariah. The governor of the province surrounding Jerusalem came to the temple site and inquired: *Who hath commanded you to build this house?* (Ezra 5:3). They replied that King Cyrus had authorized the project. The governor then sent a letter to the king asking him to produce such a decree, if indeed one existed. A search was made and the original decree was found. Darius then reinforced this decree with one of his own. *Let the governor of the Jews and the elders of the Jews build this house of God in His place.* So Darius simply reissued the decree of Cyrus authorizing that the Temple of God be rebuilt. Based upon Ezra 4:24 and biblical/archeological research, this event likely occurred in 520 BC. Again moving forward 483 years, we find an ending date of 37 BC. This was about when King Herod began to reign in Jerusalem, and is again much too early. We must search further.

The First Decree of Artaxerxes

In Ezra 7:12-26, we read that Ezra, the scribe, who was a descendent of Aaron, approached King Artaxerxes I and petitioned the king to allow him and a band of Israelites to return to Jerusalem. We will show in Chapter 8 that this occurred in the spring of 458 BC in the seventh year of Artaxerxes reign. Ezra wanted to *set magistrates and judges* in place, *teach the laws of God*, and *let judgment be executed speedily*, upon all who would not obey the laws of God (Ezra 7:25-26). The petition was granted, and Ezra left *on the first day of the first month of Artaxerxes Seventh year*, and arrived in Jerusalem *on the first day of the Fifth month*. We will show later that the departure from the city of Babylon was on Nisan 1 in 458 BC (Ezra 7:9). After a short delay to find some Levites to serve as priests, he arrived in Jerusalem after a journey of just less than five months (Ezra 7:8). Ezra assembled all of the people and read the proclamation and the law. The *decree went forth* at this time to all the people, and was put into effect. Synchronizing with Sabbatical years, the 70 weeks of Daniel would have started on a most appropriate day... *Tishri 1, 458 BC;* which was the Feast of Rosh Hashanah (Feast of Trumpets). Projecting forward in time

483 years from this date, we arrive at 26 AD. Please note that to arrive at 26 AD; we must add a total of 484 years because when one crosses from BC to AD, there is no year zero. The year 26 AD is considered by many to be when Jesus Christ came to the river Jordan and started his ministry of 3.5 years. This is a strong candidate, but we will consider the final possible decree.

The Second Decree of Artaxerxes

In the 20th year of King Artaxerxes (Neh. 1:1) word came to Nehemiah that things were not going so well in Jerusalem: *The remnant that are left of the captivity there in the province are in great affliction and reproach. The wall of Jerusalem also is broken down, and the gates thereof are burned with fire* (Neh. 1:3). Nehemiah wept, mourned, fasted and petitioned God to turn the heart of Artaxerxes to let him go to Jerusalem and rebuild the city. (Neh. 1:4-11; 2:1-5). God moved Artaxerxes' heart, and he gave Nehemiah permission to return. He also sent a letter to *Asaph* informing him to supply timber to rebuild the gates, the walls and the temple (Neh. 2:6-8). This commission was issued to Nehemiah in the month of Nisan (Neh. 2:1). If the first year of Artaxerxes reign (which we will show later) was Sept, 465 BC-Sept, 464 BC, then the 20th year of Artaxerxes was Sept, 446 BC-Sept, 445 BC. Sir Isaac Newton assumed that the decree was issued on Nisan 1, 445 BC. After a five month trip to Jerusalem and a judiciary established, Daniels 70th week would start on Tishri 1, 445 BC. If we subtract 484 years from this date we would arrive at September of 39 AD. The crucifixion of Christ would be on Nisan 14 in 43 AD. This is much too late for the death of Christ. At this point, Newton made a rectifying assumption. Using the flood account of Gen 6-8, he determined based upon Gen 7:11, 7:24 and 8:4 that a *prophetic month* was only 30 days long, and a *prophetic year* was 360 days long. He supported this theory by referring to the Book of Revelation, which equates 1260 days to 42 months (Rev 11:2-3). Using a year as 360 days, he multiplied 360 days times 483 years. He then converted this number of prophetic days into a *Gregorian* calendar year, even though the Gregorian calendar had not even been implemented in Daniel's time. The subsequent date for the crucifixion of Christ worked out to be on a Thursday, Nisan 14, in 32 AD. The 7 years remaining in Daniel's 490-year prophecy were then given to the tribulation period of John's Revelation. However, the Roman Catholic Church has decreed for many centuries that Christ was crucified on a Friday in 33 AD. To accommodate this date, Hoehner followed the same procedure but used 445 BC-444 BC as the 20th year of Artaxerxes, Hoehner arrived at Friday, April 3, 33 AD as the crucifixion date by starting one year later than Newton; enforcing some clever assumptions; and using the Julian calendar.

We can only applaud Sir Isaac Newton and Harold Hoehner for using such a clever approach to arrive at either 32 AD (Newton) or 33 AD (Hoehner) as a crucifixion year. Their assumptions have been critically assailed and claimed in error by Pickle, Ice and Jones to name a few. The assumption of a 360-day *prophetic year* is simply unwarranted. **First**, the flood account in Genesis does state that over a period of 150 days, five months elapsed, but this does not guarantee that *each month* was 30 days in duration. In fact, if anyone wants to carefully study the narrative in Gen 7 & 8 they will find that from when Noah entered the ark until he left the ark was 365 days, and it could have been exactly one solar year of 365.2422 days. **Second**, the book of Revelation would not be written for about another 620 years, so Daniel would have no access to that text. **Third**, Daniel was nearing the end of the 70-year period of Babylonian exile when he received the prophecy. He was not experiencing 360-day prophetic years during his exile, but full solar years. He was also well aware that the 10 periods of seven years exile was almost over when he petitioned God in prayer and fasting. There would be no confusion whatsoever in associating full solar years with the 70 sevens in the prophecy. **Fourth**, if Daniel *understood* that the 490-year prophecy was *not* based upon the Babylonian calendar year, which was close to a solar year, there was certainly no indication of that in his response to Gabriel and there is no proof whatsoever that a 360-day year ever existed after the flood. In fact, to keep the Passover every year in the correct month, a 360 day prophetic year could not be in use. Finally, there are those today that do have access to the book of Revelation, and there is no doubt that the last 3.5 years of the tribulation period is 1260 days, and this is equated to 42 months (Rev 11:2-3). Ah ha! They say, Daniel was told this by Gabriel and he knew it all along. After all, Gabriel told Daniel that he would *understand*. This is *high conjecture* at best. We will show in the next section that these 1260 days involving 42 months are readily seen to refer to a 365.2425 solar year, and not a 360 day lunar year.

The conclusion of the matter is that the only decree which makes logical sense, and fits all the requirements of a normal 490-solar year prophecy, is the one issued by Artaxerxes in 458 BC. We will accept this date and show that it also makes sense when the length of the tribulation period is established as 3.5 years, and not seven years. We will now show that 458 BC is indeed the correct year.

The Seventh year of Artaxerxes

We have determined that the commandment to restore and to rebuild Jerusalem (Dan 9:25), which initiated the 70-week prophecy of Daniel is most likely the decree from Artaxerxes I to the scribe Ezra. This decree *went forth* to the people of Israel when Ezra arrived in Jerusalem. As previously stated, Ezra left Babylon **on the first day of the first month** (Ezra 7:9). After gathering the people together and assembling a group of Levites to conduct temple services, he **departed from the River of A-Haya on the 12th day of the first month** (Ezra 8:31). He arrived in Jerusalem on the **first day of the 5th month.** Hence, the actual journey took almost four months. Ezra left in the first month and arrived in the fifth month of Artaxerxes seventh year. The key question is: **when was Artaxerxes seventh year?** And **when was the first month**? From the context of Ezra 7, the *first month* is most likely the first month of the 7th year of Artaxerxes reign. To determine the seventh regnal year of Artaxerxes, we need to now discuss two fundamental issues: since Artaxerxes was a Persian king. (1) In what month of the year did Persian kings begin to count their regnal years? (2) How did Persian kings transition from the death of one king to the next?

The Beginning of Regnal Years

Each ancient kingdom had their own calendar system which was used to mark the beginning of a king's reign. Each ancient kingdom employed a slightly different calendar, but most had learned that the length of a solar year was determined by the sun; which we now know is exactly 365.2422 days. A year was composed of 12 months (13 in a Leap Year), and a week of seven, 24-hour days. The number of days in each month, which was from one *new moon* to the next *new moon* varied from kingdom to kingdom, as did the actual number of months in each year. The length of a month in ancient times was usually set at either 29 or 30 days. This is because the actual length of a lunar month is determined by the rotation of the moon, and is 29.53059 days. Calendars are designed to mark time by the passage of months, with the number and initiation of each month designed so that a series of 12 or 13 months would coincide with the solar year. However, there is no combination of 30 and 29 day months that can equate to a solar year on a yearly basis. There were two common solutions to the problem: the first was to add days at the end of each year; the second is to periodically add an extra (13th) month to the normal 12-month year. For example, the Egyptians used a simple 12-month calendar consisting of 12 months of 30 days per year. This would total to 360 days per year. They then added 5 days at the end of the 12th month, so that their year was 365 days. This was close to the actual solar year, but fell short about 0.2422 days per year. Hence, the calendar *drifted backward* about one day every four years. After about 1460 years, the Egyptian year would move back in sync with a true solar year. For example, if today was Christmas using this calendar, in about 730 years Christmas would be in July! The calendar used by the Jews was also a *lunar-Solar* calendar. It consisted of 12 alternating 29 and 30 day months. Simple math shows that a Hebrew year was only 354 days, which is about 11.25 days short of a solar year. About every three years, the calendar would drift back approximately 33.75 days. To keep the lunar-based 12-month year in sync with the solar year, it was discovered that by adding seven extra months over a 19-year period of time, 19 lunar calendar years of 12 (13) months would almost exactly equal the solar calendar over the same period of time. This 19-year period of time with seven inter-calculated months is called a *Metonic cycle*. With some minor adjustments to prevent back-to-back Sabbaths and other anomalies, the same calendar is in use today. The Babylonians seem to be the first to discover the *Metonic cycle* and put it into formal use. However, it must be stressed that since the seven feasts of Israel were ordained by God, and were to be observed every year following agricultural cycles, the Hebrews after the exodus also had to keep their 12-month lunar calendar in sync with the solar year. Whether this was done by a formal method such as the one just described, or done by observation of crop maturity, is unknown. However, after the Babylonian exile, the Hebrews almost surely adopted and used a Metonic cycle. Each civilization had its own names for each month of the year, but after the 70-year Babylonian exile, the Hebrews adopted the Babylonian calendar names with only slight variations. The calendar we use today is called the *Gregorian calendar*. It was derived from the *Julian calendar*. The Gregorian calendar is very accurate, as is the modern Jewish calendar. The modern Jewish calendar was first implemented by the Patriarch Hillel II in 358 AD. Table 7.1 is a summary of the four ancient calendars.

	Julian	*Gregorian*	*Hebrew*	*(Civil)*	*Babylonian*	
Month	Name	Name	Name	Months	Name	Months
1	Januarius	Jan	Tishri	Sept/Oct	Nisanu	Mar/Apr
2	Februarius	Feb	Heshvan	Oct/Nov	Aiaru	Apr/May
3	Martius	Mar	Chislev	Non/Dec	Simanu	May/Jun
4	Aprilus	April	Tebeth	Dec/Jan	Duzu	Jun/July
5	Maius	May	Shevat	Jan/Feb	Abu	July/Aug
6	Junius	June	Adar	Feb/Mar	Ululu	Aug/Sept
7	Julius	July	Nisan	Mar/Apr	Tashritu	Sept/Oct
8	Augustus	Aug	Iyyar	Apr/May	Arahsamnu	Oct/Nov
9	Septembris	Sept	Sivan	May/Jun	Kislimu	Non/Dec
10	Octobris	Oct	Tammuz	Jun/July	Tebetu	Dec/Jan
11	Novembris	Nov	Ab/Av	July/Aug	Shabatu	Jan/Feb
12	Decembris	Dec	Elul	Aug/Sept	Addaru	Feb/Mar

Table 7.1
Ancient Calendar Years

After Medo-Persia overthrew the Babylonian empire in 539 BC, the Persian Empire also adopted the Babylonian calendar for their own use. The Babylonians, Israel, Egyptians and Persians all used a common method for determining when a king came to reign and this was to use the first day of the first month in the civil year. The Babylonians and the Persians used Nisan 1, the Egyptians used Thoth 1, and the Hebrew Southern Kingdom of Judah used Tishri 1 until the Babylonian destruction and exile. This was proved and published by Edwin Thiel, and is now widely accepted.

The Beginning of Regnal Years: First Year of Reign

There were two methods that were commonly employed to determine how a new king was credited with his first year of reign. The first method was called the *Accession Year* or *Postdating* system. The second method was called the *Non-Accession Year* or *Antedating* system. Under an accession-year system, when a king dies, the months following his death are credited to that king no matter when the new king comes to the throne. The first regnal year of the new king starts at the next regnal New Year. Under the non-accession system, the old king is given credit for his full last year, and the new king is also given credit for that partial year as his first year of reign. Clearly, using antedating the last year of a King's reign is counted twice.

It must be noted that when historical records are found which list the lengths of successive kings; in the accession year system if the regnal years of multiple sequential kings are totaled from a common start date, the sum of the regnal years will coincide with calendar years. However, if a non-accession system is used, one year must be subtracted from the reign of *each king* to have the sum of regnal years match calendar years

Consider the following diagram, using the Hebrew and Persian methods of determining regnal years.

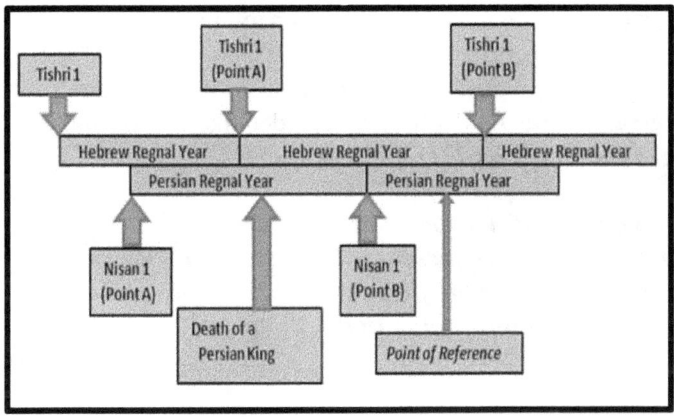

Based upon a wide range of biblical scholarly investigations, almost everyone agrees that *Persian kings used an accession year system and that Persian kings began their regnal years on Nisan 1*. It is also generally agreed that contemporary with Artaxerxes reign; *Hebrew Kings in the Kingdom of Judah also used an accession year system, but used a Tishri 1 regnal start date*. The first day of the first month in a civil calendar year is Nisan 1 on the Persian calendar and Tishri 1 on the Hebrew calendar.

Acknowledging that both the Hebrew and Persians used an accession-year system, suppose a Persian king died at the point shown. At the *point of reference*, Persian records would show that the new king was in his 1st year of reign starting at Nisan 1 (Point B), but Hebrew records would not have him reigning in his 1st year until Tishri 1 (Point B). Note that in any given year, even if both use accession systems, the Hebrew and Persian references to regnal years will *always* be off by one year between Nisan 1 (Point B) and Tishri 1 (Point B). The records will coincide the other 9 months of the year. This may all seem rather academic and confusing, but the important point to be observed is that Hebrew records at certain points in the year would show the elapsed years of reign of a Babylonian king to be one year less than the Persian records. The issue is not what month the civil year started, but which system of accounting was being used by Ezra in the Book of Ezra?

Determining the Seventh Year of Artaxerxes Reign

The Book of Ezra records that the decree which launched Daniel's 490-year prophecy occurred in the 7th year of the reign of Artaxerxes I. Ezra 7:1-10 further recorded that it was on *the first day of the first month.*

> *"...in the reign of Artaxerxes, King of Persia, the King granted him all his requests... This Ezra went up from Babylon.... for upon the first day of the first month began he to go up from Babylon... In the 7th year of Artaxerxes the King."* Ezra 7:1-10

From Ezra 7, we only know that Ezra left Babylon in the seventh year of Artaxerxes I reign, and the Biblical record is silent in recording any *calendar year* or the name of the *first month* for this event, or when the seventh year of Artaxerxes reign actually began. It is not clear from Ezra 7 that the reference of month 1 is to the 1st month of Artaxerxes regnal year, or Nisan 1 or Tishri 1. Based upon a wide range of Biblical scholarly investigations, almost everyone agrees that *Persian kings used an accession year system and that Persian kings began their regnal years on Nisan 1*. It is also generally agreed that contemporary with Artaxerxes reign; *Hebrew Kings also used an accession-year system, but used a Tishri 1 regnal start date.* So what was the first month in Ezra's Biblical records? Ezra and Nehemiah were Hebrew contemporaries, and at least according to some sources, the Biblical records of both Ezra and Nehemiah were originally one document. Whether that is true or not, the book of Nehemiah as it now stands clearly indicates that Nehemiah cross referenced Persian regnal years to a Hebrew Tishri 1-Tishri 1 regnal year system, and *NOT* the Nisan-Nisan Persian system (compare Neh. 1:1 to Neh. 2:1). If Nehemiah and Ezra were originally one document, the problem would be solved. However, no reliable data exists to prove or disprove this theory. Pragmatically, Ezra and Nehemiah were both serving in the King's court, and both were likely good friends; but this only suggests that both would use the same system to reference the reign of each king. We have already shown that depending upon which system is being used by Ezra; the seventh year of Artaxerxes as referenced by Persian records could be off by one year if measured by Jewish records. Hence, imminent scholars are divided upon exactly when Ezra left Babylon in the seventh year of Artaxerxes reign. Some defend a 458 BC date and some dogmatically defend a 457 BC date. So which is to be believed?

The most acceptable solution is to use historical and archeological records to determine what month Ezra left in the seventh year of Artaxerxes. We are quite certain that a Persian King named Xerxes preceded Artaxerxes. It is also known that the Persian King Xerxes was assassinated in the summer of 465 BC. Scribes recorded Xerxes assassination date on a clay tablet known as the *Babylonian Astronomical Text*. Scholars have translated the text and determined that the murder of Xerxes occurred sometime between August 4-August 18, 465 BC. Two other dates are recorded in ancient literature, which indicate either late July or early August of 465 BC. By all historical accounts known to exist, Xerxes was murdered before Tishri 1, 465 BC of the year in question. Xerxes was assassinated by a courtier of his court called Artabanus who wanted to assume the kingship. He also tried to assassinate Artaxerxes, but his plan was discovered and Artabanus was executed. No record has ever been found that credits Artabanus as a reigning king of Persia, but a second-century historian called Mantheo wrote that a power struggle resulted between Artabanus and Artaxerxes. However, Mantheo wrote his comments more than 500 years after the fact. Turning to archeological records, in the 20th century evidence surfaced from a community of Jews living in Egypt on the upper Nile River. They were called the *Elephantine Community*, and records of financial and social transactions were found which provides important data for this investigation. Out of a number of documents found and restored, two are of great importance: They are known as ***AP 6*** and ***AP 8***.

The Jewish document, called *AP 6* from the Elephantine community of Jews clouds the issue. Scholars all agree that *AP 6* was written on Jan 2/3, 464 BC. Unfortunately, the document is severely damaged and a key phrase is partially missing. Paleographic science has been used to reconstruct the missing

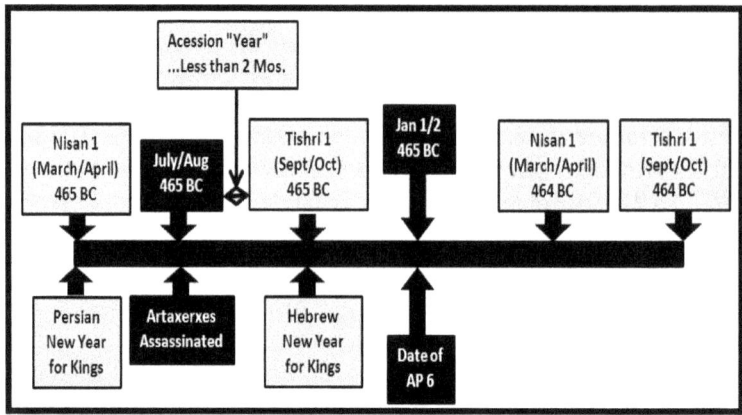

word(s), and it was found that it could be reconstructed in two ways. The first would indicate that Jan 2/3 is in the *first year* of Artaxerxes reign; the second is that it can mean in the *acession year* of Artaxerxes. We now need to determine exactly when Artaxerxes assumed the throne and started his official reign. Clearly, if AP 6 was written in early January of 465 BC, and that date is in Artaxerxes *acession year*, the first year of Artaxerxes reign would either start on Nisan 1 (March/April) of 464 BC using Persian reckoning, or on Tishri 1(Sept/Oct) of 464 BC using Babylonian rekoning. If that date is in the *first year* of Artaxerxes, then Artaxeres would have *had* to assumed the throne on Tishri 1 (Sept/Oct) of 465 BC, and the document had to have used the Hebrew regnal years The diagramon the next page graphically displays the relevant timeline. Recall that both the Persians and Hebrews used an acession year system: The Persians started their Kings reign on Nisan 1, and the Hebrews on Tishri 1. Also recall that AP 6 was written Jan 1 or Jan 2, 464 BC.

The conondrum can be stated as follows. If the throne became vacant with the assassination of Xerxes in July/August of 465 BC, regardless of the power struggle that ensued the following possibilities present themselves.

- ➢ If AP 6 recorded that Artaxerxes was in his *acession year* as of Jan 1 or Jan 2 of 464 BC, then using the *Hebrew* acession year system, something unusual would have had to occur between the death of Xerxes in July/Aug of 465 BC and Jan 2, 464 BC, such that Artaxerxes was not able to start his first year of reign until Tishri 1, 464 BC. In this case, who would get credit for the full year of reign between Tishri 1, 465 BC and Tishri 1, 464 BC ? If AP 6 is written using the Hebrew acession year viewpoint, this would also create an unlikely situation of Artaxerxes not claiming a short acession year period between July/Aug of 465 BC and Sept/Oct of 465 BC. This is very improbable, since all kings wanted to claim as many years in office as possible. Xerxes would be credited with his last year of reign ending on Tishri 1, 465 BC. So why would Artaxerexes not count this short period as his acession year, and then claim a full year of reign between Tishri 1, 465 BC and Tishri 1, 464 BC ? There is none in my opinion. Artabanus was a usurper to the throne who killed Xerxes, then Darius who was the brother of Artaxerxes Only Artaxerxes stood between Artabanus and the throne, but Artaxerxes discovered what was going on and had Artabanus killed. So, it is likely that when Artaxerxes ascended to the throne, he would remove any historical reference of him....after all, Atabanus was both a murderer and a usurper to the throne. Neither Artaxerxes or Artabanus could claim that short period of political upheavel as Year 1 of his reign under either the Hebrew or Persian acession year system, and no Persian records exist that even remotely suggeast that Artabanus ever became king. Finally, no record exists of any Persian King using a non-acession system. If AP 6 was written using the accession year system, if all traces of Artabanus were stricken from the King's records it is logical (and likely) that Artaxerxes started his first year of reign on Tishri 1, 465 BC. It is not possible for Artaxerxes first year of reign to start on Nisan 1, 465 BC using an acession year system.

- ➢ If AP 6 recorded that Artaxerxes was in his *first year of reign*, then he would have *had* to start that first year on Tishri 1, 465 BC since both the Hebrews and Persians used an acession year system.

Neither of these options can be absolutely proved using only AP 6, although several researchers have tried to do so. In particular, Horn and Wood emphatically state that only the acession year reconstruction of AP 6 makes any sense They are equally emphatic that Artaxeres first year of reign did not start until Tishri 1, 464 BC. So who is right? We will look for further information. A second document recovered from the Elaphantine community was *AP 8* . The AP 8 papyrus is well preserved and intact. In that document the following dateline is recorded.

Kislev 21= Mesore 1 in Year 6 of Artaxerxes reign

Kislev corresponds to November/December on both the Babylonian and the Julian or modern Gregorian calendar. Mesore 1 is the 12th month in the ancient Egyptian calendar that was in use in Egypt at that time. Note that the Jewish regnal New Year of Tishri 1 had occurred almost two months earlier. The Egyptian New Year at that time was a month called *Thoth,* which was at least 30 days after Mesore 1. Both the Hebrews and the Egyptians counted the reign of Artaxerxes from their own New Year day. Hence, both Kislev 21 and Mesore 1 were *within year 6 of Artaxerxes reign,* but again the question arises: Which year? From AP 8, the 6th year of Artaxerxes reign is said to contain Kislev 21. The following Table illustrates the three possible occurrence of Artaxerxes 6th year using AP 6.

Year	Hebrew System: Artaxerxes in Acession Year for Less than 2 Mos....AP 6	Persian System: Artaxerxes in Acession Year Till Nisan 1, 464 BC....AP 6	Hebrew System: Artaxerxes in Acession Year Till Tishri 1, 464 BC....AP 6
1	Tishri 1, 465 BC - 464 BC	Nisan 1, 464 BC - 463 BC	Tishri 1, 464 BC - 463 BC
2	Tishri 1, 464 BC - 463 BC	Nisan 1, 463 BC - 462 BC	Tishri 1, 463 BC - 462 BC
3	Tishri 1, 463 BC - 462 BC	Nisan 1, 462 BC - 461 BC	Tishri 1, 462 BC - 461 BC
4	Tishri 1, 462 BC - 461 BC	Nisan 1, 461 BC - 460 BC	Tishri 1, 461 BC - 460 BC
5	Tishri 1, 461 BC - 460 BC	Nisan 1, 460 BC - 459 BC	Tishri 1, 460 BC - 459 BC
6	Tishri 1, 460 BC - 459 BC	Nisan 1, 459 BC - 458 BC	Tishri 1, 459 BC - 458 BC
7	Tishri 1, 459 BC - 458 BC	Nisan 1, 458 BC - 457 BC	Tishri 1, 458 BC - 457 BC
8	Tishri 1, 458 BC - 457 BC	Nisan 1, 457 BC - 456 BC	Tishri 1, 457 BC - 456 BC

Since Kislev occurs in the month of November/December, and by AP 8 it must be in Artaxerxes 6th year of reign, then the only possible, feasible alternative is that AP 8 must be referencing the Hebrew system, and that Artaxerxes *acession year* was only between the death of Xerxes in July/Aug of 565 BC to Tishri 1 in Sept/Oct of 565 BC. While this is convincing evidence, we can show that this conclusion can be reached in another way.

Using modern computer software, the calendar date for the Egyptian Mesore 1 can be calculated for the year 460 BC. In that year, Mesore 1 occurred on Nov 11. This date must coincide with Kislev 21 by AP 8. Note that the Jews living in Egypt would most certainly know what the date was for Mesore 1, and it is highly likely that being a Jewish community they would also know the correct Hebrew calendar date. On the Hebrew calendar, every new month started with a new moon. Hence, working backwards a new moon must have occurred on Kislev 1, which would be October 21. Using new modern computers and NASA software, the new moon dates far back in time can be accurately determined, since the cycle of days from new moon to new moon is a constant. One can verify that in 460 BC, the New Moon of Kislev 1 occurred in close proximity to 3:22 AM on October 21 ! Hence, using two witnesses we have shown that Kislev 21 on November 11 occurred in the 6th year of Artaxerxes reign, and that the 6th year of his reign had to be recogned from Tishri 1, 460 BC to Tishri 1, 459 BC…using non inclusive recogning in 459 BC for convenience. Using this information relative to AP 6,

	Regnal Years of Artaxerxes
1	Tishri 1, 465 BC - 464 BC
2	Tishri 1, 464 BC - 463 BC
3	Tishri 1, 463 BC - 462 BC
4	Tishri 1, 462 BC - 461 BC
5	Tishri 1, 461 BC - 460 BC
6	Tishri 1, 460 BC - 459 BC
7	Tishri 1, 459 BC - 458 BC
8	Tishri 1, 458 BC - 457 BC
9	Tishri 1, 457 BC - 456 BC
10	Tishri 1, 456 BC - 455 BC
The 7th year of Artaxerxes Reign was Tishri 1, 459 BC to Tishri 1, 458 BC	
Ezra left Babylon on Nisan 1, 458 BC	
Ezra Arrived in Jerusalem 5 months later	
Daniel's 70 Week Prophecy started on Tishri 1, 458 BC.	
Tishri 1, 458 BC -Tishri 1, 457 BC was a Sabbatical Year	

the broken/missing segment of the AP 6 document should read *In the first year of Artaxerxes reign*, and not *in the acession year of Artaxerxes reign*. The following table shows the first 10 years of Artaxerxes reign. We have established based upon ancient documents which were double dated from a Jewish community in Egypt, that first year of Artaxeres reign was Tishri 1, 465 BC – Tishri 1, 464 BC. Starting from that date, the 7th year of his reign is Tishri 1, 459 BC to Tishri 1, 458 BC. Artaxerxes acession year was a short time between when Xerxes was murdered in July/Aug of 465 BC to Sept/Oct of 465 BC (Tishri 1).

Ezra the scribe left Babylon in the seventh year of Artaxerxes reign (Ezra 7:7) on first day of the first month (Ezra 7:9),which was Nisan 1. He arrived the first day of the fifth month…..both in the seventh year of Artaxerzes reign in the Spring of 458 BC. (Ezra 7:8). We should now note again that according to our AY chronology and the determined sabbatical years, 458 BC–457 BC *was a sabbatical year*. This is a confirming sign, since several Jewish rabbis have recorded that the first year following Ezra's departure was the year 458 BC–457 BC, and it was a sabbatical year: We agree.

The Decree of Artaxerxes

We have spent a great deal of detective work to prove that the 7th year of Artaxerxes reign was recorded by Ezra the scribe as 459 BC-458 BC. The following statements have been substantiated using Biblical records supported by archeological and historical documents.

- ➢ The decree which started the 70 Weeks of Daniel's prophecy (490 years) was that of Artaxerxes I in his 7th year of reign (Ezra 7)
- ➢ The Decree was issued sometimes just before Nisan 1 of 458 BC.
- ➢ Ezra left Babylon with a decree that authorized him to rebuild the temple (Ezra 1:1-4). It should be noted that in the 20th year of Artaxerxes, he (Nehemiah) was given permission to rebuild the walls. This second decree of

Artaxerxes was not a completely new decree: it only reinforced the one given to Ezra, which in turn was originally given by Cyrus. The decree given to Ezra certainly implied that Ezra thought that the Temple had to be protected by a new wall, and that the city inside had to have dwellings for the men and their families.

- Ezra left after Nisan 1 in 458 BC (March/April), and arrived before Tishri 1, 458 BC (Sept/Oct).
- After Ezra arrived, he gathered the people and declared a fast. After that he established the judicial system and organized the exiles. The entire decree had *gone forth* by Tishri 1, and Daniels first week of years began on Tishri 1, 458 BC....Which began a *Sabbatical year*.
- The first year of Daniel's 70 week prophecy was Tishri 1, 458 BC – Tishri 1, 457 BC.

Remember that all Sabbatical years start on Tishri 1, and not on Nisan 1. All Jubilee years are officially declared to start on Tishri 10, on the Feast of Yom Kippur. The Table on the next page is extracted from the chronology of Chapter 5.

Every entry in this table starts a Sabbatical Year, except the years shown in Column 8 which start *Years of Jubilee*. The years shown are Tishri 1 start years. For example, Row 1, Col 1 Tishri 1, is 1438 BC–Tishri 1, 1437 BC, which is the *first Sabbatical year*. Tishri 1, 458 BC–Tishri 1, 457 BC is shown as *a Sabbatical year* as previously indicated.

Recall that The Daniel prophecy predicted that there would be 69-7's = 483 years *unto Messiah the Prince*. In other words, Jesus Christ would begin His earthly ministry *immediately after* 483 years have elapsed. Starting in Tishri 1, 458 BC; 483 Solar/Julian years would elapse on Tishri 1, 26 AD. Note that 458 BC to 26 BC appears to be 484 years. This is because there is no year zero, and when passing from BC to AD, one extra year must be added. Jesus Christ came to Jordan River to be baptized when he was *about 30 years of age*. It may come as a surprise to many, but Christ was *NOT* born on December 25. This date was contrived by the Roman Catholic Church.

First Jubilee..1395-1394								
Sabbatical Years							Jubilee Yr	Cycle
1	2	3	4	5	6	7		
1438	1431	1424	1417	1410	1403	1396	1395	1
1389	1382	1375	1368	1361	1354	1347	1346	2
1340	1333	1326	1319	1312	1305	1298	1297	3
1291	1284	1277	1270	1263	1256	1249	1248	4
1242	1235	1228	1221	1214	1207	1200	1199	5
1193	1186	1179	1172	1165	1158	1151	1150	6
1144	1137	1130	1123	1116	1109	1102	1101	7
1095	1088	1081	1074	1067	1060	1053	1052	8
1046	1039	1032	1025	1018	1011	1004	1003	9
997	990	983	976	969	962	955	954	10
948	941	934	927	920	913	906	905	11
899	892	885	878	871	864	857	856	12
850	843	836	829	822	815	808	807	13
801	794	787	780	773	766	759	758	14
752	745	738	731	724	717	710	709	15
703	696	689	682	675	668	661	660	16
654	647	640	633	626	619	612	611	17
605	598	591	584	577	570	563	562	18
556	549	542	535	528	521	514	513	19
507	500	493	486	479	472	465	464	20
458	451	444	437	430	423	416	415	21
409	402	395	388	381	374	367	366	22
360	353	346	339	332	325	318	317	23
311	304	297	290	283	276	269	268	24
262	255	248	241	234	227	220	219	25
213	206	199	192	185	178	171	170	26
164	157	150	143	136	129	122	121	27
115	108	101	94	87	80	73	72	28
66	59	52	45	38	31	24	23	29
17	10	3	5	12	19	26	27	30
33	40	47	54	61	68	75	76	31
82	89	96	103	110	117	124	125	32
131	138	145	152	159	166	173	174	33

It is easy to show that Christ was born in the month of Tishri, likely on the Feast of Trumpets (Tishri 1) or on the Feast of Tabernacles (Tishri 15). He came to the Jordan River to be baptized by John the Baptizer on the Feast of Atonement, Tishri 10. In either case, Christ was *about 30 years of age* (Luke 3:23). The days between Tishri 1 and Tishri 10 are known as the *Days of Repentance*, during which every Israelite must repent of any sins committed over the last year, in order to have their name inscribed in the *Book of Life* for the coming year. It is then no coincidence that John was *preaching repentance* at that time (Mat 3:1-2). The prophecy of Daniel also predicted that Jesus Christ would be *cut off* or crucified *in the midst of the 70th week*. The duration of Christ's ministry was 3.5 years, and ended on Nisan 14, 30 AD on the cross of Calvary. Looking at the table once again, we see a remarkable thing. Christ began His ministry in a sabbatical year (Tishri 1, 26 AD–Tishri 1, 27 AD). Even more remarkable is that the next year is a Year of Jubilee. It is even more interesting when the Gospel of Luke is studied.

In Luke 4:19, Christ is attending a service in his home town of Nazareth on the next Feast of Yom Kippur. We know that this visit took place on that particular feast day because the book of Isaiah was always read on that day. He stood to read in the synagogue and the book of Isaiah the prophet was given to Him. He then turned to Is 61 and began reading.

> *"The Spirit of the Lord is upon Me, because He hath appointed me to preach the gospel to the poor: He hath sent me to heal the brokenhearted, to preach deliverance to the captives, and recovering of sight to the blind, to set at liberty them that are bruised, to preach the acceptable year of the Lord."* Is. 61:1-2(a)

Christ stopped reading in the middle of Isaiah verse 2. The next words proclaimed that a *Day of Vengeance* was coming, which will not occur until His Second Advent. The message that Jesus proclaimed is *Jubilee*. The *Jubilee* that Jesus proclaimed was at the very heart of His earthly ministry. Jesus then added: **This day is this Scripture fulfilled in your ears** (Luke 4:21). Jesus not only announced that it was time for a Jubilee. He announced that He *WAS* the Jubilee. He had come to do all of those things written by Isaiah the prophet and more. From that point on, he publically set about healing the blind, causing the deaf to hear, commanding the lame to walk, setting people free from their spiritual bondage, and proclaiming the message of salvation to Jews and Gentiles alike. The *fullness of time* had surely *arrived*.

This message was a *Jubilee message* and it was read in a *Jubilee year*, important to the efficacy of our offered chronology.

The Crucifixion of our Lord Jesus Christ
According to the prophecy of Daniel (Dan 9:26), *after threescore and two weeks* (after 483 total years had been completed), Christ would be *cut off* (crucified). Exactly when this would occur can now be determined. According to Dan 9:27; Christ was prophesied to be killed *in the midst* of the (last) week. This is perfectly consistent with the known 3.5 year ministry of Christ. The midst of this last week was on *Nisan 14, 30 AD* on a *Wednesday*, which is the *Feast of Passover*. The offered chronology points to this date, but is there other evidence that this is the correct year? The answer is, *YES*.

- The apostle Paul was converted on the road to Damascus by Jesus Christ, who appeared in his risen body shortly after he was crucified; which we have just shown is in 30 AD. Fourteen (14) years after his conversion, Paul records in Gal. 2:1 that he, Barnabus, and Titus journeyed to Jerusalem. While Paul, Barnabus, and Titus were in Jerusalem, King Herod Agrippa died. This date is known to be during or shortly after the Passover Feast of 44 BC (March/April). The apostle Luke records that John the Baptist came to the Jordan River baptizing and preaching repentance in the 15th year of Tiberius Caesar (Luke 3:1-3). Tiberius was the successor to Augustus Caesar, who became the Emperor of Rome on Jan 13, 27 BC after the assassination of Julius Caesar. The last five years of his life (AD 10-14) were untroubled by war or disaster. Augustus was aging fast, and was more and more disinclined to appear personally in the senate or in public. Yet in AD 12 he consented, reluctantly we are told, to yet one more renewal of his imperial reign for ten years. Roman emperors were appointed in January, and officially conferred in March. He consented with a demand that his stepson, *Tiberius*, now over fifty years of age, should be equated with himself, both in power and authority, in the administration of the empire. He retreated to an island villa and hardly ever appeared in public between 12 AD and his death in 14 AD. Augustus died on Aug 19, 14 AD and Tiberius became sole ruler. If Luke measured the 15 years from the co-reign of Tiberius starting in the spring of 12 BC, the 15th year would be the spring of 26 AD to the spring of 27 AD.

Christ was baptized by John in September of 26 AD. There is no reason to think that Luke would not have counted the reign of Tiberius from 12 BC. Jerusalem was effectively under the iron boot of Tiberius between 12 AD - 14 AD, when the death of Augustus occurred.

March/April		March/April	Year
12 BC	to	13 BC	1
13 BC	to	14 BC	2
14 BC	to	15 BC	3
15 BC	to	16 BC	4
16 BC	to	17 BC	5
17 BC	to	18 BC	6
18 BC	to	19 BC	7
19 BC	to	20 BC	8
20 BC	to	21 BC	9
21 BC	to	22 BC	10
22 BC	to	23 BC	11
23 BC	to	24 BC	12
24 BC	to	25 BC	13
25 BC	to	26 BC	14
26 BC	to	27 BC	15

The 15th year of Tiberius Reign was Spring of 26 AD to Spring of 27 AD. Christ came to the river Jordan to be baptixed in the Fall of 26 AD

- Just before the first Passover of Christ's ministry (John 2:13), following his baptism at the Jordan River, Christ foretold of his death and resurrection in three days.

"Destroy this temple (his body) and in three days I will raise it up" (John 2:1

But the Jews thought that Christ was referring to Herod's temple and replied:

"Forty and six years was this temple in building, and wilt thou raise it up in three days?"   John 2:20

In the Works of Josephus (Book XV: 11:1), he records that construction on the temple was begun in the 18th year of King Herod's reign, which was 20 BC-19 BC. Leaping forward 46 years, we come to 27 AD-28 AD. The first Passover in Jesus ministry was in March/April of 27 BC.

- Jesus was *about 30 years of age* when He was baptized. If the baptism of Christ took place in September of 26 AD, he would have been born around Tishri 1 (September/October) of 5 AD (remember to add one year when crossing from BC to AD). Until recently, everyone believed that Herod died in the spring of 4 BC. A new theory places the death of Herod in either 1 BC or 1 AD, but that date is not without controversy for all but those who wish to show a Friday crucifixion in 33 AD. If Herod died in 4 BC, then Christ could not have been born after that date. In that case, a September/October 5 BC date for Christ is a nice fit.

- Shortly before the last Passover of Christ's ministry at which He was crucified, Jesus was delivering the Olivet Discourse to his disciples at which time he prophesied that Herod's Temple would be destroyed and when.

"Verily I say unto you, this generation shall not pass till all these things be fulfilled." Mat 24:34

This was in the spring of 30 AD. Almost all biblical scholars agree that based upon the Exodus account where the entire generation of Hebrews who left Egypt would perish (die), a biblical generation was 40 years. Adding 40 years to the spring of 30 AD, we arrive in the spring of 70 AD, when Herod's temple was destroyed. Only a 30 AD crucifixion renders this destruction exactly one generation.

Terminating Daniels 70th Week

We have proposed and presented reasonable arguments to support a Nisan 14 (Wednesday, April 6, 30 AD) crucifixion date for Jesus Christ. The year 30 AD falls in the middle of Daniel's 70th week, that is after 486.5 years have elapsed since the 490-year prophecy started. Clearly, this leaves 3.5 years to finish the prophecy. Many modern prophecy teachers allow the

70-7's to expire on Tishri 1 (Sept/Oct) of 33 AD. The event designated to end the prophecy is proposed to be the stoning of Stephen in Acts 6. Proponents of this theory (rightly so) identify this event as the final act of rejection of Jesus Christ as the promised Messiah by the corporate nation of Israel. From this point on, the message of salvation in Jesus Christ under the new covenant passed to both Gentiles and Jews. We totally reject the logic which ends Daniel's 70th week in 33 AD based upon two platforms. *First*, we have already discussed in some detail the things which must be completed before Daniel's 70 weeks of years expires, and several things can only be accomplished at the second advent of Jesus Christ. This reason is enough to reject the *Steven hypothesis*. A *second* and more compelling reason is in the stoning of Steven. In Acts 1-2 we are told how the Holy Spirit fell on the Feast of Pentecost, 50 days after the resurrection. Chapter 3 records a post-Pentecost miracle, the healing of a lame man, followed by Peter's sermon. Chapters 4:1-6:7 are concerned with the beginning of persecutions and the preparation for spreading the gospel. Acts 6:8 records how Steven *full of faith and power* did *great wonders and miracles*. The Jewish leaders turned against him, fearing that he would *destroy this place, and change the customs*. At this point Stephen delivers perhaps the most powerful sermon ever preached (Acts 7:1-53). When he finished his discourse, the Jews *cast him out of the city and stoned him*. So, Steven became the first apostle named in the New Testament to be martyred after the day of Pentecost. Now the conclusion: the conversion of Paul (Saul) is recorded in Acts 9. However, considering the sequence and duration of the events recorded in the Book of Acts, his conversion on the road to Damascus was likely within a year after Christ was crucified. It is impossible that the stoning of Steven took place 3.5 years after the crucifixion. We therefore conclude that there has been a *gap* of almost 2000 years since the midpoint of Daniel's 70th week. The termination of Daniel's 70th week will not occur until the second coming of Jesus Christ at the end of the great tribulation period. We have already thoroughly discussed the things that were to be accomplished by the end of Daniel's 70th week, and all of those things will not be fully accomplished until the end of the age of grace, or the church age. The fact that the tribulation period described in the book of Revelation is only 3.5 years in duration, and not 7 years as is commonly taught, is not a large leap of faith. In either case, there is a gap in time which represents the church age.

Gabriel next informs Daniel that the prophecy involves a period of *70 weeks*. The interpretation is consistent across almost all scholars of prophecy. The 70 weeks of this prophecy represents 70 periods of seven years, or a total period of 490 years. The 490 years is broken into three parts. A period of seven weeks or 49 years; a period of 62 weeks or 434 years; and a final period of seven years (490 years-49 years-434 years). Almost parenthetically, Gabriel now assures Daniel that the street and the wall will be built again, but it will not be without great difficulty. The street and the wall are two integral parts of the city.

The Messiah just introduced now returns to full view. The final seven years is further subdivided into two parts. *After* threescore and two weeks (the second 434 year period of time), *the Messiah* (Jesus Christ) *will be cut off.* The phrase to be *cut off* means to be *killed*. Note again that this event occurs after the 483rd year is over, *in the midst of the week*. That is, on or near after 3.5 years have elapsed in the 70th or final week. This, of course, can only point to the crucifixion of our Lord Jesus Christ. Christ did not die for Himself; He was perfect in every way. He died for you and me so that we could be reconciled to God and saved by grace. It is one of the tragic and enigmatic events in all history. Christ died for the sins and inequities of both Jews and Gentiles, but the nation of Israel and most individuals rejected Him as their Messiah.

The next part of the prophecy deals with a ***prince to come*** and ***his people***. It is important to recognize who this *prince* represents. Many prophecy teachers identify this prince as the antichrist which will arise during the great tribulation period and persecute all who refuse to worship him. Looking back on historical events, it is almost certain that this *prince* is the Roman general Titus, and his *people* are his own countrymen, Roman legions, who would completely destroy Herod's Temple, ransack the city of Jerusalem and bring Israel into Roman submission. The end came in a *flood* - that is quickly. The last statement is extremely important. Daniel is told that: ***unto the end of the war desolations are determined.*** This short passage has a dual meaning: physical and spiritual. The Nation of Israel has been attacked and assailed by practically every nation over the past 2,500 years. The most sacred ground in modern Israel is the Temple Mount, where Herod's Temple once stood. It is now controlled by the Muslims who built the Dome of the Rock over the very place where it is claimed Abraham's binding of Isaac took place. The Jewish temple is indeed desolate, and it will remain that way until it is taken back by Israel just before the great tribulation period and a new temple is built. Until that time, Israel will be continually at war along the Gaza Strip and other lands that God gave to Israel. But the real war is *spiritual* in nature. As a nation, the Jews refuse to see that Jesus Christ has come to save the people. To them, He is still regarded today as a *prophet* only. They are still awaiting their Messiah. This spiritual war will continue until the second coming of Christ, when they will finally recognize Jesus Christ as their true and only Messiah.

The next part of the prophecy has been the most abused and misunderstood passage in the whole Bible. Interpretation of the Personal pronoun "*he*" has lead to all the confusion and misinterpretation of this important passage.

> *"And he shall confirm the covenant with many for one week: and in the midst of the week he shall cause the sacrifice and the oblation to cease, and for the overspreading of abominations he shall make it desolate, even until the consummation, and that determined shall be poured upon the desolate."* Dan 9:27

Three things are to be accomplished by the person referred to as ***He.***

- ➢ *He* shall confirm the covenant with many for one week,
- ➢ *He* shall cause the sacrifice and the oblation to cease,
- ➢ *He* shall make *it* desolate.

When James Ryrie wrote the Ryrie Study Bible in 1976, he identified this *he* as the *antichrist*. Multitudes of biblical scholars have followed his theology. The prevailing interpretation of this passage is that Daniel's 70th week, a period of seven years, is the period of time described in the Book of Revelation. The first 3.5 years represent the period of time in which the Temple will be rebuilt; the antichrist will rise to power; and a one-world government will be established. After 3.5 years, a great world leader will be *wounded unto death* by a knife, and he will miraculously come back to life and be controlled by Satanic influence. This Satanically controlled *antichrist* will become the world ruler; demand that the entire world worship him; place a statue in the temple which will talk; and martyr anyone who opposes him. He will persecute Christians and Jews alike so severely that Christ said **for then shall be great tribulation, such as was not since the beginning of the world to this time, no, nor ever shall be** (Mat 24:21). The only thing that will save mankind will be Christ himself when he returns to fight the great battle of Armageddon. All of this theology is based upon who "*he*" represents. We will now argue that *he* is identified with the *Messiah*, and not a future antichrist. It is true that a great world ruler will arise in the end times and become the antichrist, but this personage is not the *he* in Dan 9:27. ***First***, the entire focus of Dan 9:27 is to the Jewish nation and its people. ***Second***, the antecedent of *he* cannot grammatically be the prince and his people in the previous verse. ***Third***, we have already determined that this *prince* is the Roman general *Titus*. The antecedent is the Prince; the Messiah, Jesus Christ. We will now show that the three things to be accomplished by *he* were accomplished by Christ during his three-year ministry.

He **shall confirm the covenant with many for one week**
Theologians who identify *he* with the antichrist maintain that the seven-year final period of tribulation (Daniel's 70th week) will begin when the antichrist establishes a covenant with the Jewish people. The word translated *confirm* means to *strengthen, to firm up, to make strong*. There is a great deal of difference in *confirming a covenant* and *establishing a covenant*. If this

confirmation was done by Jesus Christ, what covenant was confirmed and when? The answers are clearly contained in the Holy Scriptures. The concept of a *covenant* is important to the interpretation, since it was a covenant that was confirmed. A covenant in the Bible is always a promise. What is the most important covenant or promise to the Jewish people? Every Jew will know that it is the covenant God made with Abraham.

> *"Now to Abraham and his seed were the promises made. He saith not and to seeds, as in many; but as of one. And to thy seed, which is Christ. And this I say, that the covenant that was confirmed before of God in Christ, the law, which was 430 years after, cannot disannul, that it should make the promise of none effect. .... Wherefore then serveth the law? It was added because of transgressions, till the seed should come to whom the promise made."* Gal 3:16, 17, 19

Jesus fulfilled the promise to Abraham when he came to the Jordan River to be baptized and to initiate the purpose of reconciling Jews and Gentiles alike to God.

> *"and if you be Christ's, then you are Abraham's seed and heirs according to the promise."* Gal 3:29

The promise of a Messiah which would save Israel was *confirmed for one week* (7 years). But all agree that the ministry of Christ which began at the river Jordan only lasted 3.5 years until he was *cut off* (crucified). Where are the other 3.5 weeks? We have already presented evidence that Daniel's 70th week did not end with the stoning of Steven, but the last 7 years of Daniel's prophecy was interrupted and suspended with 3.5 years remaining. These 3.5 years are the length of the Tribulation described in the Book of Revelation.

He shall cause the sacrifice and the oblation to cease

Christ came as the Son of God in the flesh to live a perfect, sinless life under the law. Jesus established a new covenant after satisfying the old. His life on earth and his work on the cross rightly divided and fulfilled the Law. A new covenant was

established by which both Jew and Gentile are saved by *grace*
When Jesus came to the Jordan River, John looked up and said:

> **"Behold the Lamb of God who taketh away the sins of the world."** John 1:29

Under the old covenant, the Levitical priesthood stood in the Temple day after day, month after month and year after year sacrificing bulls and goats to make atonement for sins. In the Old Testament, the word *atonement* meant a *covering*, temporarily satisfying God until the only sacrificial Lamb fully acceptable to God would be slain on the cross of Calvary. Only the High Priest could approach God, and then only once a year for a very short time on the Day of Atonement (Feast of Yom Kippur). There he spoke to God as he appeared in a cloud over the mercy seat in the Holy of Holies. The work of the Lamb of God, Jesus Christ, when He went to the cross abolished the Levitical sacrificial system forever, and now allows us to enter into the very presence of God Himself through our intercessor, the Lord Jesus Christ.

> **"For it is not possible that the blood of bulls and of goats could take away sins. For Christ was offered to bear the sins of many; and unto them that look for him shall he appear a second time without sin unto salvation."** Heb 9:28

Traditional and persistent teaching maintains that *he* is the antichrist, and that after he *confirms a covenant* with the Jews a seven-year tribulation period begins; the temple will finally be rebuilt on the Temple Mount; the old sacrificial system will be reinstated; and daily sacrifices renewed. This same line of teaching has the antichrist suddenly turning on the nation of Israel after 3½ years of peace. He will then cause the *sacrifice and the oblation* (daily prayers) *to cease*. Nowhere in Scripture is this shown to be true.

He shall make it desolate

The sacrificial death of Jesus Christ at the cross accomplished much more than establishing a new covenant. When the Lamb of God said *it is finished,* he not only meant that the old covenant was finished. He meant that the old Levitical sacrificial system was finished. He not only meant that living a life of fear and condemnation under the Law was finished. He declared that the entire ritualistic worship associated with the temple was finished.

Anyone who has accepted Jesus Christ as their savior is now a member of the Body of Christ, and the Holy Spirit now lives within their own temple (their body) as a guarantee of Christ's promises. Christ made the Jewish temple desolate. Jesus was not cut off for himself, for he was sinless. He who knew no sin was made sin for us. He took all of the sins of the world from Adam to the millennial kingdom and placed them upon himself. He had come to his own people, the Jews, but his own people rejected him. By rejecting his full and perfect sacrifice for all sins, the Jews as a corporate body made a mockery of his sacrificial act. Their offerings of bulls and goats are now an abomination to the Lord. Shortly before he was crucified, the Messiah uttered a passionate and final verdict against his own Jewish people.

> *"Oh Jerusalem, Jerusalem, thou that killest the prophets. And stone them that are sent unto you, how often would I have gathered thy children together, even as a hen gathers her chickens under her wings, and you would not. For I say unto you, Ye shall not see me henceforth (again) till ye shall say, Blessed is he that cometh in the name of the Lord. Behold, your house is left unto you desolate."*
> Mat 23: 37, 39 & 38

These words, in perfect agreement with Dan 9:27 should convince anyone by the Holy Scriptures that *he* in Dan 9:27 is NOT the antichrist, but Jesus Christ, the Messiah. *He* confirmed a covenant with many, *He* caused the Jewish system of sacrifice and oblation to cease, and *he* made it desolate. These are not *accomplishments* of the antichrist during *the future time of Jacob's trouble*, but the work of our Lord Jesus Christ. Finally, note that in His own words (Mat 23:37) Christ solves another *mystery:* **Oh Jerusalem, Jerusalem, thou that killeth the prophets** equates Jerusalem with those who killed the prophets. Recall that Daniel's 70-week prophecy of 490 years was directed to ***thy people and upon thy Holy City*** (Dan 9: 24). Clearly, the city of Jerusalem never killed anyone. It was the people of Jerusalem that hung Christ on the cross of Calvary and killed the prophets. This identification of the Jews with Jerusalem exactly parallels and explains a difficult passage in the book of Revelation.

> ***"And there came unto me one of the seven angels which had the seven vials full of the last seven plagues, and talked with me saying 'come hither and I will show you the bride, the Lamb's wife'. And he carried me away in the spirit to a great and high mountain, and showed me that great city, the holy Jerusalem, descending out of heaven from God."***
> Rev 21: 9-10

In several places in the New Testament, the body of Christ (those who have accepted Jesus Christ as their Lord and Savior) are called the *Bride of Christ*. But here we see that the heavenly city of Jerusalem is equated to the bride of Christ. Just as before, a city, even one with gates of pearl and streets of gold, cannot be a bride. Here as before, the city and the people are inseparable. All of those who reject Christ as their savior are equated to the earthly (fleshly) city of Jerusalem, while the body of true believers in Jesus Christ is equated to the heavenly (spiritual) city of Jerusalem. It is in this glorious city that all the saints will live forever. Words cannot be spoken, nor can the mind imagine, what glories Christ will bestow upon all who believe in His name!

It is important to understand that the prophecy of Daniels 70th week was intended to give Daniel *understanding* that the 70 years of Babylonian captivity will not end in the national establishment of the earthly kingdom promised to Abraham's descendents, but that a period of 70 times seven or 490 years is decreed to pass before Israel will inherit the promises. It is also prophesied that *in the middle* of the last week of years, after 3.5 years have passed, that the promised Messiah would not establish His kingdom at that time, but he will be *cut off* (crucified). The children of promise (Jewish people) will not be brought back into a covenant relationship with God until they finally recognize Jesus Christ as their Messiah. This time will not come until the great tribulation period has run its course of 3.5 years at the end of the age. Keep in mind that the book of Revelation would not be written for another 600 years, and the sequence of events which occurs during this period of time was completely unknown. It is seldom understood that the entire purpose of the tribulation period is not to have Christ finally cast Satan away and off of this earth. This was important, but the tribulation period is for the Gentiles and Jews who constitute the body of Christ to bring the nation of Israel back into an intimate, everlasting covenant relationship with God, and for the Jewish people to finally accept Jesus Christ as their personal Savior. This *mystery* was hidden through ages past from the Jews. A *mystery* is not something mysterious in the modern sense, but something that had remained hidden until the fullness of time in which it is finally known. Paul revealed this mystery.

"Whereby, when ye read; ye may understand my knowledge in the mystery of Christ. Which in other ages was not made known unto the sons of men, as it is now revealed unto his holy apostles and prophets by the Spirit. That the Gentiles should be fellow heirs and of the same body, and partakers of his promise in Christ by the gospel." Ephesians 3:4-6

The mystery was that Jews and Gentiles alike would be heirs to the promises of God, and that both would constitute the same body of Christ. This was completely unknown to the Old Testament saints, and was not revealed until the new covenant was set in place by Jesus Christ. Even the Apostle Peter misunderstood that the New Covenant would be established with both Jews and Gentiles heirs and joint heirs to salvation. God had to change the theology of Peter to accept this truth through a vision (Acts 10:1-15), and confirmed in Acts 10:45

Even until the consummation, and that determined shall be poured out on the desolate

The word *consummation* means *to bring to a completion or an end*. The end of the present age of grace will come to an end as the Great Tribulation Period expires and Christ comes at His Second Advent. Anyone who has not accepted Jesus Christ as the Son of God and believed upon Him by that time will find that it is too late. The phrase, *that determined*, refers to all of the events revealed and recorded in the book of Revelation. His words are true, and everything shown to the apostle John and faithfully recorded will come to pass. However, that determined is specifically directed to *the desolate*. Who are the desolate? They are those who have chosen to follow the antichrist and reject the true Messiah, Jesus Christ. This passage refers to the *Wrath of God*, which is the ultimate fate of all those who reject the free gift of eternal life by not believing in Him.

> ***"But God commendeth his love toward us, in that, while we were yet sinners, Christ died for us. Much more then, being now justified by His blood, we shall be saved from wrath through Him."*** Romans 5:8-9

> ***"For God hath not appointed us to wrath, but to obtain salvation by our Lord Jesus Christ."*** *I* Thessalonians 5:10

The concept of believers escaping wrath is almost universally misunderstood. There needs to be a distinction between *wrath* and *tribulation*. While we may not like it at the time, tribulation is a good thing. It refines us and places us in the fire that we may be more like Christ. The apostle Paul said: **We glory in tribulation, knowing that tribulation worketh patience; and patience experience; and experience hope** (Rom 5:3). Certainly the last 3.5 weeks of Daniel's prophecy will be wrought with much tribulation, but we must endure knowing the rewards which follow those who are faithful, even unto death. The Wrath of God will be poured out upon Satan's kingdom in the seven bowl judgments. Those who are alive, prepared, and seek after Christ will not experience the W*rath of God* which is the seven bowl judgments (Rev 16:1).

> ***"And I (John) heard a great voice out of the temple saying to the seven angels, go your ways, and pour out the vials (bowls) of the Wrath of God upon the earth."*** Rev 16:1

Those who overcome (true believers in Jesus Christ) will be spared this wrath. They will be raptured away as the 7th trumpet sounds before the seven bowl judgments are poured out. The rapture is coupled with rewards and the imminent reclamation of the earth by Jesus Christ.

"And the seventh angel sounded (the seventh trumpet); and there were great voices in heaven, saying, the kingdoms of this world are become the kingdoms of our Lord, and of His Christ, and he shall reign forever and ever. And the nations were angry, and thy wrath is come." Rev 11: 13, 18

We have spent a great deal of time and effort to establish three scriptural truths.

1. *Daniel 9:25-27 is a Messianic prophecy through and through. It is to the Jewish people and does not contain any reference to the antichrist.*
2. *The 70th week of Daniel is in two parts. One part of duration 3.5 years is the earthly ministry of Christ; the second 3.5 years has not occurred yet, and represents the last 3.5 years of this age (dispensation of Grace).*
3. *The 70-week prophecy of Daniel has been used to show that there is indeed a gap of time between when Christ was crucified in 30 AD and when the last half of Daniel's 70th week will begin. That gap of time is known only to the Father, but we can say with a great deal of conviction that the amount of time remaining in Daniel's prophecy is 3.5 years. The seven-year duration of the tribulation period is found to be in error, and in fact cannot be supported by the book of Revelation. The following periods of time are all given, and each one has a termination point which corresponds to the end of the tribulation period.*
    ❖ *Two witnesses will prophesy for 1260 days (Rev 10:3). They die as the seventh trumpet sounds at the end of the antichrist's reign. These 1260 days are*

> *equated to a "time, times and half a time" in Rev 12:14.*
> - *There will be a great war in heaven, and Satan will be cast down to the earth for a "short time" to persecute all those who dwell upon the earth (Rev 12:12). This short period of time corresponds to the rise and reign of the antichrist, which is 42 months (Rev 13:5).*
> - *When Satan is cast down to the earth, a "remnant of the woman's seed" will flee to the wilderness where they will be protected for 1260 days. This is equated to a "time, times and half a time" in Rev 12:6.*

All of these last three time periods are 3.5 years long, and the end of each terminate at or very near the end of Daniel's 70th week. A 3.5 year tribulation period should make everyone happy!

Chapter Eight

Finding Daniel's 70th Week

In Chapter 7, we determined that Daniel's 490-year prophecy started in the seventh year of Artaxerxes reign (Tishri 1, 459 BC – Tishri 1, 458 BC). Ezra the scribe was given permission to journey to Jerusalem (Ezra 7) with *some Israelites, including Levites* (Ezra 7:7). The journey began in the spring of 458 BC, just after Nisan 1. After a journey of less than 5 months, the decree went forth to the people; the judiciary went forth; and after addressing interfaith marriage problems, the 70 weeks of Daniel started on Tishri 1, 458 BC. This began a period of 486.5 years of the 490-year prophecy, which terminated on Nisan 14, 30 AD at the crucifixion of Jesus Christ. At that point, Daniel's 70th week was *interrupted* with 3.5 years yet remaining to terminate Daniel's 70th week of seven years duration. Where is the remaining 3.5 years? We will show that the great tribulation period which ends the age of grace is only 3.5 years long, and not seven years as is claimed by most prophecy scholars.

Traditional Theology
The most common line of teaching is that the Book of Revelation describes a 7 year tribulation period. In the European theatre a powerful, charismatic leader will emerge on the world scene who is smart, energetic, influential, and a brilliant orator. Prior to his appearance, Europe will have either consolidated into 10 major countries or alliances; or a strong 10 nation confederacy will exist for both political and economic purposes.(Dan 7, Rev 17). Either way, the charismatic leader will appear on the scene, and through supernatural powers will make war against three of the countries and emerge as their dictator. From this power base, he will then bring the entire 10-nation confederacy under his sole dictatorship. He will now become the most powerful man in the world. At this point, he will make a pact with Israel, and either by political prowess or using military strength, he will authorize the Jewish holy temple to be rebuilt in Jerusalem. This will supposedly take 3.5 years,

and is generally taught to coincide with the six seal judgments. The remaining 3.5 years would usually commence with war in heaven against Satan (Rev 12), and his being cast down to the earth. The great world leader will be wounded to death and will be miraculously revived as the Antichrist... totally controlled and empowered by Satanic forces. The last 3.5 years will represent persecution by the Antichrist, and contain both the 7 trumpet judgments and the 7 bowl judgments. Scriptural support for this pact with Israel is claimed to be in Daniel 9.

> ***"And he shall confirm the covenant with many for one week: and in the midst of the week he shall cause the sacrifice and the oblation to cease, and for the overspreading of abominations he shall make it desolate, even until the consummation, and that determined shall be poured upon the desolate"***   Dan 9:27

The *he* in Dan 9:27 is identified as the great world leader who will become the Antichrist. We have already provided arguments against this interpretation. The *he* in Dan 9:27 is NOT this new world leader, but Jesus Christ. The covenant which is confirmed by Christ at His first advent is God's promise that a Son of David will arise called the Messiah, who will redeem Israel and restore them to their land. It was Jesus Christ who caused the temple sacrifices and oblations to cease when He established the New Covenant at the cross of Calvary. When Christ died on the cross He *did* redeem any Jew or Gentile who would believe upon His Holy name, but as a nation Israel will not be completely restored to their land until the millennial kingdom is established. However, we are not refuting the fact that a great world leader will arise before the last 3.5 years of Daniel's 70th week commences, and he *will* be heralded as their long awaited messiah. By divine appointment (God is in control), he *will* somehow accomplish the restoration of Solomon's temple, and the Jewish nation *will* accept this man as their long-awaited messiah. The temple *will* be rebuilt, sacrifices and oblations reinstated and messianic expectations will run high (Rev 11:1-2). It is also true that at the height of his power and influence, this *false messiah* will suddenly turn against Israel and invade

Jerusalem just as the last 3.5 years of Daniel's 70th week commences. Another important event that will happen as the last half of Daniel's 70th week begins is that this great world leader will be ***mortally wounded*** (Rev 13:1-6). He will then be taken over by a strong demonic prince who will arise out of the bottomless pit (Rev 17:7-11). He is called a ***beast out of the sea*** (Rev 13:2). We call him by the name *antichrist*, although this name is not found in the book of Revelation. This *beast out of the Sea* will be accompanied by another ***Beast out of the Earth***. We call this second beast the *false prophet*. He will set up an image in the desecrated temple in Jerusalem that will speak and martyr anyone who fails to worship Satan and the Antichrist, and accept Satan as their god. No one will be allowed to buy or sell unless they have the ***mark of the beast*** (Rev 13:16-17) on their right hand or their forehead. The Antichrist will be supernaturally, satanically empowered to ***make war against the saints and to overcome them*** (Rev 13: 7). These important events will not take place until Satan is defeated in heaven and cast down to the earth (Rev 12).

It is important to again realize that the ***He*** which will bring an end to sacrifice and offerings has been shown to be Jesus Christ when He died on the Cross (Chapter 7). His death ended the Old Testament sacrificial system forever. However, it is almost certain that like many Old Testament prophecies, this has a *double meaning*. The primary application is to the death of Christ and its impact on sacrifices and sin offerings. Its secondary application is to when the antichrist and the false prophet will stop the renewed Jewish sacrifices and oblations after the final tribulation period of 3.5 years starts to run its course. We agree that the supernatural recovery of a deadly wound to the emerging world leader, the desecration of the newly rebuilt temple, and the cessation of oblations and sacrifices will all occur before the last 3.5 years of Daniel's 70th week begins. However, we cannot accept a limited and designated 3.5 year period of time during which Herod's Temple will be rebuilt and the old Levitical sacrificial system reinstated.

It is also recorded in Rev 13:11-15 that an image will be erected which both speaks and passes judgment on those who fail to worship the image. It does not take much imagination to recognize that Antiochus Epiphanies and the Macabees revolt was a *shadow and type* of what will happen during the last 3.5 years of the Tribulation Period, starting with the events of Rev 12 and ending when Christ returns and *restores all things* in Rev 19. This chain of future events is supported by Mat 24:15 and II Thess. 2:3-4. Christ prophesied that the temple would be desecrated in His *Olivet Discourse* which He gave shortly before His death.

> ***"Therefore when you see the abomination of desolation spoken of by Daniel the prophet, standing in the holy place, then let them that are in Judea flee to the mountains."***
> Mat 24:15-16

Christ reinforced this prophecy in Rev 12:6 and Rev 11:15-16. The ***abomination of desolation*** has long been debated by prophecy scholars. Many propose that this abomination is the satanically-indwelled antichrist as he stands in the temple. Some say that it is swine that are killed on the altar of sacrifice in the Holy Place. However, we believe that the *abomination* is an ***image of the beast; that the image of the beast should both speak and cause as many as would not worship the image of the beast to be killed*** (Rev 13:15). Imagine that, an image or a statue that can recognize a person and speak. If any person stands before the image and refuses to worship the beast (antichrist), then that person will be killed (Rev 13:15). This will happen very soon after the last 3.5 years of Daniel's 70th week starts to unfold.

Let us again make one thing clear. These events which have just been described WILL HAPPEN. The point we wish to make is that the rise of the great world leader, the unification of European countries under this person, the covenant with Israel which will rebuild the temple, the breaking of that covenant after the temple is rebuilt and the emergence of the Satanically indwelled antichrist need not take place in a 3.5 year period called the first half of Daniel's final seventh week. In fact, there is no scriptural authority whatsoever to make this assumption. The events just described definitely will happen and will precede the last 3.5 years of Daniel's 70th week, but need not be time-constrained by the first 3.5 weeks of Daniel's 70th week. They are *signs* that the end is near.

The Last Half of Daniel's 70th Week

We have already shown that the first half of Daniel's 70th week is separated from the second half of Daniel's week by now more than 2000 years and still counting. The traditional view that Daniel's 70th week is an unbroken sequence of seven years should be rejected in light of the clear and consistent biblical record which we have presented. The traditional view is based entirely upon the incorrect interpretation of the personal pronoun *he* in Dan 9:27. Proponents of this teaching will sometimes say: *"But the book of Revelation supports an elapsed seven-year period of time"* But does it? Let us examine the evidence.

In Rev 11:1-2 an angel is told to *rise and measure the Temple of God,* but leave out the court which is outside the temple for it has been given to the Gentiles. And they will *tread the holy city underfoot for 42 months.* The holy city is Jerusalem. It will be taken over and trod under foot for 42 months. When does this take place? It should be clear that this is over the last 3.5 years of the tribulation period, and after the temple has been rebuilt. Immediately following this prophecy, we are told that: *I* (God) **will give power to my two witnesses, and they will prophesy one thousand two hundred and sixty days** (Rev 11:3). From the context of Rev 11:1-10, these 1260 days coincide with the 42-month period of persecution and Gentile domination of Jerusalem.

In Rev 12: 1-17 we are told that there is a great war in the heavenlies, and that the dragon (Satan) is cast down and immediately attacks Israel. A *sun-clothed woman* (a fleeing remnant from Jerusalem) retreats into the wilderness where: **she has a place prepared by God, that they should feed her there for one thousand two hundred and sixty days** (Rev 12: 6, 12-

16). The *beast from the sea* who subsequently arises is the antichrist (Rev 13:1-4), which is the great world leader who was **mortally wounded** (Rev 13:3, 14-15). We believe that this event is reported accurately in the Ryrie Study Bible as follows.

"Apparently Satan will miraculously restore antichrist to life in an imitation of the resurrection of Christ" (Ryrie Study Bible).

The results are unrestrained persecution of all who oppose him.

"All the world marveled and followed the beast. So they worshipped the dragon who gave authority to the beast, and they worshipped the beast, saying, 'who is like the beast? Who is able to make war with him? And he was given a mouth speaking great things and blasphemies, and he was given authority to continue for 42 months." Rev 13: 3-5

The point of all this is that there are *four different passages* in the book of Revelation that refer to allocated periods of time. These passages establish that 42 months (Rev 11:2, 13:5); 1260 days (Rev 11:3); and time, times and half a time (Rev 12:14) are all the same length of time. We must emphasize that all of the above references to time in the Book of Revelation refer to the same period of elapsed time, and all end at or very near the end of the trumpet and bowl judgments, which when completed terminate the 70th week of Daniel's prophecy. Well meaning prophecy teachers have combined these time periods to start and end at different times, to accommodate a 7 year period of tribulation. The table on the following page provides a summary of this discussion.

These biblical verses establish that each of these time periods terminate at or very near the end of the tribulation period, and coincide with the termination of Daniel's 70th week. It is concluded that in the Book of Revelation there is no reason to believe that the tribulation period is anything but 3.5 years, consisting of 42 months or 1260 days.

Time Period	Initiation	Termination	Reference
42 Months	Temple is given to Gentiles	Time of the Gentiles over. End of the age.	Rev 11:2
42 Months	Reign of the beast (Antichrist)	Beast (Antichrist) is conquered by Christ at the Battle of Armageddon	Rev 13:5
1260 days	Two witnesses will start prophesying	Both killed by the Beast 3 days before the end of tribulation period	Rev 11:3
Time, times and half a time	Woman(Israel remnant) is nourished in the wilderness from the beast(antichrist)	Antichrist reign is over at the Battle of Armageddon	Rev 12:14

Dispensational Theology and a 7 Year Tribulation

In the first half of the nineteenth century a Plymouth England minister, John Nelson Darby, fathered a theory known as *dispensationalism*, which included pre-tribulation rapture theology. This theology eventually evolved into several integrated components which include the following ideas:

- Darby identified seven distinct dispensations or periods of time.
- The church age began at Pentecost and will end at the second advent of Christ
- The 70th week is claimed to be yet in the future, and is seven years in duration. The prince that confirms the covenant in Dan. 9:27 is a future antichrist who will stop the sacrifices in a rebuilt temple in Jerusalem.
- The Old Testament promises to Abraham, including the restoration of Israel to the promised land, will be fulfilled at the second coming of Christ
- We are living in the church age during which salvation is dealt with quite differently than at a previous time.

Much of the theory of modern dispensationalism and a 7 year tribulation period rests upon the assumption that we can make the first 69 weeks of Daniel's 70 weeks fit into some sort of timeline from Artaxerxes' 20th year to the death of Christ. Often when one discusses the details of the first 69 weeks with a dispensationalist, the dates and theories of Sir Robert Anderson arise, as outlined in his book, *The Coming Prince*. A critical examination of Anderson's work can be found by Bob Pickle at http://www.pickle-publishing.com/papers/sir-robert-anderson.htm).

It is important to recognize that as just discussed, there is a large group of prophesy teachers and theologians who start Daniel's 70th week in either 445 BC (Sir Robert Anderson and others) or in 444 BC (Harold Hoehner and others). As previously discussed, they resort to using a *prophetic year* based largely upon facts that are in the book of Revelation. It cannot be denied that if taken literally, 42 months can be equated to 1260 days, which seem to imply that a *prophetic month* is 30 days long and a *prophetic year* is 12 months of 30 days or 360 days long. Everyone who follows this line of thought, multiplies the number of years in Daniel's 70th week by 360 days, and then converts these prophetic years into either Julian years (360.25 days long) or to Gregorian years (360.2524 days long). To illustrate, we will show how Sir Robert Anderson first used this theory.

Anderson adopted a date of March 14, 445 BC for the initiation of Daniel's 70-week prophecy using Nehemiah 2:1. He then proposed that God intended a *prophetic* year to be 360 days rather than a solar calendar year of 365.2425 days. He then determined the number of prophetic days that must have elapsed between 445 BC and the end of 473 prophetic years; (473x360) = 173,770 days. If 173,770 days are advanced from March 14, 445 BC we arrive at April 6, 32 AD. Checking this date against a Gregorian calendar date (even though the calendar at that time was the Julian calendar), Anderson found that April 6 in 32 AD fell on a Sunday, and if it was the crucifixion week, it would be Palm Sunday. In the same week Nisan 14 fell on a Monday. This could never be true, so he declared that Thursday, April 10 was the crucifixion date of Jesus Christ. This all sounds too good to be true; and for good reason.... It is not. In a critical and scientific investigation of Anderson's calculations both Bob Pickle and later Thomas Ice have shown several errors in Anderson's calculations and in his reasoning. In 1977 Harold Hoehner corrected several errors, and published his doctoral dissertation (*Chronological Aspects of the Life of Christ*) in which he used 444 BC as the 20th year of Artaxerxes. Using the same fundamental approach as Anderson, he arrived at a crucifixion date of Friday, April 3, 33 BC. This date has been widely accepted ever since, particularly by Roman Catholics, since the Roman Catholic Church doggedly holds to a Friday crucifixion date.

Although both approaches should be highly commended for innovation and believable results, we must reject both crucifixion dates as being interesting but not acceptable. ***First***, Daniel did not have all of these complex numbers running through his mind when he received the prophecy. We have argued that he was no doubt relating the prophecy to full calendar years with sabbatical year milestones. ***Second***, to make the 445 BC or the 444 BC departure dates for Daniel's prophecy work, Daniel would have had to anticipate (or know) the exact number of days in either a Gregorian or Calendar solar year. Daniel was told that he would *understand* when he received this prophecy, and there is no hint in the biblical record that he would understand this complex system of calculation. Finally, both Anderson and Hoehner claim that the book of Revelation substantiates their approach.... But the book of revelation would not be written until about 500 years later! ***Third***, and most compelling, is that the concept of a 360-day prophetic year cannot be accepted. The only precedence that a prophetic month was to be only 30 days was from the biblical account of the flood. Using Gen 7:24 and Gen 7:11 with Gen 8:4; one can equate 5 months with 150 days... Bingo! However, the fact that it rained for 150 days over a 5 month period does not specifically prove that each month was 30 days in duration. For example, two months of 31 days, two of 29 days and one of 30 days will yield the same result. ***Finally***, to accept a Friday crucifixion of

Christ is to completely ignore the straightforward and simple statements of Christ on several occasions that He would be in the grave three days and three nights, and Christ banked the belief of his entire ministry on this statement.

> *"Then certain of the Scribes and of the Pharisees answered, saying, Master, we would see a sign from thee. But he answered and said unto them, An evil and adulterous generation seeketh after a sign; and there shall no sign be given to it, but the sign of the prophet Jonah: For as Jonah was three days and three nights in the whale's belly; so shall the son of man be three days and three nights in the heart of the earth."*   Matthew 12:37-49

It is impossible to have Christ in the grave a full three days and three nights using a Friday crucifixion and a Sunday morning resurrection without a very clever part-day accounting scheme, and even this stretches the imagination. To get three days, one must resort to counting three hours on the first day (Friday) as a 24-hour day, the next day (Saturday) as a whole day (which it was), and somewhere between 1 hour to 12 hours Saturday evening (Sunday on the Hebrew calendar) as a whole day. Things get worse. The first night is 6:00 pm-6:00 am on Friday (Saturday night actually), and the second night is obtained by counting somewhere between 1 hour and 12 hours (6:00 pm-6:00 am) Saturday Night (actually Sunday) as a whole night. So where is the third night? Simple they say. Friday afternoon between 3:00 pm and 6:00 pm was Friday, and Friday included the previous night. The entire scenario is preposterous! Christ clearly said He would be in the grave for *three days and three nights*, and He banked the validity of who He was on this statement (Mat 12:38-39, Mat 16:1-4, Luke 11:19). He was not trying to be clever or cause confusion; He meant what He said.

> *"For as Jonas was three days and three nights in the whale's belly, so shall the Son of Man be three days and three nights in the heart of the earth."*
>   Matthew 12:40

Any other interpretation is preposterous. The 30-day month, 360-day year prophetic year theory, is not based upon solid biblical evidence as we have previously discussed. However, if we concede that this theory may have some basis in the book of Genesis (flood account), can it really be supported by the periods of time just studied in which the great tribulation period was shown to last exactly 1260 days and 42 months?

Let us examine the facts that we have put forth in our chronological study. Recall that we propose a natural and plausible start of Daniel's 70th week on Tishri 1, 458 BC... a Sabbatical year (458 BC - 457 BC). It would not stretch our imagination to assume that Daniel immediately *understood* that normal years were in view, and that they were tied to Sabbatical years. Daniel's 70 week prophecy is 490 years duration; which is mathematically 49 full sabbatical cycles of 7 years. After all, violation of 70 sabbatical years by the Nation of Israel is why he was there in the first place. He (and anyone else) would simply count off 483 years to when Messiah the Prince would appear. The only confusion or **mystery** is in what Julian year would the 490 year cycle begin? Daniels 70 weeks of years is rooted in the Jewish feast days; known to everyone of that time. Daniel could easily assume that the decree which initiated the 490 year count would coincide with a Sabbatical year, since 490 years are 70, 7 day sabbatical cycles. What he could not know is the calendar year and date in which the 490 year count would begin. Looking back, we have determined that the prophecy started on the Feast of Trumpets (Tishri 1,458 BC) and would terminate 490 years later on another Feast of Trumpets. We will discuss this at length when we look at the rapture of the church in Chapter 23. For now, we repeat from Chapter 7 that (1) Christ came to the River Jordan to be baptized by John shortly after 483 years had elapsed in 26 AD ..... Just as predicted. (2) After an earthly ministry of 3.5 years, *in the middle of Daniel's 70th week* Jesus Christ was crucified on Wednesday, Nisan 14; just three hours before the Passover supper was to be observed that evening. On the afternoon of Nisan 14 the Passover lamb was to be slain at 3:00 pm, and then prepared for the Passover Feast that evening. (3) Recall that Nisan 14 ended at 6:00 pm that day, and the next day,

Nisan 15, was the first day of the Feast of Unleavened Bread. The 70th week of Daniel was interrupted at that time *in the midst of Daniels 70th week*; approximately 3.5 years into the last 7 years of the 490 year prophecy.

Note carefully that we are not suggesting that the tribulation period is anything other than 1260 days over 42 months; this is still absolutely true. However, We would also point out that this combination of time periods does not prove that during the tribulation period, each month is 30 days long…although on the surface this might be a reasonable assumption. For example, a 1260 day 3.5 year period will result if alternating years of 29 and 31 days are used.

This curious passage of time might explain a very difficult and obscure passage in Dan 7:25 in which it was prophesied that he (the antichrist) will *intend to change times and the law.* We will suggest that based upon the research contained in this book, that the 1260 day reign of Satan, the Antichrist and the False

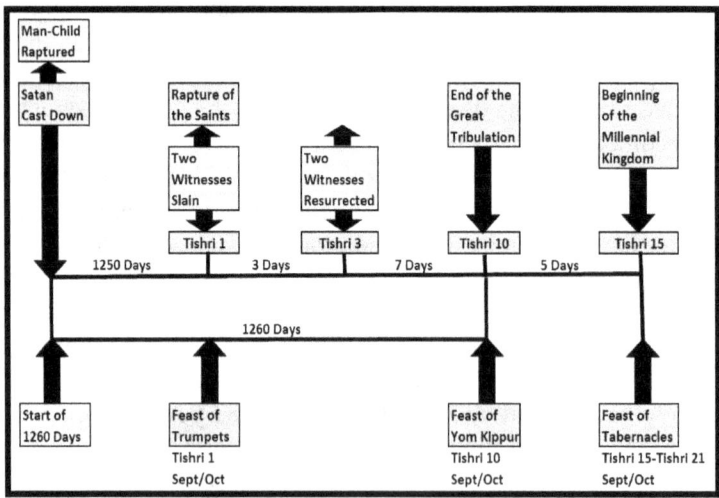

Prophet; and how this relates to the 1260 day tribulation period; are shown in the following graphic

We believe that the antichrist and the false prophet will arise on Tishri 10 after Satan and his fallen angels are cast down to the earth. The rapture of the saints will occur on Tishri 1, 1250 days later to fulfill three biblical truths.

(1) Christ said in the Olivet Discourse that:

"unless those days (the tribulation period) were shortened, no flesh would be saved, but for the elect's sake those days will be shortened." Matthew 24:22.

This is why the **elect** will be raptuired out before the 7 bowl judgments commence.

(2) No Christian is destined to go through the Wrath of God… which is the bowl judgments between Tishri 1 (Feast of Trumpets) and Tishri 10 (Feast of Yom Kippur).

(3) The antichrist, the false prophet and Satan & all his forces will be destroyed on "***The Lord's Day***", Nisan 10, the Feast of Yom Kippur.

Finding the Last Half of Daniel's 70th Week

Paul said in Colossians 2:16-17 that the Jewish feasts and celebrations were actually a *shadow* of the things to come through Jesus Christ. The Feasts of Israel provide a *blueprint* of the last seven years of Daniel's 490-year prophecy, and as we will see in the following chapters, this blueprint can be supported scripturally. Christ, the Messiah, is destined to fulfill all of the seven feasts of Israel. The first 3.5 years of the last seven years of Daniel's 70th week were the earthly ministry of Jesus Christ. His sacrificial death on the cross of Calvary perfectly fulfilled the pattern of the Feasts….. on this all theologians agree. He was the perfect *Passover Lamb* without spot or blemish; the acceptable atoning sacrifice to God; and the Lamb of God slain from the foundation of the world. He was crucified, dead and buried, and on the third day he rose from the grave on the first day of the Feast of Firstfruits. He is the *Bread of Life*, without sin. There was no *leaven* or sin upon him, except those sins he imputed to Himself of His own free will. He who knew no sin became sin for us. He was the perfect fulfillment of the Feast of

Passover, the Feast of Firstfruits and the Feast of Unleavened Bread. He is the *First of the Firstfruits*; the first of many sons and daughters to God; all who believe in his name. His resurrection from the dead was a guarantee to all of those who will become a part of His body, the same body that was victorious over death and the grave. Fifty (50) days after He rose from the grave, at the appointed time, He fulfilled His promise to send us a comforter: The Holy Spirit. The Holy Spirit fell on the disciples and all who believed on the day of Pentecost. The Day of Pentecost is the Christian name for the *Feast of Shavuot*. These four feasts (Passover, Unleavened bread, Firstfruits and Pentecost) were all in the spring of the year. There then passed many days until the last three feasts of Israel took place in the fall. These last three feasts are all observed in the month of September or October. The prophetic *clock* of Daniel's 70th week was interrupted on the day of our Lord's crucifixion. The Church Age began, and the new covenant which was established at Christ's death was now offered to Jews and Gentiles alike. The last half (3.5 years) of Daniel's 70th week will start again in some future spring month. The event which will begin the last 1260 days of Daniel's prophecy is clearly given in Rev 12:12.

"For the devil has come down to you, having great wrath, because he knows that he has a short time." Rev 12:12

That *short time* will end at the *Battle of Armageddon*, 1260 days or 42 months later: Daniel's 70th week and the battle of Armageddon will end on the Feast of Yom Kippur.

The first of the last three feasts of Israel to be fulfilled is the Feast of Rosh Hashanah or the *Feast of Trumpets* on Tishri 1 (in September or October). In Chapter 23 we will show beyond any reasonable doubt that the dead in Christ will rise on this day, and that the church will be raptured following the resurrection of the righteous dead. This very day the two witnesses will be slain after testifying for a *time, times and half a time*. The two witnesses will lie in a street of Jerusalem for three days, and then in the sight of Satan and his armies they will come to life and ascend to heaven. This event will usher in the final seven days of

Satan's rebellion and the Antichrist's reign. The apparent discrepancy between the period of time that the two witnesses are prophesying and the reign of the Antichrist is not a problem at all. There is no reason to force these two periods of time to exactly coincide. During the seven days between when the two witnesses are resurrected and the Battle of Armageddon, the *Wrath of God* will be poured out upon *all those who dwell on the earth (Rev 16:1)*. There will not be a single Christian left on earth to endure God's wrath, although there is no reason to doubt that many will accept Christ during these 7 days. In fact, this is when many Israelites will finally turn to Christ and accept Him as their long awaited Messiah. The Wrath of God is the seven bowl judgments. The seventh bowl will bring forth the great battle of Armageddon, at where Satan and all of his followers will be slain by Christ. The battle of Armageddon will occur on the *Feast of Yom Kippur* (Tishri 10). The battle will be short, and a victory celebration which follows will include the *Marriage Supper of the Lamb*, the *Bema Seat Judgment*, the *Rod Judgment*, the *Sheep and Goats judgment* and the casting of the antichrist and the false prophet into the lake of fire. We will discuss all of these in Chapter 28. Following the battle of Armageddon, Satan will be cast into the bottomless pit for 1000 years. Following these events will be the *Feast of Tabernacles*; a seven-day period of rest and celebration followed by the *last great day*; Tishri 22. The millennial kingdom of 1000 years will begin on Tishri 23 following the joyous union of Christ and all believers at the Feast of Tabernacles. Since the Feasts of Israel are the key to understanding the timing and relation of all major events in the 1260 day tribulation period, we will now devote an entire chapter to its discussion.

Thoughts and Things…..

Chapter 9

The Seven Feasts of Israel

It is impossible to correctly understand the sequence of end-time events without understanding the historical and prophetic meanings of the *Seven Feasts of Israel*. The seven feasts of Israel were ordained by God shortly after the law was given at Mt. Sinai following the exodus from Egypt. They were given for two reasons. The *first* was to commemorate the deliverance of Israel from Egyptian bondage and oppression. The *second* was to prophesy of seven events which will herald the first and second coming of Jesus Christ. The first four feasts are held in the spring, and the last three in the fall. The first four feasts were fulfilled at the death and resurrection of Jesus Christ. The last three will be fulfilled as the 70th week of Daniel and when this current age comes to a close.

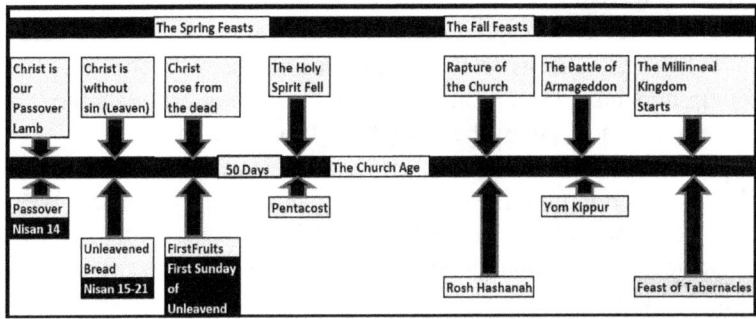

The seven feasts and their appointed time on the ancient Hebrew calendar are shown in the following table.

	Feast	Hebrew Date
1	Passover (Pesah)	Nisan 14
2	Unleavened Bread	Nisan 15-21
3	FirstFruits	Lasts 50 days, starting on 1st Sunday of Unleavened Bread
4	Pentecost (Weeks)	50th day of Feast of Weeks
5	Trumpets (Rosh Hashanna)	Tishri 1
6	Yom Kippur (Atonement)	Tishri 10
7	Tabernacles (Booths)	Tishri 15-22

The ancient Hebrew calendar was a lunar calendar. It was composed of 12 months alternating between 29 and 30 days per month. Each month started on the new moon. From new moon to new moon is approximately 29.5306 days. Since days must be whole numbers, it is obvious why they alternated between 29 and 30 days in length. Note that a 12-month year was 354 days long. This created a problem because a year is determined not by the moon, but by the sun, and a solar year is about 365 days in length (365.2422 days). Without some sort of adjustment, the Hebrew 354-day, 12-month year would *fall behind* a solar year at a rate of about 10.872 days every year. In other words, if unadjusted about every 17 years a fall festival would occur in the spring! It was determined long ago that to keep the two calendars (lunar and solar) in sync with one another, a 13th month of 29/30 days, called Adar II, was inserted seven times over a 19-year cycle. This proved to be very accurate, but because Adar II was inserted only periodically, the date of each of the seven feasts wandered through about two months. For example, Tishri 1 would some years start in September and some in October. Modern Jewish calendars use other sophisticated rules to regulate the yearly calendar and keep it in sync with a solar year, but each feast still *wanders* across two months. Modern computers have been programmed to accurately calculate the month, day and day of the week back through thousands of years. We will not elaborate further on the operation of the Jewish calendar, but it is a fascinating and rewarding study. We will now concentrate on what each festival means, both historically and prophetically, and refer to when each festival occurs by its Jewish name and Jewish calendar date. There is, however, one important historical event which we must explore: God's renumbering of the Hebrew calendar months at the exodus from Egypt. The Hebrew calendar has existed from earliest time. The ancient book of *Jubilees* records that Enoch *understood* the movement of the sun, moon and stars and was told by angels how calendars operate. In the flood account recorded in Genesis, it is clear that a calendar was in use. Moving forward in time, when the Children of Israel were in Egypt before the Exodus, there was a very good Egyptian calendar. It consisted of 12 months of 30 days, and at the end of every year five extra days were added. This made an Egyptian year 365 days long, so it only dropped back from the solar year about one day every four years. Even this made a large difference eventually. Both before and after the Exodus, we have no definitive biblical records of what calendar was used by the Hebrews. However, after the exodus from Egypt, the Feast of Firstfruits had to occur just as the barley crop was maturing in the field, because the high priest had to *wave a firstfruit* offering of barley to the Lord before anything could be harvested. It is clear that the month of Nisan was somehow started every year based upon how the crop was maturing, possibly by observing the crop of barley as it matured and inserting an extra month if the crop was not going to be ready for a firstfruits harvest on Nisan 15. Winding forward about 1000 years the nation of Israel fell to the Babylonian Empire. Virtually the whole nation was deported to Babylon for a period of 70 years for failing to observe Sabbatical and Jubilee years. The Babylonians had a deep knowledge of how calendars operated, and the Hebrews adopted both the Babylonian calindrical system and the names of each month with minor variations. We have biblical and historical records that confirm a sophisticated calendar was in effect and was being maintained by the Levitical priesthood soon after the Babylonian exile of 70 years had been completed.

As previously stated, the *Seven Feasts of Israel* are divided into two separate seasons of the year. The Feasts of Passover, Firstfruits, Unleavened Bread and Pentecost all take place in the spring. The last three Feasts of Rosh Hashanah, Yom Kippur, and Tabernacles take place in the fall. The feasts have a dual meaning; they commemorate the deliverance of the Hebrew nation from Egyptian bondage, and they also prophesy of the first and second coming of Jesus Christ. The Hebrew word for feast is *moed* which means a *set time* or an *appointed time*. God has not only set an appointed time for each feast, he has also commanded that every male in Israel must be at the place of his choice (Jerusalem) for the Feasts of Passover, Unleavened Bread, Pentecost and Tabernacles. The feasts are also called a *holy convocation*. The Hebrew word for convocation means *rehearsal*. The implication is that God has commanded the

Children of Israel to observe each feast at the *appointed time* as *a rehearsal* for seven things which will happen to Israel on those days. Looking back, it is now obvious that Jesus Christ fulfilled the first four feasts at His crucifixion between when He died on the cross of Calvary and when He sent the Holy Spirit to dwell in man on the Feast of Passover. The last three feasts will be fulfilled at the second advent of Christ. All seven feasts were divinely ordained by God and given to the nation of Israel for a perpetual observance.

The historical and physical aspects of each feast will now be briefly discussed.

The Spring Feasts

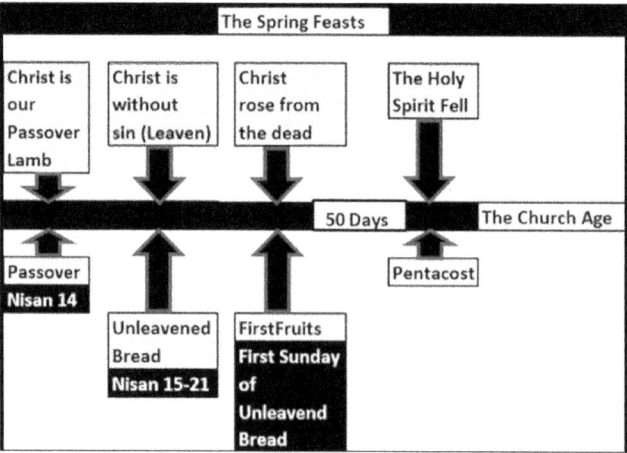

Feast of Passover (Nisan 14)

The Feast of Passover is in remembrance of the night that the Hebrew nation left Egypt on Nisan 15 (Exodus 12:2-11). On Nisan 10, God instructed the Children of Israel to select an unblemished lamb one year old and bring it into each house for four days. Each day the lamb was examined to make sure that it was still unblemished. On *Nisan 14* at 3:00 pm, they were instructed to slaughter the lamb and prepare it for the evening meal. The blood was to be caught in a bowl, and smeared over the lintel or over the door of each Hebrew house. The lamb was to be eaten that evening, which was actually the first few hours of Nisan 15. At midnight, the *Avenging Angel* of the Lord would pass over every house in Egypt. The firstborn male in any house without blood over the door would be killed, and the firstborn of all livestock outside the house would be killed (Gen 12:29). This was the event that caused the Pharaoh of Egypt to *let the people go* after his firstborn son was slain. The Feast of Passover was to commemorate and recall remembrance of this event for perpetual generations.

Spiritual Application: Jesus Christ arrived in Jerusalem on Nisan 10 (after 6:00pm) and stayed at the house of Lazarus exactly four days before He was to be crucified on Nisan 14. He was examined and scrutinized by the Sadducees and Pharisees who sought to discredit Him. He was found to be without spot or blemish. Pilate even declared: ***Then said Pilate to the chief priests and to the people, I find no fault in this man*** (Luke 23:4). Christ completely fulfilled the Feast of Passover when He was crucified on the cross of Calvary.

> *"For even Christ our Passover is sacrificed for us."*
> I Corinthians 5:7

> *"The next day John seeth Jesus coming unto him, and saith, Behold the Lamb of God, which taketh away the sin of the world."* John 1:29

The word *Passover* is literally translated *Lamb* and Christ is God's perfect Passover sacrificial lamb. He was both the sacrifice and the one who offered the sacrifice.

> *"For even Christ our Passover is sacrificed for us."*
> I Corinthians 5:7

Our Lord Jesus Christ died for our sins at 3:00 pm on Nisan 14, at exactly the same time that the High Priest was killing the Passover Lamb in the temple. At that time the veil that separated the Holy Place from the Holy of Holies was *rent in two* from top to bottom, signifying that the Levitical sacrificial system had ended. The old covenant had passed away; the new covenant had now come.

Feast of Unleavened Bread (Nisan 15-21)

The Feast of Unleavened Bread is a memorial to when the Children of Israel left Egypt in haste on the evening of Nisan 14, which was the night portion of Nisan 15. The Feast of Unleavened Bread started at 6:00 pm on Wednesday and continued for seven full days until 6:00 pm on Nisan 21. It is important to note that both Nisan 15 and Nisan 21 were designated as a *High Sabbath*. On these days there was to be no unleavened bread in any household. No servile work was to be done on these days, and if food is to be consumed it must be prepared by the family in their house. The Exodus from Egypt was sudden. In Exodus 12 we are told: ***So the people took their dough before it was leavened, having their kneading bowls bound and in their clothes on their shoulders*** (Exodus 12:34). When the Feast of Unleavened Bread was observed in subsequent years, starting with Nisan 15 there was to be no leavened bread at all in any household for seven days. All leaven was to be removed on Nisan 14. This was serious business.

> ***"For seven days no leaven shall be found in your houses, since whoever eats what is leavened, that same person shall be cut off from the congregation of Israel, whether he is a stranger or a native of the land."*** Exodus 12:19

In Exodus 16:2, the Israelites complained that they had no food, so God miraculously provided *manna* to them every day. The manna was picked in the morning on Sunday-Friday. It only lasted one day; the manna picked on Friday morning lasted two days and then spoiled on the third day to honor the Jewish Sabbath (Saturday). Moses put a *pot of manna* into the Ark of the Covenant; it *never* spoiled.

Spiritual Application: In the scriptures, *leaven* is representative of *sin*. Our Lord Jesus Christ fulfilled all of the law. His life was perfect in every way. He was the unleavened, sinless bread from heaven. Since He was sinless, He was without *spot or blemish*.

He was resurrected and lifted up to God, and He was an acceptable and perfect sacrifice to God.

> *"Your glorying is not good. Know ye not that a little leaven leaveneth the whole lump? Purge out therefore the old leaven, that ye may be a new lump, as ye are unleavened. For even Christ our Passover is sacrificed for us."*
> I Corinthians 5:6-7

Our Lord Jesus Christ said that He was the Unleavened Bread which fulfilled the feast.

> *"And as they did eat, Jesus took bread, and blessed, and brake it, and gave to them, and said, Take, eat: this is my body."* Mark 14:22

> *"And Jesus said unto them, I am the bread of life: he that cometh to me shall never hunger; and he that believeth on me shall never thirst."* John 6:35

> *"I am the bread of life. He who comes to me shall never hunger."* John 6:35

He was also the *manna that never spoiled*, eternally perfect.

> *"I am the living bread which came down from heaven: if any man eat of this bread, he shall live forever: and the bread that I will give is my flesh, which I will give for the life of the world. This is that bread which came down from heaven: not as your fathers did eat manna, and are dead: he that eateth of this bread shall live forever."*
> John 6:51, 58

Christ was crucified on Nisan 14. He *gave up the ghost* and died at 3:00 pm, at exactly the same time that the High Priest in Herod's Temple slaughtered the Passover lamb. Jesus was placed in the tomb just in time to fulfill the *Feast of Unleavened Bread* which started at 6:00 pm on Wednesday night. Jesus was our perfect Passover Lamb, without spot or blemish. He was also the perfect *Bread of Life*, without leaven (sin).

Feast of Firstfruits
The Feast of Firstfruits is also called the *Feast of Weeks*. Unlike the Feast of Passover and the Feast of Unleavened Bread, it has a specific time when it is observed, but not a specific day of the month.

> *"Speak unto the Children of Israel, and say unto them, When ye be come into the land which I give unto you, and shall reap the harvest thereof, then ye shall bring a sheaf of the firstfruits of your harvest unto the priest: And he shall wave the sheaf before the LORD, to be accepted for you: on the morrow after the Sabbath the priest shall wave it. And ye shall offer that day when ye wave the sheaf and the lamb without blemish of the first year for a burnt offering unto the LORD. And the meat offering thereof shall be two tenth deals of fine flour mingled with oil, an offering made by fire unto the LORD for a sweet savour: and the drink offering thereof shall be of wine, the fourth part of an hin. And ye shall eat neither bread, nor parched corn, nor green ears, until the selfsame day that ye have brought an offering unto your God: it shall be a statute forever throughout your generations in all your dwellings. And ye shall count unto you from the morrow after the sabbath, from the day that ye brought the sheaf of the wave offering; seven sabbaths shall be complete: Even unto the morrow after the seventh sabbath shall ye number fifty days; and ye shall offer a new meat offering unto the Lord."*   Leviticus 23:10-16

The Feast of Firstfruits starts on the *morrow after the Sabbath*. There was a raging battle between the Pharisees and the Sadducees as to what this means. The first day of the Feast of Unleavened Bread was a *Sabbath*, a High Sabbath. The Pharisees held that the Feast of Firstfruits started on Nisan 16 every year, while the Sadducees maintained that it started on the day after the *weekly Sabbath* (Saturday).The above passage says that *seven Sabbaths must be complete* in the 50-day period. This seems to refer to seven complete weeks. This will happen every year if the feast starts on the Sunday following the only Sabbath (Saturday) of Unleavened Bread. Eventually the Sadducees prevailed but the controversy remained. The real key is in the spiritual fulfillment of this feast by Jesus Christ. Christ rose early on a Sunday, and he is the *firstfruits* of the church, so the feast must also begin on a Sunday to satisfy typology. In the time of Jesus, the Feasts of Passover, Unleavened Bread and Firstfruits were considered to be one long feast season which was generally referred to as the *Passover Season*. It was not uncommon to refer to all three as simply *Passover*. The Feast of Firstfruits lasted seven days and is observed in the spring. It signified the early maturation of the barley crop. The Feast of Firstfruits was ritually observed by all Jews throughout the temple eras. The *Firstfruit Offerings* were to both please God and to support the Levitical priesthood (Lev 23:10-17, Exodus 23:19, Deut 26:1-11). On the first day of the feast, a *sheaf of barley*, which was an omer (about 2 quarts), was to be picked from the fields and offered up to God as a wave offering. It was *waved before the Lord* in a sheaf.

Spiritual Application: The firstfruits sheaf was also symbolic of the greater harvest to come, if it pleased the Lord. If the firstfruit was holy, then the entire harvest would be holy unto the Lord. Paul confirmed the spiritual intent of the firstfruit offering, and directly related it to the *root* (Israel) and the *branches* (the body of Christ).

> ***"For if the firstfruit be holy, the lump is also holy: and if the root be holy, so are the branches."***   Romans 11:16

The firstfruit offering consecrated the entire harvest to the Lord. It was an *earnest offering* or a *pledge* of the full harvest which was yet to come. It was very important, because no barley from the field could be picked or eaten until the ceremony was completed. In fact, ancient tradition held that on Nisan 1 the High Priest would inspect the *barley in the ear*. The word Nisan actually means green ear. If the crop had not matured enough by Nisan 1 to pick a *wavesheaf* on Nisan 15, then an extra month of

29/30 days called *Adar II* would be immediately added to the year. While not exact, this was elegant in its simplicity. Periodic insertion of an extra month kept the Jewish lunar-based calendar from getting very far *out of sync* with the solar calendar and the agricultural seasons. It is not known when the *Metonic cycle* was discovered, and exact insertion rules were put into place, but a sophisticated system appeared to be in operation shortly after the Babylonian exile had ended.

> **"The first of the firstfruits of thy land thou shalt bring unto the house of the LORD thy God."**   Ex 34:26

How beautiful and prophetic was the firstfruit offering! Christ is everywhere present in the typology. The offering was to be made of *green ears* of corn that would be dried in the fire. Was not our Lord Jesus Christ *tried as if in the fire* by the Pharisees and Sadducees? Was He not tempted at every turn just as we are today? After being offered to the Lord, the dried corn was then to be *beaten* out of the ear for food for the Levites. Was not our Lord Jesus Christ *beaten and bruised* for our sins, and then accepted by God as the firstfruit offering? *Oil* was also to be poured over the firstfruits offering; did Jesus not pour out the *oil* of the Holy Spirit on the day of Pentecost? Today the Feast of Firstfruits is observed by Christians for one day only and is called *Easter*. It is appropriate that Christians observe the resurrection of our risen Savior, but the modern observance called *Easter* has been corrupted. The modern observance of Easter was initiated by the Roman Catholic Church, and received its name from the Babylonian goddess, *Ishtar.* Ishtar is the pagan god of fertility, love, and sex; and that is why eggs are a part of the modern Easter celebration. The same thing is true as to why rabbits are part of the pageantry. Although children use rabbits, colored eggs and green grass to celebrate Easter, adult Christians observe Easter as the day of our Lord's resurrection from the dead. Instead of calling this celebration *Easter*, we should call it *firstfruits*. The festival is also called the *Feast of Weeks*, since it lasts exactly seven weeks (49 days) and one day. The 50th and final day is called *Shavuot* by the Jews. In 1491 BC the Children of Israel left Egypt during the night of Nisan 15 (Wednesday evening; Thursday on the Jewish calendar). Three days later they crossed the *Sea of Reeds*. They emerged on the other side a free nation, miraculously saved from the armies of the Pharaoh when God drowned all of the pursuers in the Red Sea. Fifty days later, they were given the law by God at Mt. Sinai. On the first day of the Feast of Firstfruits a remarkable thing happened. On that day, our Lord Jesus Christ rose from the grave. Christ arose just as Sunday was *dawning* or about to start just after 6:00 pm. There is no proof in the scriptures that Christ rose from the grave just before daylight on Sunday morning. This is another story that the Catholic Church instituted. To be clear, there is no problem in celebrating Christ's resurrection at a *sunrise service* on Sunday morning, it is holy that we should do so. The point is just that Christ rose early that previous evening just as Sunday began Nisan 17, and not just before sunrise.

> *"But now is Christ risen from the dead, and become the firstfruits of them that slept."* I Corinthians 15:20

Christ was the *First of the Firstfruits*. He was not the only person that had been resurrected from the dead; but he was the first to ascend to heaven, receive His glorified body, and not taste death again.

> *"For if the firstfruit be holy, the lump is also holy: and if the root be holy, so are the branches."* Romans 11:16

Christ is the vine and we are the branches. Christ spoke of this during his earthly ministry.

> *"And Jesus answered them, saying, The hour is come, that the Son of man should be glorified. Verily, verily, I say unto you, except a corn of wheat fall into the ground and die, it abideth alone: but if it die, it bringeth forth much fruit. He that loveth his life shall lose it; and he that hateth his life in this world shall keep it unto life eternal. If any man serve me, let him follow me; and where I am, there shall also my servant be: if any man serve me, him will my Father honour."* John 12:23-26

The Apostle Paul made an astonishing statement in his first letter to Corinth.

> *"But now is Christ risen from the dead, and become the firstfruits of them that slept. For since by man came death, by man came also the resurrection of the dead. For as in Adam all die, even so in Christ shall all be made alive. But every man in his own order: Christ the firstfruits; afterward they that are Christ's at his coming. Then cometh the end, when he shall have delivered up the kingdom to God, even the Father; when he shall have put down all rule and all authority and power."*   I Corinthians 15:20-24

Christ is clearly called the *firstfruits* of all that *slept* (died). He then goes on to say that following Christ there will one day be a resurrection of the dead. After that, the end (of the age) will come and all *powers, authorities and rulers* will be put under His feet. There is no indication whatsoever that there will be a seven-year period of time between when the resurrection of the dead will occur and the *end*.

Pentecost

The last day of the Feast of Firstfruits is called *Shavuot*, which we call *Pentecost*. Jewish tradition teaches that on the day of Pentecost the law was given to Israel on Mt. Sinai. There were 50 days that elapsed between when the Children of Israel emerged a new nation out of the Sea of Reeds, and when the law was given on Mt. Sinai. The word *Pentecost* is derived from the Greek word *Penta*, which means fifty. Israel departed Egypt on Nisan 15, and emerged from the Sea of Reeds three days later. This is exactly the same day that Jesus Christ emerged from the grave. In typology, a Friday crucifixion declared by the Roman Catholic Church and the subsequent resurrection from the grave on Sunday is impossible. The Israelites had to move quickly and take a full three days between when they left Egypt and when they arrived at the Red Sea. There is simply no getting around a *full* three-day journey. In order to satisfy type, Christ was in the grave for a *full* three days and three nights. The Children of Israel then traveled 47 days until they finally reached Mt. Sinai.

The Lord told the people to sanctify themselves for two days (Gen 19:10), and on the *third* day He would come down to them in a cloud. On the *50th day* after emerging from the Red Sea the Lord kept his promise and appeared to the people. A *Shofar* (trumpet made of the rams horn) was loudly sounded: louder, and louder, and louder until *fire* was seen on the mountain. A mighty wind blew and the ground shook as if an earthquake was going to occur. At that point God began to deliver the law to Moses and the nation of Israel. It is taught that every nation and every tongue heard the Lord in their own language. According to tradition, there was the Hebrew language and 69 other languages spoken throughout the world. In a miraculous and divine act, the voice of God was divided into *70 different tongues*. It is also taught by the Rabbis that as God spoke, the Children of Israel not only heard the words but actually saw each word emerging from the cloud as *tongues of fire*. The words encircled the camp and then entered each person individually. After each commandment was given, God asked: ***Do you accept upon yourself this commandment?*** and everyone present answered *yes*. The tongues of fire then fell upon stone tablets and the words of the law were recorded. The Jewish Feast of Shavuot on the 50th day commemorates these events (Joseph Good)

Spiritual Application: When Christ ascended from the grave he commanded his disciples to *go unto Jerusalem* and wait for Him to come to them.

> ***"And when the day of Pentecost was fully come, they were all with one accord in one place. And suddenly there came a sound from heaven as of a rushing mighty wind, and it filled all the house where they were sitting. And there appeared unto them cloven tongues like as of fire, and it sat upon each of them. And they were all filled with the Holy Ghost, and began to speak with other tongues, as the Spirit gave them utterance. And there were dwelling at Jerusalem Jews, devout men, out of every nation under heaven. Now when this was noised abroad, the multitude came together, and were confounded, because that every man heard them speak in his own language."***   Acts 2:1-6

What an amazing event!! On the very day that God gave the law to the people on Mt. Sinai, Jesus Christ gave the Holy Spirit to his chosen people. The falling of the Holy Spirit at Pentecost in 30 AD almost exactly paralleled the giving of the law 1500 years earlier. The law was written on tablets of stone. The *old covenant* was based upon man fulfilling the law, which was impossible. The *new covenant* was based upon grace, and written on the heart of man. The impossible task of living a perfect life under the law was fulfilled in every way by our Lord Jesus Christ, who then imputed His righteousness to all who believed in His name. Only Jesus Christ fulfilled every *"jot and tidle"* of the law. He was our *perfect Passover sacrifice for sin*, the Lamb of God. He was the *Firstfruits* offering waved before the Lord by Christ himself. He was both the *offerer* and the *offering*, our eternal High Priest. The old covenant that God had established with His people required obedience to the Old Testament Mosaic law. Because the wages of sin is death (Romans 6:23), the law required that people perform rituals and sacrifices in order to please God and temporarily cover their sins. The prophet Jeremiah predicted that there would be a time when God would make a new covenant with the nation of Israel.

> ***"The day will come" said the Lord, "when I will make a new covenant with the people of Israel and Judah… But this is the new covenant I will make with the people of Israel on that day, says the Lord. I will put my law in their minds, and I will write them on their hearts. I will be their God, and they will be my people."*** Jeremiah 31:31, 33.

Jesus Christ came to fulfill all of the Law of Moses (Matt 5:17) and create a new covenant between God and His people. He is now our High Priest who sits on the throne of God and continually intercedes for us.

> ***"This is the covenant that I will make with them after those days, saith the Lord, I will put my laws into their hearts, and in their minds will I write them."*** Hebrews 10:16

The old covenant was written in stone, but the new covenant is written on our hearts, made possible only by faith in Christ, who shed His own blood to atone for the sins of the world.

> *"And he took bread, and gave thanks, and brake it, and gave unto them, saying, This is my body which is given for you: this do in remembrance of me. Likewise also the cup after supper, saying, this cup is the new testament in my blood, which is shed for you."* Luke 22:19-20

Now that we are under the new covenant, we are not under the penalty of the law. We are now given the opportunity to receive salvation as a free gift (Eph 2:8-9). Through the life-giving Holy Spirit who lives in all believers (Romans 8:9-11), we can now share in the inheritance of Christ.

> *"For this reason Christ is the mediator of a new covenant, that those who are called may receive the promised eternal inheritance—now that He has died as a ransom to set them free from the sins committed under the first covenant."*
> Hebrews 9:15

Summary of the First Four (spring) Feasts of Israel

The spring feasts of Israel are (1) Passover, (2) Unleavened Bread, (3) First Fruits and (4) Pentecost. Each of these feasts was to provide historical and prophetic truth to the Children of Israel. Christ fulfilled each of these first four feasts at the end of his 3.5 year earthly ministry. **Passover**: Christ was the perfect Passover Lamb, slain from the foundation of the world. **Unleavened Bread**: Christ was without sin (leaven). He fulfilled the laws given to Moses by God in every way. He is our *bread of life*, and whosoever will eat of His bread will never hunger. **Firstfruits**: Christ was the perfect firstfruits offering waved before the Lord and fully accepted. He was the *first* to be raised from the grave never to die again. **Pentecost**: Christ ratified the *new covenant* on the Feast of Pentecost 50 days after he arose from the grave, He offered the Holy Spirit as our comforter and guarantee. Salvation is now offered free to all who believe that Jesus Christ is the only Son of God. The curse of the law has been replaced by amazing grace. We who are now called *Christians* can live life *more abundantly*. Every feast was a *moed*, a *set time* or an *appointed time*. The feasts are also called a *holy convocation*. The Hebrew word for convocation means *rehearsal*. Paul referred to this:

> **"Let no one judge you in food or in drink, or regarding a festival or a new moon or Sabbaths, which are a shadow of things to come, but the substance is of Christ."** Col 2:16-17

It is more than interesting that God commanded that every Jewish male appear in Jerusalem at the Feasts of Unleavened Bread; the Feast of Pentecost; and the Feast of Tabernacles (Ex 23:14, Deut 16:6). God was not only calling Israel to a time of remembrance, but he was preparing Israel for the appearance of their long-awaited Messiah in the person of Jesus Christ. All males were to witness the crucifixion of Christ (Passover) in 30 AD which was the day before the Feast of Unleavened Bread Started at 6:00 PM). The *Parakletos (*Holy Spirit) fell on the Feast of Shavuot (Pentecost); All Jewish males (and their families) who will accept Christ as their savior will be required to participate in the last Feast of Tabernacles to celebrate Christ's victory at Armageddon (Zach 14:16-19). It is strange that after all that was prophesied in the Old Testament, and all that was written by the prophets of His ministry here on earth, that the Children of Israel failed to recognize or accept Christ as their long awaited Messiah. We have shown how Christ satisfied and fulfilled each of the four spring festivals at exactly the appointed times; on exactly the appointed days; and exactly in type and substance.

Date	Feast or Event	Typology	Fulfillment
Nisan 10	The Passover Lamb is Selected. *"Bring an unblemished Lamb into the house on Nisan 10, Four days before it is to be slain And inspect it for spot or blemish"* Ex.12:3-6	God commands Israel in Egypt To select a Passover Lamb for slaughter On Nisan 14.	Jesus, the perfect Lamb of God, arrives in Bethany four days Before his crucifixion. He stood In the temple each day and was questioned by the Pharisees and Sadducees to find fault in him

Date	Feast or Event	Exodus Typology	Fulfillment by Christ
Nisan 15	First day of the Feast of Unleavened bread. A loaf of bread is baked from the Firstfruits of Barley (Old Testament Saints). It was prepared without leaven. It was offered to the Lord *"with fire"*.	The Pharaoh let *"the Children of Israel go"* after his firstborn son was slain. The departure is in haste. The bread they took with them was unleavened	Christ lay in the grave the first day. He is the *"loaf without leaven"*. He said *"I am the bread of life"*. He is the *"first"* and only to live a sinless life under the law. John said he will *"baptize you with water and fire"*
Nisan 15-21	The Feast of Unleavened Bread lasted 7 days. Both the first and last day of the feast were *"high holy"* days... Sabbath days	The Children of Israel ate unleavened bread until God gave them *"manna"* from heaven.	Christ said "I am the Bread of Life". He was the true bread without leaven. He was sinless and blameless.
First Sunday in the Feast of Unleavened Bread	Feast of Firstfruits starts on this day...always a Sunday. The Feast lasts 50 days. Every day a sheath of the emerging wheat crop is *"waved"* before the Lord. Also called the "Feast of Weeks".	On this day the Children of Israel crossed over the *"Sea of Reeds"*, and was saved from death at the Pharaoh's hand. They emerged a new Nation under God.	Christ arose from the dead on this day. He was the *"Firstfruit"* unto God of all who will someday also rise from the grave by believing upon His name.
Last Sunday of the Feast of Firstfruit	The Feast of Pentecost or Shavuot. "Penta" means fifty. Pentecost occurs 50 days after the first Sabbath (Saturday) in the Feast of Unleavened bread.	The Nation of Israel received the law from God at Mt. Sinai. The law was written on tablets of stone. The Levitical Priesthood was established. The High Priest was anointed to serve as the intercessor between man and God	On the Day of Pentecost Christ fulfilled his promise to leave with us an advocate: The Holy Spirit. On the day of Pentecost the Holy Spirit fell on the disciples and 5,000 people were saved. The new covenant based upon grace replaced the old covenant based upon the law. This new law of grace is written in the heart and not in stone

The first four feasts of Israel have been satisfied both spiritually and physically. Their implications cannot be misunderstood by either Jew or Gentile if carefully studied.

The Fall Feasts of Israel

We have seen how Christ exactly fulfilled each of the four spring feasts of Israel at his first coming. It is not difficult at all to believe that He will also fulfill each of the last three feasts of Israel at his second coming. It remains to be seen exactly when this will be accomplished, but the prophetic fulfillment and relevance of each feast can be determined. The last three feasts are partly concealed; and of course hindsight in studying the first four feasts is always better than foresight. Since all of the feasts are Jewish in nature, we would be wise to examine what Jewish tradition has to say about the last three feasts. In doing so, we will unveil a complete understanding of how we might expect this age of grace to come to an end. If Christ is going to satisfy the last three feasts at his *Second Advent*, we can say with certainty that this will come to pass at the end of Daniel's last and 70th week. The events we will describe can only occur as Christ returns to the earth to reclaim it for His eternal kingdom; set up His throne in Jerusalem; and purge all evil from the nations. The following diagram shows the relative timetable for these three final feasts. They are:

(1) ***The Feast of Rosh Hashanah*** (*Feast of Trumpets*);
(2) ***The Feast of Yom Kippur*** (*Feast of Yom Teruah*) and
(3) ***The Feast of Tabernacles*** (*Feast of Booths).*

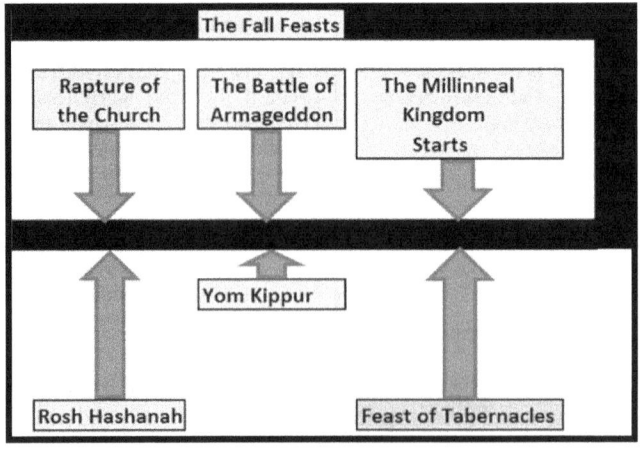

The three fall feasts all occur in the Jewish month of *Tishri*. Tishri is the first month of the *Jewish Civil Calendar* and the seventh month of the Jewish religious calendar. All three feasts will occur in a 22-day period of time in one of the Gregorian calendar months of September or October. Like the spring festivals, they are closely aligned and associated with the agricultural cycle. The month of *Nisan* brings forth the new crops of barley (Jews) and wheat (Gentiles). The month of Tishri ushers in the final harvest of wheat, corn, grapes and figs. Both the spring and fall festivals require rain to bring the precious fruit of the earth into full maturity.

> ***"Therefore be patient, brethren, until the coming of the Lord. See how the farmer waits for the precious fruit of the earth, waiting patiently for it until it receives the early and the latter rain."***   James 5:7

The early rains fell on the newborn body of Christ on the day of Pentecost in 30 AD. We have been patiently waiting for the *latter rains* to fall when Christ returns for His second advent. As previously noted, the feasts represent both historical and spiritual significance. Historically they represent significant events that occurred when God chose Moses to lead His people out of Egyptian bondage. Spiritually, each feast is a rehearsal or an appointment that God has made for Jesus Christ at His second advent.

There is an interesting correlation between the civil and the religious calendar. The civil calendar starts in September or October on Tishri 1. This is said to be the birthday of the creation of the world and the day on which Abraham was born. It is also when the wheat crop came to fullness and was harvested. The religious calendar begins in the month of March/April on Nisan 1. Nisan 1 is when the barley crop was coming into maturity and the wheat crop was starting to really grow. For those who have accepted the vicarious sacrifice of Jesus Christ on Nisan 14, the promise of resurrection from the dead and the gift of the Holy Spirit to every believer, the month of Nisan represents new beginnings in their spiritual relationship with Jesus Christ.

As we have already observed, there are almost 120 days between the Feast of *Pentecost* and the Feast of *Rosh Hashanah*. This is the long growing season for the precious crop of wheat. The wheat maturing and growing to the harvest is a shadow and type of the church age. The body of Christ is growing and one day God will declare that the harvest season is near. We will not be surprised when the **war in the heavenlies** is seen (Rev 12) and Satan is cast down to the earth. At that time we will know that the tribulation period has begun. It is a fallacy that believers will not know when the end is approaching. There will be plenty of heavenly and earthly signs for those who are watching. It is certainly true that only God will know when the tribulation period will begin and on what calendar day the church age will end, but Paul in his first letter to the Thessalonians assured them that while the end will come suddenly, they were not to be unaware of what is about to happen. If this was true then, it is true now.

> ***"But concerning the times and the seasons, brethren, you have no need that I should write to you. For you yourselves know perfectly that the Day of the Lord so comes as a thief in the night. For when they say "peace and safety" then sudden destruction comes upon them, as labor pains upon a pregnant woman. And they shall not escape. But you, brethren, are not in darkness, so that this day should overtake you as a thief.*** I Thessalonians 5:1-4

Notice that the apostle Paul is not denying that destruction and the Day of the Lord will come suddenly, but he emphatically and clearly assures them that they will not be surprised. Why would Paul assure them (and us) of this if it is not true? One thing should be pointed out which is highly relevant to our study. In the Jewish mind, the Feasts of Rosh Hashanah, Yom Kippur and Tabernacles are separate feasts, but the Jews consider this time of year to form one season containing the three feasts, just as the first four feasts were generally called Passover.

The Feast of Trumpets (Feast of Rosh Hashanah)

The next feast of Israel that Christ is appointed to fulfill is commonly known as the *Feast of Trumpets*. What will this feast ultimately accomplish according to Jewish teaching? The answer might surprise most Christian readers. Sometime in the future, the Feast of Trumpets will be a time of great joy. The following events are taught to occur on the last Feast of Trumpets.

- The long-awaited Messiah of Israel will finally come on that day,
- The dead will be raised and given a body just like that of Adam and Eve before the fall,
- The earth will be restored to its former Edenic state,
- All men will be judged at this time,
- The Wedding Feast of the Messiah will take place,
- God's covenant with Israel concerning inheriting the land of promise will finally come to pass.

According to Jewish tradition, this *final Feast of Trumpets* will be initiated by the blast of a *shofar*. The *shofar* is not a normal horn, but is said to have been reserved for this special occasion since the *binding of Isaac*. Recall that God commanded Abraham to sacrifice his only son of promise, Isaac. As Abraham raised his knife to kill his son, God stayed his hand and delivered a ram as the substitute sacrifice. The ram was to be burned completely as a *burnt offering*. The only thing left was the two ram's horns. The *first horn* was said to have been blown on Mt. Sinai when the law was given; the *second horn* is reserved for the *last trump* at the last Feast of Rosh Hashanah (Trumpets). A special season which includes the Feast of Trumpets is called *"Teshuvah"*. It begins on the first day of the month of *Elul*, which immediately precedes the month of *Tishri*. Teshuvah lasts 40 days, and ends on the Feast of Yom *Kippur* (Tishri 10). The Feast of Trumpets starts 30 days into the season of *Teshuvah* on Tishri 1. It is relevant that every morning during the month of Elul, a trumpet is sounded to warn all the people that the time has come to repent of their sins and return to God. Ask any orthodox Jew what the *last trump* means in relation to the ancient feasts of Israel and the period of Teshuvah, and he will immediately respond the last trump is the *shofar*, which will be blown at the last Feast of Rosh Hashanah. *On the last Feast of Trumpets,* it is taught that there are several books which will be opened. The first is the **Book of Remembrance**.

> ***"Then they that fear the Lord spake often to one another: and the Lord hearkened, and heard it, and a Book of Remembrance was written before him for them that feared the Lord, and that thought upon his name."*** Malachi 3:16

The second is actually *three sets of books*. Those who have committed to God and turned to righteousness are written in the *Book of the Righteous* or the **Book of Life** for the coming year. All other people living and dead are then divided into two groups. The first group is written into a book called the *Book of Rashim*, or the *Book of the Totally Wicked*. These are those who have totally rejected God and would not turn away from unrighteousness. The third or *last book* contains the names of those still alive who are not yet judged to be totally wicked, but have not yet fully repented and returned to God. Those people will have *ten more days* before their fate is sealed. These 10 days are called the *Days of Awe* and are the days between Nisan 1 and Nisan 10. The *Feast of Yom Kippur* occurs on only one day: Nisan 10. For this reason, the Feast of Yom Kippur is called the *Day of Judgment*. If these *gleanings* left in the *field* do not repent and turn away from sin by Tishri 10, their names will not be inscribed in the **Book of Life** for the coming year. If all of this sounds familiar to you, then it should. We have steadfastly maintained in this book that at the Feast of Trumpets, at the *last trump*, the rapture of the church will occur and the dead in Christ will rise to meet Christ in the air. These saints will receive their new, glorified, eternal bodies (Rev 11:15-18). This will then initiate the **Marriage of the Lamb** (Rev 19:7). The saints who are raptured and raised from the dead are those who have had their names inscribed in the **Lamb's Book of Life** (Rev 21:27). The 10 days between the Feast of Trumpets and the Feast of

Yom Kippur will be the last chance for all who remain after the rapture to escape eternal damnation. Those who reach the next feast, the *Feast of Yom Kippur*, without accepting Christ as their savior will be cast into the *bottomless pit* for 1000 years, and after the millennial kingdom they will be raised and judged at the *Great White Throne Judgment*; they will then be cast into the *lake of burning fire* (Rev 20:13). It is a sad thing, but failure of anyone to accept Jesus Christ as their personal Savior before they die is an irrevocable decision. There is no second chance.

There is yet another group of people to recognize: these are those who have missed the rapture; still alive at the Feast of Yom Kippur; and have accepted Christ as their Savior during the 10 days of repentance. This group is entirely hidden from Jewish teachings since they do not yet recognize Christ as Messiah and King. That group will pass into the millennial kingdom with the 144,000 that were sealed in Rev 7. They will have gone through the Wrath of God, which is the *seven bowl judgments* poured out on the earth between Nisan 1 and Nisan 10. Both our view of end-time events and the Jewish view of their salvation are perfectly aligned and consistent. The only difference is that the Jewish nation as a whole has been *blinded in part* until the scales are removed from their eyes and they can see. The Jewish nation as a whole is looking for their messiah to arise and save them; their conquering king is called *Messiah Ben David*, not Jesus Christ.

> *"But even if our gospel is veiled, it is veiled to those who are perishing. Whose minds the god of this age has blinded, who do not believe, lest the light of the gospel of the glory of Christ, who is the image of God should shine upon them."*
> II Corinthians 4:3-4

Christ severely rebuked the church at Laodicea for believing in the world and not Him.

> *"Because you say, I am rich, have become wealthy, and have need of nothing, and do not know that you are*

wretched, miserable, poor, blind and naked, I will spew (vomit) you out of my mouth."   Rev 3:17, 16

The Feast of Yom Kippur (Yom Teruah)

The Feast of Yom Kippur is on Tishri 10, which is also known as the *Feast of Atonement*. This day was a *holy convocation* and it was also a day of *fasting*. It was being observed when Nadab and Abihu, the two sons of Aaron, filled a censor with *profane fire* and used it to offer up incense in the Holy Place. Fire (coals) was not to be used at the Altar of Incense unless it came from the Brazen Altar. After their death, Aaron the high priest was told that he could not come before the Lord in the Holy of Holies without observing strict laws put down by God (Lev 16). The only day of the year that the high priest could come before God was on the *Day of Atonement*. On that day he would make a sacrifice for his sins, and then for the sins of the people. It was also on this day that two goats were chosen for a special offering to the Lord. One goat was for a sin offering unto the Lord, the other was to be led away into the wilderness and pushed over a high cliff outside of Jerusalem. This was called the *scapegoat*. The high priest would choose which goat would be the scapegoat by using the *Urim* and the *Thummin*. Once the scapegoat was chosen, a red scarlet cloth was tied around his horns, and the high priest would place his hands on the scapegoat, symbolically transferring the sins of the people to that goat. The scapegoat was then led away to a high cliff outside of the city and pushed to its death, symbolically representing the *removal of sin from the people*. The other goat was then sacrificed and his blood caught in a bowl. After cleansing himself again, the high priest would sprinkle the blood on the *Altar of Incense*, and then enter into the *Holy of Holies* behind the veil which separated the Holy Place from the Holy of Holies, where the Ark of the Covenant stood. The High Priest would come before the Ark and sprinkle the blood *seven times* on the *mercy seat*. The High Priest would then plead the sins of the people to God, who would come and dwell above the mercy seat in a cloud (Gaster). This is clearly a picture of Jesus Christ. He was *the scapegoat* who was led outside the city and put to death. Like the scapegoat, He took the sins of the world upon himself. *He who knew no sin became sin for us*. He was also the *sin offering* represented by the second goat. His precious blood was shed for us; it was sprinkled on everyone from Adam to the millennial kingdom, and He sprinkled it Himself before the throne of God for the sins of all mankind. Jesus was *both* the sacrifice and the one who offered the sacrifice. He is now our High Priest who continuously intercedes for us as He sits on the right hand side of God the Father on His throne. At his sacrificial death, the veil in the temple which separated man from God was rent in two, from top to bottom. This represented that there was no longer a separation of the people from God, but now by the blood of Jesus Christ we can boldly go before the Throne of God in the presence of Jesus Christ who intercedes for us. He is both our *redeemer* and our *High Priest*. In one person at one cross, Christ was both the scapegoat for all our sins, and the blood offering to God. The writer of Hebrews spoke of the necessity for a blood sacrifice.

"And almost all things are by the law purged with blood; and without shedding of blood is no remission." Heb 9:22

"Now where remission of these is, there is no more offering for sin." Hebrews 10:18

The Feast of Yom Kippur terminates a 40-day period called *Teshuvah*. It begins on the first day of the 12th Jewish month of the civil calendar called *Elul*. The 30 days in Elul which precedes the Feast of Trumpets is a time when all Jews are to repent of their sins so that their name will be inscribed in the *Book of the Righteous*. As previously mentioned, the 10 days between the Feat of Trumpets on Tishri 1 and Tishri 10 are known as the *Days of Repentance* or the *Days of Awe*. This 10 day period is the last chance that a person has to humble himself before God and repent of their sins for the previous year. On Yom Kippur, an individual's fate is sealed. At the last Feast of Yom Kippur, this will be a permanent and eternal fate. Jewish tradition teaches that at this time all persons will be held accountable for his/her sins. Perhaps of more significance to this study is the belief that on Yom Kippur the long-awaited Messiah of the Jews is expected to establish his earthly kingdom in

Jerusalem. Jewish tradition holds that the Feast of Trumpets will begin the 1000-year millennial kingdom of Christ. We believe that they have missed this date by 10 days, and that the millennial kingdom will start on Tishri 10 following the battle of Armageddon, but we will not be dogmatic about this point. It is crucial that the Jewish belief in their coming Messiah be completely understood. In the Jewish mind, there is much confusion concerning the Messiah which is mentioned many times in the Old Testament. In some passages, their Messiah is portrayed as being persecuted and scorned. In other passages He is predicted as a conquering King. To rationalize these conflicting accounts, it is taught that there would *be two messiahs* who were to appear. One is called the *Suffering Servant* or *Messiah Ben Joseph*. The other is seen as a *Conquering King* or *Messiah Ben David*. In Jewish eyes, Christ was the suffering servant. They are eagerly awaiting the appearance of the Conquering King. The arrival of Messiah Ben David will culminate in a great world battle for Jerusalem, in which the wicked will be vanquished and the righteous will inherit the land promised to them in the Abrahamic Covenant. Only after the 3.5 years of *tribulation* will Israel realize her error, the *scales will be removed from their eyes*, and they will know that Jesus Christ was both *Messiah Ben Joseph* and *Messiah Ben David*. He alone is worthy; He is the only son of the living God.

> *"And so all Israel shall be saved: as it is written, there shall come out of Zion the Deliverer, and shall turn away ungodliness from Jacob."* Romans 11:26

Jesus spoke of the error of the Jews when he spoke to His disciples on the Mount of Olives just before his crucifixion.

> *"O Jerusalem, Jerusalem, thou that killest the prophets, and stonest them which are sent unto thee, how often would I have gathered thy children together, even as a hen gathereth her chickens under her wings, and ye would not! Behold, your house is left unto you desolate. For I say unto you, Ye shall not see me henceforth, till ye shall say, Blessed is he that cometh in the name of the Lord."* Matthew 23:37-39

Hidden from their understanding is how *all Israel* will be *saved* as Christ returns to earth to fight the battle of Armageddon. It is spoken of by Zachariah.

> *"In that day shall the LORD defend the inhabitants of Jerusalem; and he that is feeble among them at that day shall be as David; and the house of David shall be as God, as the angel of the LORD before them. And it shall come to pass in that day, that I will seek to destroy all the nations that come against Jerusalem. And I will pour upon the house of David, and upon the inhabitants of Jerusalem, the spirit of grace and of supplications: and they shall look upon me whom they have pierced, and they shall mourn for him, as one mourneth for his only son, and shall be in bitterness for him, as one that is in bitterness for his firstborn. In that day shall there be a great mourning in Jerusalem, as the mourning of Hadadrimmon in the valley of Megiddon."* Zechariah 12:8-11

> *"In that day there shall be a fountain opened to the house of David and to the inhabitants of Jerusalem for sin and for uncleanness. And it shall come to pass in that day, saith the LORD of hosts, that I will cut off the names of the idols out of the land, and they shall no more be remembered: and also I will cause the prophets and the unclean spirit to pass out of the land."* Zechariah 13:1-2

> *"Behold, the day of the LORD cometh, and thy spoil shall be divided in the midst of thee. For I will gather all nations against Jerusalem to battle; and the city shall be taken, and the houses rifled, and the women ravished; and half of the city shall go forth into captivity, and the residue of the people shall not be cut off from the city. Then shall the LORD go forth, and fight against those nations, as when he fought in the day of battle. And his feet shall stand in that day upon the mount of Olives, which is before Jerusalem on the east, and the mount of Olives shall cleave in the midst thereof toward the east and toward the west, and there shall be a very great valley; and half of the mountain shall*

remove toward the north, and half of it toward the south. And ye shall flee to the valley of the mountains; for the valley of the mountains shall reach unto Azal: yea, ye shall flee, like as ye fled from before the earthquake in the days of Uzziah king of Judah: and the LORD my God shall come, and all the saints with thee. And it shall come to pass in that day, that the light shall not be clear, nor dark: But it shall be one day which shall be known to the LORD, not day, nor night: but it shall come to pass, that at evening time it shall be light. And it shall be in that day, that living waters shall go out from Jerusalem; half of them toward the former sea, and half of them toward the hinder sea: in summer and in winter shall it be. And the LORD shall be king over all the earth: in that day shall there be one LORD, and his name one. All the land shall be turned as a plain from Geba to Rimmon south of Jerusalem: and it shall be lifted up, and inhabited in her place, from Benjamin's gate unto the place of the first gate, unto the corner gate, and from the tower of Hananeel unto the king's winepresses. And men shall dwell in it, and there shall be no more utter destruction; but Jerusalem shall be safely inhabited." Zechariah 14: 1-11

There seems to be no doubt about it: **That day** is the **Day of the Lord**, and the great battle being fought is the **Battle of Armageddon**. The reader is encouraged to do a short Bible study: Look up every reference to the Day of the Lord in the Bible, and without exception it always refers to a single day. Conversely, practically all of the *pre-tribulation* advocates refer to the *day of the lord* as being seven years long. Almost every classical advocate of a *pre-wrath* rapture make the *day of the Lord* 3.5 years long. What has caused this incorrect interpretation?

Without controversy, these incorrect interpretations have been caused by four critical mistakes: (1) incorrectly assuming that the tribulation period was seven years long (2) not recognizing that the *Wrath of God* is the pouring out of the seven bowls following the sounding of the seventh trumpet (Rev 16:1), and not as the 6th seal is opened (3) failing to recognize that the seven seals only provide an overview of the tribulation period, (4) failure to distinguish between *wrath* and *tribulation* and (5) refusing to recognize that the rapture of the church occurs at the seventh trump. We will develop each of these critical issues in later chapters. For now, let us continue our discussion of the three fall feasts of Israel and their prophetic significance.

The Feast of Tabernacles

The Feast of Tabernacles is an eight-day feast. It occurs between Nisan 15-Nisan 22. King Solomon dedicated his new temple on the feast of Tabernacles. The temple of David was constructed for the Lord to come and *tabernacle* or dwell for a short time with man. It is the last of the three fall feasts, and it follows the Feast of Yom Kippur. The historical significance of the feast is well understood. It commemorates the Exodus from Egypt, and the 40 years of wandering in the wilderness, in which the Hebrew nation dwelled in temporary tents called *booths*. The feast is sometimes called the *Feast of Booths*. The English equivalent of the Latin word for tabernacle is *hut*. A third name for the full eight-day feast is the *Feast of Ingathering* (Exodus 23:16). Harvest of the fall crops of wheat, figs and grapes are all completed at this time. The Feast of Tabernacles is one of the three annual feasts at which every male Hebrew is commanded to attend in Jerusalem. The other two were the Feast of Passover and the Feast of Weeks (Exodus 23:17, 34:22, Deut 16:16). The feast is marked by celebration and praise to the Lord for both providing the crop just harvested, and for His provisions of quail, manna, and fresh water throughout the 40-year sojourn of the Exodus in the wilderness. During the seven days between Nisan 15 and Nisan 21, the people live in temporary dwellings typically constructed of palm leaves and willow branches. This is a time of great celebration and introspection of God's goodness.

During the seven days beginning on Tishri 15, there were typically three daily acts of praise; (1) the people were to wave branches before the Lord (Lev 23); (2) there were daily sacrificial offerings (Num 29); and, (3) the entire law was to be read in public gatherings. The entire 24 courses of priests were all put into service during this week. The last day of the feast is called *Shemini Atzeret,* referred to in the scriptures as simply the *eighth day of assembly* (Num 29:35). The term Shemini Atzaret is historically interpreted as *tarry or stay another day*. However, the Jewish emphasis on staying one more day as a request is not scripturally correct. The eighth day is ordained by God, and to stay is not an option but a command. The eighth day is primarily directed to the *Tefillat Geshem* or the *prayer for rain*. The months following Tishri are particularly critical to a successful planting season and a successful growing season. The *early rains* came during this time and nourished the emerging crops. According to Jewish tradition, God decides at the Feast of Tabernacles on the eighth day whether He will provide abundant rain or little rain in the coming months. The *latter rains* which occurred just before the month of Nisan enabled the crops to mature to fullness. The first and second coming of our Lord Jesus Christ was equated to the early and latter rains, which clearly reflected the Holy Spirit falling during his *first advent* and the pouring out of the Spirit of the Lord in the latter days at His *second advent*.

> **"Be patient therefore, brethren, unto the coming of the Lord. Behold, the husbandman waiteth for the precious fruit of the earth, and hath long patience for it, until he receive the early and latter rain."** James 5:7

> **"And it shall come to pass afterward, that I will pour out my spirit upon all flesh; and your sons and your daughters shall prophesy, your old men shall dream dreams, your young men shall see visions. And also upon the servants and upon the handmaids in those days will I pour out my spirit."**
> Joel 2:28-29

The requirement for the Lord to be satisfied and produce an abundance of the early and latter rains dominated the temple services each day. Every morning in the temple the High Priest would go to the Pool of Siloam and fill a pitcher full of water. He would return to the temple among the people waving palm branches and reciting Isaiah 12:3: **With joy shall ye draw water out of the wells of salvation**. He would then enter the temple and pour the water out on the Altar of Sacrifice as all the people waved palm branches in the air as an offering to the Lord for His favor. It was during this sacred ceremony on the last day of the feast that Christ arose, stood in front of all the people and shocked them all by loudly proclaiming: ***If any man thirst let him come unto me, and drink. He that believeth on me, as the Scripture hath said, out of his belly shall flow rivers of living water.*** Christ boldly spoke of when after his resurrection that the Holy Spirit would fall on all believers. This was the water that would continuously provide sustenance and never dry up.

A special season which ends on Yom Kippur is called *Teshuvah*. It begins on the first day of the month of *Elul*, which immediately precedes the month of *Tishri*. Teshuvah lasts 40 days, and ends on the Feast of Yom Kippur (Nisan 10). The Feast of Trumpets starts 30 days into the season of Teshuvah. It is relevant that every morning during the month of Elul, a trumpet is sounded to warn all the people that the time has come to repent of their sins and return to God. The first day of the feast (Tishri 15) and the last day of the feast (Tishri 22) are both *High Sabbaths*. There could be no work done on these days, and travel was limited to a Sabbath-day's journey. The cool evenings during this time were spent in a festive celebration. Every night there were torches lit everywhere to provide light. Dancing, rejoicing and banquets were enjoyed every evening into the wee hours of the morning. It was a time of pure joy. Tradition has it that no celebration in all of ancient Israel could compare to that which took place during the Feast of Tabernacles, and no single day could compare to the last day. The rabbis wrote: ***He that hath not beheld the joy of this celebration had never experienced real joy in his life*** (Joseph Good).

Jesus was undoubtedly referring to this joy when He spoke of the light that He can bring to all people who believe upon His name.

> ***"Then spake Jesus again unto them, saying, I am the light of the world: he that followeth me shall not walk in darkness, but shall have the light of life."*** John 8:12

A detailed study of the Feast of Tabernacles is both an enlightening and rewarding study. There are many shadows and types of Jesus Christ in this eight-day feast. The Feast of Tabernacles has significant application to the second coming of Jesus Christ and His initiation of the millennial kingdom. After His second advent and the battle of Armageddon, the 144,000 Hebrews who have been sealed to enter the millennial kingdom; the remnant who have survived the seven bowl judgments; survivors of the sheep and goat judgment; the Bride of Christ and all glorified believers will rest at a great Feast of Tabernacles. It is also interesting that of all the seven feasts, only the Feast of Tabernacles is mentioned as continuing over the next 1000 years.

> *"And it shall come to pass, that every one that is left of all the nations which came against Jerusalem shall even go up from year to year to worship the King, the LORD of hosts, and to keep the Feast of tabernacles. And if the family of Egypt go not up, and come not, that have no rain; there shall be the plague, wherewith the LORD will smite the heathen that come not up to keep the Feast of tabernacles. This shall be the punishment of Egypt, and the punishment of all nations that come not up to keep the Feast of tabernacles."*   Zechariah 14: 16, 18-19

Summary of the Feasts of Israel

We have given a brief overview of the four spring feasts, and the three fall feasts of Israel. All seven feasts are *rehearsals* for seven *appointments* that have been ordained since time began for our Lord Jesus Christ. The first four (spring) feasts were fulfilled at the first advent of Christ, and the last three (fall) feasts will be fulfilled at the rapture of the church and at the second advent of Christ. Collectively, all seven feasts provide a *blueprint* for the work that Christ will accomplish. They also provide a blueprint of how the tribulation period will end. In particular, it is our uncompromising belief that at the last Feast of Trumpets, Christ will appear in the air and the *rapture* will occur, and that the battle of Armageddon will occur on the Feast of Yom Kippur.

> *"Behold, I shew you a mystery; We shall not all sleep, but we shall all be changed, In a moment, in the twinkling of an eye, at the last trump: for the trumpet shall sound, and the dead shall be raised incorruptible, and we shall be changed. For this corruptible must put on incorruption, and this mortal must put on immortality. So when this corruptible shall have put on incorruption, and this mortal shall have put on immortality, then shall be brought to pass the saying that is written, Death is swallowed up in victory. O death, where is thy sting? O grave, where is thy victory?"*
> I Corinthians 15: 51-55

At the last Feast of Yom Kippur, Christ will return again, this time descending to the Mount of Olives to fight the battle of Armageddon.

> *"Behold, the day of the LORD cometh, and thy spoil shall be divided in the midst of thee. For I will gather all nations against Jerusalem to battle; and the city shall be taken, and the houses rifled, and the women ravished; and half of the city shall go forth into captivity, and the residue of the people shall not be cut off from the city. Then shall the LORD go forth, and fight against those nations, as when he fought in the day of battle. And his feet shall stand in that day upon the mount of Olives, which is before Jerusalem on the east, and the mount of Olives shall cleave in the midst thereof toward the east and toward the west, and there shall be a very great valley; and half of the mountain shall remove toward the north, and half of it toward the south. And ye shall flee to the valley of the mountains; for the valley of the mountains shall reach unto Azal: yea, ye shall flee, like as ye fled from before the earthquake in the days of Uzziah king of Judah: and the LORD my God shall come, and all the saints with thee. And it shall come to pass in that day, that the light shall not be clear, nor dark: But it shall be one day which shall be known to the LORD, not day, nor night: but it shall come to pass, that at evening time it shall be light. And it shall be in that day, that living waters shall go out from Jerusalem; half of them toward the former sea,*

and half of them toward the hinder sea: in summer and in winter shall it be. And the LORD shall be king over all the earth: in that day shall there be one LORD, and his name one. All the land shall be turned as a plain from Geba to Rimmon south of Jerusalem: and it shall be lifted up, and inhabited in her place, from Benjamin's gate unto the place of the first gate, unto the corner gate, and from the tower of Hananeel unto the king's winepresses. And men shall dwell in it, and there shall be no more utter destruction; but Jerusalem shall be safely inhabited. And this shall be the plague wherewith the LORD will smite all the people that have fought against Jerusalem; Their flesh shall consume away while they stand upon their feet, and their eyes shall consume away in their holes, and their tongue shall consume away in their mouth." Zechariah 14:1-1

"And I saw heaven opened, and behold a white horse; and he that sat upon him was called Faithful and True, and in righteousness he doth judge and make war. His eyes were as a flame of fire, and on his head were many crowns; and he had a name written, that no man knew, but he himself. And he was clothed with a vesture dipped in blood: and his name is called The Word of God. And the armies which were in heaven followed him upon white horses, clothed in fine linen, white and clean. And out of his mouth goeth a sharp sword, that with it he should smite the nations: and he shall rule them with a rod of iron: and he treadeth the winepress of the fierceness and wrath of Almighty God. And he hath on his vesture and on his thigh a name written, KING OF KINGS, AND LORD OF LORDS." Rev. 19:11-16

The Feast of Tabernacles will celebrate the second advent of Jesus Christ and His accomplished work. There will be great rejoicing and praise because: *the kingdoms of this world will have become the kingdoms of our Lord Jesus Christ*. This is the fulfillment of the angelic proclamation in Rev 11:15. There will be a great feast that will take place; the Marriage Supper of the Lamb. All believers will be at this Feast of Tabernacles. The Hebrews will inherit the land promised to them long ago; the saints will rule and reign with Christ; and the earth will return to an Edenic state. The 1000-year millennial kingdom will be populated by the *earthly seed of Abraham*, and the saints who are the *starry seed of Abraham* will rule and reign with Christ for 1000 years. We are often asked the following question: *when will the rapture of the church occur?* To the amazement of everyone listening we reply; *On some future Feast of Trumpets, in the month of September or October*. To you the reader we urge you to *watch and wait, for the time is surely near*. It is hopeless and foolish to predict a date when our Lord Jesus Christ will return for His body, which is the church of all born again believers: But it is not foolish to determine the time or season.

The Seven Feasts of Israel		
The Spring Feasts		
Feast	Date	Prophetic Significance
Passover	Nisan 14	Redemption and Salvation. Christ was our perfect Passover lamb. The New Covenant replaces the Old Covenant
Unleavened Bread	Nisan 15-Nisan 21	Justification and Sanctification. Christ was without sin. He is the bread of life
FirstFruits	First Sunday of Unleavened Bread	Resurrection and life. Christ rose from the grave and conquered death
Weeks	Starts on Feast of Firstfruits and Lasts 49 days. 50th day is Pentecost	Sanctification and spiritual maturity. The Holy Spirit fell on the Day of Pentecost
The Fall Feasts		
Trumpets	Tishri 1	Rapture of the Saints and Resurrection of the Dead. Wedding of the Lamb. Bema Seat Judgement
Yom Kippur	Tishri 10	Second Coming of Christ. Judgment of the Nations. Satan cast into Bottomless Pit for 1000 years. Antichrist and False Prophet cast into Lake of Fire
Tabernacles	Tishri 15- Tishri 21. Tishri 22 is a High Sabbath and a fast day	Beginning of 1000 year Millennial Kingdom. Tribulation Martyers Raised. Judgement of the Nations

This concludes our study of the 7 feasts of Israel and their prophetic significance.

Thoughts and Things......

Chapter 10

Seals, Bowls and Trumpets: Exposition

In the book of Revelation, there are a lot of *sevens*; seven churches (Rev 2-3), seven angels (Rev 8:2), seven seals (Rev 6:1-7 8:1-5), seven trumpets (Rev 8:6-13, 9:1-21, 11:15-19) and seven bowls (Rev 16:1-21). In this chapter we will examine the definition of the seven seals, trumpets and bowls. After these are defined and discussed, we will then show how they are chronologically linked to each other in Chapter 11.

The Seven Seals
In Rev 6 we are introduced to what is usually called *the seven seal judgments*. This term has created some confusion, since the seven seals are not *judgments*, but reflect general conditions

> "And I saw in the right hand of Him that sat on the throne a book written within and on the backside, sealed with 7 seals"
> Rev 5:1

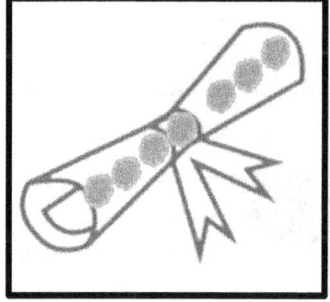

which will characterize the entire tribulation period. Understanding this is the key to unlocking the correct sequence and order of all the visions that are described by the apostle John. In Rev 5 we are introduced to *a strong angel* who asks. *Who is worthy to open the book and to loose the seals thereof?* (Rev 5:2). The angel proclaimed that *no man in heaven, or in earth, neither under the earth, was able to open the book, neither to look thereupon (*Rev 5: 3*)*. The apostle John *wept much because no man was found worthy to open and read the book, neither to look thereon* (Rev 5:4). What is in this scroll? It contains the words of God which describe the events of the tribulation period. But John and the strong angel were looking for a redeemed *man,* or an *angel* to open the scroll. One of the 24 elders which surround the throne of God (Rev 4:5) steps forward and proclaims, **Weep not: behold, the Lion of the Tribe of Judah, the root of David, hath prevailed to open the book** (Rev 5:5). Oh saints, the Lamb is worthy! He is the Son of God who sits in the heavenlies constantly intervening for us and being our advocate. **And he came and took the book out of the right hand of him that sat upon the throne** (Rev 5:7). One of the interesting things which will be noted at this point is that we will see that the seven trumpet judgments and the seven bowl judgments are executed by seven angels who **stand before God** (Rev 8:2; 16:1). Angels have eternal important duties: they offer up continual praise and worship; they convey important messages to mankind; some protect us; and some execute divine judgment. The seals are broken by our Lord Jesus Christ. Only He is worthy to do so (Rev 5:1-5). The seven seals are successively opened in Rev 6:1; 6:3; 6:5; 6:7; 6:9; 6:12, and 8:1.

We will now describe what happens when each seal is broken.

Seal 1: White Horse appears. Satan is the rider. Satan will deceive the nations with lies and deceptions. He will work through both the Antichrist & the False Prophet. Mat 24:24, Rev 13, Dan 11:36-38, I John 2:18, I Thess 5:3

The identification of this horse and rider has confused many teachers of prophecy. The rider is often identified as Christ, and the vision a preview of Christ's second coming on a white horse (Rev 19:11). However, if the rider is Christ then He rides with Death and Hell (fourth seal) and has martyred the saints

"And I saw, and behold a White Horse; and he that sat on him had a bow; and a Crown was given unto him: And he went forth conquering and to conquer" Rev 6:2

(fifth seal). This is not Christ but Satan. He rides forth looking like he is the long-awaited Jewish Messiah, but he is Satan. He will attack the world for 3.5 years in the form of a person called the antichrist. The second seal brings war and destruction.

A Fiery Red Horse appears. The rider is the Antichrist. The rider is given a great sword, and he makes war and causes nations to fight nations.
Rev 13:4,7 ; Dan11:36-43

Seal 2

This is **the Beast that arises out of the Sea** in Rev 13:1. This beast is none other than the antichrist who was **wounded to death** (Rev 13:3), and **his deadly wound was healed: and all the world wondered after this beast** (Rev 13:3). Recreating the death and resurrection of Jesus Christ, the world is deceived into thinking that surely this is

"And there went out another horse that was red: And power was given to him that sat thereon to take peace from the earth, and that they should kill one another: and there was given to him a great sword"   Rev 6:4

the long awaited Messiah. *And they worshipped the dragon (Satan, Rev 12:9) which gave power unto the beast, saying who is like unto the beast? Who is able to make war with him?* This beast is given his power by Satan. *And the Dragon gave him his power, and his seat (in the temple), and great authority* (Rev 13:2-b). This authority lasts for 1260 days or 42 months (Rev 12:9, 12:14 & 13:5). We should point out that during this 1260-day period known as the *tribulation*, that old serpent called Lucifer will reign over the earth, and he will be involved in a blasphemous triangle which is designed to mimic God, Jesus Christ and the Holy Spirit, This triumvirate (Rev 12:17, Rev 13:1-19; Rev (13:11-18, Rev 17:7-14) is Satan (the dragon), the antichrist (the beast out of the sea) and the false prophet (the beast out of the earth). They will all meet their destiny following the battle of Armageddon. Satan (the dragon) will be bound in chains for 1000 years in the bottomless pit (Rev 20:1-2); the antichrist (beast out of the sea) and the false prophet (beast out of the earth) will be cast into the lake of burning fire (Rev 19:20). Satan will join those 1000 years later (Rev 20:10). The last enemies to be destroyed will be *death and hell*, which are both also cast into the Lake of Fire (Rev 20:14).

A black horse appears. The black horse has a rider with a pair of scales in his hand. This horse and rider brings famine and pestilence.
Rev 8:7,10 ; Rev 13:16,17

As the third seal opens, a black horse appears with a rider who holds a scale in his hand. The scale is a symbol that there will be a scarcity of food, and it will be rationed out. This is a direct consequence of two things. First, we will see that when the seventh trumpet sounds, 1/3 of all the

"And I beheld, and lo a black horse, and he that sat upon him had a pair of balances in his hand. And I heard a loud voice in the midst of the four beasts say, a measure of wheat for a penny, and three measures of barley for a penny; and see that thou hurt not the oil and the wine" Rev 6:5-6

trees are burned up and *all* of the green grass. While it is not directly stated, this indicates that most if not all of the food crops will also be burned up (Rev 8:7). Second, what little food is available cannot be purchased unless one has *the mark of the beast* upon him or her (Rev 13:17). Be cautioned that if anyone takes the mark of the beast that this will seal his or her fate forever. The punishment will be that anyone who takes the mark of the beast on either their forehead or hand will be thrown into the *lake of fire* (Rev 19:20). The purchase price of a *measure of wheat for a penny* should be translated *measure of wheat for a denarius*, which was the average daily wage of a Roman worker, and was about 16 cents.

A pale horse appears. It was ridden by "Death" and is followed by Hades. One-fourth of the people on the earth are killed with sword, hunger and the beasts of the earth.
Rev 9:1-12 ; Rev 9:18 ; Rev12:7 ; Rev 13:15 ; Rev 6:10

As the fourth seal is broken, a ***pale horse*** appears. The Greek word for *pale* literally means *a sickly Green*, a yellowish-green color which seldom appear together in nature. This color is most-often seen in cases of gangrene. Gangrene is a by-product of poor medical care, famine and pestilence. Death and Hell follow the horse and rider. There are

"And I looked and behold a pale horse: And the name that sat upon him was Death, and Hell followed after him. And power was given unto them over the 4th part of the earth, to kill with sword, and hunger, and with death, and with the beasts of the earth"   Rev 6:7-8

two deaths mentioned in the Bible. The *first death* is a natural death in which the spirit departs from the body and the body lies in the grave. The Christian has no fear of natural death; it is just a gateway to eternity with our Lord and Savior Jesus Christ. The *second death* is the fate of all who refuse to accept Jesus Christ as their personal savior and reject His free gift of salvation by grace. The main resurrection of the dead is at the ***last trump***. At this time death and the grave will have been conquered by all whose bodies sleep in Christ. ***The last enemy that shall be destroyed is death*** (I Corinthians 15:26).

> *"Behold, I show you a mystery. We shall not all sleep, but we shall all be changed. In a moment at the last trump: for the trumpet will sound and the dead shall be raised incorruptible, and we shall all be changed."*
>   I Corinthians 15:51-52

The *second death* will be the casting of all unbelievers into the *lake of fire and brimstone*.

> *"He that overcometh shall inherit all things, and I will be His God, and he shall be my son. But the fearful and unbelieving, and the abominable, and murderers, and whoremongers, and sorcerers, and idolaters, and all liars, shall have their part in the lake which burneth with fire and brimstone: which is the second death."*
> Rev 21:7-8

This should forever settle the debate as to whether there is a place of everlasting torment for unbelievers. But do not be deceived, this does not mean that if you have ever lied, murdered, committed adultery, etc. that you are doomed to the second death, *for we have all sinned and fallen short of the glory of God* (Romans 3:23). What condemns anyone is not our sinful nature, but the failure to believe that Jesus Christ is the son of the living God, and that He died on the cross for *our sins*. We are delivered from eternal torment to eternal bliss by *grace*.

Note that *Death and Hell* follow closely behind. *Hell* is not well understood by most Christians. Hell is now the abode of the unrighteous dead. In the Bible, the place where departed souls reside is a Hebrew word called *sheol*, and in the New Testament it is a Greek word called *Hades*. Both words should be translated as *hell*, but in some places it is incorrectly translated as *the grave*. But the body goes to the grave, and the soul goes to *sheol*. The body dies, but the soul lives on. Sheol is composed of two parts: the first part is called *paradise*, and the second part is called *a place of torments* (Luke 16:22). The truth of this theology turns on the very words of Jesus Christ himself when He hung on the cross of Calvary. Recall that one of the two persons who hung beside Him asked Jesus to forgive his sins and save him.

> *"And he said unto Jesus, Lord, remember me when thou comest into thy kingdom."* Luke 23:42

Jesus replied:

> *"Verily I say unto thee. Today thou shalt be with Me in Paradise."* Luke 23:43

Christ died on the cross and immediately went to Paradise. There He offered the new covenant to all the departed souls who were waiting there.

> *"Wherefore he saith, when he ascended up on high, He led captivity, captive, and gave gifts unto men. Now that He ascended, what is it but that He also descended first into the lower parts of the earth?"* Ephesians 4:8-9

Those who were in Paradise were born and died under the law, the old covenant, but like Abraham they were looking forward to a coming Messiah and believed in the promises.

> *"For he (Abraham) looked for a city which hath foundations whose builder and maker is God."* Heb 11:10

Not by the law but by *faith* was Abraham, Moses, Jacob and all of the Old Testament patriarchs saved (read the great chapter of faith, Heb 11). When Christ died, He *descended* into *hell* into a compartment called *Paradise*. The apostle's creed affirms that Christ descended into *hell* and ascended from there after 3 days. For three days and three nights He presented the gospel message to those who were being held captive. When He was resurrected and ascended to Heaven, he emptied Paradise; taking *captives in His train.* It appears that at that time Paradise was moved into the third heaven, as witnessed by the apostle Paul who *ascended* there and saw things he could not reveal (II Cor 12:4). We believe that all who now die in Christ *ascend* spiritually into the third heaven where they await the final resurrection. All unbelievers still *descend* into the second compartment of Hell called the place of torments (Luke 16:23). They will be resurrected to judgment after the 1000-year millennial kingdom at the Great White Throne Judgment. As an example of the teachings of Jesus on this subject, consider the following passage in the book of Luke.

> *"There was a certain rich man...... and there was a certain beggar named Lazarus. And it came to pass that the beggar (Lazarus) died, and was carried by the angels into Abraham's bosom. (Abraham's bosom is figurative speech for paradise) (Luke 23:43, Cor 12:4). The rich man also died and was buried. And in hell he (the rich man) lifted up his eyes, being in torments. And seeing Abraham afar off and Lazarus in his bosom, the rich man begged for water for he was in torment."* Luke 16:19-23

There existed a **great gulf** which no one could cross between **Paradise** and **the place of torments**. These are the two compartments of *Ghenna or Hell* (Luke 16:26). The reply to the rich man's request for water is stunning.

> *"But Abraham said, son, remember that thou in thy lifetime received thy good things, and likewise Lazarus evil things. But now he is comforted and thou art tormented."* Luke 16:25

Do not misunderstand; the torture of the rich man was not for having worldly possessions or being rich. The reward of Lazarus was not for being poor and persecuted. The rich man obviously loved his riches and wealth more than Jesus Christ. Lazarus put his faith into the free gift of eternal life, and the salvation freely offered to all by our Lord Jesus Christ. The social status and wealth of individuals will not be worth anything in the world to come. God gives to each of us according to His pleasure, but there is an obligation.

> *"For unto whomsoever much is given, of him shall be much required "* Luke 12:48

The message is to Love Christ and not the riches of this world.
> *"Lay not up for yourselves treasures upon earth, where moth and rust doth corrupt, and where thieves break*

through and steal: But lay up for yourselves treasures in heaven where neither moth nor rust doth corrupt, and where thieves do not break through nor steal."
    Mat 6:19-20

Finally, note that during the tribulation period of 3.5 years, the animal kingdom will turn on men according to divine appointment. In Genesis Adam was given dominion over all creatures upon the earth (Gen 1:26). Now, the beasts of the earth rise to kill man.

In summary, the first four seals bring forth four horses with four different riders. These four riders are generally referred to as *the four horsemen of the apocalypse.*

The Four Horsemen of the Apocalypse

Art used by permission by Pat Marvenko Smith, copyright 1992.

As previously indicated, these four horsemen represent: (1) the false Christ; the Antichrist, (2) war over all the earth, (3) famine and a scarcity of food, and (4) Death and Hades, which kills ¼ of all the people on the earth by sword, famine, plagues and by *wild beasts* attacking mankind. The entire balance of nature is upset under the 4th horseman. Please note again, that all of these things do not occur sequentially, but will be characteristic of the last 3.5 year tribulation period.

As the 5th seal is broken, the imagery suddenly changes. During the last 3.5 years of Daniel's 70th week, Satan will persecute all who will not bow down and worship him, there will be many Christians and other people brutally murdered. Those who are martyred for refusing to abandon Christ will have a special place to rest in God's presence. This is revealed as the 5th seal is broken.

As the 5th seal opens, John sees the souls of those who have been martyred for Jesus Christ. They plead for justice and revenge. God gives each a white robe. There are more to be slain.
Rev 13:11-15, Rev 17:6

Rev 6:9-10 is a remarkable passage. It indicates that a special place *under the altar of God* has been reserved for those who have been martyred for Jesus Christ. They cry with a loud voice:

> *"How long, oh Lord, holy and true, doest thou not judge and avenge our blood on them that dwell on the earth?"*
> Rev 6:10

"And when he had opened the fifth seal, I saw under the altar the souls of them that were slain for the word of God, and for the testimony that they held: And they cried with a loud voice, saying: How long O Lord, holy and true, dost thou not judge and avenge our blood on them that dwell on the earth?" Rev 6:9-10

This reminds us that after Christ commissioned 70 followers to prepare the way for him during his earthly ministry, He said*: Go your ways; behold I send you forth as lambs among wolves* (Luke 10:3). Here are martyrs from all ages who have perished in the service of Christ. They are crying out for justice. The response to their outcry is swift and revealing. There will be many more that will be killed for believing upon Jesus Christ.

> *"And white robes were given unto every one of them; and it was said unto them, that they should rest yet for a little season, until their fellow servants also and their brethren that should be killed as they were, should be fulfilled."*
> Rev 6:1

This passage clearly states that during the tribulation period there will be martyrs who will lose their life for their belief in Jesus Christ. On the earth, nature is about to unleash devastating disasters that will make the Japanese 2011 earthquake and tsunami look like child's play. The 6th seal is about to be broken.

As the 6th seal opens, the earth is torn apart by physical disturbances. Earthquakes, meteorites and volcanoic eruptions. Earth dwellers hide in the rocks & caves. The Wrath of God has come. The end is near
Is 34:4 ; Joel 2:30-31 ; Mat 24:39 ; Rev 8:10-11 ; Rev 16:18-21

Seal 6

1.0 There is a great earthquake
2.0 The sun turns black as sackcloth
3.0 The moon becomes the color of blood
4.0 The stars (meteorites) fall upon the earth
5.0 The heavens roll up like a scroll
6.0 Every mountain is moved out of its place
7.0 Every island is dislodged

As the sixth seal is broken, there are great physical disruptions that occur all over the earth. The earth has experienced great earthquakes and volcanic eruptions, but nothing can compare to what is being described as the sixth seal is broken. The heavens are ripped apart and the earth is completely disrupted. Imagine *every* island and mountain being moved out of its place. The devastation will be unparalleled in the history of the world. Surely the events described when the sixth seal is broken indicate that the end is near. These disasters *do not* precede the seven trumpet judgments and the seven bowl judgments. They occur very near the end of the age. As this seal is broken, not only will the heavens and earth be disrupted, but the empires and kingdoms of men will collapse and be useless. Gold, silver and currency will not be enough to save mankind from the Wrath of God. Kings and rulers will cower and hide in fear.

> *"And the kings of the earth, and the great men, and the rich men, and the chief captains, and the mighty men, and every bondman, and every free man, hid themselves in the dens and in the rocks of the mountains; and said to the mountains and rocks, fall on us, and hide us from the face of Him that sitteth on the throne and from the wrath of the Lamb."* Rev 6:15-17

We will come back to the sixth seal in the next chapter when we discuss timing and chronology, but for now it is worth mentioning the context of the sixth seal. The sun is being darkened, every island is being moved out of its place and every mountain moved; the entire world is being thrown into unprecedented catastrophic events. The end of the world as we know it must be at the very door. However, common prophetic interpretation has the seals as a precursor to the entire last 3.5 years of the tribulation period. This interpretation of these events defies common logic. We will fully explore these observations in the next chapter when we discuss the chronological relationship between the seals, bowls and trumpets. Now the 7th and last seal is broken.

 As the 7th seal opens, there is "silence in Heaven". It is time to answer the martters prayers. As this seal opens, there are more thunderings, lightnings and earthquakes. Rev 16:18-21

When the seventh seal is broken, the entire contents of a scroll which is **written within and on the backside** (Rev 5:1) can now be revealed. It is time for John to witness with his own eyes the end of earth as we  know it: ***And I John saw these things, and heard them*** (Rev 22:8). The impact of what John is about to see is so destructive and comprehensive that Christ forewarned warned us:

> *"For then there shall be Great Tribulation, such as was not since the beginning of the world to this time, no, nor ever shall be. And except those days be shortened, there should be no flesh saved: but for the elect's sake, those days will be shortened."*   Matthew 24: 21-22

We will later show exactly when and how this prophecy is fulfilled.

There are ***thunderings, lightnings and earthquakes***. Since this is the last seal, we might expect that its opening describes things which will happen toward the end of the 3.5 year tribulation period… and it does. Compare what is predicted to happen as the seventh seal is broken to what will happen as the seventh bowl is poured out at the end of the tribulation period.

 Bowl 7

And the seventh angel poured out his vial into the air; and there came a great voice out of the temple of heaven, from the throne, saying, It is done. And there were voices, and thunders, and lightnings; and there was a great earthquake.   Rev 16 ; 17-18

This is *exactly* when we would expect to see these things happen as predicted by removing the seventh seal. When the seventh seal is broken, the very prospect of the terrible things that are about to happen as the tribulation period starts cause an unprecedented event in human history. There is ***silence in heaven, about the space of half an hour***. We do not know how long *half an hour* implies, and it is foolish to speculate. But when this period of silence is over, it will be time for the tribulation period of 3.5 years to begin. It is time for the seven trumpet judgments to come forth upon the earth. The seven trumpet judgments will take place sequentially, and the 7th trumpet will bring forth the devastating seven bowl judgments which radically affect the heavens and the earth.

The Seven Trumpet Judgments

Following silence of about a half an hour, a sequence of preparatory events now takes place in Heaven. *Another angel* (Rev 8:2) is summoned and comes to stand before the altar of God. He is given a *golden censor* with *much incense, that he should offer it with the prayers of all saints upon the golden altar which is before the throne. And the smoke of the incense, which came with the prayers of the saints, ascended up before God out of the angels hand* (Rev 8: 3-4). It is time for the *Wrath of Satan* to occur upon the earth as the seven trumpets are sounded by seven angels.

> "And I saw the seven angels which stood before God; and to them were given seven trumpets"   Rev 8:1

> "And the seven angels which had the seven trumpets prepared themselves to sound"   Rev 8:6

Here is a remarkable contrast between the Old and New Testament economies. In the Old Testament, there was a brazen altar of sacrifice which stood in the Holy Place, upon which the Levitical priests placed a sin offering of bulls and goats which was burned for the sins of the offerer. This altar was to have a fire burning perpetually with hot coals. It was a function of the Levitical Priesthood to make sure the fire never went out. The coals were considered to be sacred. A sacrificial animal was killed, and the blood offered as an atoning sacrifice for sins. Except for rare divine appearances by God to his servants, and to the High Priest in the Holy of Holies on the Day of Atonement, an individual had no direct access to God. Now we have access to the very throne of God through our eternal High Priest, Jesus Christ (Romans 8:34).

It appears from Rev 8:3-4, that the prayers of New Testament saints are all collected and stored near the throne of God. How marvelous that through Jesus Christ our prayers are heard and saved by God! Sometimes we feel that our prayers are not answered, but they are always heard. These prayers are offered with **much incense** upon the true Golden Altar before God's throne in heaven; the true altar of sacrifice; not a copy of the one that stood in the earthly tabernacle or the temple.

"For it is not possible that the blood of bulls and goats should take away sins." Hebrews 10:4

At this point another monumental event occurs in preparation for the seven trumpets to sound.

"And the angel took the censor, and filled it with the fire of the altar, and cast it into the earth: and there were voices, and thunderings, and lightning and earthquakes."
Rev 8:5

God is announcing by this action that the heavenly altar of sacrifice is now without sacrificial coals. The millions of prayers over thousands of years to vanquish Satan and start a new age are about to be answered. Judgment is passed to the earth by *the angel*. Execution of this judgment will be exercised by Satan, the beast and the false prophet over the last 3.5 years of Daniel's 70 week. The first trumpet now sounds.

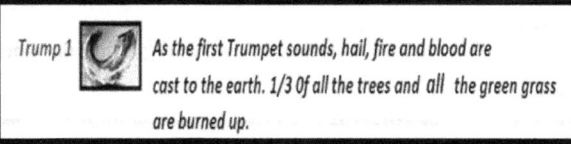
Trump 1 — As the first Trumpet sounds, hail, fire and blood are cast to the earth. 1/3 Of all the trees and all the green grass are burned up.

The famine predicted by the third seal is now come. If all of the green grass is burned up, then no animals can graze and live for

"The first angel sounded and there followed hail and fire mingled with blood, and they were cast upon the earth: And the third part of all trees was burnt up, and all the green grass burnt up" Rev 8:7

very long. It is also likely that all of the world's food crops will be burned up also. Note conclusively that the conditions *predicted* at the opening of the third seal are now in force. The third seal itself did not *cause* these conditions, but the blowing the first trump did. As the second trumpet sounds, God now causes the heavenly bodies which He created by the wave of His mighty hand to respond to His call.

> Trump 2 As the second trumpet sounds, "something like a great mountain" burning with fire was thrown into the sea.

As the second trump is blown, it appears that a gigantic meteorite *Like a great mountain* was hurled from space into the sea, or possibly one of the oceans. The result is catastrophic. A third of all the creatures which live in the sea die instantly. A third of all seagoing vessels are destroyed, 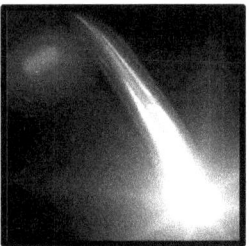 probably by a great tsunami. Not only are there effects felt worldwide from this gigantic *meteorite*, but a supernatural event also now occurs: 1/3 of *the sea* becomes blood. (Rev 8:1). As the 3rd trumpet sounds, the heavens again respond to His call.

> Trump 3 As the third trumpet sounds, a "great star" falls from the heavens.

At the sounding of the third trump, another object falls from heaven. This object is larger and is called a *great star*. It falls upon a land mass or splits and falls on all the major continents. We know this because one third of all the rivers, streams 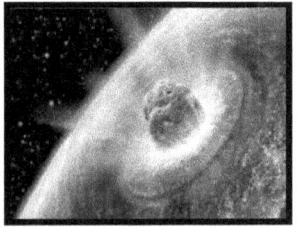 and *fountains of waters,* or the subterranean water supply, is made bitter and undrinkable (Rev 8:10). We are told the name of this star; it is called **Wormwood**. The entomology of wormwood is *to curse or make like gall.* This event was predicted by the prophet Jeremiah.

> *"Therefore, thus saith the Lord of Hosts concerning the (false) prophets; Behold I will feed them with wormwood, and make them drink the water of gaul."*   Jer 23:15

The result is death, as predicted when the fourth seal was broken (Rev 6:8): *many men died of the waters, because they were made bitter* (Rev 8:11). The fourth trumpet is now ready to sound.

Trump 4  As the fourth trumpet sounds, the sun and the moon and the stars are all affected.

As the fourth trump sounds, the heavens change the way they have operated for over 6000 years. Now the cosmos begins to change, and 1/3 of the celestial bodies are affected.

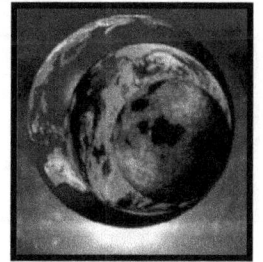

"A third part of the sun was smitten, and the third part of the moon, and a third part of the stars; so as the third part of them was darkened, and the day shown not for a third part of it, and the night likewise."   Rev 8:12

The Lord God created all of the heavens and the earth. He created the sun to govern the years and the seasons, and the moon was created to determine the days and the months. In the beginning God said:

> **"*Let* there be light, and there was light. And God saw the light, and it was good: and God divided the light from the darkness."**   Genesis 1:3-4

It is possible that the antichrist and the false prophet may use these events to fulfill a prophecy from Daniel.

> *"And he (the antichrist) will speak great words against the most High, and shall wear out the saints of the most High, and think to change times and laws."*   Daniel 7:25

Time and seasons are determined by the movement and regularity of the sun and moon. The *laws of nature* under which crops are grown may now be seriously affected. It is possible that even time may change as the end nears

At this point, an announcement is proclaimed from **an angel flying through Heaven**. The angel announces in a loud voice that although the first four trumpets have been disastrous, the worst is yet to come in the sounding of the last three trumpets. The *fifth, sixth and seventh trumpets* are so severe that they are called the *three woes* (Rev 8:13). The 5th trumpet now sounds.

Trump 5  As the fifth trumpet sounds, Satan is given a key to the bottomless pit, and demon locusts are released to torture mankind. There are soo many the "sky is darkened".

As the fifth trumpet sounds, we are given a glimpse of the underworld dungeons that are reserved for particularly bad demons and fallen angels (Rev 9:1). There are several compartments of confinement mentioned in the Holy Scriptures. The place referenced here is called *Abussos*. The Aramaic word for *Abussos* is *a-bis*, and it means *very deep,*
bottomless. The word *Abussos* is never used in translation. The King James Bible which we use in this manuscript translates the word nine times. It is translated *deep* two times (Luke 8:31, Romans 10:7); it is translated *bottomless* 2 times (Rev 9:1, Rev

9:2); and it is translated *bottomless pit* five times (Rev 9:11, Rev 11:7, Rev 17:8, Rev 20:1 and Rev 20:3). *Abussos* is an abode for evil spirits, but it is not their final resting place. Their final destination is the ***lake of fire and brimstone***, which is from the Aramaic word *Ghenna*. It is important that we stress this concept to identify what is happening when the fifth trumpet is blown. We are told that John sees:

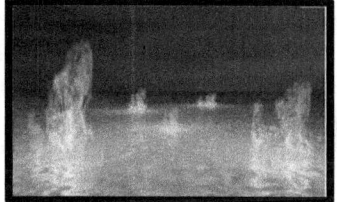

"a star fall from heaven to earth: and to him was given the key to the bottomless pit."   Rev 9:1

It is safe to assume that this key is given to Satan, for we can correlate this event with that given in Revelation Chapter 12.

"And that great dragon was cast out, that old serpent, called the Devil and Satan, which deceiveth the whole world: he was cast out into the earth and his angels were cast out with him."   Rev 12:9

In a rather obscure statement, Christ had just commissioned the 70 to go before him two-by-two into every city that He would visit to prepare the way (Like 10:1). Christ then empowered them to heal the sick (Luke 10:9) as a sign that He was coming. The seventy returned later with joy, reporting that *even the demons are subject to us in Your Name*. The reaction of Christ was undoubtedly a *mystery* at that time. He turned and said to them, *I saw Satan fall like lightning from heaven.* Christ was not impressed with their power over demons, He saw far into the future when Michael and his angels defeated Satan and all his angels and cast them out of heaven (Rev 12:7-10).

Satan has just been in a war in the heavens, and has been defeated. His defeat results in him and 1/3 of all the angels being cast out of heaven and onto the earth (Rev 12:3-4). Up until this point in time, Satan has had access to the very throne of God (Job 2:1). Satan is furious, and he now begins to persecute all who dwell upon the earth for 42 months or more precisely 1260 days (Rev 13:5). This event starts the tribulation period, the last half of Daniel's 70th week.

> **"Woe to the inhabitants of the earth and of the sea! For the devil is come down unto you, having great wrath, because he knoweth he has but a short time."** Rev 12:12

Satan uses the key that Christ has given to him and opens the bottomless pit.

> *"there arose a smoke out of the pit (Abussos), as the smoke of a great furnace; and the sun and the air were darkened by reason of the smoke from the pit."*
> Rev 9:2

This smoke is followed by a swarm of demons that have the appearance of demon locusts.

> *"and there came out of the smoke locusts upon the earth: and unto them was given power, as the scorpions of the earth have power. And it was commanded them that they should not hurt the grass of the earth, neither any green thing, neither any tree; but only those men which have not the seal of God in their forehead."* Rev 9:4

This passage is full of interesting information. *First*, notice that they cannot **hurt the grass** or any **tree** or any **green thing**. This is because the results of blowing the first trumpet have killed 1/3 of all the trees and green grass.

Trees make the oxygen that we breathe, and without them we would die. Green grass feeds many animals, and without green grass there would be mass genocide of those species. So, no further harm is allowed to

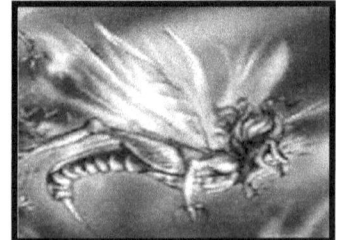

either the trees or the grass at this time. *Second*, we can be sure that the ***bottomless pit*** is a real place and that it now holds particular bad angels. It is, however, only a temporary holding place. Satan will be bound and thrown in there for the 1000-year millennial kingdom. We are told that there is a strong demon now being held in the bottomless pit which will come forth to inhabit and control the antichrist (Rev 9:11). This strong demon is called a ***beast***. This beast has evidently been a deadly and effective opponent of Jesus Christ and his gospel of salvation. He or his counterparts has also opposed all forms of Godly living and truth throughout history. We will discuss these things in great detail in Chapter 21, but for now we note that in Rev 17 we are told of *a great whore* who has committed spiritual *fornication* with kings of the earth. She is arrayed in ***purple and scarlet, decked with gold and precious stones, and pearls; and a golden cup in her hand full of abominations and the filthiness of her fornication*** (Rev 17: 4). This scarlet-arrayed woman is ***the mother of harlots and abominations of the earth*** (Rev 17:5). This harlot is sitting astride a ***scarlet colored beast, full of names of blasphemy, having seven heads and 10 horns*** (Rev 17:3). We will see that the *beast* that carries the woman during the tribulation period is the satanically- indwelled antichrist. The *seven heads* represent the great world powers (nations) who have persecuted the Jews and Christians throughout the ages, and the 10 horns represent the 10-nation confederacy over which the antichrist will reign in the end times. However, the subject of our discussion here is the *beast*. To the world, this beast is stunning and arrayed in splendor…but it is wicked. The beast is used to describe the *antichrist*, which is in fact the physical manifestation of a demonic angel, who was previously released from the bottomless pit.

> **"The beast that thou sawest** (who carries the scarlet arrayed woman) **shall ascend out of the bottomless pit, and go into perdition: and they that dwell on the earth shall wonder, whose names were not written in the book of life from the foundation of the world, when they beheld the beast that was, and is not and yet is."** Rev 17:8

Who is being persecuted as the fifth trumpet sounds? Clearly, it is anyone who does not have the *seal of God in their forehead* (Rev 9:4). What is this seal? We are not told, but we are told who is being divinely protected in Revelation 7.

> *"And after these things I saw four angels standing on the four corners of the earth, holding the four winds of the earth, that the wind should not blow on the earth, nor on the sea, nor on any tree. And I saw another angel ascending from the east, having the seal of the living God: and he cried with a loud voice to the four angels, to whom it was given to hurt the earth and the sea, saying, hurt not the earth, neither the sea, nor the trees, till we have sealed the servants of our God in their foreheads. And I heard the number of them which were sealed: and there were sealed an hundred and forty and four thousand of all the tribes of the children of Israel."*   Rev 7:1-4

There is a description of the demonic locusts and their mission in Rev 9. *And it was given that they should not kill them (those persons without the mark), but that they should be tormented five months: and their torment was as the torment of a scorpion* (Rev 9:5). They were shaped *like horses prepared for battle*; they had *crowns of gold on their head*; **and they had** *the faces of men*. Their teeth were like *Lion's teeth*; and their *hair like women*. They wore *breastplates of iron*; the sound of their wings was as *chariots rushing to battle*; and the sting was *in their tails* (Rev 9:7-10). These are awesome creatures that inflict pain but do not kill. The torture will be excruciating.

We are next given another glimpse into the spirit world and its inhabitants. In this place called *Abussos* there is an angel who is called *the* angel of the bottomless pit. His name is **Abaddon** (Hebrew) or **Apollyon** (Greek). Both words mean *the destroyer*. This very strong angel is called the *king* of the demonic locust army. Evidently, Satan has many of these strong angels at his command, for Paul told us that there are hierarchies of demonic beasts including powerful rulers.

> *"For we wrestle not against flesh and blood, but against principalities, against powers, against the rulers of the darkness of this world and against spiritual wickedness in high places."* Ephesians 6:12

The fifth trumpet is called the *first woe*. There are two more *woes* to come in the sixth and seventh trumpets. The 6th trumpet now sounds and brings worldwide demonic persecution.

Trump 6 As the sixth trumpet sounds, there are 4 mighty angels released "at the River Euphrates". Thet command an army of "200 million" "horses with riders".

As the sixth trumpet sounds, more death and destruction are unleashed upon those that dwell on the earth. The *second woe* commences as the sixth trumpet sounds (Rev 9:13). The *second woe* is announced from one of the *four horns of the golden altar which is before God*. The four horns are seen only here in the New Testament. But, in both the Old and New Testament, a *horn* is used to represent power or nations (Dan 7:24, Dan 8, Rev 12:3), individuals (Psalms 75:10) or actual horns that can be blown. The antichrist is depicted as a *little horn* (Dan 7:8); the Lord is depicted as the *horn of our salvation* (Psalm 18: 2); and Jesus Christ is called *a horn of salvation* (Luke 1:69). The Ark of the Covenant in the Old Testament had four horns, one on each corner of the lid. In context, it is better to assume that an angel in close proximity to the four horns announces what is about to occur rather than the one of the horns themselves. The agent of this announcement has been given great power, because he commanded the angel which held the sixth trumpet to *loose the four angels which are bound in the great River Euphrates* (Rev 9:14). The Euphrates River forms the border between Saudi Arabia and the countries of Syria and

Iraq. It was the principle water source for the great Babylonian Empire, and the headwaters of the Euphrates River were said to be formed from the river that flowed through the Garden of Eden (Gen 2:10-14). As the sixth trumpet sounds, we are told something quite remarkable about the four angels released from the river.

> *"And the four angels were loosed, which were prepared for an hour, and a day, and a month and a year to slay the third of men."* Rev 9:15

Imagine that! Who can doubt the omnipresence and omnipotence of Almighty God? He knows all, He sees all, and He controls all. These four angels are waiting until an exact hour to fulfill their destiny. Their mission is not mercy but death and destruction as predicted when the fourth seal was opened (Rev 6:8). We are told that their army is **200 million horsemen**. The horses are similar to the demonic locusts released when the fifth trumpet sounded, but they are more frightening both in the power to kill and in their appearance.

> *"And thus I saw the horses in the vision, and them that sat on them, having breastplates of fire, and of jacinth, and brimstone: and the heads of the horses were as the heads of lions; and out of their mouths issued smoke and brimstone."* Rev 9:17

Their command is to kill 1/3 of all mankind, and they kill by issuing fire and brimstone out of their mouths and tails. Nothing like this supernatural event has ever occurred in the history of mankind. Some have supposed that these creatures were actually attack helicopters that john described as demonic horses

> *" By these three was the third part of men killed, by the fire, and by the smoke, and by the brimstone, which issued out of their mouths. For their power is in their mouth, and in their tails: for their tails were like unto serpents, and had heads, and with them they do hurt. "* Rev 9:18-19

Amazingly, the reaction of those attacked by the demonic hoards unleashed by the fifth and sixth trumpets is not to ask for mercy or grace; but the attitude is one of scorn and defiance.

"And the rest of the men who were not killed by these plagues yet repented not of the works of their hands, that they should not worship devils, and idols of gold, and silver, and brass, and stone, and of wood: which neither can see, nor hear, nor walk. Neither repented they of their murders, nor of their sorceries, nor of their fornication, nor of their thefts." Rev 9:20-21

The time has come for the sounding of the seventh trumpet (Rev 11:15-19).

Trump 7 As the seventh trumpet sounds, the prophecies of Daniel's 70th week start to be fulfilled. The 7 Bowl judgements are imminent

We will briefly discuss the seventh trumpet, but it is so important that we will devote most of an entire chapter (Chapter 23) to its discussion.

"And the seventh angel sounded; and there were great voices in heaven, saying, The kingdoms of this world are become the kingdoms of our Lord, and of his Christ; and he shall reign for ever and ever. And the four and twenty elders, which sat before God on their seats, fell upon their faces, and worshipped God, Saying, We give thee thanks, O Lord God Almighty, which art, and wast, and art to come; because thou hast taken to thee thy great power, and hast reigned. And the nations were angry, and thy wrath is come, and the time of the dead, that they should be judged, and that thou shouldest give reward unto thy servants the prophets, and to the saints, and them that fear thy name, small and great; and shouldest destroy them which

destroy the earth. And the temple of God was opened in heaven, and there was seen in his temple the ark of his testament: and there were lightnings, and voices, and thunderings, and an earthquake, and great hail." Rev 11:15-19

The seventh angel sounds the seventh trumpet, and this gives rise to rejoicing in heaven, but on earth *the nations are angry*. This incredible reaction on the earth is because those who are angry blindly and totally follow after the Antichrist and his false prophet. Note that when the seventh angel sounds the seventh trumpet, the following things will come to pass.

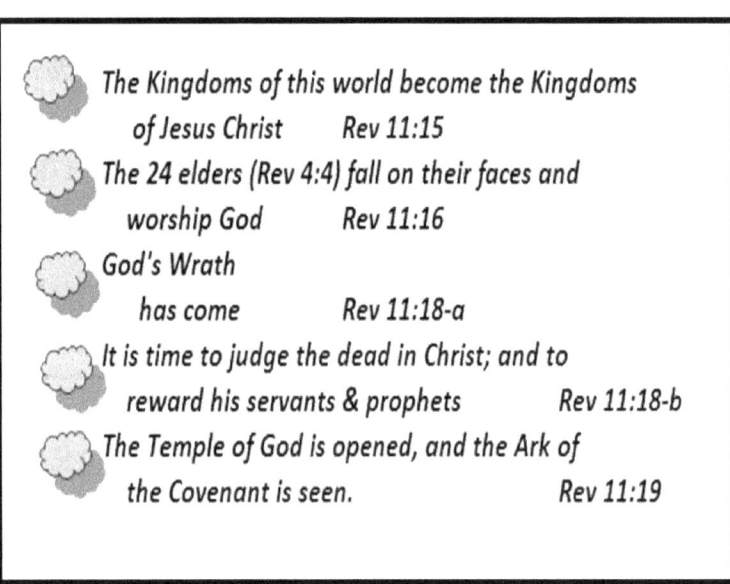

Anyone reading Rev 11:18 without a preconceived bias would immediately recognize that all believers (living and dead) will be rewarded for their deeds at the *rapture of the church*. The seventh trumpet is without controversy when this will occur.

The Seven Bowl Judgments
The seven bowls (vials) are the *Wrath of God* (Rev 15:1, 16:1). *The Wrath of God* does not fall on believers. All living

believers will be raptured out at the sounding of the seventh trumpet. The rapture of all living saints and the resurrection of the righteous dead will occur after 1250 days, 10 days short of the 1260 day period which constitutes the last

> Seven angels are summoned to pour out the *Wrath of God* upon the Kingdom of Satan…..″ And I heard a great voice out of the temple saying to the seven angels. Go your ways and pour out the vials (bowls) of the *Wrath of God* upon the earth″ Rev 16:1

half of Daniel's 70th week. Christ prophesied of this time in the Olivet Discourse.

> **"and unless those days be shortened, no flesh would be saved; but for the elects sake, those days will be shortened."** Matthew 24:22

One of the keys to understanding the sequence of events in the tribulation period, and how those events relate to the ***elect*** (the church), is to understand the concept of ***God's Wrath***. In Rev 15:1, 15:7, and Rev 16:1, we are told that the *Wrath of God* is the seven bowl judgments. We must ask the question, is the Elect (the body of Christ) expected to suffer through God's wrath? The answer is no from many scriptures. Several are given below.

> *"For God hath not appointed us to wrath, but to obtain salvation by our Lord Jesus Christ."* I Thessalonians 5: 9

> *"He that believeth on the Son hath everlasting life: and he that believeth not the Son shall not see life; but the Wrath of God abideth on him."* John 3:36

> *"Much more then, being now justified by his blood, we shall be saved from wrath through him."* Romans 9: 5
> *"Behold, the day of the LORD cometh, cruel both with wrath and fierce anger, to lay the land desolate: and he

> *shall destroy the sinners thereof out of it. Therefore I will shake the heavens, and the earth shall remove out of her place, in the wrath of the LORD of hosts, and in the day of his fierce anger."* Isaiah 13: 9, 13

> *"That day is a day of wrath, a day of trouble and distress, a day of wasteness and desolation, a day of darkness and gloominess, a day of clouds and thick darkness, Neither their silver nor their gold shall be able to deliver them in the day of the LORD's wrath; but the whole land shall be devoured by the fire of his jealousy: for he shall make even a speedy riddance of all them that dwell in the land."* Zephaniah 1: 15, 18

The *Wrath of God* is poured out upon those who have rejected salvation by not believing on his Son, Jesus Christ. Having declared that the church will not have to be subjected to God's Wrath, there needs to be a clear distinction made between *tribulation* and *wrath*. *Tribulation* is the suffering and persecution that the world and Satan will put on any true believer in Christ, while *wrath* is God's suffering and righteous justice that He will execute on unbelievers at the end of the church age. The church will be saved from God's wrath by being raptured out at the seventh trumpet Christ has told us that we will **suffer much tribulation**, but Jesus comforted us by saying that with great tribulation comes peace.

> *"These things I have spoken to you, that in Me you may have peace. In the world you will have tribulation, but take courage; I have overcome the world."* John 16:33

Tribulation is necessary to mature us and prepare us for the world to come, and to move us toward perfection: But we are not appointed to *God's Wrath*. The following verses reflect what the scriptures teach on this important concept.

> *"We glory in tribulations also: knowing that tribulation worketh patience; and patience experience; and experience, hope."* Romans 5:3-4

"For the Wrath of god is revealed from heaven against all ungodliness and unrighteousness of men who suppress the truth in unrighteousness."   Romans 1: 18

"For God hath not appointed us to wrath."   I Thess. 5:9

There will be a more detailed discussion of what happens when the seventh trump is blown in Chapter 23, but for now please note carefully what is revealed *after* the seventh trump is blown (Rev 11:15).

"And the nations were angry (Rev 9:20-21), and thy wrath is come." Rev 11:18

How could it be clearer? God's Wrath is not poured out upon the earth until the seventh trumpet has sounded. And what follows the seventh trumpet sounding? Everyone agrees that the seven bowls are poured out after the seventh trumpet has sounded.

Let us examine the seven bowl judgments that represent the *Wrath of God*. The first bowl persecutes those who have followed after Satan, the Antichrist and the False Prophet.

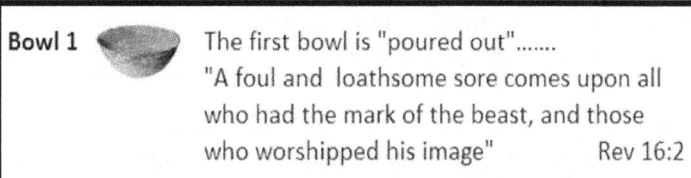

Bowl 1 — The first bowl is "poured out"……. "A foul and loathsome sore comes upon all who had the mark of the beast, and those who worshipped his image"   Rev 16:2

The first judgment upon the earth (Bowl 1) brings misery in the form of *foul and loathsome sores.* It is interesting that these sores only affect those who have received the **mark of the beast**" in either their forehead or their right hand (Rev 13:16-18). It appears that any who receives this mark will also commit to supporting Satan and the Antichrist…. They **worshipped his image.** It is important to recognize who the Wrath of God will be poured out upon. No true believer remains on earth…. The only people on earth who still remain are unbelievers and the 144,000 divinely protected and sealed group of Jews seen in Rev 7.

"And there fell a noisome and grievous sore upon the men which had the mark of the beast and upon them that worshipped his image."
Rev 13:15-16, 16:2

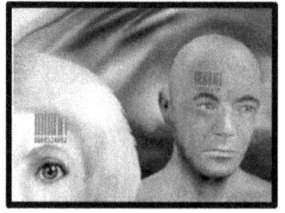

The church is gone, having been raptured out at the seventh trumpet. The only believers in Jesus Christ who remain have either been divinely protected from God's Wrath by a mark on their wrist or forehead (Rev 7:3). This group is all Jewish, not one gentile believer in the entire 144,000 (Rev 7:4). Why are they still on the earth? The answer to this question is simple once one understands the covenant that God made with Abraham in Gen 15.

"The Lord made a covenant with Abram, saying, unto thy seed have I given this land, from the River of Egypt (Nile River) to the River Euphrates." Genesis 15:18

The *Abrahamic Covenant* has always been of primary importance to the Hebrew nation. It has always been understood that God promised them all of the land from the Nile River to the Euphrates River; from the great sea (Mediterranean) to the lesser sea (Galilee). Even under the leadership of Joshua, David and Solomon; this promise was not fulfilled. Nevertheless, God's word is eternal and Israel as a nation will possess the land in the future. Numerous Old Testament passages anticipate the future blessing of Israel and her possession of the land as promised to Abraham. Ezekiel envisions a future day when Israel is restored to the land (Ezekiel 20:33–37, 40–42; 36:1–37:28). During the millennial kingdom, the Jewish nation will finally inherit and live in the land promised to them long ago. The Jewish remnant that will possess and live in the land is the 144,000 and their progeny. It is also necessary to understand that Abraham was promised many descendents. He was to produce through his loins three *seeds*. The *first* is **Jesus Christ**, the savior of the world.

> *"Now to Abraham and his seed were the promises made. He saith not, And to seeds, as of one, and to thy seed, which is Christ."* Galatians 3:16

The *second seed* is an **earthly seed**, which will inherit the earth. This is composed of the 144,000 In Rev 7, and those who survive the trumpet and bowl judgments.

> *"For all the land which thou seest, to thee will I give it, and to thy seed for ever. And I will make thy seed as the dust of the earth: so that if a man can number the dust of the earth, then shall thy seed also be numbered."* Genesis 13:15-16

The *third seed* is those throughout the ages who **will recognize Jesus Christ as their Messiah**, and enter into the new covenant. There have been many who have believed on the name of Jesus Christ down through the ages: Those of promise from the old covenant, who believed the prophets when they spoke of a coming Messiah; and those Jews born of the Holy Spirit under the new covenant. These are the *starry seed* of Abraham; they (living or dead) will join the body of Christ and be resurrected at the seventh trump. Those 144,000 who have been sealed and protected will inherit the Promised Land during the millennial kingdom. Members of the body of Christ will live above the City of Jerusalem in a glorious city with Christ called the New Jerusalem (Rev 22:1-5).The reconstituted nation of Israel will be ruled over by King David on the earth (Ez. 37:24-25). They constitute the *dusty seed* of Abraham.... the seed of the earth.

> *"For by one Spirit are we all baptized into one body, whether we be Jews or Gentiles, whether we be bond or free; and have been all made to drink into one Spirit."* I Cor. 12:1

> *"And it shall come to pass in that day, that the great trumpet shall be blown, and they shall come which were ready to perish in the land of Assyria, and the outcasts in the land of Egypt, and shall worship the LORD in the holy mount at Jerusalem."* Isaiah 27:13

"And in mercy shall his throne be established: and he shall sit upon it in truth in the tabernacle of David, judging, and seeking judgment, and hasting righteousness:" Is. 16:5

The time has now arrived for the *second bowl* to be poured out.

Bowl 2   The second bowl is "poured out".......
The sea is turned to blood and
everything in the sea dies.   Rev 16:3

As the second Bowl is poured out, every living creature in the sea dies as the seas (oceans) of the earth turn to blood. The world today lives off of the fruits of the sea. Billions of tons of fish are  consumed every day. When the second bowl is poured out and *every creature in the sea dies* as they wash ashore, the stench will be unbearable and disease will rapidly spread from decaying bodies. Sea water cannot sustain men, but now as the *third bowl* is poured out, all the fresh water comes under God's Wrath.

Bowl 3   The third bowl is "poured out".......
All of the fresh water turns to blood. Rev 16:4

When the *third bowl* is poured out upon the earth, an event takes place which is so catastrophic that just the thought of its occurrence is unbelievable. *All* fresh water turns to blood. Water is the element that is most required to sustain life. Man can go without food for long periods of time, but without water one will

280

die in a matter of days. The only fresh water left to sustain life after the third bowl is poured out upon the earth is bottled water, and it will not last long. In addition, every plant and creature is now doomed. There are many prophecy teachers who teach that the bowl judgments will take place over the last 1260 days of Daniel's 70th week. These teachers are not reading the scriptures very carefully. The end is near, possibly a matter of days when the bowls are poured out, particularly for those in rural, isolated areas. The torture of men continues when the contents of the *fourth bowl* is poured out.

Bowl 4   The fourth bowl is "poured out".......
The contents of this bowl are poured
on the sun, The angel who pours
this bowl "scorched men with fire"   Rev 16:8

The angel in charge of this bowl takes its contents and *pours it upon the sun*. This symbolically represents the power given to him by God to *scorch men with fire.* The results are predictable.

"and men were scorched with great heat, and they blasphemed the name of God who has power over these plagues, and they did not repent and give Him glory"
   Rev 16:9

One would think that the reaction of men to divine judgment would be to repent and ask God to spare them of this torture. But man is *deceitfully wicked.*

"We know that whosoever is born of God sinneth not; but he that is begotten of God keepeth himself, and that wicked one toucheth him not. And we know that we are of God, and the whole world lieth in wickedness." 1 John 5: 18-19

Remember that every living Christian who has accepted Jesus Christ as his/her savior has been raptured out before the seven angels with the seven bowls, the Wrath of God, are poured out. We will see in Chapter 11 that the seven bowl judgments will be poured out in rapid succession over a 10-day period between the Jewish Feast of Trumpets on Tishri 1, and the Feast of Yom Kippur on Tishri 10. Jewish tradition calls these days the *days of awe* and the *days of repentance*. We have already studied the prophetic significance of the last three fall feasts (Rosh Hashanah, Yom Kippur and Tabernacles) and the 10 days between Tishri 1 (Rosh Hashanah) and Tishri 10 (Yom Kippur). The earth is *reeling* as the *fifth bowl* is now poured out

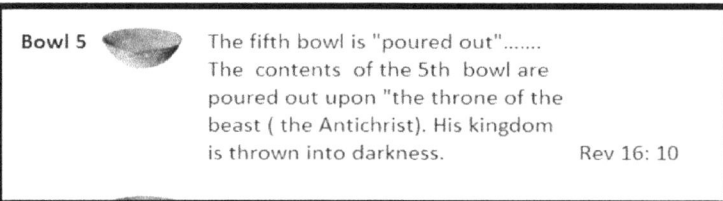

Bowl 5 — The fifth bowl is "poured out"....... The contents of the 5th bowl are poured out upon "the throne of the beast (the Antichrist). His kingdom is thrown into darkness.   Rev 16: 10

As the 5th bowl is emptied, the prophecies of Joel will finally come to pass.

> *"The sun shall be turned into darkness, and the moon into blood, before the great and the terrible day of the Lord come."*   Joel 2:31

The moon turning to blood has already been predicted as the sixth seal opened. Note that the removal of the sixth seal predicts catastrophes which will occur *very near* the end of the 1260 day period of tribulation, and *NOT* before the seven bowl judgments are executed as the majority of prophecy teachers maintain. This is because they fail to recognize that the seals provide only an *overview* of the tribulation period and show general conditions which will exist. The seals *do not* represent a sequence of events which *precede* the seven trumpets or the seven bowl judgments. They preview the devestation and catastrophies that the 7 trumpets and the 7 bowls bring.

The 6th bowl is now poured out to prepare the way for the armies of Satan to march upon Jerusalem. The Euphrates River dries up

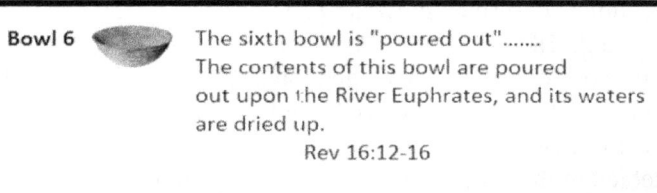

Bowl 6 — The sixth bowl is "poured out"....... The contents of this bowl are poured out upon the River Euphrates, and its waters are dried up.
Rev 16:12-16

so that the way of the kings from the East might be prepared (Rev 16:12). These are the main land armies of the antichrist. The great *Battle of Armageddon* has arrived. All who have taken the mark of the beast will join this campaign. They will be supernaturally gathered by *three unclean spirits* from all over the world by Satan, the antichrist and the false prophet.

> *"and I saw three unclean spirits like frogs coming from the mouth of the dragon (Satan), out of the mouth of the beast (antichrist) and out of the mouth of the false prophet (Beast out of the sea). For they are spirits of demons, performing signs, which go out to the kings of the earth , and of the whole world, to gather them to the battle of the great day of God Almighty."*   *Rev 16:13-14*

Satan will think that he is gathering his armies to this great final battle, but in reality it is being done according to God's eternal plan.

The word *Armageddon* appears only once in the entire Bible and is found in Revelation 16:16. No place on earth actually bears the name Armageddon. The Greek is most commonly thought to be a transliteration of the Hebrew *har Megiddo*... literally, *mountain of Megiddo*. The Mount of Megiddo is actually a *tell* or a high hill overlooking the plain of Esdraelon or Jezreel, a valley fourteen by twenty miles in size located to the southwest of Nazareth. Here, it is thought by many, that the great final battle of Armageddon will be fought.

At this point, we would like to clarify that the great battle of Armageddon is described in Ezekiel 38-39. There is an ongoing debate among Biblical scholars as to whether Ezekiel 38-39 is a description of the battle of Armageddon described in Rev 19:19-21 or whether it describes the last great battle following the 1000-year millennial reign described briefly in Rev 20:7-10. We are indebted to the following source of information for portions of this critique: http://www.gotquestions.org/Gog-Magog.html The confusion that has resulted is in the use of the terms **Gog and Magog** in both Ez. 38:1-2 and Ez. 39:39; and in Rev 20:8. The assumption that all these passages refer to the same battle is, however, just an illusion. *Magog* was a grandson of Noah (Genesis 10:2). The descendants of Magog settled to the far north of Israel, likely beyond the Black Sea just south of current day Russia. They migrated into parts of Germany, and may have even settled in southern Russia. It is important to recognize that the Gog and Magog of Ezekiel 38-39 are different from the Gog and Magog mentioned in Revelation 20:7-8. *Gog* is a title, just as *prince* is a title. Below are some of the more obvious reasons why Ezekiel 38-39 cannot describe the final great battle following the Millennial Kingdom.

1. In the battle of Ezekiel 38-39, the armies come primarily from the north and involve only a few nations of the earth (Ezekiel 38: 6, 15; 39: 2). The battle in Revelation 20:7-9 will involve all nations, so armies will come from all directions, not just from the north.
2. There is no mention of Satan in the context of Ezekiel 38-39. In Revelation 20:7 the context clearly places the battle at the end of the millennium with Satan as the primary character.
3. Ezekiel 39: 11-12 states that the dead will be buried for seven months. There would be no need to bury the dead if the battle in Ezekiel 38-39 is the one described in Revelation 20:8-9, for immediately following Revelation

20: 8-9 is the Great White Throne judgment (Rev 20: 11-15) and then the current or present heaven and earth are destroyed, replaced by a new heaven and earth (Revelation 21:1). There obviously will be a need to bury the dead if the battle takes place in the early part of the tribulation, for the land of Israel will be occupied for another 1,000 years, the length of the millennial kingdom (Revelation 20:4-6).
4. The prophecies of Ezekiel in Ez. 38-39 are immediately followed by an extensive description of the millennial kingdom in Chapters 40-44. Chronologically, this eliminates the battle described in Rev 21:8-9, since they clearly occur after the millennial kingdom has run its 1000-year course (Rev 21:7).

We will not devote any more time or space to this important issue at this time. However, the entire content of Chapter 26 is devoted to the proper identification of the battles described in Ezekiel 38-39 and Rev 21.

The seventh and last bowl is about to be poured out. This will terminate both Daniel's 70 weeks of years and the worldwide reign of the Antichrist. The Battle of Armageddon is about to take place.

Bowl 7   The seventh bowl is poured into the air........

"And the seventh angel poured out his vial into the air; and there came a great voice out of the temple of heaven, from the throne, saying, It is done. And there were voices, and thunders, and lightnings; and there was a great earthquake, such as was not since men were upon the earth, so mighty an earthquake, and so great." *Rev 16: 17-18*

When the seventh angel pours out the seventh bowl, a loud voice from out of the temple in heaven is heard from the Throne. This voice loudly proclaims that: ***It is done*** (Rev 16:17). There is immediately widespread destruction upon the earth. Although it is not revealed to us who issues this proclamation, it is altogether appropriate that the declaration It *is done* comes directly from God himself. After all, it was the voice of God who initiated the seven bowl judgments. The voice of God brought the world into existence, and only He can wreak such devastation and destruction upon His earth. It is also appropriate that the voice should come directly from His holy temple. Only one other place in the book of Revelation is the temple and the throne of God mentioned together, and that is in Revelation 7:15 when the saints of all ages are seen assembling before God. It is poignant that this is so. God sent His only begotten Son to save all who would believe upon Him, and both the work of the cross and the work of battle at Armageddon are testimonies to his majesty. However, we should not try to assign too much spiritual meaning to this declaration. The most obvious meaning is that the seven bowl judgments are the Wrath of God, and they were initiated at His word. These judgments are now finished. The following things are recorded as occurring after the seventh bowl is emptied.

	From the Temple of God there is heard "IT IS DONE"	(Rev 16:17)
	Thunderings, lightning and a great earthquake	(Rev 16:18)
	Jerusalem divided into 3 parts	(Rev 16:19)
	All cities fall	(Rev 16:19)
	"The great city" was divided into 3 parts	(Rev 16:19)
	Babylon (Seat of Satan) is destroyed	(Rev 16:19)
	Every island moves from its place	(Rev 16:20)
	Every mountain falls to the ground	(Rev 16:20)
	Hail about 100 pounds apiece fall	(Rev 16:21)

The occurrence of *thunder, lightning, earthquakes and hail* are not unique during the last 3.5 years of the tribulation period. In fact, recall that after the seventh trumpet was blown (Rev 11:19) an almost identical description of events is recorded.

> *"Then the temple of God was opened in Heaven and the Ark of the Covenant was seen in His temple. And there were lightening, noises, thunderings, an earthquake and great hail."* Rev 11:19

This scene is difficult to correlate with Rev 16:18-19. Many prophecy students have used the scene after the seventh trumpet is blown to *prove* that the seven bowl judgments *telescope* or emerge from the seventh trumpet. While there may be some apparent truth to this theory, it is clear that God himself initiates both the trumpet and bowl sequences, they are chronologically linked and separated in time. The seven trumpet judgments take place during the persecution of the antichrist, the false prophet and Satan himself over the last 3.5 years.. The bowl judgments take place immediately following this 3.5 year period of time has expired. While these two collective judgments are virtually identical in structure, they are vastly different in terms of severity. The earthquake which occurs at bowl seven is the granddaddy of all earthquakes!

> *"And there was a great earthquake, such a mighty and great earthquake as had not occurred since men were on earth."* Rev 16:18-b

> *"And there fell upon men a great hail out of heaven, every stone about the weight of a talent: and men blasphemed God because of the plague of the hail; for the plague thereof was exceeding great."* Rev 16:21

Gigantic hail *fell upon men* and *every hailstone was about the weight of a talent* (Rev 16:21). The weight of a talent is about 100 pounds. It is likely that hail of that size has never fallen on the earth.

 Hail about 100 pounds apiece fall   (Rev 16:21)

The reaction of man is unbelievable. It had never changed since the sixth trumpet sounded (Rev 9:20-21)

> *"And man blasphemed God because of the plague of the hail, since that plague was exceedingly great."*
> Rev 16:21-b

The next result of pouring out the seventh bowl is that the cities of the world fall apart.

"...*and the cities of the nations fell...*"   Rev 16:19

As we approach the end of the church age, the cities of the world spiral further and further into Satan's grasp. It is true that there are many mega churches and active congregations in every major city, but Christianity and living for Christ is definitely in the minority. Drugs, alcohol, prostitution, adultery and crime are everywhere. Recent studies have shown that only 5% of youth under the age of 18 will follow Christ and regularly attend church. At the seventh bowl, we are told that *the cities of the nations fell* (Rev 16:19). We are not told just what is meant by *fell,* but it is almost certain that due to natural or supernatural causes, multistory buildings and all skyscrapers will collapse in piles of rubble.

John also records that he saw *the great city divided into three parts* (Rev 16:19). There is no doubt that this great city is

Jerusalem, because in Rev 11:8 we are told that the dead bodies of the two witnesses that testify for 1260 days *will lie in the street of the great city which spiritually is called Sodom and Egypt where also our Lord was crucified.* We

are given no details as to how Jerusalem will be divided, but since the city will be divided into three parts, it is possible that the epicenter of the *great earthquake* might occur there and divide the city with great chasms. The destruction of cities around the world and the division of Jerusalem into three parts indicate extensive, worldwide destruction. The shock and aftershock will be supernaturally felt worldwide. Devastation is also indicated for a city called Babylon, which is the seat of Satan's world empire. It will be destroyed by a great ***millstone*** (Rev 18:21). We will devote two entire chapters (Chapters 21-22) to the destruction of physical and spiritual Babylon, and to its likely identification. For now, it is sufficient to say that there is no need to doubt that since Jerusalem has been mentioned by name immediately preceding this prophecy, that *Babylon* is the actual name of a city which has been rebuilt and occupied in the land of Shinar (Zach. 5:1-11). There is no need to spiritualize the name Babylon to secretly camouflage Rome, or Jerusalem or any other city. Babylon will be rebuilt in the end times and it will be completely and utterly destroyed by God at the end of the age (Rev 16). It is true that the ancient city of Babylon that Nimrod built was destroyed by God and the people scattered all over the world after ***confounding their language*** (Gen 11:1-9). It is also true that the city of Babylon that Nimrod built was also a seat of political and military power when the Babylonian Empire held sway over the entire known world. It held the throne of Nebuchadnezzar I, King of Babylon. The city was Conquered by the Medo-Persian empire and served as the capital city once again. However, it was eventually destroyed by invading forces. Isaiah and Jeremiah had a great deal to say about the fall of Babylon. Literalists argue that the Scriptures indicate a sudden destruction of Babylon whereas history records no such sudden destruction by which that city became desolation. Isaiah 47, for example, indicates that the *mistress of kingdoms* would suffer loss of children, and widow every man *in one day*. Furthermore,

Babylon will be destroyed *as when God overthrew Sodom and Gomorrah"* (Is 13:19). The destruction of Sodom and Gomorrah was not protracted through many centuries or destroyed by an invading army over a period of time, was made desolate suddenly by supernatural forces. Babylon's destruction is also to be  brought about suddenly, and the weapons of judgment are to be by fire just as Sodom and Gomorrah was destroyed *in a moment* by fire. The heavens and earth will come apart, and water will swallow up the site upon which the city stands (Isaiah 13:13, Jeremiah 51:42). The result of all this is found in the prophecies of Jeremiah.

> *"It shall never be inhabited, neither shall it be dwelt in from generation to generation: neither shall the Arabian pitch tent there; neither shall shepherds make their flocks to lie down there."* Isaiah 13:20; Jeremiah 50:3: 51:26

Although Babylon has been inhabited, conquered, and now lies mostly abandoned, Babylon is still being used by people and is partially inhabited. The above prophecy makes it clear *no tent will ever be pitched there* and it will be perpetually uninhabited. That is yet to be fulfilled, but it will happen at the end of this age.

Recall that as the sixth seal was broken, the vision that John saw predicted that *every mountain and island was moved out of its place (*Rev 6:14). As the effects of the seventh bowl are concluding, John now sees the fulfillment of that vision. Not only is every island and mountain moved *out of its place,* John now testifies that *every island fled away, and the mountains were not found* (Rev 16:20). Anyone who lived on an island or on a mountain is instantly killed. This will cause destruction and death in rural areas comparable to that which occurs as *the cities of the nations fell*. Although not specifically stated, it appears that only those people living on the plains or in isolated rural areas might be spared. However, they will not escape God's entire wrath.

Conclusion

We have discussed the *seven seals*, the *seven trumpets* and the *seven bowls*. The seven seals bind the outside of the scroll held by God, and as they are broken the events of the 1260 day tribulation period are *previewed. The seven seals function exactly as the preface to a good book.* The seven trumpets represented the **Wrath of Satan** on those who refuse to worship him or his image that will stand in the rebuilt temple in Jerusalem, or those who have refused to take the *mark of the beast*. These judgments are allowed by God. Why does God allow this persecution of the earth to take place after Satan is cast down? The purpose of the tribulation period is to fulfill Daniel's 70th week, and to bring Israel back into a covenant relationship with God by showing Israel that their long-awaited Messiah is none other than his only begotten Son, Jesus Christ. The *seven trumpets* serve to purify and refine both the precious wheat (the church) and the nation of Israel who will inherit the land during the millennial kingdom. The *seven bowls* represented the *Wrath of God* poured out upon Satan and all of his followers, following the rapture of the church at the sounding of the seventh trumpet before the seven bowl judgments occur. The seven trumpets are blown over a 1250-day period of time known as the **Tribulation**. Some call this period *the Time of Jacob's Trouble* (Jer 30:7), but this is incorrect. A careful study of Jer. 30 will establish that the phrase **Time of Jacob's Trouble** is referring to the **Day of the Lord;** and that day is exactly what it says.... The day that our Lord returns to fight the Battle of Armageddon. The last 10 days of the 1260 days that Satan is confined to the earth immediately follow the seventh trumpet. Christ referred to this time as one of **great tribulation.**

> *"For then shall be great tribulation, such as was not since the beginning of the world to this time, no, nor ever shall be."* Matthew 24:21

The bowl judgments are rapidly poured out over a seven-day period of time following the rapture of the church and the death of God's two witnesses, which lie in the street for three days and then are raised up. It remains to be shown that these statements are scripturally sound, and that is the subject of Chapter 13.

Finally, note from Rev 16:14 that the armies of the world are gathered to the Battle of Armageddon. As previously stated it is time for the ***Day of the Lord"*** to commence. The Day of the Lord is not a protracted period of time consisting of 7 years or even 3.5 years... it is exactly what the scriptures say it is.... One day. The Day of the Lord is widely misunderstood and misinterpreted by almost all prophecy teachers. *It is a literal Day, the day of Christ's Second Advent*, when He will return to fight the Battle of Armageddon. The source of confusion is universally attributed to Revelation 6:17. It specifically states that as the sixth seal is broken, the Day of Lord has come.

> *"For the great day of the Lord has come, and who is able to stand."* Rev 16:17

We believe that the seventh bowl judgments will *terminate* the 70th week of Daniel. They are so severe that the *seven bowls* will be poured out over a very short period of time. This period of time will be *seven consecutive days* between when the Church is raptured out at the Feast of Trumpets on Tishri 1, and when the Battle of Armageddon occurs on the Feast of Yom Kippur, Tishri 10. The *first three days* of this 10-day period of time are the three days that the two witnesses of God remain in the streets of Jerusalem after being killed (Rev 11:7-11). Chronologically, they start witnessing in the Jerusalem Temple three days *before* Satan is cast down and starts his 1260-day reign of terror. They are slain on the *same day* that the church is raptured out. *No living Christian* remains on the earth immediately after the rapture occurs, but during this short 10-day period of time during which the seven bowls are poured out, salvation will be offered to all those remaining. It appears that many will not repent.

> ***"And they*** (*who remained and follow Satan*) **blasphemed the God of heaven… And did not repent of their deeds."**
> Rev 16:11

It is important to recognize that the 10-day period of time in which a last chance for salvation will be offered is totally consistent with the scriptural *Pattern of the Harvest.* The rapture of the church is the *Great Wheat Harvest* that Christ predicted at the end of the age in the Parable of the Wheat and Tares.

> *"Let both grow together until the harvest: and in the time of harvest I will say to the reapers, Gather ye together first the tares, and bind them in bundles to burn them: but gather the wheat into my barn. The enemy that sowed them is the devil; the harvest is the end of the world; and the reapers are the angels."* Matthew 13: 30, 39

Wheat is the crop that sustained and fed the nation of Israel. It is such an important staple, that one would assume that it would be harvested very carefully, leaving none behind. However, when the harvest was completed a strange thing was commanded by God which was a spiritual *"Mystery"* under the old covenant.

> *"And when ye reap the harvest of your land, thou shalt not wholly reap the corners of thy field, neither shalt thou gather the gleanings of thy harvest."* Leviticus 19: 9

When Ruth came to Boaz seeking redemption, it was *following* the main harvest. Ruth came to pick the *gleanings* that were left in the field, but wound up being saved, her and her entire family, by Boaz, the kinsman redeemer. The entire story of Ruth and Boaz is prophetic and foreshadowed the restoration and salvation of Israel. The *mystery* of this story is that the remnants of the nation of Israel that enter into the bowl judgments are the *gleanings* of the main harvest at the seventh trumpet. They have not been raptured out due to disbelief, but God in His mercy will give them 10 more days to recognize Christ as their Messiah and fulfill the words of the prophet Isaiah.

> *"Who hath heard such a thing? who hath seen such things? shall the earth be made to bring forth in one day? or shall a nation be born at once? for as soon as Zion travailed, she brought forth her children."* Isaiah 66:8

The *time of travail* is the last 10 days of the Church Age and the New Covenant promises; after that time there will be no more grace. This *is the time of restoration for the Nation of Israel*. It is this time when there is apparently no hope, that hope and grace will be found. Our hope and salvation is in Jesus Christ. A Jewish remnant will finally accept Jesus Christ as their long awaited Messiah.

> *"For I would not, brethren, that ye should be ignorant of this mystery, lest ye should be wise in your own conceits; that blindness in part is happened to Israel, until the fullness of the Gentiles be come in. And so all Israel shall be saved: as it is written, There shall come out of Sion the Deliverer, and shall turn away ungodliness from Jacob."* Romans 5:26

Jewish rabbinical writings teach that the 10 days between the feast of Trumpets and the feast of Yom Kippur are the *Days of Awe* (Yamim Noraim) or the *Days of Repentance*. These are the days given to Israel to prepare to meet the Lord. One of the ongoing themes of *the Days of Awe* is the concept that God has *books* that he writes our names in, writing down who will live and who will die, who will have a good life and who will have a bad life during the next year. Actions during the *Days of Awe* can alter God's decree. The Jews believe that the actions that change the decree are *teshuvah, tefilah and dakahtze* or *repentance, prayer, and good deeds.* However, the gift of eternal life is free, and cannot be earned by works or mental attitude. All books are sealed on Yom Kippur. The Abrahamic Covenant finds its ultimate fulfillment in connection with the return of the true Messiah to rescue and bless Israel. That ultimate blessing will be the gift of eternal life to all of Israel who believes during this 10-day period of time. They will join the 144,000 from the 12 tribes of Israel who will populate the millennial kingdom here on earth. Satan and the armies of the Antichrist will now be supernaturally gathered to Jerusalem for that last great Battle of Armageddon (Rev 14: 1-20).

We will now show that all the confusion results from not recognizing that the seals, trumpets and bowls are *not successive events occurring over a seven-year period of time*, but that the seals are a *preview of conditions* which will exist during a total tribulation period of 3.5 years or 1260 days. The sixth seal is predicting those events which occur following the seventh bowl at the Battle of Armageddon. It is **the Lords Day**. We are now ready to show how the trumpets and bowls fit together chronologically, and how the 1260 days are allocated to the trumpet and bowl judgments.

Thoughts and things…….

Chapter 11

Seals, Trumpets and Bowls: Chronology

The Mystery of the Seven Seals
In Chapter 10 we described the seven seals, the seven trumpets and the seven bowls. How are the seals, trumpets and bowls chronologically related in the apocalypse? It is appropriate to briefly discuss the traditional view of how the seals, bowls and trumpets are related through time. The most widely-accepted view is that the seals represent events which will occur over a fixed period of time immediately preceding the seven trumpet judgments, which occur immediately after the seventh seal is broken. In turn, the seven bowl judgments immediately follow the seventh trumpet judgments. The most common period of time for the *seven seals* to occur is over the first 3.5 years of Daniel's 70th week. The *trumpets and bowls* occur sequentially over the next 3.5 years. The total time period is seven years, which is the exact time period of Daniel's 70th week. The last seven years of Daniel's 70th week are separated from the 69th year by an undetermined period of time, usually starting at the crucifixion of Christ and continuing today. It is generally taught under this scenario that the first 3.5 years of Daniel's 70th week correspond to the rise of a *great world leader*. Europe will be dominated by a powerful *10-nation confederacy*, and this great world leader will arise from among these nations. He will be the most influential man and the most dynamic speaker who ever lived. By *supernatural power*, he will manage to form his own army and *conquer three nations* in the 10-nation confederacy. From this power base, he will ascend to a dictatorship over the entire 10-nation alliance. In this role, he will manage to **confirm a covenant** with Israel and somehow have *Herod's temple rebuilt*. Jewish Messianic expectations are that only their long-awaited Messiah will be able to re-establish temple worship in Jerusalem on the Temple Mount where the Muslim Dome of the Rock now stands. By accepting this man as their Messiah, the nation of Israel will agree to a *covenant of peace* which will lead to *destruction and death*. At the height of his adoration and

power, this world leader will suddenly turn on Israel. He will march against *Jerusalem*, and successfully conquer the city. He will enter the newly-built temple, desecrate the holy places, and erect a statue which will be called the ***abomination of desolation.*** When Jerusalem is invaded, 2/3 of all inhabitants will be killed, and most of the remaining 1/3 of the people will flee for their lives into the deserts of *Moab*, probably to an area in Moab called *Petra*. This entire scenario is played out against fulfillment of the prophetic words of Jesus Christ in Matthew 24:1-16. These events are also said to be initiated as the 7 seals are broken. These events are all forced into an initial 3.5 year period of time, followed by the last 3.5 years of tribulation (Bowls and Trumpets). This theology rests upon several critical assumptions which we have partially discussed in Chapter 10.

> - The crucifixion of Jesus Christ occurs immediately after the 69-sevens's, or 483 years; not ***In the middle*** of the 70th week.
> - The tribulation period is seven years in duration.
> - The ***he*** in Daniel 9:27 is not Jesus Christ, but is the antichrist.
> - Opening of the seven seals occurs over an initial 3.5 year period called *birth pains*, and are immediately followed by a 3.5 year period called the *Lords Day*, which contain the trumpet and bowl judgments. This supposedly parallels Matthew 24:1-8.
> - The tribulation period described by John commences with the opening of the first seal, and terminates after the pouring out of the seventh bowl judgment.
> - The saints will be raptured out before the 70th week of Daniel starts (pre-tribulation rapture); or after the sixth seal is opened (pre-wrath rapture); after 3.5 years but before the trumpet judgments (mid–trib rapture); or after the bowl judgments (post-trib rapture).

Examining the Seven Seals

Let us examine the logic involved in having Seals one through seven open over the first 3.5 years of a final seven-year period of time. Throughout the book of Revelation, the apostle John repeatedly affirmed that God told him; *What you see, write in a book* (Rev 1:11). John *actually saw* everything that he wrote. John records:

> *"And I saw in the right hand of Him who sat on the throne scroll written inside and on the back, sealed with seven seals."* Rev 5:1

Picture the scene which John saw: God has in His right hand a scroll with seven seals. As these seven seals are broken, the words in the scroll are enacted for John; he sees what is taking place.

The scroll would have looked like the one shown on the left. The scroll would have had one seal on the outside, and when it was broken, a portion of its internal contents would be revealed. As the scroll is unrolled, six other seals inside the scroll are opened and more visions are presented to John. Now ask yourself the following question: *How many seals does the scroll in this picture contain?* The answer is obvious… There is no way to tell at all! The only way that John could have seen seven seals is if the scroll would have been sealed as that one shown on the right. Since the scroll *was in the right hand* of God (Rev 6:1), it is clear that John must have seen all the seals on the outside. The point being made is that most

Revelation scholars hold to the scenario that as each seal is broken, more of the scroll's narrative is read and revealed to John until the seventh seal is broken; time passes until 3.5 years have elapsed. All Revelation scholars agree that the scroll contains a written record of the tribulation period. What we are questioning is whether or not 3.5 years passes as the seals are broken. The apparent fact that all seven seals are external to the Revelation record indicates that another interpretation could be correct.

What we intend to show is that the seals are very much like a *preface* to a good book. The preface provides a summary of what the book contains from start to finish. The book is not started until the overview is finished. We will show beyond a reasonable doubt that this is exactly what the seals do also. In order to discover the truth, there must be scriptural evidence, and there is within the description of the seals in Revelation Chapters 6 and 8.

From our detailed description of the seals, trumpets and bowls in Chapter 10, we have pointed out that the first five seals are not sequential judgments, but only describe general conditions which will exist during the tribulation period. *Seal One* depicts a rider on a white horse (Rev 6:1-2). In Chapter 10 we showed that this is Satan who rides with death and hell. It was then shown that the rider of the second horse is Satan's agent of destruction…the antichrist. Satan is shown riding a white horse because he is mimicking Christ who will return on a white horse to fight the battle of Armageddon in Rev 19:11. However, we know from Rev 12 and 13, the antichrist will not arise until there are only 42 months or 1260 days left in the tribulation period. If the first and second seal depicts Satan and the antichrist arising to wreak havoc on mankind, this creates an impossible. The remaining seals involve widespread death, famine and destruction… which are the result the trumpet and bowl judgments which occur over the last 3.5 years of the 7 year period of tribulation.. not the first 3.5 years. *Seals Two through Four* depict widespread wars, famine and death (Rev 6:3-8). These are certainly descriptive of what is happening during the seven trumpet and the seven bowl judgments. *Seal Five* depicts a group of martyrs who are beneath the throne of God crying for vengeance (Rev 6:9-11); and there will be widespread martyrdom of the saints during the period of the trumpet judgments. *Seal Six* describes a great earthquake; the moon turns to blood; the sun becomes black; stars fall to the earth; and every mountain and island is moved out of its place. These events occur when the bowl judgments are poured out during the very last days of the antichrist's reign (Rev 12-14). It is also clearly stated that the **Wrath of God** is coming (Rev 6:16), which is without a doubt referring to the seven bowl judgments (Rev 15:1, 16:1). Traditional teaching holds that the first 3.5 years of the seven-year tribulation period are characterized by peace and tranquility, hardly what is described here. When the 7th seal is opened, there is silence for half an hour. This signals that the scroll can now be unrolled, and the contents shown; not that these events have already occurred. The entire scenario of the seals occurring lock-stepped through time over the first 3.5 years borders on unbelievable.

Conversely, the events and conditions just described are ideally matched to the sequential execution of the trumpet judgments followed by the seven bowl judgments, which will take place over the last 3.5 years. This is exactly what one might expect if the seals are only providing an overview. In fact, if the seals actually did precede the trumpets and bowls over a period of time, and take place over an initial 3.5 year period of time, the impact of opening seal six after a time delay of 3.5 years of peace is completely out of context (Rev 6: 12-17).

Note what happens during the trumpet and bowl judgments. A *great earthquake* is said to occur after the sixth seal is broken (Rev 12); but a great earthquake is not seen until after the sixth trumpet sounds (Rev 11:13) at the earliest, or until the seventh bowl is poured out (Rev 16:18) as the tribulation period comes to a close. We believe that the sixth seal simply warns and previews two devastating earthquakes.

In Rev 6:12, John records that *the sun becomes black and the moon becomes as blood.* Are we to believe that during the last 3.5 years that the sun will not shine? How ridiculous. The sun loses its light only after the fifth bowl is poured out (Rev 16:10), and the moon turns black just before the battle of Armageddon (Rev 16:10) as predicted by the prophet Joel (Joel 2:31). Both events occur just where they should, in the last days of Daniel's 70th week. The sixth seal is again just predicting and previewing these two events.

The *stars of Heaven fall* and the heavens *roll up like a scroll.* (Rev 6:14). This must also be an *end of days event*. The heavens churn and stars (meteorites) fall. Are we to believe that there are no stars and heavenly bodies for at least 3.5 years?

Every mountain and every island are moved out of their place. This is the most catastrophic event ever experienced by mankind. The recent tsunami in Japan (2011) will seem like a swimming pool wave compared to these disastrous events! This will happen, as it is seen and recorded by John, when the last bowl (seventh bowl) is poured out (Rev 16:20). This is almost proof positive that the seals simply describe this event, as we have steadfastly maintained. But there is more convincing evidence.

Just before the 7th and last seal is broken, the kings of the earth are seen hiding under rocks in caves because the ***great day of His wrath has come.*** We have pointed out scripturally that this *day* is not 7 years or 3.5 years long, but is exactly as stated, *one day*. It is the day that the Lord Jesus Christ returns and fights the battle of Armageddon, the last event of Daniel's 70th week. Traditional teaching that the seals, trumpets and bowls are executed sequentially through time necessitate that the *Day of the Lord* must be a protracted period of time, usually 3.5 years. It is *exactly* this dilemma presented by Rev 6:17 that has caused all Pre-Wrath rapture teachers to declare the Day of the Lord as the time over which the trumpet and bowl judgments are executed. Such an interpretation ignores the clear teaching of scripture but *must* be assumed. Do we need more scriptural or logical proof that the seals when broken consume no time, but that they preview events that are about to take place? The revelation given to John, which he is told to record for the saints to read, is written *inside* the scroll and will not be revealed until the scroll can be unrolled and read.

The evidence seems convincing, logical and perfectly in line with Scripture, that the seals only provide an overview and preview of the last 3.5 years of Daniel's 70th week, just as does the preface of any good book. The trumpets and bowls describe actual, time sequenced events which *follow* Satan being cast down to earth in Rev 12; and this is exactly what one would expect. The catastrophic events which occur when seal six is opened now harmonize perfectly with end of time events.

Revelation 6:16 reveals the reason why those who dwell upon the earth are hiding in caves in Rev 6:1.

"And said to the mountains and rocks, fall on us, and hide us from the face of him that sitteth on the throne, and from the wrath of the Lamb."   Rev 6:16

The key to this verse is in noting that the kings are hiding from the *Wrath of the Lamb*. This is the only place in the Revelation record that this phrase occurs. It is clear from several passages already studied that the *Wrath of God* is the outpouring of the seven bowl judgments (Rev 15:1, 16:1). So why is this wrath called the Wrath of the Lamb, who is undoubtedly Jesus Christ? The answer is both scripturally correct and logical. Immediately following the pouring out of the seventh bowl, Christ will return to fight the battle of Armageddon. This is the Day of the Lord…His day… and *His* wrath will be such that:

"That day is a day of wrath, a day of trouble and distress, a day of wasteness and desolation, a day of darkness and gloominess, a day of clouds and thick darkness, A day of the trumpet and alarm against the fenced cities, and against the high towers. And I will bring distress upon men that they shall walk like blind men, because they have sinned against the LORD: and their blood shall be poured out as dust, and their flesh as the dung. Neither their silver nor their gold shall be able to deliver them in the day of the LORD's wrath; but the whole land shall be devoured by the fire of his jealousy: for he shall make even a speedy riddance of all them that dwell in the land."   Zep 1:15-18

The great theologian Matthew Rosenthal observed that as the sixth seal is broken, wrath is about to fall on mankind. Since the elect are to be *saved from the wrath to come* (Romans 5:9), Rosenthal built a theology called the *pre-wrath rapture* around that one verse. He reasoned that since the elect were to be saved from wrath that the church had to be raptured out as the sixth seal is broken. Since he presented and developed that position, many have adopted a *pre- wrath rapture* theology. The problem with that theology is twofold; (1) we have repeatedly stated and attempted to prove from the scriptures, that the *wrath* referenced as the sixth seal is breaking points to no earlier than until after the sixth trumpet sounds (Rev 11:13), and no later than when the seventh bowl is poured out (Rev 16:18): (2) those who have accepted Jesus Christ as their Savior, are *not* appointed to wrath, on that we agree. This is the basis for all pre-tribulation rapture and pre-wrath theology. The *Wrath of God* from which every saint is exempt is clearly stated in Rev 15:1 and 16:1 to be the seven bowl judgments. This does not *necessitate* that the rapture of all the saints occur after the sixth seal as Rosenthal and others propose, but if the rapture is at the seventh trump as we have argued elsewhere, the saints (as stated in Scripture) will all be taken out just before the seven bowl judgments fall and escape God's wrath: (3) Anyone who seriously reads Rev 11:15-18 with an open mind cannot deny that this is describing the rapture after the seventh trumpet sounds.

The *pre-wrath rapture* theory of Rosenthal and his followers is theologically correct, but it is misplaced because they fail to recognize the real role of the seal judgments. We propose that the rapture of the church occurs exactly where it should, at the sounding of the seventh trump before God's wrath begins. Because the seals are merely descriptive, there is no conflict with Rev 6:16. The real problem that arises out of all forms of a pre-tribulation teaching is the failure to understand the difference in *tribulation* and *wrath*, and the failure to explain Rev 12:17. In Rev 12:17, the following events have already come to pass.

> ➢ A great war in the heavenlies has just taken place (Rev 12:7),
> ➢ Satan and 1/3 of all the angels are defeated and cast down to the earth (Rev 12:8),

John the revelator records that Satan is angry and announces:

> *"Woe to the inhabitants of the earth and the sea for the devil is come down to you having great wrath because he knoweth he hath but a short time"* (Rev 12:12).

The wrath spoken of here is Satan's wrath against those who will not worship him or take his mark (Rev 13:1-18). This corresponds to the seven trumpet judgments allowed by God, after the great protector of Israel, the Archangel Michael, has turned away. Satan's ***short time*** is 3.5 years.

The great world leader that prefigures the antichrist is ***wounded to death*** (Rev 13:3) and he miraculously recovers from his wound and assumes the role of a ***beast*** that ***arises out of the sea*** (Rev 13:1-4). This individual is then totally controlled by *Satan* and becomes possessed by a demonic Prince out of the bottomless pit (Rev 17:8).

A ***false prophet*** arises ***out of the earth*** (Rev 13:11*)* immediately after the ***beast*** (Antichrist) arises ***out of the sea*** (Rev 13:1). This *false prophet* establishes and enforces worship of the beast (Rev 13:1-18)

This discussion is so important that we will again restate our beliefs and their relationship to pre-wrath rapture theories. Rosenthal created a new pre wrath theological position that he felt would resolve all the chronological difficulties in the book of Revelation. His basic contribution to eschatological theories was that the rapture of the church is neither pre-tribulation, mid-tribulation nor post-tribulation; but what he calls *pre-wrath*. Rosenthal and his followers are dead right! The only problem is that he fails to recognize, as we have repeatedly pointed out, that it is the pouring out of the seven bowl judgments that constitute the *Wrath of God*, as clearly recorded in Rev 15:1, Rev 15:7 and Rev 16:1 by the words of God himself. This is reiterated in Rev 11:18 after the seventh trumpet is sounded and in Rev 14:19 as the followers of the beast are gathered to Armageddon. Matthew Rosenthal recognized the problem, but failed to see that the solution was not to place the rapture at the opening of the sixth seal, but to recognize that the six seals have no direct time delays; they only provide an overview of the last 3.5 years of Daniel's 70th week, as we have repeatedly pointed out. His *pre-wrath* theology is to be highly commended, because it opened the door to the correct interpretation of *wrath vs. tribulation.* The saints are not exempted from tribulation, which occurs during the seven trumpet judgments. Tribulation is necessary to achieve spiritual maturity.

> *"Confirming the souls of the disciples, and exhorting them to continue in the faith, and that we must through much tribulation enter into the kingdom of God."* Acts 14:22

> *"And not only so, but we glory in tribulations also: knowing that tribulation worketh patience; And patience, experience; and experience, hope: And hope maketh not ashamed; because the love of God is shed abroad in our hearts by the Holy Ghost which is given unto us."* Romans 5:3-5

Finally, we wish to solve a problem which has almost universally confounded theological students of the book of Revelation since it was written. Between the opening of the sixth and seventh seal, we are shown 144,000 Jewish people; 12,000 from each of 12 tribes of Israel; who are being sealed for protection. We will discuss this in greater detail in Chapter 14, but for now it is sufficient to note that:

- They are being sealed before the trumpet judgments can sound. Four angels who have been chosen to bring forth the first four trumpet judgments are being withheld from their assignments until the 144,000 can be protected. (Rev 7:1-3, Rev 8:7, Rev 8:8, Rev 8:10 and Rev 8:12).
- The seal is a visible mark upon their forehead (Rev 7:3). This is a sign for protection verified in Rev 9:4, from death and the torture of demon locusts which are released from the bottomless pit (Rev 9:1-2) to torment mankind for five months.
- 12,000 from each of 12 tribes of Israel are being protected (Rev 7:4-8).

But we ask: *Why is a select group of Jewish believers being divinely protected and from what?*

The 144,000 are all Hebrews who have been chosen to fulfill the Abrahamic covenant, which promised that the land would be physically populated by Hebrews during the millennial kingdom. God Himself made this promise (covenant) to Abraham, and He will make sure that it is kept. The fact that a select group is being called out and protected may offend some who say that God is no respecter of persons, and He does not show *favoritism*. The fallacy of this logic is recorded throughout the Holy Scriptures. Israel itself was chosen by God from all of the nations of the world to be *His chosen people*. The 12 apostles were chosen from all others. David was chosen to conquer Goliath, and so on. It is generally taught that this select group would be divinely protected for a period of seven years, through the entire sequence of sequential seals, bowls and trumpets. The real truth is that this group will be divinely-protected from the death sentence that will be carried out by an image erected to the antichrist which will stand in the rebuilt temple. Death is pronounced upon all who will not take the mark of the beast and worship the Antichrist (Rev 13:15). However, the false prophet who enforces the mark of the beast (Rev 13:1-4) does not arise until *after* the last 3.5 years starts (Rev 13:5). The seven trumpet judgments are executed over the last 3.5 years only, consistent with *when and why* the 144,000 are sealed and protected. We also wish to again point out that no Christian or Jew is ever exempt from tribulation, and there is no indication whatsoever that either group will escape the impact of Satan's wrath over the last 3.5 year period of tribulation. All will suffer.

John the revelator next records an amazing scene. He sees:

"a great multitude which no man could number of all nations, and kindreds, and people, and tongues standing before the throne of God in heaven". They are clothed in "white robes with palm branches in their hands" (Rev 7:9).

One of the elders who stand before God's throne asks John: ***Who are these that are arrayed in white robes and where did they come from?*** (Rev 7: 13). John is bewildered and responds ***Sir, thou knowest*** (Rev 7:14). Why does John not recognize those who are before the throne? It is not hard to understand. These standing there are all who have believed on the Lord Jesus Christ since the foundation of the world. They are the resurrected dead and the raptured saints. The angel tells John who these people are: ***these are they which have come out of great tribulation.*** This cannot be only a large number of believers who come out of the 3.5 year tribulation period, since John declares that this group is so large that ***no one could number this multitude*** (Rev 7:9). In the context of this scene, this group is again recognized as the believers of all ages. These are those who have lived and died in Christ and have experienced tribulation in one form or another, but certainly a large number of them have come out of the last 3.5 years of persecution by Satan and his forces. Oh saints, here is a great truth which must be stated in the strongest possible terms. The tribulation period represents a time in which thousands, possibly millions, of people will accept Christ as their Savior. I want to be there, and you should want to be there also. There will be many *crowns of righteousness* won during this period of time. Oh you say, *But I might be martyred or crucified*. You mean just as our Lord Jesus Christ was crucified for our sins on Calvary? If you are martyred, a wonderful fate is guaranteed; you will be taken by angels to just beneath God's throne, to await your rewards. That is also the message of the sixth seal (Rev 6:9-11) for all who lose their life for Christ during the tribulation period.

We now wish to point out the real difficulty of failing to recognize that as the seals are opened, John is only shown the general conditions under which the seven trumpets and the seven bowl judgments take place. We believe that it is crystal clear that the 144,000 are sealed for the last 3.5 years of Daniel's 70th week (or seven years if you persist); we are equally convinced that the multitude standing before the throne represent the saved (alive and dead) from all ages that will ascend in the air to meet Christ (I Cor. 15:20-24, 50-55). We will later show beyond all reasonable doubt that this occurs at the seventh trump in Chapter 23. Now the dilemma: if the seals, trumpets and bowls all happen consecutively over a seven-year period of tribulation, and a rapture occurs either before the first seal is broken (classic pre-trib rapture) or after the sixth seal is broken (classic pre-wrath rapture), why are the 144, 000 in Rev 7 shown being sealed and the raptured saints shown together between the sixth and seventh seals? Here traditional chronological teaching *throws in the towel* and offers the following solution. The explanation is that somehow either these verses are out of place, or they represent a purely parenthetical vision. The pre-tribulation rapture teachers place the events of Revelation 7 before the entire seven-year period. The post-tribulation teachers claim that the 144,000 are sealed either before a seven-year period begins, or after the sixth seal is broken to save them from wrath. The mainstream pre-wrath teachers place both the sealing of the 144,000 and the rapture just after the sixth seal is broken. Most simply pass over these visions by saying that the 144,000 are shown sealed before the tribulation period starts, and that the *great multitude* is all the saved people who respond to teachings of 144,000 Jews during the entire tribulation period. The absurdity of this last teaching is obvious. None of these explanations preserve the continuity of John's visions. A particularly obvious problem is that all of these theories blatantly ignore the following passage after the seventh trumpet is sounded.

> *"And the seventh angel sounded; and there were great voices in heaven, saying, the kingdoms of this world are become the kingdoms of our Lord, and of his Christ; and he shall reign for ever and ever. And the four and twenty elders, which sat before God on their seats, fell upon their faces, and worshipped God, saying, We give thee thanks, O Lord God Almighty, which art, and wast, and art to come; because thou hast taken to thee thy great power, and hast reigned. And the nations were angry, and thy wrath is come, and the time of the dead, that they should be judged, and that thou shouldest give reward unto thy servants the prophets, and to the saints, and them that fear thy name,*

small and great; and shouldest destroy them which destroy the earth."
    Rev 11:15-18

As the seventh angel sounds his trumpet............

- ➢ The Lord now takes back the earth which Adam gave up to Satan in the Garden of Eden.
- ➢ The church will be raptured out
- ➢ God's wrath has now come (not at the sixth seal).
- ➢ It is time for the dead (in Christ) to be judged (not for salvation).
- ➢ It is time to reward the saints (for acceptable works).
- ➢ It is time to destroy those on the earth who have followed after Satan, the antichrist and the false prophet. This will happen at the Battle of Armageddon.

In Chapter 23 we will carefully discuss the rapture issue. For now we will simply state that any honest student of the Scriptures who wishes to take Rev 11:15-18 literally will have great difficulty believing that this is something other than the rapture, followed by the Bema seat judgment for rewards of all believers. The Bema seat judgment will take place immediately after all the saints, living and dead, meet Christ in the air. On the other hand, we again with great conviction declare that the sealing of the 144,000 and the rapture of the church are described in Rev 7:1-17, exactly where they should, provided we accept the fact that the seven seals only reveal conditions and descriptive events over the last half of Daniel's 70th week. It is perfectly acceptable to see now exactly why the 144, 000 are sealed - to protect them from both death under the *wrath of Satan* (the seven trumpet judgments) and from the *Wrath of God* (the seven bowl judgments), so that they can inherit the millennial kingdom. It is our conviction that they are *not* exempted from tribulation.

"And not only so, but we glory in tribulations also: knowing that tribulation worketh patience; And patience, experience; and experience, hope" Romans 5:3-4

Paul believed that tribulation was an integral part of Christian maturity. It should be reiterated that it is difficult to believe that the entire tribulation period is called the *Time of Jacob's Trouble*, since Jer. 30:7 clearly calls it a *day*, and in Jer. 30:8 that day is without a doubt equated to the Battle of Armageddon. The last 3.5 years is when Satan executes his wrath upon the earth. The rapture of the Church will occur at the seventh trumpet consistent with both Rev 11:18 and Rev 6:16. The messianic expectations of how the Feast of Trumpets will be fulfilled perfectly aligns with this pre-wrath theological position (See Chapters 9 & 23). The seven bowl judgments are the *Wrath of God*, they are not poured out upon a single person who has accepted Jesus Christ as their Savior prior to the blowing of the 7th trump. A pre-wrath rapture as the 7th trumpet sounds brings the entire contents of the Revelation record into perfect harmony.

Part II: The Olivet Discourse

All prophecy teachers rely upon the *Olivet Discourse* to explain the seven seals. We will now show that the very words of Jesus Christ support the positions just presented. Shortly before His crucifixion, Christ and several of His disciples were departing the beautiful temple of Herod. As they left, Christ made an amazing prophecy:

> ***"See ye not all these things? Verily I say onto you, there shall not be left here one stone upon another that shall not be thrown down."*** Matthew 24: 2

Christ revealed to His disciples that Herod's Temple would be completely destroyed, and the prophecy came true almost exactly 40 years later in 70 AD by the Roman General Titus. After exiting Herod's Temple, they walked to the Mount of Olives. At that time the disciples came to him privately and asked three questions (Mat 24:3): (1) *When shall these things be?* (2) *What shall be the sign of thy coming?* and (3) *What shall be the sign(s) of the end of the world* (age)?

> *(1)* Christ did not answer the first question, but did respond to the last two. Our focus here is to compare the main

prophecies of the Olivet Discourse to the seals, trumpets and bowls. The following tables summarize the main issues.

The Olivet Discourse	The Book of Revelation
The "Beginning of Sorrows"	
False Christs & Deceptions	
Mat 24; 4-5 Take heed that no man deceives you, for many will come in my name saying, I am the Christ and shall deceive many	SEAL1.....and behold a white horse: and and he that sat on him had a bow, and a crown was given unto him: and he went forth conquering and to conquer...Rev 6: 2 I saw a beast (antichrist) rise up out of the sea(humanity) ..and all the world wondered after the beast. Rev 13: 4 And they worshipped the dragon which gave power to the beast..And all that dwell on the earth shall worship him, whos names are not written in the Lamb's book of life...Rev 13:8
Wars and Rumors of Wars	
Mat 24: 6-7 Ye shall hear of Wars, and Rumours of wars For nation shall rise against nation, and Kingdom against Kingdom.	SEAL 2 ...and there went out another horse that was red: and power was given to him that sat thereon to take peace from the earth, and that they should kill one another: and there was given unto him a great sword...Rev 6: 4 And it was given unto him (the antichrist) to make war with the saints, and to overcome them: and power was given unto him over all kindreds, and tongues, and nations...Rev 13:7
Famine and Pestilence	

Mat 24: 7
   Famines, pestilence
   and earthquakes
	SEAL 3......When he had opened the third seal, I beheld, and lo a black horse, and he that sat on him had a pair of balances in his hand... a measure of wheat for a penny,..and three measures of barley for a penny..Rev 6:5-6
	SEAL 4 ......and beheld a pale horse and Death sat upon him, followed by Hell. And power was given unto them over the fourth part of the earth to kill...with hunger....Rev 6: 8
	SEAL 6....and Lo, there was a great earthquake
	    Rev 6:12
	Trumpet 7... And there was an earthquake.
	    Rev 7: 19
	Bowl 7... And there was a great earthquake.
	    Rev 16: 18

And THEN.....Mat 24: 10	
Persecution and Death	
Mat 24: 9-12 They shall deliver you up to be, afflicted and shall kill you, and you	SEAL 5... I saw under the alter the souls of them that were slain...and it was said unto them that they should rest a little season, until after fellow servants also and their brethren , that should be killed as they were, should be fulfilled...Rev 6: 9-11
you will be hated for my name's sake	And I stood upon the sand of the sea, and saw a beast rise up out of the sea.. (The Antichrist)....Rev 13: 1
Many False Prophets will arise and Love will wax cold	And I beheld another beast coming up out of the earth: and he had two horns like a (The False Prophet)..Rev 13: 11

Gosple preached throughout the world	
Mat 24: 14 And this gosple of The Kingdom shall be preached in all the world... THEN shall the end come	Before Trumpet 1.... And I saw another angel fly in the midst of heaven, having the everlasting gosple to preach unto them that dwell on the earth, and to every nation and kindred, and tongue and people...Rev 14: 6
The Abomination that Causes Desolation	
Mat 24: 15 When you see the Abomination of Desolation Spoken of by Daniel the prophet standing in the Holy Place,	Before Trumpet 1 ....The Abomination that causes Desolation is an image set up in the Temple by the Antichrist...This is not directly described in Revelation, but is found in the Book of Danial...And from the timethat the daily sacrifice shall be taken away (by the Antichrist), and the abomination that makes desolate is set up, there shall be a thousand two hundred and ninetydays...Dan 12: 11

The Warning to Flee Destruction	
Warning to flee applies to the Middle of Danial's 70th Week	
Mat 24:16-20 Jesus warns people to flee to the mountains. Destruction comes swiftly and Christ laments that it should not be in Winter or on the Sabbath. ...Woe to them with child	And , the woman fled into the wilderness (Mountains of Petra) , where she has a place prepared of God...Rev 12: 6

The Time of Jacob's Trouble...The last 3 1/2 Years of the Tribulation	
Mat 24: 21-22 For then there shall be "Great Tribulation", and except those days be shortened, No flesh would be saved.... But those days shall be shortened	Woe to the inhabitors of the earth and of the sea, for the devil is come down unto you, having great wrath, because he knoweth that he hath but a short time...Rev 12: 12 And there was given unto him a mouth speaking great things and blasphemies; and power was given unto him to continue forty and two months...Rev 12: 5
A warning by Christ..	
False Christ and False Prophet Appear	
Mat 24: 23-26 Christ again warns the elect about "False Prophets and False Christs"	And I stood upon the sand of the sea, and saw a beast rise up out of the sea..(The Antichrist). ....Rev 13: 1 And I beheld another beast coming up out of the earth: and he had two horns like a lamb, and he spake like a man....Rev 13:11

A warning by Christ....	
Second Advent comes Suddenly...	
Mat 24: 27 For as Lightning Cometh out of the East, and Shineth even unto the West, so shall also the Coming of the Son of Man be. Mat 24: 28 For wherever the carcass, is there will the eagles be gathered together	The suddenness of Christ's coming in Mat 24:27 does NOT refer to the rapture of the church but refers to the sudden arrival of Jesus Christ at the second advent. And I saw an angel standing in the sun; and he cried with a loud voice, saying to all the fowls that fly in the midst of heaven, come and gather yourselves together unto the supper of the great God....Rev 19:17

The Sign of His Coming	
IMMEDIATELY AFTER the Tribulation of Those Days...	
Mat 24: 29 The Sun shall be Darkened, The Moon will not give (any) Light... Stars will fall from Heaven...and the Powers of Heaven will be shaken	Seventh Bowl ....And the seventh angel poured out his vial into the air...Rev 16: 17 And there were voices, and thundrs, and lightnings; and there was a great earthquake. ...Rev 16: 18 And there fell upon men a great hail out of heaven...Rev 16: 21

The Second Coming of Christ	
Mat 24: 30-31 The Sign of the Son of Man will appear in the Heavens	I saw heaven opened, and behold a White Horse and he that sat upon him was called Faithful and True...Rev 19:11
THEN shall the Son of Man be seen in Clouds of Glory and with Power	And the armies which were in heaven followed him upon white horses, clothed in fine linen, white and clean …...Rev 19:14
He will send his Angels with a great Trumpet Sound and THEY (The Angels) shall gather his ELECT from the four winds, from one end of Heaven to another	Not recorded in Revelation, but in Mat 13.. in the Parable of the Wheat and Tares… Let both (the wheat & tares) grow together until the HARVEST; and in the time of harvest I will say to the REAPERS (angels) ...Gather you together first the tares, and bind them in bundles to burn them; but gather the WHEAT into my barn .....Mat 13: 30

In the Parable of the Sower...
so shall it be in the end of this world... The Son of Man shall send forth his
angels, and thet shall gather out
of his kingdom all things that offend,
and them that do iniquity..Mat 13: 40-41

We will leave a detailed study of the comparison of the Olivet Discourse to the events of the tribulation period to the reader. It is sufficient to point out here that the Olivet Discourse covers the entire sequence of end time events Christ's response to the three questions posed by the disciples addressed only the second question: (2) *what shall be the sign of thy coming?* His answer spanned the entire course of the revelation record from Rev 12 to the battle of Armageddon in Rev 19. Note that the sign of his coming was preceded by a series of catastrophic cosmic and earthly events leading up to His Second Advent. However, Christ did indicate that there would be a specific sign.

> *"Immediately after the tribulation of those days shall the sun be darkened, and the moon shall not give her light; and the stars shall fall from heaven."*   Matthew 24:29

This almost exactly parallels the description given as the sixth seal is broken.

> *"And I beheld when he had opened the sixth seal, and lo there was a great earthquake; and the sun became black as sackcloth of hair, and the moon became as blood. And the stars of heaven fell onto the earth. Then the sky receded as a scroll when it is rolled up, and every island and mountain was moved out of its place."* Rev 6:12-14

As expected, when the sixth seal is broken it almost exactly describes what happens just before the Second Advent of Christ as the fifth, sixth, and seventh bowls rapidly end the last 3.5 years of the *tribulation* period (Rev 16:10, Rev 16:15, and Rev 16:18-21).

The key thing to note is that these events occur *IMMEDIATELY AFTER THE TRIBULATION OF THOSE DAYS*. This is exactly where they should occur if the sixth seal (and all the seals) do not chronologically precede the trumpet and bowl judgments. If our hypothesis is true, then the very words of Christ make perfect sense. It is interesting that Christ did not fully address the third question either: what shall be the sign(s) of the end of the world (age)? The reason for this is that the immediate signs of the end of the age are those signs manifested as the bowl judgments are executed upon Satan's kingdom. These signs remained completely hidden until John the revelator was shown them and told to record those events, which was over 60 years later. Christ also told His disciples that:

> *"But of that day and hour know no man, no, not the angels of heaven, but my Father only."* Rev 24:36

After Christ told this to his disciples, He then gave the parable of the *Wise and Foolish Virgins* (Mat 25:1-12), and again told them that the time was yet future and unknown (Rev 25:13). We encourage the reader to carefully study Mat 24 and Mat 25. The content and meaning of this Parable is fully discussed in Chapters 24 and 25.

Part III: The Rapture of the Church

Anytime the Book of Revelation or prophecy is mentioned, the first question that usually arises is *When will the Rapture occur?* There are basically five different answers to this question.

Pre-Tribulation Rapture

A Pre-tribulation rapture position is held by most dispensationalists today, and is the most popular theology among prophecy teachers. It is a relatively new view that seems to have been popularized by Cyrus Scofield (1843-1921) who published his widely-read *Scofield Reference Bible* in 1909. In his margin notes and in his footnotes he presented his belief that the tribulation period was seven years long, and that the church would be raptured out before the tribulation period would begin. The origination of his beliefs seems to have been spawned by a Scottish girl named *Margaret McDonald* in the early 1830's. She had a *vision* and an *utterance* in a Presbyterian church pastored by Edward Irvin (1792-1834). John Nelson Darby, pastor of the *Church of Ireland*, accepted the vision as divine prophecy from God and began to preach its acceptance. Scofield was greatly influenced by Darby and also adopted the belief. So there you have it; the pre-tribulation position held by most modern day prophecy teachers was spawned by the vision and utterance of a young Scottish girl in the 1800's and has no solid scriptural support. In fact, prior to the mid-19th century, the predominant position was a post-tribulation rapture which is completely unscriptural. The *pre-tribulation* rapture theory puts the rapture of the church before the tribulation period starts, which is generally taught to be 7 years in duration; consisting of the 7 seals, the 7 trumpets and the 7 bowls being completed sequentially across a 7 year period of time. The basic belief is that the church will be *swept away to heaven* in a secret event, and no Christian will experience any tribulation or wrath whatsoever.

Post-Tribulation Rapture

A pre-tribulation rapture was not taught or held by the ancient church fathers. The predominant position was that of a post-tribulation rapture. This belief places the rapture of the church immediately *following* a seven-year period of tribulation; and after the seven bowls have been poured out. The post–tribulation belief has largely disappeared among modern prophecy teachers because of scriptural problems which we will not address. A *post-tribulation rapture* position assumes that the church is not promised any protection from either wrath or tribulation. It occurs immediately before the 1000-year millennial kingdom.

Mid-Tribulation Rapture

The mid-tribulation rapture theory is exactly as the name indicates. It it also rooted in a 7 year tribulation belief, but will occur after 3.5 of the last seven years have elapsed. The belief was spawned by (properly) recognizing that the *man-child* of Rev 12 is not Christ, but is rapture. The problem is a failure to properly identify the man-child as a rapture of 144,000 *firstfruit harvest overcomers* (Rev 14). The *mid-tribbers* arrive there because they cannot harmonize Scripture to support either a pre-trib or a post-trib view, and they correctly recognize that Satan persecutes the earth dwellers for 42 months or 1260 days after being cast out of the heavenly realms to earth. Like the *pre-tribbers*, they hold to a seven-year tribulation period consisting of 3.5 years of peace and 3.5 years containing the trumpet and bowl judgments. Their rapture theory takes all believers out *after* the 7 seals are broken over the first 3.5 years of a 7 year period of time. Hence, this position exempts all believers from *both* the trumpet and bowl judgments. Their primary failure, as with classical pre tribulation supporters, is the total disregard for Rev 11:15-18 as previously discussed. The *mid-trib* position has only a few supporters.

Pre-Wrath Rapture

The most recent rapture theory to surface is called a *pre-wrath rapture*. It was popularized by Matthew Rosenthal, a Jew by birth and training who converted to Christianity. This position was also popularized by Robert Van Kampen, a lay teacher who wrote a book called ***The Sign***. The pre-wrath position correctly distinguishes between tribulation and wrath. It also correctly identifies that no Christian is exempt from tribulation, but that we are not destined to experience the Wrath of God. In a classical pre-wrath theology, the rapture takes place somewhere between when a seven-year period of tribulation begins and when the Wrath of God is perceived to occur. Classic pre-wrath proponents place the rapture after the 6th seal is broken.. Rosenthal placed his entire belief in a pre-wrath rapture on the premise that Christians (the church) would be spared from all wrath, but he saw the 7 seals as actual events occurring through time. His beliefs led him to the opening of the sixth seal in Rev 6:17, which clearly states that the day of wrath has come. He had no choice but to declare that the rapture of the Church occurred following the breaking of the sixth seal. His basic premise is we believe correct. Where he met an impasse in scriptural harmonization was when he failed to recognize what we have presented as scriptural truth - that the seals simply provide an overview of the tribulation period. Realizing this, all scriptural conflicts disappear between Rev 6:17 and Rev 16:1.

Scriptural Truth

For years and years this author has tried to sort through theological debates, challenge all the theories, try to resolve scriptural conflicts and adopt the correct position. Like most prophecy teachers, I started with a classic *post-trib* position; I moved to a *pre-trib* position; and finally I believed that a *pre-wrath* position met the path of least conflict. Only after years of wasted time did I conclude that there was only one authority by which Scriptural truth can be established, and that is by Scripture itself. In what follows we will simply let Scripture speak for itself, and let it lead us to what we believe is the only logical decision. When Jewish tradition, ancient teachings, or modern theology support our final position, we accept complete harmonization. However, these are only secondary confirmations. Although secular beliefs, archeological discoveries and Jewish tradition sometimes provide very strong support; the final authority must be scriptural harmonization. So let us begin.

Paul's Revelation Knowledge

The apostle Paul provides the foundation of all scriptural truth concerning what we call the *rapture*. The word rapture does not appear in the Holy Scriptures. It is taken from the Greek word

Harpazo, which means to be *caught up* or *taken away*. Harpazo appears only three times in Scripture: in Acts 8:38, I Thessalonians 4:17 and in Rev 12:5. In I Thessalonians Paul spoke of a time at which all living believers would be *caught up* to meet our Lord Jesus Christ in the air.

> **"For the Lord himself will come down from heaven, with a loud command, with the voice of the archangel and with the trumpet call of God, and the dead in Christ will rise first. After that, we who are still alive and are left will be caught up** (Harpazo) **together with them in the clouds to meet the Lord in the air. And so we will be with the Lord forever."**
> I Thessalonians 4:16

Paul tells us that this event will be preceded by a ***trumpet call of God***. In the following passage, he is more specific about *which* trump is being referenced.

> **"Listen, I tell you a mystery: We will not all sleep** (die), **but we will all be changed, in a flash, in the twinkling of an eye, at the last trumpet. For the trumpet will sound, the dead will be raised imperishable, and we will all be changed."**
> I Corinthians 15:51-52

Paul reveals to the saints at Corinth the ***mystery***: ***We will all be changed***, whether we are alive or dead, at the ***last trump***. Now that is fairly specific, but when would the *last trump* be sounded? The term *last trump* is a Jewish eschatological term which is connected to the Feast of Rosh Hashanah or the Feast of Trumpets, which always occurs in the seventh Jewish month on Tishri 1. Jewish people see Rosh Hashanah as the beginning of a 10-day period of introspection, confessing of sins, and individual repentance leading up to the Feast of Yom Kippur on Tishri 10. There are also 30 days of blowing the trumpet preceding Tishri 1 called *Teshuvah*; and finally a *last trump* is blown on the Feast of Trumpets. But there is also a trumpet blown on Tishri 10, so again, when is the last trumpet? Here we must dig deeper into Jewish Rabbinical teachings. According to the ancient Jewish rabbis and teachers, the *last trump* is related to the *binding of*

Isaac. Recall that Abraham was called by God to sacrifice his only natural son Isaac, and he went up onto the mountain to do so. Ancient teachings say that Abraham went to where the *Dome of the Rock* now stands. Just as he was about to kill his son, God stayed his hand and produced a *ram* for a suitable sacrifice. This ram was offered as a *burnt offering* to the Lord and totally consumed upon a fire. The only thing that survived was the two ram's horns. Tradition holds that the first horn was blown when the law was given at Mt. Sinai; the second horn, the *last horn*, is to be blown at a future *Feast of Rosh Hashanah*.

The average Christian does not take the time to research Biblical principles (so we read books! to try and resolve difficulties based upon personal beliefs. There are several different types of trumpets that are sounded in the Biblical records. There are silver trumpets, gold trumpets and goat horn trumpets. A trumpet made of a ram's horn is called a **shofar**. The shofar was sounded to initiate or call Israel to battle; it was sounded to inaugurate a new king; and it was to be sounded to announce a Year of Jubilee. But the *trumpet blast* that was sounded when the law was given (*first trump*), and the one that will be sounded at the last Feast of Trumpets (*second trump*) are uniquely reserved for those two special occasions and are also called *Shofars*. They are very special trumpets, and in this context represent when the Jewish nation received God's law at Mt. Sinai, and when the Jewish nation will finally receive their promised Messiah at a future Feast of Trumpets. Indeed, Rosh Hashanah is called *Yom T'ruah* or *Yom Teruah* which means *the day of the shofar blast*. The use of two ram's horns are deeply rooted in Jewish Rabbinical writings. This is all interesting, but is it substantiated anywhere else in God's word? Once again, notice what Christ says in the *Olivet Discourse*.

> ***"Immediately after the tribulation of those days shall the sun be darkened, and the moon will not give her light, and the stars shall fall from heaven, and the powers of heaven shall be shaken: And then shall appear the sign of the Son of Man in heaven: and then shall all the tribes of the earth mourn, and they shall see the Son of Man coming in the***

clouds of heaven with great power and great glory. And He shall send his angels with a great sound of a trumpet, and they shall gather together His elect from one end of heaven to the other." Matthew 24:29-31

Notice several extremely important *clues* in this discourse.

- ➢ This is clearly the rapture of the church.
- ➢ It occurs *after* the tribulation of those days (not before, not in the middle).
- ➢ The sun is darkened, moon loses her light, and the heavens are disturbed. These are events which occur *after the seventh trumpet is sounded.*
- ➢ *Everyone* will see this happening
- ➢ He (Christ) will send his angels to *gather the elect to him* in the air.

The inescapable conclusion is that the rapture occurs immediately after what Christ called the *tribulation* period at the *sound of a trumpet.* This event perfectly aligns with Rev 11:15-18 and corresponds to the 7th *trumpet*. The seven bowl judgments are yet to be poured out. Why does the rapture occur before the first bowl is poured out? Listen carefully and open your mind. Christ answered this question also.

"For THEN there shall be GREAT TRIBULATION, such as was not from the beginning of the world to this time (blowing of the seventh trumpet), no, nor ever shall be. And except those days be shortened, there should no flesh be saved: but for the elects' sake those days shall be shortened." Matthew 24:21-22

"And I saw another sign in heaven, great and marvelous, seven angels having the seven last plagues; for in them is filled up the Wrath of God." Rev 15:1

"And I heard a great voice out of the temple saying to the seven angels, Go your ways and pour out the vials of the Wrath of God upon the earth." Rev 16:1

We have already pointed out that all believers are not destined to experience God's Wrath, and God's Wrath is clearly stated as occurring when the bowls are poured out (Rev 15:1,16:1) There are several important things to note in these parallel passages.

- ➢ Christ uses the term **great tribulation** to describe what *follows* the rapture. It is important to recognize that the 3.5 years of Satan's wrath against mankind and the saints we call *The Tribulation Period*. The time (10 days) over which the seven bowl judgments are poured out is so severe and devastating that we will follow the words of Christ and call this *The Great Tribulation*. Christ will *shorten these times* or there might not be any Christians left alive.

- ➢ The **shortening of time** which Christ references is the rapture of the church (The Body of Christ) at the 7th trumpet. The Body of Christ will be removed and not have to experience God's Wrath which is poured out in the seven bowl judgments over ten days between Rosh Hashanah and Yom Kippur. (Rev 16:1).

Another sign now appears. What was the first sign? The *first sign* was the sign of his coming that Christ predicted in Mat 24:30. This is *another sign*. Why another sign? Because all of the people on earth who remain alive have 10 more days to accept Christ as their Messiah and they will be warned.

The Scriptures which we have presented should be enough to convince anyone with an open mind, not cluttered with secular teaching that the rapture will occur on the Feast of Trumpets, Tishri 1, as the seventh trumpet of God is sounded. Chapter 23 will provide a more detailed discussion of this belief.

The following graphic provides a visual overview of how the seven seals simply provide an overview of the events which transpire as the seven trumpets are blown followed by the wrath of God; the seven devastating bowl judgments.

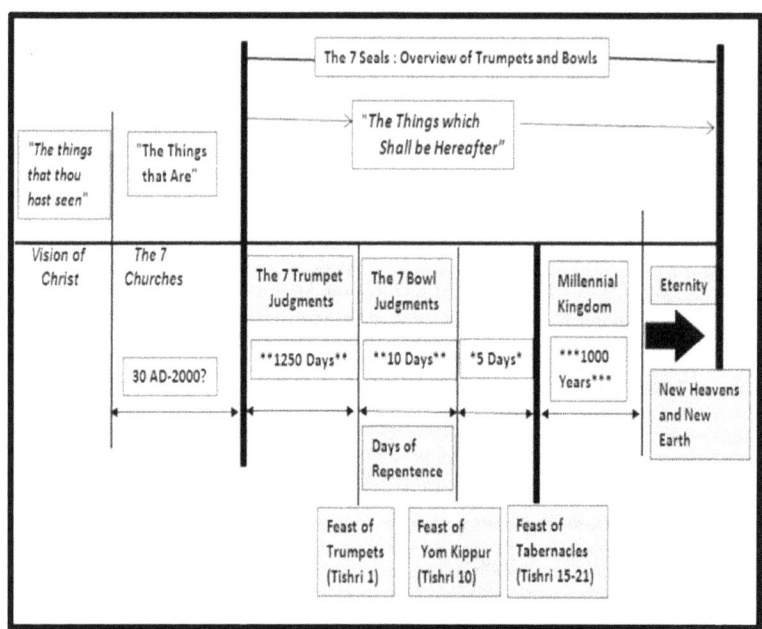

Thoughts and Things…….

Chapter 12

The Little Scroll

Between when the sixth and seventh trumpet sounds, there is a parenthetical interlude in which a little scroll and the appearance of two witnesses are described. This type of parenthetical insertion is not unique to the literary structure in the Book of Revelation. Between the opening of the sixth and seventh seal, the sealing of the 144,000 and the great multitude seen in heaven also were an interlude. In this chapter we will discuss the little scroll, and in Chapter 13 we will discuss the two witnesses. Revelation 10 is one of the most difficult chapters to interpret in the entire book. It is composed of two parts: the first part concerns a *Little Scroll* which is brought down from heaven to the earth by **another mighty angel** (Rev 10:1-10) and the second part is a *command to John* (Rev 10:11).

> *"And I saw another mighty angel come down from heaven, clothed with a cloud: and a rainbow was upon his head, and his face was as it were the sun, and his feet as pillars of fire: And he had in his hand a little book open: and he set his right foot upon the sea, and his left foot on the earth."*
> Rev 10:1-2

The scene has now shifted from heaven to the earth. The mighty angel has one foot on the sea and one foot on the land, which signifies that the message contained in the scroll must be worldwide in scope. Who is this mighty angel? Some have identified this angel as Gabriel or Michael. Another possibility is to equate him with the **strong angel** of Rev 5:2 who was previously present when the seven-sealed scroll was opened. A number of noted theologians have said that this is Christ. The description given here is similar to that given of Christ in Rev 1:12-16, which was in a vision given to John when he saw the seven-sealed scroll. However, there are several key differences to the previous vision of the larger scroll and the current vision where he sees a *little scroll*. The first, larger scroll was being held by God until He gave it to Christ. This little scroll is being held by an angel until he gives it to John. It is not likely that this strong angel is Christ, since Christ is never called an angel in the entire bible. What reinforces this opinion is that in Rev 10:6 the angel that holds the little scroll *swears by Him* (God or Christ), and if this is Christ this sort of utterance would never come from the Son referring to His Father. The conclusion is that any identification would be pure conjecture, but it is likely that this is just another angelic creature of great power and authority who serves God.

He has in his hand a *Little Book* which in the Greek is best interpreted as a *Little Scroll*. The word *little* seems to indicate smaller in either content or size to the seven-sealed scroll of Rev 5. The fact that this angel has his foot on both the sea and the land indicates that the message is affecting the whole world. Since one foot is on the sea, the angel is not subject to sinking and is obviously a spirit being.

> *"And cried with a loud voice, as when a lion roareth: and when he had cried, seven thunders uttered their voices. And when the seven thunders had uttered their voices, I was about to write: and I heard a voice from heaven saying unto me, seal up those things which the seven thunders uttered, and write them not."* Rev 10:3-4

The loud voice that sounds like the roaring of a lion is symbolic of the authority and power that the angel carries with him. When the lion roars; *seven thunders* speak. Who or what are these seven thunders? This is not the noise of seven claps of thunder, but an extrapolation of the previous statement that the proclamation is *loud*. It is not only loud; it must be overwhelming to sound like thunder. An association to the seven-fold voice of the thunderstorm in Psalm 29:3-9 is possible, but the association is weak. A better explanation is that these *thunders* are the sound of seven angelic beings that speak in unison. The best conclusion is that these seven thunders cannot be identified with any precedence in Scripture, and they are possibly unique to this vision. Whatever the source might be,

John is able to clearly hear what is being said and prepares to write it down. Another voice from heaven is then heard which instructs John to *not write down* what he has heard. This is a highly unusual scenario. John has previously been instructed to record the things which he sees and hears; now he is silenced. It is interesting but futile to conjecture why John would be allowed to hear the *seven thunders* in the first place if he cannot reveal the message.

> ***"And the angel which I saw stand upon the sea and upon the earth lifted up his hand to heaven, And sware by him that liveth for ever and ever, who created heaven, and the things that therein are, and the earth, and the things that therein are, and the sea, and the things which are therein, that there should be time no longer. But in the days of the voice of the seventh angel, when he shall begin to sound, the mystery of God should be finished, as he hath declared to his servants the prophets."*** Rev 10: 5-7

The mighty angel now reveals that he receives his authority to speak and act directly from God. The right hand is raised, which is always the sign of a covenant or an oath. The declaration is astounding. For every creature in the sea and every inhabitant of the earth, time as we know it is going to cease to exist. The direct implication is that the 1260 days, 42 months, time/times/half-a-time are preparing to come to a close, and whatever is contained in the *little scroll* is a record of something that will come to pass *after* Daniel's 70th week has ended. There are two statements which follow that require careful exegesis and interpretation. *The mystery of God will be finished in the days of the voice of the seventh angel.* The first question is which 7th angel? There are two possibilities: the 7th angel who sounded the 7th trumpet or the seventh angel who pours out the 7th bowl? The Greek word translated **sound** is *solpizo*, which is to sound or blast a trumpet. This 7th angel is sounding the 7th trumpet. The Greek word for word *days* is *Hemerai*, which denotes a period of time, as in Mat 24:29. The natural interpretation in context of what follows is that *days* would include the ten days between Tishri 1 and Tishri 10 during which the bowl judgments are poured out upon the

Antichrist and his forces. The sounding and days which follow complete a ***mystery of God.*** What is this *mystery*?

The Greek word for mystery is *Mysterion*. A mystery in the Scriptures is not like our modern interpretation of something which cannot be explained, but rather something which has been *hidden* from understanding until it is divinely revealed in the Word of God. The word mystery cannot be found in the Old Testament, but it is difficult to exclude the Old Testament prophets from being implicated in this declaration. The apostle Paul twice associates a *mystery* with his teachings to both Jews and Gentiles.

> ***"For I would not, brethren, that ye should be ignorant of this mystery, lest ye should be wise in your own conceits; that blindness in part is happened to Israel, until the fullness of the Gentiles be come in."***
> Romans 11:25

> ***"This is a great mystery: but I speak concerning Christ and the church."*** Ephesians 5:32

The promise to Abraham and his dusty seed to inherit the land has always been known and accepted by Israel, but the fulfillment of this promise through Jesus Christ has been almost completely hidden from the Jews. Paul recorded a great *mystery*.

> ***"What then? Israel hath not obtained that which he seeketh for; but the election hath obtained it, and the rest were blinded"*** Romans 11:7

After the seventh trumpet sounds and the church is taken out, the bowls will be poured out in the *Wrath of God*. During the time that the 7 bowls are poured out, when all else has failed, Israel will turn to Jesus Christ as their Messiah, and *all of Israel* (that are left alive) *will be saved*. This is all consistent with this vision; the bowl judgments seem to be *contained* within the *days* of the seventh angel's actions. Those who have been previously raptured out and resurrected will now be joined to a believing remnant that will constitute the full body of Christ. We believe that this is primarily the *mystery* being spoken of here.

However, another equally valid interpretation of this ***mystery now revealed*** is the eternal purpose of God. Why has He allowed Satan to persecute and lead God's creation to sin and destruction for thousands of years? The Old Testament prophets came to Israel over and over again warning them of what would happen (corporately) if their cries were ignored. The promise to Abraham and his dusty seed to inherit the land has always been known and accepted by Israel, but the fulfillment of this promise through Jesus Christ has been almost completely rejected by the Jews. The voice from heaven speaks again and tells John to *take the little book and eat it.*

> *"And the voice which I heard from heaven spake unto me again, and said, go and take the little book which is open in the hand of the angel which standeth upon the sea and upon the earth. And I went unto the angel, and said unto him, give me the little book. And he said unto me, Take it, and eat it up; and it shall make thy belly bitter, but it shall be in thy mouth sweet as honey. And I took the little book out of the angel's hand, and ate it up; and it was in my mouth sweet as honey: and as soon as I had eaten it, my belly was bitter"*
> Rev 10:8-10

The position of the angel standing on the sea and the earth once again speaks of the great authority of the angel, but it also probably speaks to the universal application of whatever is contained in the little book. The instruction to *eat the scroll* brings the force of actually eating the scroll to completely understand the meaning and to completely digest its contents. The angel understands the result of this action. He declares to John that it will be *sweet as honey* in his mouth, but once eaten it will be *bitter* in his stomach. The action is not unique in the Biblical records. The prophet Ezekial once played out a similar scene.

> *"Moreover he said unto me, Son of man, eat that thou findest; eat this roll, and go speak unto the house of Israel. So I opened my mouth, and he caused me to eat that roll. And he said unto me, Son of man, cause thy belly to eat, and fill thy bowels with this roll that I give thee. Then did I eat it; and it was in my mouth as honey for sweetness. And he said unto me, Son of man, go, get thee unto the house of Israel, and speak with my words unto them. For thou art not sent to a people of a strange speech and of an hard language, but to the house of Israel."* Ezekiel 3:1-5

The Message given to Ezekiel is to speak to the apostate house of Israel. This may indicate that whatever is contained in this *little scroll* was also to the house of Israel, but there is no indication whatsoever as to what the contents of the scroll might conceal. John now is reassured that there are more future events for him to see and record.

> *"And he said unto me, Thou must prophesy again before many peoples, and nations, and tongues, and kings."* Rev 10:11

The last part of this vision is not a request but a command to John. He *must* prophesy. Perhaps the angel was afraid that John would understand the secrecy of the little scroll to mean that anything he sees from now on cannot be revealed. In any case, John will prophesy again and the words of what he sees will span the rapture of the church at the seventh trump to eternity following the millennial kingdom. Since John penned this great book, **many peoples, nations, tongues and kings** have been comforted and reassured in knowing how the world as we know it will end. Christ will rule and reign as **King of Kings and Lord of Lord"**, and all who believe in Him will be co-heirs to this promise.

Chapter 13

The Two Witnesses

During the 1260 days that the antichrist reigns over the earth and the trumpet judgments are sounded, God will anoint two witnesses who will stand in the desecrated temple and proclaim the Gospel of Jesus Christ. They will stand in stark contrast to the image that the antichrist will erect in the temple that will both supernaturally speak and destroy anyone who refuses to worship the beast and take the mark of the beast (Rev 13:11-15). Before these two witnesses are described, John is commanded to measure the temple where the two witnesses will reside.

> *"And there was given me a reed like unto a rod: and the angel stood, saying, Rise, and measure the temple of God, and the altar, and them that worship therein. But the court which is without the temple leave out, and measure it not; for it is given unto the Gentiles: and the holy city shall they tread under foot forty and two months."*   Rev 11:1-2

The conjunction *and* connects the vision that John has just seen concerning a description of the *Little Scroll* with a command to *measure* the *Temple of God*. John is now seeing a vision of things that are happening on the earth. Rev 11:1-2 confirms with certainty that there will be a third Jewish temple rebuilt upon some site in Jerusalem prior to the tribulation period. It is not revealed whether or not it is on the site where the Dome of the Rock now sits, but Jewish expectation and hope is that it will be rebuilt on the same site where Herod's temple stood. John's account also reassures us that there will be an *altar* and that there will be a renewal of Jewish temple worship. The heart of Jewish Temple worship was and undoubtedly will be the old Levitical sacrificial system, and the *altar* is then most likely to be the *Altar of Sacrifice*. The graphic on the next page shows how Herod's temple was constructed. This is a picture of a scaled model taken in the Israel Museum.

Model of Herod's Temple - currently in the Israel Museum

The temple consisted of five main areas: (1) court of the Gentiles (2) court of the Women (3) court of Israel (4) Holy Place and (5) Holy of Holies. The Gentiles were not allowed in the temple complex proper, but they could mingle in two large areas East and West of the Temple. Women were not allowed to gather just outside of the Holy Place, but had an intermediate court. The Court of Israel was where the men would approach the Holy Place with their sacrifices, but only the Levitical priesthood was allowed in the Holy Place. The High Priest was singularly allowed in the Holy of Holies, and then only once a year on the Day of Atonement. The Altar of Sacrifice stood before the Court of Israel in the Holy Place. John the revelator reveals that the temple will be desecrated, and that the *Court without the Temple* is not to be measured. This would not only include the Court of the Gentiles, but must include both the Court of Women and possibly the Court of Israel. The measurement commanded to be taken will likely include both the Holy Place and the Holy of Holies. Why the other courts are excluded is a *mystery* not explained; only that it has been **given unto the Gentiles**. In one of the courts the antichrist will erect the statue which will speak and demand that the he and Satan be worshipped as God. Both the prophet Daniel and Christ spoke of this desecration.

> *"And from the time that the daily sacrifice shall be taken away, and the abomination that maketh desolate set up, there shall be a thousand two hundred and ninety days. Blessed is he that waiteth, and cometh to the thousand three hundred and five and thirty days."* Daniel 12:11-12

> *"And this gospel of the kingdom shall be preached in all the world for a witness unto all nations; and then shall the end come. When ye therefore shall see the abomination of desolation, spoken of by Daniel the prophet, stand in the holy place, (whoso readeth, let him understand:) Then let them which be in Judaea flee into the mountains."*
> Matthew 25:14-16

John confirms that the *"the holy city shall they tread under foot forty and two months"*. The *Holy City* is undoubtedly the city of Jerusalem, identified in Rev 11:8. The 42 months is also identical to the time that Satan will persecute the saints aided by the antichrist and the false prophet; the last half of Daniel's 70th week. The narrative now immediately shifts to *two witnesses.*

> *"And I will give power unto my two witnesses, and they shall prophesy a thousand two hundred and threescore days, clothed in sackcloth. These are the two olive trees, and the two candlesticks standing before the God of the earth."*
> Rev 11:3-4

These two witnesses are to prophesy for 1260 days, which is identical to the period of time that the Abomination in Dan 12:11 stands in the temple. This period of time also is over the last half of Daniel's 70th week, and it terminates on or near the blowing of the last trumpet when the rapture occurs. The two witnesses are identified as *the two olive trees* and *the two candlesticks* standing before God; but who are they? This question has sparked considerable controversy. The two witnesses are killed by the *beast* that is the antichrist (Rev 11:7) after they have finished their testimonies. Because they experience death, and a believer in Christ only experiences death once (Heb 9:27); the popular choice has been Enoch and Elijah who were both translated to heaven and never died (Gen 5:24, II Kings 2:11). It is almost certain that one of the witnesses is Elijah, since Christ stated that:

> *"And they asked him, saying, why say the scribes that Elias must first come? And he answered and told them, Elias verily cometh first, and restoreth all things."* Mat 9:11-12

Malachi predicted that Elijah would return before the *"Day of the Lord"* (Mal 4:5), which we believe is the single day on which the battle of Armageddon will be fought. Another equally popular choice is Moses and Elijah. This is because when Christ took Peter, James and John up on a *high mountain*, Moses and Elijah appeared before them. In addition, note what John next records in Rev 11.

> *"And if any man will hurt them, fire proceedeth out of their mouth, and devoureth their enemies: and if any man will hurt them, he must in this manner be killed. These have power to shut heaven that it rain not in the days of their prophecy: and have power over waters to turn them to blood, and to smite the earth with all plagues, as often as they will."* Rev 11:5-6

Elijah both called fire down from heaven (II King 1:10) and withheld rain on the earth for 3.5 years. (I King 17:1). Moses turned water into blood and struck the earth with plagues (Exodus 7:14-11:10). For these reasons, many identify the two witnesses as Moses and Elijah. We are also told that the two witnesses are *the two olive trees and the two lampstands* standing before God. These two witnesses, whoever they may be, are shadowed and typed by Zerubbabel and Joshua.

> *"What are these two olive trees upon the right side of the candlestick and upon the left side thereof? And I answered*

again, and said unto him, what be these two olive branches which through the two golden pipes empty the golden oil out of themselves? And he answered me and said, knowest thou not what these be? and I said, no, my lord. Then said he, these are the two anointed ones that stand by the LORD of the whole earth."   Zechariah 4:14-17

The resemblance is striking, but it stretches the context to assume that they would be called again to witness to the new covenant saints. In conclusion, no matter how much evidence is accumulated, the truth is that the identity of the two witnesses has been withheld from us, and it is impossible to be dogmatic as to who they might be. We are, however, not left to any doubt as to how their testimony comes to an end.

"And when they shall have finished their testimony, the beast that ascendeth out of the bottomless pit shall make war against them, and shall overcome them, and kill them. And their dead bodies shall lie in the street of the great city, which spiritually is called Sodom and Egypt, where also our Lord was crucified. And they of the people and kindreds and tongues and nations shall see their dead bodies three days and an half, and shall not suffer their dead bodies to be put in graves."   Rev 11:7-9

After testifying for 1260 days, the beast (antichrist) will overcome both of them and kill them. The two witnesses will be slain very near the Feast of Trumpets. The 1260 day period that they witness will coincide with the reign of the antichrist, but will start 10 days earlier than when he arises. The beginning of this period of witness will either immediately precede or start at the time that there is war in heaven (Rev 12). The fact that they will have to endure a violent death is an unexplained enigma, since both of the witnesses possess great power and were ordained by God. They have also faithfully discharged their duties, and rather than be translated out they are killed. The place of their death is clearly identified as Jerusalem. The extent of antichrist's influence and corruption is clearly indicated by the scope of their representation. They witness to **peoples, kindreds,** *tongues and nations*. The antichrist will not allow their bodies to be buried, and they will lie in the street for 3.5 days, which is an interesting play on the 3.5 years that they witnessed and the 3.5 years of Christ's earthly ministry. When they are killed, there will be a great party in the antichrist's camp.

> *"And they that dwell upon the earth shall rejoice over them, and make merry, and shall send gifts one to another; because these two prophets tormented them that dwelt on the earth."* Rev 11:10

There will be rejoicing and gifts sent to one another because the two witnesses have **tormented them**. It is paradoxical to recognize that those who celebrate are oblivious to the torture which will be heaped upon them in the lake of burning fire (Rev 20:15). From Rev 11:9, we are told that **many nations** will see their dead bodies lying in the street. This is no doubt made possible by modern satellite communications. All over the world, the followers of the antichrist will **make merry** and **rejoice** while watching on CNN. However, the two witnesses have one more appointment with destiny.

> *"And after three days and an half the Spirit of life from God entered into them, and they stood upon their feet; and great fear fell upon them which saw them. And they heard a great voice from heaven saying unto them, Come up hither. And they ascended up to heaven in a cloud; and their enemies beheld them."* Rev 11:11-12

Just as the party is really underway, the two witnesses rise from the street and stand. The phrase ***Spirit of Life*** is best translated as ***Breath of Life***, and is reminiscent of God breathing the life of man into existence in Genesis 2:7. The *dry bones* prophecy in which Israel is resurrected from the dead is also called to remembrance.

> *"Again he said unto me, Prophesy upon these bones, and say unto them, O ye dry bones, hear the word of the LORD. Thus saith the Lord GOD unto these bones; behold, I will*

cause breath to enter into you, and ye shall live: And I will lay sinews upon you, and will bring up flesh upon you, and cover you with skin, and put breath in you, and ye shall live; and ye shall know that I am the LORD. So I prophesied as I was commanded: and as I prophesied, there was a noise, and behold a shaking, and the bones came together, bone to his bone. And when I beheld, lo, the sinews and the flesh came up upon them, and the skin covered them above: but there was no breath in them. Then said he unto me; prophesy unto the wind, prophesy, son of man, and say to the wind, thus saith the Lord GOD; Come from the four winds, O breath, and breathe upon these slain, that they may live." Ezekiel 37:4-9

Many modern prophecy teachers relate the *dry bones* prophecy to the re-gathering of the Jewish people to Israel after Israel became a nation on May 14, 1948. However, we believe that this interpretation is in error. The dry bones prophecy involves a resurrection from the dead. *New life* will be granted to long dead sinews and bones. This is not a migration of Jews to the State of Israel. These bones will rise, consistent with Messianic expectations, at the *last trump*. This is a resurrection of dead Jewish believers from both the New Covenant, and those that saw Christ coming under the Old Covenant. Abraham was typical of all these resurrected Old Testament saints: **For he looked for a city which hath foundations, whose builder and maker is God**" (Heb 11:10); The bones of Abraham will someday arise. Hence, the analogy extends beyond the fact that the two witnesses will rise from the dead and ascend to heaven in a cloud. We believe that they will be preceded 3.5 days earlier by by the alive and dead in Christ. Notice how all of this ends.

"And the same hour was there a great earthquake, and the tenth part of the city fell, and in the earthquake were slain of men seven thousand: and the remnant were affrighted, and gave glory to the God of heaven." Rev 11:13

There is a *great earthquake* which kills 7,000 men. A tenth part of the city (Jerusalem) is destroyed and the remnant is **affrighted**. The Greek word for affrighted means to be *terrified, or afraid*. Those who are left alive are affrighted (terrified) and called the *remnant*. The remnant of what? The word remnant is used over 90 times in both the Old and New Testament, and in all but a few instances it refers to the Jewish nation.

> *"Yet will I leave a remnant that ye may have some that shall escape the sword among the nations, when ye shall be scattered through the countries. And they that escape of you shall remember me among the nations whither they shall be carried captives, because I am broken with their whorish heart, which hath departed from me, and with their eyes, which go a whoring after their idols: and they shall lothe themselves for the evils which they have committed in all their abominations. And they shall know that I am the LORD."* Ezekiel 6:8-10

> *"And it shall come to pass, that in the place where it was said unto them, Ye are not my people; there shall they be called the children of the living God. Esaias (Elijah) also crieth concerning Israel, though the number of the children of Israel be as the sand of the sea, a remnant shall be saved."* Romans 9:26-27

Notice that the apostle Paul associates Elijah with a remnant that will be saved. Although not conclusive, we suggest that the remnant that repented was the Lost Sheep of Israel, and not a remnant of antichrist's apostate followers. If anyone follows after the antichrist and receives the *mark of the beast*, they are beyond redemption (Rev 20:20). This closes the scene of the two witnesses. The seventh trumpet is about to sound. We will devote Chapter 23 to this sounding, but first there are many more wonderful things that we will explore in Chapters 14-22.

Chapter 14

The Sun Clothed Woman, the Man child and the Dragon

It is generally agreed that Revelation Chapter 12 is the most difficult chapter to explain in the book of Revelation. If we are to understand how the 3.5 year period of tribulation will begin, then it is imperative that a correct interpretation be given to the events that transpire between Rev 12:1 and Rev 13:18.

> *"And there appeared a great wonder in heaven; a woman clothed with the sun, and the moon under her feet, and upon her head a crown of twelve stars. And she being with child cried, travailing in birth, and pained to be delivered. And there appeared another wonder in heaven; and behold a great red dragon, having seven heads and ten horns, and seven crowns upon his heads. And his tail drew the third part of the stars of heaven, and did cast them to the earth: and the dragon stood before the woman which was ready to be delivered, for to devour her child as soon as it was born. And she brought forth a man child, who was to rule all nations with a rod of iron: and her child was caught up unto God, and to his throne."* Rev 12:1-5

The Man child
A beautiful sun-clothed woman appears in heaven. She is bearing a child and travails in birth pains. A ***Great Red Dragon*** who is Satan (Rev 12: 9) is waiting for the *child* to be born, and has in mind to *devour* the child at birth. The woman births a *man*

child, who is destined to rule all nations with a *rod of iron*. But before Satan can kill the *man child* it is caught up to the throne of God. The traditional interpretation of this vision holds that the *woman* is *Mary* the mother of Jesus, and that the *child* is *Jesus Christ*. The *dragon* that wishes to kill the child is *King Herod*, who tried to kill the baby Jesus by executing all male children under the age of two years after the visit of the Magi. This interpretation is so convoluted that no justification exists for it at all. The following observations will establish this beyond any doubt whatsoever.

- Mary was not the glorious figure depicted here in spite of her deification by the Roman Catholic Church. She is seen clothed with the sun and the moon under her feet, a position of domination. It is never recorded anywhere in Scripture that she exercised such authority. Mary was certainly blessed above all women to give birth to the son of God, but she was a sinner and a mother like every other woman who has ever lived.
- If the sun-clothed woman is Mary, then the Dragon would be Herod. But Rev 12:9 specifically identifies the dragon as Satan. It is true that Herod was a wicked and cruel king beyond belief, but he was not possessed by Satan as was Judas and will the antichrist. Jesus Christ was the first child born of Mary, a virgin, but Rev 12:17 clearly states that this sun-clothed woman *already* had other *seed* or offspring.
- The **man child** is immediately **caught up unto God and to his throne** (Rev 12:5), but Christ did not ascend to His Father until he was about 33.5 years old.
- Mary and Joseph, hearing that Herod sought to kill her child, fled to Egypt for protection. The man child does not flee anywhere, and this *woman* flees into the wilderness without the child.
- Immediately after the woman **flees into the wilderness** (Rev 12:6), there is **war in heaven** (Rev 12:7) and *Satan* is **cast down to the earth** (Rev 12:9) for a period of 3.5 years. Satan is still the *ruler of this earth*; he has never

> been cast out of the heavens where even today he accuses us before the throne of God.
> - The woman flees into the wilderness *alone* for **1260 days** (Rev 12:6). There is no such event even hinted at in the Holy Scriptures for Mary the mother of Jesus.
> - The Archangel Michael is involved in this scene (Dan 12:1). Michael will not appear until **the time of the end.**
> - Satan pursues the man child immediately after birth, but Herod had some time elapse before slaughtering the infants. Christ had already returned to Nazareth with Joseph and Mary, and then left for Egypt after having been warned of the slaughter by the Magi. Herod was not even aware that a Messiah had been born until the wise men told him. The dragon is waiting to kill the child even before it is born.

We could list even more reasons to reject persistent teaching that the woman is Mother Mary; the child is Jesus Christ; and the dragon is King Herod. *So who is this woman and what does she represent?* In the Bible there have been two great encounters between a woman and Satan; the first was in the Garden of Eden and the second is in Rev 12:1-12. Satan won the first encounter, but Christ will win the second. This **Sun-Clothed Woman** is the true woman of God, the Bride of Christ, those who have accepted Jesus Christ as their Lord and Savior. She is, in spirit, the same woman who was in the garden, and she is battling *that old serpent* for the last time victorious.

> ***"And the great dragon was cast out, that old serpent, called the Devil."*** Rev 12:9.

It is the same serpent, the same woman, engaged in the same warfare from the beginning of this world; her seed against his seed. What God prophesied in the opening act in the Garden of Eden between the woman and that old serpent is now being played out again in this heavenly scene. It is a different time and a different place, but the same warfare.

Before the kingdom of heaven can fully and completely manifest itself in heaven, it must first be established on the earth - *on earth as it is in heaven.* Her seed is now victorious over the serpent, preparing the way for the kingdom to become a literal, physical reality upon the earth.

> **"Now is come salvation, and strength, and the kingdom of our God, and the power of his Christ: for the accuser of our brethren is cast down, which accused them before our God day and night."** Rev 12:10

From the very first verse, we see who this woman is. We see her shining in the righteousness of which she is clothed. We see her place of authority, and her relationship to the God of creation. The woman is not a singular woman but a corporate body. She is not the full and completed Body of Christ, but only a portion. She is composed of both Jews and Gentiles which have matured and now become one in Christ. This is the *Starry seed* of Abraham (Gen 15:5). We will subsequently see that this man-child is a firstfruit portion of the body of Christ.

The sun, the moon, and the 12 stars are inseparably connected to this woman. The *first reference* to this trinity is found in Joseph's second dream, with Joseph being the twelfth star. From this we discover their prophetic significance.

> *"And he dreamed yet another dream, and told it his brethren, and said, Behold, I have dreamed a dream more; and, behold, the sun and the moon and the eleven stars made obeisance to me."* Genesis 37:9

From Joseph's dream we understand that in Gen 37 the sun, the moon, and the 11 stars represent his father, mother and 11 brothers (tribes), respectfully. There is no 12th star, since Joseph is that *star*. This vision prefigured the church age by almost 4000 years. The image which Joseph saw in his dream was a prophecy of how one day the entire family of Joseph and all of their descendents would be subject to Joseph. This came true when Joseph was put in charge of all the grain in Egypt, and Jacob moved the entire nation of Israel into Egypt during the famine. The glorious sun clothed woman in Rev 12 represents the *corporate body of Christ*, which will include the redeemed from Abraham to the end of the church age. In Romans 11, Paul explained how the *gentiles* would be heirs to salvation through the Nation of Israel. Paul represented Israel as a *holy lump*... a *trunk* which had many *holy branches*. When Israel rejected Christ as their Messiah, Christ commissioned Paul to offer salvation to the Gentiles. The branches of Israel were broken off and the branches of the Gentiles *grafted* into the tree. The Gentile branches were called those from a *wild olive tree*, while the branches of the original tree were from a *cultivated olive tree*. The *root* was the promises to Israel, now given to both Jews and Gentiles alike. Paul further warned the gentiles not to boast; and revealed that the original branches would one day be *grafted back* (at the end of the age).

In Joseph's dream, there was no woman. But, in the image before us, the *sun* represents the promised *Messiah*, Jesus Christ: **unto us a child is born**; **unto us a son is given**, the seed of the woman. The *light* of the sun is the righteousness of God: **But to you who fear My name, the Sun of Righteousness shall arise** (Mal 4:2). The *moon* is the *body of Christ*, now composed of both Jews and gentiles. The moon only reflects the light of the Sun; and so we inherit righteousness from our Lord Jesus Christ and shine with His glory when we receive the Holy Spirit. The 12 stars now represent the offspring of the 12 tribes of Israel, *and* the sons and daughters birthed by the 12 apostles and the gospel message that they spread throughout the world. The glorious sun clothed woman represents the believers of all ages that will inherit the Kingdom of God. In the millennial kingdom, after the tares have been removed, the *mature wheat* will gloriously stand in the fields of the earth during the millennial kingdom: **Then shall the righteous shine forth as the sun in the kingdom of their Father. Who hath ears to hear, let him hear** (Mattew 13:43). This man-child is the firstfruit harvest of the full body of Christ which has matured first.

The Sun Clothing Her Head
As previously indicated, this woman is seen clothed with the glorious garment of light in which she once walked in Eden's bliss. She no longer needs to sew her *filthy rags* of leaves to hide her shame, for what her works could never provide in the Garden of Eden, Grace has so wondrously tailored. Restoration is complete in our savior Jesus Christ: **For he hath made him to be sin for us, who knew no sin; that we might be made the righteousness of God in him** (2 Corinthians 5:21).

This woman who is clothed with the sun is the sanctified, glorified body of Christ; no spots in her garments, no tares in her field. She is the *good fruit*, the maturity of the *good seed* (Christ in you) ready for harvest. She is clothed in the righteousness of God. In Revelation Chapter One, Christ stands in the midst of his glorious church (*seven lamp stands*); soon the glorious church will stand around our Lord Jesus Christ.

> ***"That they all may be one; as thou, Father, art in me, and I in thee, that they also may be one in us."*** John 17:21

The Tares, **them of the synagogue of Satan, which say they are Jews, and are not, but do lie** (Rev 2:9) have been bundled for a *future* burning. They will join themselves, like Cain, to the beast in Revelation Chapter 13 and will come to persecute the woman; **but behold, I will make them to come and worship before thy feet, and to know that I have loved thee** (Rev. 3:9).

The Moon Under Her Feet
The moon represents the body of Christ, receiving the New Covenant. The New Covenant is freedom and liberty from sin. Christ was a perfect reflection of His father and His Father's will. Those who follow after Christ and totally submit to His will are a reflection of Him. Paul without a doubt clarifies for us the basis of this woman's standing, *GRACE*. The New Covenant is the *New* Jerusalem; it is above all, not earthly. It is free and not in bondage to the *Old* Jerusalem – the *law*. There can be no dispensational connection herebetween this woman and the old covenant. There has appeared a great wonder in heaven. This

woman of wonder is of above. She stands in the heavens with the moon under her feet. The moon is the lesser light, it reflects the greater light while darkness rules. The greater light is that which is reflected upon this woman; she is clothed with the *sun*. Herein we see the intentions of the new covenant, to clothe us with his righteousness.

> **"Consider the lilies how they grow: they toil not, they spin not; and yet I say unto you, that Solomon in all his glory was not arrayed like one of these. If then God so clothe the grass, which is to day in the field, and tomorrow is cast into the oven; how much more will he clothe you, O ye of little faith?"** Luke 12:27-28

While the darkness of the night (the tribulation of this world caused by Satan) still rules, this woman stands clothed in *the light of Jesus Christ*. Her garments are also symbolic of a *wedding dress*; it grants her the right to attend His wedding (Rev 19:7-9).

The old covenant and its curse reign during the night, but if we will stand upon **grace** and not become entangled in the *law*, we can be clothed with the sun. God has appointed us to rule and reign with him and not to suffer the *Wrath of God*.

> **"For when they shall say, peace and safety; then sudden destruction cometh upon them, as travail upon a woman with child; and they shall not escape. But ye, brethren, are not in darkness, that that day should overtake you as a thief. Ye are all the children of light, and the children of the day: we are not of the night, nor of darkness. Therefore let us not sleep, as do others; but let us watch and be sober. For they that sleep, sleep in the night; and they that be drunken, are drunken in the night** *(foolish virgins)*. **But let us, who are of the day, be sober, putting on the breastplate of faith and love; and for an helmet, the hope of salvation. For God hath not appointed us to wrath, but to obtain salvation by our Lord Jesus Christ."** I Thessalonians 5:3-9

To fully comprehend what is happening in this vision, we must also understand what authority and destiny that Jesus Christ has given to His church.

> *"For the preaching of the cross is to them that perish foolishness; but unto us which are saved it is the power of God."* I Corinthians 1:18

> *"For the kingdom of God is not in word, but in power."* I Corinthians 4:20

> *"Now unto him that is able to do exceeding abundantly above all that we ask or think, according to the power that worketh in us."* Ephesians 3:20

> *"For our gospel came not unto you in word only, but also in power, and in the Holy Ghost, and in much assurance; as ye know what manner of men we were among you for your sake."* I Thessalonians 1:5

Our Lord Jesus Christ has been anointed by the Father to give authority and power to whom He chooses (Rev 28:18). All power and authority over Satan comes to us by Jesus Christ through the Holy Spirit which abides in all Christian believers. It is up to us to appropriate this power and authority. Our Lord Jesus Christ could conquer Satan and all of his demonic forces with only a wave of His mighty hand, but He has chosen not to do so. He has instead chosen to exert authority over Satan through His body on earth, the individual members of His church. In Ephesians 3: 8-12, Paul revealed a *mystery* unknown from the foundation of the world, that the **manifold wisdom of God** would be revealed in the church, **according to the eternal purpose that He purposed in Christ Jesus our Lord** (Eph. 3:10-11). All power and authority is given to the saints in Jesus Christ, and it is up to us (*the saints*) to claim and appropriate that power and authority. Paul's mystery was that both Jews and Gentiles alike would be chosen for this high calling, all who believe in the promises. Our Lord Jesus Christ is now seated at the right hand of God the Father waiting for the church to claim the victory over Satan. The ultimate destiny of Satan and his forces is to be completely destroyed and put away by Christ himself at the battle of Armageddon, but before that can happen it is the destiny of the body of Christ to exercise authority over Satan.

> *"For I reckon that the sufferings of this present time are not worthy to be compared with the glory which shall be revealed in us. For the earnest expectation of the creature waiteth for the manifestation of the sons of God."*
> Romans 8:18-19

The man child in Rev 12: 5 is the manifestation spoken of by the apostle Paul: **In the fullness of time** there will be brought to completion a *glorious church without spot or wrinkle* (Eph 5:27). This glorious church is not now sinless, but is composed of all Christians who have *followed after Christ.* Like in the Parable of the Seeds, some will grow in Christ and bring forth much fruit; some will accept Christ as their savior but never produce fruit. Both will inherit the Kingdom of Heaven, but each will have special assignments and duties consistent with their maturity. In both groups, all *spots and wrinkles* will be washed away by the *blood of Christ* when we stand before the throne of God.

> *"Then said Jesus unto his disciples, If any man will come after me, let him deny himself, and take up his cross, and follow me."* Matthew 16:24

Those who follow after Christ and move on to maturity are the *overcomers* spoken of in every church letter in Rev 2 and Rev 3. At a time when only God knows, this group will come to fullness and will be *caught up unto God and to His throne* (Rev 12:5). Paul was speaking of this when he said:

> *"For we know that the whole creation groaneth and travaileth in pain together until now."* Romans 8:22

The Revelation record says that this *man child* is to be **caught up** (Rev 12:5). The Greek word used here and translated *caught up* is *Harpazo,* and is exactly the same word used by Paul in I Thessalonians 4.

> *"...and the dead in Christ shall rise first: Then we which are alive and remain shall be caught up (*Harpazo*) together with them in the clouds, to meet the Lord in the air."*
> I Thessalonians 4:17

Rev 12:5 verifies that the man-child will be caught up in *a rapture* beyond any reasonable doubt. In fact, there is no way that it can be anything else. We have already shown that the general resurrection of the dead and rapture of the living will occur as the seventh trumpet is blown. The setting of Rev 12 is before the tribulation period starts, not at the end. Once this conclusion is reached, it then becomes clear that this group of raptured saints is the *firstfruit harvest* of the overcoming, mature saints before the tribulation period starts. This group will escape both the wrath of Satan (7 trumpet judgments) and the wrath of God (7 bowl judgments).

> *"Watch ye therefore, and pray always, that ye may be accounted worthy to escape all these things that shall come to pass, and to stand before the Son of man"* Luke 21:36

The man-child is seen standing on the heavenly Mt. Zion in Rev 14:1-5. They have been caught up to God and His throne (rev 12:5). We confirmed this in Chapter 15 when we examined the great multitude described in Rev 7:9-17. We have also shown in Chapter 15 that this is *not* the 144,000 being exempted (sealed) from wrath in Rev 7:1-8. The 144,000 in Revelation Chapter 7 are from 12 tribes of Israel, and will live in the Promised Land during the millennial kingdom. The 144,000 raptured out in Revelation Chapter 12 are later shown to be in heaven in Revelation Chapter 14. Rev 14:5 confirms that if the man-child of Rev 12:5 is identical to the 144,000 of Rev 14:5, they are a *firstfruits harvest*. They are destined to be in heaven during the entire tribulation period; they will be part of the Bride of Christ; and they will rule and reign with Christ during the millennial kingdom. They are those who will **rule all nations with a rod of iron** (Rev. 12:5). This is a promise made to the overcomers in Rev 2:27. This group has submitted to Christ as a *Child*, but has matured as a full grown spiritual *Man*. For those who may think that this is very strange, remember that maturity and purity do not save anyone, but it will distinguish each individual from another as believing Christians. The difference between individual Christians was clearly taught by Christ in the *Parable of the Seeds* in Mat 13:3-23, Mark 4:13-20 and Luke 8:4-15. The *sower* of the seed (*gospel message*) is *Jesus Christ*; the *seed* is the call to salvation heard by three distinct groups but only two believe and bring forth fruit; those who represent *stony ground* and those that represent *good ground*. The *third group* hears the call of Christ but is *only offended*. Those who receive the seed on *good ground* respond fully and move on to maturity. They produce *much fruit*. Those whose ground is *stony* never mature and never bring forth *fruit*. We must stress that those who hear the call but reject the offer of eternal life are bound for perdition; these are the ones who receive the seed but their *ground* was *hard*, and the seed *withered and died*. Christ spoke of this:

> **"For many are called, but few are chosen."** Matthew 22:14

Please understand that the two groups that received the seed are both saved, but they will have different roles in the kingdom to come. Some of the *good ground* saints will mature to a point where they will be a part of the *firstfruits harvest*; the *overcomers* in each of the seven churches. They will be raptured out before Satan begins to reign on this earth through the Antichrist and the False Prophet. This group of Christians will experience neither tribulation nor God's wrath.

> **"These are they which were not defiled with women; for they are virgins. These are they which follow the Lamb whithersoever he goeth. These were redeemed from among men, being the firstfruits unto God and the Lamb."**
> Rev 14:4

It is also true that the overcomers of Revelation 12 will be *intimate with the Lord* (Rev 14:4). The general multitude of saved people in Rev 7: 9-17 will include all of these 144,000; the raptured saints at the seventh trumpet; and the resurrected saints from all ages past. Because of the failure of most Revelation teachers to recognize that the **man-child** of Rev 12:5 is raptured out, they are forced to identify the man-child as Jesus Christ in the first century. We have pointed out the errancy of this interpretation. The *mystery* is easily solved and everything in Rev 12 comes into complete harmony with the rest of the Revelation record as soon as the man-child is shown to be identical to the 144,000 standing in heaven that have been **redeemed from the earth** and are clearly called *firstfruits* (Rev 14:3-5). They are in fact the firstfruits of the *wheat harvest* to come at the 7th trumpet. When the main resurrection and rapture occurs at the seventh trumpet, *all* believers will meet Christ in the air; not just a portion. No believer in Christ will be left behind at the main rapture of the body of Christ. Not one!

The 144,000 are a fulfillment of the firstfruits principle set forth by God when He gave the law and initiated the Feasts of Israel. The firstfruits were always only a portion of the entire harvest, and they were that portion that matured first. Note that the firstfruits were picked from the field by the high priest, and then *waved before God*. This was done long before the main harvest, and was a *guarantee and down payment* of the larger harvest to come. This principle will be fulfilled by Jesus Christ. He will gather the man-child to Himself, and *wave* this group of firstfruits before the Lord. How wonderful is the full council of God's word! Everything in the Old Testament was a *shadow and type* of things to come in Jesus Christ.

Finally, notice that the sun-clothed woman is a **great sign** (Rev 12:1). If God gives us a sign, we had best listen carefully. Once this *great sign* has been clearly understood, the imagery of the woman, her man child, the sun and the moon all come together harmoniously to depict the eternal plan of God to show his *manifold wisdom* to Satan. In Gen 17: 1-8, God made a covenant with Abraham. He promised Abraham, who had no sons at age

90, that the earth would be full of the *seeds* of his loins. He was told that he would be the *father of many nations*. Then God promised Abraham that the Land of Canaan would be the possession of his seed forever. Later, in Gen 22:17 the lord told Abraham that his seed (descendents) would be of two types: an earthly seed, and a starry seed: ***I will bless thee, and in multiplying I will multiply thy seed as the stars of the heaven, and as the sand which is upon the sea shore*** (Gen 22:17). Finally, the apostle Paul verified that Abraham would spawn from the seed of his loins the Messiah, our Lord Jesus Christ.

> *"Now to Abraham and his seed were the promises made. He saith not, And to seeds, as of many; but as of one, And to thy seed, which is Christ."*   Galatians 3:16

The *starry seed* of Abraham will be that seed who will accept Christ as their long-awaited Messiah and the Son of God. They will be a part of the body of Christ. The *earthly seed* will fulfill the promise of inheriting the Land of Canaan in the Millennial Kingdom. God has not forsaken Israel nor will He forget his Covenant promises to Abraham. The following figure is a graphic depiction of the *Seeds of Abraham* and the course of history from Abraham to the millennial kingdom.

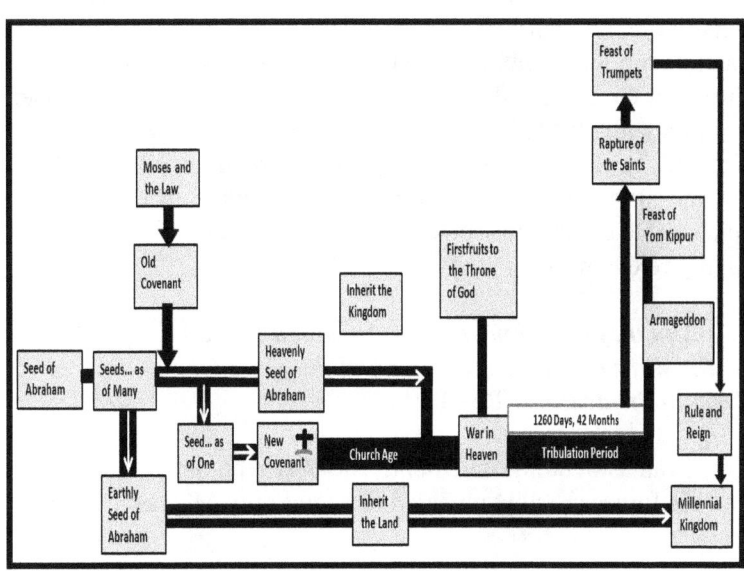

The Dragon

There is no doubt what the dragon represents. We are told in Rev 12:9 that the dragon is that old serpent, called the devil and Satan. The symbolism of Satan as a dragon is found in several Old Testament records and in older manuscripts. In ancient Egypt, Satan is pictured as living in the Nile River as a mighty dragon. The power of this dragon was thought by the Israelites to be manifested through the Pharaoh of Egypt, who oppressed them unmercifully.

> *"Behold, I am against thee, Pharaoh King of Egypt, the great dragon that lieth in the midst of his rivers, which hath said, my river is mine on, and I have made it for myself."*
> Ezekial 29:3

As previously discussed, the sun-clothed woman (the corporate body of Jesus Christ) is ***travailing in birth pains*** (Rev 12:2). She is *pained* to be delivered. The original word translated pained is *basaniste*, it is only used once in the entire New Testament. The base meaning is to *be tormented or vexed*. The tribulation period will be immediately preceded by the rapture of 144,000 saints that comprise the ***man-child*** travailing to be berthed. Satan is trying to prevent this from happening; he is *that old serpent* from the Garden of Eden, and he has never changed his relentless pursuit of Christians trying to keep them from maturing. But he cannot stop this event, and the man-child is raptured to the throne of God (Rev 14:1-3). At that time, the Archangel Michael appears with all of his angels and there is a great ***war in heaven*** (Rev 12:7). But Satan and his angels ***prevailed not*** (Rev 12:8). He and his angels were ***cast out into the earth*** (Rev 12:9). It is remarkable to note how this victory is accomplished, and it is highly relevant to our study.

> *"And they overcame him by the blood of the Lamb, and by the word of their testimony; and they loved not their lives unto the death."* Rev 12:11

This is an astounding statement! The ***they*** who defeated Satan and his forces are now revealed to be not only Michael and his angels, but also a group of resurrected saints. This conclusion is inescapable. *They* overcame Satan by the **blood of the Lamb**, and *they* were not afraid to die for their belief in Jesus Christ. Angels do not need the blood…. They were created in purity. Note that it does not say that they all died physically for Christ (martyrs), but that they have refused to yield to Satan's temptations in this world. They have not died spiritually. Again, they have come to maturity and have completely *sold out* to Christ and have followed Him; they have *died* to the world.

> ***"Set your affection on things above, not on things on the earth. For ye are dead, and your life is hid with Christ in God"***   Colossians 2:2-3

In his first letter to the church at Corinth, the apostle Paul was correcting some false doctrine which had crept into the church. That false doctrine was that there was no resurrection of the dead. They believed in the immortality of the soul, but not the resurrection of the body. Paul said that ***if the dead do not rise, then Christ is not risen*** (I Cor. 15:16). He then goes on to say:

> ***"For He must reign (in heaven) until He hath put all enemies under His feet. The last enemy that shall be destroyed is death (Rev 20:14). Else what shall they do which are baptized for the dead, if the dead rise not at all? Why are they then baptized for the dead? And why stand we in jeopardy every hour? I die every hour."***
>   I Corinthians 15: 26, 29-31

In Paul's mind, he is already dead though he lives. He has been crucified with Christ just as surely as if he had hung on the cross.

> ***"For to me to live is Christ, and to die is gain".***   Phil 1:21

It appears that the 144,000 *firstfruits* will join Michael and his angels in defeating Satan. What a time this will be! Satan is now cast down to the earth and he is full of *great wrath* (Rev 12:12). There is a warning that goes forth:

> *"Rejoice to you that are now in heaven, but woe to the inhabitants of the earth and of the sea! ...Because he (Satan) knoweth that he hath but a short time."* Rev 12:12.

This *short time* is a *time, times and half-a-time* or 1260 days (Rev 12:14). We note also that Michael, the great archangel protector of Israel, has led the successful battle against Satan and his angels. The prophet Daniel had also received a vision of this conflict and adds the following:

> *"And at that time (time of the end) shall Michael stand up, the great prince which standeth for the children of thy people: and there shall be a time of trouble, such as never was since there was a nation even to that same time."*
> Daniel 12:1

The Hebrew phrase *stand up* is a mistranslation of the Aramaic text. It should be translated as *stand aside* or to *stand down*. This is exactly what will happen over the 1260-day persecution of those who dwell upon the earth. This permission from God for Satan to persecute His people was given in shadow and type in the book of Job. God let Satan test and persecute Job to prove his faith and bring him into a stronger covenant relationship with Him. Job's faith in God and his refusal to abandon his faith is a shadow and type of how the believers will need to resist Satan in the tribulation period: ***For they did not love their lives to the death*** (Rev 12:11). God will allow Satan to persecute both Israel and the church during this period of time. The reason why Israel is persecuted is explained by the apostle Paul.

> *"For I would not, brethren, that you should be ignorant of this mystery, lest you should be wise in your own conceits; that blindness in part has happened to Israel until the fullness of the Gentiles has come in. And so all Israel shall be saved as it is written. There shall come out of Zion the Deliverer and shall turn away ungodliness from Jacob. For this is My covenant unto them, when I shall take away their sin."* Romans 11:26

God's eternal purpose was to send His Son, the Lord Jesus Christ, to *take away the sins of the world* (John 1:29). The Jewish nation as a whole refused His offer. The purpose of the 1260 days persecution by Satan and the reason that God permits it is to use the church to bring Israel back into a covenant relationship with God, accept Jesus Christ as their savior, and fulfill God's promise to Abraham that His *seed* will inherit the land promised to them after the Exodus. This period of persecution contains the *seven trumpet judgments* which are part of *His wrath* as previously discussed.

When the dragon *saw that he was cast onto the earth* (Rev 12:12) he turns on the city of Jerusalem to persecute those who live there.

> *"And when the dragon saw that he was cast unto the earth, he persecuted the woman which brought forth the man child. And to the woman were given two wings of a great eagle, that she might fly into the wilderness, into her place, where she is nourished for a time, and times, and half a time, from the face of the serpent."*   Rev 12:13:14

Once Michael *stands aside*, the dragon will then try to destroy *the woman* who berthed the man child, and he will start by attacking the city of Jerusalem. Following the teachings of the late Robert Van Kampen, we will call this the *Jerusalem Campaign*. We will discuss this invasion of Jerusalem in Chapter 26. Like all demons, Satan must have a *human body* in which he or one of his strong princes of darkness will reside. He will have his man in the powerful world leader who is at this time ruler of the eighth great world kingdom, a 10-nation end-time confederacy which must arise before Satan is cast down. Once the antichrist arises as Satan incarnate, he will assemble his army to attack Jerusalem and persecute the nation of Israel (Rev 17:11). As he enters Jerusalem he will find that many have heeded the warning of Christ in His Olivet Discourse, and have already fled from the city.

> *"And when the dragon saw that he was cast unto the earth, he persecuted the woman which brought forth the man child. And to the woman were given two wings of a great eagle, that she might fly into the wilderness, into her place, where she is nourished for a time, and times, and half a time, from the face of the serpent."*   Rev 12:13-14

Christ had already forewarned the people who will be in Jerusalem that they should flee, quickly; and He gave them a sign.

> *"When ye therefore shall see the abomination of desolation, spoken of by Daniel the prophet, stand in the holy place, (whoso readeth, let him understand:) Then let them which be in Judaea flee into the mountains: Let him which is on the housetop not come down to take any thing out of his house: Neither let him which is in the field return back to take his clothes. And woe unto them that are with child, and to them that give suck in those days! But pray ye that your flight be not in the winter, neither on the sabbath day."*
> Matthew 24:14-20

Christ had warned that *the sign* will be an *abomination of desolation* that will stand in the Holy Place. This implies that the temple will be completely overrun and the sacrifices stopped. Remember that no one is allowed into the Holy of Holies except for the High Priest; and then only once a year on the Feast of Yom Kippur. Evidently, the antichrist will stand in the Holy of Holies and demand that he be worshipped as God. In his letter to the church at Thessalonica, Paul was speaking to the saints about the second coming of the Lord. It seems that someone had been preaching and spreading the word that the rapture had already occurred, and that they had missed it.

> *"Let no man deceive you by any means: for that day shall not come, except there come a falling away first, and that man of sin be revealed, the son of perdition; Who opposeth and exalteth himself above all that is called God, or that is*

> *worshipped; so that he as God sitteth in the temple of God, shewing himself that he is God."* II Thessalonians 2:3-4

The ***man of sin*** of which Paul spoke of is the same as the man seen in Daniel 12:10-11 and the same as in Rev 13.

> *"Many shall be purified, and made white, and tried; but the wicked shall do wickedly: and none of the wicked shall understand; but the wise shall understand. And from the time that the daily sacrifice shall be taken away, and the abomination that maketh desolate set up, there shall be a thousand two hundred and ninety days."* Danial 12:11-12

Here we are introduced to a 1290-day period of time. The reign of the beast and the antichrist will only be for 1260 days, over the last half of Daniel's 70th week. They will be defeated and cast into the lake of burning fire (Rev 19:20) at the end of these 1260 days. This period of 1260 days will end at the Battle of Armageddon. Evidently, there will be an additional 30 days after the battle of Armageddon to have the wedding feast; judge the nations; clean up after the great battle; and to recover the 144,000 from *the wilderness* of Bozra where they have been protected. (Isaiah 63:1).

When Satan finds that a remnant is escaping from Jerusalem, he pursues and tries to kill them as they flee.

> *"And the serpent cast out of his mouth water as a flood after the woman, that he might cause her to be carried away of the flood. And the earth helped the woman, and the earth opened her mouth, and swallowed up the flood which the dragon cast out of his mouth."* Rev 12:15-16

For a reason not explained, rather than encounter this fleeing remnant with the antichrist's army, Satan will try to drown the *woman* with some type of supernatural flood. In the Exodus, the pharaoh, who was a shadow and type of Satan, pursued Israel. But before he could harm them, the Red Sea swallowed up him and his armies; and the children of Israel emerged a new nation from the Red Sea. In Revelation 12:13-16, we again see the antichrist, Satan in the flesh, pursuing God's people. Once again we see a *flood,* and again God's people are delivered. In the passage above, it is recorded that *the earth swallowed up the flood.* The earth also *swallowed up* Korah and his family when he trespassed God's law by offering *strange fire* in the Holy Place. (Num 16: 28-33). How exactly the earth opens her mouth and saves the fleeing remnant is not revealed to us, but it is likely that an earthquake opened up the earth and an unknown force called the *flood* was carried away.

> *"And the dragon was wroth with the woman, and went to make war with the remnant of her seed, which keep the commandments of God, and have the testimony of Jesus Christ."*   Rev 12:17

Here we have a confirmation that the man-child is just a portion of the saints which is still alive and remain on the earth when this event occurs. The dragon now turns to **make war with the remnant of her seed.** Who is this remnant? They are those who *keep the commandments of God and have the testimony of Jesus Christ.* Since Satan will execute his wrath upon the followers of Christ and on the nation of Israel over the last 3.5 years of the tribulation period, this is proof that there will be Christians that will be persecuted and killed during the last half of Daniel's 70th week.

We now need to take a closer look at the antichrist and the false prophet in Chapters 17 and 18; who are the agents of Satan's political, military and religious systems over the last 1260-days of Daniel's 70th week.

Chapter 15

The Two Groups of 144,000

Between the opening of the sixth and the seventh seals we see in Rev 7 a group of 144,000 Jews from 12 tribes of Israel who are sealed in their forehead (Rev 7:1-8). In Revelation Chapter 14 we again see a group of 144,000 (Rev 14:1-7). Are these the same groups? We will show that they are not. Each has its place in the millennial kingdom and each has certain distinguishing characteristics. The following biblical descriptions provide a contrast between the two groups.

The 144,000 in Revelation Chapter 7

"And after these things I saw four angels standing on the four corners of the earth, holding the four winds of the earth, that the wind should not blow on the earth, nor on the sea, nor on any tree. And I saw another angel ascending from the east, having the seal of the living God: and he cried with a loud voice to the four angels, to whom it was given to hurt the earth and the sea, saying, Hurt not the earth, neither the sea, nor the trees, till we have sealed the servants of our God in their foreheads. And I heard the number of them which were sealed: and there were sealed an hundred and forty and four thousand of all the tribes of the children of Israel. Of the tribe of Juda were sealed twelve thousand. Of the tribe of Reuben were sealed twelve thousand. Of the tribe of Gad were sealed twelve thousand. Of the tribe of Aser were sealed twelve thousand. Of the tribe of Nepthalim were sealed twelve thousand. Of the tribe of Manasses were sealed twelve thousand. Of the tribe of Simeon were sealed twelve thousand. Of the tribe of Levi were sealed twelve thousand. Of the tribe of Issachar were sealed twelve thousand. Of the tribe of Zabulon were sealed twelve thousand. Of the tribe of Joseph were sealed twelve thousand. Of the tribe of Benjamin were sealed twelve thousand."   Rev 7:1-7

The 144,000 in Revelation Chapter 14

"And I looked, and, lo, a Lamb stood on the mount Sion, and with him an hundred forty and four thousand, having his Father's name written in their foreheads. And I heard a voice from heaven, as the voice of many waters, and as the voice of a great thunder: and I heard the voice of harpers harping with their harps: And they sung as it were a new song before the throne, and before the four beasts, and the elders: and no man could learn that song but the hundred and forty and four thousand, which were redeemed from the earth. These are they which were not defiled with women; for they are virgins. These are they which follow the Lamb whithersoever he goeth. These were redeemed from among men, being the firstfruits unto God and to the Lamb. And in their mouth was found no guile: for they are without fault before the throne of God."   Rev 14:1-5

The following table summarizes and compares the characteristics of each group.

The 144,000 In Chapter 14	The 144,000 In Chapter 7
There is no indication that they are all Jewish. They are from "among men". They are redeemed "from the earth" Rev 14:4	They are all Jewish from 12 tribes of Israel Rev 7:4
All are standing before God's throne in heaven Rev 14:5	All are "on the earth" Rev 7:1-2
They have God's name on their foreheads Rev 14:1	They are being "sealed" on their foreheads Rev 7:3
They are with "the Lamb of God" Rev 14:1	There is no mention that they are with Christ or God as they are sealed
The 144,000 are accompanied by harpists and harps before the throne Rev 14:2	There is no mention of music as they are sealed
The 144,000 are called "Firstfruits" unto God Rev 14:14	These are not a firstfruit assembly
They follow the Lamb wherever He goes. Rev 14:4	This group is on the earth. They are not with Christ
They have been taken to Heaven	They are on the earth

It seems apparent that when a comparison is made between these two groups of 144,000, they cannot be the same. The most popular view of these two groups of 144,000 is that they are one and the same, but viewed at different times. By necessity, most prophecy students have the 144,000 of Rev 7 *protected* from the *seals, trumpets and bowls* which are overwhelmingly taught to sequentially occur over a period of 7 years. Pre-tribulation supporters cannot have the same group of 144,000 being sealed for the entire tribulation period, and also have the same group standing on the Heavenly Mt. Zion anytime during the first 6 seals and the first 5 trumpet judgments. This is impossible since the 144,000 of Rev 7 are seen being exempt from the torment of demon locust after the fifth trumpet sounds (Rev 9:4). However, there is a line of reasoning that both Pre-tribulation and Pre-wrath supporters can use to claim that the 144,000 in Rev 7 and in Rev 14 are one and the same. They propose that the vision recorded in Rev 14 is not in sequence with Rev 12 and 13, but take place *after* the tribulation period has ended: The 144,000 sealed in Rev 7 are shown after having been taken to the Millennial Throne by Christ. This position can, in fact, be supported by either a 7 year or a 3.5 year tribulation period. It is clearly understood that in either case, then those that are sealed in Rev 7 are exempt from martyrdom during both the seven trumpet judgments and the seven bowl judgments. They will inherit the Millennial Kingdom on earth. Some have these 144,000 in Rev 14 standing on the heavenly Mt. Zion and others have them standing on the earthly Mt. Zion in preparation for the Millennial Kingdom. Hence, the interpretation of whether these two groups are *identical* hinge on whether or not the 144,000 of Rev 14 are the same as those in Rev 7, but simply seen at different points in time.

We conclude by comparing scripture to scripture, that they must be *different* groups. Both are coexisting at the same time: One is on the earth and one is in heaven before the throne of God. We will present scriptural evidence to support our position in this chapter. However, if the 144,000 of Rev 7 are the *Jewish remnant* that will populate the millennial kingdom, it makes perfect sense to protect them from death during both the trumpet and bowl judgments to come.

So what is the truth? The truth lies exactly where it should be found, in the scriptures. There is no need to conjecture or postulate about who these two groups represent if we will simply open our spiritual eyes. We have conclusively shown in Chapter 14 two very important things: (1) The *Man-Child* of Rev 12 is *not* Jesus Christ, and (2) the Man-Child was *raptured* out. So a partial rapture *must* occur as Satan is cast down before the last 3.5 years of tribulation. The man-child is revealed in Rev 12:5, and they are *caught up to God and to His throne*. They are the same as the 144,000 which are then seen standing in heaven before the throne of God (Rev 14:1, 3, 5). They follow Christ wherever He goes (Rev 14:5). This 144,000 is a *firstfruits rapture*, just as the scriptures say they are in Rev 14:4. They are the *overcomers* out of each of the seven churches in Rev 2-3. It is easy to identify this 144,000 with the promise to the overcomers in the Church at Philadelphia, long identified as an end-time church. It is the only church that was not rebuked. The overcomers in this church (and by extension to the other six churches) are promised that **they would no more leave the temple of God** and that they would receive a **new name** (Rev 3:12). Christians in the church at *Smyrna* are told to **Be faithful unto death** (Rev 2:10). The *Man-Child* in Rev 12:11 **loved not their lives to the death**. Overcomers in the church at *Thyatira* were told that **They would rule with a rod of iron** (Rev 2:27). The Man-Child in Rev 12:5 are told they will **rule with a rod of iron**. Some in the church of *Laodicea* were to **sit on God's throne**. The throne is where God rules and reigns. The man-child is to **rule all the nations** and was **caught to God's throne**. The identification of the Man-child with the *overcomers* in each of the seven churches in Rev 2-3 is strong.

> *"He who overcomes I will… write on Him the name of my God and the name of the city of my God, the New Jerusalem, which comes down from out of heaven from my God. And I will write on him my new name."* Rev 3:12.

In order to properly discern the difference in the two groups of 144,000 (Rev 7:1-8 and Rev 14:1-5 it is necessary to understand that the 144,000 in Rev 14:1-5 are called *firstfruits*; the 144,000 in Rev 7:1-8 are *not* firstfruits. Firstfruits are associated with the four spring Feasts of Israel, which are not only held in remembrance of how God delivered them from Egypt, but they are *appointments and rehearsals* of things to come. What does this mean prophetically?

Firstfruits and the 144,000 of Rev 14:1-5

The concept of a Firstfruits harvest is deeply rooted in the Holy Scriptures. The study of Firstfruits is too rich and extensive to be covered here in any great detail, but the general prophetic implications will be briefly discussed. There were three times during the year that all males were required to be in Jerusalem. These three times of the year correspond to three feasts of Israel: (1) The Feast of Weeks (Feast of Unleavened Bread) ,(2) The Feast of Shavaot (Pentecost), and (3) The Feast of Tabernacles (Feast of Ingathering). Each of these 3 feasts are to remember how God saved the Children of Israel from Egyptian bondage, but they are also a *moed* (rehearsal) for the redemption of Jews and Gentiles who accept Jesus Christ as their Savior. These three feasts of Israel are each associated with a different harvest. The *barley* ripens first around the time of Passover in Nisan (Spring); the *wheat* ripens next around the time of Pentecost; and the *fruits which grow on the vine* ripen last in the fall in the month of Tishri (Fall). The three Feast periods or harvests, picture the start of a *ripening* of three groups of people.

These three crops depict three types of people. The barley represents the pre-Christ Children of Israel who believed in a coming Messiah; the wheat represents the rest of the believers (Jews and Gentiles) after the 1st advent of Christ; and the grapes represent the unbelievers.

Feast of Unleavened Bread

The Feast of Unleavened Bread started on Nisan 15 and continues for 7 full days through Nisan 21 (See Chapter 9). The 1st and 7th days of this feast are a Sabbath day (a High Holy Day) no matter what day of the week they might fall on. The Hebrews were an agricultural society that depended heavily upon two main grain crops; barley and wheat. These two crops were planted together in the fall: Wheat and Barley. The *barley crop* matured first, and then the wheat. The first of the barley harvest occurred at the time of the Passover and Feast of Unleavened Bread. The wheat crop came into fullness about the time of Pentecost or the Feast of Ingathering. The following instructions were given as to what must be done to harvest the barley.

In the fourteenth day of the first month at even is the LORD's Passover. And on the fifteenth day of the same month is the feast of unleavened bread unto the LORD: seven days ye must eat unleavened bread. Leviticus 23:5-6.

Ye shall bring a sheaf of the firstfruits of your harvest unto the priest: And he shall wave the sheaf before the LORD, to be accepted for you: on the morrow after the sabbath the priest shall wave it. And ye shall offer that day when ye wave the sheaf a he lamb without blemish of the first year for a burnt offering unto the LORD. Leviticus 23:10-12

Since the feast of the Unleavened beard was seven days long it would have contained only one Sunday, and that Sunday would be when the firstfruits of the barley harvest were waved to the Lord.

The *barley* symbolizes a group of Old Testament saints who believed that Christ would arise as the Messiah of Israel. The fulfillment of the Feast of Firstfruits can now be understood.

> (1) Christ was our firstfruit offering to the Lord. He was the *First of the Firstfruits*. He was without leaven (no sin was upon him). He was our Passover Lamb, slain from the foundation of the world without blemish.

(2) The *sheaf of barley* is presented to the High Priest, who then waves it before the Lord. Christ is our eternal High Priest.

(3) This *wave sheath* is a group of *firstfruit Jewish believers* that must be waved (presented) before the Lord. This wave sheath is the *firstfruits of the Children of Israel*. They are the *best portion* of all the Old Testament saints who believed in faith that Christ the Messiah would someday come to forgive their sins. Can this interpretation be supported by Holy Scripture? ... Yes. In Matthew 27 the following event is recorded.

Jesus, when he had cried again with a loud voice, yielded up the ghost. And, behold, the veil of the temple was rent in twain from the top to the bottom; and the earth did quake, and the rocks rent; And the graves were opened; and many bodies of the saints which slept arose, and came out of the graves after his resurrection, and went into the holy city, and appeared unto many.
Matthew 27:50-53

Note that *many* (not all) of the Old Testament saints arose from the grave *after* his resurrection. Christ was crucified, dead and buried. On the third day He arose from the dead. THIS WAS EXACTLY THE SAME DAY THAT THE SHEATH OF BARLEY WAS TO BE WAVED BEFORE THE LORD. Christ fulfilled the Feast of Passover and the Feast of Firstfruits in every way. On the first day of the Feast of Weeks (Sunday; during the Feast of Firstfruits) he became the sinless firstfruit offering to His father. (Some of) the Old Testament recipients of His New Covenant saving grace were then collected from the grave. He then presented (waved) them to His Father. Christ was the *first of the firstfruits*, This small group of Jewish Christian believers were the *firstfruits* of many sons and daughters that would be raised or raptured to glory. The physical and spiritual firstfruit offerings were a guarantee or promise of the larger harvest yet to come.

Note that nothing could be harvested and used from the field until this wavesheaf of barley was presented to the Lord. Why was the firstfruit barley ritual a shadow and type of redeemed Old Testament saints? Because barley was not the precious wheat that represented the church saints… the wheat had not yet matured, but the barley had already come forth. Mat 27:52-53 can now be fully understood. The resurrection of many Old Testament believers was a ***Firstfruits Rapture.*** There must be a similar firstfruits rapture that corresponds to the New Covenant saints. So where is the Firstfruits of the New Covenant saints (Jews and Gentiles) that will also be redeemed from the earth?

Feast of Pentecost

Following the resurrection of Christ (on Sunday, the first day after the 1st Jewish Sabbath in the 7 day Feast of Firstfruits), the Lord gave instructions to mark off 49 days. The 50th day would be the Feast of Pentecost. This is also called the Feast of Weeks and the Feast of Ingathering.

And ye shall count unto you from the morrow after the sabbath, from the day that ye brought the sheaf of the wave offering; seven sabbaths shall be complete: Even unto the morrow after the seventh sabbath shall ye number fifty days; and ye shall offer a new meat offering unto the LORD. Ye shall bring out of your habitations two wave loaves of two tenth deals: they shall be of fine flour; they shall be baken with leaven; they are the firstfruits unto the LORD. Lev 23:15-17

On this day there is to be a ***new meat offering unto the Lord***. The designation of a meat offering should be translated a *meal offering*. This ***new*** *meal **offering*** consists of two wave loafs of two tenth deals. These loafs by context are made from a *sheaf* (about 2 quarts) of *wheat*, not barley. The two loafs are for the LORD. Here we see a very strange thing: The two loaves are to be ***baked with leaven***. In the scriptures *leaven* always represents *sin*. Note that this is the only offering ever presented to God with leaven. Further, and very important, is that no grain from the field could be picked and consumed until this firstfruit offering had been presented to the Lord. The symbolism is clear. Jesus often referred to those whom He called as precious wheat. Wheat was often used by Jesus Christ to represent the body of Christ. The Parable of the Wheat and Tares best demonstrates this analogy (Mat 13). Just as the *firstfruits* of the barley harvest represented Old Testament saints, the *firstfruits* of the wheat harvest were to be presented to the Lord as two loaves of wheat cooked with leaven.. One loaf represents the gentiles, the other the Jews. Both contain leaven because all are full of sin but are saved by grace.

The Firstfruit Harvest of Wheat

We have proposed that (1) the two loaves represent two groups of believers, Jews and Gentiles.

> *For there is no difference between the Jew and the Greek: for the same Lord over all is rich unto all that call upon him.* Romans 10:12

> *That the blessing of Abraham might come on the Gentiles through Jesus Christ; that we might receive the promise of the Spirit through faith.* Galatians 3:14

(2) Lev 23:17 makes it clear that that this is a *firstfruits offering*.

We have shown that the barley firstfruits offering were fulfilled after Christ arose from the grave when many Old Testament saints were raised and seen by many. So when is the Pentecost firstfruits resurrection and where is it in the Holy Scriptures? .... the answer is found in the Book of Revelation. In order to understand this *mystery* we must understand how this all fits into the Daniel prophecy of 70 weeks. We have presented much evidence that the last week (7 years) of Daniel's prophecy was interrupted with 3.5 years remaining. We have shown this period of time to be the duration of the tribulation period. We have shown that the last 3.5 years will commence when Satan and his fallen angels are cast down to the earth (Rev 12). The antichrist and the false prophet then arise (Rev 13). What happens next? It is obvious that almost 2000 years have now elapsed since

Daniel's 70th week was suspended. In Rev 14 we see 144,000 saints standing on the heavenly Mt. Zion.

And I looked, and, lo, a Lamb stood on the mount Sion, and with him an hundred forty and four thousand, having his Father's name written in their foreheads. And I heard a voice from heaven, as the voice of many waters, and as the voice of a great thunder: and I heard the voice of harpers harping with their harps: And they sung as it were a new song before the throne, and before the four beasts, and the elders: and no man could learn that song but the hundred and forty and four thousand, which were redeemed from the earth. Rev 14:1-3

These were redeemed from among men, being the firstfruits unto God and to the Lamb. Rev 14:4

How could this be any clearer if read without preconceived conclusions. (1) These can only be the **man-child** of Rev 12:5 who was caught up unto God and His throne (Rev 14:1-3) *before* the reign of the antichrist and the false prophets begins. They are a *firstfruit*s harvest **unto God and to the Lamb** (Rev 14:4-b). The remaining question is why did this not occur in 30 AD on the Feast of Pentecost? The answer is obvious: The gift of eternal life by believing in Jesus Christ as their promised Messiah was offered to the Jews and rejected. After the Feast of Pentecost in 30 AD, Paul was called by Christ on the road to Damascus and sent to the gentiles. This had not yet come to pass. All Christians understand that the Holy Spirit fell on the day of Pentecost in 30 AD. Paul was sent to present the gospel to the gentiles, and later Peter. At this time, the 70th week of Daniel had been interrupted. When will it resume? As soon as Satan is cast out of the heavenlies in Rev 12, and the antichrist and false prophet arise. Note that to God *one day is like a thousand years*. To him the church age is merely a blink of the eye in eternity. The firstfruit harvest of Rev 14:1-4 fulfills the shadow and type of Pentecost in 30 AD within a blink of Gods eternal eye. Here is wisdom and understanding.

The Feast of Tabernacles

The Feast of Pentecost marks the beginning of the wheat harvest. The main harvest is yet to come. We have previously presented scriptural evidence that the main harvest will occur on Tishri 1, the Feast of Trumpets or Rosh Hashanah (Rev 11:15-19). This is the rapture and resurrection of all believers (Mat 24:29-31, I Thess. 4:16-18, I Cor. 15:51-53).

And I looked, and behold a white cloud, and upon the cloud one sat like unto the Son of man, having on his head a golden crown, and in his hand a sharp sickle. And another angel came out of the temple, crying with a loud voice to him that sat on the cloud, Thrust in thy sickle, and reap: for the time is come for thee to reap; for the harvest of the earth is ripe. And he that sat on the cloud thrust in his sickle on the earth; and the earth was reaped. Rev 14:14-16

This is the *main harvest*. After the main harvest, the principle of the **gleanings** now becomes clear.

And when ye reap the harvest of your land, thou shalt not wholly reap the corners of thy field, neither shalt thou gather the gleanings of thy harvest. Lev 19:9

The gleaning is the wheat that is left in the field after the main harvest. The gleanings will be the Jews and Gentiles who remain on the earth after the rapture occurs on Tishri 1 and had not accepted Christ as their savior. These individuals will not escape the **Wrath of God** (Rev 15:1 & Rev 16:1). However, they will have the 10 days between Tishri 1 and Tishri 10 to accept Christ and escape eternal damnation. These 10 days are known as the *Days of Awe*, the *Days of Repentance* and the *Days of Redemption* by Jewish believers. The Feast of Yom Kippur will come on Tishri 10, which we have shown is the great *Battle of Armageddon*. On this day, the **grapes** of the field will be harvested by Jesus Christ our Lord and Savior. This is also clearly revealed in the scriptures.

And another angel came out from the altar, which had power over fire; and cried with a loud cry to him that had the sharp sickle, saying, Thrust in thy sharp sickle, and gather the clusters of the vine of the earth; for her grapes are fully ripe. And the angel thrust in his sickle into the earth, and gathered the vine of the earth, and cast it into the great winepress of the wrath of God. And the winepress was trodden without the city, and blood came out of the winepress, even unto the horse bridles, by the space of a thousand and six hundred furlongs.
Rev 14:17-20

Note that the **grapes** clearly represent the wicked followers of Satan who have refused to accept Christ as their savior. They have been gathered between Tishri 1-Tishri 10 to a place **without the city**. This is clearly the *City of Jerusalem* and the place outside the city is where the *Battle of Armageddon* will take place. This is the fulfillment of the **Wrath of God**. Again we see allusions and allegories to a harvest, but not a harvest of wheat (believers). The grape harvest is a harvest of unbelievers.

The period of time between Tishri 10 and Tishri 15 will be discussed in some detail in later chapters, but for now we note that the Feast of Tabernacles will start on Tishri 15 and end on Tishri 22. It is the most joyous occasion in the Jewish religious year. Rabbis have written that *you have not seen joy or celebration until you attend the Feast of Tabernacles.* The Jews cannot even imagine the joy of this last Feast of Tabernacles. Satan, the antichrist, the false prophet and all of their followers have been destroyed at the Battle of Armageddon: The 144,000 who have been divinely protected (Rev 7) will be there: the remnant who fled Jerusalem to hide in Petra: the 144,000 firstfruits who were raptured out as the man-child: those who were in the main harvest at the last trump: and those who accepted Christ during the bowl judgments ... all will be gathered to this Feast of Tabernacles. The work of Christ during the church age is finished. The millennial kingdom is now come.

In Biblical times the wheat was harvested by shodding oxen with *brass* shoes. Brass in the scriptures is used to represent purification and separation. The oxen would tread the wheat and separate the precious wheat from the husks. The barley is then thrown into the air with a winnowing fork and the wind blows the chaff away. This is beautifully illustrated in the Book of Ruth. Ruth comes to Boaz (the kinsman redeemer) at the time of *wheat harvest*. She lies at his feet on the *threshing floor* and is redeemed.

In the three spring feasts we see the redemptive grace of our Savior reaching from the fall of Adam and Eve to the Battle of Armageddon. Our Lord Jesus personally fulfilled all three of the spring feasts. They were fulfilled down to the minutest detail and on the very day of the lunar calendar that they were supposed to be fulfilled. Christ was crucified on Passover, in the grave by the first day of Unleavened Bread and rose on the first day of the Feast of Weeks. On some future Feast of Pentecost /Feast of Ingathering another firstfruit harvest of New Covenant saints will be caught up to God's throne. This is exactly what one might expect out of a fair and equitable God… if there was an Old Testament firstfruit harvest there will be a New Testament firstfruit harvest.

Firstfruits of the Body of Christ
The bread with no leaven from the feast of Unleavened Bread represented the very first maturity of grain, which was the barley. This is *Israel* under the law… that remnant of Israel who listened to the prophets and knew that a Messiah was coming to take away their sins. The only way to enter heaven under the law was to live a sinless life, *no leaven*. Only Christ fulfilled the law and lived a sinless life, and so Paul called Him *the first of the firstfruits*. After His resurrection, He ascended to heaven, *waved himself*, and was fully accepted by God. At that time, **many** (Mat 27:52)old testament saints were raised from the grave as a *firstfruits barley offering* and **appeared to many** (Mat 27:53). After 50 more days, which constituted the *Feast of Weeks*, the *Feast of Ingathering* was held. The two loaves previously mentioned were *baked with leaven*, to be accepted by the Lord as

a *sin offering*. What an exact picture and type of what we have just studied in the two groups of 144,000. The *two loaves* with leaven represented *Jews and Gentiles* alike. The 144,000 seen before the throne in heaven are the *firstfruits of the New Covenant*. The first group (*Jewish*) is the *dusty seed of the earth* that God promised Abraham; they will inherit the Land during the millennial kingdom. The second group is *believing Jews and Gentiles*, who are the *starry seed* that has become a *firstfruits offering* from the body of Christ. Finally, the first 3.5 years of Daniel's 70th week ended in 30 AD. There has been a *long maturation and growing* season of now over 2000 years in which the full body of Christ (*wheat*) is coming to full maturity. Not every Christian will mature to an *overcomer*. Those who are alive and ready will be raptured out as the man-child in Revelation Chapter 12.

> *"And there she being with child cried, travailing in birth, and pained to be delivered... And his tail drew the third part of the stars of heaven, and did cast them to the earth: and the dragon stood before the woman which was ready to be delivered, for to devour her child a soon as it was born. And she brought forth a man child, who was to rule all nations with a rod of iron: and her child was caught up unto God, and to his throne."* Rev 12: 2, 4, 5

The 144,000 of Rev 14 are collectively the *man-child* of Rev 12. They are the *firstfruits* of the larger wheat harvest unto God. The Mt. Zion of Rev 14:1 is the *heavenly Mt. Zion*. The Mt. Zion on earth will be in control of Satan and the antichrist for the next 3.5 years.

In Rev 14:3 these 144,000 are seen *before the 24 elders and the four living creatures*. In Rev 14:4 we are told that they were *purchased from among men*, not from the 12 tribes of Israel as in Rev 7. The firstfruit harvest is not *left in the field* but are brought immediately to the temple and offered up to God (Exodus 23:19, 34:26). The *field* is the *world* and these 144, 000 are the *wheat* which has matured before the rest of the *harvest*. There are several observations which can be made.

- Since the 144,000 in Rev 7 are literally (12x12, 000) = 144,000 Hebrews; the 144,000 in Rev 14 are also literally 144,000.
- The *man child* is raptured out to heaven before the 1260-day tribulation period starts. The 144,000 of Rev 7 are also shown before the 1260-day period of time starts, but they will be divinely protected and will enter the millennial kingdom to fulfill God's promise to Abraham. The 144,000 of Rev 14 are called *virgins*. The 144,000 sealed Hebrew are not *virgins* in a physical or a spiritual sense. They must experience tribulation on earth and grow to maturity. The 144,000 of Rev 14 have not defiled themselves with the world. They are **spiritual virgins** (Rev 14:4).They *follow the Lamb* wherever He goes (Rev 14: 4). They are the *firstfruits (Rev 14:4)*. There is a strong association to the *overcomers* described in each of the seven church letters. The members of Christ's church are destined to be kings and priests who rule and reign with Christ throughout the earth (Rev 1:6). The 144,000 of Rev 14 is a special group with a special assignment.
- The group of 144,000 in Rev 7 are again in view in Rev 9:4 at the blowing of the fifth trumpet. The demon locusts that are loosed from the *bottomless pit* to torment men are told to attack **only those men who do not have the seal of God** (Rev 7:3). How can these 144,000 of Rev 7 be the same as the 144,000 *firstfruits* of Rev 14, which are clearly seen in heaven before God's throne before the trumpet judgments fall (Rev 14: 1-5)? They cannot.

The Main *Wheat* Harvest

The main harvest on a future Feast of Trumpets will include all believers from all ages; Jews and Gentiles alike. We will explore this further in Chapter 23. The Marriage supper of the Lamb is about to take place and the 1000 year millennial kingdom is about to begin. The shadows and types of all the 7 Feasts of Israel and the fulfillment of the firstfruits have come to pass. I will hope to see you there.

Wrath vs Tribulation

Finally, let us again note the timing and position of when the 144,000 sealed Hebrews appear, and what immediately follows. Rev 7 is an *interlude* between *after* when the sixth seal is broken (Rev 6:12) and *before* when the seventh seal is broken (Rev 8:1). We again remind the reader that the seals provide a general overview of the last 1260 days and span the entire period of time. The opening of the sixth seal predicts *His wrath*.

> *"And said to the mountains and rocks, Fall on us, and hide us from the face of him that sitteth on the throne, and from the wrath of the Lamb: For the great day of his wrath is come; and who shall be able to stand?"* Rev 6:16-17

Here we must be very careful to determine what is the meaning of *wrath* . Both the seven bowl judgments and the seven trumpet judgments are actually wrath initiated by God, because it is by His authority and power that both the trumpet and the bowl judgments come forth. All are issued by His command and initiated by His angels. Just as God allowed Satan to persecute Job, God allows Satan and the revived antichrist to rule over the earth during the last 3.5 years of this age. But the agent of the wrath experienced under the seven trumpet judgments is Satan, executed by his minions the antichrist and the false prophet. The seven trumpet judgments are executed upon the earth by Satan over this period of time and God allows this to happen over a *short time*, which is 42 months or 1260 days. Note that Rev 12:12 confirms that Satan executes this *wrath*.

> *"Therefore rejoice, ye heavens, and ye that dwell in them. Woe to the inhabiters of the earth and of the sea! for the devil is come down unto you, having great wrath, because he knoweth that he hath but a short time."* Rev 12:12

After the church is raptured out at the seventh trumpet the severe *wrath of God* will be executed over a ten-day period of time upon Satan and all who *dwell upon the earth*. The agent of the wrath poured out upon Satan's kingdom is God, executed by **the seven angels.**

> *"And I heard a great voice out of the temple saying to the seven angels, Go your ways, and pour out the vials of the wrath of God upon the earth."* Rev 16:1

Both the seven trumpet judgments and the seven bowl judgments are called *His wrath*. The seven trumpet judgments can also properly be called the *Wrath of Satan*, allowed by God. The seven bowl judgments can be properly called the *Wrath of God*, executed by the *seven angels of His presence* at the direct command of God.

Summary and Conclusions

There are two groups of 144,000 which are shown in Rev 7:1-8 and Rev 14:1-5. These are not the same group of 144,000; we have identified many differences. The 144,000 in Rev 14 are all Hebrews from 12 tribes of Israel; 12,000 from each tribe. There is no need to spiritualize these groups and say the numbers are symbolic. By some unknown divine choice, God has identified the 144,000 Jews of Rev 7 and placed a seal of protection on their foreheads. This group is seen protected from demon locusts after the fifth trumpet sounds (Rev 9:4), so this is the latest that this sealing could occur. However, this would beg the question of *when and how* the 144,000 seen in heaven were sealed before the first trumpet sounds. We believe that the 144,000 of Rev 14 are sealed before the last 3.5 years of the tribulation period starts. Those sealed are all Jewish that have accepted Christ as their Savior; they are the *earthly* seed of Abraham and will inherit the land promised to Abraham long ago during the Millennial Kingdom. If this all sounds strange, stop and consider how and when God will fulfill His covenant with Abraham. Recall that this was an *unconditional covenant*, and it must be fulfilled by a living, earthly remnant.

The 144,000 in Rev 14 were **redeemed from the earth**. These 144,000 are both Jews and Gentiles who have been previously identified as *firstfruit* overcomers. They are standing before the throne of God and are special servants who **follow the Lamb** wherever He goes (Rev 14:4). They have not defiled themselves; they are spiritually dedicated *virgins*. They are identical to the *man-child* in Rev 12 who is ***caught up to God's throne***. The failure to identify these two groups properly has been typical of most prophecy teachers. Pre-tribulation rapture supporters who hold to a 7 year period of tribulation cannot support a firstfruits rapture after 3.5 years have passed. They cannot understand a firstfruit rapture which precedes a full rapture at the sounding of the 7th trumpet because they have not recognized the significance of the *blueprint* offered by the Seven Feasts of Israel and the prophetic significance of the firstfruits principles. The vision of the sealing of the 144,000 of Rev 7:1-8 is immediately followed by a vision (Rev 7:9-17) of every redeemed saint standing ***before the throne and before the Lamb*** in heaven (Rev 7:9). There are 3.5 years separating these two visions, and we have shown in Chapter 11 that this is perfectly acceptable, since the seals are only providing an overview of this same period of time.

Chapter 16

The Great Multitude

In the first part of Revelation Chapter 7 (Rev 7:1-8), John saw 144,000 Hebrews that had been sealed; 12,000 from each of 12 tribes of Israel. They were sealed before the last 3.5 years of Daniel's 70th week commenced. Now John sees another group which is a *great multitude* standing in heaven before the throne of God.

> *"After this I beheld, and, lo, a great multitude, which no man could number, of all nations, and kindreds, and people, and tongues, stood before the throne, and before the Lamb, clothed with white robes, and palms in their hands; And cried with a loud voice, saying, Salvation to our God which sitteth upon the throne, and unto the Lamb. And all the angels stood round about the throne, and about the elders and the four beasts, and fell before the throne on their faces, and worshipped God, Saying, Amen: Blessing, and glory, and wisdom, and thanksgiving, and honour, and power, and might, be unto our God forever and ever. Amen. And one of the elders answered, saying unto me, What are these which are arrayed in white robes? and whence came they? And I said unto him, Sir, thou knowest. And he said to me, These are they which came out of great tribulation, and have washed their robes, and made them white in the blood of the Lamb. Therefore are they before the throne of God, and serve him day and night in his temple: and he that sitteth on the throne shall dwell among them. They shall hunger no more, neither thirst any more; neither shall the sun light on them, nor any heat. For the Lamb which is in the midst of the throne shall feed them, and shall lead them unto living fountains of waters: and God shall wipe away all tears from their eyes."* Rev 7: 9-17

There is a great deal of difference between the vision of the 144,000 who are sealed and protected in Rev 7:1-8 and the group seen here. The 144,000 are seen on the earth; this multitude is in heaven. The previous group of 144,000 is from 12 tribes of Israel; this group is from *all nations, kindreds, people and tongues*. The 144,000 are numbered; this group can possibly be numbered, but it is a *great multitude*. This multitude has been taken to heaven since they are seen standing before the throne of God and before *the Lamb*, who is Jesus Christ. The crowd that has been gathered to greet them is comprehensive; all the angels are there; the *24 elders* are there; and the *four living beasts* or *zoa* are there. This multitude has all been given *white robes* and they have *palms* in their hands. Who are these that John sees? Christ has been seen wearing white in Rev 1:14; angels evidently wear white garments (John 20:12, Acts 1:10); and the saints will be given white robes (Rev 3:4-5). It is worth noting that garments of white are promised to all believers including the overcomers in each of the 7 churches of Rev 2 and 3. White robes are also promised to the martyrs seen underneath the throne of God as when the fifth seal was broken (Rev 6:9-11).

Before we identify this great multitude, note that one of the elders approaches John and asks two questions: (1) who are these? And (2) where did they come from? Perhaps John could answer that question; but he responds, *Sir, thou knowest*. In other words, John is really saying *I have no idea; but I bet that you can tell me*. The question that first needs to be addressed is why did John not recognize those standing in front of him? Perhaps he was terrified or out of sorts. Perhaps if there were some that he should recognize, they had changed in appearance. Recall that after the crucifixion, Christ appeared to two men (Rev 16:12-13) on a country road just after His resurrection; He walked with them, but they did not know who He was until He spoke. As John sees this vision, it seems most likely that there were so many standing there in white garments that he simply could not identify the few that he might have known on earth. In any case, the elder immediately answered both questions. These are followers of Christ who have *washed their robes and made them white in the blood of the Lamb*. They have *come out of great tribulation*. This term, *great tribulation*, was first used by Jesus Christ in the Olivet Discourse (Rev 24:21). If one carefully studies the context and position of this statement by Christ, it is clear that He was referring to the last 1260 days of Daniel's 70th week as the *great tribulation* since this statement immediately followed His warning to watch for the *abomination of desolation* (Rev 24:15) that will appear in the Jerusalem temple shortly after Satan is cast down to the earth in Rev 12. We cannot say that this entire multitude went through the tribulation period. In fact, we are quite sure that there are saints from all ages past that have been redeemed by the blood of the Lamb and are now standing before the throne of God. Certainly, a large number will have have come out of that period of time. Many will come to Christ over the last 3.5 years of the Church age. It is interesting that there are three groups of believers that are promised to be given *garments of white*. The first are **martyrs** (Rev 6:9-11); the second are the **overcomers**; and the third are **believers** of all ages (Rev 3:4-5). We believe that this group can be positively identified - they are the complete body of Christ. The following passage provides strong evidence that this is correct.

> *"And after these things I heard a great voice of much people in heaven, saying, Alleluia; Salvation, and glory, and honour, and power, unto the Lord our God: For true and righteous are his judgments: for he hath judged the great whore, which did corrupt the earth with her fornication, and hath avenged the blood of his servants at her hand. And again they said, Alleluia. And her smoke rose up for ever and ever. And the four and twenty elders and the four beasts fell down and worshipped God that sat on the throne, saying, Amen, Alleluia. And a voice came out of the throne, saying, Praise our God, all ye his servants, and ye that fear him, both small and great. And I heard as it were the voice of a great multitude, and as the voice of many waters, and as the voice of mighty thunderings, saying, Alleluia, for the Lord God omnipotent reigneth. Let us be glad and rejoice, and give honour to him: for the marriage of the Lamb is come, and his wife hath made herself ready. And to her was granted that she should be arrayed in fine linen, clean and white: for the fine linen is the righteousness of saints."*
> Rev 19:1-9

Rev 7:9-17 opens with a ***great multitude*** and Rev 19:1-9 opens with ***much people***: both are in heaven. Both groups declare ***Salvation, glory, honor and power***. The ***24 elders and the four living creatures*** are both in the throng. Both groups ***are praising and worshipping God***. Both groups are ***arrayed in white linen***. The group in Rev 19 is composed of both the bride of Christ (Rev 19:7) and the wedding guests (Rev 19:9). This group has been redeemed to the Lamb and comes from the rapture of the Church at the seventh trumpet.

By scriptural association, we believe that the ***great multitude*** of Rev 7:9 is the same group. They clearly represent the body of Christ, and they have been given ***white linen garments*** which are promised to all believers. The 144,000 of Rev 7:1-8 are not a part of this great multitude. The 144,000 of Rev 7:1-8 are in the earth and are all from 12 tribes of Israel. They have been sealed so that they can survive the *great tribulation* period and the seven bowl judgments; they will inherit the land during the millennial kingdom. However, the 144,000 of Rev 4:1-5 are a part of this group. We have discussed this in some detail in Chapter 14. The ***great multitude*** of Rev 7: 8-17 are both Jewish and Gentile believers from all ages who have been resurrected or raptured at the seventh trumpet, and now stand in heaven. These two groups are separated in time by 3.5 years. However, this is perfectly acceptable since the seal judgments are only providing an overview of this period of time. Both groups are parenthetically described between the sixth and seventh seal. The last 3.5 years of the church age and the reign of antichrist is about to commence. We will now see what sign is shown to all on the earth and heaven that reign of the Antichrist is about to begin.

Chapter 17

The Beasts of Revelation

There are three beasts that are described in the book of Revelation. The first beast arises *out of the Sea* (Rev 13:1-10); the second beast arises *out of the earth* (Rev 13:11-18); and the third is a *beast that carries a scarlet-clad woman* (Rev 17). We will see that the beast out of the sea and the beast that carries the scarlet-clothed woman are one and the same. This beast will inherit all of the power and characteristics of the *dragon* who is Satan (Rev 12:9). The beast out of the sea is also a man that will be inhabited and totally controlled by a powerful Prince of Darkness who will arise out of the bottomless pit (Rev 17:8). The resulting beast-man is known as the *antichrist*.

The Beast out of the Sea

In Revelation Chapter 13 there is a *beast* that arises out of the sea.

"And I stood upon the sand of the sea, and saw a beast rise up out of the sea, having seven heads and ten horns, and upon his horns ten crowns, and upon his heads the name of blasphemy. And the beast which I saw was like unto a leopard, and his feet were as the feet of a bear, and his mouth as the mouth of a lion: and the dragon gave him his power, and his seat, and great authority. And I saw one of his heads as it were wounded to death; and his deadly wound was healed: and all the world wondered after the beast. And they worshipped the dragon which gave power unto the beast: and they worshipped the beast, saying, who is like unto the beast? Who is able to make war with him? And there was given unto him a mouth speaking great things and blasphemies; and power was given unto him to continue forty and two months. And he opened his mouth in blasphemy against God, to blaspheme his name, and his tabernacle, and them that dwell in heaven. And it was given unto him to make war with the saints, and to overcome them: and power was given him over all kindreds, and tongues, and nations. And all that dwell upon the earth shall worship him, whose names are not written in the book of life of the Lamb slain from the foundation of the world. If any man have an ear, let him hear."   Rev 13:1-9

John is said to be **standing upon the shore of the sea**, and as he is watching he sees a beast **rise up out of the sea.** In ancient non-biblical literature the *sea* was often referred to as the reservoir of evil. Dragons and sea serpents were believed to have dwelled in their great depths. Another interpretation is that the *sea* stands for the sea of humanity. We will see later that this beast is the antichrist, and as a man he will arise out of the sea of a 10 nation European confederacy. There is no reason not to accept both interpretations, for the final form of the antichrist will be satanically-controlled. It is difficult to interpret this imagery until we realize just what comprises this *beast*. At first glance, it appears that this *beast out of the sea* is Satan, but we are immediately told that this is not so.

> *"....having seven heads and ten horns and upon his horns ten crowns, and upon his heads the name of blasphemy. And the beast which I saw was like unto a leopard, and his feet were as the feet of a bear, and his mouth as the mouth of a lion: and the dragon gave him his power, and his seat, and great authority."* Rev 13:1-2

The *dragon* who is Satan (Rev 12) *gives him* (the beast out of the sea) *his power, throne and authority.* This beast has been given all of the characteristics, power and authority of Satan. This beast has *seven heads and ten horns*. The seven heads indicate that this beast possesses attributes of all of *seven great world empires* which preceded him and persecuted Israel. The beast also has *10 horns*, all of which have been crowned. The ten horns represent the final 10-nation confederacy which will arise before the  tribulation period begins (Dan 2:42, 7:23-24). The crowns are important since they symbolize that each is in full power and each have a king when the antichrist arises in the end times. The *heads* have *blasphemous names*. Since this beast has the characteristics of all seven kingdoms which preceded him, he will have unbelievably blasphemous authority and power. We are told what this beast looks like in appearance.

> *"the beast which I (John) saw was like a leopard, his feet were like a bear, and his mouth was like a Lion."* Rev 13:2

A *leopard* was the national symbol of the Grecian Empire; the *bear* was the national symbol of the Medo-Persian Empire; and the *lion* was the national symbol of the Babylonian Empire. This beast is a combination of all of these previous empires, indicating that it has more power and military might than any one of these previous kingdoms (Rev 7:1-7). The leopard represents speed and swiftness; the bear ferocity and terrifying appearance in battle; and the lion, the mightiest of all ravenous creatures, is the recognized monarch of the animal kingdom. Is this a real beast, or is this image simply meant to describe a man? Let us examine his description.

> *"I saw one of his heads as it were wounded to death; and his deadly wound was healed: and all the world wondered after the beast. And they worshipped the dragon which gave power unto the beast: and they worshipped the beast, saying, Who is like unto the beast? who is able to make war with him? And there was given unto him a mouth speaking great things and blasphemies; and power was given unto him to continue forty and two months. And he opened his mouth in blasphemy against God, to blaspheme his name, and his tabernacle, and them that dwell in heaven. And it was given unto him to make war with the saints, and to overcome them: and power was given him over all kindreds, and tongues, and nations. And all that dwell upon the earth shall worship him, whose names are not written in the book of life of the Lamb slain from the foundation of the world. If any man have an ear, let him hear."* Rev 13: 3-9

This *beast* cannot represent a country or a kingdom. It must be a man.

- ➢ It has a *mouth*,
- ➢ *power* was given to *him*,
- ➢ He speaks *blasphemy against God*,
- ➢ He makes *war against the saints*,
- ➢ He is *worshipped*,
- ➢ He has a *head wounded to death*,
- ➢ His wound was *healed*,
- ➢ The wound was done by a *sword* (Rev 13:14).

There is no need to spiritualize this *beast out of the sea*. These characteristics are best interpreted to render this image one of a *man*. However, even a casual examination of this description will cause the *beast-man* to command wonder and amazement. This is a man, but it is not a normal man. Comparing scripture to scripture, there is no doubt that this is the *little horn* of Daniel

9:23-26. He is a man with *fierce countenance* (Dan 8:23); He understands *dark sentences (Dan 8:23)*; his *power will be mighty, but not by his own power*. The power of this beast-man comes from Satan. The dragon (Satan) is the source of the beast's power and authority, and this power is manifested through the mortal body of the antichrist. Satan has already tried to rule the world once before. After Christ was baptized in the Jordan River, He went to the wilderness for 40 days and 40 nights to be tested and tried by Satan. Satan offered Christ all the nations of the world, and all of his power and authority (Mat 4:9, Luke 4:6). He would not have done so if he could not back up his offer. Here he once again unleashes everything he has against the world when his anointed, the beast out of the sea, emerges as the most powerful man in the world. He (the antichrist) will *destroy fearfull*; he will *prosper and thrive;* he will also destroy *the holy people*; and he is *cunning and deceitful.* But he will not be able to escape the inevitable fate which awaits him.

> **"He shall magnify himself in his heart, He shall destroy many in their prosperity, He shall even rise against the Prince of Princes. But he shall be broken without human hand."**   Dan 8:23-25

Our Lord Jesus Christ will appear after his 42-month reign of terror has ended and destroy him *"**with the sword of his mouth**"* (Rev 19:15). Christ is the "***destroying stone***" of Dan 2: 44-45.

The Seven Heads and the Ten Horns

The *seven heads* are seven kingdoms, but kingdoms must have kings ruling over them. John the revelator sees *seven diadems* (crowns) on the heads. This clearly reveals that these seven kingdoms have already come into existence and that the kings of each kingdom have come to power. These seven kingdoms no longer exist, but Satan has seven heads and seven horns because he has been active in each and every one. He possesses the power and characteristics of each, so he is seen carrying all seven heads. The 10 horns can only be understood by carefully studying the prophecies of Daniel. In Dan 2:31-35 we can identify these *ten horns* as representing a latter day *10-nation confederacy of countries* which will arise in the end times. These ten horns are identical to the ten toes in Nebuchadnezzar's dream-image of a great colossus (Dan 2:41-44).

Rev 13: 1-10	Like a....	Features	Description
Beast out of the Sea	Leopard	Bear feet Lion mouth	Beast is a *Man* Number is *666* Puts his *Number*, his *Mark*, or his *Name* on people to allow them to buy or sell. Refusal is Death
		7 Heads 10 Horns	All Crowned (Stephanos)

In the book of Daniel, we are told the meaning of the *seven heads and ten horns* that are seen upon the dragon (Rev 10:3). Horns in prophecy are *nations* and heads are *kings*. A nation or group of nations (*horn*) must have a king (*head*), and a king must have a *crown*. Each head is full of *blasphemy*. The vision that John saw is not the beast itself, but a representation of what constitutes the beast. It is pure imagery. The beast is representative of seven kingdoms (nations) which have persecuted Israel down through the ages. Almost all expositors agree that the first six *nations* were:

1. The *Egyptian Empire*…Oppressed Israel for 215 years
2. The *Assyrian Empire*…..Caused the fall of the Northern Kingdom in 723 BC
3. The *Babylonian Empire*…Destroyed David's Temple and deported all of Israel to Babylon for 70 years over a period of time between 605 BC and 586 BC.
4. The *Medo-Persian Empire* … Conquered Babylon in 538 BC.
5. The *Grecian Empire*…. Conquered the Medo-Persian Empire in 330 BC
6. The *Roman Empire*….. Ruled over Israel for almost 400 years. Destroyed Herod's Temple in 70 AD and treated Israel as a vassal state

Since there are seven empires represented by the *beast out of the sea* can we identify the seventh kingdom?

The Mysterious Seventh-Beast Empire

There have been several excellent descriptions of the seventh-beast empire offered by multiple scholars of prophecy. For example, the classic works of Clarence Dakin, Finis J. Dake and Charles Ryrie to name just a few. Most modern scholars claim that the eighth world empire to persecute and rule over Israel is the end time 10-nation confederacy that will be conquered and then ruled by the *antichrist* who is called the Beast out of the Sea (Rev 13:1-10.

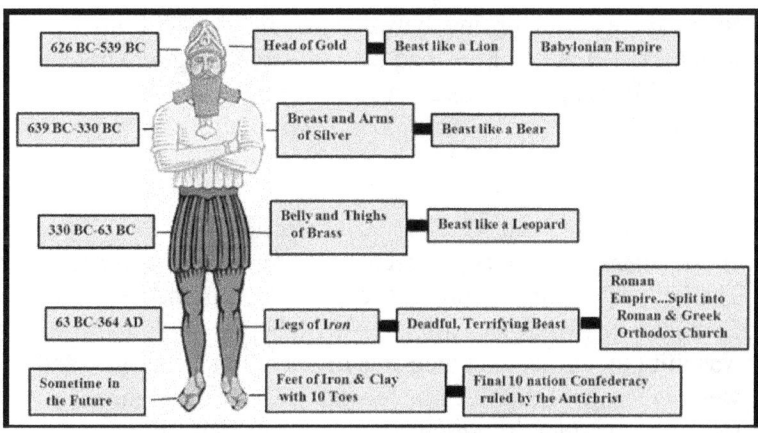

"And here is the mind which hath wisdom. The seven heads are seven mountains, on which the woman sitteth. And there are seven kings: five are fallen, and one is, and the other is not yet come; and when he cometh, he must continue a short space. And the beast that was, and is not, even he is the eighth, and is of the seven, and goeth into perdition. And the ten horns which thou sawest are ten kings, which have received no kingdom as yet; but receive power as kings one hour with the beast. These have one mind, and shall give their power and strength unto the beast. These shall make war with the Lamb, and the Lamb shall overcome them: for he is Lord of lords, and King of kings: and they that are with him are called, and chosen, and faithful."   Rev 17:9-14.

The seven mountains are the seven empires which have ruled over Israel. We are told that when John sees this vision, that: ***five are fallen, and one is, and the other is not yet come; and when he cometh, he must continue a short space***. From above, the five that have fallen are the (1) *Egyptian* (2) *Assyrian* (3) *Babylonian* (4) *Medo-Persian* and (5) *Grecian* Empires. The sixth which *is* when John saw the vision is the great *Roman Empire*. On this, most scholars agree. Who or what was the seventh empire that will persecute the nation of Israel? First, the only reference to a seventh empire followed by an eighth *beast* empire is in Rev 17:10-11. There are several important clues to consider. In Daniel 2:20, he wrote of a great Colossus which spanned the period of time between the Babylonian Empire which existed at that time, and the millennial kingdom of Christ. The Colossus appeared as a warrior prepared for battle. (*http://www.revelationscrolls.com/Battle%20of%20Armageddon.htm*)

The head of gold is the *Babylonian Empire* (Dan 2:38). The chest and arms of silver represents the *Medo-Persian Empire*. The belly and thighs of brass (bronze) represent the *Grecian Empire*. The two legs of iron represent the *Roman Empire*, which was initially unified and then was divided into the eastern and western Roman Empires. The *feet* have *10 toes*, and these represent the *final 10-nation confederacy* which will be taken over and ruled by the antichrist. Now carefully note something important: *the 10 toes represent the eighth world empire* ruled by the antichrist over the last half of Daniel's 70th week. What happened to the seventh world empire? The seventh world empire was completely hidden from both Daniel and the Old Testament prophets. We hope it is clear that the seventh empire must appear *after* the Roman Empire and *before* the eighth beast empire. We now quote *Robert Van Kampen*.

> ➢ The seventh empire which persecutes Israel *must appear before the last 3.5 years* of the Church age begins in order to precede the eighth Beast Empire.
> ➢ It will persecute the people of Israel when "*they are out of their land*".

- It must remain only *"a little while"*.
- It will be *hideously cruel* .
- It must exist *before Israel* begins to return to their land.

This seventh empire *cannot* be the end-time 10-nation confederacy. This confederacy was never a unified empire, but consisted of separate countries with separate kings. Looking back, there is only one empire which has existed since the Roman Empire which perfectly fits all requirements. It is the **Third Reich** of Hitler. The Third Reich was incredibly anti-Semitic, and was responsible for the genocide of over 10 million Jews. This has not previously been recognized as the Seventh Empire because most of the classic prophecy scholars wrote before the rise of *Hitler's Third Reich*, which occurred in the late 1930's and early 1940's. We are convinced that the seventh world empire which corresponds to the seventh head of the beast is the Third Reich of Hitler. This kingdom is identical to the seventh head of the *beast* which carries *religious Babylon* on its back in Rev 17:3.

Crowns of the Beast

In Rev 12:1 we saw the dragon (Satan) appearing in heaven and the dragon had **seven heads and seven horns and seven crowns upon his heads.** The crowns which Satan wears are *stephanos* crowns. Stephanos crowns are those crowns that are placed upon gladiators or on those individuals who had won events in the Roman games. They were temporary crowns made out of things like flowers and sometimes soft metal. They are not permanent crowns. The crown that God will give us is a *diadem*. This is a crown that will never fade away and will last for all eternity.

> *"Henceforth there is laid up for me a crown* (diadems) *of righteousness, which the Lord, the righteous judge, shall give me at that day: and not to me only, but unto all them also that love his appearing."*   2 Timothy 4:8

In Rev 19:12 we are given a description of our Lord Jesus Christ at His Second Advent. He is seen with *many crowns* on His head. These crowns are also *diadems*! The gift of crowns speaks of the relationship between Christ and those *sons and daughters* who have believed in His name. The same type of crown worn by Jesus Christ at His second coming is the same type of crown He gives to his saints. The crown marks their relationship to Christ and their kingdom authority in Him.

> *"Fear none of those things which thou shalt suffer: behold, the devil shall cast some of you into prison, that ye may be tried; and ye shall have tribulation ten days: be thou faithful unto death, and I will give thee a crown of life."* Rev 2:10

> *"To him that overcometh will I grant to sit with me in my throne, even as I also overcame, and am set down with my Father in his throne."* Rev 3:21

The sons and daughters of Christ who faithfully follow him in this life will rule and reign with Him on this earth. This is a fundamental promise to those who have *died in Christ*, yet they live.

The Beast out of the Earth

Following this detailed description of a *beast out of the sea*, we are now told of a second *beast out of the earth*.

> *"And I beheld another beast coming up out of the earth; and he had two horns like a lamb, and he spake as a dragon. And he exerciseth all the power of the first beast before him, and causeth the earth and them which dwell therein to worship the first beast, whose deadly wound was healed. And he doeth great wonders, so that he maketh fire come down from heaven on the earth in the sight of men."* Rev 13:11-13

This *beast out of the earth* reminds us of Rev 5:6 when John saw Jesus Christ standing in the middle of God's throne room, appearing as a *lamb*. But this is a *beast* who only appears to be a Lamb. He is called the *false prophet* (Rev 16:13; 19:20, 20:10) because he will serve Satan and head up an apostate one-world religion that demands worship of the Satanic-indwelled antichrist. He looks like a lamb, but he *speaks* like *a dragon*. The significance of this beast having only two horns, as contrasted to the first beast which has ten horns, is not explained. It could mean that his seat of authority is in two countries rather than one, but to speculate without scriptural justification is meaningless. It should be noted that the entire structure of Revelation 13 is based upon false and counterfeit images. There is a *counterfeit trinity*: the beast out of the sea, the beast out of the earth, and Satan. This is to mimic Christ, the Holy Spirit and God the Father. The charade does not end here. There is a counterfeit resurrection from death of the great world leader (Rev 13:14); there is a counterfeit mark of deity in either the forehead or the hand (Rev 13:16); and there is a counterfeit image of God standing in the Holy Place of the temple (Mat 24:15, Dan 11:31, Dan 12:11). This image will actually speak, and command anyone standing there to worship Satan and the antichrist. Failure to do so will result in instant death. The beast has a counterfeit outwardly image, but inside he is demonically-possessed and serves Satan. His counterpart, the beast out of the earth (Rev 13:11) has special power over fire (Rev 13:13); he claims to have a connection with a divine resurrection (Rev 13:12), and he has power over life or death (Rev 13:15.

Rev 13:11-17	Appearance	Features	Description
Beast out of the Earth	Like a lamb	Speaks like a dragon	Exercises all of the power of the beast out of the sea
	Two large horns		
			Causes the whole world to worship the beast out of the sea
			Brings fire from the heavens
			Performs great miracles
			Creates an image that speaks and commands all to worship the image or die
			Puts the *Mark of the Beast* on all who worship the image

The Beast Which Carries a Scarlet-Clothed Woman

The third beast which we will study is actually not a third beast at all, but is another description of the **beast out of the Sea** in Rev 13:1-11. In Rev 17:1-7 we are introduced to a **great harlot who sits on many waters**. The idiom for *waters* is scripturally referring to peoples and nations of a wide variety. This *woman* (harlot) is sitting on *a scarlet beast* (Rev 17:3). In Chapter 21 we will have much to say about this woman; for now our interest is in the *scarlet beast* upon which she sits.

> *"The beast that thou sawest was, and is not; and shall ascend out of the bottomless pit, and go into perdition: and they that dwell on the earth shall wonder, whose names were not written in the book of life from the foundation of the world, when they behold the beast that was, and is not, and yet is. And here is the mind which hath wisdom. The seven heads are seven mountains, on which the woman sitteth. And there are seven kings: five are fallen, and one is, and the other is not yet come; and when he cometh, he must continue a short space. And the beast that was, and is not, even he is the eighth, and is of the seven, and goeth into perdition. And the ten horns which thou sawest are ten kings, which have received no kingdom as yet; but receive power as kings one hour with the beast. These have one mind, and shall give their power and strength unto the beast. These shall make war with the Lamb, and the Lamb shall overcome them: for he is Lord of lords, and King of kings: and they that are with him are called, and chosen, and faithful. And he saith unto me, The waters which thou sawest, where the whore sitteth, are peoples, and multitudes, and nations, and tongues. And the ten horns which thou sawest upon the beast, these shall hate the whore, and shall make her desolate and naked, and shall eat her flesh, and burn her with fire. For God hath put in their hearts to fulfil his will, and to agree, and give their kingdom unto the beast, until the words of God shall be fulfilled."* Rev 17:8-17

Who or what is this *beast* that carries the *scarlet-clothed woman?* By comparing scripture to scripture, it is not difficult to identify the *beast of Revelation Chapter 17* as identical to the *beast of Revelation 13*. Specifically, the beast that carries the woman is the Antichrist, who in purpose and power is Satan. The beast out of the sea and the beast that carries the woman are two different characterizations of the same person. There are several identifying characteristics that make conjecture near certainty.

1. Both beasts have Seven Heads and Ten Horns

   "And I stood upon the sand of the sea, and saw a beast rise up out of the sea, having seven heads and ten horns, and upon his horns ten crowns, and upon his heads the name of blasphemy." Rev 13:
   "So he carried me away in the spirit into the wilderness: and I saw a woman sit upon a scarlet colored beast, full of names of blasphemy, having seven heads and ten horns." Rev. 17:3

2. There is common *wonder* using identical phrases

   "And I saw one of his heads as it were wounded to death; and his deadly wound was healed: and all the world wondered after the beast." Rev 13: 8

   "The beast that thou sawest was, and is not; and shall ascend out of the bottomless pit, and go into perdition: and they that dwell on the earth shall wonder, whose names were not written in the book of life from the foundation of the world, when they behold the beast that was, and is not, and yet is." Rev 17: 8

3. Both Beasts are full of Blasphemy

   "And I stood upon the sand of the sea, and saw a beast rise up out of the sea, having seven heads and ten horns, and upon his horns ten crowns, and upon his heads the name of blasphemy. And there was given unto him a mouth speaking great things and blasphemies; and power was given unto him to continue forty and two

months. And he opened his mouth in blasphemy against God, to blaspheme his name, and his tabernacle, and them that dwell in heaven." Rev 13: 1, 5-6

"So he carried me away in the spirit into the wilderness: and I saw a woman sit upon a scarlet colored beast, full of names of blasphemy, having seven heads and ten horns." Rev 17: 3

4. Both are followed by those whose names are not written in the Book of Life

"And all that dwell upon the earth shall worship him, whose names are not written in the book of life of the Lamb slain from the foundation of the world." Rev 13: 8
"The beast that thou sawest was, and is not; and shall ascend out of the bottomless pit, and go into perdition: and they that dwell on the earth shall wonder, whose names were not written in the book of life from the foundation of the world, when they behold the beast that was, and is not, and yet is." Rev 17:8

5. Both beasts have dominion over nations and tongues

"And it was given unto him to make war with the saints, and to overcome them: and power was given him over all kindreds, and tongues, and nations." Rev 13: 7

"And he saith unto me, The waters which thou sawest, where the whore sitteth, are peoples, and multitudes, and nations, and tongues. " Rev 17: 15

6. Both Require Wisdom to Understand

"Here is wisdom. Let him that hath understanding count the number of the beast: for it is the number of a

man; and his number is Six hundred threescore and six" Rev 13:18

"And here is the mind which hath wisdom. The seven heads are seven mountains, on which the woman sitteth." Rev 17: 9

These similarities should be enough to establish that the *beast of Rev 13* and the *beast of Rev 17* are one and the same. However, the vantage point from which we observe the beast is different. The beast of Rev 13 describes a demonically-possessed *man* who we call the antichrist. The beast of Rev 17 describes a *system* that Satan creates to support both the religious and political components of the antichrist's reign. We will devote Chapter 18 to a detailed description and analysis of the antichrist, and all of Chapter 21 to the scarlet-clothed woman and the beast that carries her.

Rev 17: 1-18	Features	Description	Other Information	Empires
A Scarlet colored Beast carrying a Scarlet and purple clothed woman covered with gold & jewels holding a golden cup full of abominations.	7 Heads	7 Mountains or Kingdoms Also 7 Kings		Egyptian, Assyrian, Babylonian, Medo-Persia, Greece, Roman, Natzi 3rd Reich
			5 are Fallen	***5 are Fallen***** Egyptian, Assyrian, Babylonian, Medo-Persia, Greece, Roman
			1 "is"	*** 1 is***** Roman Empire
			1 is yet to come and will continue a "Short Space"	*** 1 is yet to come Natzie Third Reich,
	10 Horns	None Crowned Yet	No crowns mean that the 10 nation end time confederacy has not yet been conquered and energized by the Antichrist	The Scarlet Beast is an 8th King

Summary
In this short chapter we found it necessary to clearly distinguish between *the Beast out of the Earth* (Rev 13:11-18) and the

Beast out of the Sea (Rev 13:1-10. The beast out of the sea is none other than the satanically-empowered antichrist (Rev 13:20, who had previously arisen as a great world leader (Dan 11:36-39); he will fight against and conquer three of the nations in an end time 10-nation confederacy which will exist in Europe (Dan 7:24), and become dictator over all of these previously independent nations (Dan 7:23-25). Somewhere very near the beginning of the final 3.5 years of Daniel's 70th week, he will be wounded unto death by a sword or a knife (Rev 13:14). He will then be resurrected from certain death (Rev 13:12) and taken over by a strong demonic prince who is now being held in the bottomless pit for this assignment (Rev 17:5-8). After this *demonic prince* takes over his mind and body, the great world leader is transformed into a *beast* (Rev 17:17). We call this satanically-controlled individual the *antichrist*, a name not actually found anywhere in scripture but commonly used in the literature. This ***Beast out of the Sea*** (Rev 13:1-10) is identical to the beast in Rev 17:17:3-4 that carries a ***woman robed in purple and scarlet*** (Rev 17: 3-4) on its back. The purple- and scarlet-robed woman represents the universal world religion created by the antichrist to worship only his image and by association Satan. The ***beast out of the earth*** (Rev 13:11-18) is head of the worldwide religious system represented by the purple- and scarlet-robed woman. This *false prophet* is supernaturally powerful, and sets up an image of the antichrist that both speaks and causes all who refuse to worship its image to be killed (Rev 13:14-15) , and then forces everyone who capitulates to take a *mark of the beast* in their right hand or forehead (Rev 13:16-17). In Chapter 22, we will examine a city which will be set up by the antichrist as the worldwide economic and trade center of the world. That great city is called ***Babylon the Great*** (Rev 18).

Chapter 18

The Antichrist

The term *antichrist* is known to practically every Christian, but few people take the time or effort to fully characterize or identify this individual. Strangely enough, the word antichrist never appears in the Holy Scriptures. Who is this individual? When will he appear? What are his motives and from where will he come? We will attempt to answer all of these questions using biblical clues. It is impossible to answer these questions without some help from the prophet Daniel. We will see that between the visions shown to Daniel and John, we can put together all the information we need.

Nebuchadnezzar's Dream Image
In Dan 2: 36-45, Daniel interprets a dream which King Nebuchadnezzar had in which he saw a mighty colossus which was composed of various metals and resembled a man.

> *"Thou, O king, sawest, and behold a great image. This great image, whose brightness was excellent, stood before thee; and the form thereof was terrible. This image's head was of fine gold, his breast and his arms of silver, his belly and his thighs of brass, His legs of iron, his feet part of iron and part of clay. Thou sawest till that a stone was cut out without hands, which smote the image upon his feet that were of iron and clay, and brake them to pieces. Then was the iron, the clay, the brass, the silver, and the gold, broken to pieces together, and became like the chaff of the summer threshingfloors; and the wind carried them away, that no place was found for them: and the stone that smote the image became a great mountain, and filled the whole earth. This is the dream; and we will tell the interpretation thereof before the king. Thou, O king, art a king of kings: for the God of heaven hath given thee a kingdom, power, and strength, and glory. Thou art this head of gold."*
> Daniel 2: 31-35, 38-b

Daniel was then given the meaning of this image by God.

> *"And after thee shall arise another kingdom inferior to thee, and another third kingdom of brass, which shall bear rule over all the earth. And the fourth kingdom shall be strong as iron: forasmuch as iron breaketh in pieces and subdueth all things: and as iron that breaketh all these, shall it break in pieces and bruise. And whereas thou sawest the feet and toes, part of potters' clay, and part of iron, the kingdom shall be divided; but there shall be in it of the strength of the iron, forasmuch as thou sawest the iron mixed with miry clay. And as the toes of the feet were part of iron, and part of clay, so the kingdom shall be partly strong, and partly broken. And whereas thou sawest iron mixed with miry clay, they shall mingle themselves with the seed of men: but they shall not cleave one to another, even as iron is not mixed with clay. And in the days of these kings shall the God of heaven set up a kingdom, which shall never be destroyed: and the kingdom shall not be left to other people, but it shall break in pieces and consume all these kingdoms, and it shall stand for ever. Forasmuch as thou sawest that the stone was cut out of the mountain without hands, and that it brake in pieces the iron, the brass, the clay, the silver, and the gold; the great God hath made known to the king what shall come to pass hereafter: and the dream is certain, and the interpretation thereof sure."*   Daniel 2: 41-45

Daniel was able to relate this dream image to King Nebuchadnezzar of Babylon, but he did not at this time understand all of the details. More remarkable details are given to Daniel later, and they are recorded in Dan 7 and Dan 8. This great image represented four successive empires which would persecute the nation of Israel, and each would reign over much of the known world. Daniel was not immediately told any kingdom but the first: Oh King (Nebuchadnezzar); *you are the head of gold* (Dan 2:38). This confirms that the first kingdom is the *Babylonian Empire.* The other kingdoms which would follow the Babylonian Empire were not revealed to Daniel, but looking forward to Dan 7-8 we can identify the other kingdoms with near certainty. We know that this vision spanned a period of time from about 605-604 BC to sometime far into the future. The *Babylonian Empire* was succeeded by the *Medo-Persian, Greek* and *Roman Empires*. The original unified Roman Empire fractured into what was called the Eastern and Western Roman empires in AD 364, and then through time it was divided into many smaller countries. These countries form much of what we call southern and Western Europe today. Eventually (still future), a final 10-nation confederacy will arise out of the old Roman Empire which is represented by the 10 toes of the colossus. This 10-nation confederacy is often called the *revived* or *revised* Roman Empire, but this is incorrect. Although the land mass associated with each country can be traced to within the boundaries of the original Roman Empire, these are ten separate countries which will unite in a functioning coalition for either economic or military reasons. A great world leader will then arise in the end times, and through conquest and political prowess will conquer three of these 10 nations; he will then establish himself as a dictator over all 10 nations (Dan 7: 23-25). This dictator will receive a near fatal wound by the sword (Rev 13:3), be taken over by a third beast from the bottomless pit (Rev 17:8) and become what we call the antichrist. The antichrist will rule for 3.5 years, and after that time a ***mighty stone*** will ***strike the image*** and crush it so severely (Dan 2:33-35, Dan 7:26) that the iron (Roman empire), clay (10 nation confederacy), bronze (Grecian empire) silver (Median & Persian empire) and gold (Babylonian empire) become like ***chaff*** (Dan 2:35). Note that every remnant of every world empire is completely destroyed. The ***wind*** will carry it away and it will be found no more (Dan 2:35).

The composite image represents a series of kingdoms that will persecute and rule over Israel until her *deliverer* comes. This deliverer is none other than our Lord Jesus Christ at the end of the age. He is the ***mighty stone*** and the ***cornerstone that the builders*** (Israel) ***rejected*** (Is 28:16, Mat 21:42, I Peter 2:6). He is also the ***mountain*** that will completely destroy any remnants of all these empires (Dan 2:35). He will ***fill the whole earth***

(Dan 2:35) with his righteous, everlasting kingdom following the battle of Armageddon when He will *strike the image*. With this short background, we will now concentrate on the *ten toes* of the image.

The Feet and Ten Toes of Nebuchadnezzar's Colossus

The feet and the *ten toes* of the image represent the last great united empire which will arise out of the old Roman Empire. It is composed of 10 nations as previously discussed. We are told that the last form of this 10-nation confederacy will be partly strong and partly broken; some nations will be strong as *iron* and some weak as *clay*. This probably refers to the seven nations which remained intact (strong) and the three which were conquered by the antichrist (weak), but we cannot say for sure what this means. God will completely destroy this last 10-nation empire (through his son the Lord Jesus Christ), and the new kingdom which He will establish (a kingdom of righteousness) will endure forever. Daniel only knew at this time that the first kingdom was the Babylonian Empire, because it was revealed to him that: ***You*** (Nebuchadnezzar, King of Babylon) ***are the head of gold*** (Dan 2:38). The dream which Nebuchadnezzar had of this great colossus was in the second year of his reign, which is known to have occurred in 604 BC. It was not until the first year of his successor, Belshazzar in 553 BC, did Daniel receive more information about the other world empires to come.

The Four Beasts of Belshazzar's Dream

Daniel's thoughts were *troubled*, and rightly so. He now understood that Israel would not be delivered until far into the future. About 51 years later God revisited Daniel to give him more understanding of what this all meant. The setting was another dream which came to King Belshazzar, who succeeded Nebuchadnezzar. This time Daniel was only asked to interpret the dream, and not to reveal it as he did with Nebuchadnezzar.

> *"In the first year of Belshazzar king of Babylon Daniel had a dream and visions of his head upon his bed: then he wrote the dream, and told the sum of the matters. Daniel spake and said, I saw in my vision by night, and, behold, the four*

winds of the heaven strove upon the great sea. And four great beasts came up from the sea, diverse one from another. The first was like a lion, and had eagle's wings: I beheld till the wings thereof were plucked, and it was lifted up from the earth, and made stand upon the feet as a man, and a man's heart was given to it. And behold another beast, a second, like to a bear, and it raised up itself on one side, and it had three ribs in the mouth of it between the teeth of it: and they said thus unto it, Arise, devour much flesh. After this I beheld, and lo another, like a leopard, which had upon the back of it four wings of a fowl; the beast had also four heads; and dominion was given to it. After this I saw in the night visions, and behold a fourth beast, dreadful and terrible, and strong exceedingly; and it had great iron teeth: it devoured and brake in pieces, and stamped the residue with the feet of it: and it was diverse from all the beasts that were before it; and it had ten horns." Daniel 7:1-7

This vision further explains the four components of the great colossus that Daniel had seen previously. The colossus was presented as stunning, made of various metals and spectacular in its appearance. In this vision, the four empires represented by the colossus now become *ravenous beasts*. As we study this vision, we have the advantage of looking back across 2600 years. From historical records, we can clearly identify the nations that were involved, represented by *four great beasts from the sea* of humanity.

Beast One*: *Like a lion with eagles wings. A lion was the symbol of the ***Babylonian Empire*** (Jer. 4:7, 13). This is the first *beast* kingdom, the *head of gold* in Dan 2:32.

Beast Two*: *Like a bear*.** This is the ***Medo-Persian Empire (Is 13:17-18) which was known for its ferociousness and strength. It was raised up on one side because the Persians dominated the Medes. The beast has three ribs in its mouth. These three ribs represent the three main conquests of the Medo-Persian Empire: the nations of Lydia, Babylon and Egypt .These are the breast and arms of silver in Dan 2:32.

Beast Three: *Like a leopard* with *four wings on its back.* This is the ***Grecian Empire*** which was known for its swiftness and speed of conquest. Alexander the Great conquered the entire known world in just 3.5 years. He died at the age of only 33 lamenting that he had no more kingdoms to conquer. Upon his death, his kingdom was split into four smaller kingdoms: *Asia Minor, Syria, Egypt and Macedonia (Greece).* This is the meaning of the four heads upon the beast. The four wings likely represent the swiftness by which Alexander flew to conquer the known world; East, West, North and South. It was said that as Alexander was dying he wept and lamented that he had no more worlds to conquer around the Mediterranean Sea. This third beast is the belly and thighs of brass in Dan 2:32.

Beast Four: *Dreadful, terrifying and strong with teeth of iron.* It was different from all the beasts before it, and ***it had 10 horns***. This is not the powerful and ravaging Roman Empire as some have proposed, but the final 10-nation confederacy previously discussed. These 10 horns represent ten kings (Dan 7:24). But kings must rule a kingdom, so this also represents a ten- nation confederacy that will arise in the end times out of the old Roman Empire. These 10 horns are identical to the 10 toes on the colossus of Dan 2; they are the same as the 10 horns seen on the beast that arises out of the sea in Rev 13:1; and they are the same as the 10 horns shown on the beast of Rev 17:16-17 that carries the woman. We will discuss this woman in Chapter 21.

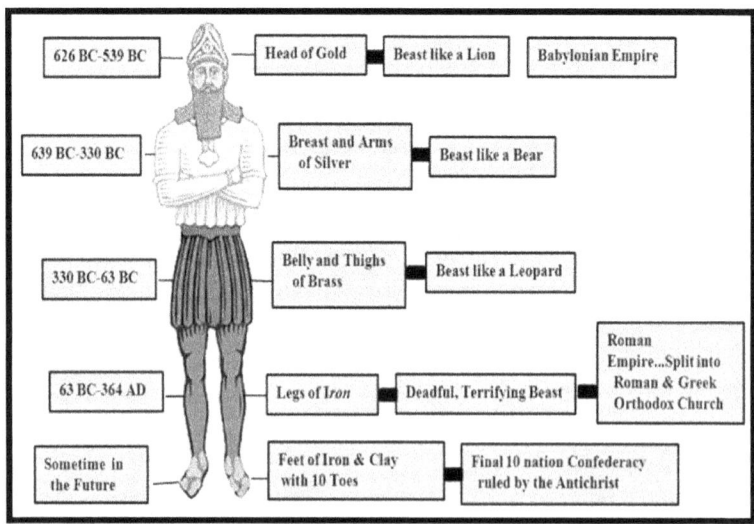

The vision continues, and Daniel is given more information about the *10 horns* on the fourth beast.

The Little Horn

> *"I considered the horns, and, behold, there came up among them another little horn, before whom there were three of the first horns plucked up by the roots: and, behold, in this horn were eyes like the eyes of man, and a mouth speaking great things."*   Daniel 7:8

This confirms the interpretation given previously; the *ten horns* are *ten nations* which correspond to the *ten toes* on the Colossus. We are now introduced to a *little horn*. We will show that this *little horn* is the antichrist. This ten-nation confederacy will arise out of the boundaries of the old Roman Empire. After this confederacy is formed, a great world leader will emerge, likely from the old province of Asia Minor (Greece). Daniel was *considering* the 10 horns and suddenly a *little horn* arose among the other 10 horns. Suddenly three of the ten horns (nations) were *plucked out by the roots*.

The *little horn* began to speak *pompous* words. There is no doubt that the 10 horns are 10 kings (Dan 7:24) and kingdoms. The three nations *plucked out by the roots* clearly indicate that this *little horn* has slain three other kings and completely destroyed their identity. He now becomes dictator over the entire set of nations, and they become unified under the *little horn* (Dan 7:24). Note the sudden change in operation. He will now **persecute the saints of the most high** for a **time and times and half a time** (Dan 7:25). This is exactly the same amount of time given to the antichrist in Rev 13: 5. As previously discussed, recall that the 10 horns represent an end time 10-nation confederacy. A little horn arises *from among the 10 horns* and this *horn* immediately *plucks up* or destroys the kingdoms of three of the horns. The interpretation is as follows: The *little*

horn is the antichrist. He will arise from *among* the 10 nations (Dan 7:24) and he will conquer three of the 10 nations with little or no apparent opposition. After the vision in Dan 7 is seen, Daniel was *greatly troubled* (Dan 7:28). Daniel was uncertain about the *little horn* and would know more of what this meant. Two years later, the Lord sent the same angel (Dan 8:1) to enable understanding.

Daniel's Vision of The Ram and the Goat

"In the third year of the reign of King Belshazzar a vision appeared unto me, even unto me Daniel, after that which appeared unto me at the first. And I saw in a vision; and it came to pass, when I saw, that I was at Shushan in the palace, which is in the province of Elam; and I saw in a vision, and I was by the river of Ulai. Then I lifted up mine eyes, and saw, and, behold, there stood before the river a ram which had two horns: and the two horns were high; but one was higher than the other, and the higher came up last. I saw the ram pushing westward, and northward, and southward; so that no beasts might stand before him, neither was there any that could deliver out of his hand; but he did according to his will, and became great. And as I was considering, behold, an he goat came from the west on the face of the whole earth, and touched not the ground: and the goat had a notable horn between his eyes. And he came to the ram that had two horns, which I had there seen standing before the river, and ran unto him in the fury of his power. And I saw him come close unto the ram, and he was moved with choler against him, and smote the ram, and brake his two horns: and there was no power in the ram to stand before him, but he cast him down to the ground, and stamped upon him: and there was none that could deliver the ram out of his hand. Therefore the he goat waxed very great: and when he was strong, the great horn was broken; and for it came up four notable ones toward the four winds of heaven. And out of one of them came forth a little horn, which waxed exceeding great, toward the south, and toward the east, and toward the pleasant land. And it waxed great,

even to the host of heaven; and it cast down some of the host and of the stars to the ground, and stamped upon them. Yea, he magnified himself even to the prince of the host, and by him the daily sacrifice was taken away, and the place of his sanctuary was cast down. And an host was given him against the daily sacrifice by reason of transgression, and it cast down the truth to the ground; and it practised, and prospered. Then I heard one saint speaking, and another saint said unto that certain saint which spake, How long shall be the vision concerning the daily sacrifice, and the transgression of desolation, to give both the sanctuary and the host to be trodden under foot? And he said unto me, Unto two thousand and three hundred days; then shall the sanctuary be cleansed. And it came to pass, when I, even I Daniel, had seen the vision, and sought for the meaning, then, behold, there stood before me as the appearance of a man. And I heard a man's voice between the banks of Ulai, which called, and said, Gabriel, make this man to understand the vision. So he came near where I stood: and when he came, I was afraid, and fell upon my face: but he said unto me, Understand, O son of man: for at the time of the end shall be the vision."   Daniel 8: 1:-17

Daniel now has a vision that he was by the Ulai River when an angel appeared before him (Dan 8:2). Standing beside the river he saw a ram with two horns, and one horn was higher than the other. This ram was the Medo-Persian Empire; one (shorter) horn was the Medes and the other (higher) horn the Persians who dominated the combined empire. The ram *pushed* west, north and south, and nothing could stand against it (Dan 8:4). At the height of its power, a *male goat* with a *notable single horn* suddenly came from the West (Dan 8:5). The *he-goat* attacked the ram and broke off both horns. The he-goat quickly *cast him* (the ram) *down and trampled over him* (Dan 8:7). This *male goat* was *Alexander the Great*, who attacked and destroyed the *Medo-Persian Empire* in a short span of time. The male goat became *very strong*, but at the height of his power the *single notable horn was broken off*, and it was replaced by *four other horns*. The single horn was Alexander the Great, and it being broken off refers to his sudden death at age 33. Alexander's death caused his empire to be split into four smaller empires. *One* of these four new horns grew *exceedingly great*, and it moved to the south and east into *the Glorious Land* (Israel). It grew stronger, even to *the host of heaven* and it *cast some of the stars to the ground and trampled them*. He even *exalted himself high to the Prince of the Host* (Jesus Christ); and by him (the single notable horn) the *daily sacrifices were taken away, and the place of his sanctuary was cast down*. A vast army was given to the *little horn*, and he *cast truth to the ground*. Here we have an extremely important declaration by the angel who came to Daniel.

> ***"..understand, O son of man, that the vision refers to the time of the end."*** Daniel 8:17,

> ***"...at the latter time of the indignation."*** Daniel 8:19

It is important that we understand that this last prophecy is what is called a *near-far* prophecy. It was first fulfilled beginning when the Grecian Empire of Alexander the Great came to power, followed by the breaking up of his kingdom into four smaller empires. Here we again see that in prophecy a horn represents a ***seat of power***, and is usually a nation. However, a kingdom must have a king and here we see an individual in view, not a country. Who is this individual that waxed greatly, invaded the Holy Land and exalted himself to be like Jesus Christ? It is none other than the antichrist in Rev 13.

We now expand and clarify our previous comments concerning the two goats and their horns. The *Ram* with the *two horns* that first appeared represented the *Kingdom of Medo-Persia*. The *he-goat* that next appeared represents the *Kingdom of Greece*.

- ➢ The "*single large horn*" is Alexander **the Great.**

- ➢ The **single horn broken off** is the sudden **death of Alexander the Great**. Alexander died when only 33 years old after conquering much of the known world

➢ The *four horns* that arise to replace the single horn are the ***division of the Grecian Empire*** into four new, smaller empires reigned by four of Alexander's Generals.

Macedonia .... Ruled by ***Cassandra***
Thrace and Asia Minor (Turkey).... Ruled by ***Lysimachus***
Syria...... Ruled by ***Seleucus***
Egypt..... Ruled by ***Ptolemy***

Following the separation of Macedonia, a vile and evil king called Antiochus Epiphanies arose from *out of the horn* of Greece. History has shown that this all came to pass, but it *IS NOT* what this prophecy ultimately represents. How can we ignore the straightforward words of Gabriel: ***"the vision refers to the time of the end"*** (Dan 8:17, 19). It should be clearly understood that the overthrow of Babylon by the Medo-Persian Empire; the conquests of Alexander the Great; his early death at age 33; the division of the Grecian empire into four parts; and the rise to power of Antiochus Epiphanies in 175 BC all actually took place. Antiochus conquered Jerusalem in 171 BC, desecrated the temple by sacrificing swine in the holy place, and demanded they worship him as a god. A brave band of rebels led by Judas Maccabeus fought against Antiochus for 3.5 years and finally defeated Antiochus on December 25, 168 BC. The Macabees cleansed the temple and reinstated the daily sacrifices. This event is still remembered today as the *Feast of Hanukkah*. However, the fulfillment of this prophecy still lies in the future; Antiochus was just a *shadow and type* of the real focus of the visions shown to John, which is the rise and fall of the *beast out of the sea* in Rev 13:1 or the *antichrist*. The man we know as the antichrist is further described in Dan 8:19-25. We will now let the scriptures speak as to how the antichrist will be revealed and recognized as he arises with 3.5 years left in the church age.

Descriptions of the Antichrist

"And he said, Behold, I will make thee know what shall be in the last end of the indignation: for at the time appointed the end shall be. The ram which thou sawest having two

horns are the kings of Media and Persia. And the rough goat is the king of Grecia: and the great horn that is between his eyes is the first king. Now that being broken, whereas four stood up for it, four kingdoms shall stand up out of the nation, but not in his power. And in the latter time of their kingdom, when the transgressors are come to the full, a king of fierce countenance, and understanding dark sentences, shall stand up. And his power shall be mighty, but not by his own power: and he shall destroy wonderfully, and shall prosper, and practise, and shall destroy the mighty and the holy people. And through his policy also he shall cause craft to prosper in his hand; and he shall magnify himself in his heart, and by peace shall destroy many: he shall also stand up against the Prince of princes; but he shall be broken without hand."   Daniel 8: 19-25

Here we are clearly told that the *ram with two horns* is the *Kingdom of Medo-Persia*, and the *rough goat* with one prominent horn is *Greece* and *Alexander the Great*. The prominent horn is broken off (death of Alexander) and his kingdom is divided into *four nations* as previously described. This vision clearly equates the *little horn* of Dan 8:9, which arose from one of the four horns shown on the he-goat of Dan 8:5, with a king of *fierce countenance*. To prove that this prophecy also describes the end time antichrist, we offer the following observations. He will: (1) understand *dark sentences*; (2) he will be demonically possessed, (3) His power shall be mighty; he will dominate the entire world with his commercial, military and religious systems, (4) His power does not come from his own strength but from someone else (Satan), (5) He shall *wonderfully destroy;* anyone who refuses to worship *the beast* will be killed, (6) He will destroy the *holy People*, the people of Israel, (7) He will cause *craft* to prosper; worldly goods and commerce, (8) By *peace* he will destroy many, likely by convincing many to take the mark of the beast which is fatal, (9) He will stand up against the *Prince of Princes*, Jesus Christ, but in the end (10) He will be *broken without hand*. This is clearly an end-time prophecy of the antichrist. There is no indication that Antiochus created a vast financial and commercial system, he was a deranged warrior. No ruler at any point in time in the Old Testament has *stood up* against Jesus Christ. Antiochus was also not *broken without hand*. History records after his defeat in 167 BC, Antiochus died of an unknown disease in 164 BC. The antichrist will not die of some disease; he will be supernaturally destroyed by a sword that proceeds out of the mouth of Christ at the battle of Armageddon (Rev 19).

Origin of the Antichrist

We will now assimilate all the prophecies in Daniel and attempt to determine the origin of the antichrist. To do so, it would be enormously helpful if we are to watch and discern the times of the end approaching. *First*, we have determined from Dan 2 that the antichrist will arise from *among* a ten-nation confederacy that will be formed at the time of the end, just before the last 3.5 years of the tribulation period begins. *Second*, from Dan 7 we were told that the antichrist will arise from within the boundaries of the old Roman Empire. *Third*, in Dan 8: 21 we were told that the antichrist would arise out of one of the old 4 divisions of Alexander the Great's empire. In addition, Dan 8:8-9 restricted his origin to one of the four divisions of Alexander the Great's World Empire: (1) Greece, (2) Egypt, (3) Syria, and (4) Turkey. This narrows the origin of the antichrist to one of these four countries. But, from which of these will the antichrist arise? We believe that the answer is given in the 8th chapter of Daniel.

> *And out of one of them (Greece, Egypt, Syria and Turkey) came forth a little horn, which waxed exceedingly great, toward the South, and toward the east, and toward the pleasant land.* Daniel 8:9

Now note that Dan 8:1-14 is referring to Antiochus Epiphanes, who came to the throne in 175 BC; plundered the temple in Jerusalem; stopped the daily sacrifices; and descecrated the alter of sacrifice and the Holy Place by butchering swine in the temple. But,what does that tell us about the Antichrist? In Dan 8:15-16 we are told that the angel Gabriel was sent to Daniel to understand the full *meaning of this vision*. Gabriel now makes an astounding statement: ***Understand that the vision refers to the time of the end*** (Dan 8:17). Gabriel is telling Daniel that this is another *near-far prophecy*. It describes *both* the actions of Antiochus and those of the antichrist !

In Daniel 11:36 we are told of a ***willful King*** who all agree is the Antichrist. In Dan 7:8; 8:9-12 we are introduced to a ***little horn*** who we have identified as the Antichrist. Comparing scripture to scripture, the little horn is proved to be the end time Antichrist. The actions of the little horn and the directions of his conquests indicate that the Antichrist will likely come from *Syria*. By searching other Old Testament prophecies, we find even stronger indications that the Antichrist will arise from Syria. The Antichrist is referred to as *The Assyrian* (Isa 10:5,12, 24; 30:27-33), the *King of Assyria* (Isa 10:12), the *King of Babylon* (Isa 14:4-17) and the *King of Tyrus*. Babylon and Tyrus are known to be in the modern country of Syria.

Taken as a unified description of the Antichrist, conjecture approaches near certainty. Finally, two great prophecy teachers (Arthur W. Pink and Clarence Larkin) believed that the *King of the South* is Egypt, the *King of the East* is Greece, and the *Pleasant Land* is Israel. Since all prophetic directions are relative to Jerusalem, we are left with the north and the west. To the west is Turkey. Note that there is no mention of the north; Pink concludes that the north is not mentioned because it is from the north where the antichrist will arise. We agree and conclude that the antichrist will arise from the north and the country will be *Syria*. This belief is also held by Clarence Larkin. We quote Larkin from his book "*Dispensational Truth*".

> "*While Daniel foresaw that the Kingdom of Alexander the Great would be divided into Four Kingdoms and that out of one of them would come the antichrist, He was not told at that time which one it would be, but 20 years later in 533 BC, he had another vision in which he saw two kings warring against each other. One was called the "King of the North" and the other the "King of the South". This chapter (Dan 11:1-45) is one of the most wonderfully minute as to prophetic details of*

any chapter in the Bible. It corresponds exactly with the profane history of the Kings of Egypt and Syria for over 350 years. From verse 5 to verse 31 we have an account of what is called the "wars" of the "Kings of the North" (Syria) and the "Kings of the South" (Egypt). These end with the close of the rein of Antiochus Epiphanes, 164 BC. Verses 32-35 cover the whole period from 164 BC down to the "Time of the End". At verse 36 "The Willful King" (antichrist) appears, and from that verse down to the end of the book, we have an account of what is to befall Daniel's people in the "latter days". This vision of the "King of the North" (Syria) and of the "King of the South" (Egypt), in which the "King of the North" prevailed, revealed to Daniel that antichrist would arise in the "Syrian" division of Alexander's kingdom, for the description of the "King of the North" corresponded with the description of the "Little Horn" that came up on one of the "Four Horns" of the He-Goat, and also with the "Little Horn" that came up among the "Ten Horns" on the head of the Fourth Beast."

Our research confirms these concise words of Clarence Larkin. The question of which nations will form the basis of the antichrist's ten-nation confederacy will now be addressed.

The End Time 10 Nation Confederacy
We know from Daniel's image of the Colossus in Daniel Chapter 2 that all ten nations will arise out of the old Roman Empire. The antichrist's ten-nation confederacy will now be addressed. The map on the next page shows the extent of the old Roman Empire at the height of its power. More than 40 modern countries of varying size and power currently exist within the boundaries of the old Roman Empire shown in a dark shade. It is impossible to definitively state which countries will form the final 10-nation confederacy over which Satan and the antichrist will rule. However, it is certain that a 10-nation confederacy will arise in the European theatre in the end times. It is worth mentioning that at this time (2011) an interesting federation of countries has been formed called the European Economic Community. Since 2007 there have been 27 countries in this economic alliance. It is

possible that a new 10-country coalition could be formed out of these countries, or from a combination of these and others. Only time will tell. We only mention this because it demonstrates that such a coalition can be formed, and will be sometime in the future.

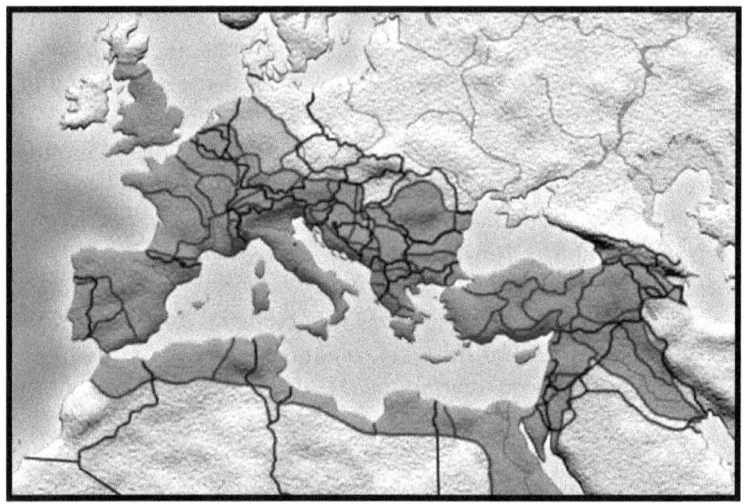

By comparing scripture to scripture, we have shown that the *beast that arises out of the sea* in Rev 13 is the same as the *beast that carries the Scarlet-Clothed Woman* in Rev 17. We can also now state that the *little horn* of Dan 7 and the beasts of Rev 13 and Rev 17 are all the same individual, the antichrist; who will arise just as the last 3.5 years of the tribulation period begins. From Rev 17:7-14 we learn why this *antichrist* is so powerful.

Stitching Prophecy Together

"And the angel said unto me, Wherefore didst thou marvel? I will tell thee the mystery of the woman, and of the beast that carrieth her, which hath the seven heads and ten horns. The beast that thou sawest was, and is not; and shall ascend out of the bottomless pit, and go into perdition: and they that dwell on the earth shall wonder, whose names were not written in the book of life from the foundation of the world,

when they behold the beast that was, and is not, and yet is. And here is the mind which hath wisdom. The seven heads are seven mountains, on which the woman sitteth. And there are seven kings: five are fallen, and one is, and the other is not yet come; and when he cometh, he must continue a short space. And the beast that was, and is not, even he is the eighth, and is of the seven, and goeth into perdition. And the ten horns which thou sawest are ten kings, which have received no kingdom as yet; but receive power as kings one hour with the beast. These have one mind, and shall give their power and strength unto the beast. These shall make war with the Lamb, and the Lamb shall overcome them: for he is Lord of lords, and King of kings: and they that are with him are called, and chosen, and faithful." Rev 7: 7-14

In the books of Revelation and Daniel, a *horn* is a symbol of power, usually a king. A *mountain* represents a kingdom or nation. The *mystery* (Rev 17:7) of the antichrist is as follows. The time frame of this vision starts *prior* to when the great world leader arises from *among* a ten-nation confederacy, and ends in his total defeat at the battle of Armageddon. The vision starts before his body, mind and soul are taken over by a powerful demonic prince (Rev 13:3), and before he unifies his kingdom. We know this because Rev 17:12 specifically states without controversy that *the ten horns which you saw are ten Kings who have received no kingdom as yet, but they receive authority for one hour as kings with the beast.* Notice that after the world leader arises and conquers three kingdoms, he will establish himself as the dictator and appoint new kings or a mixture of old and new kings to their leadership positions. It is not clear if this is shortly before the world leader is wounded to death, or shortly after. What is clear is that the existence of the antichrist's kingdom will last for *one hour*. It seems clear that *one hour* is 3.5 years. Recall that the church at Philadelphia was the only church with absolutely no rebuke; she is regarded as the church of end time *overcomers.* In Rev 3:10 Christ promises that: *Because you have kept my command to persevere, I also will keep you from the HOUR OF TRIAL which shall come upon the whole world to test those who dwell upon the earth*

(Rev 3:10). In Rev 12:12 after Satan has been cast down to the earth he declares: ***Woe to the inhabitants of the earth***, and he pursues the saints that remain on the earth for 42 months or 3.5 years (Rev 12:12). While this is not proof, it certainly provides strong evidence that the *hour of trial* is 42 months or 1260 days.

This *beast* that John saw: ***was, and is not, and will ascend out of the bottomless pit*** (Rev 17:8). Most commentators try to put this description around 91 AD when John received his revelations. We believe that this destroys the context of the entire vision. John is commenting on what he sees. The time frame of this vision places it exactly where it should be to satisfy this prophecy: between when the great world leader is ***wounded to the death*** and when he miraculously recovers. As John looks far into the future to receive this vision, this individual *was*. He had been on the world scene for a number of years when he rose to power as a great world leader. After he receives his deadly wound, he is for all practical purposes, and possibly literally, dead - or apparently wounded so severely he cannot recover. At this point in time, he *is not*. He has ceased to exist as a charismatic and powerful world leader, and will from this point forward become the antichrist. He will also become identical to the ***Beast out of the sea*** in Rev 13:1. When the great world leader is ***mortally wounded*** (Rev 13:3), he will be taken over by a strong demon *prince* from the bottomless pit, and given all the power of Satan. The *bottomless pit* is an underworld domain where extremely dangerous and powerful angels are being held. The **nephillim** of Gen 6:1-2 which cohabitated with earthly women are there. In Rev 9:11 we are told that ***Abaddon*** will arise out of the bottomless pit to serve as king over persecuting demonic locusts (Rev 9:11). This dramatic transformation and demonic character of the antichrist is the reason that ***those who dwell upon the earth will marvel, whose names are not written in the Book of Life.*** (Rev 7:8). Note that they marvel not because of the beast that takes over his body, but because everyone will recognize this person as the world leader *slain as to death* who miraculously recovers. All of this harmonizes perfectly with our scriptural interpretation.

A second interpretation which is equally valid and makes perfect sense is that John is using double imagery, referring to the antichrist as not a normal man but a *beast*, which is what he has become. The *man* that was once a mighty world leader as a human has now become a *beast* in human form. The cause of this transformation is the strong angel from the bottomless pit who has taken over the human body. This *beast* existed previously as a *prince* (Dan 10:13-20) and inhabited another body. He *was* the real power and strength of some prior kingdom, but not to the extent that he will be now. When his kingdom perished, this bad angel was sent to the bottomless pit to wait for this assignment. He is *not* when he is called out of the bottomless pit to assume the role of the *antichrist*, which is identical to the *beast out of the sea*. He *will ascend* to take over the wounded body of the world leader. This is perfectly consistent with Rev 17:11.

"And the beast that was, and is not, even he is the eighth, and is of the seven, and goeth into perdition. And the ten horns which thou sawest are ten kings, which have received no kingdom as yet; but receive power as kings one hour with the beast. These have one mind, and shall give their power and strength unto the beast." Rev 17:11-13

We are also told that the 10-nation confederacy will be of *one mind* with the *beast* and follow him to the end. The (new) antichrist/beast and his (new) 10-nation confederacy comprise the eighth world kingdom to persecute Israel (Rev 17:11). The newly energized *beast* will fully mobilize all of his forces and turn on the holy city of Jerusalem. He will also try to kill every person who will not worship him and take his mark (Rev 13: 13-17). His mission on earth is to eradicate the offspring of the sun-clothed woman **who keep the commandments of God and have the testimony of Jesus Christ** (Rev 12:17).

We *summarize* the rise of antichrist and his major activities as follows.

- A great world leader will emerge out of the European political theatre. He will be a charismatic speaker, effective politician, and will exert tremendous influence on European political and economic activity.
- This world leader will likely arise out of Syria.
- We know that Herod's Temple will somehow be rebuilt (Rev 11:1-2). While not directly stated in scripture, it is possible that this great leader will manage to get this done. This will cause many in the nation of Israel to hail him as their promised messiah. Traditional teaching using a seven-year tribulation period will have the new temple rebuilt during the first 3.5 years of the seven years. We agree that the temple will be rebuilt (Rev 11:1-2) prior to when the antichrist will arise, but there is no need whatsoever to assume that this is part of a seven-year tribulation period. In fact, the extent and size of a modern temple the size of Herod's temple would likely take longer than 3.5 years. Our theology of limiting the tribulation to 3.5 years actually supports the rise of a 10-nation confederacy, a great world leader, and temple reconstruction without any time limitations.
- In the end times, a ten-nation confederacy will arise in Europe from within the boundaries of the old Roman Empire.
- The power base of the world leader will enable him to build enough military strength to attack and topple three of the nations within the 10-nation confederacy.
- After conquering these three nations, the other seven will unite with him under one military and economic system. It will likely be the most powerful military and economic confederation ever formed.
- Either during these military campaigns or shortly afterward, this world leader will be *"**wounded onto death**"* by *"**a sword**"* (Rev 13 14). The Greek word for a sword literally means *a long knife*. When he is wounded and expected to die, he will at this point be taken over by a great demonic prince, and through all the power that Satan can give him he will emerge as what we call *the antichrist"*. This is the *beast out of the sea* described in

Rev 13: 1-10. This will happen after Satan has been cast out of heaven onto the earth (Rev 12). The reign of antichrist will be 42 months or 1260 days. We believe that his seat of power will be in the city of Babylon, rebuilt for his reign.

- ➤ Immediately following emergence of the antichrist, a second equally-powerful and evil individual will emerge. This new personage is called *the beast out of the earth*. He is **"*like a lamb but speaks like a dragon*"** (Rev 13:11). This *beast* will be the religious counterpart of the warrior-beast, antichrist. He is a powerful and influential (*false*) prophet and religious leader, mimicking Jesus Christ, but he has all of the motives and power of the Dragon (*Satan*). Read what John the revelator has to say about this *beast out of the earth*.

"And I beheld another beast coming up out of the earth; and he had two horns like a lamb, and he spake as a dragon. And he exerciseth all the power of the first beast before him, and causeth the earth and them which dwell therein to worship the first beast, whose deadly wound was healed. And he doeth great wonders, so that he maketh fire come down from heaven on the earth in the sight of men, and deceiveth them that dwell on the earth by the means of those miracles which he had power to do in the sight of the beast; saying to them that dwell on the earth, that they should make an image to the beast, which had the wound by a sword, and did live. And he had power to give life unto the image of the beast, that the image of the beast should both speak, and cause that as many as would not worship the image of the beast should be killed. And he causeth all, both small and great, rich and poor, free and bond, to receive a mark in their right hand, or in their foreheads: and that no man might buy or sell, save he that had the mark, or the name of the beast, or the number of his name. Here is wisdom. Let him that hath understanding count the number of the beast: for it is the number of a man; and his number is Six hundred threescore and six." Rev 13: 11-18

The first action of the *false prophet* will likely be to join the antichrist in an invasion of Israel, and set up the ***abomination that causes desolation*** in the temple. It is well within reason that prior to construction of the new temple in Jerusalem, a covenant will have been made with the Jewish people to allow them to freely worship Yahweh in their new temple. He (the antichrist) will suddenly turn on Jerusalem and nullify the promise made years earlier by the charismatic world leader. The prophet Isaiah seems to have written of this day.

> ***"Because ye have said, We have made a covenant with death, and with hell are we at agreement; when the overflowing scourge shall pass through, it shall not come unto us: for we have made lies our refuge, and under falsehood have we hid ourselves: Therefore thus saith the Lord GOD, Behold, I lay in Zion for a foundation a stone, a tried stone, a precious corner stone, a sure foundation: he that believeth shall not make haste. Judgment also will I lay to the line, and righteousness to the plummet: and the hail shall sweep away the refuge of lies, and the waters shall overflow the hiding place. And your covenant with death shall be disannulled, and your agreement with hell shall not stand; when the overflowing scourge shall pass through, then ye shall be trodden down by it."*** Isaiah 28:15-18

He (the beast) will break his covenant with Israel, conquer Jerusalem, invade and desecrate the temple, and demand an *abomination that causes desolation* be set up in the Holy Place. The desecration is an image that supernaturally speaks and requires all who look upon the image to worship the antichrist and take the *mark of the beast* (666). Here we must with much trepidation issue a stern warning to anyone who reads this book. If you are still on the earth at this time, a supernatural event will occur that may cost you your life.

> ***"And he (the Beast out of the earth) deceives those who dwell on the earth by those signs which he was granted to do in the sight of the beast (the beast out of the sea), telling those who dwell on the earth to make an image to the beast***

> *who was wounded by the sword and lived. He was granted power to give breath to the image of the beast, that the image of the beast should both speak and cause as many as would not worship the image of the beast to be killed."*
> Rev 13:14-15

What is happening here is unprecedented in all of history. This *false prophet* is given the power to tell *all those who dwell on earth to make an image to the beast*. Reading this passage literally, everyone who is alive will be instructed to make an image just like the one standing in the Jerusalem temple. It will be like a *bobble doll,* but it *CAN SPEAK*. It commands anyone within its line of sight to worship the antichrist as God. Failure to do so will result in *DEATH*. Once anyone yields to this image, each person is sealed with the *mark of the beast* and is allowed to roam freely, buy and sell, etc.

> *"And he (the false prophet) causes all (who worship the antichrist) to receive a mark on their right hand or on their foreheads. And no one can buy or sell except one who has the mark or the name of the beast or the number of his name. Here is wisdom. Let him who has understanding calculate the number of the beast, for it is the number of a man. His number is 666."* Rev 13: 16-18

The result of capitulation is too severe to even imagine. Those who do so will be sentenced to eternal damnation in the lake of fire and brimstone (Rev 19:20). ***DO NOT WORSHIP THE IMAGE - DO NOT TAKE THE MARK OF THE BEAST.*** No wonder the martyred saints seen under the throne of God after the fifth seal is broken cry out:

> *"How long, oh Lord, holy and true until you judge and avenge our blood on those who dwell on the earth?"*
> Rev 6:10

Do not give in to this apostasy! You will be trading a few moments of agony for an eternity with God. We have issued this warning, just as Christ did:

"For then there will be great tribulation, such as there has not been since the beginning of the world until this time, nor ever shall be. See, I have told you beforehand."   Rev 24:21

Christ has issued a warning to those in Jerusalem to flee immediately when this occurs.

"Therefore when you see the 'abomination of desolation spoken of by Daniel the prophet, standing in the holy place (whosoever reads let him understand), then let them that are in Judea flee to the mountains."   Rev 24: 15-16

Those that *flee* are the *woman* in Rev 12:6. It is now time to reveal the end of this age, and show how Christ will harvest the earth, separating the *wheat* from the *tares*.

Chapter 19

The Three Angels

In Revelation 14:1-5 John the revelator saw a group of 144,000 firstfruit saints standing before the throne of God in heaven. They have been called to heaven from *among men*. They are *firstfruits to God and to the lamb*, and they *follow the Lamb wheresoever He goeth* (Rev 14:4). On the earth, there are several groups left: (1) many Christians who are not a part of this firstfruits harvest who will have to endure the seven trumpet judgments, (2) a vast number of non-Christians who embrace apostate religions, (3) Jewish individuals who have not been sealed as part of the 144,000 who are divinely protected, (4) Those who are atheists or who are agnostics, (5) those who are of the age of reason who have not yet accepted Christ as their savior, and (6) those who fervently follow after Satan, the antichrist and the false prophet. All of these earth dwellers will be offered salvation by the worldwide proclamations of an *angel* who boldly and loudly proclaims the gospel of Jesus Christ to everyone on the earth.

> *"And I saw another angel fly in the midst of heaven, having the everlasting gospel to preach unto them that dwell on the earth, and to every nation, and kindred, and tongue, and people, saying with a loud voice, Fear God, and give glory to him; for the hour of his judgment is come: and worship him that made heaven, and earth, and the sea, and the fountains of waters."* Rev 14:6-7

We are told that *another angel* now enters the scene. There has been much speculation as to what is meant by *another angel*, but positive identification is impossible. An angelic being was shown in Rev 11:15 when an angel blew the seventh trumpet. In Rev 12:7, Michael was mentioned as he led a group of angels in a cosmic conflict with Satan and his angels. Whoever this angelic being, it is certain that this angel is given the responsibility to preach the gospel message to **every nation,**

kindred and tongue and people. Once before, a message was given to the entire known world. This was when the law was given by God on Mt. Sinai to the nation of Israel. We are also reminded of when the Holy Spirit fell on the day of Pentecost, and the gift of tongues was given to those who would proclaim the risen Christ in all of the languages of the people who were there. The message of this angel fulfills the words of Christ when He delivered the Olivet Discourse in 30 AD.

> *"And many false prophets shall rise, and shall deceive many. And because iniquity shall abound, the love of many shall wax cold. But he that shall endure unto the end, the same shall be saved. And this gospel of the kingdom shall be preached in all the world for a witness unto all nations; and then shall the end come."* Matthew 24:11-14

This gospel message is full of admonitions and warnings.

> *"Saying with a loud voice, Fear God, and give glory to him; for the hour of his judgment is come: and worship him that made heaven, and earth, and the sea, and the fountains of waters."* Rev 14:7

The angel speaks with a *loud voice*; a voice of authority. The angel commands those who hear its voice to **fear God**. In the pulpit today, we hear a great deal of love, mercy and grace, as well we should: But this is rarely balanced with the message that God is to be feared.

> *"Wherefore, my beloved, as ye have always obeyed, not as in my presence only, but now much more in my absence, work out your own salvation with fear and trembling."* Phil 2:12

> *"It is a fearful thing to fall into the hands of the living God."* Hebrews 10:31

The fear of God can only be quenched by placing our faith in the hands of Jesus Christ. Through Him and by Him we are able to stand boldly in the presence of the Living God with reassurance that the Grace of Jesus Christ is sufficient. Those whose fears will be realized are those who will refuse to accept Christ as their Lord and Savior. The punishment is not unfair; all unbelievers will have their chance to be given eternal peace and salvation: ***And because iniquity shall abound, the love of many shall wax cold.*** The angel commands that anyone who hears the message should ***worship Him.*** Inherent in salvation by grace through Jesus Christ is the fear of eternal damnation. No one in their right mind would want to be thrown into the Lake of Burning Fire. The gift of eternal life is almost too simple to be believed… all we have to do is to place our faith in Jesus Christ and acknowledge His saving work on the cross. No one can buy, work or talk their way into salvation. Simply believe on His name. It is only by Him and through Him that anyone can stand in God's holy presence without being cast away. This message is directed to unbelievers who without childlike faith are incapable of understanding grace. Once one surrenders to Christ, the old man becomes a new man, and sins are no longer remembered. To give God glory is a part of Christian repentance and self surrender. Christ said that those who have known Him also know the Father.

The timing of this message and when it is delivered appears at first to be at the beginning of the tribulation period, but a closer examination reveals the fallacy of this assumption. A *second angel* appears who proclaims that the end time city of Babylon has fallen.

> "***And there followed another angel, saying, Babylon is fallen, is fallen, that great city, because she made all nations drink of the wine of the wrath of her fornication.***" Rev 14:8

The City of Babylon will not be destroyed (Rev 18) until after the body of Christ has been raptured out at the seventh trumpet, and this is very near the end of the tribulation period and Satan's reign. A ***third angel*** now appears who identifies an act from which there can be no redemption.

> *"And the third angel followed them, saying with a loud voice, If any man worship the beast and his image, and receive his mark in his forehead, or in his hand, the same shall drink of the wine of the wrath of God, which is poured out without mixture into the cup of his indignation; and he shall be tormented with fire and brimstone in the presence of the holy angels, and in the presence of the Lamb: And the smoke of their torment ascendeth up for ever and ever: and they have no rest day nor night, who worship the beast and his image, and whosoever receiveth the mark of his name"*
>   Rev 14:9-11

The mark of the beast will be a mark in either the forehead or their right hand (Rev 13:16). Those who refuse to take the mark will be a part of the first resurrection, and they will rule and reign with Christ upon the earth for 1000 years (Rev 20:4). Those who take the mark will be cast into the lake of burning fire after the millennial kingdom (Rev 20:11-15). The context of when this message is delivered has been to place it between the rapture of all living believers at the seventh trumpet, and the battle of Armageddon on the Feast of Yom Kippur. This period of time coincides with the last ten days of the 1260 day reign of the Antichrist, which are when the seven bowls of God's wrath are poured out. Those who turn to Jesus Christ during this period of time and accept Him as their savior and Messiah will be *blessed*. Some will survive this period of great tribulation, and some will not; many will be martyred and slain for their faith.

> *"Here is the patience of the saints: here are they that keep the commandments of God, and the faith of Jesus. And I heard a voice from heaven saying unto me, Write, Blessed are the dead which die in the Lord from henceforth: Yea, saith the Spirit, that they may rest from their labours; and their works do follow them."*   Rev 14:12-13

Let anyone be forewarned that if they enter this terrible period of time they may well suffer a horrible death. However, be assured that they will *rest*, and their *works* will follow them. Even during this short period of time, there will be works worthy of reward.

This final conflict between Satan and Christ provides all unbelievers still alive at that time one last opportunity to gain eternal life. It is far better to suffer death at the hand of the antichrist than it will be to face the second death of all unbelievers (Rev 20:12-15). Those who accept Christ during this period of time are those individuals who have refused to take the mark of the beast or to worship its image, and were not raptured out at the 7th trump. These are unbelievers who will finally accept Christ as their savior. Many will be from the House of Israel.

Every person on the earth has now been warned. All will now be separated into only two groups: those who have accepted Jesus Christ as their savior, and those who have not. The next chapter will describe how these two groups will be gathered together at the end of the age.

Thoughts and Things……..

Chapter 20

The Harvests of the Earth

In Chapters 17 and 18 we studied the rise of antichrist and his false prophet. The time that these two *beasts* persecute the saints will be a *time, times and half a time; 24 months; or 1260 days.* In Rev 14:7-14 we receive a vision of how the saints are to be gathered to the rapture, and in Rev 14:15-20 we are given a prophecy of how the followers of Satan are gathered to the Battle of Armageddon.

Harvest of the Saints

> *"And I looked, and behold a white cloud, and upon the cloud one sat like unto the Son of man, having on his head a golden crown, and in his hand a sharp sickle. And another angel came out of the temple, crying with a loud voice to him that sat on the cloud, Thrust in thy sickle, and reap: for the time is come for thee to reap; for the harvest of the earth is ripe. And he that sat on the cloud thrust in his sickle on the earth; and the earth was reaped."*   Rev 14: 14-16

The scene unfolds as John sees **one like unto the Son of Man** sitting on a white cloud. The term *son of man* was used by Christ on many occasions to describe his earthly presence. Here we see it again used in a heavenly setting. Is this Christ or some angel? The term used in the second sentence **and another angel** came out of God's temple seems to indicate that he who sits on the cloud is an *angel* but not Christ. In Rev 1:7 we are told that Christ will come again **with clouds** (Mat 24:30), but this angelic being is simply sitting on a cloud. It is likely that this is another strong angel who has been sitting on a cloud holding a sickle, and waiting until he is commanded to stand and act. We are then told that yet **another angel** comes out of God's temple. The term in the Greek used here means *another of the same kind; of similar rank and authority*. This angel cries out in **a loud voice** to the other angel: **Thrust in thy sickle and reap**. This reminds us that Christ often taught his disciples by using parables and illusions from agricultural analogies. The sickle continues this analogy. The angel further announces that *the time is come to reap.* The reason why is again an agricultural analogy; *the harvest of the earth is ripe.* What is being reaped? Christ said:

> *"But, when the grain ripens, immediately he puts in the sickle, because the harvest has come."* Mark 4:29

The angel said *the time has come*: the grain has ripened in the stalk, and the reaping is to commence. This is the rapture of the church and resurrection of believers from all ages. The precious grain is now to be gathered into the barn, but the wheat must be separated from the chaff. When does this *reaping of the harvest* occur? We have shown that this will occur at the sounding of the seventh trump, and immediately preceding the seven bowl judgments. In the *Olivet Discourse*, Christ referred to this harvest.

> *"And He will send His angels with a great sound of a trumpet, and they will gather together His elect from the four winds, from one end of heaven to another."*
> Matthew 24:31

Harvest of the Wicked

The vision that John is now being shown depicts how all unbelievers and those who have taken the mark of the beast will be called to the 2cd advent of Christ. This gathering will supernaturally take place concurrent to the seven bowl judgments. Satan, the antichrist, the false prophet and their followers will all be gathered to the Battle of Armageddon.

> *"And another angel came out of the temple which is in heaven, he also having a sharp sickle. And another angel came out from the altar, which had power over fire; and cried with a loud cry to him that had the sharp sickle, saying, Thrust in thy sharp sickle, and gather the clusters of the vine of the earth; for her grapes are fully ripe. And the angel thrust in his sickle into the earth, and gathered the*

> *vine of the earth, and cast it into the great winepress of the wrath of God. And the winepress was trodden without the city, and blood came out of the winepress, even unto the horse bridles, by the space of a thousand and six hundred furlongs."* Rev 14:14-16

As John continues to look at the scene, ***another*** (third) ***angel*** comes forth out of the temple of God. The angel in the previous scene harvested the righteous saints from the earth; the angel in this scene will harvest those who have chosen to follow Satan, the antichrist and the false prophet. The angel who emerges from the temple of God has another ***sharp sickle*** in his hand. The sharpness of both sickles speaks to the completeness of the harvest. No one alive will escape these two harvests; every living human will be in one group or another. At this point a fourth angel emerges from ***the altar*** of God. The altar reminds us of the scene in Rev 6: 9, where the martyred saints were seen waiting *under* the altar and crying out for justice. Their cries were: ***How long, oh Lord, Holy and True, until you avenge our blood?*** Now their cries are answered with action. This must be an angel of either a higher order or one with greater authority, because it comes directly from the altar of God. The importance of this angel is underscored by the fact that it has ***power over fire***. It might be tempting to associate this angel with the altar of sacrifice which stood in the earthly temple, but this seems unlikely. Why would there be a need for an altar of sacrifice? Jesus Christ was the perfect and final sacrifice under the Old Testament economy. The answer is probably found by precedence in Rev 8:1-5.

> *"And when he had opened the seventh seal, there was silence in heaven about the space of half an hour. And I saw the seven angels which stood before God; and to them were given seven trumpets. And another angel came and stood at the altar, having a golden censer; and there was given unto him much incense, that he should offer it with the prayers of all saints upon the golden altar which was before the throne. And the smoke of the incense, which came with the prayers of the saints, ascended up before God*

> *out of the angel's hand. And the angel took the censer, and filled it with fire of the altar, and cast it into the earth: and there were voices, and thunderings, and lightnings, and an earthquake."* Rev 8:1-5

This scene reveals several important things.

- ➤ This scene is *immediately after* the seventh seal is broken. As we have pointed out, the seals provide an overview of the tribulation period. Since this is the last seal, this is one of the last things which happen in the tribulation period. Indeed! This is exactly when the harvest of the wicked occur, at the Feast of Yom Kippur in the 7th month of (Tishri), on the last day of this age (Yom Kippur).
- ➤ This angel is before a *golden altar*.
- ➤ The altar contains *fire*.
- ➤ There are *thunderings, lightning and an earthquake*. This exactly corresponds to what happens as the last (seventh) bowl is poured out immediately before the battle of Armageddon (Rev 16:18).

Comparing scripture to scripture, it is almost certain that the angel of Rev 8:1-5 is the same angel who has ***power over fire*** in this scene. This angel has the authority to order the second angel in this scene to: ***Thrust in thy sharp sickle, and gather the clusters of the vine of the earth; for her grapes are fully ripe. And the angel thrust in his sickle into the earth, and gathered the vine of the earth, and cast it into the great winepress of the wrath of God*** (Rev 14:15-16). The harvest of the wicked is illustrated as reaping the grapes with a sharp sickle (knife) and casting them into the winepress of God. We are reminded of two Old Testament passages:

> *"I have trodden the winepress alone; and of the people there was none with me: for I will tread them in mine anger, and trample them in my fury; and their blood shall be sprinkled upon my garments, and I will stain all my raiment."*
> Isaiah 63:3

> *"Therefore prophesy thou against them all these words, and say unto them, The LORD shall roar from on high, and utter his voice from his holy habitation; he shall mightily roar upon his habitation; he shall give a shout, as they that tread the grapes, against all the inhabitants of the earth."*
> Jeremiah 25:30

The fact that this represents the final gathering of the wicked to the battle of Armageddon is confirmed by the following scripture.

> *"And out of his mouth goeth a sharp sword, that with it he should smite the nations: and he shall rule them with a rod of iron: and he treadeth the winepress of the fierceness and wrath of Almighty God."* Rev 19:15

The reason for this command to an angel to go forth at this time is that ***her*** (the earth's) ***grapes are fully ripe***. The fullness of time is at hand. Every Christian echoes the same lamentation; *Why has God waited this long?*

> **"The Lord is not slack concerning his promise, as some men count slackness; but is longsuffering to us-ward, not willing that any should perish, but that all should come to repentance"** II Peter 3:9

The precious wheat (saints) has been harvested from the earth at the 7th trump (rapture of the saints), and now the crucible of wickedness has reached its limit; the *grapes* are not just ripe, they are ***fully ripe***. In a seeming paradox, Christ said to his elect that ***you are the fruit and I am the vine*** (John 15:2, 4-5).

Just as Christ's children are his *fruits of righteousness*, the grapes of the earth are from Satan's vineyard, which produces evil fruit. This fruit of iniquity has now come to fullness and it is time for Christ to become conquering King. The angel responds to this authoritative command and immediately ***thrusts his sickle into the earth***. With this sharp sickle, he ***gathers the vine of the earth and casts it into the great winepress of the Wrath of God***.

In Rev 14:1-13 we saw that the saints had been raptured out prior to this harvest to meet our Lord Jesus Christ in the air. Now we see that there is a harvest of grapes (all unbelievers) which are being gathered to meet our Lord Jesus Christ at the Battle of Armageddon. Large armies will come from the *North* and cross the Euphrates River, which has been supernaturally *dried up* to allow the ground forces to easily march to Jerusalem when the 6th bowl was poured out.

> *"And the sixth angel poured out his vial upon the great river Euphrates; and the water thereof was dried up, that the way of the kings of the east might be prepared. And I saw three unclean spirits like frogs come out of the mouth of the dragon, and out of the mouth of the beast, and out of the mouth of the false prophet. For they are the spirits of devils, working miracles, which go forth unto the kings of the earth and of the whole world, to gather them to the battle of that great day of God Almighty."* Rev 16: 12-14

Here we also see that the agents of the *sickle* harvesting the earth are *three unclean spirits*; they *go forth unto the kings of the earth and of the whole world* to gather all of the unbelievers to Jerusalem. How ironic! The armies and followers of the antichrist are led to Armageddon and certain destruction by *unclean spirits* from Satan himself!! They foolishly think that these unclean spirits are leading them to victory over Christ, but they are being led to death and destruction. The closing words in the Book of Revelation now ring true.

> *" He who is unjust, let him be unjust still; he who is filthy, let him be filthy still; he who is righteous, let him be righteous still; he who is holy, let him be holy still'* Rev 22:11

As the *grapes* are gathered (Rev 19:19, Rev 16:12) to the earthly winepress in the valley of Meddigo just outside of Jerusalem, they will experience the judgment of Christ, which is *righteous and true* (Rev 19:2). The church is gone; she will not experience God's wrath (the bowls) or the wrath of Christ when He returns. Finally, the role of angels in destroying the wicked is given in

Mat 13:41-42, 49-50. In these verses we again see the meaning of the angel appearing with fire; fire is always a symbol of wrath. The fact that this winepress is trodden outside of Jerusalem at the battle of Armageddon is obvious from the events described in Rev 19.

> *"And I saw heaven opened, and behold a white horse; and he that sat upon him was called Faithful and True, and in righteousness he doth judge and make war. His eyes were as a flame of fire, and on his head were many crowns; and he had a name written, that no man knew, but he himself. And he was clothed with a vesture dipped in blood: and his name is called The Word of God. And the armies which were in heaven followed him upon white horses, clothed in fine linen, white and clean. And out of his mouth goeth a sharp sword, that with it he should smite the nations: and he shall rule them with a rod of iron: and he treadeth the winepress of the fierceness and wrath of Almighty God."* Rev 19:11-15

The result of this battle is too devastating to imagine.

> *"Behold, the day of the LORD cometh, and thy spoil shall be divided in the midst of thee. For I will gather all nations against Jerusalem to battle; and the city shall be taken, and the houses rifled, and the women ravished; and half of the city shall go forth into captivity, and the residue of the people shall not be cut off from the city. Then shall the LORD go forth, and fight against those nations, as when he fought in the day of battle. And his feet shall stand in that day upon the mount of Olives, which is before Jerusalem on the east, and the mount of Olives shall cleave in the midst thereof toward the east and toward the west, and there shall be a very great valley; and half of the mountain shall remove toward the north, and half of it toward the south. And ye shall flee to the valley of the mountains; for the valley of the mountains shall reach unto Azal: yea, ye shall flee, like as ye fled from before the earthquake in the days of Uzziah king of Judah: and the LORD my God shall come, and all the saints with thee. And it shall come to pass in that*

day, that the light shall not be clear, nor dark: But it shall be one day which shall be known to the LORD, not day, nor night: but it shall come to pass, that at evening time it shall be light. And it shall be in that day, that living waters shall go out from Jerusalem; half of them toward the former sea, and half of them toward the hinder sea: in summer and in winter shall it be. And the LORD shall be king over all the earth: in that day shall there be one LORD, and his name one. All the land shall be turned as a plain from Geba to Rimmon south of Jerusalem: and it shall be lifted up, and inhabited in her place, from Benjamin's gate unto the place of the first gate, unto the corner gate, and from the tower of Hananeel unto the king's winepresses. And men shall dwell in it, and there shall be no more utter destruction; but Jerusalem shall be safely inhabited. And this shall be the plague wherewith the LORD will smite all the people that have fought against Jerusalem; Their flesh shall consume away while they stand upon their feet, and their eyes shall consume away in their holes, and their tongue shall consume away in their mouth."   Zechariah 14: 1-12

We are told that *blood came out of the winepress, even unto the horse bridles, by the space of a thousand and six hundred furlongs*. This statement reflects the massive slaughter and loss of human life that will occur on that day. Blood will flow *up to the horses' bridles* for 1600 furlongs. A *horse's bridal* is usually 15 hands up to the withers, or about 5 feet; 1600 furlongs is about 184 miles, which is approximately the length of Palestine. Many theologians have questioned God's word, but we dare not do so. The phrase probably means that in some places it will reach the height of a horses bridle, and that blood will flow to some extent for over 184 miles. We believe that this is made possible by another contemporary judgment. Immediately preceding this massacre, the seventh bowl will have been poured out and *great hail the weight of 100 pounds apiece* will fall (Rev 16:21). Hail of this magnitude falling over an extended period of time will result in massive flooding and water runoff as it melts. This water will carry with it blood for 184 miles. Joel spoke of this day long ago. The similarities are striking.

"For, behold, in those days, and in that time, when I shall bring again the captivity of Judah and Jerusalem. I will also gather all nations, and will bring them down into the valley of Jehoshaphat, and will plead with them there for my people and for my heritage Israel, whom they have scattered among the nations, and parted my land." Joel 3:1-2

"Assemble yourselves, and come, all ye heathen, and gather yourselves together round about: thither cause thy mighty ones to come down, O LORD. Let the heathen be wakened, and come up to the valley of Jehoshaphat: for there will I sit to judge all the heathen round about. Put ye in the sickle, for the harvest is ripe: come, get you down; for the press is full, the fats overflow; for their wickedness is great. Multitudes, multitudes in the valley of decision: for the day of the LORD is near in the valley of decision." Joel 3:12-14

The harvest of the earth is complete. The *wheat* has been harvested and taken to God's *barn*, and the *grapes* have been gathered to Armageddon to be trodden under in the winepress of Christ's wrath. The next vision to be described is the corresponding destruction of both the political and commercial centers of Satan's activities.

Thoughts and Things………..

Chapter 21

Mystery: Babylon the Great

In Revelation Chapter 17 we were introduced to a woman who is sitting on a scarlet beast. Who is this woman, and what is the beast that she rides? These two questions have perplexed biblical scholars for over 2000 years. In this chapter we will attempt to answer these questions consistent with Biblical truth.

"And there came one of the seven angels which had the seven vials, and talked with me, saying unto me, Come hither; I will shew unto thee the judgment of the great whore that sitteth upon many waters: With whom the kings of the earth have committed fornication, and the inhabitants of the earth have been made drunk with the wine of her fornication. So he carried me away in the spirit into the wilderness: and I saw a woman sit upon a scarlet coloured beast, full of names of blasphemy, having seven heads and ten horns. And the woman was arrayed in purple and scarlet colour, and decked with gold and precious stones and pearls, having a golden cup in her hand full of abominations and filthiness of her fornication: And upon her forehead was a name written,

MYSTERY, BABYLON THE GREAT, THE MOTHER OF HARLOTS AND ABOMINATIONS OF THE EARTH.

And I saw the woman drunken with the blood of the saints, and with the blood of the martyrs of Jesus: and when I saw her, I wondered with great admiration." Rev 17:1-6

The imagery which John now sees is spectacular in its appearance. There is a woman *arrayed in splendor and wearing garments of purple and scarlet*. Purple and scarlet are colors worn by royalty. She is adorned with *gold and precious stones and pearls*. This woman is rich with worldly wealth and displays it for all to see. She carries in her hand a *golden cup*. We would expect to find expensive, vintage wine in this cup, but it is *full of abominations and the filthiness of her abominations*. She is not intoxicated with wine but she is drunk with *the blood of the saints and with the blood of the martyrs of Jesus*. Not only is she drunk with the blood of the saints, but her influence and power is so great that she sits (as a hen sets over her offspring) upon *many waters*, which are identified as *peoples, multitudes, nations and tongues* (Rev 17:15). These have *committed fornication* (with the world through her) and indulged in her adulterous practices. This is not an actual woman, but pure imagery. The adultery she commits is not physical but spiritual.

What is *spiritual adultery*? The Bible describes the relationship that God desires with each of us in extremely personal terms. According to Paul, when we receive Christ, we become *betrothed* to him. In ancient Israel, when it comes time for a man to marry, he will go to the house of his proposed bride and approach the father of that house with a marriage proposal. If accepted, he is betrothed to his future bride. Unlike modern society, once a man and a woman were betrothed, they were considered to already be married even though the marriage had not taken place. So it is with those who believe in our Lord Jesus Christ. When we accept Jesus Christ as our savior, we are also *betrothed to Him*. This relationship will not fully be consummated until just before Christ's return and the Marriage of the Lamb takes place, but we have already entered into a permanent covenant relationship—one in which we are pledged to give our deepest devotion and service to him alone (2 Cor. 11:2-3). Christ views this commitment with complete seriousness; He gives us his Holy Spirit to show how committed He is, and He expects us to be faithful to Him until that day. Spiritual adultery was not only a problem in the Old Testament; it was an ongoing problem in the New Testament as well. In the

Old Testament the Children of Israel habitually transgressed against God's laws by taking up the ways of the heathen nations around them and by adopting their abominable customs.

"For of old time I have broken thy yoke, and burst thy bands; and thou saidst, I will not transgress; when upon every high hill and under every green tree thou wanderest, playing the harlot." Jeremiah 2:20

God likened these practices to a whorish wife committing adultery against her husband, and regularly warned his people against committing such acts. Jesus said:

"I will cast her into a bed, and them that commit adultery with her into great tribulation, except they repent of their deeds." Rev 2:22

The **inhabitants of the earth** refer to those who choose to follow Satan, the antichrist and the false prophet. They have been **made drunk with the wine of her fornication.** This woman who supplies the *wine* is evil and represents apostasy in the highest form. She also represents spiritual infidelity and has a mindset to kill the saints and figuratively drink of their blood. This woman is seen **in the wilderness, sitting on a scarlet beast which was full of names of blasphemy.** Why she is seen *in the wilderness* is not known, but possibly this represents her real position in the world. Prostitutes, drug dealers, pedophiles and other *purple and scarlet* people of this world hide in the shadows and love the darkness. Conversely, it may just be symbolism to reflect the position of this woman relative to those who follow Jesus Christ, because those who follow after Christ walk in the light and not darkness. This woman represents a false religious system that will force all people to worship the antichrist in the latter days. Its chief progenitor will be the *beast out of the sea* that arises in Rev 13:1. The false prophet:

"…exercises all of the authority of the Beast out of the Sea (antichrist) and causes the earth and those who dwell in it to worship the Beast". Rev 13:12

Characteristics of "Mystery Babylon the Great"
1. She sits on peoples, multitudes, nations and languages.
2. The world is intoxicated with the wine of her physical and spiritual adulteries.
3. She sits on a Beast that has seven heads and ten horns.
4. She is drunk with the blood of the saints.
5. John was greatly astonished when he saw her.
6. The ten horns, a 10-nation confederacy, will eventually hate her.
7. These 10 nations will bring her to ruin and burn her with fire.
8. She is symbolically the great city that rules over the kings of the earth. (See Chapter 22).

Satan knows much of the plan of God. He knows that according to the word of God in Genesis 3:15, one day he would *bruise a heel* that would in turn one day *bruise his head*. So Satan formulated a plan and devised a religious system that people would believe in, kill for, even be willing to die for. This religious system would is an occult system, centering upon *Mystery Babylon*. This is meant to elevate man to the level of God, eventually control the world, and deify Satan as lord.

A person which prefigured and influenced the propagation of this self-serving, self-seeking society was *Semiramis*. Together with Nimrod, she ruled Babel, one of the first major cities constructed after the flood (Genesis 11:1-9). According to the nineteenth century historian, *Alexander Hyssop*, Babel (Babylon) was the primal source from which all idolatry spread to the ancient world. Also according to Hyssop, Shem the son of Noah killed Nimrod because of his iniquitous practices. Semiramis however, moved quickly. She became pregnant and gave birth to a son called Tammuz. She let it be known that this was Nimrod reincarnate. This was the first imitation of the *Holy trinity* (Father, Son and Holy Ghost), which is the Christian godhead (*The Two Babylons*, Alexander Hyssop). Another historian, Ralph Woodrow, concluded that even to this present time, evidence of Babylonian worship exists in **all the false religions of the earth** (*Babylon, Mystery Religio*n, Ralph Woodrow) http://kenraggio.com . It must be clearly understood that most of the book of Revelation is clothed in mystery and symbolism. The *great whore that sits on many waters* is not a real woman, but a symbol of wickedness, false religion and idol worship. She has been made **drunk with the blood of the saints and with the blood of the martyrs of Jesus**. It should be noted that many apostate religions and satanic practices employ blood sacrifices as part of their religious rites. Although the symbolism of the woman is representative of an apostate religious system, the following passage is also true.

> *"And the woman whom you saw is that great city which reigns over the kings of the earth."* Rev 17:18

One must keep in mind that a basic and fundamental truth concerning the book of Revelation is that from Rev 4:1 to Rev 22:21 everything seen by John is prophetic and will not occur until the last 42 months, 1260 days of the final tribulation period. This woman is called a *great city* which *reigns over the Kings of the earth*. This statement has created enormous confusion. Biblical teachers have identified this woman as modern Jerusalem and even New York City. However, there should not be any confusion at all. John calls this city by name, and he calls it **Babylon** (Rev 17:5, 18:2, 18:10, 18:21 and 14:8). The ancient city of Babylon will one day be restored to her former glory and will serve as the world capital of the antichrist. If this is not true, then nothing in Rev 18 makes any sense (Rev 18:1-24). Many who reject this plain and straightforward interpretation maintain that *Babylon* is a secret word for *Rome*. A theory put forth by those who equate this woman to modern day Rome is that Rome was the seat of world power in John's day, and had cast him onto the Island of Patmos for preaching the gospel. The idea is that John was too scared to identify the real city by its name, so he used Babylon symbolically. How utterly crazy this thought is! John, the beloved disciple, was not scared of Rome, Satan or any other place or person. He knew that glory in Christ Jesus awaited him for his faithfulness. Like Paul, John was not scared of death or persecution. In Rev 18 the future glory, influence and permanent destruction of this great city is covered in detail, and it is also called *Babylon* in that vision. Remember that John actually saw these things and was told what to write in a book by Jesus Christ either directly or indirectly. John was told to call this city Babylon, and he called it Babylon. The City described in Revelation 18 is a real city that will be a major world power in the end times. Some may try to allegorize or spiritualize the name Babylon, but if this belief is held then Rev 18 is not to be believed at all.

You would think that John the apostle, who personally witnessed the crucifixion of our Lord Jesus Christ, would be physically sickened as he views this woman, but instead he **wondered with great admiration**. In possibly a spirit of disappointment, the angel who is showing him this beast-woman asks John; **Why do you marvel?** Without waiting for an answer, the angel immediately says that he will **tell you** (John) **the mystery of the woman and of the beast that carries her**.

> *"And the angel said unto me, Wherefore didst thou marvel? I will tell thee the mystery of the woman, and of the beast that carrieth her, which hath the seven heads and ten horns. The beast that thou sawest was, and is not; and shall ascend out of the bottomless pit, and go into perdition: and they that dwell on the earth shall wonder, whose names were not written in the book of life from the foundation of the world, when they behold the beast that was, and is not, and yet is. And here is the mind which hath wisdom. The seven heads are seven mountains, on which the woman sitteth. And there are seven kings: five are fallen, and one is, and the other is not yet come; and when he cometh, he must continue a short space. And the beast that was, and is not, even he is the eighth, and is of the seven, and goeth into perdition. And the ten horns which thou sawest are ten kings, which have received no kingdom as yet; but receive power as kings one hour with the beast. These have one mind, and shall give their power and strength unto the beast. These shall make war with the Lamb, and the Lamb shall overcome them: for he is Lord of lords, and King of kings: and they that are with him are called, and chosen, and faithful. And he saith*

unto me, The waters which thou sawest, where the whore sitteth, are peoples, and multitudes, and nations, and tongues." Rev 17:7-15

The angel's explanation illustrates the power and allure of Satan's world. The way of Satan glitters like diamonds and shines like gold, but it can only lead to spiritual death. The apostle Paul called this the ***Mystery of Iniquity***. Paul warned us of this deception.

"For the mystery of iniquity doth already work: only he who now letteth will let, until he be taken out of the way."
II Thessalonians 2:7

The *Mystery of Iniquity* that Paul identified is manifested as ***Mystery, Babylon the Great.*** This woman is a false religious system that opposes Jesus Christ, promotes the ways of the world and is described as a *harlot*. The beast that carries the woman is unmistakably the antichrist, and his worldwide commercial and military system.

The scarlet beast that the woman is riding upon has ***7 heads and 10 horns***. In Rev 12:3 John saw a ***dragon*** appear with ***seven heads and 10 horns***. This dragon was identified as Satan. In Rev 13:1 a ***beast out of the sea*** arises with ***seven heads and 10 horns***. This beast was identified as the antichrist. The beast which carries the woman is one and the same. The antichrist is Satan in the flesh... one cannot be separated from the other. The image which John is seeing is the true character of the satanically-controlled antichrist. In Rev 17:9 John is told that:

"Here is the mind that has wisdom. The seven heads are seven mountains upon which the woman sits." Rev 17:9

In previous chapters we have identified these ***seven mountains*** as seven world empires that have now come and gone.

1. Egypt
2. Assyrian

3. Babylonian
4. Medo-Persian
5. Babylon
6. Roman
7. The Third Reich

The beast which carries the woman has the characteristics, power and strength of all these previous kingdoms. In a real sense, Satan has actually been a part of all these kingdoms. He is the *Chief Prince of this World*. He has appointed one of his strong angels to dominate the personality and thoughts of each king in each kingdom. Daniel was told about two of these angels by Gabriel; the Prince of Persia in Dan 10:10-13 and the Prince of Greece in Dan 10:20. This final beast empire will be a mosaic of all the seven empires before it. This beast also has **10 horns**. These 10 horns symbolize 10 countries. We cannot say for sure who these 10 countries are, but we can say that they all are a member of the current European community. We can further narrow down their origin. In the end times, a 10 nation confederacy will arise from out of the boundaries of the *old Roman Empire*. All prophecy teachers prior to World War II, in which millions of Jews were eradicated by Hitler, associated this *10-nation confederacy* with the seventh kingdom. This view is now untenable because there is no indication whatsoever in the scriptural records that this confederacy will exist as a world empire that will persecute or rule over Israel. After it is formed, 3 nations in this 10 nation confederacy will be conquered or submit to the antichrist, and this new Satanically controlled economic, political and military world power will be the 8th and final world kingdom ruled by the antichrist (Dan 7:23-25, Rev 17:11). The original 10 nation confederacy is part of this 8th and final world kingdom, but it is not the separate 7th world empire. So what is this mysterious 7th world empire?

The Third Reich of Hitler caused more deaths and persecution of the Jews than any other empire in world history, and cannot now be ignored. It is reported that Hitler eradicated over six million Jews. This viewpoint is perfectly consistent with what John is told in Rev 17:11-14. It can now be assumed that the 7th world empire that persecuted and dominated the Jews was none other than Hitler's 3rd Reich.

In spite of this straightforward historical interpretation, the *seven heads* which are identified as *seven mountains* have been the subject of much debate. A prevailing view is that this *beast* is Rome. Rome is famous for being *the city of seven hills*. The woman is often equated with the Roman Catholic Church. Of course, the Roman Catholic Church is in Rome, but it is a separate city state.

Many have gone so far as to not only assign this religious system to the Roman Catholic Church, but to also claim that the Pope will be the antichrist. This view is bolstered by Rev 17:19, which states:

> **"And the woman whom you saw is that great city which reigns over the Kings of the earth."**   Rev 17:19

We do not believe that this interpretation will pass the test of scrutiny. *First*, while it is true that Rome is surrounded by seven hills, there is a great deal of difference in *mountains* and *hills*. *Second*, the seven mountains are a part of the beast that supports the woman, and not a part of the woman herself. *Third*, Rome is not the Vatican and the Pope does not control any nations. The Vatican is its own city state, and it is not the same as the city of Rome. It is not likely that the Pope will ever assume the role of a dictator over a ten-nation confederacy and assemble a mighty army devoted to war and conquest. *Fourth*, in prophecy *mountains* are often representative of kingdoms, and in the book of Daniel they never represent *a real mountain* but a political and economic entity called a *nation* or an *empire*. *Fifth*, the Vatican has never *ruled over all of the kings of the earth* and likely never will.

The Roman Catholic Church is certainly full of questionable spiritual practices.

- The veneration and exalted state of the Pope as the infallible source of all scriptural truth ignores the Holy Spirit.
- The worship and veneration of Mother Mary, and the prayers submitted to God through her image and name.
- The mysterious transubstantiation of bread and wine into the actual body and blood of Christ, administered only by a priest, cannot be sustained by Scripture.
- The Roman Catholic Church has been responsible for killing thousands of people in the Dark Ages and during the crusades. In the name of Christ and the church, the conquistadores practically eradicated the Mayan Empire in Yucatan and the nation of Peru in the Andes.

However, despite the questionable history and practices of the Roman Catholic Church, one thing is highly commendable: the church does faithfully preach salvation through Jesus Christ. She clearly does not fit the *mother of harlots*, the progenitor of all false religions, but rather she is just one of many religious systems that have engaged in harlotry.

So who or what is the city that is said to represent the harlot in Rev 17:19? Who or what is this *mother of all harlots*? There is only one physical city that qualifies for this title and that is the ancient city of Babel. The name *Babel* is a conjugation of two root words; *bab* meaning *gate* and *el* meaning *god*; hence, *the gate of god*. The ancient city of Babel was founded by Nimrod in a land called Shinar, which is now the country of Iraq, between 100 and 500 years after the flood. Nimrod was a son of Cush, who was a son of Ham. Nimrod was said to be a *mighty hunter*. Nimrod wanted to build a great tower which would *reach to the heavens*. His purpose was not to worship and glorify God, but to *exalt himself to the heavens* and *be like God* (Gen 11). For this rebellion, God destroyed this tower and the city of Babel. He scattered all of the people to the *four winds of the world* and he *confused the languages* (Gen 11:9). Recall that *Semiramis* was the goddess-queen of this city.

"And the whole earth was of one language, and of one speech. And it came to pass, as they journeyed from the east, that they found a plain in the land of Shinar; and they dwelt there. And they said one to another, Go to, let us make brick, and burn them thoroughly. And they had brick for stone, and slime had they for mortar. And they said, Go to, let us build us a city and a tower, whose top may reach unto heaven; and let us make us a name, lest we be scattered abroad upon the face of the whole earth. And the LORD came down to see the city and the tower, which the children of men builded. And the LORD said, Behold, the people is one, and they have all one language; and this they begin to do: and now nothing will be restrained from them, which they have imagined to do. Go to, let us go down, and there confound their language, that they may not understand one another's speech. So the LORD scattered them abroad from thence upon the face of all the earth: and they left off to build the city. Therefore is the name of it called Babel; because the LORD did there confound the language of all the earth: and from thence did the LORD scatter them abroad upon the face of all the earth."   Genesis 11:1-9

The ancient city of Babel was destroyed by God, but it was eventually rebuilt and was named *Babylon*. King Nebuchadnezzar built one of the mightiest cities the world has ever seen on this ancient site, and he mimicked the Tower of Babel with the *Hanging Gardens of Babylon*, one of the seven wonders of the ancient world. Although the site of Babel is mostly in ruins today, it will again be rebuilt in the end times and serve as Satan's seat of religious and commercial power for Satan's minion; the *antichrist*. It is this great city that either in situ or in influence has for over 4000 years made the inhabitants of this earth *drunk*. Babel was without a doubt the fountainhead of all false religions and spiritual corruption. The wickedness of Babel spread throughout the entire world and still exists today as *a mystery*. Kings and kingdoms have *gone to bed with her* and committed *fornication* with her. She is;

> **"Mystery Babylon the Great, the Mother of Harlots and Abominations of the Earth."** Rev 17:5

But neither the plan of Nimrod nor his false religion perished. Every country of the world has historical remnants of Babel and its religious system. The pyramids in Egypt, the Yucatan Peninsula and the Peruvian Empires were all patterned from the Tower of Babel, if not by historical connection, then by the influence of Satan. Even the mounds in Kentucky, USA are a mute testimony to his progeny. Accompanying all of these mighty structures was always a false religion which worshipped foreign gods. *Everywhere* the symbols and records are the same. It is generally believed by all biblical scholars that Babel and Nimrod was the fountainhead of all apostate world religions, and spawned many wicked spiritual practices. His actions so displeased God that he scattered the people of Babel all over the world, and confounded their language. This resulted in the hundreds of different languages spoken throughout the world, and solves the mystery of how the Americas and other remote regions of the world were populated. However, the dream and purpose of Nimrod and his *Tower of Babel* did not die. Without a doubt, the city of Babylon was the *Mother of Harlots and Abominations of the Earth*. In conclusion, the **great city that ruled over the Kings of the Earth** was Babel. It will again rise as the city of Babylon, and it will be the seat of power for the future Antichrist. The *mystery* is how this apostate city will be rebuilt and rise to the greatest commercial center in the world. This *mystery* is not explained, but it will come to pass. This is exactly what John saw and recorded in Rev 17 & 18; why should we doubt it? We now again turn to the *beast* which carries the woman. Who or what is this *beast*?

> ***"And the beast that was, and is not, even he is the eighth, and is of the seven, and goeth into perdition. And the ten***

horns which thou sawest are ten kings, which have received no kingdom as yet; but receive power as kings one hour with the beast. These have one mind, and shall give their power and strength unto the beast. These shall make war with the Lamb, and the Lamb shall overcome them: for he is Lord of lords, and King of kings: and they that are with him are called, and chosen, and faithful." Rev 17:11-15

Here we are given some important information about this *beast*. Remember that the beast is twofold in nature. The beast is a *kingdom* and the beast is also a *king*. The kingdom is the ten-nation confederacy from which the pre-antichrist, great world leader, will emerge. He will overthrow three of the ten nations and assume a dictatorship over the entire political military and economic system. Daniel saw this beast as

"dreadful and terrible, exceedingly strong beast. It had huge iron teeth (military power); it was devouring, breaking in pieces and trampling the residue with its feet. It was different from all the beasts that were before it, and it had ten horns" Daniel 7:7

"I (Daniel) was considering the (10) horns, and there was another horn, a little one, coming up among them, before whom three of the first horns were plucked out by the roots." Daniel 7:8

Daniel **wished to know the truth of the beast,** *and of the ten* **horns that were on his head, and about the other horn (little horn) which came up, before which three fell** (Dan 7:19-20). Daniel observed the same horn **making war with the saints, and prevailing against them** (Daniel 7:21).

"Thus he said, the fourth beast shall be the fourth kingdom upon earth, which shall be diverse from all kingdoms, and shall devour the whole earth, and shall tread it down, and break it in pieces. And the ten horns out of this kingdom are ten kings that shall arise: and another shall rise after them; and he shall be diverse from the first, and he shall subdue

> *three kings. And he shall speak great words against the most High, and shall wear out the saints of the most High, and think to change times and laws: and they shall be given into his hand until a time and times and the dividing of time."*
> Daniel 7:23-25

By comparing scripture to scripture, there should be no doubt that the beast that carries the woman is the antichrist and his empire. From Daniel 23-27 there can also be no doubt as to how this kingdom will end. Christ will return and completely destroy the antichrist and his empire.

> *"But the judgment shall sit, and they shall take away his dominion, to consume and to destroy it unto the end. And the kingdom and dominion, and the greatness of the kingdom under the whole heaven, shall be given to the people of the saints of the most High, whose kingdom is an everlasting kingdom, and all dominions shall serve and obey him."* Daniel 7:26-27

However, there is another passage that must be considered

> *"The beast that thou sawest was, and is not; and shall ascend out of the bottomless pit, and go into perdition: and they that dwell on the earth shall wonder, whose names were not written in the book of life from the foundation of the world, when they behold the beast that was, and is not, and yet is."* Rev 17:11

This passage cannot be applied to the antichrist. The beast is said to **ascend out of the bottomless pit**. The bottomless pit is a subterranean chamber reserved for the imprisonment of particularly bad angels. The fallen angels that cohabitated with man (Gen 6:1-6) are confined there (Jude 1:6). The demon locusts of Rev 9:2-3 will be released from the pit to torment men, and a powerful demonic angel called *Abaddon* will emerge from there (Rev 9:11). But how can a *kingdom* ascend out of the *pit* and go into *perdition*? Clearly this cannot happen. As this *beast* is studied carefully, it becomes clear that the entire vision is symbolic of the nature and operation of the antichrist. The beast is *a person*; the beast is *an empire* and the beast is *a religious system*. But even beyond those three characterizations, the actual antichrist is a revived great world leader who was **wounded by the sword and lived** (Rev 13:14). After being *mortally wounded* (Rev 13:3), a demonic *prince* (Dan 10:13) will be released out of the bottomless pit (Rev 9:1) and take over the mind and body of the world ruler, just as Judas was taken over when he betrayed Christ. When John records that **the beast that you saw was, and is not and will ascend out of the bottomless pit** (Rev 17:8), it is in reference to the demonic prince that inhabits the antichrist's body. In a real sense, the antichrist is transformed into a *demonic beast*. He receives his power from Satan. (Rev 13:5-7). At the end of his reign his fate is predetermined; he will be cast into the *lake of burning fire*.

> *"And I saw the beast, and the kings of the earth, and their armies, gathered together to make war against him that sat on the horse, and against his army. And the beast was taken, and with him the false prophet that wrought miracles before him, with which he deceived them that had received the mark of the beast, and them that worshipped his image. These both were cast alive into a lake of fire burning with brimstone."*   Rev 19:19-20

Rev 17:12 provides us with the approximate time that this beast will begin to dominate the world.

> *"And the ten horns which thou sawest are ten kings, which have received no kingdom as yet; but receive power as kings one hour with the beast."*   Rev 17:12

In Rev 12: 3 John observed **war in the heavens**. The result of this Great War was that **Satan and all his angels were cast down to the earth** (Rev 12: 9). When Satan first appears in Rev 12:3, he is shown with **ten horns, and seven diadems (crowns) on his heads**. These 10 horns are of course 10 kings and 10 kingdoms, so at that time each of the 10 nations existed and each had a king. In Rev 17: 12, these 10 kings have **received no kingdom as** *yet*, so this was before Satan and his angels were cast to the earth. These 10 nations existed as political and possibly economic partners; after the antichrist unites these 10 nations into one political, social, economic and military empire they will *receive this kingdom*. Evidently, the *mystery of iniquity* was already in full swing and the one-world apostate religion had already begun to form. The truth is that the world today is ready for such a religion. Any religion that will allow adultery, homosexual ministers, drug use and sinful practices while guaranteeing eternal salvation will be widely accepted. These churches will learn too late what the Holy Scriptures say about these practices. Timothy was very specific about the state of religion in the end times.

> *"This know also, that in the last days perilous times shall come. For men shall be lovers of their own selves, covetous, boasters, proud, blasphemers, disobedient to parents, unthankful, unholy, Without natural affection, trucebreakers, false accusers, incontinent, fierce, despisers of those that are good, Traitors, heady, highminded, lovers of pleasures more than lovers of God; Having a form of godliness, but denying the power thereof: from such turn away. For of this sort are they which creep into houses, and lead captive silly women laden with sins, led away with divers lusts, Ever learning, and never able to come to the knowledge of the truth."* II Timothy 3:1-7

> *"For the time will come when they will not endure sound doctrine; but after their own lusts shall they heap to themselves teachers, having itching ears; And they shall turn away their ears from the truth, and shall be turned unto fables."* II Timothy 4:3-4

Returning to the vision which John saw, recall that the Harlot rides upon a beast which we have now fully characterized. The beast supports both the *false prophet* and the one-world *religious system*. What is the fate of the Harlot, which represents the false religious system of the beast?

> *"And the ten horns which thou sawest upon the beast, these shall hate the whore, and shall make her desolate and naked, and shall eat her flesh, and burn her with fire. For God hath put in their hearts to fulfil his will, and to agree, and give their kingdom unto the beast, until the words of God shall be fulfilled."* Rev 17:18

The *beast* upon which this woman rides is the antichrist, who is totally controlled by Satan; his system is composed of all of the strength, persecution and personalities of all the seven kingdoms which preceded it. This person, with his 10-nation confederacy, his commercial system and his false religion will dominate the entire world. The religious system which his minion the *false prophet* (Rev 13:1) initiates and enforces is represented in its entirety by the *woman arrayed in purple and scarlet* who sits astride the beast. In Rev 17:18 we are shown an incredible prophecy. The *10 horns* which represent the countries in the antichrist's final *eighth kingdom* will *hate the whore*! Not only will they hate the woman (*her religious system*) they will *make her desolate*. They figuratively, and possibly literally, will *eat her flesh* and *burn her with fire*. This is all in accord with the wishes of the *beast*. This is not logical, but it does not need to be. This is something that God will cause to happen. The harlot is initially supported by the protection and motives of the antichrist, but according to God's eternal plan, Satan will not be able to stand anything worshipped in body or spirit but him. So he will turn upon this *woman* and totally destroy her *religious system*. He will then demand that he alone be worshipped. This is the ultimate fulfillment of Satan's original rebellion before God. Sometime long before God created Adam and Eve, Satan rebelled against God intending to either replace Him or establish his own reign in the third heavens. It is almost unbelievable, but 1/3 of all the angels followed Satan in this rebellion (Rev 12:3-4). In a battle which is not described in the bible, Satan and his angels fought against God and lost. At that time, he (Satan) and all of his followers (angels) were expelled from heaven and God's presence.

> *"How art thou fallen from heaven, O Lucifer, son of the morning! how art thou cut down to the ground, which didst weaken the nations! For thou hast said in thine heart, I will ascend into heaven, I will exalt my throne above the stars of God: I will sit also upon the mount of the congregation, in the sides of the north: I will ascend above the heights of the clouds; I will be like the most High."* Isaiah 14:12-14

For some unknown reason, Satan was allowed continued access to God and he is there today condemning the saints.

> *"Now there was a day when the sons of God came to present themselves before the LORD, and Satan came also among them. And the LORD said unto Satan, Whence comest thou? Then Satan answered the LORD, and said, From going to and fro in the earth, and from walking up and down in it."*
> Job 1:6-7

In this remarkable passage, the *Sons of God* are the *good angels* who did not rebel against God. It is also revealed that Satan is allowed to address God even now, and that he roams over all of the earth seeking to destroy all those who refuse to worship him.

> *"Be sober, be vigilant; because your adversary the devil, as a roaring lion, walketh about, seeking whom he may devour:"* I Peter 5:8

It is very interesting that while Satan is directing the antichrist to destroy the worldwide religious system that he has created by his *false prophet*, his influence is so great that the system is actually destroyed not supernaturally, but by the 10 nation confederacy.

> *"The waters which thou sawest, where the whore (the false religious system) sitteth, are peoples, and multitudes, and nations, and tongues. And the ten horns (the 10 nation confederacy of the antichrist) which thou sawest upon the beast, these shall hate the whore, and shall make her desolate and naked, and shall eat her flesh, and burn her with fire (destroy the*

*religious system). **For God hath put in their hearts to fulfil his will, and to agree, and give their kingdom unto the beast (the antichrist), until the words of God shall be fulfilled.*"* Rev 17:15-17

How this will happen we do not know, but it will. Exactly when this will happen is not revealed either, but in the context of the antichrist's reign, it must be very near the end of the last 1260 days of his reign. After this happens, the rebuilt city of Babylon in the plains of Shinar will still remain. However, God himself will destroy this city, as we will see in Chapter 22.

Thoughts and Things......

Chapter 22

Commercial Babylon

The apostle John has just seen a woman clothed in *purple and scarlet* sitting astride a *beast* with seven heads and 10 horns. The woman represents the religious system which is created to force all people to worship the beast out of the sea, who is Satan incarnate in the form of the Antichrist. John has watched with *great amazement* as the woman was described. In Rev 18:1-25, John is now shown a vision concerning the rise and fall of a great city. It is called the **Great city of Babylon** (Rev 18:10). The city is a center of commercial and economic wealth (Rev 18:12-13), but she will become **desolate** (Rev 18:19), and a **habitation for foul creatures and unclean birds** (Rev 18:2). The vision is presented in three parts: (1) an angelic pronouncement of judgment (Rev 18:1-3), (2) predictions from heaven that Babylon is sure to fall (Rev 18:4-24), and (3) voices heard in heaven which praise God for executing judgment on this wicked city. (Rev 19:1-3)

> *"And after these things I saw another angel come down from heaven, having great power; and the earth was lightened with his glory. And he cried mightily with a strong voice, saying, Babylon the great is fallen, is fallen, and is become the habitation of devils, and the hold of every foul spirit, and a cage of every unclean and hateful bird. For all nations have drunk of the wine of the wrath of her fornication, and the kings of the earth have committed fornication with her, and the merchants of the earth are waxed rich through the abundance of her delicacies. And I heard another voice from heaven, saying, Come out of her, my people, that ye be not partakers of her sins, and that ye receive not of her plagues. For her sins have reached unto heaven, and God hath remembered her iniquities. Reward her even as she rewarded you, and double unto her double according to her works: in the cup which she hath filled fill to her double. How much she hath glorified herself, and*

lived deliciously, so much torment and sorrow give her: for she saith in her heart, I sit a queen, and am no widow, and shall see no sorrow. Therefore shall her plagues come in one day, death, and mourning, and famine; and she shall be utterly burned with fire: for strong is the Lord God who judgeth her. And the kings of the earth, who have committed fornication and lived deliciously with her, shall bewail her, and lament for her, when they shall see the smoke of her burning, standing afar off for the fear of her torment, saying, Alas, alas, that great city Babylon, that mighty city! for in one hour is thy judgment come. And the merchants of the earth shall weep and mourn over her; for no man buyeth their merchandise any more: The merchandise of gold, and silver, and precious stones, and of pearls, and fine linen, and purple, and silk, and scarlet, and all thyine wood, and all manner vessels of ivory, and all manner vessels of most precious wood, and of brass, and iron, and marble, And cinnamon, and odours, and ointments, and frankincense, and wine, and oil, and fine flour, and wheat, and beasts, and sheep, and horses, and chariots, and slaves, and souls of men. And the fruits that thy soul lusted after are departed from thee, and all things which were dainty and goodly are departed from thee, and thou shalt find them no more at all. The merchants of these things, which were made rich by her, shall stand afar off for the fear of her torment, weeping and wailing, And saying, Alas, alas, that great city, that was clothed in fine linen, and purple, and scarlet, and decked with gold, and precious stones, and pearls! For in one hour so great riches is come to nought. And every shipmaster, and all the company in ships, and sailors, and as many as trade by sea, stood afar off, And cried when they saw the smoke of her burning, saying, What city is like unto this great city! And they cast dust on their heads, and cried, weeping and wailing, saying, Alas, alas, that great city, wherein were made rich all that had ships in the sea by reason of her costliness! for in one hour is she made desolate. Rejoice over her, thou heaven, and ye holy apostles and prophets; for God hath avenged you on her. And a mighty angel took up a stone like a great millstone, and cast it into the sea, saying, Thus with violence shall that great city Babylon be thrown down, and shall be found no more at all. And the voice of harpers, and musicians, and of pipers, and trumpeters, shall be heard no more at all in thee; and no craftsman, of whatsoever craft he be, shall be found any more in thee; and the sound of a millstone shall be heard no more at all in thee; And the light of a candle shall shine no more at all in thee; and the voice of the bridegroom and of the bride shall be heard no more at all in thee: for thy merchants were the great men of the earth; for by thy sorceries were all nations deceived. And in her was found the blood of prophets, and of saints, and of all that were slain upon the earth."

Rev 18:1-24

"And after these things I heard a great voice of much people in heaven, saying, Alleluia; Salvation, and glory, and honour, and power, unto the Lord our God: For true and righteous are his judgments: for he hath judged the great whore, which did corrupt the earth with her fornication, and hath avenged the blood of his servants at her hand. And again they said, Alleluia. And her smoke rose up for ever and ever."

Rev 19:1-3

The scene which John now sees is launched by **another angel**. This is not an ordinary angel; it must be an archangel of the same rank and position of Gabriel and Michael. This angelic being speaks with a **strong voice**, has **great power.** The message which this angel brings is to pronounce that Babylon the Great has fallen. Babylon is clearly identified as a **mighty city**, but is described in terms as if it was alive and a beautiful wicked woman.

The fall of this great city called Babylon has already been predicted in Rev 14:8. The message of Babylon's destruction is an *angel* that *illuminates the earth with His glory*. We are reminded of when Ezekiel saw an image of God that **caused the earth to shine with his glory** (Ez. 43:2-5). This is an angelic being of the highest rank. This angel is not the agent of destruction himself, but is the source of a proclamation that *Babylon the Great is fallen*. There is no doubt that this Babylon is the same as that city referred to by the woman in Rev 17:18 which was **that great city which reigns over the kings of the earth**. The *great city* is called Babylon and there are 356 references to a city by that name in the Old Testament, and 12 times in the New Testament. We have already established that the Old Testament City of Babylon arose from the ashes of Babel. It is likely that this city of Babylon will arise in the same geographical location. In the book of Revelation, the city is identified as Babylon six times in five different places (Rev 14:8, 16:19, 17:5, 18:10 and 18:25). Biblical non-literalists often claim that *Babylon* is just a synonym for Rome, and cites I Peter 5:13 as proof. We will again state that our God is not afraid to call this city *Babylon*, and neither was the apostle John. If the Revelation record actually meant Rome or any other city, then that name would have been used.

It is clear that there will be a great economic and commercial city arise in the end times, and that city will serve as a seat of influence and power for the antichrist; it will dominate the world economic system. All the merchants of the earth will become rich through the abundance of her luxury: and in the fullness of time God will destroy that great city (Rev 18:8, 10, 18). The prophet Isaiah prophesied the destruction of this city long ago.

> ***"And Babylon, the glory of kingdoms, the beauty of the Chaldees' excellency, shall be as when God overthrew Sodom and Gomorrah. It shall never be inhabited, neither shall it be dwelt in from generation to generation: neither shall the Arabian pitch tent there; neither shall the shepherds make their fold there. But wild beasts of the desert shall lie there; and their houses shall be full of doleful creatures; and owls shall dwell there, and satyrs shall dance there. And the wild beasts of the islands shall cry in their desolate houses, and dragons in their pleasant palaces: and her time is near to come, and her days shall not be prolonged."***   Isaiah 13:19-22

Many expositors maintain that this prophecy was fulfilled long ago when Babylon was completely destroyed. But Babylon has never vanished. Even today, there is a town of about 10,000 people on or near the site. Before his demise, Sadaam Hussein had even rebuilt some of the ancient city. Although Babylon is now almost deserted, the prophecies of Isaiah have never been completely fulfilled: ***Only wild beasts shall lie there, owls and creatures; it shall never be inhabited neither shall it be dwelt in from generation to generation.*** Its destruction will be as when God overthrew *Sodom and Gomorrah*. Sodom and Gomorrah was destroyed so fast that Lot and his family were not even out of sight when total destruction occurred. The devastation was so complete, that only in recent years have archeologists found the site. Further, Isaiah without a doubt affirms that this same manner of destruction will fall upon Babylon in the end times.

> *"Howl ye; for the day of the LORD is at hand; it shall come as a destruction from the Almighty….. Behold, the day of the LORD cometh, cruel both with wrath and fierce anger, to lay the land desolate: and he shall destroy the sinners thereof out of it. For the stars of heaven and the constellations thereof shall not give their light: the sun shall be darkened in his going forth, and the moon shall not cause her light to shine. And I will punish the world for their evil, and the wicked for their iniquity; and I will cause the arrogancy of the proud to cease, and will lay low the haughtiness of the terrible."*   Isaiah 13:6, 9-10

If you will read all of Isaiah 13, it should be clear that the fall of Babylon will be swift and complete, just after the seventh bowl is poured out. If we compare this passage to Rev 16:19, it is clear that the city of Babylon will fall just before the second advent of Christ. Although this passage does not specifically identify the city of Babylon, there is one other passage in the Old Testament which speaks to an end-time city called Babylon.

The fifth chapter of Zechariah has a curious and previously obscure prophecy. The book of Zechariah is largely devoted to end-time prophecies, and like the book of Revelation it is full of symbolism.

> *"Then the angel that talked with me went forth, and said unto me, Lift up now thine eyes, and see what is this that goeth forth. And I said, What is it? And he said, This is an ephah that goeth forth. He said moreover, This is their resemblance through all the earth. And, behold, there was lifted up a talent of lead: and this is a woman that sitteth in the midst of the ephah. And he said, This is wickedness. And he cast it into the midst of the ephah; and he cast the weight of lead upon the mouth thereof. Then lifted I up mine eyes, and looked, and, behold, there came out two women, and the wind was in their wings; for they had wings like the wings of a stork: and they lifted up the ephah between the earth and the heaven. Then said I to the angel that talked with me, Whither do these bear the ephah? And he said unto me, To build it an house in the land of Shinar: and it shall be established, and set there upon her own base."*
>   Zechariah 5:4-11

An angel came to Zechariah and showed him a *scroll* which we are told is **the curse which goeth forth over the whole earth"** (Zach. 5:3). He sees a *woman* sitting in the midst of an ***ephah***. An angel tells Zechariah that ***this is wickedness***. There is a **weight of lead** which is temporarily holding back the wickedness. Suddenly two more women appear and they lift up the wickedness and transport it to the Land of Shinar. This is Mesopotamia, and the land of Shinar is where the ancient city of Babylon once stood. (Gen 10:10). This fact has never been disputed among biblical scholars or archeologists. Zechariah then asks the angel to explain where the ephah of wickedness is being taken and why. The answer is unmistakable: ***To build a house in the Land of Shinar: it shall be established.*** There you have it! As far as Zechariah is concerned, a *house* or a *city* will be built in the Land of Shinar (Gen 11:2). We propose that this city is the end time commercial city called Babylon. This rebuilt city of Babylon will house all forms of wickedness. The evil woman who is sealed in the ephah is the same woman as that described in Revelation Chapter 21. This woman is shown in great splendor and wealth.

> *"The woman was arrayed in purple and scarlet, and adorned with gold and precious stones and pearls, having in her hand a golden cup full of abominations and the filthiness of her fornications."*   Rev 17:4

The location of her operations appears to be the rebuilt city of Babylon. If this woman represents the false religious system of Revelation Chapter 17, then the *house* in which she resides certainly fits all the requirements of the city called *Babylon* in Rev 17:18. This woman arrayed in purple and scarlet is given a name which is written on her forehead:

> *"Mystery, Babylon the Great,*
> *The Mother of Harlots*
> *And of the Abominations*
> *Of the Earth"*

Here is another *mystery* which is not fully revealed in the Revelation record. The *mystery* of the woman is how she manages to seduce the world into idolatry, fornication and adultery: The *mystery* is how people can be completely controlled and dominated by the wealth of this world: The *mystery* is why God has waited so long to finally destroy this woman and reclaim this earth through his Son, Jesus Christ. But vindication, judgment and justice are coming soon.

> *"After these things* (the fall of religious and commercial Babylon) *I heard a loud voice of a great multitude in heaven* (Rev 7:9 and Rev 19:1*), saying "Alleluia! Salvation and glory and honor and power to the Lord our God! For true and righteous are His judgments, because He hath judged the great Harlot who corrupted the earth with her fornication; and He has avenged on her the blood of His servants shed by her."*   Rev 19:1-2

At last the prayers of the martyred saints crying out for vengeance beneath the throne of God are answered! (Rev 6:9) This all perfectly fits the visions shown to John in Rev 17-18. Babylon is going to be rebuilt and will serve as the commercial center of the antichrist's kingdom. It is not clearly stated, but it seems that this city will also serve as the seat of power for the false prophet and his religious system. The woman is typed by two Babylons: one is religious and one is commercial. It is interesting to note that just before the Second Advent of Christ, we were told that the sixth bowl is poured out *on the great river Euphrates, and its water was dried up, so that the way of the kings from the east might be prepared* (Rev 16:14). Prepared for what and why? This obscure passage reveals that the ground forces of the antichrist will cross the dried up Euphrates River from the east and advance toward Jerusalem for the final battle of Armageddon. With modern equipment, the advance will be swift. Now another *mystery* is solved! They (the antichrist and his armies) are coming from the East of the River Euphrates which geographically points to the *land of Shinar*; which is where the ephah of Zach 5:5-11 will stand. It is likely that the city is destroyed shortly after the armies depart.

Wealth, gold, silver and social status have become the goals of today's people in this world. It is little wonder that *another voice from heaven* cries out a warning; *Come out of her, my people, lest you share in her sins* (Rev 18:4). Just like the Tower of Babel; economic, social and many religious systems have been elevated to an ungodly position. The *"true gospel"* and the life of following after Christ have been sacrificed to the needs and wants of this evil world. *For her sins have reached to heaven and God has remembered her iniquities* (Rev 18:5). Her cup is full of *abominations and the filthiness of her fornication* (Rev 17:4, Rev 18:7). In the ruins of Babel and in the long ago shadows of the tower that Nimrod build long ago, we can still hear the cries of those who have suffered and died over all the years.

> *"And in her was found the blood of prophets, and of saints, and of all that were slain upon the earth."* Rev 18:24

The phrase *in her* is not directed to the rebuilt city of Babylon, but to the progeny of Nimrod's city of Babylon and the blood that has been spilled down through the ages in the name of religious systems. The near extinction of the Peruvian Empire; the slaughter of innocent people in the Mayan Empire; the Crusades of the 17th century; and the eradication of over six million Jews by Hitler are testimonies to the destructive forces of false religious practices. But she will reap what she has sown. Christ warned his sheep:

> *"But lay up for yourselves treasures in heaven, where neither moth nor rust doth corrupt, and where thieves do not break through nor steal."*   Matthew 6:20

This city must be larger and more powerful than any that has ever existed. There will be great riches there beyond belief.

> *"The merchandise of gold, and silver, and precious stones, and of pearls, and fine linen, and purple, and silk, and scarlet, and all thyine wood, and all manner vessels of ivory, and all manner vessels of most precious wood, and of brass, and iron, and marble; And cinnamon, and odours, and ointments, and frankincense, and wine, and oil, and fine flour, and wheat, and beasts, and sheep, and horses, and chariots, and slaves, and souls of men. And the fruits that thy soul lusted after are departed from thee, and all things which were dainty and goodly are departed from thee, and thou shalt find them no more at all. …..that great city, that was clothed in fine linen, and purple, and scarlet, and decked with gold, and precious stones, and pearls!"*
>   Rev 18:12-14, 16

It is clear that this great city will be completely destroyed, and it will be sudden.

> *"Alas, alas, that great city Babylon, that mighty city! for in one hour is thy judgment come"*   Rev 18:10

> *"for in one hour is she made desolate.*   Rev 18:19

"For in one hour so great riches is come to nought."
    Rev 18:17

The destruction will not only be swift but complete.

"And the fruits that thy soul lusted after are departed from thee, and all things which were dainty and goodly are departed from thee, and thou shalt find them no more at all."   Rev 18:14

The city will be destroyed by a violent, supernatural event.

"Therefore shall her plagues come in one day, death, and mourning, and famine; and she shall be utterly burned with fire: for strong is the Lord God who judgeth her."
    Rev 18:8

"And a mighty angel took up a stone like a great millstone, and cast it into the sea, saying, Thus with violence shall that great city Babylon be thrown down, and shall be found no more at all. And the voice of harpers, and musicians, and of pipers, and trumpeters, shall be heard no more at all in thee; and no craftsman, of whatsoever craft he be, shall be found any more in thee; and the sound of a millstone shall be heard no more at all in thee; And the light of a candle shall shine no more at all in thee; and the voice of the bridegroom and of the bride shall be heard no more at all in thee: for thy merchants were the great men of the earth; for by thy sorceries were all nations deceived."
    Rev 18:21-23

The agent of destruction has been long debated. We are told that *a mighty angel took up a stone like a great millstone and cast it into the sea*. It appears that this is a celestial object similar to an asteroid which is called out of the heavens by this mighty angel and caused to strike the great city. This completely destroys everything in one moment of time. The reaction of the entire world to this total destruction is predictable: **the Kings of the earth lament and weep for her** (Rev 18:9). They cry out; **alas,**

alas (Rev 18:10), and **mourn** (Rev 18:11). The merchantmen of the world that make their living from seafaring vessels will *stand at a distance* (Rev 18: 15) and *cry out, What is like this great city?*

> *"And cried when they saw the smoke of her burning, saying, what city is like unto this great city! And they cast dust on their heads, and cried, weeping and wailing, saying, Alas, alas, that great city, wherein were made rich all that had ships in the sea by reason of her costliness!"*
> Rev 18:18-19

Oh, the corrupting influence of Satan and his false religious beliefs. The people of the earth stand and lament for the destruction of a wicked city, but when Christ was crucified the people cried out: *He is deserving of death. Then they spat in his face and beat Him* (Mat 26:66-67). The people of this world weep over losing their gold and silver, but never wept over our crucified Lord and Savior. Oh what tears this brings to our eyes, oh how we love Him. We, like the martyred saints of Rev 6:9 cry out, *how long O Lord? How Long !!!*

In stark contrast to the merchants of the world, there is great joy in heaven. The angelic hosts cry out:

> *"Rejoice over her, thou heaven, and ye holy apostles and prophets; for God hath avenged you on her."* Rev 18:20

The fall of a great end-time commercial city has been described in detail, a result of the ego and purpose of the Antichrist to be worshipped as God, and have no other religious competition. In the end, Satan will not be able to tolerate any religious system; he and he alone must be worshipped. The followers of this system are completely under the power of Satan and his minion the antichrist; they blindly follow him. But, at the height of his religious and commercial power Christ will completely and utterly destroy his rebuilt city of Babylon. In fury and under a false hope of still ruling over the world, he unwittingly plans an all-out attack and destruction of Jerusalem. He will think that this is his idea, but it is not. The time has come for the final showdown, the *battle of Armageddon*.

Thoughts and Things......

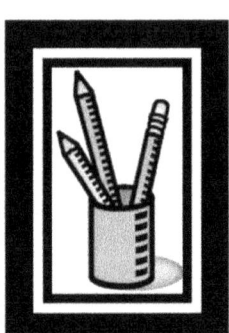

Chapter 23

Rapture of the Saints on Rosh Hashanah

Throughout this book we have stressed the close connection between the Seven Feasts of Israel and the First and Second Coming of our Lord Jesus Christ. In this chapter we will summarize our belief that the rapture and the resurrection of the righteous dead will occur as the seventh trumpet is blown, on Tishri 1, the Feast of Rosh Hashanah. The modern Jewish calendar observes Rosh Hashanah over a two day period: Tishri 1 – Tishri 2, but there is no scriptural authority or license for a two-day feast. God ordained only Tishri 1. The word Rosh means *head* and Hashanah means *year*. The Feast of Rosh Hashanah is commonly known as the *Feast of Trumpets*, and we will usually use that identification in our discussion. In Jewish writings the Feast of Trumpets has many themes and secular titles. A list of names that particularly relate to this discussion are:

- Yom Turah............. The Day of an Awakening Blast
- Yom ha-Dim........... The Day of Judgment
- Ha Melech.............. The Coronation of the Messiah
- Yom ha-Zikkaron......The Day of Remembrance
- Kiddushin...............The Wedding Day

Jewish Rabbinical teaching holds that several important things happened on the Feast of Trumpets. Tradition holds that Abraham was born on Tishri 1; the world was created on Tishri 1; the law was read on Tishri 1; and on some future Feast of Trumpets their long-awaited Messiah will return to restore all things. Jewish Rabbinical writings also record that on a future Tishri1, the dead will be resurrected and receive new bodies like those of Adam and Eve in the Garden of Eden. It is also commonly believed that on the final feast day of Rosh Hashanah a special *Shofar* horn will be sounded to usher in a new age.

Hebrew tradition venerates the faith and obedience of Abraham when God instructed him to go up to a place where the Dome of the Rock now stands to sacrifice his son of promise, Isaac. Just as Abraham was about to kill his son, God stayed his hand and provided a ram caught in a thicket as a substutionary sacrifice. The ram was then sacrificed as a burnt offering, and was totally consumed except for the two ram's horns. These two horns of the sacrificial ram were called *holy shofars*, and both were to play a significant role in God's eternal plan for mankind. One was blown on Mt. Sinai when Moses and the children of Israel received the law. Tradition says that the blast of this shofar was heard all over the world in all known languages. The second ram's horn will be blown at the last Feast of Trumpets, and it too will be heard all over the world. In previous discussions we have identified the blowing of this *shofar* with the seventh trumpet in the book of Revelation, and with the sounding of a *trumpet* that Paul called a *mystery*.

> **"For this we say unto you by the word of the Lord, that we which are alive and remain the coming of the Lord shall not prevent (precede) them which are asleep. For the lord Himself shall descend from heaven with a shout, with the voice of the archangel, and with the trump of God: and the dead in Christ will rise first: Then we which are alive and remain shall be caught up together with them in the clouds, to meet the Lord in the air: and so shall we ever be with the Lord."** I Thessalonians 4:15-17.

A natural question to ask is *what trump*? In his letter to the Corinthians, Paul also revealed this mystery and provided other details.

> **"Behold, I shew you a mystery; we shall not all sleep, but we shall all be changed, in a moment, at the twinkling of an eye, at the last trump: for the trumpet shall sound, and the dead shall be raised incorruptible, and we shall all be changed. For this corruptible must put on incruption, and this mortal must put on immortality."** I Cor 15:51-53

Note that in his letter to the Thessalonians, Paul identified a sign of this event as the *trump of God*. In his letter to the Corinthians he further explained that this was the *last trump*. If there is a *last trump* then there must be others that precede it. In Rev 11, John records something revealed to him by the 24 elders who stand before the throne of God.

> *"The nations were angry, and your wrath has come. And the time of the dead that they should be judged, And that You should reward Your servants the prophets and the saints, and those who fear Your name, small and great, and should destroy those who destroy the earth."* Rev 11:18

There are several clues in Rev 11:18 that equate this event beyond any reasonable doubt with the rapture described by Paul in the previous passages.

- ➤ The **Wrath of God has come**. This is clearly identified with the seven bowl judgments in Rev 15:1,15:7 and 16:1. The seventh trumpet immediately precedes the Wrath of God (the seven bowl judgments), which in turn precedes the Battle of Armageddon.
- ➤ The **nations were angry**. After the 7th trumpet has sounded and people have disappeared everywhere, one would think that the people who follow Satan would bow down and seek mercy; but just the opposite is true. *And they blasphemed the God of heaven because of their pains and sores, and did not repent of their deeds* (Rev 16:11).
- ➤ It is **time to judge the dead**. The time to judge the dead is only at the Bema Seat Judgment and at the Great White Throne Judgment. In context, this is the Bema Seat Judgment: which will be held immediately following the rapture of the church. The Bema Seat Judgment closely follows the Feast of Trumpets and is before the throne of God. The Great white Throne Judgment occurs at the end of the Millennial Kingdom and is for unbelievers.
- ➤ It is **time for rewards**. Note those who are rewarded: **Prophets and saints who fear His name**. After the

rapture occurs, saints and prophets who are dead or alive will be rewarded for their deeds.
- It is time to ***destroy those who would destroy the earth***. This cannot speak of any event but the great battle of Armageddon.

If any student of prophecy is reading God's word without a preconceived notion or an agenda to prove, there can be no doubt that the rapture that Paul reveals as a *mystery,* and the words which John records in Revelation 18:11, both converge to the same point in time…… the rapture of the saints at the sounding of the seventh trumpet and the rewards for the saints.. Everything is also in complete harmony with ancient Jewish Messianic expectations, although they (the Jews) do not recognize it.

When the rapture occurs at the seventh trumpet, the ***dead In Christ will rise first***, and then those ***which are alive and remain*** will be caught up to meet Christ in the air. With the exception of the 144,000 who have been sealed to escape death and enter the millennial kingdom, and the remnant of the Jerusalem Campaign (see Chapter 26) who have fled to Petra, the only people left on the earth are unbelievers. In the Olivet Discourse Jesus taught that: **And this gospel of the kingdom will be preached to all the world as a witness to all the nations, and then the end will come** (Mat 24:14). After the destruction of the city called Babylon (Rev 14:8) and just prior to the rapture of the church, an angel is sent to preach the gospel throughout the world.

> *"Then I (John) saw another angel flying in the midst of heaven, having the everlasting gospel to preach to those who dwell on the earth—to every nation, tribe, tongue and people."*   Rev 14:6

When the rapture does occur, it will come as a complete surprise to all unbelievers. They will be doing what they have always done.

> *"For as in the days before the flood, they were eating and drinking, marrying and giving in marriage, until the day*

that Noah entered the ark. And did not know until the flood came and took them all away, so also will the coming of the Son of Man be." Rev 24: 39.

This is a warning by Christ to be *watchful*. There is nothing wrong with marrying and eating; Christ is simply saying that it will be a sudden and unexpected event. It is interesting that Christ immediately followed this warning with a glimpse into how it will be.

"Then two men will be in the field: one will be taken and the other left. Two women will be grinding at the mill: one will be taken and the other left." Rev 24: 40-41

Some may possibly realize what has happened, but very few; after the seventh trumpet is blown it is too late to be included in the Bride of Christ (Chapter 24).

Finally, we need to address the most commonly-held belief of when the rapture of the saints will occur, and that is *before* the seven seals are broken. This theology is based entirely upon three platforms: (1) the church is not to go through the wrath of God, (2) the wrath of God starts with the seven seals, and (3) the tribulation period is composed of two equal parts of 3.5 years duration. During the first 3.5 years the seals are broken, and during the last 3.5 years the seven trumpet judgments and the seven bowl judgments occur. We have previously addressed all of these assumptions and shown them to be questionable. This is called a pre-tribulation rapture, and is major part of modern dispensational teaching. The passage which supposedly supports this theology is Rev 4:1.

"After these things I looked, and behold, a door standing open in heaven. And the first voice which I heard was like a trumpet speaking with me, saying "Come up here, and I will show you things which must take place after this."
Rev 4:1

All pre-tribulation theologians and teachers point to this verse as representing the rapture of the church as revealed by Paul. In Rev 1 John is told to: **Write the things which thou hast seen, and the things which are, and the things which shall be hereafter** (Rev 1:19). *The things which are* refer to the condition and evaluation of the seven churches in Asia. Rev 4 provides a rare glimpse of the heavenly throne room of God and His attendants. Rev 5 introduces the scroll written on both front and back, which will reveal the things which will happen after the tribulation period begins. The scroll also includes a description of the millennial kingdom and eternity to follow. Christ is given the scroll to reveal its contents. The *things which shall be hereafter* are the events which frame the tribulation period and the revelation record of Rev 6-Rev 22. To equate Rev 4:1 with the rapture of the church is stretching one's imagination to the limit. John, in the spirit, is being called into heaven to *see* the things which *shall be hereafter*. He sees an open door, and he is commanded to *come up here*.

John is not being bodily translated out of the earth. His body is still on Patmos, and he has been supernaturally called to heaven *in the Spirit* (Rev 4:2). The calling of John is through an *open door*. Nowhere in scripture is a door associated with the rapture of the saints to meet Christ in the air. The events recorded in Rev 4-5 all took place around 90 AD. There is not a verse of prophecy that relates to what is happening to the apostle John and the rapture of the saints. The following arguments support this position.

> - The apostle John is not meeting Christ in the air; he is being transported to the throne room of God, as Rev 4:2-11 attests.
> - He does not receive a new, incorruptible body; he returns to Patmos where he writes what he has seen. Historical records tell us that he was later released and died in Ephesus.
> - A voice commands John to *come up here*. At the rapture of the saints, all called forth will meet Christ in the air, not in heaven. The call will be with a *shout* and the *sound*

of a trump. The rapture will be accompanied by the blowing of a trumpet, not something that *sounds like a trumpet*.
- John hears someone speaking to him who is not identified, but who has a voice *like a trumpet*. This is not *the last trump* spoken of by Paul. In fact, it is not a trumpet at all! There is not the slightest indication of a trumpet being sounded which is calling John forth in Rev 4:1.
- The apostle Paul clearly teaches that at the rapture of the saints the **dead in Christ** will rise *first*, then those who are alive will follow. There is no indication whatsoever that the ascension of John in the spirit represents the dead in Christ.
- Pre-tribulation rapturists all claim that John is representing the entire body of Christ. There is no scriptural authority to assume this whatsoever. The assumption that Rev 4:1 corresponds to the rapture of the church and the resurrection of the saints from all ages is simply unfounded and has no basis in scripture.
- Finally, all who propose and persist in a pre-tribulation rapture will not discuss or even try to harmonize Rev 11:18 with Rev 4:1. That is because they cannot.
- If a pre-tribulation rapture does occur, it will be by chronological sequencing have to occur *shortly after* the *gap in time* which started in 30 AD. In God's time, He would see the 70th week of Daniel immediately following the termination of the 69th week of Daniel. Since the 69th week ended at Passover, the 70th week would begin during the Passover season. Since a seven-year period of tribulation would immediately follow a pre-tribulation rapture, it would by necessity *end* on or near the Feast of Passover. This scenario would negate any relationship to the last three feasts in the month of Tishri, which occurs six months after Nisan. Every feast of Israel was ordained by God to reflect upon historical events, but the main reason that God ordained the seven feasts was to show Israel the substance and reality of Jesus Christ. Christ had *appointments* to *be* at every feast. As we have shown, the

Feasts of Passover, Unleavened Bread, Firstfruits and the Feast of Weeks (Pentecost) were all fulfilled in every way when Christ was crucified and rose from the grave at His First Advent. The Feasts of Rosh Hashanah (Trumpets), Yom Kippur (Atonement) and Tabernacles (Booths) will all be fulfilled at the Second Advent of Christ.

➢ There is no indication whatsoever that Christ was involved in the ascension of John in Rev 4:1. He is not even seen by John until He receives the seven sealed scroll in Rev 5:6-7. In the rapture revealed by Paul, Christ will personally receive all unbelievers *in the air*, alive or dead

The last Feast of Trumpets will fulfill the rapture of the church and the resurrection of all the dead saints on Tishri 1 (September or October). The *last trump* or the second Ram's horn (Shofar) will be blown on that day, and Christ will call us to meet Him in the air with a *shout* from an archangel, possibly Gabriel. It is interesting that Jewish Messianic expectations are that at some future Rosh Hashanah the Shofar will be blown, and all of the dead patriarchs will be *awakened*. They will then be given resurrection bodies as those that Adam and Eve had in the Garden of Eden.

Paul refers to these dead bodies as Christians who are *asleep* (I Cor. 15:51). It is a scriptural New Covenant principle taught by Paul that the only dead raised at the **last trump** will be those who have accepted Christ as their Savior… Jews or Gentiles. Whether the dead in Christ will be awakened with a *shout* or by a *blast* of the second ram's horn or *shofar* is a moot point. The dead in Christ will be awakened at the *last trump* and be called to meet Christ in the air; then those who are alive and remain will also join Christ *in the air*. Paul reinforces this scriptural principle in his letter to the believers at Ephesus.

> **"Awake, you who are asleep, arise from the dead, and Christ will give you light."** Ephesians 5:14

On this day, we will all be redeemed from sin into everlasting righteousness. We have been sealed with the gift of the Holy Spirit until that day when our redemption is complete.

> *"And do not grieve the Holy Spirit of God, by whom you were sealed for the day of redemption."* Ephesians 4:31

On the last Feast of Trumpets, Jews also believe that the gates of heaven will be opened, so that the righteous may enter.

> *"In that day…. Open the gates, that the righteous nation which keeps the truth may enter in."* Isaiah 26:1-2

Summary

Both Jewish Messianic expectations and the New Testament are in harmony as to when the rapture of the church and the resurrection of the dead in Christ will occur. All scripture supports that this event will most likely occur at the sounding of the seventh trumpet as described by both Paul (I Cor. 15:51-53, I Thess. 4:15-17) and by John the revelator (Rev 11:18). Those who are in Christ when the seventh trumpet sounds will not have to go through the *Wrath of God*, which are the seven bowl judgments (Rev 15:7, Rev 16:1). The words of Jesus Christ in Mat 24:22 now make perfect sense:

> *"And unless those days be shortened, no flesh (the elect) would be saved; but for the sake those days will be shortened."* Matthew 24:22.

Once the righteous are taken out of the earth, the devastating seven bowl judgments of God's wrath (Rev 15:1, 16:1, 16:19) will be poured out upon all who remain. The Feast of Trumpets and the rapture will occur on Tishri 1, exactly 1250 days after Satan is cast out of heaven (Rev 12:7-9). The 1260-day tribulation period (last half of Daniel's 70th week) will be *cut short* for all *flesh* who have accepted Christ as their savior. The battle of Armageddon on the Feast of Yom Kippur (Tishri 10) will terminate the church age and begin the millennial kingdom. The bowl judgments between Tishri 1 and Tishri 10 were described in Chapters 10 and 11. It is now time for Christ to bodily return at His Second Advent and fight at the battle of Armageddon. However, before we discuss this great battle we will first look at the *Wedding of the Lamb* and the *Wedding Feast*.

Thoughts And Things……..

Chapter 24

The Bride of Christ Wedding of the Lamb & The Wedding Supper

Revelation 19:1-10 provides a bridge between the rapture of the church, the destruction of Babylon the Great and the Battle of Armageddon. An announcement now takes place that the Wedding of the Lamb has arrived. It is preceded by four *"hallelujah's"* (Alleluia's). The *first three* praise God for the destruction of that great city, Babylon the Great, and the religious system that worshipped the beast (Rev 19:1-4). The *fourth* praises God because the time has come for Him to rule and reign as a conquering King over all the earth (Rev 19:5-6). Following these four hallelujahs, an announcement is made that it is time for the *Marriage of the Lamb* (Rev 19:7-8). The final announcement concerns the *Marriage Supper of the Lamb* (Rev 9:9).

The First Three Halleluiahs: Praising God for the Destruction of Babylon

> *"And after these things I heard a great voice of much people in heaven, saying, Alleluia; Salvation, and glory, and honor, and power, unto the Lord our God: For true and righteous are his judgments: for he hath judged the great whore, which did corrupt the earth with her fornication, and hath avenged the blood of his servants at her hand. And again they said, Alleluia. And her smoke rose up forever and ever. And the four and twenty elders and the four beasts fell down and worshipped God that sat on the throne, saying, Amen; Alleluia."*   Rev 19:1-4

As Babylon fell, there was weeping and lamentations from the kings of the earth over her complete destruction (Rev 18:9-11), while in heaven there is rejoicing and praise to God (Rev 18:20).

The *three halleluiahs* in Rev 19:1-4 continue this heavenly praise and rejoicing. This celebration begins with a **hallelujah** from **much people**. This is obviously a unique and important scene that John sees. The Greek word translated *hallelujah* occurs only in Chapter 19 of all the New Testament. This great multitude is not identified, but a clue may be found in the phrase *much people*; it is essentially the same as a translation rendered **multitud**e in Revelation 7.

> *"After this I beheld, and, lo, a great multitude, which no man could number, of all nations, and kindreds, and people, and tongues, stood before the throne, and before the Lamb, clothed with white robes, and palms in their hands."*
> Rev 7:9

The praise of *much people* is undoubtedly led by angels as elsewhere (Rev 4:8. 4:11 and 5:12-14), but is likely that they are now joined by the resurrected and raptured saints who ascended at the seventh trumpet. This is chronologically correct, because sounding of the seventh trump initiated the rapture of the church and the resurrection of the righteous dead. This great multitude of saints has been sanctified and glorified, and now stand before the throne of God in their robes of white. This first hallelujah tells us why there is such enthusiasm and joy; it is because **salvation, power, honor, and glory** have finally come unto **the Lord our God.** The reference to *Lord our God* is to Jesus Christ, because in Rev 19:2 the object of this praise is because He has **avenged on her the blood of His servants shed by her**. It is He who through His sacrificial death on the cross offers salvation and glory to all who believe upon His name. It is His servants who have suffered and died down through the ages; and it is His servants that have been martyred over the last 3.5 years. His judgments are **righteous and true** .The first halleluiah celebrates God's final judgment on the harlot. Babylon has fallen and in a short time Satan and his followers will be completely destroyed at the Battle of Armageddon. The destruction of Babylon the Great in Rev 18, along with all of her unholy inhabitants, are also vindicated by the declaration that His judgments are *true and righteous*. God has always been in control of His creation, although we sometimes cannot see His eternal purpose or plan. The reason for all the destruction and death that fell on Babylon is that she has *corrupted the earth with her fornication*. Her fornication is not just physical adulterous behavior, but it is also *spiritual fornication*. Destruction of the harlot was spiritually completed by His sacrificial work on the cross of Calvary; we now have the promise of eventual victory over Satan and his earthly kingdom. God has never changed His hatred and condemnation of spiritual and physical adultery. The wording of Rev 19:2 is very similar to that recorded in II Kings 9:7 in which judgment was pronounced upon King Ahab for his adulterous union with Jezebel.

> *"And thou shalt smite the house of Ahab thy master, that I may avenge the blood of my servants the prophets, and the blood of all the servants of the LORD, at the hand of Jezebel. For the whole house of Ahab shall perish: and I will cut off from Ahab him that pisseth against the wall, and him that is shut up and left in Israel."* II Kings 9:7-8

It is interesting that in Rev 19:3 it is recorded that the *smoke* of Babylon will rise up *forever and ever*. This is the fulfillment of Rev 18:2 and a prophecy concerning Babylon by the prophet Jeremiah.

> *"And he cried mightily with a strong voice, saying, Babylon the great is fallen, is fallen, and is become the habitation of devils, and the hold of every foul spirit, and a cage of every unclean and hateful bird."* Rev 18:2

> *"Therefore the wild beasts of the desert with the wild beasts of the islands shall dwell there, and the owls shall dwell therein: and it shall be no more inhabited for ever; neither shall it be dwelt in from generation to generation."* Jer 50:39

The false religions of this world have finally been judged and found wanting. The apostate religions of the world will finally come to an end, and Christ alone will be worshipped as **King of**

Kings and Lord of Lords. David wrote of this over 3000 years ago.

> *"Thine, O LORD, is the greatness, and the power, and the glory, and the victory, and the majesty: for all that is in the heaven and in the earth is thine; thine is the kingdom, O LORD, and thou art exalted as head above all."*
> I Chronicles 29:11

Christ has finally avenged the *blood of His servants*, answering the pleas of the martyred saints which were seen under the throne of God in Rev 6:10: ***How long, O Lord, holy and true, dost thou not judge and avenge our blood on them that dwell on the earth?*** Now the praise reaches a mounting crescendo as the *24 elders and the four beasts* fall down before God and cry *Alleluia*. Another voice is now heard *from the throne*, saying: ***Praise our God, all ye his servants, and ye that fear him, both small and great.*** This voice is difficult to identify. It is not from God the father, because the phrase ***our God*** would be a reference to Himself; it is not from Jesus Christ because He would not refer to the Father as *our God*. In Rev 3:2 he addressed the Father as ***my God***. The declaration could have come from another high ranking angel such as that identified as a ***strong angel*** in Rev 5:2; or possibly from one of the 24 elders or the 4 living creatures who surround the throne of God (Rev 11:15-17). One solution is to attribute this voice to an *overcomer*. In the letter to Laodicea, the following promise was made to the overcomers:

> ***"To Him that overcometh will I grant to sit with me in my throne."*** Rev 3:21

One of these overcomers might have become overwhelmed with joy, and loudly proclaimed this spontaneous praise. We are best left to consider and note the various alternatives rather than venture an unsupported guess.

The Fourth Halleluiah: The King is about to Rule and Reign

> *"And a voice came out of the throne, saying, Praise our God, all ye his servants, and ye that fear him, both small and great. And I heard as it were the voice of a great multitude, and as the voice of many waters, and as the voice of mighty thunderings, saying, Alleluia: for the Lord God omnipotent reigneth."* Rev 19:5-6

The source of the fourth halleluiah is also hard to determine. It comes *out of the throne*. The voice does not come from within the throne, or necessarily from someone sitting on the throne, but likely from its context it comes from the direction of the throne. It could also possibly be one of the four living creatures or one of the 24 elders, but it is impossible to say. Whatever the source of the voice, it is authoritative. The voice commands *all His servants*, both *great and small* to worship Him. The antecedent to *him* is *God*, which we believe is God the Father. The qualification is *ye that fear Him*. As Christians, we are to fear God since He is without sin and will not tolerate any form of sin in His heavenly presence. Our fears are answered by His Son and our Savior, Jesus Christ. It is through him and by Him that we can stand in the presence of God.

> *"Let us therefore come boldly unto the throne of grace, that we may obtain mercy, and find grace to help in time of need."* Hebrews 4:16

The command is once again answered by a great multitude that we have tentatively identified as the raptured and resurrected saints who now stand before God's throne. This fourth alleluia is brought forth by the *great multitude*. However, they are evidently now joined by everyone and everything present. The familiar *thunderings* heard on two previous occasions (Rev 6: 10, 14) emerge from the throne room, and the sound is as *many waters*. Once the author stood beside Niagara Falls, and the sound was not only overwhelming, but it penetrated both body and mind. This must be how it sounded as this fourth *halleluiah* was proclaimed. This time it is qualified; *for the Lord God omnipotent reigneth.* Once again, the scriptures seem to confirm that our offered chronology in which the rapture and resurrection of all believers at the seventh trumpet seems to be verified by scripture. When the seventh trumpet sounds in Rev 11 it is immediately followed by the following declaration which completely fits the context of Rev 19:6.

> *"And the seventh angel sounded; and there were great voices in heaven, saying, the kingdoms of this world are become the kingdoms of our Lord, and of his Christ; and he shall reign for ever and ever."* Rev 11:15

Christ is now ready to fight the battle of Armageddon and then assume his earthly reign for 1000 years. The Age of Grace and Daniel's 70th week is about to end, and only the destruction of the antichrist, the false prophet, Satan and all of his followers is yet to be fulfilled. At the seventh trumpet, the body of Christ has been raptured to meet Christ in the air and the righteous dead have been raised. While the seven bowl judgments are being poured out upon the earth, events of enormous importance will take place in heaven. The saints of all ages who have longed for the glorious appearance of their Lord Jesus Christ have been either raised from the dead or translated to the throne of God, where they will be rewarded for their good deeds at the *Bema Seat Judgment*; they will be given new glorified, incorruptible bodies and robes of righteousness. The *Bride of Christ* has been made ready for the Wedding Ceremony of the Lamb.

The Marriage of the Lamb

> *"Let us be glad and rejoice, and give Him glory, for the marriage of the Lamb has come, and his wife has made herself ready. And to her it was granted to be arrayed in fine linen, clean and bright, for the fine linen is the righteous acts of the saints."* Rev 19:7-8

Christ has gathered to Himself a bride *without spot or wrinkle (Eph 5:27)*. The purity of the bride is not due to the perfection of the bride on this earth, for ***all have sinned and fallen short of the Glory of God*** (Rom 3:23). The righteousness of the saints has been imputed to all believers by Christ our redeemer. It is through Him that we attain a glorious state without spot or wrinkle. We now come to a declaration that the ***Marriage of the Lamb has come and the bride has made herself ready***.

In the Old Testament, *Israel* was portrayed as the *Bride of God*. She has forsaken her marriage vows and been unfaithful throughout the ages, but God will not abandon or forsake her for his *mercy endureth forever*. In the book of Hosea God declares:

> ***"I will bring her into the wilderness, and speak comfort to her... And it shall be, in that day, Says the Lord, that you will call me My Husband, and no longer call me My Master... I will betroth you to me forever."***
> Hosea 2:14,16,19

The Lord will call Israel His bride, and Jesus Christ will also have a bride. Paul revealed a *mystery* to the church at Ephesus that the Church is the bride of Christ.

> ***"Wives, submit yourselves unto your own husbands, as unto the Lord. For the husband is the head of the wife, even as Christ is the head of the church: and he is the saviour of the body. Therefore as the church is subject unto Christ, so let the wives be to their own husbands in every thing. Husbands, love your wives, even as Christ also loved the church, and gave himself for it; That he might sanctify and cleanse it with the washing of water by the word, that he might present it to himself a glorious church, not having spot, or wrinkle, or any such thing; but that it should be holy and without blemish. So ought men to love their wives as their own bodies. He that loveth his wife loveth himself. For no man ever yet hated his own flesh; but nourisheth and cherisheth it, even as the Lord the church: For we are members of his body, of his flesh, and of his bones. For this cause shall a man leave his father and mother, and shall be joined unto his wife, and they two shall be one flesh. This is***

a great mystery: but I speak concerning Christ and the church." Ephesians 5:22-32

The Bride of Christ is the corporate body of all believers, both Jews and Gentiles, who have accepted Christ as their savior; all will be arrayed in *fine linen, clean and white.* There is a strange analogy given that equates the clothing of the saints to their privilege of wearing fine linen, clean and white. The *fine linen* is the *righteousness of the saints*. Paul explained it like this:

"For if by one man's offence (Adam) *death reigned by one; much more they which receive abundance of grace and of the gift of righteousness shall reign in life by one, Jesus Christ. Therefore as by the offence of one judgment came upon all men to condemnation; even so by the righteousness of one the free gift came upon all men unto justification of life. That as sin hath reigned unto death, even so might grace reign through righteousness unto eternal life by Jesus Christ our Lord."* Rev 5:17-22

Sinful man has no righteousness in him at all, except that imputed to us by our Lord Jesus Christ. *As it is written, There is none righteous, no, not one* (Rom 3:10).

The Marriage Supper of the Lamb

"And he saith unto me, Write, Blessed are they which are called unto the marriage supper of the Lamb. And he saith unto me, These are the true sayings of God." Rev 19:9

The scene now shifts to the *Marriage Supper* of the Lamb. The Wedding takes place in heaven, immediately following the rapture and resurrection of the bride of Christ. The Wedding Supper will take place on earth. The personal pronoun *He* is not capitalized in the King James Bible, so we cannot be sure that this command to write is given by Jesus or some strong angel. It is impossible to tell, but the message is one of declaring beatitude: *Blessed are they which are called to the Marriage Supper of the Lamb*. Who are those that will be called to the

Marriage Supper? We must first understand that the Marriage of the Lamb and the Marriage Supper of the Lamb are not two immediately successive events as they usually are today. The concept of a Jewish couple being married in the time of Christ is almost completely unknown to modern Christians. It is impossible to understand the Marriage of the Lamb in Rev 19:7-8 without understanding Jewish customs concerning marriage. The Marriage of the Lamb and the Marriage Supper of the Lamb are seldom taught in churches today, but it is an event in which all Christians will participate as either the bride or the wedding guests (Mat 22:10). There are four major parts of the marriage ceremony. There are: (1) *the betrothal,* (2) *the preparation,* (3*) the marriage and its consummation,* and (4) the *wedding supper.* Only the last two parts are mentioned in Rev 19: 7-9. To understand what is going to happen at the wedding of Christ and the subsequent marriage supper, we need to examine all four parts.

The Betrothal

The Jewish wedding rituals at the time of Christ were quite different from those in the western world today. The marriage between a man and a woman was usually initiated by the father of the groom. Often, long before the son came to maturity, the father would pick a special bride for his son. When the time came to initiate the wedding rituals, the father would discuss the arrangement with his son, and after notifying the father of the bride, they would set out to seal the marriage contract. The son would then make a journey to the bride's house and make the price known to the bride's father. After much discussion, a dowry was agreed upon between the groom and the bride's father. A covenant was then made between the groom and the father of the prospective bride. The groom would bring with him a bottle of the finest wine, and to ratify the covenant a glass of wine would be poured. The bride would then be called, and the cup of wine offered. If the prospective bride took the glass and drank from it, they were at that point officially engaged. In contrast to the engagement in western civilization today, even though this was just a ratification of the covenant, from that moment on they were officially married (Gen 29:21, Deut 22:

22-30). This is why Joseph, when he found that she was with child, considered *putting Mary away* (Mat 1:19). Joseph had never been intimate with Mary, he was only betrothed. But according to Jewish custom, they were already considered to be married and Joseph thought she had committed *adultery*. Even though they were considered to be married, the prospective bride and groom could not yet live together as husband and wife.

God has an eternal plan for man which has never changed. When *his bride*, Israel, went off and *committed adultery* with foreign gods and foreign marriages, God did not *put her away* either. In the fullness of time, being foreknown by both the Father and the Son, He sent his only begotten Son into the world to establish a *new covenant* by which both Jews and Gentiles could be saved. Jesus Christ came into the world and presented himself to His bride. The price was high. One can well imagine the Hebrew son asking his father about the dowry that had been proposed. He might have asked his Father if another price could be paid. If He did, the father would respond: *We have both set the price and it must be paid*. Christ also agonized over the *price* that he had to pay while on the Mount of Olives.

> *"And he went a little further, and fell on his face, and prayed, saying, O my Father, if it be possible, let this cup pass from me: nevertheless not as I will, but as thou wilt."*
> Matthew 26:39

> *"And being in an agony he prayed more earnestly: and his sweat was as it were great drops of blood falling down to the ground."* Luke 22:44

He went to the cross of Calvary and willingly paid the price for His bride. All who accept Jesus Christ before the rapture; accept Him as the only begotten Son of God; and believe that He has been raised from the dead is the Bride of Christ. This *New Covenant* was established at the Lord's Last Supper when He poured the *wine* and offered it to those who were there.

> *"And as they were eating, Jesus took bread, and blessed it, and brake it, and gave it to the disciples, and said, Take, eat; this is my body. And he took the cup, and gave thanks, and gave it to them, saying, Drink ye all of it; For this is my blood of the new testament, which is shed for many for the remission of sins."* Matthew 26: 26-28

Note that Christ proclaimed that the wine was *my blood of the New Testament*. Christ went to the cross the next day and poured His own blood out into the cup of the New Covenant. He had paid the price for His new bride. Christ is our pure and spotless Passover Lamb; Christ is the Unleavened Bread, sinless and without leaven; Christ is the Firstfruit offering to God and the first of *many sons and daughters* (II Cor 6:18). In Paul's letter to the Hebrews he made it clear that Christ had paid the price for our sins by shedding his blood for us.

> *"And almost all things by the law are purged with blood; and without shedding of blood there is no remission of sins."* Hebrews 9:22

The Preparation

Once the marriage contract had been accepted, the groom returned to his father's home. The son now began to build a house for his new bride under the watchful eye of the father. All things had to be complete before the groom could go and claim his bride. The preparations could take up to two years. The groom could not just say *it is time* and leave to claim his bride. That decision was up to his father. When the groom was asked how long it might be until he would return he could only reply, *only my father knows*. In the meantime, all things needed to insure that a perfect wedding would take place were done. The groom would choose two of his close friends to be with him when he went to retrieve his bride. These two are the *friends of the groom*. One would assist the groom and one would assist the bride. In addition to choosing his two friends, it would now be announced to all that the bride had been officially betrothed and all of the *bridesmaids* would be assembled. The bride and the bridesmaids would make ready their wedding garments, white and without spot or wrinkle for the great event. One of the wonderful romantic customs was that when the father said *go*, the groom and his close friends would leave that very night, planning to arrive around midnight. The bride would then be *stolen away* in the night by the groom. Of course, the bride knew that this was going to happen, she just did not know exactly when. Having been warned that the time was near, every night she and her bridesmaids would stay up very late saying *perhaps this could be the night*. The blessed day now came, and as the groom approached her house, he would loudly sound a trumpet to let her know that he had arrived. The wedding gown had been carefully prepared, and the bride with all her friends each slept with a lamp nearby so that they could leave at a moment's notice. Except for the sound of a trumpet, the actual arrival of the groom was sudden and unannounced. However, as the day approached the bride and her bridesmaids would be expecting every night that the groom would arrive. Perhaps they had been told to be ready any day, or perhaps they had been given an approximate number of days until the groom would return. The bride would have prepared herself for this event by making sure that she would have a lamp filled with oil to use in the night journey. It was also necessary that all the bridesmaids would have their lamps ready for the joyous occasion. It was not uncommon for the entourage to wait several days, even weeks. Suddenly, at the *midnight hour* (Mat 25:6) the trumpet would sound and the groom would appear. Those that were prepared to go would gather up their belongings, trim their lamps and begin the journey. The groom would lead the procession back to his father's property where he had so carefully prepared his honeymoon chamber. That special place was called a *Chupah*.

We are told that Christ has gone to His father's house to prepare a place for us. He testified to this himself.

> **"Let not your heart be troubled: ye believe in God, believe also in me. In my Father's house are many mansions: if it were not so, I would have told you. I go to prepare a place for you. And if I go and prepare a place for you, I will come**

again, and receive you unto myself; that where I am, there ye may be also." Joel 14:1-3

The time between when the groom established the wedding covenant and the actual wedding takes place could take a long time. It has now been almost 2000 years and we earnestly travail for His return.

"For we know that the whole creation groaneth and travaileth in pain together until now." Romans 8:22

Just as in the ancient Jewish wedding, the Son cannot go to claim his bride until God said *it is time to return* .

"But of that day and hour knoweth no man, no, not the angels of heaven, but my Father only." Matthew 24:36

The Jewish belief is that there will be a specific day when their Messiah will arrive. On that day, there will also be a resurrection of the dead. Daniel spoke of this event long ago.

"And at that time shall Michael stand up, the great prince which standeth for the children of thy people: and there shall be a time of trouble, such as never was since there was a nation even to that same time: and at that time thy people shall be delivered, every one that shall be found written in the book. And many of them that sleep in the dust of the earth shall awake, some to everlasting life, and some to shame and everlasting contempt. And they that be wise shall shine as the brightness of the firmament; and they that turn many to righteousness as the stars for ever and ever."
Daniel 12:1-3

This is a classical example of what is called a *near-far prophecy*. There are two resurrections revealed here; one will be a resurrection of the righteous on the Feast of Trumpets near the end of the tribulation period. The other resurrection is a resurrection of the unrighteous 1000 years later. This exactly parallels what we are proposing in this book. According to

Strong's Concordance, the accurate Greek translation that Michael will *stand up* should be translated Michael will *stand aside*. After Michael and his heavenly forces have defeated Satan (Rev 12) and cast Satan and his angels down to the earth, Michael, that great protector of Israel, will *stand aside* for 3.5 years as the trumpet judgments sound. Why is Michael standing aside? Because the last 3.5 years of Daniel's 70th week is to bring the Children of Israel back into a covenant relationship with God, and cause them to finally recognize that Christ is their long- awaited Messiah. Michael cannot make this decision for anyone; each individual has to accept Christ on their own. These 3.5 years will be a time of trouble unprecedented in all of Jewish history. The persecution of believers by Satan acting through the antichrist will even exceed that experienced under Hitler and the Third Reich. What will be the end of these things? Daniel is told that *thy people shall be delivered*, but not all. Many will rise to everlasting life, but some (at the end of the millennial kingdom) will arise to shame and contempt. The *wise* are those who will be raised from the dead; they will precede those who are still alive at the seventh trumpet.

The Jewish expectation is that their long-awaited Messiah would come and restore all things as they were in the Garden of Eden. At that time, all Jewish believers will be given an *incorruptible new body*. It is taught that this would occur at the *sound of a trumpet* on the *Feast of Rosh Hashanah*. If this all sounds familiar, then it should. We have already presented evidence that the rapture of the church and the resurrection of the dead will occur on some future *Tishri 1* on the *Feast of Rosh Hashanah.* Jewish believers will be a part of the rapture of the church. Both Jews and Gentiles alike will be part of the bride of Christ on that glorious day. We need to understand that at the rapture of the church *all* who have accepted Jesus Christ as their savior, living and dead, will be caught up to meet Christ. Not one will be left behind. The apostle Paul was quite clear on this issue.

> ***"We shall not all sleep, but we shall ALL be changed, In a moment, in the twinkling of an eye, at the last trump."***
> I Corinthians 15:51-52

When this occurs, the words spoken by Christ will certainly be true.

> *"Then two men will be in the field: one will be taken and the other left. Two women will be grinding at the mill: one will be taken and the other left."*   Matthew 24:40 41

The Consummation

Both the *friend of the groom* and the *friend of the bride* would accompany the couple from the bride's house to the groom's wedding chamber where they would enter to consummate their marriage. The consummation typically lasted seven days. The *friend of the groom* would stand or stay near the door of the Chupah listening for the joyous announcement that the bride and groom were coming forth from the chamber. The groom would whisper to his *best man* that the marriage had been consummated and that they were almost ready to emerge from the *Wedding Chamber* (Is 26:20). All of the *wedding guests* would be assembled to welcome the bride and groom. At that point, the best man would loudly shout, *let us begin the wedding feast* and the bride and groom would appear. There was then a joyous celebration followed by a wedding feast. All of the bride and groom's friends would have come to the feast.

Who are the two *friends of the groom*? We believe that they are Elijah and John the Baptist. Elijah was prophesied to be one who would appear in the end times (Mat 17:9-11), and John the Baptist seemed to confirm that he was a friend of the groom.

> *"He that hath the bride is the bridegroom: but the friend of the bridegroom, which standeth and heareth him, rejoiceth greatly because of the bridegroom's voice: this my joy therefore is fulfilled. He must increase, but I must decrease."*   John 3:29-30

Recall that the *friend of the groom* is appointed to stand watch as the marriage is consummated over a (typical) seven-day period of time. This is perfectly consistent with our teaching that the 7 bowls of God's Wrath will be poured out over 10 days between the Feast of Trumpets and the Feast of Yom Kippur. After seven days, the (1) marriage will have been completed; (2) the saints who have been caught up to heaven in the rapture have escaped the Wrath of God, and (3) the seven bowl judgments are over. The entire group will then return to earth) for the *Wedding Supper of the Lamb* following the battle of Armageddon.

> *"...and He said to me* (John), *write: Blessed are those who are called to the marriage supper of the Lamb ! And He said to me, These are the true sayings of God."* Rev 19:7-9

> *"..and I saw heaven opened, and behold a white horse, and He that sat upon him was called Faithful and True, and in righteousness He doth judge and make war."* Rev 19:11

Christ is riding out of heaven; heaven has been closed for ten days, but now it is opened again: He is emerging from His wedding with vengeance and justice to make war at the great Battle of Armageddon. After the battle, it will then be time to judge the nations (sheep and goat judgment, Mat 25:31-46)); receive the 144,000 who were sealed in Rev 7:1-8; Journey to Bozrah to retrieve those who fled from Jerusalem to Petra(Is 63:1-3 Micah 2:12); judge the Jewish remnant with God (rod judgment, Ezekiel 20:33-37)); hold the Wedding Feast; and then observe the Feast of Tabernacles in Jerusalem between Tishri 15-Tishri 22.

The Wedding Feast: The Marriage Supper of the Lamb

As we have just explained the betrothal of Christ to His bride, the church, will culminate in a wonderful ceremony in which Christ will be eternally joined to His body of believers. This great union is called the *Wedding of the Lamb*, and will be held in heaven following the resurrection of all who fell asleep in Christ and all who are alive as the last trumpet sounds. Seven days later, Christ will return with his bride and his holy angels to fight the battle of Armageddon. Sometime shortly after the battle is over, there will be a great **wedding feast** on the earth. The bride will be there along with all of the honored guests.

There will be *two feasts* which will occur on the earth following the battle of Armageddon. The first is a feast at which all the birds of prey and carrion will be called to the *Valley of Jezreel* to feed upon the multitudes of dead who will lie on the ground.

> **"Then I saw an angel standing in the Sun; and he cried with a loud voice, saying to all of the birds that fly in the midst of heaven, come and gather together for the supper of the great God. That you may eat the flesh of kings, the flesh of captains, the flesh of mighty men, the flesh of horses and of those who sat on them."** Rev 19: 17-18

This explains a curious and obscure statement by Christ as He sat upon the Mount of Olives.

> *"For wherever the carcass is, there the eagles will be gathered together."* Matthew 24: 28

Summary and Conclusions

Many Christians today have never heard of the marriage of Jesus Christ to His bride or of the Wedding Feast from the pulpit. Of those that have heard of these wonderful events, there is widespread confusion concerning the difference between the *Wedding of the Lamb* and the *Wedding Supper of the Lamb*. In a Jewish wedding, these two events are separated in time. They are not held in one day as in western culture. In Rev 19:9, John the revelator records: **Blessed are those who are invited to the marriage supper of the lamb.** Blessed indeed! But, the group who actually attended the wedding ceremony in heaven is even more blessed. These two groups are not the same. The *Wedding of the Lamb* will take place in heaven after the Bride of Christ has been raptured out or resurrected from the grave. The *Wedding Feast* will take place on the earth following the battle of Armageddon. The *wedding guests* will include the Bride of Christ and all of those who are alive and remain (those who have accepted Christ during the ten-day period of redemption between the Feast of Trumpets and the Feast of Yom Kippur and didn't take the mark of the beast). This will be discussed in detail in the next chapter. It will be a joyous occasion that Christ spoke of as

He ate the last supper with His disciples in the upper room on the evening before He was crucified. He had just broken the bread which represented His body and drank of the wine which represented His blood which was shed for the remission of our sins.

> **"But I say to you, I will not drink of this fruit of the vine from now until that day when I drink it new with you in my Father's Kingdom."**   Matthew 26:29

This *new cup* will be filled with *new wine*; it will be a cup of gladness, joy and new life. This cup will be drunk at the Wedding Feast of our Lord Jesus Christ. It will initiate a new age: the 1000-year millennial kingdom. The wedding ceremony will be in heaven; the wedding feast will be on the earth.

However, in the Marriage Supper planned by God for His Son Jesus Christ, something will go tragically wrong. In order to complete the exegesis of the wedding feast we will need to carefully examine what Christ predicted would happen as He spoke to His disciples. This discourse by Christ is presented as the *Parable of the Wise and Foolish Virgins* on the Mount of Olives.

Chapter 25

The Wise and Foolish Virgins

Christ was about to be betrayed by Judas Iscariot. He was sitting on the Mount of Olives speaking to His disciples, and possibly to others in His inner circle, who had gathered there on the night before He was to be crucified. Earlier, He had been asked to describe the things which would take place at the end of the age (Mat 24:1-3). As He sat there, he delivered what has been called the *Olivet Discourse*, which was recorded in Matthew 24:3-51 and Matthew 25. The Parable of the Wise and Foolish Virgins has been interpreted by many to illustrate what will happen at the rapture of the church, but we will show that this is not the correct interpretation of this parable. It actually describes the *Wedding of the Lamb*, which will be held in heaven shortly after the rapture and resurrection of all believers. In Chapter 24 we discussed the Wedding of the Lamb and the Wedding Supper of the Lamb. These two great end time events only involve the body of Christ; all those (Jews and gentiles) who have accepted Christ as their savior before the 7th trumpet sounds. Christ has just revealed to those around Him that He will return to claim those who believe upon His name. Christ revealed a period of great tribulation upon the whole earth, which will end in the destruction of the wicked. In Mat 24:45-51, Christ then turns to those who are there and ask the question: *Who then is the faithful and wise servant who will be given meat in due season?* In other words, which Jewish people will inherit the kingdom and what are the requirements to do so? Christ did not immediately answer that question, but He reinforced the warning that He would come unexpectedly when the inhabitants of this earth will not be expecting Him. Christ then warns them that at that hour there will be *"weeping and gnashing of teeth"* (Matthew 24:51).

First, we note that the Olivet Discourse was addressed to Jewish listeners and the Jewish nation. Of course, we who now live in the Church Age should heed his warnings and we can better understand His words. At the time of the end, both Jews and

Gentiles will both be redeemed. However, we need to again note that these followers of Jesus Christ were all Jewish and were just becoming fully aware of what was about to happen. They may have already accepted the fact that Christ was about to be crucified but did not completely understand how their Messiah would return and redeem His followers. The gospel message had not yet been passed on to the gentiles, and the entire concept of a church and the body of Christ was completely unknown. The burning question on everyone's mind was what would happen to the Jewish nation and those who continued to follow the Old Testament law? Christ next addressed this question in the Parable of the *Wise and Foolish Virgins* in Matthew 25:1-13.

The setting of Matthew 25 is that Christ was at the very end of His earthly ministry. He had known from time eternal that God's chosen people, the nation of Israel, would reject him as their Messiah and crucify Him in their final act of denial. In a previous parable (Mat 21: 33-44) called the *Parable of the Vineyard* Christ had addressed the question of what would happen to Israel after His rejection. In this parable, Christ revealed that He would be crucified and the mantle of anointing would pass to the Gentiles (a nation bearing fruits, Mat 21:43). The question of whether or not the Jewish nation would have a path to salvation was not addressed in that parable. The parable of the **Wedding Banquet** in Matthew 22 was to partly address that unanswered question.

> *"And Jesus answered and spake unto them again by parables, and said, The kingdom of heaven is like unto a certain king, which made a marriage for his son, and sent forth his servants to call them that were bidden to the wedding: and they would not come. Again, he sent forth other servants, saying, Tell them which are bidden, Behold, I have prepared my dinner: my oxen and my fatlings are killed, and all things are ready: come unto the marriage. But they made light of it, and went their ways, one to his farm, another to his merchandise: And the remnant took his servants, and entreated them spitefully, and slew them. But when the king heard thereof, he was wroth: and he sent*

forth his armies, and destroyed those murderers, and burned up their city. Then saith he to his servants, The wedding is ready, but they which were bidden were not worthy. Go ye therefore into the highways, and as many as ye shall find, bid to the marriage. So those servants went out into the highways, and gathered together all as many as they found, both bad and good: and the wedding was furnished with guests. And when the king came in to see the guests, he saw there a man which had not on a wedding garment: And he saith unto him, Friend, how camest thou in hither not having a wedding garment? And he was speechless. Then said the king to the servants, Bind him hand and foot, and take him away, and cast him into outer darkness; there shall be weeping and gnashing of teeth. For many are called, but few are chosen." Matthew 22: 1-14

Let us examine this parable carefully and open our ears to hear and our eyes to see. In the Old Testament, *Israel* was depicted as *God's Bride* in several prophecies. In Jeremiah 31:31 there is a prophecy that the Lord will make a New Covenant with the Houses of Israel and Judah. God then clearly declared that he was a husband to Israel.

"Behold, the days come, saith the LORD, that I will make a new covenant with the house of Israel, and with the house of Judah: Not according to the covenant that I made with their fathers in the day that I took them by the hand to bring them out of the land of Egypt; which my covenant they brake, although I was an husband unto them, saith the LORD: But this shall be the covenant that I will make with the house of Israel; After those days, saith the LORD, I will put my law in their inward parts, and write it in their hearts; and will be their God, and they shall be my people." Jeremiah 31:31-32.

This is an extremely important passage in understanding the Parable of the Wise and Foolish Virgin and we will return to it later. God declared that He was a husband to Israel (Jeremiah 31:32; Ezekiel 16:30-34), but Israel broke the marriage covenant.

She became a spiritual adulteress. *"So it came to pass, through her casual harlotry, that she defiled the land and committed adultery with stones and trees"* (Jeremiah 3:9). God's invitation for Israel to be his bride was rejected by corporate Israel, and so God instituted a new plan. He would send his only Son to the lost house of Israel and offer them salvation. Let us now examine the *Parable of the Wedding Banquet* in Matthew 22: 1-14.

- *The kingdom of heaven is like unto a certain king, which made a marriage for his son; and sent forth his servants to call them that were bidden to the wedding: and they would not come.*

The **king** is *God the Father*, and His **son** is *Jesus Christ*. In the New Testament, those who accept Jesus Christ as the only Son of God and believe upon His name is depicted as the **Bride of Christ.**

"Husbands, love your wives, just as Christ also loved the church and gave Himself for her, that He might sanctify and cleanse her with the washing of water by the word, that He might present her to Himself a glorious church, not having spot or wrinkle or any such thing, but that she should be holy and without blemish" Ephesians 5:25-27.

Although this parable was directly addressing the lost house of Israel, Paul was anxious to win both Gentiles and the Jews over to Christ, and he declared that *all who would believe* would stand as a virgin bride before Christ.

"For I am jealous for you with godly jealousy. For I have betrothed you to one husband, that I may present you as a chaste virgin to Christ" II Corinthians 11:2

The parable reveals that God joyously sent His only Son to save Israel, and He prepared for the wedding; but when Christ came as the Son of Man He was rejected; they refused to come to the marriage.(believe that He was their Messiah and the Son of God).

- *Again, he sent forth other servants, saying, Tell them which are bidden, Behold, I have prepared my dinner: my oxen and my fatlings are killed, and all things are ready: come unto the marriage. But they made light of it, and went their ways, one to his farm, another to his merchandise: And the remnant took his servants, and entreated them spitefully, and slew them.*

God gave the house of Israel another chance. Even after they had crucified His Son, God was still not willing to reject His chosen people. He *is longsuffering* and His word is true. He sent the 12 chosen disciples to preach the gospel to the Jewish people, offering a New Covenant in which the law would be written on their hearts and salvation would be a free gift by grace. Sadly, they killed Stephen and continued to persecute the disciples. Every disciple suffered severe persecution, and all except the apostle John met a violent death. Finally, God acted against Israel for her repeated transgressions. We should note that after Stephen was stoned, Christ met Paul on the road to Damascus and specifically instructed him to take the message of salvation by grace to the gentiles.

- *But when the king heard thereof, he was wroth: and he sent forth his armies, and destroyed those murderers, and burned up their city.*

God gave the house of Israel 40 years to repent and turn to Christ, but they (corporately) refused to do so. God moved the Roman Legions under the command of Titus to attack and destroy Jerusalem in 70 AD. Herod's temple was completely destroyed; the city was burned; and all of the people were put under the subjugation of the Roman Empire. Their fate was sealed... they had made their choice.

- *Then saith he to his servants, The wedding is ready, but they which were bidden were not worthy. Go ye therefore into the highways, and as many as ye shall find, bid to the marriage. So those servants went out into*

> *the highways, and gathered together all as many as they found, both bad and good:*

Here we have the doctrine of immanency combined with the call for Jews and Gentiles alike to be saved. The ***wedding is ready***; for almost 2000 years now Christians have been crying out: ***How long oh Lord?*** The wedding will take place when God tells His servants the angels to *go* and fetch His bride. All are bid to go to the Wedding of the Lamb: Jews and Gentiles, good and bad; they are all offered eternal life by the Grace of Jesus Christ.

- *So those servants went out into the highways, and gathered together all as many as they found, both bad and good: and the wedding was furnished with guests.*

Here we have a wonderful truth revealed about who will be the Bride of Christ and what qualifications are needed. Oh what grace! Those invited will be ***good and bad***. Here is a truth often totally misunderstood by most Christians. No one can buy their way into heaven by being good. Salvation is offered to all by grace…rich or poor; young or old; good or bad. Who are His *servants* that issue the invitation? Why, they are you and me. They are every Christian fulfilling the great commission. Christ commanded us to: ***Go ye into all the world, and preach the gospel to every creature*** (Mark 16:15). It is clear that the Wedding Feast which precedes the millennial kingdom of 1000 years will be attended by ***all… as many as could be found***, which include the nation of Israel. And the wedding guests will be a great number. Now something tragic happens. One of the guests is discovered which does not have on *garments of white, without spot or wrinkle*.

- *And when the king came in to see the guests, he saw there a man which had not on a wedding garment: And he saith unto him, Friend, how camest thou in hither not having a wedding garment? And he was speechless.*

This man was stunned to hear that he was not invited. He was no doubt a leader in the community, a good father, a good citizen and a decent person. For all of his good deeds it is apparent that he was never found on his knees… spiritually or physically… acknowledging to the Father that Jesus Christ was his Lord and Savior. It would have been so easy, because the gift of eternal life is free. *Friend, how camest thou in hither not having a wedding garment?* Evidently, he was surprised *(speechless)* to learn that he did not have the garments to attend the feast.

> *"For in this we groan, earnestly desiring to be clothed upon with our house which is from heaven: If so be that being clothed we shall not be found naked. For we that are in this tabernacle do groan, being burdened: not for that we would be unclothed, but clothed upon, that mortality might be swallowed up of life"* II Corinthians 5:2-4

> *"He that overcometh, the same shall be clothed in white raiment; and I will not blot out his name out of the book of life, but I will confess his name before my Father, and before his angels. I counsel thee to buy of me gold tried in the fire, that thou mayest be rich; and white raiment, that thou mayest be clothed, and that the shame of thy nakedness do not appear; and anoint thine eyes with eyesalve, that thou mayest see"* Rev 3:5,18

It was not that he had not been forewarned or told. This wedding banquet will take place at the end of the age. The gospel message will have been preached throughout the world. He knew what needed to be done, and he knew the consequences of rejecting Jesus Christ. Where did all of the other guests get their wedding garments? They are the garments given to the Bride of Christ after they are raptured to heaven, before the Marriage of the Lamb occurs. The wedding garments were promised to all overcomers in the letter to the *Church at Laodicea*, the end time church with no rebuke. These garments are white, without spot or wrinkle. Only Christ can award such garments. This man was not clothed in these garments, and when he was found, he was speechless! There will be many on this day that will expect to be a part of either the bride of Christ or later be invited to the wedding feast as a guest…. But they will inherit neither. Without robes of righteousness, with no spots or wrinkles, no one can stand before Christ and participate in either the wedding or the wedding feast. The fate of this unworthy guest is too terrible to even comprehend.

> ***"Then said the king to the servants, Bind him hand and foot, and take him away, and cast him into outer darkness; there shall be weeping and gnashing of teeth. For many are called, but few are chosen."***   Matthew 22:13-14

The result is final and everlasting. The unwanted guest is cast into **darkness** *where there is* **weeping and gnashing of teeth**. Too harsh you say? A loving God would not do such a thing? Do not be deceived: this is the fate of all who will not accept Jesus Christ as their savior. Finally, Christ issued a stern warning.

> ***"For many are called but few are chosen."***   Matthew 22:14

Sadly, Satan and the world will engulf many, and the gift of eternal life will be lost. The Wedding of the Lamb will take place in heaven immediately after Crist has called of the saints to Him in the rapture at the last trump.. The call has gone out to everyone. Salvation is now offered to Jews and Gentiles alike. In the Age of Grace, there are only two types of people who will ever live upon the earth: those who accept Christ as their savior, and those who do not. The door is now open, but one day in the future it will be too late. It will be closed

We *must* in the strongest possible way restate what has just been presented. Many pastors today preach only love and grace. Many will not preach everlasting damnation for those who refuse Christ. They say that a loving, gracious and merciful God could not do such a thing; they are wrong. The God of mercy and grace had to stand aside as His only Son was beaten beyond recognition, nailed to a cross, suffered and died. This was the redeeming work of Jesus Christ and He paid all to become sin for us. The work is finished and acceptable to the Father; our sins are no longer remembered and they are removed as far as the east is from the west as we stand at the judgment seat. What do we have to pay to receive eternal life? Salvation is offered as a free gift to all who will believe upon His name. While salvation is by grace and is freely given, every Christian will have to pay the price as they live on this earth. Those in Christ will not be accepted by the world, for they are not part of this world. We only sojourn here for a short while. There will be persecution, rejection, ridicule and tribulation as we journey towards eternity. It is a small price to pay, but many will not believe. Their fate is to be *cast... into outer darkness; there shall be weeping and gnashing of teeth.* Let everyone be warned. This parable is clearly describing how salvation by grace was first presented to the nation of Israel, and when they corporately refused, it was offered to the Gentiles. The setting is clearly the rapture followed by the Wedding of the Lamb. We now return to the Parable of the **Wise and Foolish Virgins.**

The Parable of the Wise and Foolish Virgins

"Then shall the kingdom of heaven be likened unto ten virgins, which took their lamps, and went forth to meet the bridegroom. And five of them were wise, and five were foolish. They that were foolish took their lamps, and took no oil with them: But the wise took oil in their vessels with their lamps. While the bridegroom tarried, they all slumbered and slept. And at midnight there was a cry made, Behold, the bridegroom cometh; go ye out to meet him. Then all those virgins arose, and trimmed their lamps. And the foolish said unto the wise, Give us of your oil; for our lamps are gone out. But the wise answered, saying, Not so; lest there be not enough for us and you: but go ye rather to them that sell, and buy for yourselves. And while they went to buy, the bridegroom came; and they that were ready went in with him to the marriage: and the door was shut. Afterward came also the other virgins, saying, Lord, Lord, open to us. But he answered and said, Verily I say unto you,

> *I know you not. Watch therefore, for ye know neither the day nor the hour wherein the Son of man cometh."*
> Matthew 25:1-13

There are several key components of this parable that must be carefully noted. First, the Parable of the Wise and Foolish Virgins is immediately *preceded* by the following verse which can only refer to the rapture of the church, both from context and content.

> *"Then shall two be in the field; the one shall be taken, and the other left. Two women shall be grinding at the mill; the one shall be taken, and the other left. Watch therefore: for ye know not what hour your Lord doth come."*
> Matthew 24: 40-42

We again must realize that when Christ spoke this parable on the Mount of Olives, he was speaking to His Jewish disciples and by extension to all Jews. Except for glimmerings of the church age to come, there was no established or immediate concept of the Church at all. This was a *mystery* hidden from Israel. However, they would be given every opportunity to accept Christ as their Messiah. It was not until well after the day of Pentecost that the apostle Paul was commissioned to take the gospel to the Gentiles. After that point in time, the corporate body of Christ would consist of all who would believe in Christ as the Son of God, Gentiles and Jews alike. The door to salvation was still to be open to the Jewish people, but it was to be under the New Covenant and not the Old. The Law would now be written on an individual's heart, and not in stone. Hence, this parable was addressed to Jewish listeners and it was about the Nation of Israel; how they would be dealt with at the end of the age; and how Israel could participate in the Marriage of the Lamb. Most of the theological confusion is due to the fact that the story revolves around 10 virgins, who are usually all identified as part of the body of Christ. The 10 virgins are assumed to all be born again Christians, of which 5 somehow slipped away from salvation. Such a theological position cannot be sustained. Christ made it clear that all who accepted Him as Lord and Savior and experienced a new birth in Christ would receive eternal life. This is the fundamental promise of John 3:16.

There are several key concepts in this parable which must be clearly understood before the true meaning of the parable can be found.
1. Who are the *virgins* in this parable?
2. Who is the *bridegroom*?
3. What is the meaning of the *oil* and the *lamps*?
4. What is the *light* ?
5. What are the *primary warnings* in this parable?

The Virgins

The Greek word translated as a virgin or virgins in this parable is *parthenos*, which means simply a maiden or an unmarried daughter. It is used here to represent Jews. The Greek work *parthenos* is never used to describe redeemed saints except in one place. In Rev 14:4 the word *parthenos* is translated *virgins* and it is used to describe the 144,000 firstfruit overcomers standing on Mount Zion. This exception is, however, easily explained. The 144,000 *firstfruits* seen in heaven in Rev 14 will not become a bride until 3.5 years later. There is no compelling reason not to think that in this parable the word virgin is being used in generic terms to describe a group of Jews, some who will miss the rapture and some who will not.

There is no need to spiritualize the term *virgins*. The virgins simply represent those who expect to go to the Wedding ceremony. However, five of the virgins will be denied. The parable should be read in context. Remember that Christ gave this parable on the Mount of Olives just before His death to His disciples.

Note that a Parable was meant to convey meaning to only His disciples: *"And he said, Unto you it is given to know the mysteries of the kingdom of God: but to others in parables; that seeing they might not see, and hearing they might not understand."* (Luke 8:10). As we read this parable today, we have the Holy Spirit to give us wisdom and understanding. We will shortly see that the separation of the virgins occurs at what the apostle Paul revealed as the Rapture. All expected to be a part of the Bride of Christ and go to the Wedding Ceremony, but there were five *foolish virgins* who were left behind.

The Bridegroom
The bridegroom is Jesus Christ and He has come to invite all of the 10 virgins to His Wedding, but five were not prepared. The failure to be invited to the Wedding seems to be directly related to some not having *oil in their lamps* when the bridegroom came.

The Oil and the Lamps
The 10 virgins in this parable represent the potential bride. It is clear that the only thing that separated the wise from the foolish virgins was the lack of *oil*. All had **lamps** but *"those who were foolish took their lamps but took no oil with them"* (Mat 25:3). So what is the *oil* in this parable? Most commentators boldly assert that the oil represents the Holy Spirit which dwells within us, but this interpretation is not correct. *First*, oil in the Old Testament scriptures is never used to represent the Holy Spirit. It is used for (1) anointing (2) for light and for (3) cooking and baking. *Oil* in the New Testament was mentioned in: (1) Healing the sick (James 5:14, Mark 6:13) (2) honoring Christ (Luke 7:46) (3) Helping a neighbor (Luke 10:36) (4) Paying debts (Luke 16:16) and (5) To impart gladness (Heb 1:9). Nowhere in the New Testament is oil directly used to represent the Holy Spirit. This appears to be modern theology stretching the truth of scripture.

The Holy Spirit was given in the New Testament to all believers as a guarantee of our future redemption; as our comforter; as a source of understanding and wisdom; and as a power gift. This is a New Covenant gift, and was unknown as Christ gave the Olivet Discourse. The Holy Spirit would not fall on man until after the death of Christ on the day of Pentecost. So what is this oil that all 10 virgins had initially, and when the bridegroom finally arrived that five of the virgins did not have? We must search the scriptures to determine what the oil represents.

> *"Behold, I have taught you statutes and judgments, even as the LORD my God commanded me, that ye should do so in the land whither ye go to possess it. Keep therefore and do them; for this is your wisdom and your understanding in the sight of the nations, which shall hear all these statutes, and say, Surely this great nation is a wise and understanding people.*
> Deuteronomy 4:5-6

Here we are told that the Lord imparted statutes to the Nation of Israel to give them **wisdom** and **understanding**.

> *"The fear of the LORD is the beginning of wisdom: a good understanding have all they that do his commandments: his praise endureth for ever."* Psalms 111:10

Remember that Christ was speaking to the Jews, and that except for those Jews who had turned to Christ during His earthly ministry, all were living under the Old Testament Law. In Proverbs 21:20, we are told that *"**There is....oil in the dwelling of the wise**"* So *oil* brings *wisdom*. Wisdom comes from (1) fearing the Lord (2) keeping His commandments.

So the oil which is in every *Jewish believer* is the **Word of the Lord**. The Torah, the commandments given to Israel by God, and the Law is the *oil* which all of the 10 virgins possessed. But living only under the Old Testament law caused the lamps of the Old Testament Jewish believers in the law to go out. The reason is clear: Only Christ can rescue man from the curse of the law. So Paul continued:

> *"Christ hath redeemed us from the curse of the law, being made a curse for us: for it is written, Cursed is every one that hangeth on a tree: That the blessing of Abraham might come on the Gentiles through Jesus Christ; that we might receive the promise of the Spirit through faith. Brethren, I speak after the manner of men; Though it be but a man's covenant, yet if it be confirmed, no man disannulleth, or*

addeth thereto. Now to Abraham and his seed were the promises made. He saith not, And to seeds, as of many; but as of one, And to thy seed, which is Christ. And this I say, that the covenant, that was confirmed before of God in Christ, the law, which was four hundred and thirty years after, cannot disannul, that it should make the promise of none effect. For if the inheritance be of the law, it is no more of promise: but God gave it to Abraham by promise. Wherefore then serveth the law? It was added because of transgressions, till the seed should come to whom the promise was made; and it was ordained by angels in the hand of a mediator" Gal 3:13-16

But here is a paradox. In Paul's letter to the Galatians, he addressed the character of the law and how it was simply a taskmaster, given to show Israel that it was impossible to find salvation under the law. Only believing in Christ and being redeemed from sin can anyone be saved… Jew or Gentile.

"For as many as are of the works of the law are under the curse: for it is written, Cursed is every one that continueth not in all things which are written in the book of the law to do them. But that no man is justified by the law in the sight of God, it is evident: for, The just shall live by faith. And the law is not of faith: but, The man that doeth them shall live in them. Christ hath redeemed us from the curse of the law, being made a curse for us" Galatians 3:10-13

This provides us the scriptural confirmation of what the *oil* represented in this parable. The *oil* is the *laws of God*. The wisdom of the saints is in knowing the law and obeying the law. The paradox is that no one can find salvation and redemption under the law. The good news is that Christ came not to abolish the law but to fulfill the law. Every Christian is commanded to follow Christ and be conformed to His image. Christ came that the law might be fulfilled, and when He became the perfect sacrificial Lamb of God the burden of being condemned under the law was lifted.

The Light from the Lamps
But there is something else here…When the bridegroom came to claim His guests, the Wise Virgins had *light* and the foolish virgins did not. What is this light?

> *"Thy word is a lamp unto my feet, and a light unto my path."*   Psalms 119:105

So the *word* is the *oil*, the *lamp* and the *light*! How can this be true? The answer is given in the first verse of the Gospel of John.

> *"In the beginning was the Word, and the Word was with God, and the Word was God. The same was in the beginning with God."*   John 1:1-4

> *"All things were made by him; and without him was not anything made that was made. In him was life; and the life was the light of men."*   John 1:3-4

Here is the true meaning of this Parable. Our Lord and Savior Jesus Christ came into the world to save the world, fulfill the law, and offer salvation by grace to all who believe upon His name. He is the *oil* (the living word)…He is the *light* (source of all power and good works)….We are the vessel (*Lamp*) that can proclaim the good news… salvation and redemption by grace for all who believe upon His name. It is interesting that when Christ returns at His 2cd advent to fight the Battle of Armageddon; *"His name is called The Word of God!"* How wonderfully all scripture hangs together if we will just open our eyes to see.

> *"Then spake Jesus again unto them, saying, I am the light of the world: he that followeth me shall not walk in darkness, but shall have the light of life."*   John 8:12

> *"I am come a light into the world, that whosoever believeth on me should not abide in darkness."*   John 12:46

> *"Ye are all the children of light, and the children of the day: we are not of the night, nor of darkness"* I Thess. 5:5
>
> *"Ye are the light of the world. A city that is set on an hill cannot be hid. Neither do men light a candle, and put it under a bushel, but on a candlestick; and it giveth light unto all that are in the house. Let your light so shine before men, that they may see your good works, and glorify your Father which is in heaven. Think not that I am come to destroy the law, or the prophets: I am not come to destroy, but to fulfil. For verily I say unto you, Till heaven and earth pass, one jot or one tittle shall in no wise pass from the law, till all be fulfilled. "*
> Matthew 5:14-18

Here we have scriptural confirmation that Christ, the hope of glory living in us, is the source of New Covenant *light*. Letting His light shine through us lets our *lamp* shine brightly. Without Christ, the living word (the *Oil*) in us, our lamps will go out…. We cannot in and of our mortal, sinful bodies produce *light* unless Christ lives within us.. Christ was the only living man who lived a perfect and sinless life, and it was through his sacrificial death that the Law was perfectly satisfied. In the Old Testament the blood of bulls and goats was shed daily to cover the sins of the people; Christ was our perfect sacrificial Lamb. It is by Him and through Him that we are able to conquer death and be seen sinless before God in the final judgment. The *mystery* is that the Jewish nation has continued to reject the saving grace of Jesus Christ for almost 2000 years. They are still looking for a messiah to arise to be their deliverer. So the *oil* in *all* of the 10 virgins was knowledge of the Law. They all had this knowledge, so all of their lamps were initially burning. The *extra oil* or the *new oil* is obtained by accepting Christ as our savior and letting His light shine in us. The old oil will burn completely burn out without the new oil.

The Meaning of the Parable

In this Parable Christ is telling his Jewish listeners (and by extension all who would listen over the next 2000 years) that He is the ***word***.... the ***Oil*** of Gladness......That He is the ***Light***... that lifts us from darkness into the Sun of Righteousness. In Him and by Him ***all things*** are now made complete. He is the source of all power, works and deeds that will be rewarded and not be burned up like wood, hay and stubble... He is the *New Oil*. So the wise virgins have accepted Christ as their savior, they are not condemned to death under the Old Covenant but now live in the grace and redemption of the New Covenant. They will be part of the Wedding Ceremony. The *living word*...Christ Jesus the hope of glory is now in them...this is the ***extra oil*** that keeps their lights burning forever. The lamps of the Foolish Virgins are going out...they have not accepted Chris as their messiah and redeemer... they are condemned and dying under the weight of the law. Oh saints... today we need to pray for millions of Jews who will not accept our Lord Jesus Christ as their long awaited Messiah. We must work to make ***Wise Virgins*** out of ***Foolish Virgins.*** Christ is giving his Jewish followers the path to salvation and redemption.

When Christ spoke this parable on the Mount of Olives, the notion of the New Covenant church, the Body of Christ and the gift of the Holy Spirit was probably almost completely unknown. However, His words would echo down through the ages to every Jew who would be born after the Olivet discourse, and these words would need to be understood by every member of the Body of Christ who would follow his death, burial and resurrection. The meaning of this parable will be given in common language and simple language.

1. ***Then*** (Mat 25:1, 24:29:31, 24:31), when Christ returns for His Bride, the Parable of the 10 virgins will be fulfilled.
2. The ***virgins*** are all Jewish
3. These virgins are waiting for the ***Bridegroom*** to return. To orthodox Jews, this is the return of their long awaited messiah who will save them and restore all things. To the Body of Christ, this is the Rapture of the Church described in I Thess 4: 15-17. It is interesting that Paul tells the

>   Thessalonicans that they *are not in darkness*,
>   but that they were all the *sons of light*
>   I Thessalonians 5:4-5
> 4. The 10 Virgins all had *lamps*. The word of God is both the oil and a *light*.
> 5. The *wise virgins* had extra oil in their lamps. These Jews had accepted Christ as their Savior and were prepared to go when the Bridegroom arrived. The Foolish Virgins had not accepted Christ as their Savior. They were still clinging to the law and awaiting their promised Messiah. They did not have the light of Christ in them… their Lamps were going out.

The laws and commandments of God compel us…demand of us…that we live under the Law. The Law was not evil, but it resulted in sure death For as many as are of the works of the law are under the curse: *"for it is written, Cursed is every one that continueth not in all things which are written in the book of the law to do them."* (Gal 3:10). The only way that anyone can find salvation and eternal life is to believe upon Jesus Christ. *No one is justified by the law, for the just shall live by faith"* (Gal 3:11). If any Jew wants to receive eternal life, it must be by faith…faith that believes Christ is the only son of God who has died on the cross for our sins. *"Christ has redeemed us from the curse of the law, having become a curse for us"* (Gal 3:13). All Jewish believers in the world today are born under the curse of the law, and unless they accept Jesus Christ as their Savior they are doomed to destruction.

> *"Do we then make voit the law by faith? Certainly not! On the contrary, we establish the law."*   Romans 3:31

Salvation is given by the grace of Jesus Christ, and grace is propitiated by faith. Abel, Noah, Enoch and Abraham all were redeemed from the law by faith (Hebrews 11). So are we (the Gentiles) free to do anything we want to do? …. No! Christ has freed us from the bonds of the law and by doing so we can now live without fear or condemnation under the law. Paul posed the same question to the Roman Christians.

> *" What then? shall we sin because we are not under the law but under grace? Certainly not!*" Romans 7:7

> *"Wherefore, my brethren, ye also are become dead to the law by the body of Christ; that ye should be married to another, even to him who is raised from the dead, that we should bring forth fruit unto God."*
> Romans 7:4

Note that Romans 7:4 clearly states that if we are freed from the curse of the law by believing in our Lord Jesus Christ, that we (the body of Christ) will be *married* to Him (Christ). This is the fundamental message of the Parable of the Wise and Foolish Virgins. Paul continues:

> *"For when we were in the flesh, the motions of sins, which were by the law, did work in our members to bring forth fruit unto death. But now we are delivered from the law, that being dead wherein we were held; that we should serve in newness of spirit, and not in the oldness of the letter. What shall we say then? Is the law sin? God forbid. Nay, I had not known sin, but by the law: for I had not known lust, except the law had said, Thou shalt not covet. But sin, taking occasion by the commandment, wrought in me all manner of concupiscence. For without the law sin was dead. For I was alive without the law once: but when the commandment came, sin revived, and I died. And the commandment, which was ordained to life, I found to be unto death. For sin, taking occasion by the commandment, deceived me, and by it slew me. Wherefore the law is holy, and the commandment holy, and just, and good. Was then that which is good made death unto me? God forbid. But sin, that it might appear sin, working*

> *death in me by that which is good; that sin by the commandment might become exceeding sinful."*
> Romans 7: 5-13

It is interesting to note that in reading through this parable, there are two important themes which emerge as part of the mainstream message: (1) watchfulness, and (2) being prepared. It should also be noted that *all* of these virgins slumbered and slept. They had become complacent and their state was one of slothfulness. The Foolish Virgins were undoubtedly living a good life; they were not murderers or thieves; they might have even been faithful Orthodox Jews. But they not only failed to be watchful and ready, they had not accepted Christ as their long awaited Messiah and deliverer. Since they were *all slumbering*, all 10 had become complacent.

> *"For as in the days that were before the flood they were eating and drinking, marrying and giving in marriage, until the day that Noe entered into the ark, And knew not until the flood came, and took them all away; so shall also the coming of the Son of man be."*
> Matthew 24: 38-39

One of the themes of this book is to present scriptural evidence that the rapture will not rescue the Body of Christ from 3.5 years of **tribulation**, but all who have accepted Jesus Christ as their savior will escape the **Wrath of God**. It should also be stressed that while most Christians will be **slumbering**, if the Book of Revelation and prophecy is carefully studied, those who are *wise* will not be surprised when the rapture does occur. There are plenty of signs which have been discussed in this book. The Apostle Paul addressed this same issue in his letter to the Christians at Thessalonica. In both I Thess.13-17 and I Cor. 15:51-54 He had revealed the **mystery** of what we now call the rapture. Word reached Paul that one or more people in the church were declaring that Christ had already returned and the rapture of His church had already occurred. Paul corrected this erroneous teaching in II Thessalonians 2: 1-17. He reminded them that as the **Sons of Light** they would not be left behind or taken by surprise. These things he had previously asserted in his 1st letter to the Thessalonicans.

> *"But of the times and the seasons, brethren, ye have no need that I write unto you. For yourselves know perfectly that the day of the Lord so cometh as a thief in the night. For when they shall say, Peace and safety; then sudden destruction cometh upon them, as travail upon a woman with child; and they shall not escape. But ye, brethren, are not in darkness, that that day should overtake you as a thief. Ye are all the children of light, and the children of the day: we are not of the night, nor of darkness. Therefore let us not sleep, as do others; but let us watch and be sober. For they that sleep sleep in the night; and they that be drunken are drunken in the night. But let us, who are of the day, be sober, putting on the breastplate of faith and love; and for an helmet, the hope of salvation. For God hath not appointed us to wrath, but to obtain salvation by our Lord Jesus Christ...."*
> I Thessalonians 5:1-9

We who have found the Pearl of Great Price, our Lord and Savior Jesus Christ, and believed upon His name will not be surprised. In II Thess. 1-9 the Apostle Paul gave them *signs* to look for as that day approached, and these signs are also for us today.

1. There will be a great *falling away* before that day (II Thessalonians 2:3).

> *"This know also, that in the last days perilous times shall come. For men shall be lovers of their own selves, covetous, boasters, proud, blasphemers, disobedient to parents, unthankful, unholy, Without natural affection, trucebreakers, false accusers, incontinent, fierce, despisers of those that are good, traitors, heady, highminded, lovers of pleasures more than lovers of God; Having a form of godliness, but denying the power*

thereof: from such turn away. For of this sort are they which creep into houses, and lead captive silly women laden with sins, led away with divers lusts, Ever learning, and never able to come to the knowledge of the truth." II Timothy 3:1-7

2. The antichrist (***Man of Sin, Son of Perdition***) will be revealed (II Thessalonians 2:3).
3. He will sit in the rebuilt Jewish Temple in Jerusalem and declare himself to be God (II Thessalonians 2:4)
4. The antichrist will be satanically powered, and will show ***power, signs and lying wonders.*** Today there is little doubt that these ***signs*** will be seen by the whole world on the internet, CNN News, CBS, NBC and Fox network.

The Bridegroom Arrives

The bridegroom (Christ) now arrives to invite them to His Wedding. Carefully note that the Wedding of the Lamb and the Wedding Supper both have one thing in common: no one will be at either celebration unless they have accepted Jesus Christ as their Savior. There are five wise virgins and five foolish virgins. What separates the wise from the foolish? And what do they all have in common?

1. They all have **lamp**s. The lamps which they all had was their mortal body. The fuel for their lamps was the oil of God's word and the light was Christ Jesus in them.

> *"Let your light so shine before men, that they may see your good works, and glorify your Father which is in heaven."* Matthew 5:16

> *"But now the righteousness of god apart from the law is revealed, being witnessed by the law and the prophets."* Romans 3:21

2. ***"Thy word is a lamp unto my feet and a light unto my path"*** (Psalms 119:105). Everyone can understand the 10 commandments, whether they are part of their religion or not. All have heard the word.
3. Christ said that **I am the word made flesh, and I am the light of the world.**

"Whosoever therefore shall be ashamed of me and of my words in this adulterous and sinful generation; of him also shall the Son of man be ashamed, when he cometh in the glory of his Father with the holy angels"
Mark 8:38

4. All had *some oil* in their lamps. Oil in this case does not necessarily represent the indwelling of the Holy Spirit as most have proposed. In fact, a word search of the New Testament does not provide concrete support for this concept at all. If *oil* in this parable is symbolic of the Holy Spirit, it is completely out of context. First, the foolish virgins who were low on oil were told to go and buy some more. The Holy Spirit cannot be bought and sold; it is imputed to every born-again Christian freely and in full measure. Second, the wise virgins were asked to *give away some of their oil*. The Holy Spirit cannot be transferred from one to the other. We are best advised to interpret the meaning of the word oil to symbolically represent the main themes of this parable: to be watchful and prepared. The foolish virgins were not prepared; the wise virgins were prepared. This is consistent with interpreting the word virgin to simply represent a group of ten, and not to be interpreted as born again Christians. With this foundation, we see that: A cry was made: ***the bridegroom cometh***. In the parable, all arose and ***trimmed their lamps***; they tried to light their lamps. The *wise virgins* were ready; the *foolish virgins* were not ready.
5. The foolish virgins immediately recognized that they were in deep trouble, and tried to *buy some oil* from the wise virgins. Their reply was devastating: ***Not so, lest there be not enough for us and you, but go ye rather to them that sell and buy for yourselves.*** At first glance, this

seems very out of place. Salvation and being ready, being prepared, and being watchful is a personal decision, and no one can accept Christ as savior for anyone else. In addition to this parable focusing on being ready and prepared, the parable stresses the urgency of accepting Jesus Christ as their savior before it is too late. Millions of unbelievers have died without being prepared for eternity… they have passed from life into eternal damnation by not being prepared…they have never really accepted Jesus Christ as their savor. ***Go to them that sell…*** in other words, seek Christ and He will find you. But, in this case it is too late. The foolish virgins go to find oil (salvation) but the door is shut…Christ said ***I don't know you.*** What a horrible tragedy. We are told to ***watch always***; always be ***prepared*** and ***be ready***; we must go about the business of winning souls to Christ as if today was the last day.

6. While they went to ***buy***, the bridegroom arrived, and those who were ready and prepared went to the wedding. The concept of *buying* in this parable is exactly what Christ told the Church at Philadelphia.

   I counsel thee to buy of me gold tried in the fire, that thou mayest be rich; and white raiment, that thou mayest be clothed, and that the shame of thy nakedness do not appear; and anoint thine eyes with eyesalve, that thou mayest see." Rev 3:18

7. They now return and plead: ***Lord, Lord ,open to us***. But they hear a terrible pronouncement: ***I Know you not***. It has been almost 2000 years since Christ established the New Covenant of salvation by grace; the door to eternal life has been wide open. After the Battle of Armageddon it will be closed. There will be no second chance, the fate of all who are still alive at this time has been determined: eternal life or eternal damnation. The tragic ending to this parable is that the foolish virgins now try to enter into and take part in the wedding feast. Christ's response is swift and final. *"I know you not."*

The words of Christ echo through the ages:

> *Not everyone who saith unto Me , Lord, Lord, shall enter into the Kingdom of Heaven* Matthew 7:21

Further Explanation of the Parable

It is the opinion of this author that the Parable of the Wise and Foolish Virgins is the most difficult of all Kingdom Parables in the Book of Matthew. We have proposed that the setting and context of this parable is the rapture of all living believers at the last trump immediately followed by the *Wedding of the Lamb* in heaven (Rev 19:7). The Battle of Armageddon will occur 10 days later on the Feast of Yom Kippur, and following that great battle the *Wedding Supper* of the Lamb will take place on the earth (Rev 19:9); most likely during the *Feast of Tabernacles*. However, as we have pointed out, the bride of Christ is never even mentioned in this parable. The bride of Christ is not separately identified in this parable because the Bride of Christ is many and not one. All of the Wise Virgins will be a part of the Bride of Christ. The bride is the body of Christ.

> *"For as the body is one, and hath many members, and all the members of that one body, being many, are one body: so also is Christ. But now hath God set the members every one of them in the body, as it hath pleased him. But now are they many members, yet but one body."* I Corinthians 12:12, 18, 20

This parable is a description of those who will be invited to the *Wedding of the Lamb*. The Wise Virgins will attend; the Foolish Virgins will not. The *Wedding Supper* will have *guests;* all of those be all of those who were not at the Wedding of the Lamb, but have turned to Jesus Christ as the Son of God and survived the Wrath of God..... the seven bowl judgments. A large part of this group will be the Foolish Virgins.

For years I believed that since the Bride of Christ was never mentioned in this parable, that the parable must be describing the Wedding Feast on Earth. This conclusion cannot be sustained by carefully examining the scriptures. *First,* note that the arrival of the bridegroom (Christ) is both sudden and unexpected. This would hardly be the case if this parable is describing the *Wedding Supper* of the Lamb, because if this is true the rapture of the saints would have occurred sometime before the Wedding Supper of the Lamb and no one would be surprised. *Second*, the Foolish Virgins are told to ***go and find oil*** for their lamps which had gone out. They did so and even returned some time later. This could not be true if this occurred at the Wedding Supper because the church age and the age of grace ends at the Battle of Armageddon; which **precedes** the Wedding Supper. *Third*, it may be significant to note that Christ denied them entry to the Wedding Ceremony by saying; "I ***know you not***". He did not say that He would never know them.

A fundamental truth in scripture is that no one who has accepted Christ as their savior before the seventh trumpet sounds and the rapture occurs will have to go through the Wrath of God. They will all be participating in the heavenly wedding ceremony of the Lamb. This fundamental truth is maintained throughout the New Testament, and in the sequence of end time events and when they occur as presented in this book. In a final act of grace, many who will have to go through the 7 bowl judgments will accept Christ as their Messiah and be saved. Sadly, many others will not take this last opportunity to receive eternal life and accept Jesus Christ as their savior. These will blindly follow the Antichrist and his false prophet to the Battle of Armageddon where they will be destroyed by a ***sharp sword*** which ***comes out of His*** (Christ's) ***mouth*** (Rev 19:15). Christ predicted this would happen; some will continue to follow the antichrist and Satan to their destruction.

> **"He that is unjust, let him be unjust still: and he which is filthy, let him be filthy still: and he that is righteous, let him be righteous still: and he that is holy, let him be holy still."**   Rev 22:11

Some of the Jewish foolish virgins will never turn to Christ, but some will. These and the Jewish wise virgins will enter into all of the joys and wonders of the millennial kingdom. Some may think that this last minute redemption is unfair. Many Christians have endured persecution and tribulation throughout their entire life; some will have just gone through the tribulation period and suffered greatly; and at the wedding feast they will sit next to someone who has just been saved. The question of whether or not anyone can be saved at the *last hour* is settled by what happened at Calvary. Just before he died, one of the sinners which hung on a cross next to Christ finally recognized that he was the Son of God and asked to be remembered when Christ came into His kingdom. Christ replied that: *"today thou wilt be with me in Paradise"*. That very hour the thief was saved. He will be at both the Wedding of the Lamb and the Wedding Feast. This is exactly what will happen to the wise virgins during the last seven days of this age.

Recall that the two primary messages of this parable were to be *watchful* and be *prepared*. This cannot be denied, but there is an equally-important message that follows these two commands. The time for salvation is now: not tomorrow or the next day. In this same discourse, Christ twice reinforced the importance of not delaying this decision.

> *"Watch, therefore: for ye know not what hour your Lord doth come."*   Matthew 24:42

> *"Watch, therefore, for you know neither the day nor the hour wherein the Son of Man cometh."*
> Matthew 25:13

As the Wedding Feast is celebrated, it is time to rest and be joyful. It is our belief that this feast will be held during the Feast of Tabernacles, which will be held between Nisan 15-Nisan 22. We have discussed this in Chapter 9: (The Seven Feasts of Israel) and in Chapter 24. It is now time to begin the millennial kingdom, but first we will discuss the greatest battle in history, the battle of Armageddon.

Thoughts and Things…………

Chapter 26

The Three Invasions of Jerusalem

Everyone who has even casually studied prophecy and the Book of Revelation is familiar with the final invasion of Jerusalem which is called the Battle of Armageddon. However, few casual students of prophecy (and some experienced prophecy teachers) have failed to recognize that there will be three major invasions of Jerusalem in the end times.

- ➤ The first will take place either immediately preceding or just after the 3.5 year tribulation period begins. We will call this invasion *The Jerusalem Campaign* (Van Kampen).
- ➤ The second will occur on the *last day* of the tribulation period; *The Battle of Armageddon*.
- ➤ The third will mark the *last event* in the 1000 year millennial kingdom. We will call this *Satan's Last Stand*

We will now discuss each of these three invasions in some detail.

The Jerusalem Campaign

We believe that the first invasion of Jerusalem will take place very early in the 1260 day tribulation period. The exact time that this invasion takes place is relatively unimportant, but the results are of great interest to prophecy studies. We will call this initial invasion the *Jerusalem Campaign* to distinguish it from the other two invasions. This identification was first suggested by Robert Van Kampen in his book *The Sign*.

The Jerusalem Campaign will follow a series of events which will likely initiate the last 3.5 years of tribulation. These events have previously been discussed in other chapters, but they will be summarized here for continuity.

- A great world leader will emerge out of the old Roman Empire who will by divine appointment be the most charismatic and influential individual to ever live. He will arise out of a European 10 nation confederacy, and by military strength he will conquer 3 of these nations and become the sole dictator.
- By supernatural influence, he will then do something which will seem strange to prophecy students. He will initiate a pact with Israel, and place them in a position of peace and security. The wars which are now raging between Muslims, Palestine and other nations will cease. Peace will reign over Israel. However, this covenant of peace will be in reality a covenant with death. This is a covenant made with Satan and not with God.

"Wherefore hear the word of the LORD, ye scornful men, that rule this people which is in Jerusalem. Because ye have said, We have made a covenant with death, and with hell are we at agreement; when the overflowing scourge shall pass through, it shall not come unto us: for we have made lies our refuge, and under falsehood have we hid ourselves:" Is. 28:14-15

- By supernatural power he will do an astounding thing: He will manage to rebuild Herod's Temple and restore the Old Testament rituals to the Jewish people (Rev 11:1-2). This will result in Israel exalting this world leader to the position of their long awaited deliverer. They will be deluded into thinking that this is their prophesied Messiah. The Nation of Israel will be *blinded in Part* (Romans 11:7) until they see the truth.

"Even him, whose coming is after the working of Satan with all power and signs and lying wonders, and with all deceivableness of unrighteousness in them that perish; because they received not the love of the truth, that they might be saved. And for this cause God shall send them strong delusion, that they should believe a

lie: That they all might be damned who believed not the truth, but had pleasure in unrighteousness."
II Thessalonians 9-12

- Immediately before the Jerusalem Campaign, a war between Satan and the heavenly hosts, led by the Archangel Michael, will take place. Satan and his angels will be cast out of heaven (Rev 12:7-9).
- Satan will be furious, and immediately cause the great world leader to initiate death and destruction (Rev 6:4,8). Either just before or just after Satan is cast down, the world leader will attack and conquer three of the nations, and by political and military power he will assume control and unify all 10 nations (Dan 7:24). We believe that it is during these military invasions that the great world leader will be *wounded as to death* (Rev 13:3,14): His body and mind will then be taken over by a strong Satanic Prince; he will be dedicated to serve Satan; and he will live only to eradicate all Jews and Christians. He will be the prophesied antichrist.
- He will assume the role of *sole dictator* over the original 10 nation confederacy and unify all military power under his leadership.
- His first satanic act will be to break the covenant of peace with Israel and invade the Holy City of Jerusalem.

"And your covenant with death shall be disannulled, and your agreement with hell shall not stand; when the overflowing scourge shall pass through, then ye shall be trodden down by it." Isaiah 28:18

The Jerusalem Campaign is described by the prophet Zechariah.

"Awake, O sword, against my shepherd, and against the man that is my fellow, saith the LORD of hosts: smite the shepherd, and the sheep shall be scattered: and I will turn mine hand upon the little ones. And it shall come to pass, that in all the land, saith the LORD, two parts therein shall be cut off and die; but the third

> *shall be left therein. And I will bring the third part through the fire, and will refine them as silver is refined, and will try them as gold is tried: they shall call on my name, and I will hear them: I will say, It is my people: and they shall say, The LORD is my God."*
> Zechariah 13:7-9

The prophecy is staggering. It reveals that 2/3 of all the people will be killed, and only 1/3 will survive. This remnant will flee to the mountains and canyons of Western Israel, where they will be divinely protected. Most prophecy scholars identify their place of refuge as Petra.

The destruction of Jerusalem and the death of 2/3 of the people will also be associated with another act of apostasy. After the invasion, the temple will be desecrated and an image of the antichrist will be erected in the temple. All who see this image will be forced to worship it or face death. Christ spoke of all these things in the Olivet Discourse.

> *"When ye therefore shall see the abomination of desolation, spoken of by Daniel the prophet, stand in the holy place, (whoso readeth, let him understand) Then let them which be in Judaea flee into the mountains: Let him which is on the housetop not come down to take any thing out of his house: Neither let him which is in the field return back to take his clothes. And woe unto them that are with child, and to them that give suck in those days! But pray ye that your flight be not in the winter, neither on the sabbath day: For then shall be great tribulation, such as was not since the beginning of the world to this time, no, nor ever shall be."* Matthew 24:15-21

It is interesting to note that Christ was living under the law when He spoke these words, and He knew that when this happened, every Jew who would not accept Him as Lord and Savior would also be under the law. One of the prohibitions was that if this occurred on Saturday (the Jewish Sabbath) no one would be able to flee on foot more than about ½ mile without breaking the law of Moses (Acts 1:12, Ex 16:29, Num 35:5). It is also noteworthy that in this warning, this event would be followed by severe tribulation.

> *"For then shall be great tribulation, such as was not since the beginning of the world to this time, no, nor ever shall be".* Matthew 24:21

This is exactly correct following our belief that the tribulation period is only 3.5 years, and that it begins with the Jerusalem Campaign.

The Battle of Armageddon

The ***Battle of Armageddon*** is referred to by that name only once in the Holy Scriptures (Rev 16:16). This phrase is used to refer to that last great battle between Satan and Christ in Rev 19: 11-21. Christ will return to earth to fight this epic battle with Satan, the antichrist, the false prophet and all of their followers. The armies of the antichrist, or at least the main body, will cross the Euphrates River which has been dried up when the sixth bowl is poured out (Rev 16:12). The antichrist and his armies will rapidly advance to Jerusalem, and camp near the city in the *Valley of Jezreel* where they will mobilize to attack Jerusalem. The word *Armageddon* comes from a Hebrew phrase *Har-Magedone*, *Har* means *hill* and *Megedone* is a *location name*. The exact location of Armageddon is unclear because there is no known hill or mountain called Megiddo. The most likely reference is to the general hill country surrounding the *plain* of Megiddo, some sixty miles north of Jerusalem. Everyone on the earth who worships the antichrist will also be gathered to this place by three *unclean spirits* called demons (Rev 16:13-14). The *whole world* of antichrist's followers will be assembled by Satan (Rev 16:13). This is his last chance to destroy God's eternal plan, and he will use all of his deception and power to mobilize his forces. Suddenly, without warning Christ will ascend from heaven. The arrival of Christ and the total destruction of Satan and his followers are described below.

> *"And I saw heaven opened, and behold a white horse; and he that sat upon him was called Faithful and True, and in righteousness he doth judge and make war. His eyes were as a flame of fire, and on his head were many crowns; and he had a name written, that no man knew, but he himself. And he was clothed with a vesture dipped in blood: and his name is called The Word of God. And the armies which were in heaven followed him upon white horses, clothed in fine linen, white and clean. And out of his mouth goeth a sharp sword, that with it he should smite the nations: and he shall rule them with a rod of iron: and he treadeth the winepress of the fierceness and wrath of Almighty God. And he hath on his vesture and on his thigh a name written,*
>
> *KING OF KINGS, AND LORD OF LORDS.*
>
> *And I saw an angel standing in the sun; and he cried with a loud voice, saying to all the fowls that fly in the midst of heaven, Come and gather yourselves together unto the supper of the great God; That ye may eat the flesh of kings, and the flesh of captains, and the flesh of mighty men, and the flesh of horses, and of them that sit on them, and the flesh of all men, both free and bond, both small and great. And I saw the beast, and the kings of the earth, and their armies, gathered together to make war against him that sat on the horse, and against his army."*   Rev 19: 11-21

Christ will arrive on the *Feast of Yom Kippur* on a white horse. This is the second time that a rider on a white horse has arrived on earth. The first (Rev 6:2) was Satan riding out *conquering and to conquer*. The second is none other than our Lord Jesus Christ riding out to conquer Satan and his followers. *He is called faithful and true* for the third time (Rev 1:5, 3:7, 19:11). His eyes are like a *flame of fire*, and have not changed since John first saw Him in Rev 1:14. He is descending from heaven (Rev 19:11) with a heavenly entourage. On his head are *many crowns*. These are *diadem crowns* worn by heavenly creatures and redeemed saints, and not *stephanos crowns* worn by earthly rulers. In Rev 19:13 we are told something very unusual: he is clothed in a *robe dipped in blood*. Since the battle of Armageddon has not begun yet, from where did this blood come? The meaning is not explained and is difficult to determine. ***It has been suggested*** that Christ has just come from *Bozrah* where those who fled Jerusalem following the Jerusalem Campaign have been hiding and protected for 42 months. As Christ escorts them to Jerusalem he is vanquishing His enemies along the way (Isaiah 63:1-6).

> *"Who is this that comes from Eden with dyed garments from Bozrah? Why is your apparel red, and your garments like one who treads in the winepress? I have trodden the winepress alone; and from the peoples no one was with me. For I have trodden them in My anger, and trampled them in My fury; their blood is sprinkled upon My garments and I have stained all My robes."*   Isaiah 63:1-3

This interpretation is compelling, but does not fit the context of Rev 19:11. In fact, it is more likely that Christ would not go to Bozrah until ***after*** the battle of Armageddon is over. Where is this described in the Book of Revelation?

In Rev 14:1-20 we have seen that an angel appears out of the temple and upon command thrusts a *sharp sickle* into the earth and reaps. The fruit that is reaped is unbelievers, who are thrown into the *winepress of the Wrath of God*. This is referencing the *Wrath of God* which is clearly the seven bowl judgments, but the climax of the winepress is at the battle of Armageddon. Note that *the winepress was trampled outside the city* (Jerusalem) in the battle of Armageddon (Rev 14:20). His robe is not *sprinkled* as one might expect in battle, but *dipped* (Rev 19:13). This is the same Greek word used when Christ *dipped or sopped* his bread at the last supper. In addition, in Rev 19:13 the Battle of Armageddon has not even begun yet. We can offer no sustainable interpretation of why the robe of Christ is *dipped in blood* when Christ comes down from heaven, but is seen wearing robes *sprinkled in blood* when returning from Bozrah. It is our belief that this robe of white is symbolically dipped in His own precious blood which was shed at Calvary. Note that the prophet Isaiah writes that ***I*** (Jesus Christ) ***have trodden the winepress alone.*** We cannot believe that Is 63:1-3 occurs *before* the Battle of Armageddon, since this would require a second advent well before the triumphant return described in Rev 11:19. Our best conclusion is that Is 6:1-3 is describing an event immediately following the Battle of Armageddon, but we cannot be dogmatic on this interpretation.

Christ will fight the battle of Armageddon with only one weapon: ***a sharp sword out of His mouth***. Using this sword, ***he alone will tread the winepress of the fierceness and wrath of God almighty***. This is Christ's personal battle and He treads the winepress alone. Christ needs no help. The battle is not protracted but is won supernaturally in a short period of time. Zechariah describes it in gory detail.

> ***"Behold, the day of the LORD cometh, and thy spoil shall be divided in the midst of thee. For I will gather all nations against Jerusalem to battle; and the city shall be taken, and the houses rifled, and the women ravished; and half of the city shall go forth into captivity, and the residue of the people shall not be cut off from the city. Then shall the LORD go forth, and fight against those nations, as when he fought in the day of battle. And his feet shall stand in that day upon the mount of Olives, which is before Jerusalem on the east, and the mount of Olives shall cleave in the midst thereof toward the east and toward the west, and there shall be a very great valley; and half of the mountain shall remove toward the north, and half of it toward the south. And ye shall flee to the valley of the mountains; for the valley of the mountains shall reach unto Azal: yea, ye shall flee, like as ye fled from before the earthquake in the days of Uzziah king of Judah: and the LORD my God shall come, and all the saints with thee. And it shall come to pass in that day, that the light shall not be clear, nor dark: But it shall be one day which shall be known to the LORD, not day, nor***

night: but it shall come to pass, that at evening time it shall be light. And it shall be in that day, that living waters shall go out from Jerusalem; half of them toward the former sea, and half of them toward the hinder sea: in summer and in winter shall it be. And the LORD shall be king over all the earth: in that day shall there be one LORD, and his name one. All the land shall be turned as a plain from Geba to Rimmon south of Jerusalem: and it shall be lifted up, and inhabited in her place, from Benjamin's gate unto the place of the first gate, unto the corner gate, and from the tower of Hananeel unto the king's winepresses. And men shall dwell in it, and there shall be no more utter destruction; but Jerusalem shall be safely inhabited. And this shall be the plague wherewith the LORD will smite all the people that have fought against Jerusalem; their flesh shall consume away while they stand upon their feet, and their eyes shall consume away in their holes, and their tongue shall consume away in their mouth." Zechariah 14: 1-12

The armies which are in heaven, clothed in fine linen, white and clean, followed Him on white horses (Rev 19:14). Who are those who follow Him on white horses? There are many who say that these followers are angels. There are many passages that associate the coming of Jesus Christ with His angels. Angels are assigned various duties in the scriptures, but in no single passage are they said to war with Satan at the battle of Armageddon. There are, however, several passages which seem to indicate that those following Christ on white horses are the Bride of Christ and the overcomers of Rev 2-3. They are also clothed in **white, clean, fine linen** (Rev 3:4, 18; 19: 14). In Rev 17:14 those with him are called **chosen and faithful**. These terms apply to those who have faithfully followed and served Christ. In Rev 3:5, Christ promises those who overcome that they will be *clothed in white garments*. The great multitude that John saw standing before the throne in Rev 7: 9, 13; who are identified as the raptured and resurrected saints, are wearing *white robes*. Based upon these supporting scriptures, it is safe to conjecture that the saints who have been with Christ at the Marriage of the Lamb now return with him to the Battle of Armageddon. It is certain that the 144,000 *firstfruits* taken into heaven before the last 1260 days of the tribulation period are with Christ, since these are the ones *who follow the Lamb wherever He goes* (Rev 14:4*)*.

We are now given some identifying characteristics of Christ as He will appear at His second advent. In Rev 19:12, He has *many crowns* and a name written *that no one knew except Himself.* It is not revealed where this name was written. It is interesting that the overcomer (Philadelphia) is promised that he will be given the *name of My God*, and the name of the *city of my God*, and Christ will write on him ***My new name*** (Christ's) (Rev 3:12). Every overcomer will also be given a ***white stone*** (Rev 2:17) with a new name that *no one knows except him who receives it.* The average Christian understands the basic principle of a covenant relationship with Christ, but few understand what this initiated in the Old Testament. When a covenant was made between two people, two things happened: (1) they exchanged a portion of their garments, and (2) each was given a new name that only they knew. How revealing this custom is to our relationship with Christ! We will be given a new name and new garments of white by Jesus Christ. In Rev 19: 16 Christ has *on his robe and on his thigh a name written* **King of Kings and Lord of Lords.**

The carnage from the battle of Armageddon will be unprecedented in all of history. There will probably be millions of people killed, and thousands of horses. Blood will run to the *horses' bridals.* This is probably after being mixed with millions of gallons of water from melting 100-pound hailstones that have just fallen from heaven (Rev 16:21).The carnage will obstruct all movement of people (Ezekiel 39:11) in the *Valley of Hamon Gog*, which simply means *the valley of Gog*, or the valley of a ruler; who in this case is the antichrist. It will take seven months for Israel to cleanse the land of bones and dead bodies (Ezekiel 39:12-15). Before Christ comes, the city of Jerusalem and its inhabitants will be on the brink of extinction. *Two-thirds* of the people will be *cut off and die*, and only *one-third* will survive (Rev 9:15-18). At that time Israel will turn to the only one who can save them. They will finally call upon Jesus Christ and recognize Him as their long-awaited Messiah. Jesus Christ prophesied of this before He went to the cross of Calvary.

> *"O Jerusalem, Jerusalem, the one who kills the prophets and stones those who are sent to her! How often I wanted to gather your children together, as a hen gathers her chicks under her wings, but you were not wiling! See! Your house is left to you desolate; for I say to you, you shall see Me no more till you say, Blessed is He who comes in the name of the Lord."* Rev 23:37-39

Following the Battle of Armageddon, the covenant made to Abraham will be fulfilled (land, seed and blessing) and a new covenant will be established with all of Israel; and so *all of Israel* (those who are left alive) *will be saved.*

> *"For I would not, brethren, that ye should be ignorant of this mystery, lest ye should be wise in your own conceits; that blindness in part is happened to Israel, until the fulness of the Gentiles be come in. And so all Israel shall be saved: as it is written, There shall come out of Sion the Deliverer, and shall turn away ungodliness from Jacob: For this is my covenant unto them, when I shall take away their sins."*
> Romans 11:25-27

> *"Behold, the days come, saith the LORD, that I will make a new covenant with the house of Israel, and with the house of Judah: Not according to the covenant that I made with their fathers in the day that I took them by the hand to bring them out of the land of Egypt; which my covenant they brake, although I was an husband unto them, saith the LORD: But this shall be the covenant that I will make with the house of Israel; After those days, saith the LORD, I will put my law in their inward parts, and write it in their hearts; and will be their God, and they shall be my people."*
> Jeremiah 31: 31-33

The *day of the Lord* will finally come to its long awaited conclusion. The beast (antichrist) and the false prophet will be cast alive into the lake of fire and brimstone.

> *"And I saw the beast, and the kings of the earth, and their armies, gathered together to make war against him that sat on the horse, and against his army. And the beast was taken, and with him the false prophet that wrought miracles before him, with which he deceived them that had received the mark of the beast, and them that worshipped his image. These both were cast alive into a lake of fire burning with brimstone."* Rev 19:19:20

That old serpent the devil, called Satan, will be cast into the bottomless pit where he is confined and bound for 1000 years.

> *"And I saw an angel come down from heaven, having the key of the bottomless pit and a great chain in his hand. And he laid hold on the dragon, that old serpent, which is the Devil, and Satan, and bound him a thousand years, And cast him into the bottomless pit, and shut him up, and set a seal upon him, that he should deceive the nations no more, till the thousand years should be fulfilled: and after that he must be loosed a little season."* Rev 20: 1:3

All of the followers of Satan… *every one* … are *killed with the sword which proceeded from the mouth of Him (Christ) who sat on the horse*. The Wrath of God is now complete.

After the battle, there will be two great feasts on the earth. The *first* will be on the fields of Armageddon, and the guests will be all of the birds of prey and carrion to feast upon the dead bodies.

> *"And I saw an angel standing in the sun; and he cried with a loud voice, saying to all the fowls that fly in the midst of heaven, Come and gather yourselves together unto the supper of the great God; That ye may eat the flesh of kings, and the flesh of captains, and the flesh of mighty men, and*

the flesh of horses, and of them that sit on them, and the flesh of all men, both free and bond, both small and great." Rev 19:17-18

The birds of prey feasting on dead bodies explain another mysterious statement made by Christ just prior to his crucifixion:

"For wherever the carcass is, there the eagles will be gathered together" Rev 24:28

The second feast will be the *Marriage Supper of the Lamb.*

"Let us be glad and rejoice, and give honour to him: for the marriage of the Lamb is come, and his wife hath made herself ready. And to her was granted that she should be arrayed in fine linen, clean and white: for the fine linen is the righteousness of saints. And he saith unto me, Write, Blessed are they which are called unto the marriage supper of the Lamb. And he saith unto me, These are the true sayings of God." Rev 19:7-9

Our Lord Jesus Christ is now victorious, and the 1000-year millennial kingdom is at hand.

Satan's Last Stand
Every Christian can be comforted and reassured of one fundamental truth: God is in control of His creation, and His Son Jesus Christ will conquer Satan; do away with all sin; usher in a new world of peace and righteousness; and banish Satan to an eternity of torture in the Lake of Burning Fire. All of these things will not take place until *after* the 1000 year millennial kingdom has come to an end. A common misconception is that after the Church age is over and Christ returns for the second time to rule and reign over the earth, that there will be no sin and no sinners for 1000 years. There are two biblical passages which negate this common belief.

> *"And it shall come to pass, that every one that is left of all the nations which came against Jerusalem shall even go up from year to year to worship the King, the LORD of hosts, and to keep the feast of tabernacles.] And it shall be, that whoso will not come up of all the families of the earth unto Jerusalem to worship the King, the LORD of hosts, even upon them shall be no rain. And if the family of Egypt go not up, and come not, that have no rain; there shall be the plague, wherewith the LORD will smite the heathen that come not up to keep the feast of tabernacles. This shall be the punishment of Egypt, and the punishment of all nations that come not up to keep the feast of tabernacles."* Zechariah 14:16-19

Two things are obvious from this prophecy. The first is that even after the Battle of Armageddon and the millennial kingdom begins, there will be rebellion and disregard for Christ and His ordinances. The people will be required to go to Jerusalem every year to attend the Feast of Tabernacles (Zechariah 16:14-19) ..... no doubt to celebrate and remember their deliverance at the Battle of Armageddon. Some are called **heathen**, and they will be punished for their disobedience. The punishment will be **no rain** and an unknown **plague** (Zechariah 14:18).

This conclusion is made certain by the last event of the millennial kingdom.

> *"And when the thousand years are expired, Satan shall be loosed out of his prison, and shall go out to deceive the nations which are in the four quarters of the earth, Gog and Magog, to gather them together to battle: the number of whom is as the sand of the sea. And they went up on the breadth of the earth, and compassed the camp of the saints about, and the*

> *beloved city: and fire came down from God out of heaven, and devoured them. And the devil that deceived them was cast into the lake of fire and brimstone, where the beast and the false prophet are, and shall be tormented day and night for ever and ever."* Rev 20:7-10

This is the third and last military campaign against Jerusalem. It will be referred to as *Satan's Last Stand*. Satan will be loosed from heaven and will again ***deceive the nations*** from the ***four quarters of the earth***. If it was not written by John it would be hard to believe….. There will be as many as the ***sand of the sea*** that joins Satan. This is the only place in Holy Scripture that this battle is recorded, and the end is swift and final: ***Fire came down from heaven and devoured them.***

Why was Satan released to do this horrible thing? Why did so many people march against Christ? The answer is both revealing and true. First, it is clear that just as in Noah's day, the world had become wicked and sinful. The people who perished in this last battle were descended from the seed of Adam and they carried with them the old man… the sin nature. These are a physical remnant of Abraham who have inherited the land… the Jewish remnant that fulfilled the Abramic Covenant. Most of this earthly population have been born of Israelites who were living in the land, but some may have lived since the millennial kingdom began. Evidently, since the land will be restored to an Edenic state man will live a very long time…possibly longer than Methuselah.

> *"There shall be no more thence an infant of days, nor an old man that hath not filled his days: for the child shall die an hundred years old; but the sinner being an hundred years old shall be accursed."* Isaiah 65:20

The prophet Isaiah is referring to real people, with earthly bodies. Hence, they were each born with the original curse of sin that was passed down from Adam. If man returning to a rebellious and sinful state seems too hard to believe since Christ is ruling and reigning over them, one only needs to remember what happened only 50 days after God had Moses lead his people from Egypt. Moses arrived at Mt Sinai on the 47th day, and went up to receive the law. When he returned, the people were engaged in adulterous acts and worshipping idols... only 47 days after crossing the Red Sea, and within the very sight of God's shekinah light!! Second, the intention of God has always been to establish a new heaven and a new earth, and restore man to the Edenic state. The *passport* to this new kingdom is simple: Accept His Son Jesus Christ as lord and savior, and receive eternal life by amazing grace. However, before eternity can begin which is totally free from sin, the covenant given to Abraham by God himself must be completed. Israel must be in the land. Since the curse of a sinful nature is inherited by anyone born of the flesh; it had to be removed forever. The final battle of Jerusalem will accomplished this goal.

Gog and Magog

We would like to conclude this discussion with an examination of *Gog* and *Magog.* The names of Gog and Magog appear in only three places in the Authorized King James bible: Ezekiel 38:1-3, Ezekiel 39:1 and in Revelation 20:7-8. The relationship between these three passages of scripture has been a subject of debate for over 2000 years. There are three major issues which are in debate: The *first* is exactly who or what do the nouns Gog and Magog represent? The *second* is whether or not Ezekiel 38 and Ezekiel 39 refer to the same battle or different battles? The *third* is which of the three *Jerusalem Invasions* does Ezekiel 38 and Ezekiel 39 describe? The reader is asked at this time to read Ezekiel 38 and 39 before proceeding. These are lengthy chapters and will not be duplicated here.

Magog was a grandson of Noah and a son of Japheth. His name appears in the *table of nations* In Gen 10-11, which detail the generations of the sons of Noah, Shem, Ham, and Japheth. From this genealogy, the entire world was populated, so we are all descended from Noah. We have not evolved from apes! Magog is not referring to a reincarnated son of Japheth, but to the nations and people that he spawned out of his loins. The descendants of Magog migrated to the land north of the Caucasus Mountains in an area between the Black and Caspian Seas. Magog, Meshach and Tubal are all mentioned by Ezekiel. They spawned the Russians, Muscovites, Germans, Siberians and other people who formed modern northern Europe (Dake). Some claim that by this genealogy, Russia will be the leader of those who invade Jerusalem and will be the main force led by **Gog**. Even if Russia is included in this invasion force, it does not prove in any way that she (Russia) will be the dominating force. Dan 11:44 plainly predicts that Russia and the Northern nations will be conquered by the antichrist and his forces as the last 3.5 years of Daniel's 70th week unfolds. In conclusion, Magog is referring to a group of Northern countries that will be led by a person called *Gog*. There is no person called John Gog, or Paul Gog or even Gog; Gog is a title for the leader of these invading forces. In context of our previous discussion, the leader of the invasion described in Ezekiel 38 is called **Gog**, The *chief prince* of the invasion described in Ezekiel 39 is also called **Gog**, but hese are not the same person as we will shortly see.

The third question is the one to which we will devote the most analysis: What is the relationship between Ezekiel 38, Ezekiel 39 and Rev 20:7-8? We believe that by carefully examining all of these scriptures that the only conclusion that satisfies the scriptural accounts is to identify the following correlations.

- ➢ Ezekiel 38 is describing the *Jerusalem Campaign*, which takes place in the first few days of the last 3.5 years of tribulation.
- ➢ Ezekiel 39 is describing the *Battle of Armageddon* which closes the tribulation period.
- ➢ Rev 20:7-8 describe the final assault of Satan against Christ, and stands independent of Ezekiel 38 and 39. The appearance of the nouns Gog and Magog in Rev 20:8 are referring to the leader (Gog) and the lands or nations (Magog) that will form to attack Christ. This leader is in fact Satan, which proves that the term *Gog* is simply describing a vile and evil person.

Comparing Ezekiel 38 to Ezekiel 39

The fact that Ezekiel 38 is describing a different battle from Ezekiel 39 is not unique to this exegesis. The great biblical scholar Finis Jennings Dake reached this same conclusion, and provides extensive scriptural support for this position in his *Dake's Reference Bible*. It was also suggested in the *Ryrie Study Bible*, as a footnote accompanying Ezekiel 38-39. Again, recognize that there are *three* invasions of Jerusalem in the end times: (1) The *Jerusalem Campaign* as the tribulation period begins (2) the great *Battle of Armageddon* as the tribulation period ends and (3) The *Last Stand of Satan* following the Millennial Kingdom.

> - In both Ezekiel 38 and Ezekiel 39, the invading armies come from the **remote parts of the North**; (Ezekiel 38:15) and from the **north parts** (Ezekiel 39:2). Both simply identify nations north of Israel (Ezekiel 38:15). This is true of both the Jerusalem Campaign and the Battle of Armageddon, and is consistent with the antichrist and his armies. This is not true in Rev 20:8; Satan and his forces come from the *four corners of the earth* (Rev 20:8).
> - In Ezekiel 38:11, we are told that Israel is *dwelling safely*. This can only be true just prior to the Jerusalem Campaign or at the end of the Millennial kingdom; but *not* at the Battle of Armageddon.
> - In Ezekiel 38:12 we are told that the purpose of this invasion is to **take a spoil** and to turn upon the people of Israel that have been gathered **out of the nations**. This cannot be applied to either the Battle of Armageddon or Satan's Last Stand; and is best meant to describe the *Jerusalem Campaign*. The Battle of Armageddon is when the Antichrist attacks a desolate and partially destroyed Jerusalem; The Battle of Satan's Last Stand is against Christ as he reigns in Jerusalem.

- In Ezekiel 39:12, there is a detailed description of a post-battle clean-up operation. It will take 7 months to bury the dead and cleanse the land. This ***cannot*** refer to Satan's Last Stand, because after that battle a new heaven and a new earth will be formed… all of the old earth will be burned with fire. It could refer to the Jerusalem campaign, but who would clean up the carnage? Certainly not the armies of the antichrist or those who remain in Jerusalem. This can only logically apply to a period of time following the Battle of Armageddon. Both the temple and the land will need to be cleansed for the Millennial Kingdom.
- In Ezekiel 39:17-20 there is a description of the ***feathered fowl*** which will come to the battleground, and feast on the dead that are laying there. In Rev 19: 17 almost the exact words are used: After the battle of Armageddon, ***all the fowls*** are invited to eat the flesh of the slain armies of antichrist (Also see Ezekiel 39:4 and Mat 24:28).This is a very strong indication that Ezekiel 39 is describing the Battle of Armageddon.
- In Ezekiel 38:20 there is an interesting description of ***mountains being thrown down*** and ***steep places falling***. At first, this would seem to indicate that this is associated with the pouring out of the 7th bowl (Rev 16:20), and would link Ezekiel 38 to Armageddon. However, this could very well explain a *mystery*. We know that when the Jerusalem Campaign takes place, the fleeing Children of Israel would be supernaturally saved. The *mystery of how this might happen* can now possibly be explained. In Rev 12 we are told:

> ***"And the serpent cast out of his mouth water as a flood after the woman, that he might cause***

> *her to be carried away of the flood. And the earth helped the woman, and the earth opened her mouth, and swallowed up the flood which the dragon cast out of his mouth"*
> Rev 12:15-16

The earth opening its mouth is almost certainly an earthquake. If this observation is correct, then Ezekiel 38 could well be linked to the Jerusalem Campaign since this is exactly when this miracle occurred.

➢ Ezekiel 39:25-29 provides a statement of *why* the events of Ezekiel 39 occurred, and what they accomplished. It is also stated there that ALL of Israel had been gathered into the land after this battle, and this was done only after *"they have borne their shame and all their trespasses, whereby they have trespassed against me"*. This **cannot be true** following the *Jerusalem Campaign* or at *Satan's Last Stand*. This can only be true after the Battle of Armageddon, when Israel will finally realize that Christ is their long awaited Messiah and lament their transgressions and disbelief. Then all of Israel will be regathered to the land of promise.

There are many other scriptures in Ezekiel 38 and Ezekiel 39 that could be discussed, but those just given fully support the following conclusions

- Ezekiel 38 and Ezekiel 39 describe two separate battles. Ezekiel 38 is describing the *first* invasion of Jerusalem by the Antichrist and his armies. This is what we have previously called the *Jerusalem Campaign*.
- Ezekiel 39 is describing the *second* assault on Jerusalem called the *Battle of Armageddon*.

The only question not yet completely explained is why Gog and Magog are mentioned in Rev 20:7-8 if Ezekiel 38 and Ezekiel 39 describe two prior battles.

Satan's Last Stand
The following discussion relies heavily upon conclusions reached by Dake. As the Millennial Kingdom comes to a close, it will be necessary to purge all evil and sin from the earth. Satan will be loosed from his 1000 year exile in the Bottomless Pit, and he will go out to *"deceive the nations which are in the four quarters of the earth, Gog and Magog, to gather them together for battle"* (Rev20:8). As we have previously pointed out, there is no mention here of any armies being formed from the North as there are in Ezekiel 38-39. It defies all logic to assume that Satan's forces in this last battle would be confined to only areas north of Jerusalem. The purpose of Satan' defeat at this last battle is to purge all the earth of sin and vanquish Satan forever to prepare for eternity. This assault on Jerusalem and Christ will be led by Satan. He will surround the *camp of the saints* and the *beloved city*. The *camp of the saints* is no doubt referring to the area in which the believing remnant of Israel will be living during the Millennial Kingdom. The *beloved city* is Jerusalem. The reference to Gog and Magog has a straightforward explanation. As always, satan must have an earthly body from which to operate. We are not told who or where this body will represent, so the physical Satanically controlled leader of this last invasion of Jerusalem is simply called *Gog*. Magog represents the lands from which the forces of Satan are called. The two terms are used here as symbolic of all who will follow after Satan at the end of the millennial kingdom, and the four corners of the world from which they come. Neither Ezekiel 38 or Ezekiel 39 describe this final assault. The battle is barely mentioned in Rev 20:7-9 … this final battle will be swift and complete.

"and fire came down from God out of heaven and devoured them" Rev 20:9

Following this battle, all those who have rejected Christ and have followed Satan to this battle will have been destroyed. The final event which will now take place is the *Great White Throne Judgment*, in which those who have died without accepting Christ as their savior… living and dead… will be judged. (Rev 20: 11-15). This earth and its sinful nature; the curse of Adam; the corruption, temptation and disbelief caused by Satan; and all the evil that now is present will all come to an end. The end of all things is immediately described.

"And I saw a new heaven and a new earth: for the first heaven and the first earth were passed away; and there was no more sea" Rev 21:1

Before we close our look into the future, we will now discuss the Millennial Kingdom.

Thoughts and Things………..

Chapter 27

The Millennial Kingdom

The word *millennial* is not found in the book of Revelation. It is a word derived from the Latin which appears in Rev 20:2. 20:5 and 20:7. It is derived from the Latin words *mille*; thousand, and *annus*; year. The millennial kingdom was virtually hidden from both the Old and New Testament saints; even though once the Biblical Book of Revelation was composed by John one can recognize references to it in the words of the prophets. Except for Chapter 20 in the book of Revelation, the entire concept of a 1000 year span of time following Daniel's 70th week would have likely remained a *mystery*. The sequence of events leading up to the millennial kingdom is as follows.

- The Church will have been raptured out as the seventh trumpet sounds (Tishri 1, Feast of Trumpets)
- The two witnesses who have proclaimed the gospel of Jesus Christ and were slain after their testimony will rise from the dead and ascend to heaven.
- The *Bema Seat Judgment* of rewards takes place in Heaven
- The *Wedding of the Lamb* takes place in Heaven
- The *Wrath of God* is poured out upon the kingdoms of this world as the seven bowl judgments rapidly occur (Tishri 1-10)
- The *Battle of Armageddon* is fought against Satan and his followers. This is the **Day of the Lord** spoken of by many Old Testament prophets. This ends the Age of Grace; it is the last day of Daniel's 70th Week; and it is the last day of the great tribulation. At this time, the fate of all living persons has been sealed (Tishri 10, Feast of Yom Kippur)

Before the 1000 year millennial kingdom can begin, there are some incredible events which must take place.

- The 144,000 sealed Jews from 12 tribes of Israel are recovered and the remnant that had fled Jerusalem at the Jerusalem campaign are recovered from the wilderness and from Bozrah where they have been hiding from the Antichrist and Satan.
- The Judgment of the *Sheep and Goats* takes place in Jerusalem to judge the nations
- The Lord God executes the *Rod Judgment* in the wilderness
- The *antichrist and the false prophet* have been cast into the lake of burning fire
- *Satan* is cast into the bottomless pit where he is bound for 1000 years
- The *Feast of Tabernacles* is held in Jerusalem. It is a time of rest, joy and celebration (Tishri 15-22)
-

We believe that the Millennial Kingdom will begin on Tishri 15, the Feast of Tabernacles; but it could well begin on Tishri 11, the first day after the Battle of Armageddon takes place.

Daniel's Inquiry

The prophet Daniel is advanced in years, having led a full and righteous life in Babylon. He has been rewarded by being shown visions and dreams that project almost 2500 years into the future. In Daniel 12:5-6, he was standing by a river (probably the Hiddekel River (Dan 10:4), and he saw two angels standing on each side (of the river). Standing upon the river was a man in linen. One of the angels asked the man:

> ***"And one said to the man clothed in linen, which was upon the waters of the river, How long shall it be to the end of these wonders?"*** Daniel 12:6

The reply was swift and definitive.

> ***"And I heard the man clothed in linen, which was upon the waters of the river, when he held up his right hand and his left hand unto heaven, and sware by him that liveth for ever that it shall be for a time, times, and an half; and when he***

shall have accomplished to scatter the power of the holy people, all these things shall be finished." Daniel 12:7

The *he* in this passage is the antichrist. Here we have confirmation that he will reign for *a time, times and half a time,* which all agree is 42 months or 1260 days. Daniel heard but was still confused. He asked: ***What shall be the end of these things?*** (Dan 12:8). Daniel is not told of what events will end the reign of the antichrist, but he is given a time frame.

"And I heard, but I understood not: then said I, O my Lord, what shall be the end of these things? And he said, Go thy way, Daniel: for the words are closed up and sealed till the time of the end. Many shall be purified, and made white, and tried; but the wicked shall do wickedly: and none of the wicked shall understand; but the wise shall understand. And from the time that the daily sacrifice shall be taken away, and the abomination that maketh desolate set up, there shall be a thousand two hundred and ninety days. Blessed is he that waiteth, and cometh to the thousand three hundred and five and thirty days. But go thou thy way till the end be: for thou shalt rest, and stand in thy lot at the end of the days."
Daniel 12:9-13

Here is a remarkable prophecy.

- ➢ The antichrist will set up an *abomination that causes desolation* (Mat.24:15) in the rebuilt millennial temple (Rev 11:1-2).
- ➢ We know from Dan 12:7 that the antichrist will reign under Satan's influence for 1260 days, then ***all these things shall be finished*** (the reign of antichrist and Satan).
- ➢ There will be a period of 1290 days from when the abomination is set up until *"these things will end"*. What are *these things*? By comparing last days events described in Daniel to those recorded in the book of Revelation, this can only mean the consummation and fulfillment of all end time prophecies.

Daniel is also told that those who *come to the 1235th day* are *blessed*. This prophecy identifies two periods of time which will follow Daniel's 70th week: one of 30 days (1260-1290) and one of 45 days (1291-1335). Daniel did not understand and so he again asked for wisdom.

"And I (Daniel) heard, but I understood not: then said I, Oh my Lord what shall be the end of these things?"   Dan 12:8

The answer given to Daniel is not informative.

"Go the way, Daniel: for the words are closed up and sealed until the end of time"   Daniel 12:9

So there we have it! If Daniel is having a private conversation with a mighty angel sent from God and cannot fully comprehend these things, what hope do we have to fully understand all of these things? It would be foolish (as some have) to be confident in describing what is being explained here. Daniel is told not to concern himself with these things, because the words which would describe these post-tribulation events are *sealed till the time of the end*.

The 1290 Day Prophecy

We are not specifically told what will take place over these two additional periods of time, but the following scenario will be proposed. The first 30 day period immediately following the Feast of Yom Kippur and the end of the 1260 day reign of the antichrist will involve several necessary tasks. During this 30 day period, we propose that Christ (1) will establish His throne in Jerusalem, (2) Execute the Bema Seat judgment, the judgment of the Sheep and the Goats (3) the wilderness Rod Judgment with the Father (5) Judgment and sentencing passed on the antichrist, the false prophet and Satan (6) dividing the land and place the living Israelites in their allocated portion, and (7) initiating His kingdom (See Chapter 28). The next 45 day period of time will likely involve (1) cleansing the land, (2) establishing the people and placing King David on his throne and (3) rebuilding the Millennial Temple on the new Mt. Zion. (4) In addition, Jerusalem will have been destroyed during the bowl judgments and will need to be prepared for the Millennial Kingdom following the battle of Armageddon.

The people on earth (Children of Israel) will see in the flesh all of these things come to pass. They will inherit the land promised to them under the Abramic Covenant. All who inter into God's rest in the Millennial Kingdom will be called *blessed*.

> *"Blessed is he that waiteth, and cometh to the thousand three hundred and five and thirty days"* Daniel 12:12

They are called *blessed* because they have refused to worship the Antichrist and Satan, and have survived the bowl judgments. Of all the Children of Israel that have suffered and died, theirs alone is the privilege and Joy to fulfill God's covenant to Abraham. Not only that, they will actually see and talk to Moses, David and Daniel. Blessed indeed!!

It is worth reviewing what the prophet Zechariah wrote concerning what will happen in Jerusalem as the Battle of Armageddon unfolds.

> *"Behold, the day of the LORD cometh, and thy spoil shall be divided in the midst of thee. For I will gather all nations against Jerusalem to battle; and the city shall be taken, and the houses rifled, and the women ravished; and half of the city shall go forth into captivity, and the residue of the people shall not be cut off from the city. Then shall the LORD go forth, and fight against those nations, as when he fought in the day of battle. And his feet shall stand in that day upon the mount of Olives, which is before Jerusalem on the east, and the mount of Olives shall cleave in the midst thereof toward the east and toward the west, and there shall be a very great valley; and half of the mountain shall remove toward the north, and half of it toward the south."*
> Zechariah 14:2-4

When the seventh bowl judgment was executed upon the earth, the city of Jerusalem was split into three parts (Rev 16:19). The Holy Mount and the abomination that caused desolation were caused to fall when *the mountains were not found* (Rev 16:19-20). Here we see amazing geological changes. At His second advent, our Lord Jesus Christ will descent to stand upon the Mount of Olives. The Mount of Olives is actually a *tell* or *high hill* just across the Kidron Valley from the temple. It was there that Christ delivered the Olivet Discourse during His last night on this earth as the *Son of Man*. He will return triumphantly as the King of King and Lord of Lords: The only Son of God. The Mount of Olives will split into two pieces! This will form a new, *great* valley running east and west.

> *"Then shall the LORD go forth, and fight against those nations, as when he fought in the day of battle. And his feet shall stand in that day upon the mount of Olives, which is before Jerusalem on the east, and the mount of Olives shall cleave in the midst thereof toward the east and toward the west, and there shall be a very great valley; and half of the mountain shall remove toward the north, and half of it toward the south."* Zechariah 14:3-4

> *"But in the last days it shall come to pass, that the mountain of the house of the LORD shall be established in the top of the mountains, and it shall be exalted above the hills; and people shall flow unto it. And many nations shall come, and say, Come, and let us go up to the mountain of the LORD, and to the house of the God of Jacob; and he will teach us of his ways, and we will walk in his paths: for the law shall go forth of Zion, and the word of the LORD from Jerusalem."* Micah 4:1-2

After the battle ends, Christ will need to cleanse and rebuild the temple in Jerusalem, for it will be the center of worship during the Millennial Kingdom. The Temple Mount and the Holy Temple will rise again. Christ Himself will rebuild the temple in Jerusalem.

> *"Behold the man whose name is The BRANCH; and he shall grow up out of his place, and he shall build the temple of the LORD: Even he shall build the temple of the LORD; and he shall bear the glory, and shall sit and rule upon his throne; and he shall be a priest upon his throne: and the counsel of peace shall be between them both."*
> Zech 6:12-13

It should also be again noted that following the Battle of Armageddon, those of Israel who remain alive from the nations, and the sealed 144,000 of Rev 7, will be re-gathered to Jerusalem where they will be allocated the land (Ezekiel 45:1, 48).

> *"Therefore thus saith the Lord GOD; Now will I bring again the captivity of Jacob, and have mercy upon the whole house of Israel, and will be jealous for my holy name; After that they have borne their shame, and all their trespasses whereby they have trespassed against me, when they dwelt safely in their land, and none made them afraid. When I have brought them again from the people, and gathered them out of their enemies' lands, and am sanctified in them in the sight of many nations; Then shall they know that I am the LORD their God, which cause them to be led into captivity among the heathen: but I have gathered them unto their own land, and have left none of them any more there. Neither will I hide my face any more from them: for I have poured out my spirit upon the house of Israel, saith the Lord GOD."* Ezekiel 39:25-29

Immediately following a description of the Battle of Armageddon, the prophet Ezekiel next gave a detailed description of what Jerusalem will look like during the millennial kingdom (Ezekiel 38-45).

- ➢ Mount Zion will be restored and anointed as a Holy Mountain (Ezekiel 43:12)

- An Altar of Sacrifice to the Lord will be placed there (Ezekiel 38:13-17)
- In the middle of Mount Zion there will be a Most Holy Place (Ezekiel 45:3)
- The new city of Jerusalem will be rebuilt by the Israelites and the hills will be *full of grapes and vineyards* (Amos 9:13-15)

The Little Scroll and Prophetic Blueprints

Finally, we will propose to solve one of the great *mysteries* in the Book of Revelation. In Chapter 12 we discussed a **little scroll** which John the revelator saw in the hand of **another mighty angel** (Rev 10:1). The angel that held the scroll stood (Rev 10:2) upon the earth and the sea (symbolic that the message in the scroll was worldwide in scope), and **seven thunders spoke** (Rev 10:3-4). As John reached to record their message, he was told: **Seal up these things and write them not.** (Rev 10:4). This command is nearly identical to the words which Daniel heard... both revelations are *sealed until the time of the end* (Rev 10:6, Dan 12:9). We believe that the contents of the little scroll describe what will take place *after* the 70th week of Daniel and the tribulation period is over. This period of time would be 75 days, consisting of one 30 day period and one 45 day period.

We have also suggested that the key to understanding the sequence and timing of end-time events is to use the *Feasts of Israel* as a *blueprint*. We have also proposed that the 75 days following the battle of Armageddon will be filled with a series of judgments and restoration activities preparing Jerusalem for the Millennial Kingdom. It is very interesting that 75 days from the feast of Yom Kippur, which ends the tribulation period, will take us to an important Jewish holiday: the *Feast of Hanukkah*! The Feast of Hanukkah is also known as the *Festival of Lights*. It is an eight-day Jewish holiday commemorating the rededication of the Holy Temple (the second temple) in Jerusalem at the time of the Maccabean Revolt in the second century BC. Hanukkah is observed for eight nights and days, starting on the 25th day of Kislev according to the Hebrew calendar, which may occur at any time from late November to late December on the Gregorian calendar. What a fitting occasion to dedicate the restored Millennial Temple and praise Christ.

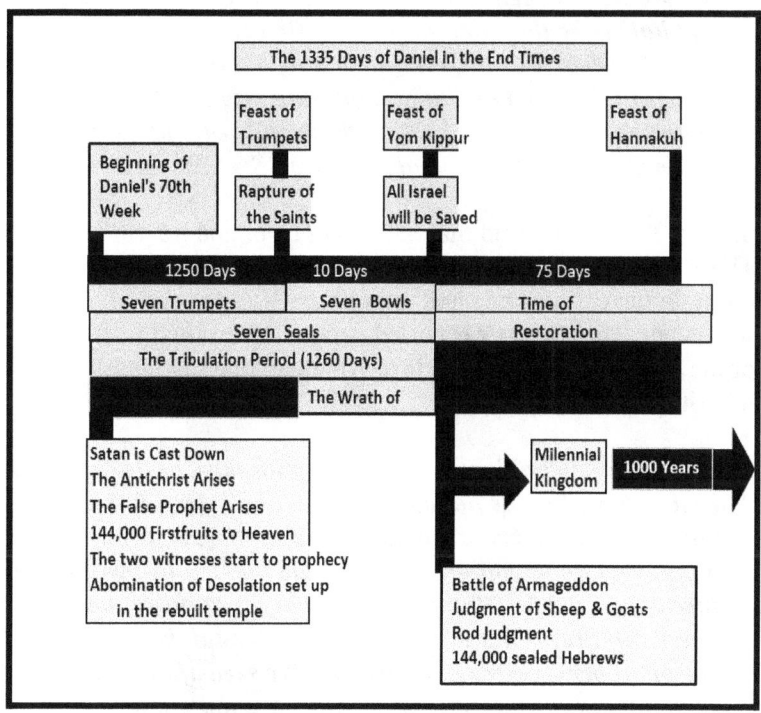

The Millennial Kingdom

"And I saw an angel come down from heaven, having the key of the bottomless pit and a great chain in his hand. And he laid hold on the dragon, that old serpent, which is the Devil, and Satan, and bound him a thousand years, And cast him into the bottomless pit, and shut him up, and set a seal upon him, that he should deceive the nations no more, till the thousand years should be fulfilled: and after that he must be loosed a little season. And I saw thrones, and they sat upon them, and judgment was given unto them: and I saw the souls of them that were beheaded for the witness of Jesus, and for the word of God, and which had not worshipped the beast, neither his image, neither had received his mark upon their foreheads, or in their hands;

and they lived and reigned with Christ a thousand years. But the rest of the dead lived not again until the thousand years were finished. This is the first resurrection. Blessed and holy is he that hath part in the first resurrection: on such the second death hath no power, but they shall be priests of God and of Christ, and shall reign with him a thousand years. And when the thousand years are expired, Satan shall be loosed out of his prison." Rev 20:1-3

In Rev 22:2 we are told that Satan will be bound for *1000 years*. The 1000 years following the church age is when Christ will return to the earth to rule and reign over His world from Jerusalem. This 1000-year period is the long awaited fulfillment of the covenant that God made to Abraham that his *seeds* would inherit the Promised Land.

"As for me, behold, my covenant is with thee, and thou shalt be a father of many nations. Neither shall thy name any more be called Abram, but thy name shall be Abraham; for a father of many nations have I made thee. And I will make thee exceeding fruitful, and I will make nations of thee, and kings shall come out of thee. And I will establish my covenant between me and thee and thy seed after thee in their generations for an everlasting covenant, to be a God unto thee, and to thy seed after thee. And I will give unto thee, and to thy seed after thee, the land wherein thou art a stranger, all the land of Canaan, for an everlasting possession; and I will be their God. And God said unto Abraham, Thou shalt keep my covenant therefore, thou, and thy seed after thee in their generations." Genesis 17: 4-8

The prophets Isaiah and Zechariah also prophesied of this coming to pass.

"The word that Isaiah the son of Amoz saw concerning Judah and Jerusalem. And it shall come to pass in the last days, that the mountain of the LORD's house shall be established in the top of the mountains, and shall be exalted above the hills; and all nations shall flow unto it. And many

people shall go and say, Come ye, and let us go up to the mountain of the LORD, to the house of the God of Jacob; and he will teach us of his ways, and we will walk in his paths: for out of Zion shall go forth the law, and the word of the LORD from Jerusalem. And he shall judge among the nations, and shall rebuke many people: and they shall beat their swords into plowshares, and their spears into pruning hooks: nation shall not lift up sword against nation, neither shall they learn war any more."   Isaiah 2:1-4

"And it shall be in that day, that living waters shall go out from Jerusalem; half of them toward the former sea, and half of them toward the hinder sea: in summer and in winter shall it be. And the LORD shall be king over all the earth: in that day shall there be one LORD, and his name one. All the land shall be turned as a plain from Geba to Rimmon south of Jerusalem: and it shall be lifted up, and inhabited in her place, from Benjamin's gate unto the place of the first gate, unto the corner gate, and from the tower of Hananeel unto the king's winepresses. And men shall dwell in it, and there shall be no more utter destruction; but Jerusalem shall be safely inhabited."   Zechariah 14: 8-11

(http://www.lamblion.com/articles/articles_jews12.php

The earth will at last be restored to a place of peace and harmony between man and the animal kingdom just as it was in the Garden of Eden.

> *"The wolf also shall dwell with the lamb, and the leopard shall lie down with the kid; and the calf and the young lion and the fatling together; and a little child shall lead them. And the cow and the bear shall feed; their young ones shall lie down together: and the lion shall eat straw like the ox. And the sucking child shall play on the hole of the asp, and the weaned child shall put his hand on the cockatrice' den. They shall not hurt nor destroy in all my holy mountain: for the earth shall be full of the knowledge of the LORD, as the waters cover the sea."*   Isaiah 11:6-9

The millennial kingdom is prophesied to last 1000 years in Rev 20: 2, 3, 4, 5, 6 and 7. Rev 20: 4-6 and Rev 20: 11:15. We will concentrate on the following verses.

> *"And I saw an angel come down from heaven, having the key of the bottomless pit and a great chain in his hand. And he laid hold on the dragon, that old serpent, which is the Devil, and Satan, and bound him a thousand years, And cast him into the bottomless pit, and shut him up, and set a seal upon him, that he should deceive the nations no more, till the thousand years should be fulfilled: and after that he must be loosed a little season." ….. And when the thousand years are expired, Satan shall be loosed out of his prison, And shall go out to deceive the nations which are in the four quarters of the earth, Gog and Magog, to gather them together to battle: the number of whom is as the sand of the sea. And they went up on the breadth of the earth, and compassed the camp of the saints about, and the beloved city: and fire came down from God out of heaven, and devoured them. And the devil that deceived them was cast into the lake of fire and brimstone, where the beast and the false prophet are, and shall be tormented day and night for ever and ever."*   Rev 20: 1-3, 7-10

An angel descends from heaven with a key to the bottomless pit. This is the same key that Christ has in His possession in Revelation 1:18, for these are the keys to *Death and Hades*. The *bottomless pit* is a temporary holding place for bad angels. It was opened in Rev 9:1 to release demon locusts upon mankind, and to release their leader, the angel *Abaddon*. The angel who has the key is probably the same one who opened the pit in Rev 9:1. The beast that controls the will, body and mind of the antichrist will ascend out of this pit. After the battle of Armageddon, Satan will be cast into the bottomless pit and sealed up for 1000 years so that *he should deceive the nations no more* for *1000 years*. The angel is also carrying a *great chain* in his hand. It is not certain, but comparing Scripture to Scripture it is likely that this chain is used to securely lock and close the entrance to the bottomless pit. This is indicated because in Rev 20:3 Satan has a *seal set on him*. It appears that this seal constrains Satan in some mysterious way. It could mean a great chain, although we cannot be certain about this interpretation. However, one thing is perfectly clear. After the battle of Armageddon the beast who inhabited the antichrist will be forced to leave his body, just as the demons were forced to leave the Gadarene (Mark 5:1-13) This powerful angel will be cast into the *lake of fire and brimstone* along with the false prophet (Rev 19:20).

Although we have covered this before, it is important that the fate of the person we call the antichrist is completely understood. The antichrist will be the great world leader who emerged in Europe and rose to be dictator of a powerful end-time 10-nation confederacy. In Rev 13:1 and 17:8 this same *man* is called a *beast*. This beast is identical to the satanically controlled *antichrist*; although he is never called that in the book of Revelation. The *man* is transformed into a *beast* after he is wounded by a sword (Rev 13:14); they are one and the same. His *deadly wound was healed* (Rev 13:12) to enable a *prince of darkness* (Dan 10:10-13) to rise from the *bottomless pit* (Rev 17:8) and take over his mind and body. Satan has done this once before when Satan caused Judas to betray Christ. The *beast* is identical to the a*ntichrist* in all ways, but the mystery is that one part is a man, and the other part is a powerful demonic prince who receives all his power and authority from Satan. What is the final fate of this multifaceted individual? All theologians point to the following passage of scripture.

> *"And the beast was taken, and with him the false prophet that wrought miracles before him, with which he deceived them that had received the mark of the beast, and them that worshipped his image. These both were cast alive into a lake of fire burning with brimstone."*   Rev 19:20

Paul speaks of the antichrist being *consumed* by the Lord with the *spirit* (breath) *of His mouth*.
> *"And then shall that Wicked be revealed, whom the Lord shall consume with the spirit of his mouth, and shall destroy with the brightness of his coming."*   II Thessalonians 2:8

As previously revealed, the *beast* that is identical to the *antichrist* will be cast into the *lake of fire and brimstone* with the false prophet (Rev 19:19-20). However, we have a strange and seemingly conflicting statement in Ezekiel 39.

> *"And it shall come to pass in that day, that I will give unto Gog a place there of graves in Israel, the valley of the passengers on the east of the sea: and it shall stop the noses of the passengers: and there shall they bury Gog and all his multitude: and they shall call it The valley of Hamon-gog."*   Ezekiel 39:11

How can the same person be *cast alive into the lake of fire and brimstone*, and also be *slain by the Lord* and buried in the *valley of Hamon Gog*? This question has perplexed many. The answer is, of course, consistent with all Biblical truth, as it should. The *beast* and the a*ntichrist* are one and the same. The *beast* is a powerful demonic demon from the bottomless pit (Rev 17:8). When Christ slays the antichrist at the battle of Armageddon, the living *demonic prince* who controls him will also be subdued by Christ and thrown into the lake of fire and brimstone. The physical, earthly body of the antichrist will remain in the Valley of Megiddo with the rest of the dead. Just like Judas, he will be raised and judged at the *Great White Throne Judgment.*

> *"And I saw a great white throne, and him that sat on it, from whose face the earth and the heaven fled away; and there was found no place for them. And I saw the dead, small and great, stand before God; and the books were opened: and another book was opened, which is the book of life: and the dead were judged out of those things which were written in the books, according to their works. And the sea gave up the dead which were in it; and death and hell delivered up the dead which were in them: and they were judged every man according to their works."* Rev 20: 11-13

These two prophecies, separated by almost 4,000 years are both correct. There is no inerrancy in Scripture, only inerrant interpretation by well-meaning Christians.

Thoughts and Things………..

Chapter 28

Resurrections and Judgments

Most Christians understand that once Christ is accepted as their Lord and Savior; salvation by grace is a guarantee of eternal life. Associated with that guarantee is resurrection from the dead if you die. Following a resurrection at the *last trump* is a judgment for rewards, not to determine eternal life.

"For we must all appear before the judgment seat of Christ; that every one may receive the things done in his body, according to that he hath done, whether it be good or bad."
II Corinthians 5:10

However, the average Christian does not understand that there are multiple resurrections and judgments. To guide us in this

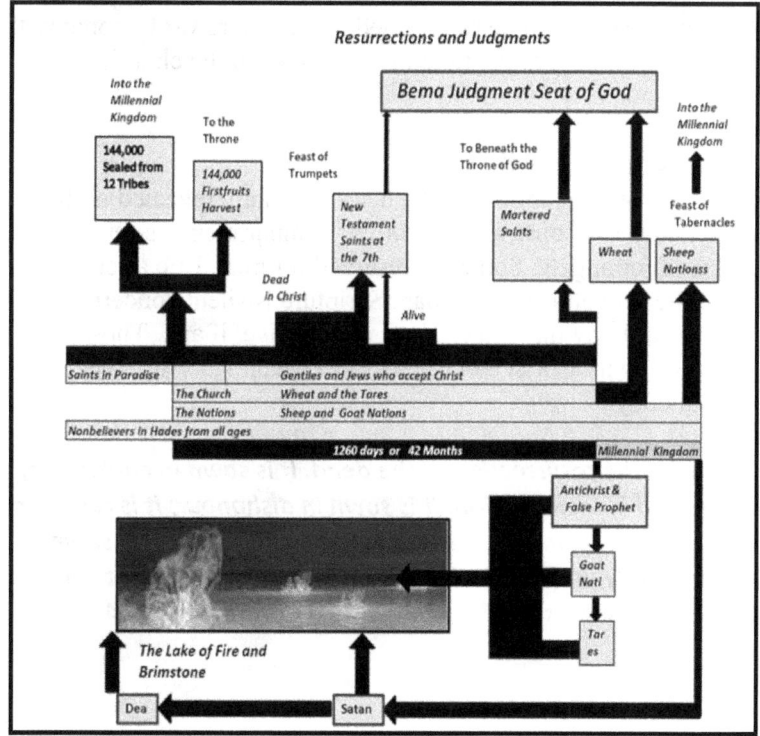

discussion, study the previous graphic. This graphic shows all resurrections and judgments in a chronological sequence beginning with the resurrection of Christ and ending with the judgment of all unbelievers after the millennial kingdom.

Abodes of the Dead

In a discussion of resurrections and judgments, it should be understood that every person who ever lived will be judged before God. All will be judged for their deeds in the flesh. Good deeds which are done under the guidance of the Holy Spirit, those which please God, will be rewarded. Those deeds which are done out of servitude and in the flesh will be cast away like *wood, hay and stubble* (I Corinthians 11-13).

> *"If any man's work abide which he hath built thereupon, he shall receive a reward. If any man's work shall be burned, he shall suffer loss: but he himself shall be saved, yet so as by fire."*   I Corinthians 3: 14-15

It is not necessary to be resurrected to receive rewards; some will be caught up alive at the time of the end when the church is raptured out.

Abodes of the Dead

There are several abodes of the dead which are revealed in the Scriptures. The spirit world is full of compartments: some are reserved for angels: Some are reserved for man. Life after death is for the soul and spirit of man. Scripture is silent concerning the *type* of body that unbelievers will receive, if any. Those who will dwell with Christ forever will receive an incorruptible, eternal body.

So also is the resurrection of the dead. It is sown in corruption; it is raised in incorruption: It is sown in dishonour; it is raised in glory: it is sown in weakness; it is raised in power: It is sown a natural body; it is raised a spiritual body. There is a natural body, and there is a spiritual body.   I Corinthians 15: 42-44

After death, the body goes to the grave and the soul and spirit go to *Sheol* or *Hades*. In the Old Testament, the Hebrew word for Hell is *Sheol*. In the New Testament the Greek word for hell is *Hades*. Both of these words are usually mistranslated as simply *Hell*. The concept of *hell* runs throughout the entire Biblical record. Christ gave us a glimpse of what happens after physical death in the story of the rich man and Lazarus. There are some that maintain this story is a parable, but if so it is the only parable that uses a proper name (Lazarus) in its story. Even so, parables are intended to reveal *mysteries* of the kingdom and convey biblical truth. In any case, we accept the story as true. We are told that the underworld of the dead is made up of two compartments; one is called *Paradise* and the other is called a *place of torments*. Collectively these two compartments are referred to as *Hell*. In the Apostles Creed, Christ was said to be **crucified, dead and buried; he descended into Hell and on the third day He arose from the dead.** More correctly, Christ descended into *Paradise* where he preached to those confined there (Acts 2:31, Eph 4:7-12, Phil. 1:23). While on the cross, He told the repent tent thief that **today thou shalt be with me in Paradise**. Before Christ ascended on the third day, all righteous dead were sent to *Paradise*, and all the unrighteous dead went to *the place of torments*. On the day of His resurrection Christ resurrected *some* from this place: they were seen in Jerusalem for several days. We believe that the rest were transferred to another place also called *Paradise* in the third heaven, where they and all the righteous dead that have died from that time until now are being held waiting for their glorified, resurrection bodies which they will receive at the *last trump* (Eph. 4:7-12). This conclusion is supported by Paul. He wrote that: **he knew a man (which was actually Paul) that was caught up into Paradise, and heard unspeakable words** (II Cor.12: 2-4). Since Christ *descended* into Paradise, and Paul *ascended* into Paradise, most theologians believe that after the resurrection of Christ, that Paradise was moved *up* to the *third heaven* (II Cor. 12:2) near the presence of God and Christ. The unrighteous dead from all ages remained in the place of torments to await their final resurrection and sentencing at the Great White Throne Judgment, which will take place after the 1000-year millennial kingdom. Prior to the ascension of Christ, *Paradise* and the *place of torments* were separated by a *great gulf* which could not be crossed, but one place could be seen from the other. Far below the place of torments is another compartment called the *bottomless pit* or the *abyss*. The abyss is reserved for the most evil and vile angels. We know that demons in the form of locusts are now there imprisoned (Rev 9:1-2), and they have a wicked prince called Abaddon ruling over them (Rev 9:11). Satan will be confined in the bottomless pit for 1000 years after the Second Advent of Christ (Rev 20:2). There is another underworld compartment called "*Tartarus*". Tartarus is contained in the lowest region of the underworld. The angels who cohabitated with man and had sexual relations with women on this earth are being held in this place (2 Peter 2:4). Finally, there is a place of everlasting torment called *the lake of fire and brimstone*. The antichrist and the false prophet will be cast into this place following the battle of Armageddon (Rev 19:20). Satan and all whose names are not written in the **Book of Life** will be cast into the lake of burning fire immediately following the millennial kingdom (Rev 20:10). With this short introduction to the underworld and the abodes of the dead, we will now discuss all the resurrections and judgments.

Resurrections and Judgments

The hope of resurrection from the dead is the cornerstone of a Christian's belief. Christ was approached by the Pharisees and the Sadducees, and testing his claim to be the Son of God they asked Him to show them a sign from heaven. Christ had healed the sick, made the lame to walk, cured lepers and performed great miracles. His reply probably surprised them, particularly the Sadducees, who did not believe in the resurrection of the dead.

> "*A wicked and adulterous generation seeks after a sign, and no sign shall be given to it except the sign of the prophet Jonah.*"   Matthew 16:4

The sign that Christ would give to them and the entire world was shadowed and typed by the story of Jonah and the whale. Recall that Jonah was instructed by God to go to Nineveh to preach repentance. Jonah refused the Lord and fled to Joppa where he was to board a ship bound for Tarshish. As he crossed the Mediterranean Sea, the Lord brought a great storm against the ship and Jonah was cast into the sea by the crew of the ship. The Lord *prepared a great fish.* It is commonly taught that this great fish was a whale, but this cannot be found in the scriptures. Jonah was swallowed by the *great fish* and spent 3 days and 3 nights in its belly. If Jonah was to satisfy type for our Lord Jesus Christ, I believe that he actually died there. The scriptures record that *the floods (water) compassed me about and the waves passed over me…the weeds were wrapped about my head* (Jonah 2:1-9). Jonah was redeemed by the great fish, who vomited Jonah out upon the dry land (Jonah 2:10).The sign of Jonah which Christ gave to the Pharisees and the Sadducees was actually fulfilled in two ways. Just as Jonah was in the belly of the whale for three days and three nights, Christ would be in the heart of the earth for three days and three nights; then He would be raised from the dead and ascend to the Father. Paul put the hope of our resurrection from the dead in stronger terms.

> *"For if the dead do not rise, then Christ is not risen. And if Christ is not risen, your faith is futile; you are still in your sins! Then also those who have fallen asleep in Christ have perished. If in this life only we have hope in Christ, we are of all men the most pitiable."*   I Corinthians 15:16-19

Most Christians are not aware and have not been taught the theological and multiple biblical concepts of resurrection and judgment. Resurrections and judgments result in eternal rewards for all believers, or in eternal punishment of unbelievers. Some pastors and teachers simply refuse to accept that a loving and compassionate God could possibly torment anyone forever. As we shall see, they are wrong.

There are *ten* different Resurrections and/or judgments which have occurred or will occur surrounding the First and Second Advent of Jesus Christ. It is interesting that in the bible the number ten ten is one of the perfect numbers, and signifies the perfection of Divine order. The number 10 implies that nothing is wanting; that the number and order are perfect; that the whole cycle is complete.

1. *Christ, the First of the Firstfruits*
2. *The Firstfruits of Israel*
3. *The Firstfruits of the Church*
4. *The Resurrection of the Saints immediately before the rapture*
5. *The Rod Judgment*
6. *The Sheep and Goats Judgment*
7. *Survivors of the Bowl Judgments*
8. *Martyrs' of the Tribulation*
9. *The Great White Throne judgment*
10. *Inhabitants of the Millennial Kingdom*

It may seem obvious, but to be resurrected one must be dead. In the Holy Bible, there are two types of resurrected persons. The first is the *righteous dead* and the second is the *unrighteous dead*. There are two distinct resurrections spoken of in the Bible; the *first resurrection* and the *second resurrection*. The first resurrection is composed of several phases, while the second resurrection occurs at a single point in time. The first resurrection is restricted to those who believe in Jesus Christ as their savior; the second resurrection is composed of all unbelievers. The second resurrection will take place at the end of the 1000-year millennial kingdom. The first resurrection began with the resurrection of Jesus Christ and ends following the rapture of the church at the seventh trumpet. The martyrs are uniquely dealt with after the battle of Armageddon (Rev 20:4). An anomaly which has been included in our discussion is the Firstfruits rapture of the saints. This has been included for continuity. We will see that this Firstfruits rapture corresponds to the Man Child of Rev 12:5, and balances the Firstfruits resurrection of Matthew 25:52.

Christ, the First of the Firstfruits
We have pointed out in Chapter 9 that the death, burial and resurrection of Jesus Christ fulfilled the Feast of Passover, the Feast of Unleavened Bread and the Feast of Firstfruits.

> *"Forasmuch as ye know that ye were not redeemed with corruptible things, as silver and gold, from your vain conversation received by tradition from your fathers; But with the precious blood of Christ, as of a lamb without blemish and without spot:"*   I Peter 1: 18-19

> *"Purge out therefore the old leaven, that ye may be a new lump, as ye are unleavened. For even Christ our Passover is sacrificed for us:"*   I Corinthians 5:7

> *"But now is Christ risen from the dead, and become the firstfruits of them that slept."*   I Corinthians 15:20

The *firstfruit* is an important concept that runs throughout both the Old and New Testament.

> *"For as in Adam all die, even so in Christ shall all be made alive. But every man in his own order: Christ the firstfruits; afterward they that are Christ's at his coming."*
> I Corinthians 15:22-23

This verse provides a key to understanding New Testament resurrections. In the original version of the Holy Bible, there were no punctuation marks; they were added by the translators. We believe that this verse should be punctuated as follows.

> *"For as in Adam all die, even so in Christ shall all be made alive. But every man in his own order: Christ, the firstfruits, and afterward they that are Christ's at his coming."*
> I Corinthians 15:22-23

When Christ arrived in Jerusalem just before the fourth and last Passover of His earthly ministry, His final days were to finish fulfilling all Old Testament prophecy. He was crucified on a *Wednesday*, died and was buried. After the third day (Jewish Sabbath, Saturday) He rose from the grave. In Mat 28:1 we are told that Mary Magdalene and the other Mary came to the grave of Jesus *in the end of the Sabbath*.... our Lord had already risen just as the *Feast of Firstfruits* was beginning. There had been many others raised from the dead before Christ, but Christ was the first to be raised, receive a glorified, eternal, non-corruptible body, and ascend into heaven. Christ was the *First of the Firstfruits* (Exodus 23:19) to be offered up to God. The concept of a *Firstfruits offering* is given in Leviticus.

"Speak unto the children of Israel, and say unto them, When ye be come into the land which I give unto you, and shall reap the harvest thereof, then ye shall bring a sheaf of the firstfruits of your harvest unto the priest: And he shall wave the sheaf before the LORD, to be accepted for you: on the morrow after the sabbath the priest shall wave it. And ye shall offer that day when ye wave the sheaf an he lamb without blemish of the first year for a burnt offering unto the LORD."   Leviticus 19:10-12

The *Feast of Firstfruits* started on the first Sunday following the only Sabbath (Saturday) during the *Feast of Unleavened Bread*. Christ was crucified on the *Feast of Passover*; Nisan 14; a Wednesday. He rose from the grave on Nisan 17, three days later, just as Sunday was *dawning* (Mat 28:1-2). Sunday, Nisan 17 was the first day of the *Feast of Firstfruits*, sometimes called the *Feast of weeks*. It lasted 49 days, and on the 50th day the *Feast of Pentecost* or *Shavuot* was held. Both the first day and the 50th day was a *high Sabbath*, and both were always on a Sunday. On Nisan 17 several interesting events occurred.

- ➢ Noah's ark rested on Mt Sinai.
- ➢ Israel crossed the Red sea during the Exodus.
- ➢ Israel ate of the *firstfruits* of Canaan after crossing the river Jordan. Manna ceased on Nisan 16.
- ➢ Israel was saved by Esther when Haman is hanged.

In the *Pattern of the Harvest*, the wheat and barley were both planted in *early fall*. If the early rains came following the planting season, both would be nearing harvest time by the season of Passover in the spring. The month of Nisan was in ancient times also known as *Aviv*, which means *green in the ear*. At that time, the barley would just be maturing and springing forth in the ear. Wheat would not yet be in the ear. Barley matured faster and could be harvested sooner. During the 49-day count to Pentecost, a firstfruit offering would be made every day. The first of the firstfruits of the grain offered on Nisan 17 was barley. The firstfruit offering on Nisan 17 is carried out in the following manner. A Levite would go to the field and collect a sheaf of barley. A single sheaf would be carried directly to the High Priest, who would offer it up to God. This sheaf was not just a holy offering to God, but it was a guarantee or down payment that represented faith in God to produce the latter harvest and send the latter rains. The firstfruit offerings were always the first, the best and the fullest. They were *holy onto the Lord*. Our Lord Jesus Christ was the *first of the firstfruits*, the first harvest of all the saints. He was both the high priest who made the offering to God, and the offered wave sheaf. He was the *lamb without spot or blemish* that was a meat offering on that day. He was the *single barley cake* that was without leaven, which represents sin. Only Christ could possibly fulfill all of these requirements.

The Firstfruits of Israel
We will now discuss an important ordinance which took place on the Feast of Firstfruits. From the firstfruit harvest, a single cake of barley was to be baked without leaven, and offered up as a burnt offering to the Lord. The *single sheaf offered up as the first of the firstfruits* would not be enough to bake a loaf of barley bread, there had to be more. So enough firstfruits were subsequently gathered in to make a loaf. Remember, no produce of the spring crops could be eaten until this ritual was completed. So additional barley sheaths were picked, offered to God as a *wave offering*, and then a loaf was baked. Christ is the *first of the firstfruits*. Is there a corresponding resurrection that represents this additional barley? Yes there is! And it is usually either

ignored or overlooked. First, the barley represents that portion of the grain which matures first; it is not holier than the wheat which takes longer to mature. The *barley* represents the nation of *Israel*, which came first. The *wheat* represents the *church*, which matured later. Recall in Mat 27 there was a resurrection recorded immediately *after* Christ had *risen* from the grave.

> *"And the graves were opened; and many bodies of the saints which slept arose, And came out of the graves after his resurrection, and went into the holy city, and appeared unto many."*   Matthew 27: 52-53

This is a resurrection of **many** (Mat 27: 52-53) Old Testament saints who had lived under the law, but believed the prophets and believed in the promise of a Messiah who would arise and resurrect them to eternal life. These Old Testament saints were the *Barley Firstfruits Harvest* onto God, and came to life after our Lord Jesus Christ had been *waved* and accepted unto God as the *first of the firstfruits*. This mysterious ritual was symbolic of two things: (1) The Lord was to be praised and blessed for providing the early and latter rains (Hosea 6:3, James 5:7), which was necessary to mature the entire crop (2) the Firstfruit offering , accepted by God, was a guarantee and promise of the larger harvest yet to come. This has both *physical* and *spiritual* implications. This was revealed by Paul in his letter to the Romans.

> *"For if the firstfruit be holy, the lump is also holy: and if the root be holy, so are the branches."*   Romans 11:16

Paul here compares all believers to a **lump** *of bread.* If any part of the loaf is leavened, it is all leavened. If any part of the loaf is unleavened, it is all unleavened. Leaven is always a symbol of sin. Since we are in Christ and He is in us, if Christ the firstfruit is holy… we are also holy. This is a great principle of justification, sanctification and glorification in Christ Jesus. Paul immediately expands this analogy to the salvation of both Jews and Gentiles. He calls Christ the *root* of an olive tree. The natural branches of this olive tree are the *Jews*. These branches were broken off and the *gentiles* grafted into the tree. The analogy is beautiful in its message. The Gentiles were grafted into the wild olive tree to receive salvation under the New Covenant, but the Jewish branches will also be offered salvation. Paul concludes by revealing that if the ***root is holy***, so would be ***all the branches***. In John 15, Christ is typed as a ***vine*** and believers as ***branches***. John and Paul are both revealing that the grace of Christ and his shed blood on the cross of Calvary is sufficient to save all… Jews and gentiles alike.

> ***"I am the vine, ye are the branches: He that abideth in me, and I in him, the same bringeth forth much fruit: for without me ye can do nothing."***   John 15:5

The Firstfruits of the Church

To understand the third resurrection, it is necessary to understand what happened on the Feast of Pentecost, on the 50th day since the resurrection of Christ. Every Christian knows that on that day the Holy Spirit fell on those in the upper room, and then on everyone else who had been gathered there and in Jerusalem waiting for Christ to appear (Acts 2:38). It was a great day, and 3000 people were saved (Acts 2:41). However, there were no resurrections recorded on that day. What we want to focus on is that on Nisan 17, day 1 of the *Feast of Weeks*, there was a *single cake* baked with *no leaven* from the firstfruit *harvest of barley*. This firstfruits loaf was *waved before the Lord by the high priest* for acceptance.

> **"Speak unto the children of Israel, and say unto them, When ye be come into the land which I give unto you, and shall reap the harvest thereof, then ye shall bring a sheaf of the firstfruits of your harvest unto the priest: And he shall wave the sheaf before the LORD, to be accepted for you: on the morrow after the sabbath the priest shall wave it."**
> Leviticus 23:10-11

During the next 49 days the wheat matured in the field, and by the *Feast of Pentecost* it was ready to harvest. However, recall that one of the *laws of the harvest* was that no fruit of the field (wheat or barley) could be consumed without a wave sheath offering to the Lord (Leviticus 23:20). Note carefully what the Lord commanded.

> *"Even unto the morrow after the seventh sabbath shall ye number fifty days; and ye shall offer a new meat offering unto the LORD. Ye shall bring out of your habitations two wave loaves of two tenth deals: they shall be of fine flour; they shall be baken with leaven; they are the firstfruits unto the LORD. And the priest shall wave them with the bread of the firstfruits for a wave offering before the LORD, with the two lambs: they shall be holy to the LORD for the priest."*
> Leviticus 23: 16-17, 20

There is a remarkable thing here. Note that from the firstfruit sheaves of the latter (wheat) harvest, there were to be *two loaves* baked, and they were both to contain *leaven,* which is representative of *sin*. How can something sinful be consecrated and accepted by the Lord? Why are there two loaves baked and offered up? How do these ordinances relate to a resurrection? The *two loaves* represent both *Jews and the Gentiles*. The leaven is the sinful nature of man in both Jews and Gentiles. The *leaven of sin* which is in all of us is covered by the blood of Christ, and our salvation is assured by our belief that He is the Son of God and that He died for our sins. From the cross until today, there is no difference in Jew or Gentile. There are only those who believe in Christ's name and those who do not.

> *"Is he the God of the Jews only? is he not also of the Gentiles? Yes, of the Gentiles also."*   Romans 3:29

> *"Even the righteousness of God which is by faith of Jesus Christ unto all and upon all them that believe: for there is no difference: For all have sinned, and come short of the glory of God; Being justified freely by his grace through the redemption that is in Christ Jesus."*   Romans 3:22-24

Paul made it clear that Christ does not distinguish between any person. This is the mystery of what Peter said in the book of Acts:

> **"Then Peter opened his mouth, and said, Of a truth I perceive that God is no respecter of persons"** Acts 10:34

We have discussed a *firstfruit resurrection* of some (not all) Jewish believers which took place immediately following the resurrection of Christ. These were all *Old Covenant* believers. It follows that somewhere in time after this event took place, that there would be a firstfruit resurrection of *New Covenant* believers. Can we find such an event in the Scriptures? The answer is yes.

> *"And I looked, and, lo, a Lamb stood on the mount Sion, and with him an hundred forty and four thousand, having his Father's name written in their foreheads. And I heard a voice from heaven, as the voice of many waters, and as the voice of a great thunder: and I heard the voice of harpers harping with their harps: And they sung as it were a new song before the throne, and before the four beasts, and the elders: and no man could learn that song but the hundred and forty and four thousand, which were redeemed from the earth. These are they which were not defiled with women; for they are virgins. These are they which follow the Lamb whithersoever he goeth. These were redeemed from among men, being the firstfruits unto God and to the Lamb."*
> Rev 14:1-4

The four beasts and 24 elders were discussed in Chapter 3. The 144,000 sealed Jews from 12 tribes of Israel were discussed in Chapter 15. We now observe that these 144,000 are:

- Standing on the heavenly Mount Zion,
- Standing with *a lamb*… which is undoubtedly Christ,
- They sing a *new song*… the song of believers in heaven,
- They are before God's throne, before the 4 beasts & the 24 elders,

- They are *redeemed from the earth*,
- They *follow the Lamb* wherever He goes,
- They were *redeemed from among men*,
- They are the *firstfruits* offering to God and the Lamb,

Here we have a *firstfruits offering* standing before God (Rev 14:1). They have been *translated* from the earth (Rev 12:5) and now stand before the throne in heaven. This is a reasonable assumption, since they parallel the 144,000 Israelites who are still on the earth and have been sealed from the trumpet and bowl judgments in Rev 7: 1-8. This heavenly 144,000 is not *protected*, they are *redeemed*. These 144,000 are in *heaven* not on the *earth*; the 144,000 in Rev 7 *follow Christ* wherever He goes (Rev 14:4). If the clear and definitive record of John that they were: (1) Caught up (translated) to the throne of god (Rev 12:5), *before* Satan is cast to the earth and before the antichrist arises and *(2)* they are following Christ wherever He goes (Rev 14:4), then this must represent a harvest of 144,000 followers of Christ *immediately preceding* the tribulation period. This occurs 42 months before the tribulation period is over, and after Satan has been *cast to the earth* in Rev 12:1-9. This heavenly firstfruit offering is clearly composed of *both* Jews and Gentiles because they come from *the earth*, not strictly Israel. But why is there almost a 2000-year *gap* between the Jewish firstfruit offering and this firstfruit offering of the New Testament saints? The answer is obvious if we consider the way God sees time. The 70-week prophecy of Daniel spans time between when the prophecy started in 458 BC until it ends. We have shown in Chapters 7 and 8 that 70 weeks is 490 years, and that between when the prophecy started in 458 BC until Christ was crucified was 486.5 years. This leaves 3.5 years unfulfilled in the last week of Daniel's prophecy. The last 3.5 years of Daniel's 70th week is initiated when that old serpent, Satan, is cast down to the earth in Rev 12:9. This is when the 144, 000 from 12 tribes of Israel are sealed, and when the 144,000 firstfruits are seen in heaven. The *gap in time* started following the Feast of Passover in 30 AD. The last half of Daniel's 70th week will resume its count at some future Feast of Passover, when Satan is cast down. In God's eyes, there is no *gap* in time at all. **But, beloved, be not ignorant** *of this one thing, that one day is with the Lord as a thousand years, and a thousand years as one day.* (II Peter 3:8). Time is eternity, and to the Lord time has not passed at all!

> *"Watch ye therefore, and pray always, that ye may be accounted worthy to escape all these things that shall come to pass, and to stand before the Son of man."*
> Luke 21:36

The 144,000 shown in Rev14:1 on Mt. Zion are the *firstfruits* of all the *main wheat harvest*. We will now discuss the main harvest, which we call the *rapture,* but this is a limiting term as we will see.

The Rapture and the Resurrection of the Dead Saints

Paul gives us almost everything we know about what is called the *rapture* of the saints. The word *rapture* is not found in the Bible, but it has been adapted from the Latin word *rapiemur*, which means to be *caught up* or *snatched away*.

> *"But I would not have you to be ignorant, brethren, concerning them which are asleep, that ye sorrow not, even as others which have no hope. For if we believe that Jesus died and rose again, even so them also which sleep in Jesus will God bring with him. For this we say unto you by the word of the Lord, that we which are alive and remain unto the coming of the Lord shall not prevent them which are asleep. For the Lord himself shall descend from heaven with a shout, with the voice of the archangel, and with the trump of God: and the dead in Christ shall rise first: Then we which are alive and remain shall be caught up together with them in the clouds, to meet the Lord in the air: and so shall we ever be with the Lord. Wherefore comfort one another with these words."* I Thessalonians 4:13-18

Paul indicated that this event will be initiated by the ***trump of God***. Paul further clarified this trump in I Corinthians 15.

> *"Behold, I shew you a mystery; We shall not all sleep, but we shall all be changed, In a moment, in the twinkling of an eye, at the last trump: for the trumpet shall sound, and the dead shall be raised incorruptible, and we shall be changed."* I Corinthians 15:51-52

It is strange that theologians ignore two facts: (1) if there is a last trump, it must have been preceded by a series of other trumpet blasts. (2) Jewish rabbinical teachings hold that the long-awaited Jewish Messiah will return at some future Feast of Trumpets, and that the nation of Israel will be given glorified bodies. If there is some truth to these two observations, it must be revealed somewhere in the Holy Scriptures as the end time comes to a close. We find absolute confirmation in Rev. 11:19

> *"And the seventh angel sounded; and there were great voices in heaven, saying, The kingdoms of this world are become the kingdoms of our Lord, and of his Christ; and he shall reign for ever and ever. And the four and twenty elders, which sat before God on their seats, fell upon their faces, and worshipped God, Saying, We give thee thanks, O Lord God Almighty, which art, and wast, and art to come; because thou hast taken to thee thy great power, and hast reigned. And the nations were angry, and thy wrath is come, and the time of the dead, that they should be judged, and that thou shouldest give reward unto thy servants the prophets, and to the saints, and them that fear thy name, small and great; and shouldest destroy them which destroy the earth. And the temple of God was opened in heaven, and there was seen in his temple the ark of his testament: and there were lightnings, and voices, and thunderings, and an earthquake, and great hail."* Rev 11:19

Observe what John records in these Scriptures.

- ➢ The seventh angel sounds the seventh trumpet, which is the last in a sequence of seven.
- ➢ The Kingdoms of this world now become the kingdoms of Jesus Christ.

- ➢ Thy wrath is come. The wrath of God is the seven bowl judgments which immediately follow (Rev 15:7; 16:1).
- ➢ It is time to reward the saints.
- ➢ The ark of His covenant is seen in heaven.

We cannot escape with any rational argument other than these passages point to the rapture of the church at the sounding of the seventh trumpet. No other interpretation is possible. We call this event the *rapture* because all of the saints alive and on the earth at that time will be *caught up* to meet Christ in the air. However, ascension of the living is preceded by all of those who have died in Christ and await this glorious event. A *resurrection* of all the *dead in Christ* will take place *before* the alive are caught up. All will receive *robes of righteousness, clean and white* to cover their resurrected bodies. Those who are translated alive to heaven will also receive robes of righteousness, clean and white. The saints who are alive at this time will *not* experience God's wrath, which are the seven bowl judgments.

> *"For God hath not appointed us to wrath, but to obtain salvation by our Lord Jesus Christ."* I Thessalonians 5:9

> *"Much more then, being now justified by his blood, we shall be saved from wrath through him."* Romans 5:9

Those who have been rewarded and now appear without spot or wrinkle will accompany Christ at His Second Advent.

> *"And I saw heaven opened, and behold a white horse; and he that sat upon him was called Faithful and True, and in righteousness he doth judge and make war. His eyes were as a flame of fire, and on his head were many crowns; and he had a name written, that no man knew, but he himself. And he was clothed with a vesture dipped in blood: and his name is called The Word of God. And the armies which were in heaven followed him upon white horses, clothed in fine linen, white and clean."* Rev 19:11-14

It is now easy to understand the words of Christ in the Olivet Discourse which described this same event.

> *"Immediately after the tribulation of those days shall the sun be darkened, and the moon shall not give her light, and the stars shall fall from heaven, and the powers of the heavens shall be shaken: And then shall appear the sign of the Son of man in heaven: and then shall all the tribes of the earth mourn, and they shall see the Son of man coming in the clouds of heaven with power and great glory. And he shall send his angels with a great sound of a trumpet, and they shall gather together his elect from the four winds, from one end of heaven to the other."* Matthew 24:29-31

The rapture of the church, and the resurrection of the dead at the seventh trumpet, brings to a close a 1250 day reign of terror which included the seven trumpet judgments. The rapture takes place *immediately after the tribulation of those days* caused by the persecution of Satan and the Antichrist. The cosmic disturbances in Mat 24:29 are described by John the Revelator as the seventh trumpet sounds. The description is almost identical to that given by Christ in the Olivet Discourse.

> *"And the temple of God was opened in heaven, and there was seen in his temple the ark of his testament: and there were lightnings, and voices, and thunderings, and an earthquake, and great hail."* Rev 11:19

The opening of the sixth seal predicts this event.

> *"And I beheld when he had opened the sixth seal, and, lo, there was a great earthquake; and the sun became black as sackcloth of hair, and the moon became as blood; And the stars of heaven fell unto the earth, even as a fig tree casteth her untimely figs, when she is shaken of a mighty wind. And the heaven departed as a scroll when it is rolled together; and every mountain and island were moved out of their places. And the kings of the earth, and the great men, and the rich men, and the chief captains, and the mighty men,*

and every bondman, and every free man, hid themselves in the dens and in the rocks of the mountains." Rev 6:12-15

In the *Pattern of the Harvest*, we call this the *main harvest*. It occurs on *Tishri 1*, which is the *Feast of Trumpets*. It is the time of year when all of the *wheat harvest* is gathered into God's *barn*, threshed and the *husks* separated to the winds. This is the fulfillment of the parable that Christ told about in the parable of the W*heat and the Tares*.

> *"Another parable put he forth unto them, saying, The kingdom of heaven is likened unto a man which sowed good seed in his field: But while men slept, his enemy came and sowed tares among the wheat, and went his way. But when the blade was sprung up, and brought forth fruit, then appeared the tares also. So the servants of the householder came and said unto him, Sir, didst not thou sow good seed in thy field? from whence then hath it tares? He said unto them, An enemy hath done this. The servants said unto him, Wilt thou then that we go and gather them up? But he said, Nay; lest while ye gather up the tares, ye root up also the wheat with them. Let both grow together until the harvest: and in the time of harvest I will say to the reapers, Gather ye together first the tares, and bind them in bundles to burn them: but gather the wheat into my barn."* Mat 13:24-30

In Revelation 19, immediately before the millennial kingdom starts, we are told that the *first resurrection* had been completed.

> *"And I saw thrones, and they sat upon them, and judgment was given unto them: and I saw the souls of them that were beheaded for the witness of Jesus, and for the word of God, and which had not worshipped the beast, neither his image, neither had received his mark upon their foreheads, or in their hands; and they lived and reigned with Christ a thousand years. But the rest of the dead lived not again until the thousand years were finished. This is the first resurrection. Blessed and holy is he that hath part in the first resurrection: on such the second death hath no power,*

> *but they shall be priests of God and of Christ, and shall reign with him a thousand years."*   Rev 20: 4-6

The judgment associated with this main harvest is called the *Bema Seat* judgment (http://www.allaboutgod.com/bema-seat.htm): also called the *Judgment Seat of Christ*. The concept of the *Bema Seat* comes from the ancient Olympics, where a judge would sit on a Seat called the *bema* at the finish line. The judge's purpose was to determine what position the runners came in-first, second, and so on-and then to give out the appropriate rewards. That is the imagery behind what is known as the Bema Seat Judgment. It is not a judgment of life or death, but one of rewards. The Bema Seat judgment is described by Paul in I Corinthians 3.

> *"If any man builds on this foundation using gold, silver, costly stones, wood, hay or straw, his work will be shown for what it is, because the Day will bring it to light. It will be revealed with fire, and the fire will test the quality of each man's work. If what he has built survives, he will receive his reward. If it is burned up, he will suffer loss; he himself will be saved, but only as one escaping through the flames."*
>   I Corinthians 3:12-15

Here we have a fundamental truth that underlies all service to our Lord and Savior. Your *gold, silver, and costly stones* are works that may seem done for the glory of God, but they are not done with the right motive, and under the guidance of the Holy Spirit. Please read Mat 7:13-27 and pray over these words of Christ. The Bema Seat judgment does not determine salvation. Rather, it is when believers must give an account of their lives to Christ. The magnitude of their rewards and their place in the millennial kingdom is determined at this time. It is very important to not confuse the *Bema Seat* judgment with the *Great White Throne* judgment, which follows the 1000-year millennial kingdom. The Great White Throne is where those who *do not* believe in Jesus Christ are judged and condemned. In contrast, the Bema Seat is for believers whose salvation has already been secured by faith in Jesus Christ (John 3:16; Romans 10:9-10).

> *"For we must all appear before the judgment seat of Christ, that each one may receive what is due him for the things done while in the body, whether good or bad."* II Cor. 5:10

Paul is teaching us that all Christians will stand before the Bema Seat of Christ. At the Bema Seat, Jesus Christ will bring to light every deed, good or bad, that each believer has done on this earth since he or she became a Christian. Every Christian will be rewarded for his/her good works, deeds, and faithfulness.

There is a first and second resurrection recorded in the Book of Revelation. The *first resurrection* which will conclude at the Bema Seat Judgment (Rev 20:4-6). While it is not obvious, the *first resurrection* will take place in several phases over a period of time which has now been almost 2000 years. Just as there is a *first resurrection*, then there will be a second. The *second resurrection* is revealed in Rev 20:11-15.

> *"And I saw the dead, small and great, stand before God; and the books were opened: and another book was opened, which is the book of life: and the dead were judged out of those things which were written in the books, according to their works. And the sea gave up the dead which were in it; and death and hell delivered up the dead which were in them: and they were judged every man according to their works. And death and hell were cast into the lake of fire. This is the second death. And whosoever was not found written in the book of life was cast into the lake of fire."*
> Rev 20:11-15

This is called the *Great White Throne Judgment*, and it takes place after the 1000-year millennial kingdom has run its course. At this judgment, all of the unrighteous dead, all who have refused to accept Jesus Christ as their savior, will be raised from the dead and judged. This will include all of the Old Testament Hebrews who ignored the words of the prophets. Daniel was told of this judgment long ago.

> *"And many of them that sleep in the dust of the earth shall awake, some to everlasting life, and some to shame and everlasting contempt. And they that be wise shall shine as the brightness of the firmament; and they that turn many to righteousness as the stars for ever and ever."*   Dan 12: 2-3

Here is an example of how prophecy can span large periods of time in the Old Testament within only a few words. From when this prophecy was given to Daniel, almost 2500 years have elapsed. In addition, the prophecy clearly states that *some* will awake from the grave to *everlasting life*; and *some* will awaken to *shame and everlasting contempt*. This is called a *near-far* prophecy. Those who wake to everlasting life are resurrected at the rapture; those who awake to everlasting shame will not be resurrected until the end of the millennial kingdom 1000 years later. Their fate is to be thrown into the *lake of fire* (Rev 20:12-15).

When Christ was raised from the dead He was the *first of the firstfruits*. Another *firstfruit resurrection* occurred when many of the Old Testament saints rose from the grave after Christ was risen (Mat 27:52-53). These two resurrections were the *first two parts* of the *first resurrection*. The final stage of the first resurrection has yet to occur. It will precede what we commonly call the *rapture*. Before we discuss the second resurrection, we will discuss several judgments which will take place before the millennial kingdom starts.

Judgment of the Antichrist and the False Prophet

Following the rapture, the *seven bowls of God's wrath* will be poured out on the earth, and all of Satan's forces, the antichrist and the false prophet will be gathered to the *Battle of Armageddon* where all will be vanquished by Christ himself.

> *"And I saw heaven opened, and behold a white horse; and he that sat upon him was called Faithful and True, and in righteousness he doth judge and make war. His eyes were as a flame of fire, and on his head were many crowns; and he had a name written, that no man knew, but he himself. And*

> *he was clothed with a vesture dipped in blood: and his name is called The Word of God. And the armies which were in heaven followed him upon white horses, clothed in fine linen, white and clean. And out of his mouth goeth a sharp sword, that with it he should smite the nations: and he shall rule them with a rod of iron: and he treadeth the winepress of the fierceness and wrath of Almighty God. And he hath on his vesture and on his thigh a name written, KING OF KINGS, AND LORD OF LORDS."* Rev 19:11-16

The battle will not last long. Zechariah recorded its outcome in graphic detail.

> *"Behold, the day of the LORD cometh, and thy spoil shall be divided in the midst of thee. For I will gather all nations against Jerusalem to battle; and the city shall be taken, and the houses rifled, and the women ravished; and half of the city shall go forth into captivity, and the residue of the people shall not be cut off from the city. Then shall the LORD go forth, and fight against those nations, as when he fought in the day of battle. And his feet shall stand in that day upon the mount of Olives, which is before Jerusalem on the east, and the mount of Olives shall cleave in the midst thereof toward the east and toward the west, and there shall be a very great valley; and half of the mountain shall remove toward the north, and half of it toward the south."*
> Zechariah 14:1-4

> *"And this shall be the plague wherewith the LORD will smite all the people that have fought against Jerusalem; Their flesh shall consume away while they stand upon their feet, and their eyes shall consume away in their holes, and their tongue shall consume away in their mouth."*
> Zechariah 14:12

When the battle is over, Christ will personally pass sentence upon the antichrist and the false prophet. Both will be cast alive into the *lake of fire and brimstone*.

> *"And I saw the beast, and the kings of the earth, and their armies, gathered together to make war against him that sat on the horse, and against his army. And the beast was taken, and with him the false prophet that wrought miracles before him, with which he deceived them that had received the mark of the beast, and them that worshipped his image. These both were cast alive into a lake of fire burning with brimstone."* Rev 19:19-20

Satan will be cast into the bottomless pit, where he will be confined for 1000 years until the millennial kingdom has run its course. He will then return for one final battle (Rev 20:7-10).

The Rod Judgment

Immediately following the battle of Armageddon, Christ will go to the desert with His Father and there God will execute what is called the *rod judgment* upon all of the people of Israel that have survived.

> *"As I live, saith the Lord GOD, surely with a mighty hand, and with a stretched out arm, and with fury poured out, will I rule over you: And I will bring you out from the people, and will gather you out of the countries wherein ye are scattered, with a mighty hand, and with a stretched out arm, and with fury poured out. And I will bring you into the wilderness of the people, and there will I plead with you face to face. Like as I pleaded with your fathers in the wilderness of the land of Egypt, so will I plead with you, saith the Lord GOD. And I will cause you to pass under the rod, and I will bring you into the bond of the covenant: And I will purge out from among you the rebels, and them that transgress against me: I will bring them forth out of the country where they sojourn, and they shall not enter into the land of Israel: and ye shall know that I am the LORD."* Ezekiel 20:33-38

Here we see that God will cause all of the children of Israel who have survived the last half of Daniel's 70th week to come into the wilderness to *pass under the rod*. What is this rod? In ancient times the sheepherder would line up all of his flock and cause them to pass under a rod. As they came under the rod, he would count them and separate the ones who were blemished and unfit from those who had not failed the test. Those who pass under God's *rod of judgment* will enter into the *land* to fulfill the covenant He made with Abraham. While God is bringing His bride back into a covenant relationship with Him, Christ is also preparing to judge the nations. Before Christ can judge the nations, He travels south toward Edom and Petra to reclaim the remnant that had fled there after the antichrist and his armies attacked Jerusalem in what Van Kampen called the *Jerusalem Campaign*. They have likely retreated to the ancient fortress city of *Petra* to hide in the wilderness for a *time, times and half a time* (Rev 12:6). This act is recorded in a strange and obscure passage found in Isaiah 63.

> *"Who is this that cometh from Edom, with dyed garments from Bozrah? this that is glorious in his apparel, travelling in the greatness of his strength? I that speak in righteousness, mighty to save. Wherefore art thou red in thine apparel, and thy garments like him that treadeth in the winefat? I have trodden the winepress alone; and of the people there was none with me: for I will tread them in mine anger, and trample them in my fury; and their blood shall be sprinkled upon my garments, and I will stain all my raiment."*   Isaiah 63:1-3

From this prophecy, we see that Christ is:

- ➢ Coming from Edom and Bozrah.
- ➢ He is displaying great strength.
- ➢ He speaks righteously.
- ➢ His apparel is stained red with (sprinkled) blood.

The best interpretation of this passage is that Christ has already *trodden the winepress*, and it is this act which has stained His garments with blood. In Rev 14:18-19 we were told:

> *"And another angel came out of the temple which is in heaven, he also having a sharp sickle. And another angel*

> *came out from the altar, which had power over fire; and cried with a loud cry to him that had the sharp sickle, saying, Thrust in thy sharp sickle, and gather the clusters of the vine of the earth; for her grapes are fully ripe. And the angel thrust in his sickle into the earth, and gathered the vine of the earth, and cast it into the great winepress of the wrath of God. And the winepress was trodden without the city, and blood came out of the winepress, even unto the horse bridles, by the space of a thousand and six hundred furlongs."* Rev 14:18-20

Who *treads the winepress*? In language very similar to that used in Isaiah (Is 63:3), we are told it will be Jesus Christ.

> *"And he was clothed with a vesture dipped in blood: and his name is called The Word of God. And the armies which were in heaven followed him upon white horses, clothed in fine linen, white and clean. And out of his mouth goeth a sharp sword, that with it he should smite the nations: and he shall rule them with a rod of iron: and he treadeth the winepress of the fierceness and wrath of Almighty God."* Rev 19:13-15

The Greek phrase translated ***dipped in blood*** could also be translated *splattered in blood*. Comparing scripture to scripture, it is not conclusive but it is convincing that this person who is *coming from Edom and Bozrah* (Is 63:1) is our Lord Jesus Christ. His garments are splattered with the blood of the antichrist and his armies which were totally annihilated. It appears that this trip to Bozrah takes place immediately *following* the battle of Armageddon on Tishri 10, and *before* the Feast of Tabernacles on Tishri 15-22. *After* he returns, the nations of the world will be gathered to Jerusalem before the throne of Christ, and all will take place in the judgment of the *Sheep and the Goats*.

The Sheep and Goats Judgment

"When the Son of man shall come in his glory, and all the holy angels with him, then shall he sit upon the throne of his glory: And before him shall be gathered all nations: and he shall separate them one from another, as a shepherd divideth his sheep from the goats: And he shall set the sheep on his right hand, but the goats on the left. Then shall the King say unto them on his right hand, Come, ye blessed of my Father, inherit the kingdom prepared for you from the foundation of the world. Then shall he say also unto them on the left hand, Depart from me, ye cursed, into everlasting fire, prepared for the devil and his angels."
Matthew 25:31-34, 41

The judgment of the *sheep and goats* will separate all the people from all of the other nations who have survived into two groups: One group will go into the millennial kingdom, and the other group will be cast into the lake of burning fire. The criteria are given by Christ Himself in Matthew 25:35-46. It is how the people of the nations treated **my brethren** during the *Time of Great tribulation and persecution.* Who **are** **my brethren**?

"For I was an hungred, and ye gave me meat: I was thirsty, and ye gave me drink: I was a stranger, and ye took me in: Naked, and ye clothed me: I was sick, and ye visited me: I was in prison, and ye came unto me. Then shall the righteous answer him, saying, Lord, when saw we thee an hungred, and fed thee? or thirsty, and gave thee drink? When saw we thee a stranger, and took thee in? or naked, and clothed thee? Or when saw we thee sick, or in prison, and came unto thee? And the King shall answer and say unto them, Verily I say unto you, Inasmuch as ye have done it unto one of the least of these my brethren, ye have done it unto me. Then shall he say also unto them on the left hand, Depart from me, ye cursed, into everlasting fire, prepared for the devil and his angels: For I was an hungred, and ye gave me no meat: I was thirsty, and ye gave me no drink: I was a stranger, and ye took me not in: naked, and ye clothed

me not: sick, and in prison, and ye visited me not. Then shall they also answer him, saying, Lord, when saw we thee an hungred, or athirst, or a stranger, or naked, or sick, or in prison, and did not minister unto thee? Then shall he answer them, saying, Verily I say unto you, Inasmuch as ye did it not to one of the least of these, ye did it not to me. And these shall go away into everlasting punishment: but the righteous into life eternal."   Matthew 25:35-40

Martyrs' of the Tribulation

Following the casting of antichrist and the false prophet into the lake of fire, and the banishing of Satan into the bottomless pit, the following judgment is briefly mentioned.

"And I saw thrones, and they sat upon them, and judgment was given unto them: and I saw the souls of them that were beheaded for the witness of Jesus, and for the word of God, and which had not worshipped the beast, neither his image, neither had received his mark upon their foreheads, or in their hands; and they lived and reigned with Christ a thousand years. "   Rev 20:4

This group of martyrs has already been seen in Rev 6:9-11. The martyrs were underneath the throne of God; they were given *white robes* and told to *rest* a little longer. It may seem strange that there will be a judgment of martyrs who have given their life rather than reject Christ, but understand that these were mortal men who were not sinless.. so they too must be judged. It certainly follows that their ultimate reward will be great.

By carefully reading Rev 20:1-6, it appears that this scene immediately follows the millennial kingdom. The thrones are occupied by *martyrs*, who have lost their lives for refusing to take the **mark of the beast** or worship **his image**. There is a *mystery* yet to be solved; who are **they** that sit on thrones and pass judgment. *They* who are sitting on thrones and passing judgment are not told to us, but there are several interesting possibilities.

Some have identified those who sit on these thrones of judgment as the 24 elders previously seen in Rev 4:4, Rev 5:10 and Rev 11:16. This belief is based upon Rev 5:9-10, where the 24 elders sing a *new song* and declare that they are part of the saints who will rule and reign upon the earth. However, this interpretation will not withstand biblical scrutiny. The 24 elders are seen occupying thrones before the tribulation period begins in Rev 4:4 .... they have not been subjected to the beast of Revelation.

Others maintain that this group of judges is the apostles in Mat 19:28 and Luke 22:30, who are promised to *sit on thrones and judge the 12 tribes of Israel*. All of the apostles except for John were said to have been martyred. This is a possibility if the scene in Rev 20:4 is *after* the millennial kingdom as we have proposed. All believers have already been previously resurrected or raptured; and all unbelievers will not be judged until after the 1000-year millennial kingdom is over. If these are the apostles sitting in fulfillment of Mat 19:28 and Luke 22:30, they are taking part in the Great White Throne judgment and not the Bema Seat judgment.

Finally, some have suggested that those sitting in judgment are a part of the *overcomers* from each of the seven churches in Rev 2-3. This is very unlikely, since this would be a select group of 12 from a select group of 144,000... possible but not likely.

We are left with no clear indication of who these judges might be, and the Revelation record is silent, so we best admit that this is an *unsolved mystery*.

In any case, this is the fulfillment of a promise that God made to the martyrs who were seen beneath the throne in Rev 6 as the *sixth seal* was opened. This martyrs *cried with a loud voice*.

> **"And when he had opened the fifth seal, I saw under the altar the souls of them that were slain for the word of God, and for the testimony which they held: And they cried with a loud voice, saying, How long, O Lord, holy and true, dost**

> *thou not judge and avenge our blood on them that dwell on the earth? And white robes were given unto every one of them; and it was said unto them, that they should rest yet for a little season, until their fellowservants also and their brethren, that should be killed as they were, should be fulfilled."*   Rev 6:9-11

These martyrs have made the ultimate sacrifice; they have given their lives rather than deny Jesus Christ. Because of their faithfulness *unto death*, they *shall be priests of God and of Christ, and shall reign with him a thousand years.*

> *"But the rest of the dead did not live again until the thousand years were finished…. Blessed and holy is he who has a part in the first resurrection. Over such the second death has no power, but they will be priests of God and of Christ; and shall reign with Him for 1000 years."*
>   Rev 20:5-6

The resurrection and reward of the martyrs beneath God's throne complete the seven phases of the *first resurrection* and judgments. The *second resurrection* and judgment is not for another 1000 years. *Seven* is the Biblical number of *completeness* and eight is the Biblical number of *new beginnings.*

There is an old saying: *"Anyone who believes in Christ as their savior is born twice, and dies only once. Anyone who refuses Christ as their savior is born once, but dies twice".*

The Great White Throne Judgment

The *second death* is for all *unbelievers* from the first Adam to the end of the 1000-year reign of Jesus Christ in the millennial kingdom. They have made their choice, and their fate is to be judged and found wanting at the *Great White Throne Judgment*, immediately following the millennial kingdom. Their fate is to be thrown into the *lake of burning fire*. At this time, Satan will make one last, futile attempt to reign. When the battle of Armageddon ended, Satan was cast into the bottomless pit for

1000 years (Rev 20:1-3), and when the thousand years are over Satan will be loosed out of his prison for *a little while* (Rev 20:3) to gather his forces from all over the world.

> *"And when the thousand years are expired, Satan shall be loosed out of his prison, And shall go out to deceive the nations which are in the four quarters of the earth, Gog and Magog, to gather them together to battle: the number of whom is as the sand of the sea. And they went up on the breadth of the earth, and compassed the camp of the saints about, and the beloved city: and fire came down from God out of heaven, and devoured them. And the devil that deceived them was cast into the lake of fire and brimstone, where the beast and the false prophet are, and shall be tormented day and night forever and ever."* Rev 20:7-10

The battle must be brief, because it is barely given mention in Rev 20:9. However, the *Great White Throne* Judgment is described in some detail.

> *"And I saw a great white throne, and him that sat on it, from whose face the earth and the heaven fled away; and there was found no place for them. And I saw the dead, small and great, stand before God; and the books were opened: and another book was opened, which is the book of life: and the dead were judged out of those things which were written in the books, according to their works. And the sea gave up the dead which were in it; and death and hell delivered up the dead which were in them: and they were judged every man according to their works. And death and hell were cast into the lake of fire. This is the second death. And whosoever was not found written in the book of life was cast into the lake of fire."* Rev 20:11-15

Following the Great White Throne Judgment, Death and Hell were *cast into the Lake of Fire*. The apostle Paul spoke of this when he asserted: *The last enemy that shall be destroyed is death* (I Corinthians 15:26).

Inhabitants of the Millennial Kingdom

The last judgment to be passed before eternity begins is to judge, condemn or reward all of those people who entered the 1000 year millennial kingdom and lived or died to the end; and all of those who were born during this period of time and lived or died. It is clear that these people must be judged: ***for we shall all stand before the judgment seat of Christ*** (Romans 14:10). However, this is yet another *unsolved mystery* in the Biblical record. There is no mention of how or where the earthly inhabitants of the millennial kingdom will be judged. We can only assume that these individuals will be judged after the 1000 year millennial kingdom is over… possibly but not necessarily at the Great White Throne Judgment. The only thing we know is recorded in Rev 20: 11-15

And so the world as we know it comes to an end. All sin and all those who have not accepted eternal life by believing in our Lord Jesus Christ have been purged from the earth. It is now time for eternity to begin, with new heavens and a new earth.

Thoughts And Things……..

Chapter 29

A New Heaven and a New Earth

The millennial kingdom is over, and Satan has been cast into the lake of fire and brimstone. The earth has been purged of all sin and it is now time to establish new heavens and a new earth. The earth will not be recreated, but will be completely renovated. Peter revealed to us that following the *Day of the Lord* the earth will be renovated with fire.

> *"the heavens shall pass away with a great noise, and the elements shall melt with fervent heat, the earth also and the works that are therein shall be burned up."* II Peter 3:10

By comparing scripture to scripture, this radical transformation of the earth must take place following the millennial kingdom; just prior to eternity. It is necessary for God to renovate the old earth. The physical earth was put under a curse by God after Adam and Eve fell, and it must be cleansed (Gen 3:17) Sin and death spoiled the first creation, but both have now been removed (Rev 20:14). The old earth is now replaced with one in which there will be no more death, sorrow, crying, pain or sin (Rev 21:3). Evidently, the saints who will inherit the kingdom will not remember the old world or anything in it. There will also be no more oceans or seas.

> *"For behold, I create new heavens and a new earth: and the former will not be nor come to mind"* Isaiah 65:17

> *"And I saw a new heaven and a new earth: for the first heaven and the first earth were passed away; and there was no more sea."* Rev 21:1

There will be no more sea because in Rev 22:1-2 we are told that there will be *a pure river of water of life, clear as crystal,* which will flow out of the earthly throne of God. Along this river on both sides there will grow a tree of life which will yield 12 different fruits every month. God promises those who come into this new creation that: I ***will give unto him that is athirst of the fountain of life freely*** (Rev 21:6). John was told that: ***it is done. I am Alpha and Omega, the beginning and the end***. This reiterates and fulfills what John heard in Rev 1:8 when Christ first spoke to him: ***I am Alpha and Omega, the beginning and the ending***. John is now reassured that all those who overcome the world by placing their trust and faith in our Lord Jesus Christ will now be his son.

"I will be his God and he shall be my son." Rev 21:7

There is no person who is now alive that does not have the opportunity to live in this new world forever and be a son or daughter of Christ. There are many in the world today who think that being good and kind are all that is needed to insure eternal life in the world to come: There are those who believe that they will be reincarnated: and there are those who believe in placing their eternal soul in the hands of people like Mohammed. It must be stated in the strongest possible way that there is only one way to obtain eternal life. Place your faith in the resurrected Son of God who is Jesus Christ and accept eternal life as a free gift by His grace. No amount of good deeds or works can obtain eternal life. Christ issued the following warning.

"But the fearful, and unbelieving, and the abominable, and murderers, and whoremongers, and sorcerers, and idolaters, and all liars, shall have their part in the lake which burneth with fire and brimstone: which is the second death."
Rev 21:8

According to these words, we are all doomed. Who has not experienced unbelief in moments of weakness and told *little white lies*? But be of good cheer and know the truth. Paul said that: ***For all have sinned, and come short of the glory of God*** (Rom 3:23). No one is sinless and *without spot or wrinkle* until it is imputed to them by Jesus Christ. This passage clearly means that anyone who has not been washed in the blood and imputed the righteousness of Christ will ever enter eternity. This is the true gospel message:

> *"For God so loved the world, that he gave his only begotten Son, that whosoever believeth in him should not perish, but have everlasting life. For God sent not his Son into the world to condemn the world; but that the world through him might be saved. He that believeth on him is not condemned: but he that believeth not is condemned already, because he hath not believed in the name of the only begotten Son of God."* John 3:16-18

Make no mistake about it; the lake of burning fire is a real place, and eternal torment is also real (Rev 20:10).

We are now told where everyone who is the Bride of Christ will spend eternity… it is in the *new Jerusalem*.

> *"And I John saw the holy city, new Jerusalem, coming down from God out of heaven, prepared as a bride adorned for her husband. And I heard a great voice out of heaven saying, Behold, the tabernacle of God is with men, and he will dwell with them, and they shall be his people, and God himself shall be with them, and be their God. And God shall wipe away all tears from their eyes; and there shall be no more death, neither sorrow, nor crying, neither shall there be any more pain: for the former things are passed away."* Rev 21:2-4

(1) This new city is Holy onto the Lord
(2) This is the *New Jerusalem*… **But Jerusalem which is above is free, which is the mother of us all** (Gal 4:26)
(3) It is prepared as a *bride for her husband*
(4) At this time, God will move his throne (tabernacle) to the new earth (Rev 22:3)
(5) God will dwell with the saints who reside in the new Jerusalem
(6) All of the former things will now pass away

It is necessary to establish a *new Jerusalem* because the old, earthly Jerusalem was full of sin and disbelief. It would not be fit for God's presence. This New Jerusalem is superior to the old Jerusalem in every way. Recall that in the letter written to the Church of Philadelphia, the overcomers were promised that they would have the name of the New Jerusalem written upon them, and that they would receive a new eternal name. This will be visible proof that the recipient has the right to dwell in this city and eternally commune with God. John is given the vision of this city *coming down from out of Heaven*. From whence did this city emerge? This is the ultimate fulfillment of a promise that Christ made when He ascended into heaven.

> *"In my Father's house are many mansions: if it were not so, I would have told you. I go to prepare a place for you. And if I go and prepare a place for you, I will come again, and receive you unto myself; that where I am, there ye may be also."*   John 4:2-3

What does this city look like and how has it been prepared for us?

- The *light* in the city was like a Jasper stone. This is the light of God that John saw in Rev 4:3. It is a transparent, light green color (Rev 21:11)
- The city had 12 gates (Rev 21:12). These 12 gates were formed out of gigantic *pearls* (Rev 21:21)
- Each gate had the *name* of one of the 12 tribes of Israel written upon it (Rev 21:12)
- The city was a *cube*; 12,000 furlongs (15,000 miles) on each side (Rev 21:17)
- The city was surrounded by a *wall great and high* (Rev 21:12). Each wall was 144 cubits wide (Rev 21:17). An ancient cubit was said to be the length of a man's forearm, or about 18 inches. This would make the wall about 216 feet wide.

- ➤ The city had **12 foundations** (Rev 21:14), and each one had the name of one of the 12 *apostles* written upon it. (The original 12 minus Judas plus Matthias, Acts 1:26)
- ➤ The wall was made of ***Jasper*** (Rev 21:18)
- ➤ The city itself was made of pure, transparent ***gold*** (Rev 21:18)
- ➤ The 12 foundations were inlaid with all manner of ***precious stones*** (Rev 21:19-20)
  - *First*-Jasper- A transparent green stone
  - *Second*-Sapphire- A hard blue stone
  - *Third*-Chalcedony- A transparent stone; most likely a yellowish, red color
  - *Fourth*-Emerald-A beautiful green stone
  - *Fifth*-Sardonyx-A bluish-white and red stone
  - *Sixth*-Sardius-a blood red stone
  - *Seven*th-chrysolyte-A goldish-yellow stone
  - *Eighth*-Beryl-A transparent bluish-green
  - *Ninth*-Topaz-A pale green stone
  - *Tenth*-Chrysoprasus-A yellow-green stone
  - *Eleven*th-Jacinth-A reddish-yellow stone
  - *Twelfth*-Amethyst-A deep purple and violet color
- ➤ The City will have ***no temple*** in it. The Lord God and Jesus Christ are themselves the temple (Rev 21:22)
- ➤ Inside the city there was no sun shining during the day, or a moon visible during the night. The ***glory of God*** and the ***Glory of Christ*** provide the light (Rev 21:23)
- ➤ The ***gates*** to the city will never be shut (Rev 21:25).
- ➤ The ***kings of the earth*** will visit the city and give glory and honor to it. (Rev 21:24)

John is now told who will be entering into the city to honor Christ and worship.

"He that overcometh shall inherit all things; and I will be his God, and he shall be my son. But the fearful, and unbelieving, and the abominable, and murderers, and whoremongers, and sorcerers, and idolaters, and all liars, shall have their part in

the lake which burneth with fire and brimstone: which is the second death." Rev 21:7-8

Almost parenthetically, John records that no one who lies, defiles or performs the works of abomination will ever be allowed in the city (Rev 21:27). It is certain that none of these things exist in God's perfect world; it is likely a reinforcing statement that if anyone who reads these words ever expects to enter the city in the future must accept the atoning grace of Jesus Christ now. Anyone who passes into this eternal state of happiness will have his/her name written into a book called the ***Lambs Book of Life*** (Rev 21:27). It is assumed that anyone who accepts Christ as their savior will have their name recorded in this sacred book.

Christ has finished His atoning work for mankind: God is pleased with His new creation, and we cannot even imagine what eternity will bring. Perhaps there will be another earth somewhere that God will create, and perhaps He will create another Adam and Eve and try again. Perhaps we (the saints) will be involved in this new venture…. It is impossible to tell.

"And he that sat upon the throne said, Behold, I make all things new. And he said unto me, Write: for these words are true and faithful. And he said unto me, It is done. I am Alpha and Omega, the beginning and the end. I will give unto him that is athirst of the fountain of the water of life freely. He that overcometh shall inherit all things; and I will be his God, and he shall be my son." Rev 21:5-7

Chapter 30

Come Quickly, Lord Jesus

Like a holy bookend, the closing words of Rev 22:6-17 closely parallel and reinforce the message of Rev 1:1-8.

- The things in the book of Revelation are from ***God himself*** (Rev 1:1, 22:6)
- The things revealed to us are ***faithful and true*** (Rev 22:6, 1:5)
- These things will ***soon come to pass*** (Rev 22:6, 1:1)
- There are seven special ***blessings*** (beatitudes) for all who read and study His words
  1. ***Blessed*** is he that ***readeth,*** and they that ***hear*** the words of this prophecy, and ***keep*** those things which are written therein (Rev 1:3)
  2. ***Blessed*** are the dead which die in the Lord from henceforth: *Yea, saith the Spirit, that they may rest from their labors; and their works do follow them* (Rev 14:13)
  3. Behold, I come as a thief. ***Blessed*** is he that watcheth, and keepeth his garments, lest he walk naked, and they see his shame (Rev 16:15)
  4. ***Blessed*** are they which are called unto the marriage supper of the Lamb. And he saith unto me, These are the true sayings of God (Rev 19:9)
  5. ***Blessed*** and holy is he that hath part in the first resurrection: on such the second death hath no power, but they shall be priests of God and of Christ, and shall reign with him a thousand years (Rev 20:6)
  6. Behold, I come quickly; ***blessed*** is he that keepeth the sayings of the prophecy of this book (Rev 22:7)
  7. ***Blessed*** are they that do his commandments, that they may have right to the tree of life, and may enter in through the gates into the city (Rev 22:15)

There is no other book in the Bible that calls a Christian to its study and understanding more than the book of Revelation. Its content is meant to be understood, but not without prayerful and long study. ***Blessed is he who keeps the sayings of the prophecy of this book.*** Blessed indeed!! All Christians should be prepared for the tribulation described in this book. ***Seal not the sayings of the prophecy of this book, for the time is at hand*** (Rev 22:10).

Twice Christ warns us of the immanency attached to the words of this book: ***Behold I come quickly*** (Rev 22:7): ***And behold I come quickly, and my reward is with Me to give every man according as his work will be*** (Rev 22:12). The warning of immanency and impending judgment is closely associated to our eternal relationship with Jesus Christ. We are sternly warned:

> ***"He that is unjust, let him be unjust still: and he which is filthy, let him be filthy still: and he that is righteous, let him be righteous still: and he that is holy, let him be holy still."***
> Rev 22:11

This is a warning against anyone delaying the decision to accept Christ as their personal savior. This is a warning to anyone who thinks that Christ is not watching and waiting…*He knows…He sees*. This present world could end at any time, and once the Age of Grace has run its course, there will be no second chance. The entire course of human history, beginning in the Garden of Eden and ending at Satan's Last Stand, has been a cosmic conflict between Satan and God. Everyone who will have reached the age of reason must choose between Satan and his worldly promises, or God and His eternal promises. Today we are truly blessed to be living in the Age of Grace, in which eternal life is freely given to all of those who believe that Jesus Christ is the Son Of God and died for our sins. We are sanctified, glorified and justified under the cross of Calvary.

To those who anxiously wait for His glorious appearing, Christ issues a call.

> *"And, behold, I come quickly; and my reward is with me, to give every man according as his work shall be. I am Alpha and Omega, the beginning and the end, the first and the last. Blessed are they that do his commandments, that they may have right to the tree of life, and may enter in through the gates into the city."*   Rev 22:12

Salvation cannot be bought, earned or borrowed from anyone. Salvation and eternal life is a personal decision that each person must make for themselves. Good works cannot guarantee salvation any more that *being good* can guarantee eternal life.

> *"Knowing that a man is not justified by the works of the law, but by the faith of Jesus Christ, even we have believed in Jesus Christ, that we might be justified by the faith of Christ, and not by the works of the law: for by the works of the law shall no flesh be justified."*   Galatians 2:16

However, James said that *faith without works is dead.*

> *"What doth it profit, my brethren, though a man say he hath faith, and have not works? can faith save him? Even so faith, if it hath not works, is dead, being alone. Yea, a man may say, Thou hast faith, and I have works: shew me thy faith without thy works, and I will shew thee my faith by my works. But wilt thou know, O vain man, that faith without works is dead? Seest thou how faith wrought with his works, and by works was faith made perfect? Ye see then how that by works a man is justified, and not by faith only. For as the body without the spirit is dead, so faith without works is dead also."*   James 2:14-26

Is there a contradiction here? What does the Apostle James mean when he says that *faith without works is dead*? There is no contradiction. Salvation and eternal life are guaranteed by Jesus Christ to be a free gift. He has paid the price by being the perfect Passover Lamb, slain from the foundation of the world. He has taken all of our sins away from us *as far as the east is from the west*; through Him and by Him we are made pure and white as we stand before God in His glorious light. Salvation is not an issue of works; it never was and never will be. However, our position in the eternal kingdom, how we will serve Christ, what we will be assigned to do, and our responsibilities in the kingdom are determined by works …. *Righteous works*. If anyone really accepts Christ as their personal Lord and Savior, works will follow: Not out of servitude or out of trying to repay Christ, but out of genuine love for Him. Real faith will always manifest itself in works. Halfhearted faith, even that which started out burning inside, can never be manifested in acceptable works. This is the straightforward message of the ***Parable of the Sower*** in Mark 4:14-20, and is the heart of the condemnation of the church at Ephesus; who had ***lost their first love of Christ***. Service and responsibility in the kingdom follow works on this earth. Salvation is a free gift. Works are manifested by the gifts of the spirit (I Corinthians 14:1-12). Paul revealed this truth to us:

> *"Now he that planteth and he that watereth are one: and every man shall receive his own reward according to his own labour. For we are labourers together with God: ye are God's husbandry, ye are God's building. According to the grace of God which is given unto me, as a wise masterbuilder, I have laid the foundation, and another buildeth thereon. But let every man take heed how he buildeth thereupon. For other foundation can no man lay than that is laid, which is Jesus Christ. Now if any man build upon this foundation gold, silver, precious stones, wood, hay, stubble; Every man's work shall be made manifest: for the day shall declare it, because it shall be revealed by fire; and the fire shall try every man's work of what sort it is. If any man's work abide which he hath built thereupon, he shall receive a reward. If any man's work shall be burned, he shall suffer loss: but he himself shall be saved; yet so as by fire."*   I Corinthians 3: 8-15

Jesus confirmed these truths and gave us many more when He sent the apostle John to record in a book:

> *"The Revelation of Jesus Christ, which God gave unto him, to shew unto his servants things which must shortly come to pass; and he sent and signified it by his angel unto his servant John: Who bare record of the word of God, and of the testimony of Jesus Christ, and of all things that he saw."* Rev 1:1-2.

> *"I Jesus have sent mine angel to testify unto you these things in the churches. I am the root and the offspring of David, and the bright and morning star."* Rev 22:16

The identification of *I Jesus* appears nowhere else in the Holy Scriptures. It is a unique and personal identification that affirms the source of these words. No other book in the Holy Bible was completely recorded by comprehensive visions. John repeatedly stated that he *saw these things*. God revealed these things to Christ who sent and signified it to his servant John (Rev 1:1). Christ assures us that the words in his book of Revelation are true and accurate.

> *"For I testify unto every man that heareth the words of the prophecy of this book, If any man shall add unto these things, God shall add unto him the plagues that are written in this book: And if any man shall take away from the words of the book of this prophecy, God shall take away his part out of the book of life, and out of the holy city, and from the things which are written in this book."* Rev 22:18-19

Christ reaffirms His authority and position to claim the truthfulness of these words by declaring that He is *the root and offspring of David* and that He is the *bright and morning star*. King David is venerated by the Jews as the king of Israel. Here in a strange but powerful declaration Christ establishes that He was the *root of David*; all things were made *by and for Him*. He preexisted before the world was formed, and David was part of His manifold creative powers. Simultaneously, He affirms that He is from the Davidic line by natural birth and owns the right of kingship through His genealogy. He is the King of Kings and

Lord of Lords by both his heavenly position as the Son of God, and by His earthly position as the greater Son of David. He completely fulfills all of the Jewish Messianic expectations and will fulfill all their promises. Christ also declares Himself to be the ***bright and morning star***. The overcomers in the letter to Thyatira were promised that ***I will give him the morning star***. That promise is reaffirmed at this time. Imagine, Christ *IS* the bright and morning star; He is the light of the world. He is the brightest star in the galaxy and He is giving Himself to us! He will give us salvation, eternal life, a mansion to live in forever, and white robes without spot or wrinkle. He will make us kings and priests. He also will give us His name. *HE WILL GIVE US HIMSELF*. Surely:

> "..... *Eye hath not seen, nor ear heard, neither have entered into the heart of man, the things which God hath prepared for them that love him*"   I Corinthians 2:9

> "*He which testifieth these things saith, Surely I come quickly. Amen. Even so, come, Lord Jesus*"   Rev 22:20

The Grace of our Lord Jesus Christ

be with you all

Amen   (Rev 22:21)

Bibliography

Africanus, Julius, ***Chronographies***, Grand Rapid, Michigan: 1978 reproduction of 1867 version.

Agee, M. J., ***The End of the Age***, Avon Books, New York, NY, 1994.

Albright, W. F., T***he Chronology of the Divided Monarchy of Israel***, American School of Oriental Research, 1945

Anderson, Sir Robert, ***The Coming Prince***, 1882

Anderson, Sir Robert, ***The Coming Prince***, Kregel Publications, Grand Rapids, Michigan, 1988.

Anstey, M., ***The Romance of Biblical Chronology***, London Marshall Brothers, 1913.

Archer, Gleason, ***A survey of the Old Testament***, Moody Press, Chicago, 1974

Babylonian Talmud, Rosh Hashana and Arakin Tract.

Barnhouse, Donald Grey, ***Revelation***, Zondervan Publishing House, Grand Rapids, Michigan, 1871.

Booker, Richard, *Jesus in the Feasts of Israel*, Destiny Image Publishers, Shippinsburg, Penn., 1987.

Bright, J., ***A History of Israel***, Westminister Press, Chicago, Illinois, 1959.

Bullinger, E. W., ***The Companion Bible***, Kregal Publishing Co., Grand Rapids, Michigan, 1990.

Finis Jennings Dake,, ***Dake's Annotated Reference Bible***, Dake Bible Sales, Inc., Lawrenceville, Georgia, 1974.

DeHaan, M.R., ***Daniel the Prophet***, Zondervan Publishing House, Grand Rapids , Michigan, 1947.

Dewitt, Roy Lee, ***Teaching From the Tabernacle***, Baker Book House, Grand Rapids, Michigan, 1991.

Encyclopedia Judaica, Keter Publishing House, Jerusalem, Israel, 1971.

Finnegan, Jack, ***Handbook of Biblical Chronology***, Revised Edition, Hendrickson Publishing Co., Peabody, Maryland, 1998.

Faulstich, Eugene, http://biblechronologybooks.com/

Fuchs, Daniel, ***Israel's Holy Days***, Loizeaux Brothers, Neptune, New Jersey, 1985.

Galil, Gershon, *The Chronology of the Kings of Israel & Judah*, E. J. Brill Publishing Co., New York, NY, 1996.
Gaster, Theodore H, *Festivals of the Jewish New Year*, Morrow Quill Paperbacks, New York, NY, 1978.
Glaser, Zhava and Mitch Glaser, *The Fall Feasts of Israel*, Moody Bible Institute, Chicago, Illinois, 1977.
Good, Joseph, *Rosh Hashanah and the Messianic Kingdom to Come*, Hatikva Ministries, Port Arthur, Texas, 3rd Edition, 1970.
Hales, William, *A New Analysis of Chronology*, 2cd Edition, London, England, 1830.
Hislop, Alexander, *The Two Babylons*, Loizeaux Press, New Jersey, 1916.
Hoehner, Harold W., *Chronological Aspects of the Life of Christ*, Zondervan Press, Grand Rapids, Michigan, 1977.
Horn, H. H., and L. H. Wood, *The Chronology of Ezra 7*, TEACH Services, Inc., Second Edition, www.TEACHServices.Com, 1970.
Http://www.olive-tree.net, *A Summary of Edwin Theil's Work*, 5/3/2007
Ice, Thomas, http://www.pre-trib.org/
Ironside, Henry A., *Daniel,* Loizeaux Brothers Inc., Oakland, California, 1920.
Jeffrey, Grant R., *Armageddon: Appointment with Destiny*, Toronto, Canada, Frontier Research, Inc., 1988.
Jones, Floyd Nolan, **The Chronology of the Old Testament**, Master Books, Third Printing,: May,2007
Josephus, Flavius, *The Works of Josephus*, Hendrickson Publishing Company, 1987.
Lahaye, Tim, *Revelation*, Lamplighter Books, Zondervan Publishing House, Grand Rapids, Michigan,1975.
Larkin, Clarence, *The Greatest Book on Dispensational Truth in the World*, The Clarence Larkin Estate, Glenside, California, 1918.
Lenski, R. C. H., *Lenskie's Commentary on the New Testament*, Augsbury Fortress Press, 1964.
Levitt, Zola, *The Seven Feasts of Israel*, Zola, P. O. Box 12268, Dallas,Texas, 75225, 1979.
Lindsay, Gordon, *16 Volume Revelation Series*, Published by Christ for the Nations, Dallas, Texas, 1982.

Lindsey, Hal, *The Late Great Planet Earth*, Zondervan Publishing Company, Grand Rapids, Michigan, 1970.
Lukenbill, D.D., *Ancient Records of Assyria and Babylon*, Greenwood Press, New York, N.Y., 1968.
Newton, Sir Issac, *The Chronology of Ancient Kingdoms*, London, England, 1728.
McDowell, Josh, *Prophecy: Fact or Fiction*, Here's Life Publishing Company, San Bernadino, California, 1981.
McFall, Leslie, http://www.btinternet.com/~lmf12/
McGee, J. Vernon, *Daniel*, Thomas Nelson Publishers, Nashville, Tenn., 1975.
Morris, L.C., *The Gospel According to Luke*, William B. Eerdmans Publishing Company, Grand Rapids, Michigan, 1982.
Nee, Watchman, *Come Lord Jesus*, Christian Fellowship Publishers, New York, NY, 1976.
Pentecost, Dwight D., *Parables of Jesus*, Zondervan Publishing,
Pentecost, Dwight J., *Things to Come*, Zondervan Publiishing, Grand Rapids, Michigan, 1973.
Phillips, Don T., *The Book of Revelation: Mysteries Explained, Revised Edition* ,2012,Virtualbookworm.com Publishing Co., PO Box 9949, College Station, Texas, 2004
Phillips, John, *Exploring Revelation*, Moody Press, Chicago, Illinois, 1987.
Pickle, Bob, http://www.pickle-publishing.com/papers/
Pink, A. W., *The Antichrist*, Kregel Publishing, Grand Rapids, Michigan, 1988.
Pratt, John P., *Divine Calendars Testify of Abraham, Isaac and Jacob*, Meridian Magazine, Sept 11, 2003.
Prideaux, Humphrey, *The Old and New Testament: History of the Jews*, 25th Edition, London, England, 1858.
Rawlinson, George, http://en.wikipedia.org/wiki/George_Rawlinson
Rice, John R., *The King of the Jews (Matthew)*, Sword of the Lord Publishers, Murfreesboro, Tenn, 1971.
Rice, John R., *The Son of Man (Luke)*, Sword of the Lord Publishers, Murfreesboro, Tenn, 1971.
Ritchie, John, *Feasts of Jehovah*, Kregel Publications, Grand Rapids, Michigan, 1982.
Rosenthal, Marvin, *The Pre-Wrath Rapture of the Church*, Thomas Nelson Publishers, Nashville, Tenn., 1990.

Ryrie, Charles C., ***Ryrie Study Bible***, King James Version, Moody Press, Chicago, Illinois, 1978.

Ryrie, Charles C., ***Ryrie Study Bible***, New King James Version, Moody Press, Chicago, Illinois, 1985.

Salerno, Donald A., ***Revelation Unsealed***, Virtualbookworm.com Publishing Co., PO Box 9949, College Station, Texas, 2004

Sedar Olam, Roman & Littlefield Publishing Company, New York, New York, 2005.

Shea, William H., Andrews University Seminary Studies, Summer 1988, Vol. 26, No. 2, 171-180.

Shepard, Coulso, ***Jewish Holy Days***, Loizeaux Brothers Publishing Co., 1961.

Shodde, George H., ***The Book of Jubilees***, Artisan Publishers, 1980.

Spurgeon, Tommie, ***The 7 Spirits of God***, http://www.americaisraelprophecy.com/thesevenspiritsofgod.html

Strauss, Lehman, ***God's Prophetic Calendar***, Loizeaux Brothers http://www.google.com/Publishing Co.,1987.

Strong, James, ***Strong's Concordance of the Bible***, World Bible Publishers, Iowa Falls, Iowa, 1986.

Thiele, Edwin R., ***The Mysterious Numbers of the Hebrew Kings***, Zondervan Press, Grand Rapids, Michigan, 1983.

Thiele, Edwin R., ***A Summary of Edwin Thiele's Work***, http://www.olive-tree.net

Thomas, Robert, ***Revelation 1-7: An Exegetical Commentary***, Moody Press, Chicago, Illinois, 1992.

Thomas, Robert, ***Revelation 8-23: An Exegetical Commentary***, Moody Press, Chicago, Illinois, 1992.

Ussher, James, ***Annals of the World***, Master Books, London, England, 1658.

Van Kampen, Robert, ***The Sign***, Crossway Books, Inc., 1992.

Vine, W.E., ***The Expanded Vines Dictionary of New Testament Words,*** Bethany House Publishers, Minneapolis, Minn.,1994.

Wacholder, Ben Zion, ***The Calendar of Sabbatical Cycles During the Second Temple and the Early Rabbinic Period***, Hebrew Union College Annual 44 (1973), pp. 153-196

www.ingramcontent.com/pod-product-compliance
Lightning Source LLC
Chambersburg PA
CBHW060055190426
43202CB00030B/1580